Advanced Electronic Communications Systems

Advanced Electronic Communications Systems

Fourth Edition

Wayne Tomasi
Mesa Community College

Prentice Hall
Upper Saddle River, New Jersey   Columbus, Ohio

Library of Congress Cataloging-in-Publication Data

Tomasi, Wayne.
    Advanced electronic communications systems / Wayne F. Tomasi. —
4th ed.
      p. cm.
    Includes index.
    ISBN 0-13-750986-3
     1. Digital communications.   2. Telecommunication systems.
I. Title.
TK5103.7.T65   1998
621.382—dc21
                                      97-20675
                                        CIP

Cover photo: Mike Agliolo/Photo Researchers, Inc.
Editor: Charles E. Stewart, Jr.
Production Coordinator: Betty O'Bryant, Publishers' Production Services
Production Editor: Christine M. Harrington
Design Coordinator: Julia Zonneveld Van Hook
Text Designer: ETP Harrison
Cover Designer: Brian Deep
Production Manager: Pamela D. Bennett
Marketing Manager: Debbie Yarnell

This book was set in Times Roman by Carlisle Communications, Ltd. and was printed and bound by Courier/Kendallville, Inc. The cover was printed by Phoenix Color Corp.

© 1998, 1994, 1992, 1987 by Prentice-Hall, Inc.
Simon & Schuster/A Viacom Company
Upper Saddle River, New Jersey 07458

Printed in the United States of America

10 9 8 7 6 5 4 3 2 1

ISBN: 0-13-750986-3

Prentice-Hall International (UK) Limited, *London*
Prentice-Hall of Australia Pty. Limited, *Sydney*
Prentice-Hall of Canada, Inc., *Toronto*
Prentice-Hall Hispanoamericana, S. A., *Mexico*
Prentice-Hall of India Private Limited, *New Delhi*
Prentice-Hall of Japan, Inc., *Tokyo*
Simon & Schuster Asia Pte. Ltd., *Singapore*
Editora Prentice-Hall do Brasil, Ltda., *Rio de Janeiro*

In loving memory of my father,
Harry Tomasi

electronics communications and data

Preface

The purpose of this book is to extend and update the knowledge of the reader to more modern digital and data communications systems, microwave radio communications systems, satellite communications systems, and optical fiber communications systems. The book was written so that a reader with previous knowledge in basic electronics, electronics communications principles, and an understanding of mathematics through trigonometry will have little trouble understanding the concepts presented. Within the text, numerous examples emphasize the most important concepts, and questions and problems are included at the end of each chapter. Answers to selected problems are included at the end of the book.

Advanced Electronic Communications Systems, Fourth Edition, provides a comprehensive and modern coverage of the field of digital and data communications. The most important and extensive changes and additions to this edition occur in the chapters that deal primarily with digital and/or data communications such as Chapters 2, 3, and 8. This edition also includes more end of chapter problems. The major new topics and enhancements incorporated into this edition, by chapter number, are

1. A new section on digital amplitude modulation has been added and the section "Frequency Shift Keying" has been rewritten.
2. In addition to a rewritten introduction and updated section on serial interfaces, new sections on bar codes, echoplex, checksum, RS-232D and RS-530 interface standards, Centronics parallel interface, IEEE 488 bus, telephone network, telephone circuit, telephone circuit transmission parameters, modem control (the AT command set), and CCITT modem recommendations have been provided.
3. The sections "Local Area Networks," "Token Passing Ring," and "Ethernet" have been rewritten. New sections on data transmission modes, asynchronous transfer mode, Synchronous Optical Network (SONET), 10BASE-5 Ethernet, 10BASE-2 Ethernet, 10BASE-T Ethernet, 100BASE-T Ethernet, Fiber Distributed Data Interface (FDDI), and the Fibre Channel Systems Initiative expand the coverage.

4. A new section on signal power in binary digital signals has been added.
5. The section on digital biphase has been rewritten and expanded and a new section on statistical time-division multiplexing added.
6. Chapter 6 remains essentially the same as in the previous edition.
7. Chapter 7 remains essentially the same as in the previous edition.
8. The section on multiple accessing has been rewritten to extend the coverage, and a comprehensive section on satellite radio navigation, including detailed coverage of the Navstar Satellite System and the Global Positioning System (GPS), has been added.
9. Chapter 9 remains essentially the same as in the previous edition.

ACKNOWLEDGMENTS

I would like to thank Betty O'Bryant for her efforts in the production of this book. Her knowledge and expertise are greatly appreciated. I would also like to thank the following reviewers: Thomas Young, Rochester Institute of Technology; Mike Rodriguez, Rochester Institute of Technology; Peter Risdahl, Southern Alberta Institute of Technology; Donald Stelzer, DeVry Institute of Technology, Phoenix; Eugene Staiger, SUNY College of Technology; Bill Lin, DeVry Institute of Technology, Woodbridge; Merle Parmer, DeVry Institute of Technology, Phoenix; Robert E. Greenwood, Ryerson Polytechnical Institute; James W. Stewart, DeVry Institute of Technology, Woodbridge; Susan A. R. Garrod, Purdue University; James C. Chapel, Lincoln Land Community College; James Fisk, Northern Essex Community College; Allan Shapiro, Northern Virginia Community College; William H. Maxwell, Nashville State Technical Institute; and Ladimer S. Nagurney, University of Hartford.

Wayne Tomasi

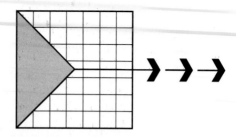

Contents

3 DATA COMMUNICATIONS PROTOCOLS AND NETWORK CONFIGURATIONS   127

4 DIGITAL TRANSMISSION   191

5 MULTIPLEXING   227

6 MICROWAVE RADIO COMMUNICATIONS AND SYSTEM GAIN   273

7 SATELLITE COMMUNICATIONS   301

8 SATELLITE MULTIPLE-ACCESS ARRANGEMENTS   333

9 OPTICAL FIBER COMMUNICATIONS   359

CHAPTER 1

Digital Communications

INTRODUCTION

During the past several years, the *electronic communications* industry has undergone some remarkable technological changes. Traditional electronic communications systems that use conventional analog modulation techniques, such as *amplitude modulation* (AM), *frequency modulation* (FM), and *phase modulation* (PM), are gradually being replaced with more modern *digital communications systems*. Digital communications systems offer several outstanding advantages over traditional analog systems: ease of processing, ease of multiplexing, and noise immunity.

In essence, electronic communications is the transmission, reception, and processing of *information* with the use of electronic circuits. Information is defined as knowledge or intelligence communicated or received. Figure 1-1 shows a simplified block diagram of an electronic communications system, which comprises three primary sections: a *source,* a *destination,* and a *transmission medium.* Information is propagated through a communications system in the form of symbols that can be *analog* (proportional), such as the human voice, video picture information, or music, or *digital* (discrete), such as binary-coded numbers, alpha/numeric codes, graphic symbols, microprocessor op-codes, or database information. However, very often the source information is unsuitable for transmission in its original form and must be converted to a more suitable form prior to transmission. For example, with digital communications systems, analog information is converted to digital form prior to transmission, and with analog communications systems, digital data are converted to analog signals prior to transmission.

FIGURE 1-1 Simplified block diagram for an electronic communications system

DIGITAL COMMUNICATIONS

The term *digital communications* covers a broad area of communications techniques, including *digital transmission* and *digital radio*. Digital transmission is the transmittal of digital pulses between two or more points in a communications system. Digital radio is the transmittal of digitally modulated analog carriers between two or more points in a communications system. Digital transmission systems require a physical facility between the transmitter and receiver, such as a metallic wire pair, a coaxial cable, or an optical fiber cable. In digital radio systems, the transmission medium is free space or Earth's atmosphere.

FIGURE 1-2 Digital communications systems: (a) digital transmission; (b) digital radio

Figure 1-2 shows simplified block diagrams of both a digital transmission system and a digital radio system. In a digital transmission system, the original source information may be in digital or analog form. If it is in analog form, it must be converted to digital pulses prior to transmission and converted back to analog form at the receive end. In a digital radio system, the modulating input signal and the demodulated output signal are digital pulses. The digital pulses could originate from a digital transmission system, from a digital source such as a mainframe computer, or from the binary encoding of an analog signal.

SHANNON LIMIT FOR INFORMATION CAPACITY

The *information capacity* of a communications system represents the number of independent symbols that can be carried through the system in a given unit of time. The most basic symbol is the *binary digit* (bit). Therefore, it is often convenient to express the information capacity of a system in *bits per second* (bps). In 1928, R. Hartley of Bell Telephone Laboratories developed a useful relationship among bandwidth, transmission time, and information capacity. Simply stated, *Hartley's law* is

$$I \propto B \times T \qquad (1\text{-}1)$$

where I = information capacity (bps)
         B = bandwidth (Hz)
         T = transmission time (s)

From Equation 1-1 it can be seen that the information capacity is a linear function of bandwidth and transmission time and is directly proportional to both. If either the bandwidth or the transmission time is changed, a directly proportional change in information capacity will occur.

In 1948, C. E. Shannon (also of Bell Telephone Laboratories) published a paper in the *Bell System Technical Journal* relating the information capacity of a communications channel to bandwidth and signal-to-noise ratio. Mathematically stated, the *Shannon limit for information capacity* is

$$I = B \log_2 \left(1 + \frac{S}{N}\right) \qquad (1\text{-}2a)$$

or

$$I = 3.32 \, B \log_{10} \left(1 + \frac{S}{N}\right) \qquad (1\text{-}2b)$$

where I = information capacity (bps)
         B = bandwidth (Hz)
         $\dfrac{S}{N}$ = signal-to-noise power ratio (unitless)

For a standard voice-band communications channel with a signal-to-noise power ratio of 1000 (30 dB) and a bandwidth of 2.7 kHz, the Shannon limit for information capacity is

$$I = 2700 \log_2 (1 + 1000)$$
$$= 26.9 \text{ kbps}$$

Shannon's formula is often misunderstood. The results of the preceding example indicate that 26.9 kbps can be transferred through a 2.7-kHz channel. This may be true, but it cannot be done with a binary system. To achieve an information transmission rate of 26.9 kbps through a 2.7-kHz channel, each symbol transmitted must contain more than one bit of information. Therefore, to achieve the Shannon limit for information capacity, digital transmission systems that have more than two output conditions (symbols) must be

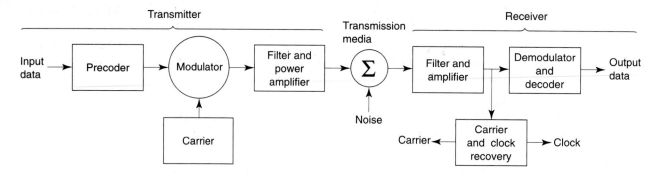

FIGURE 1-3 Simplified block diagram of a digital radio system

used. Several such systems are described in the following chapters. These systems include both analog and digital modulation techniques and the transmission of both digital and analog signals.

DIGITAL RADIO

One property that distinguishes a digital radio system from a conventional AM, FM, or PM radio system is that in a digital radio system the modulating and demodulating signals are digital pulses rather than analog waveforms. Another difference between digital and analog radio systems is the type of modulation used. Digital radios, however, use analog carriers just as conventional systems do.

Figure 1-3 shows a simplified block diagram for a digital radio system. In the transmitter, the precoder encodes or groups the incoming data into a control word that modulates the carrier signal. The modulated carrier is shaped (filtered), then amplified. In the receiver, the pulse shaping network further filters the modulated wave, rejects out-of-band noise, and suppresses interference from adjacent channels.

DIGITAL AMPLITUDE MODULATION

The simplest digital modulation technique is double-sideband, full-carrier amplitude modulation with a binary modulating signal. Mathematically, amplitude modulation by a binary signal is

$$v(t) = \frac{A}{2}[1 + m(t)](\cos \omega_c t) \tag{1-3}$$

where $\omega_c t$ = carrier angular frequency (rad/s)
           $m(t)$ = binary modulating signal

In Equation 1-3, if the modulating signal is a standard binary data waveform, $m(t) = \pm 1$. Thus, for 100% modulation $v(t)$ is either on or off; what is referred to as on-off keying (OOK) modulation.

It is generally recognized that with amplitude modulation the carrier itself contains no information. Consequently, suppression of the carrier yields DSB-SC (double-sideband, suppressed-carrier) modulation, which is stated mathematically as

$$v(t)_{\mathrm{dsb}} = Am(t)(\cos \omega_c t)$$

When $m(t)$ equals either 0 or 1, again we have OOK modulation. An OOK waveform can be demodulated either coherently or noncoherently with little difference in performance. The use of amplitude modulated analog carriers to transport digital information is a relatively low-quality, low-cost method of digital radio and is seldom used in high-capacity, high-performance systems.

FREQUENCY SHIFT KEYING

Frequency shift keying (FSK) is another relatively simple, low-performance form of digital modulation. Binary FSK is a form of constant-amplitude angle modulation similar to conventional frequency modulation except that the modulating signal is a binary pulse stream that varies between two discrete voltage levels rather than a continuously changing analog waveform. The general expression for a binary FSK signal is

$$v(t) = V_c \cos\left[\left(\omega_c + \frac{v_m(t)\,\Delta\omega}{2}\right)t\right] \qquad (1\text{-}4)$$

where $v(t)$ = binary FSK waveform
           V_c = peak unmodulated carrier amplitude
           ω_c = radian carrier frequency
        $v_m(t)$ = binary digital modulating signal
         $\Delta\omega$ = change in radian output frequency

From Equation 1-4 it can be seen that with binary FSK the carrier amplitude V_c remains constant with modulation. However, the output carrier radian frequency (ω_c) shifts by an amount equal to $\pm\Delta\omega/2$. The frequency shift ($\Delta\omega/2$) is proportional to the amplitude and polarity of the binary input signal. For example, a binary 1 could be +1 volt, and a binary zero could be −1 volt, producing frequency shifts of $+\Delta\omega/2$ and $-\Delta\omega/2$, respectively. In addition, the rate at which the carrier frequency shifts is equal to the rate of change of the binary input signal $v_m(t)$ (that is, the input bit rate). Thus, the output carrier frequency deviates (shifts) between $\omega_c + \Delta\omega/2$ and $\omega_c - \Delta\omega/2$ at a rate equal to f_m.

FSK Transmitter

With binary FSK, the center or carrier frequency is shifted (deviated) by the binary input data. Consequently, the output of a binary FSK modulator is a step function in the time domain. As the binary input signal changes from a logic 0 to a logic 1, and vice versa, the FSK output shifts between two frequencies: a *mark* or *logic 1 frequency* and a *space* or *logic 0 frequency*. With binary FSK, there is a change in the output frequency each time the logic condition of the binary input signal changes. Consequently, the output rate of change is equal to the input rate of change. In digital modulation, the rate of change at the input to the modulator is called the *bit rate* and has the units of bits per second (bps). The measure of the rate of change at the output of the modulator is called *baud* and is equal to the reciprocal of the time of one output signaling element. In essence, baud is the line speed in symbols per second. In binary FSK, the input and output rates of change are equal; therefore, the bit rate and baud rate are equal. A simple binary FSK transmitter is shown in Figure 1-4.

Bandwidth Considerations of FSK

As with all electronic communications systems, bandwidth is one of the primary considerations when designing a binary FSK transmitter. FSK is similar to conventional frequency modulation and so can be described in a similar manner.

Figure 1-5 shows a binary FSK modulator, which is very similar to a conventional FM modulator, and is very often a voltage-controlled oscillator (VCO). The fastest input rate of change occurs when the binary input is a series of alternating 1s and 0s: namely,

FIGURE 1-4 Binary FSK transmitter

a square wave. Consequently, if only the fundamental frequency of the input is considered, the highest modulating frequency is equal to one-half the input bit rate.

The rest frequency of the VCO is chosen such that it falls halfway between the mark and space frequencies. A logic 1 condition at the input shifts the VCO from its rest frequency to the mark frequency, and a logic 0 condition at the input shifts the VCO from its rest frequency to the space frequency. Consequently, as the input binary signal changes from a logic 1 to a logic 0, and vice versa, the VCO output frequency *shifts* or *deviates* back and forth between the mark and space frequencies.

In a binary FSK modulator, Δf is the peak frequency deviation of the carrier and is equal to the difference between the rest frequency and either the mark or space frequency (or half the difference between the mark and space frequencies). The peak frequency deviation depends on the amplitude of the modulating signal. In a binary digital signal, all logic 1s have the same voltage and all logic 0s have the same voltage; consequently, the frequency deviation is constant and always at its maximum value.

The output of a FSK modulator is related to the binary input as shown in Figure 1-6 where a logic 0 corresponds to space frequency f_s, a logic 1 corresponds to

FIGURE 1-5 FSK modulator, t_b, time of one bit = $1/f_b$; f_m, mark frequency; f_s, space frequency; T_1, period of shortest cycle; $1/T_1$, fundamental frequency of binary square wave; f_b, input bit rate (bps)

FIGURE 1-6 FKS frequency deviation

mark frequency f_m, and f_c is the carrier frequency. The required peak frequency deviation, Δf, is given as

$$\Delta f = \frac{|f_m - f_s|}{2} = \frac{1}{4t_b} \quad \text{(Hz, minimum)} \tag{1-5}$$

where t_b is the time of one bit in seconds and f_m and f_s are expressed as

$$f_m = f_c - \Delta f = f_c - \frac{1}{4t_b} \tag{1-6a}$$

$$f_s = f_c + \Delta f = f_c + \frac{1}{4t_b} \tag{1-6b}$$

From Figure 1-6 it can be seen that FSK consists of two pulsed sinusoidal waves of frequency f_m and f_s. Pulsed sinusoidal waves have frequency spectrums that are sin x/x functions. Consequently, we can represent the output spectrum for an FSK signal as shown in Figure 1-7. Assuming that the zero crossings contain the bulk of the energy, the bandwidth for FSK can be approximated as

$$BW = f_m + \frac{2\pi}{t_b} - \left(f_s - \frac{2\pi}{t_b}\right) = f_m - f_s + \frac{2}{t_b} = 2\left(\Delta f + \frac{1}{t_b}\right) \tag{1-7}$$

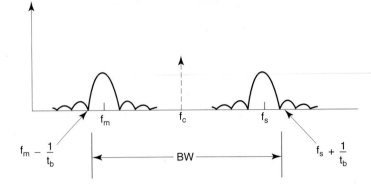

FIGURE 1-7 FSK frequency spectrum

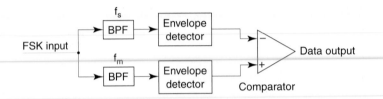

FIGURE 1-8 Noncoherent FSK demodulator

Example 1-1

Determine the bandwidth and baud for an FSK signal with a mark frequency of 49 kHz, a space frequency of 51 kHz, and a bit rate of 2 kbps.

Solution

$$t_b = 1/4000 = 0.25 \text{ ms}$$

Substituting into Equation 1-7 gives

$$BW = 51{,}000 - 49{,}000 + 2/0.25 \text{ ms} = 2000 + 4000 = 6000 \text{ Hz}$$

With FSK, the baud is equal to the input bit rate or

$$\text{baud} = 2000$$

FSK Receiver

FSK demodulation is quite simple with a circuit such as the one shown in Figure 1-8. The FSK input signal is applied to the inputs of both bandpass filters (BPFs). The respective filter passes only the mark or only the space frequency on to its respective envelope detector. The envelope detectors, in turn, indicate the total power in each passband and the comparator responds to the largest of the two powers. This type of FSK detection is referred to as noncoherent detection; there is no frequency involved in the demodulation process that is synchronized either in phase, frequency, or both with the incoming FSK signal.

Figure 1-9 shows the block diagram for a coherent FSK receiver. The incoming FSK signal is multiplied by a recovered carrier signal that has the exact same frequency and phase as the transmitter reference. However, the two transmitted frequencies (the mark and space frequencies) are not generally continuous; it is not practical to reproduce a local reference that is coherent with both of them. Consequently, coherent FSK detection is seldom used.

The most common circuit used for demodulating binary FSK signals is the *phase-locked loop* (PLL), which is shown in block diagram form in Figure 1-10. A

FIGURE 1-9 Coherent FSK demodulator

FIGURE 1-10 PLL-FSK demodulator

PLL-FSK demodulator works similarly to a PLL-FM demodulator. As the input to the PLL shifts between the mark and space frequencies, the *dc error voltage* at the output of the phase comparator follows the frequency shift. Because there are only two input frequencies (mark and space), there are also only two output error voltages. One represents a logic 1 and the other a logic 0. Therefore, the output is a two-level (binary) representation of the FSK input. Generally, the natural frequency of the PLL is made equal to the center frequency of the FSK modulator. As a result, the changes in the dc error voltage follow the changes in the analog input frequency and are symmetrical around 0 V.

Binary FSK has a poorer error performance than PSK or QAM and, consequently, is seldom used for high-performance digital radio systems. Its use is restricted to low-performance, low-cost, asynchronous data modems that are used for data communications over analog, voice-band telephone lines (see Chapter 2).

Minimum Shift-Keying FSK

Minimum shift-keying FSK (MSK) is a form of *continuous-phase* frequency shift keying (CPFSK). Essentially, MSK is binary FSK except that the mark and space frequencies are *synchronized* with the input binary bit rate. Synchronous simply means that there is a precise time relationship between the two; it does not mean they are equal. With MSK, the mark and space frequencies are selected such that they are separated from the center frequency by an exact odd multiple of one-half of the bit rate [f_m and $f_s = n(f_b/2)$, where n = any odd integer]. This ensures that there is a smooth phase transition in the analog output signal when it changes from a mark to a space frequency, or vice versa. Figure 1-11 shows a *noncontinuous* FSK waveform. It can be seen that when the input changes from a logic 1 to a logic 0, and vice versa, there is an abrupt phase discontinuity in the analog output signal. When this occurs, the demodulator has trouble following the frequency shift; consequently, an error may occur.

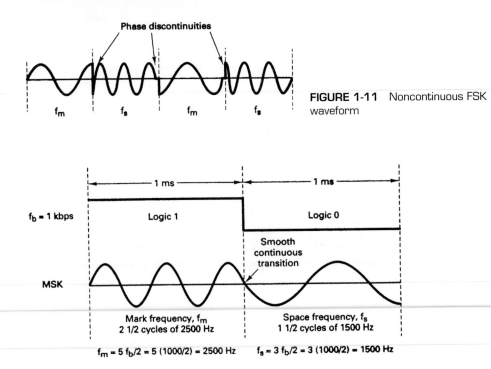

FIGURE 1-11 Noncontinuous FSK waveform

FIGURE 1-12 Continuous-phase MSK waveform

Figure 1-12 shows a continuous phase MSK waveform. Notice that when the output frequency changes, it is a smooth, continuous transition. Consequently, there are no phase discontinuities. MSK has a better bit-error performance than conventional binary FSK for a given signal-to-noise ratio. The disadvantage of MSK is that it requires synchronizing circuits and is, therefore, more expensive to implement.

PHASE SHIFT KEYING

Phase shift keying (PSK) is another form of angle-modulated, constant-amplitude digital modulation. PSK is similar to conventional phase modulation except that with PSK the input signal is a binary digital signal and a limited number of output phases are possible.

Binary Phase Shift Keying

With *binary phase shift keying* (BPSK), two output phases are possible for a single carrier frequency ("binary" meaning "2"). One output phase represents a logic 1 and the other a logic 0. As the input digital signal changes state, the phase of the output carrier shifts between two angles that are 180° out of phase. Other names for BPSK are *phase reversal keying* (PRK) and *biphase modulation*. BPSK is a form of suppressed-carrier, square-wave modulation of a continuous wave (CW) signal.

BPSK transmitter. Figure 1-13 shows a simplified block diagram of a BPSK modulator. The balanced modulator acts as a phase reversing switch. Depending on the logic condition of the digital input, the carrier is transferred to the output either in phase or 180° out of phase with the reference carrier oscillator.

Figure 1-14a shows the schematic diagram of a balanced ring modulator. The balanced modulator has two inputs: a carrier that is in phase with the reference oscillator and the binary digital data. For the balanced modulator to operate properly, the digital input voltage must be much greater than the peak carrier voltage. This ensures that the

FIGURE 1-13 BPSK modulator

FIGURE 1-14 (a) Balanced ring modulator; (b) logic 1 input; (c) logic 0 input

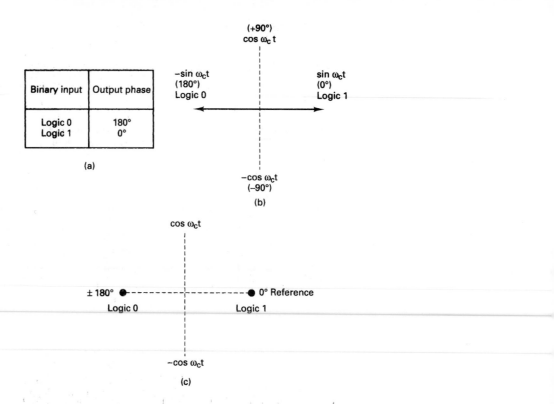

Binary input	Output phase
Logic 0 Logic 1	180° 0°

(a)

(b)

(c)

FIGURE 1-15 BPSK modulator: (a) truth table; (b) phasor diagram; (c) constellation diagram

digital input controls the on/off state of diodes D1–D4. If the binary input is a logic 1 (positive voltage), diodes D1 and D2 are forward biased and on, while diodes D3 and D4 are reverse biased and off (Figure 1-14b). With the polarities shown, the carrier voltage is developed across transformer T2 in phase with the carrier voltage across T1. Consequently, the output signal is in phase with the reference oscillator.

If the binary input is a logic 0 (negative voltage), diodes D1 and D2 are reverse biased and off, while diodes D3 and D4 are forward biased and on (Figure 1-14c). As a result, the carrier voltage is developed across transformer T2 180° out of phase with the carrier voltage across T1. Consequently, the output signal is 180° out of phase with the reference oscillator. Figure 1-15 shows the truth table, phasor diagram, and constellation diagram for a BPSK modulator. A *constellation diagram,* which is sometimes called a *signal state-space diagram,* is similar to a phasor diagram except that the entire phasor is not drawn. In a constellation diagram, only the relative positions of the peaks of the phasors are shown.

Bandwidth considerations of BPSK. A balanced modulator is a *product modulator;* the output signal is the product of the two input signals. In a BPSK modulator, the carrier input signal is multiplied by the binary data. If +1 V is assigned to a logic 1 and −1 V is assigned to a logic 0, the input carrier ($\sin \omega_c t$) is multiplied by either a + or −1. Consequently, the output signal is either + 1 $\sin \omega_c t$ or −1 $\sin \omega_c t$; the first represents a signal that is *in phase* with the reference oscillator, the latter a signal that is 180° out of phase with the reference oscillator. Each time the input logic condition changes, the output phase changes. Consequently, for BPSK, the output rate of change (baud) is equal to the input rate of change (bps), and the widest output bandwidth occurs when the input binary data are an alternating 1/0 sequence. The fundamental frequency (f_a) of an alternative 1/0 bit sequence is equal to one-half of the bit rate ($f_b/2$). Mathematically, the output phase of a BPSK modulator is

FIGURE 1-16 Output phase-versus-time relationship for a BPSK modulator

$$\text{output} = \underbrace{(\sin \omega_a t)}_{\substack{\text{fundamental frequency} \\ \text{of the binary} \\ \text{modulating signal}}} \times \underbrace{(\sin \omega_c t)}_{\substack{\text{unmodulated} \\ \text{carrier}}} \qquad (1\text{-}8)$$

or

$$\frac{1}{2} \cos(\omega_c - \omega_a)t - \frac{1}{2} \cos(\omega_c + \omega_a)t$$

Consequently, the minimum double-sided Nyquist bandwidth (f_N) is

$$\begin{array}{ccc} \omega_c + \omega_a & & \omega_c + \omega_a \\ -(\omega_c - \omega_a) & \text{or} & -\omega_c + \omega_a \\ \hline & & 2\omega_a \end{array}$$

and because $f_a = f_b/2$,

$$f_N = 2\left(\frac{f_b}{2}\right) = f_b$$

Figure 1-16 shows the output phase-versus-time relationship for a BPSK waveform. The output spectrum from a BPSK modulator is simply a double-sideband, suppressed-carrier signal where the upper and lower side frequencies are separated from the carrier frequency by a value equal to one-half of the bit rate. Consequently, the minimum bandwidth (f_N) required to pass the worst-case BPSK output signal is equal to the input bit rate.

Example 1-2

For a BPSK modulator with a carrier frequency of 70 MHz and an input bit rate of 10 Mbps, determine the maximum and minimum upper and lower side frequencies, draw the output spectrum, determine the minimum Nyquist bandwidth, and calculate the baud.

Solution Substituting into Equation 1-8 yields

$$\text{output} = (\sin \omega_a t)(\sin \omega_c t)$$
$$= [\sin 2\pi(5 \text{ MHz})t] [\sin 2\pi(70 \text{ MHz})t]$$
$$= \underbrace{\frac{1}{2} \cos 2\pi(70 \text{ MHz} - 5 \text{ MHz})t}_{\text{lower side frequency}} - \underbrace{\frac{1}{2} \cos 2\pi(70 \text{ MHz} + 5 \text{ MHz})t}_{\text{upper side frequency}}$$

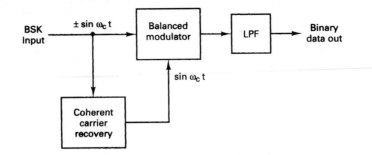

FIGURE 1-17 BPSK receiver

Minimum lower side frequency (LSF):

$$LSF = 70 \text{ MHz} - 5 \text{ MHz} = 65 \text{ MHz}$$

Maximum upper side frequency (USF):

$$USF = 70 \text{ MHz} + 5 \text{ MHz} = 75 \text{ MHz}$$

Therefore, the output spectrum for the worst-case binary input conditions is as follows:

(Suppressed)

The minimum Nyquist bandwidth (f_N) is

$$f_N = 75 \text{ MHz} - 65 \text{ MHz} = 10 \text{ MHz}$$

and the baud = f_b or 10 megabaud.

BPSK receiver. Figure 1-17 shows the block diagram of a BPSK receiver. The input signal may be $+\sin \omega_c t$ or $-\sin \omega_c t$. The coherent carrier recovery circuit detects and regenerates a carrier signal that is both frequency and phase coherent with the original transmit carrier. The balanced modulator is a product detector; the output is the product of the two inputs (the BPSK signal and the recovered carrier). The low-pass filter (LPF) separates the recovered binary data from the complex demodulated signal. Mathematically, the demodulation process is as follows.

For a BPSK input signal of $+\sin \omega_c t$ (logic 1), the output of the balanced modulator is

$$\text{output} = (\sin \omega_c t)(\sin \omega_c t) = \sin^2 \omega_c t \qquad (1\text{-}9)$$

(filtered out)

or

$$\sin^2 \omega_c t = \frac{1}{2}(1 - \cos 2\omega_c t) = \frac{1}{2} - \frac{1}{2} \cos 2\omega_c t$$

leaving

$$\text{output} = +\frac{1}{2} \text{V} = \text{logic 1}$$

It can be seen that the output of the balanced modulator contains a positive voltage [+(1/2)V] and a cosine wave at twice the carrier frequency ($2\omega_c$). The LPF has a cutoff frequency much lower than $2\omega_c$ and, thus, blocks the second harmonic of the carrier and passes only the positive constant component. A positive voltage represents a demodulated logic 1.

For a BPSK input signal of $-\sin \omega_c t$ (logic 0), the output of the balanced modulator is

$$\text{output} = (-\sin \omega_c t)(\sin \omega_c t) = -\sin^2 \omega_c t \qquad (1\text{-}10)$$

(filtered out)

or

$$-\sin^2 \omega_c t = -\frac{1}{2}(1 - \cos 2\omega_c t) = -\frac{1}{2} + \frac{1}{2}\cos 2\omega_c t$$

leaving

$$\text{output} = -\frac{1}{2}V = \text{logic } 0$$

The output of the balanced modulator contains a negative voltage [$-(1/2)V$] and a cosine wave at twice the carrier frequency ($2\omega_c$). Again, the LPF blocks the second harmonic of the carrier and passes only the negative constant component. A negative voltage represents a demodulated logic 0.

M-ary encoding. *M-ary* is a term derived from the word "binary." *M* is simply a digit that represents the number of conditions possible. The two digital modulation techniques discussed thus far (binary FSK and BPSK) are binary systems; there are only two possible output conditions. One represents a logic 1 and the other a logic 0; thus, they are *M*-ary systems where *M* = 2. With digital modulation, very often it is advantageous to encode at a level higher than binary. For example, a PSK system with four possible output phases is an *M*-ary system where *M* = 4. If there were eight possible output phases, *M* = 8, and so on. Mathematically,

$$N = \log_2 M \qquad (1\text{-}11)$$

where N = number of bits
         M = number of output conditions possible with N bits

For example, if 2 bits were allowed to enter a modulator before the output were allowed to change,

$$2 = \log_2 M \quad \text{and} \quad 2^2 = M \quad \text{thus,} \quad M = 4$$

An *M* = 4 indicates that with 2 bits, four different output conditions are possible. For *N* = 3, *M* = 2^3 or 8, and so on.

Quaternary Phase Shift Keying

Quaternary phase shift keying (QPSK), or *quadrature PSK* as it is sometimes called, is another form of angle-modulated, constant-amplitude digital modulation. QPSK is an *M*-ary encoding technique where *M* = 4 (hence, the name "quaternary," meaning "4"). With QPSK four output phases are possible for a single carrier frequency. Because there are four different output phases, there must be four different input conditions. Because the digital input to a QPSK modulator is a binary (base 2) signal, to produce four different input conditions, it takes more than a single input bit. With 2 bits, there are four possible conditions: 00, 01, 10, and 11. Therefore, with QPSK, the binary input data are combined into groups of 2 bits called *dibits*. Each dibit code generates one of the four possible output phases. Therefore, for each 2-bit dibit clocked into the modulator, a single output change occurs. Therefore, the rate of change at the output (baud rate) is one-half of the input bit rate.

QPSK transmitter. A block diagram of a QPSK modulator is shown in Figure 1-18. Two bits (a dibit) are clocked into the bit splitter. After both bits have been serially inputted, they are simultaneously parallel outputted. One bit is directed to the I channel and the other to the Q channel. The I bit modulates a carrier that is in phase with the reference oscillator (hence, the name "I" for "in phase" channel), and the Q bit modulates a carrier that is 90° out of phase or in quadrature with the reference carrier (hence, the name "Q" for "quadrature" channel).

FIGURE 1-18 QPSK modulator

It can be seen that once a dibit has been split into the I and Q channels, the operation is the same as in a BPSk modulator. Essentially, a QPSK modulator is two BPSK modulators combined in parallel. Again, for a logic 1 = +1 V and a logic 0 = −1 V, two phases are possible at the output of the I balanced modulator (+sin $\omega_c t$ and −sin $\omega_c t$), and two phases are possible at the output of the Q balanced modulator (+cos $\omega_c t$ and −cos $\omega_c t$). When the linear summer combines the two quadrature (90° out of phase) signals, there are four possible resultant phasors given by these expressions: +sin $\omega_c t$ + cos $\omega_c t$, +sin $\omega_c t$ − cos $\omega_c t$, −sin $\omega_c t$ + cos $\omega_c t$, and −sin $\omega_c t$ − cos $\omega_c t$.

Example 1-3

For the QPSK modulator shown in Figure 1-18, construct the truth table, phasor diagram, and constellation diagram.

Solution For a binary data input of Q = 0 and I = 0, the two inputs to the I balanced modulator are −1 and sin $\omega_c t$, and the two inputs to the Q balanced modulator are −1 and cos $\omega_c t$. Consequently, the outputs are

$$I \text{ balanced modulator} = (-1)(\sin \omega_c t) = -1 \sin \omega_c t$$

$$Q \text{ balanced modulator} = (-1)(\cos \omega_c t) = -1 \cos \omega_c t$$

and the output of the linear summer is

$$-1 \cos \omega_c t - 1 \sin \omega_c t = 1.414 \sin(\omega_c t - 135°)$$

For the remaining dibit codes (01, 10, and 11), the procedure is the same. The results are shown in Figure 1-19.

In Figure 1-19b it can be seen that with QPSK each of the four possible output phasors has exactly the same amplitude. Therefore, the binary information must be encoded entirely in the phase of the output signal. This constant amplitude characteristic is the most important characteristic of PSK that distinguishes it from QAM, which is explained later in this chapter. Also, from Figure 1-19b it can be seen that the angular separation between any two adjacent phasors in QPSK is 90°. Therefore, a QPSK signal

Binary input		QPSK output phase
Q	I	
0	0	−135°
0	1	−45°
1	0	+135°
1	1	+45°

(a)

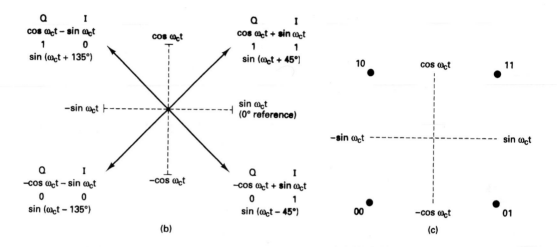

(b)

(c)

FIGURE 1-19 QPSK modulator: (a) truth table; (b) phasor diagram; (c) constellation diagram

FIGURE 1-20 Output phase-versus-time relationship for a QPSK modulator

can undergo almost a +45° or −45° shift in phase during transmission and still retain the correct encoded information when demodulated at the receiver. Figure 1-20 shows the output phase-versus-time relationship for a QPSK modulator.

Bandwidth considerations of QPSK. With QPSK, because the input data are divided into two channels, the bit rate in either the I or the Q channel is equal to one-half of the input data rate ($f_b/2$). (Essentially, the bit splitter stretches the I and Q bits to twice their input bit length.) Consequently, the highest fundamental frequency present at the data input to the I or the Q balanced modulator is equal to one-fourth of the input data rate (one-half of $f_b/2 = f_b/4$). As a result, the output of the I and Q balanced modulators requires a minimum double-sided Nyquist bandwidth equal to one-half of the incoming bit rate (f_N = twice $f_b/4 = f_b/2$). Thus, with QPSK, a bandwidth compression is realized (the minimum bandwidth is less than the incoming bit rate). Also, because the QPSK output signal does not change phase until 2 bits (a dibit) have been clocked into the bit

FIGURE 1-21 Bandwidth considerations of a QPSK modulator

splitter, the fastest output rate of change (baud) is also equal to one-half of the input bit rate. As with BPSK, the minimum bandwidth and the baud are equal. This relationship is shown in Figure 1-21.

In Figure 1-21 it can be seen that the worse-case input condition to the I or Q balanced modulator is an alternative 1/0 pattern, which occurs when the binary input data has a 1100 repetitive pattern. One cycle of the fastest binary transition (a 1/0 sequence) in the I or Q channel takes the same time as 4 input data bits. Consequently, the highest fundamental frequency at the input and fastest rate of change at the output of the balanced modulators is equal to one-fourth of the binary input bit rate.

The output of the balanced modulators can be expressed mathematically as

$$\text{output} = (\sin \omega_a t)(\sin \omega_c t)$$

where
$$\omega_a t = 2\pi \frac{f_b}{4} t \quad \text{and} \quad \omega_c t = 2\pi f_c t$$

$$\underbrace{\phantom{\omega_a t = 2\pi \frac{f_b}{4} t}}_{\substack{\text{modulating} \\ \text{phase}}} \qquad \underbrace{}_{\substack{\text{unmodulated} \\ \text{carrier phase}}}$$

Thus,
$$\text{output} = \left(\sin 2\pi \frac{f_b}{4} t\right)(\sin 2\pi f_c t)$$

$$\frac{1}{2} \cos 2\pi \left(f_c - \frac{f_b}{4}\right)t - \frac{1}{2} \cos 2\pi \left(f_c + \frac{f_b}{4}\right)t$$

The output frequency spectrum extends from $f_c + f_b/4$ to $f_c - f_b/4$ and the minimum bandwidth (f_N) is

$$\left(f_c + \frac{f_b}{4}\right) - \left(f_c - \frac{f_b}{4}\right) = \frac{2f_b}{4} = \frac{f_b}{2}$$

Example 1-4

For a QPSK modulator with an input data rate (f_b) equal to 10 Mbps and a carrier frequency of 70 MHz, determine the minimum double-sided Nyquist bandwidth (f_N) and the baud. Also, compare the results with those achieved with the BPSK modulator in Example 1-2. Use the QPSK block diagram shown in Figure 1-18 as the modulator model.

Solution   The bit rate in both the I and Q channels is equal to one-half of the transmission bit rate or

$$f_{bQ} = f_{bI} = \frac{f_b}{2} = \frac{10 \text{ Mbps}}{2} = 5 \text{ Mbps}$$

The highest fundamental frequency presented to either balanced modulator is

$$f_a = \frac{f_{bQ}}{2} \quad \text{or} \quad \frac{f_{bI}}{2} = \frac{5 \text{ Mbps}}{2} = 2.5 \text{ MHz}$$

The output wave from each balanced modulator is

$$(\sin 2\pi f_a t)(\sin 2\pi f_c t)$$

$$\frac{1}{2} \cos 2\pi (f_c - f_a)t - \frac{1}{2} \cos 2\pi (f_c + f_a)t$$

$$\frac{1}{2} \cos 2\pi [(70 - 2.5) \text{ MHz}]t - \frac{1}{2} \cos 2\pi [(70 + 2.5) \text{ MHz}]t$$

$$\frac{1}{2} \cos 2\pi (67.5 \text{ MHz})t - \frac{1}{2} \cos 2\pi (72.5 \text{ MHz})t$$

The minimum Nyquist bandwidth is

$$f_N = (72.5 - 67.5) \text{ MHz} = 5 \text{ MHz}$$

The symbol rate equals the bandwidth; thus,

$$\text{symbol rate} = 5 \text{ megabaud}$$

The output spectrum is as follows:

(Suppressed)

$$f_N = 5 \text{ MHz}$$

It can be seen that for the same input bit rate the minimum bandwidth required to pass the output of the QPSK modulator is equal to one-half of that required for the BPSK modulator in Example 1-2. Also, the baud rate for the QPSK modulator is one-half that of the BPSK modulator.

QPSK receiver.   The block diagram of a QPSK receiver is shown in Figure 1-22. The power splitter directs the input QPSK signal to the I and Q product detectors and the carrier recovery circuit. The carrier recovery circuit reproduces the original transmit carrier oscillator signal. The recovered carrier must be frequency and phase coherent with the transmit reference carrier. The QPSK signal is demodulated in the I and Q product detectors, which generate the original I and Q data bits. The outputs of the product detectors are fed to the bit combining circuit, where they are converted from parallel I and Q data channels to a single binary output data stream.

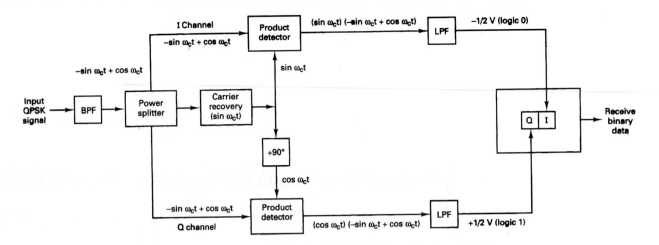

FIGURE 1-22 QPSK receiver

The incoming QPSK signal may be any one of the four possible output phases shown in Figure 1-19. To illustrate the demodulation process, let the incoming QPSK signal be $-\sin \omega_c t + \cos \omega_c t$. Mathematically, the demodulation process is as follows.

The receive QPSK signal $(-\sin \omega_c t + \cos \omega_c t)$ is one of the inputs to the I product detector. The other input is the recovered carrier $(\sin \omega_c t)$. The output of the I product detector is

$$I = \underbrace{(-\sin \omega_c t + \cos \omega_c t)}_{\text{QPSK input signal}} \underbrace{(\sin \omega_c t)}_{\text{carrier}}$$

$$= (-\sin \omega_c t)(\sin \omega_c t) + (\cos \omega_c t)(\sin \omega_c t)$$

$$= -\sin^2 \omega_c t + (\cos \omega_c t)(\sin \omega_c t)$$

$$= -\frac{1}{2}(1 - \cos 2\omega_c t) + \frac{1}{2}\sin(\omega_c + \omega_c)t + \frac{1}{2}\sin(\omega_c - \omega_c)t$$

$$\qquad\qquad\qquad\qquad \underset{\text{(filtered out)}}{} \qquad\qquad \underset{\text{(equals 0)}}{}$$

$$I = -\frac{1}{2} + \frac{1}{2}\cos 2\omega_c t + \frac{1}{2}\sin 2\omega_c t + \frac{1}{2}\sin 0$$

$$= -\frac{1}{2} \text{ V (logic 0)}$$

Again, the receive QPSK signal $(-\sin \omega_c t + \cos \omega_c t)$ is one of the inputs to the Q product detector. The other input is the recovered carrier shifted 90° in phase $(\cos \omega_c t)$. The output of the Q product detector is

$$Q = \underbrace{(-\sin \omega_c t + \cos \omega_c t)}_{\text{QPSK input signal}}\underbrace{(\cos \omega_c t)}_{\text{carrier}}$$

$$= \cos^2 \omega_c t - (\sin \omega_c t)(\cos \omega_c t)$$

$$= \frac{1}{2}(1 + \cos 2\omega_c t) - \frac{1}{2}\sin(\omega_c + \omega_c)t - \frac{1}{2}\sin(\omega_c - \omega_c)t$$

$$\qquad\qquad\qquad\qquad \underset{\text{(filtered out)}}{} \qquad\qquad \underset{\text{(equals 0)}}{}$$

$$Q = \frac{1}{2} + \frac{1}{2}\cos 2\omega_c t - \frac{1}{2}\sin 2\omega_c t - \frac{1}{2}\sin 0$$

$$= \frac{1}{2} \text{ V (logic 1)}$$

Chapter 1   Digital Communications

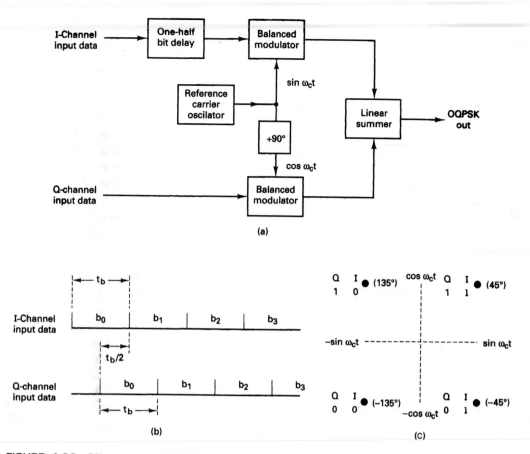

FIGURE 1-23 Offset keyed (OQPSK): (a) block diagram; (b) bit alignment; (c) constellation diagram

The demodulated I and Q bits (0 and 1, respectively) correspond to the constellation diagram and truth table for the QPSK modulator shown in Figure 1-19.

Offset QPSK. *Offset QPSK* (OQPSK) is a modified form of QPSK where the bit waveforms on the I and Q channels are offset or shifted in phase from each other by one-half of a bit time.

Figure 1-23 shows a simplified block diagram, the bit sequence alignment, and the constellation diagram for a OQPSK modulator. Because changes in the I channel occur at the midpoints of the Q-channel bits, and vice versa, there is never more than a single bit change in the dibit code, and therefore, there is never more than a 90° shift in the output phase. In conventional QPSK, a change in the input dibit from 00 to 11 or 01 to 10 causes a corresponding 180° shift in the output phase. Therefore, an advantage of OQPSK is the limited phase shift that must be imparted during modulation. A disadvantage of OQPSK is that changes in the output phase occur at twice the data rate in either the I or Q channels. Consequently, with OQPSK the baud and minimum bandwidth are twice that of conventional QPSK for a given transmission bit rate. OQPSK is sometimes called OKQPSK (*offset-keyed QPSK*).

Eight-Phase PSK

Eight-phase PSK (8-PSK) is an *M*-ary encoding technique where *M* = 8. With an 8-PSK modulator, there are eight possible output phases. To encode eight different phases, the incoming bits are considered in groups of 3 bits, called *tribits* (2^3 = 8).

FIGURE 1-24 8-PSK modulator

I	C	Output
0	0	−0.541 V
0	1	−1.307 V
1	0	+0.541 V
1	1	+1.307 V

Q	C̄	Output
0	1	−1.307 V
0	0	−0.541 V
1	1	+1.307 V
1	0	+0.541 V

+1.307 V
+0.541 V
0 V
−0.541 V
−1.307 V

(a)   (b)   (c)

FIGURE 1-25 I- and Q-channel 2-to-4-level converters: (a) I-channel truth table; (b) Q-channel truth table; (c) PAM levels

8-PSK transmitter. A block diagram of an 8-PSK modulator is shown in Figure 1-24. The incoming serial bit stream enters the bit splitter, where it is converted to a parallel, three-channel output (the I or in-phase channel, the Q or in-quadrature channel, and the C or control channel). Consequently, the bit rate in each of the three channels is $f_b/3$. The bits in the I and C channels enter the I channel 2-to-4-level converter, and the bits in the Q and C̄ channels enter the Q channel 2-to-4-level converter. Essentially, the 2-to-4-level converters are parallel-input *digital-to-analog converters* (DACs). With 2 input bits, four output voltages are possible. The algorithm for the DACs is quite simple. The I or Q bit determines the polarity of the output analog signal (logic 1 = +V and logic 0 = −V), whereas the C or C̄ bit determines the magnitude (logic 1 = 1.307 V and logic 0 = 0.541 V). Consequently, with two magnitudes and two polarities, four different output conditions are possible.

Figure 1-25 shows the truth table and corresponding output conditions for the 2-to-4-level converters. Because the C and C̄ bits can never be the same logic state, the outputs from the I and Q 2-to-4-level converters can never have the same magnitude, although they can have the same polarity. The output of a 2-to-4-level converter is an *M*-ary, *pulse-amplitude-modulated* (PAM) signal where *M* = 4.

Example 1-5

For a tribit input of Q = 0, I = 0, and C = 0 (000), determine the output phase for the 8-PSK modulator shown in Figure 1-24.

Solution The inputs to the I channel 2-to-4-level converter are I = 0 and C = 0. From Figure 1-25 the output is −0.541 V. The inputs to the Q channel 2-to-4-level converter are Q = 0 and $\overline{C}$ = 1. Again from Figure 1-25, the output is −1.307 V.

Thus, the two inputs to the I channel product modulators are −0.541 and sin $\omega_c t$. The output is

$$I = (−0.541)(\sin \omega_c t) = −0.541 \sin \omega_c t$$

The two inputs to the Q channel product modulator are −1.307 V and cos $\omega_c t$. The output is

$$Q = (−1.307)(\cos \omega_c t) = −1.307 \cos \omega_c t$$

The outputs of the I and Q channel product modulators are combined in the linear summer and produce a modulated output of

$$\text{summer output} = −0.541 \sin \omega_c t − 1.307 \cos \omega_c t$$
$$= 1.41 \sin(\omega_c t − 112.5°)$$

For the remaining tribit codes (001, 010, 011, 100, 101, 110, and 111), the procedure is the same. The results are shown in Figure 1-26.

From Figure 1-26 it can be seen that the angular separation between any two adjacent phasors is 45°, half what it is with QPSK. Therefore, an 8-PSK signal can undergo almost a ±22.5° phase shift during transmission and still retain its integrity. Also, each phasor is of equal magnitude; the tribit condition (actual information) is again contained only in the phase of the signal. The PAM levels of 1.307 and 0.541 are relative values. Any levels may be used as long as their ratio is 0.541/1.307 and their arc tangent is equal to 22.5°. For example, if their values were doubled to 2.614 and 1.082, the resulting phase angles would not change, although the magnitude of the phasor would increase proportionally.

It should also be noted that the tribit code between any two adjacent phases changes by only one bit. This type of code is called the *Gray code* or, sometimes, the *maximum distance code*. This code is used to reduce the number of transmission errors. If a signal were to undergo a phase shift during transmission, it would most likely be shifted to an adjacent phasor. Using the Gray code results in only a single bit being received in error.

Figure 1-27 shows the output phase-versus-time relationship of an 8-PSK modulator.

Bandwidth considerations of 8-PSK. With 8-PSK, because the data are divided into three channels, the bit rate in the I, Q, or C channel is equal to one-third of the binary input data rate ($f_b/3$). (The bit splitter stretches the I, Q, and C bits to three times their input bit length.) Because the I, Q, and C bits are outputted simultaneously and in parallel, the 2-to-4-level converters also see a change in their inputs (and consequently their outputs) at a rate equal to $f_b/3$.

Figure 1-28 shows the bit timing relationship between the binary input data; the I, Q, and C channel data; and the I and Q PAM signals. It can be seen that the highest fundamental frequency in the I, Q, or C channel is equal to one-sixth of the bit rate of the binary input (one cycle in the I, Q, or C channel takes the same amount of time as six input bits). Also the highest fundamental frequency in either PAM signal is equal to one-sixth of the binary input bit rate.

With an 8-PSK modulator, there is one change in phase at the output for every 3 data input bits. Consequently, the baud for 8-PSK equals $f_b/3$, the same as the minimum bandwidth. Again, the balanced modulators are product modulators; their outputs are the product of the carrier and the PAM signal. Mathematically, the output of the balanced modulators is

$$\theta = (X \sin \omega_a t)(\sin \omega_c t) \qquad (1-12)$$

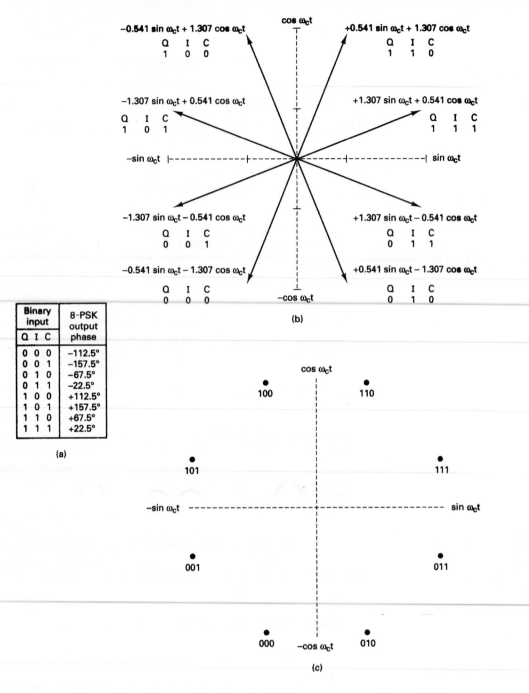

Binary input	8-PSK output phase
Q I C	
0 0 0	−112.5°
0 0 1	−157.5°
0 1 0	−67.5°
0 1 1	−22.5°
1 0 0	+112.5°
1 0 1	+157.5°
1 1 0	+67.5°
1 1 1	+22.5°

(a)

FIGURE 1-26 8-PSK modulator: (a) truth table; (b) phasor diagram; (c) constellation diagram

| Tribit input | QIC 000 | QIC 001 | QIC 010 | QIC 011 | QIC 100 | QIC 101 | QIC 110 | QIC 111 |

8-PSK output phase

−112.5°   −157.5°   −67.5°   −22.5°   +112.5°   +157.5°   +67.5°   +22.5°

FIGURE 1-27 Output phase-versus-time relationship for an 8-PSK modulator

FIGURE 1-28 Bandwidth considerations of an 8-PSK modulator

where
$$\omega_a t = 2\pi \frac{f_b}{6} t \quad \text{and} \quad \omega_c t = 2\pi f_c t$$

$\underbrace{\qquad\qquad\qquad}_{\text{modulating signal}} \quad \underbrace{\qquad\qquad}_{\text{carrier}}$

and
$$X = \pm 1.307 \quad \text{or} \quad \pm 0.541$$

Thus,
$$\theta = \left(X \sin 2\pi \frac{f_b}{6} t \right)(\sin 2\pi f_c t)$$

$$= \frac{X}{2} \cos 2\pi \left(f_c - \frac{f_b}{6} \right)t - \frac{X}{2} \cos 2\pi \left(f_c + \frac{f_b}{6} \right)t$$

The output frequency spectrum extends from $f_c + f_b/6$ to $f_c - f_b/6$ and the minimum bandwidth (f_N) is

$$\left(f_c + \frac{f_b}{6} \right) - \left(f_c - \frac{f_b}{6} \right) = \frac{2f_b}{6} = \frac{f_b}{3}$$

Example 1-6

For an 8-PSK modulator with an input data rate (f_b) equal to 10 Mbps and a carrier frequency of 70 MHz, determine the minimum double-sided Nyquist bandwidth (f_N) and the baud. Also, compare the results with those achieved with the BPSK and QPSK modulators in Examples 1-2 and 1-4. Use the 8-PSK block diagram shown in Figure 1-24 as the modulator model.

Solution   The bit rate in the I, Q, and C channels is equal to one-third of the input bit rate, or

$$f_{bC} = f_{bQ} = f_{bI} = \frac{10 \text{ Mbps}}{3} = 3.33 \text{ Mbps}$$

Therefore, the fastest rate of change and highest fundamental frequency presented to either balanced modulator is

$$f_a = \frac{f_{bC}}{2} \quad \text{or} \quad \frac{f_{bQ}}{2} \quad \text{or} \quad \frac{f_{bI}}{2} = \frac{3.33 \text{ Mbps}}{2} = 1.667 \text{ Mbps}$$

The output wave from the balance modulators is

$$(\sin 2\pi f_a t)(\sin 2\pi f_c t)$$

$$\frac{1}{2} \cos 2\pi(f_c - f_a)t - \frac{1}{2} \cos 2\pi(f_c + f_a)t$$

$$\frac{1}{2} \cos 2\pi[(70 - 1.667) \text{ MHz}]t - \frac{1}{2} \cos 2\pi[(70 + 1.667) \text{ MHz}]t$$

$$\frac{1}{2} \cos 2\pi(68.333 \text{ MHz})t - \frac{1}{2} \cos 2\pi(71.667 \text{ MHz})t$$

The minimum Nyquist bandwidth is

$$f_N = (71.667 - 68.333) \text{ MHz} = 3.333 \text{ MHz}$$

Again, the baud equals the bandwidth; thus,

$$\text{baud} = 3.333 \text{ megabaud}$$

The output spectrum is as follows:

(Suppressed)

$$f_N = 3.333 \text{ MHz}$$

It can be seen that for the same input bit rate the minimum bandwidth required to pass the output of an 8-PSK modulator is equal to one-third that of the BPSK modulator in Example 1-2 and 50% less than that required for the QPSK modulator in Example 1-4. Also, in each case the baud has been reduced by the same proportions.

   8-PSK receiver.   Figure 1-29 shows a block diagram of an 8-PSK receiver. The power splitter directs the input 8-PSK signal to the I and Q product detectors and the carrier recovery circuit. The carrier recovery circuit reproduces the original reference oscillator signal. The incoming 8-PSK signal is mixed with the recovered carrier in the I product detector and with a quadrature carrier in the Q product detector. The outputs of the product detectors are 4-level PAM signals that are fed to the 4-to-2-level *analog-to-digital converters* (ADCs). The outputs from the I channel 4-to-2-level converter are the I and C bits, whereas the outputs from the Q channel 4-to-2-level converter are the Q and $\overline{C}$ bits. The parallel-to-serial logic circuit converts the I/C and Q/$\overline{C}$ bit pairs to serial I, Q, and C output data streams.

FIGURE 1-29 8-PSK receiver

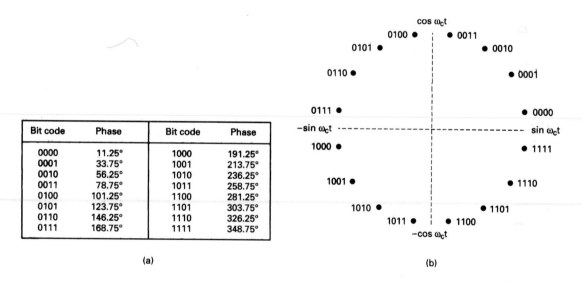

Bit code	Phase	Bit code	Phase
0000	11.25°	1000	191.25°
0001	33.75°	1001	213.75°
0010	56.25°	1010	236.25°
0011	78.75°	1011	258.75°
0100	101.25°	1100	281.25°
0101	123.75°	1101	303.75°
0110	146.25°	1110	326.25°
0111	168.75°	1111	348.75°

(a)   (b)

FIGURE 1-30 16-PSK: (a) truth table; (b) constellation diagram

Sixteen-Phase PSK

Sixteen-phase PSK (16-PSK) is an *M*-ary encoding technique where $M = 16$; there are 16 different output phases possible. A 16-PSK modulator acts on the incoming data in groups of 4 bits ($2^4 = 16$), called *quadbits*. The output phase does not change until 4 bits have been inputted into the modulator. Therefore, the output rate of change (baud) and the minimum bandwidth are equal to one-fourth of the incoming bit rate ($f_b/4$). The truth table and constellation diagram for a 16-PSK transmitter are shown in Figure 1-30.

With 16-PSK, the angular separation between adjacent output phases is only 22.5°. Therefore, a 16-PSK signal can undergo almost a ±11.25° phase shift during transmission and still retain its integrity. Because of this, 16-PSK is highly susceptible to phase impairments introduced in the transmission medium and is, therefore, seldom used.

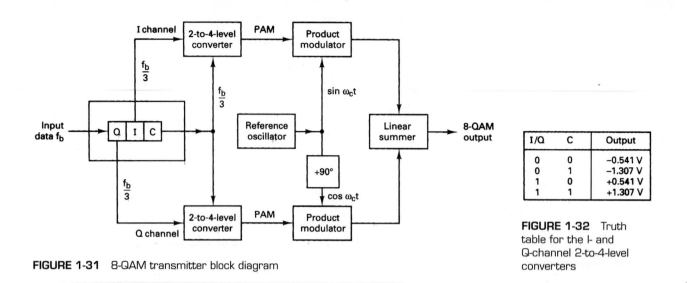

FIGURE 1-31 8-QAM transmitter block diagram

I/Q	C	Output
0	0	−0.541 V
0	1	−1.307 V
1	0	+0.541 V
1	1	+1.307 V

FIGURE 1-32 Truth table for the I- and Q-channel 2-to-4-level converters

QUADRATURE AMPLITUDE MODULATION

Quadrature amplitude modulation (QAM) is a form of digital modulation where the digital information is contained in both the amplitude and phase of the transmitted carrier.

Eight QAM

Eight QAM (8-QAM) is an *M*-ary encoding technique where *M* = 8. Unlike 8-PSK, the output signal from an 8-QAM modulator is not a constant-amplitude signal.

8-QAM transmitter. Figure 1-31 shows the block diagram of an 8-QAM transmitter. As you can see, the only difference between the 8-QAM transmitter and the 8-PSK transmitter shown in Figure 1-24 is the omission of the inverter between the C channel and the Q product modulator. As with 8-PSK, the incoming data are divided into groups of three bits (tribits): the I, Q, and C bit streams, each with a bit rate equal to one-third of the incoming data rate. Again, the I and Q bits determine the polarity of the PAM signal at the output of the 2-to-4-level converters, and the C channel determines the magnitude. Because the C bit is fed uninverted to both the I and Q channel 2-to-4-level converters, the magnitudes of the I and Q PAM signals are always equal. Their polarities depend on the logic condition of the I and Q bits and, therefore, may be different. Figure 1-32 shows the truth table for the I and Q channel 2-to-4-level converters; they are identical.

Example 1-7

For a tribit input of Q = 0, I = 0, and C = 0 (000), determine the output amplitude and phase for the 8-QAM transmitter shown in Figure 1-31.

Solution The inputs to the I channel 2-to-4-level converter are I = 0 and C = 0. From Figure 1-32 the output is −0.541 V. The inputs to the Q channel 2-to-4-level converter are Q = 0 and C = 0. Again from Figure 1-32, the output is −0.541 V.

Thus, the two inputs to the I channel product modulator are −0.541 and sin $\omega_c t$. The output is

$$I = (-0.541)(\sin \omega_c t) = -0.541 \sin \omega_c t$$

The two inputs to the Q channel product modulator are −0.541 and cos $\omega_c t$. The output is

$$Q = (-0.541)(\cos \omega_c t) = -0.541 \cos \omega_c t$$

The outputs from the I and Q channel product modulators are combined in the linear summer and produce a modulated output of

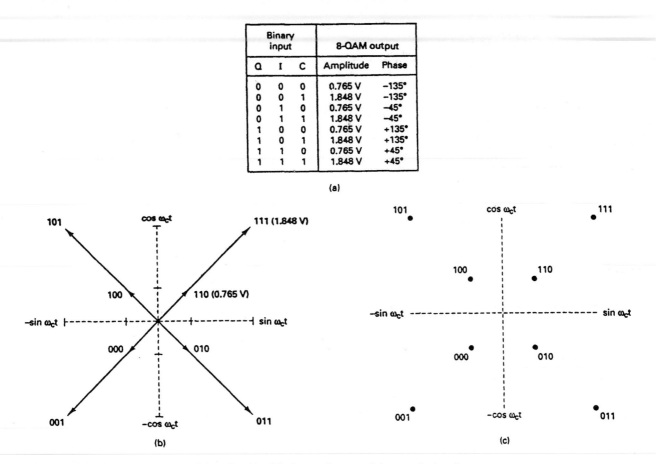

Binary input			8-QAM output	
Q	I	C	Amplitude	Phase
0	0	0	0.765 V	−135°
0	0	1	1.848 V	−135°
0	1	0	0.765 V	−45°
0	1	1	1.848 V	−45°
1	0	0	0.765 V	+135°
1	0	1	1.848 V	+135°
1	1	0	0.765 V	+45°
1	1	1	1.848 V	+45°

(a)

(b)

(c)

FIGURE 1-33 8-QAM modulator: (a) truth table; (b) phasor diagram; (c) constellation diagram

$$\text{summer output} = -0.541 \sin \omega_c t - 0.541 \cos \omega_c t$$
$$= 0.765 \sin(\omega_c t - 135°)$$

For the remaining tribit codes (001, 010, 011, 100, 101, 110, and 111), the procedure is the same. The results are shown in Figure 1-33.

Figure 1-34 shows the output phase-versus-time relationship for an 8-QAM modulator. Note that there are two output amplitudes and only four phases are possible.

Bandwidth considerations of 8-QAM. In 8-QAM, the bit rate in the I and Q channels is one-third of the input binary rate, the same as in 8-PSK. As a result, the highest fundamental modulating frequency and fastest output rate of change in 8-QAM are the same as with 8-PSK. Therefore, the minimum bandwidth required for 8-QAM is $f_b/3$, the same as in 8-PSK.

8-QAM receiver. An 8-QAM receiver is almost identical to the 8-PSK receiver shown in Figure 1-29. The differences are the PAM levels at the output of the product detectors and the binary signals at the output of the analog-to-digital converters. Because there are two transmit amplitudes possible with 8-QAM that are different from those

FIGURE 1-34   Output phase and amplitude-versus-time relationship for 8-QAM

FIGURE 1-35   16-QAM transmitter block diagram

achievable with 8-PSK, the four demodulated PAM levels in 8-QAM are different from those in 8-PSK. Therefore, the conversion factor for the analog-to-digital converters must also be different. Also, with 8-QAM the binary output signals from the I channel analog-to-digital converter are the I and C bits, and the binary output signals from the Q channel analog-to-digital converter are the Q and C bits.

Sixteen QAM

As with the 16-PSK, 16-QAM is an M-ary system where $M = 16$. The input data are acted on in groups of four ($2^4 = 16$). As with 8-QAM, both the phase and amplitude of the transmit carrier are varied.

16-QAM transmitter.   The block diagram for a 16-QAM transmitter is shown in Figure 1-35. The input binary data are divided into four channels: The I, I', Q, and Q'. The bit rate in each channel is equal to one-fourth of the input bit rate ($f_b/4$). Four bits are serially clocked into the bit splitter; then they are outputted simultaneously and in parallel with the I, I', Q, and Q' channels. The I and Q bits determine the polarity at the output of the 2-to-4-level converters (a logic 1 = positive and a logic 0 = negative). The I' and Q' bits determine the magnitude (a logic 1 = 0.821 V and a logic 0 = 0.22 V). Consequently, the 2-to-4-level converters generate a 4-level PAM signal. Two polarities and two magnitudes are possible at the output of each 2-to-4-level converter. They are ±0.22 V and ±0.821 V. The PAM signals modulate the in phase and quadrature carriers in the product modulators. Four outputs are possible for each product modulator. For the I product modulator they are +0.821 sin $\omega_c t$, −0.821 sin $\omega_c t$, +0.22 sin $\omega_c t$, and −0.22 sin $\omega_c t$. For the Q product modulator they are +0.821 cos $\omega_c t$, +0.22 cos $\omega_c t$, −0.821 cos $\omega_c t$, and −0.22 cos $\omega_c t$. The linear summer combines the outputs from the I and Q channel

I	I′	Output
0	0	−0.22 V
0	1	−0.821 V
1	0	+0.22 V
1	1	+0.821 V

Q	Q′	Output
0	0	−0.22 V
0	1	−0.821 V
1	0	+0.22 V
1	1	+0.821 V

FIGURE 1-36 Truth tables for the I- and Q-channel 2-to-4 level converters; (a) I channel; (b) Q channel

product modulators and produces the 16 output conditions necessary for 16-QAM. Figure 1-36 shows the truth table for the I and Q channel 2-to-4-level converters.

Example 1-8

For a quadbit input of I = 0, I′ = 0, Q = 0, and Q′ = 0 (0000), determine the output amplitude and phase for the 16-QAM modulator shown in Figure 1-35.

Solution The inputs to the I channel 2-to-4-level converter are I = 0 and I′ = 0. From Figure 1-36 the output is −0.22 V. The inputs to the Q channel 2-to-4-level converter are Q = 0 and Q′ = 0. Again from Figure 1-36, the output is −0.22 V.

Thus, the two inputs to the I channel product modulator are −0.22 V and $\sin \omega_c t$. The output is

$$I = (-0.22)(\sin \omega_c t) = -0.22 \sin \omega_c t$$

The two inputs to the Q channel product modulator are −0.22 V and $\cos \omega_c t$. The output is

$$Q = (-0.22)(\cos \omega_c t) = -0.22 \cos \omega_c t$$

The outputs from the I and Q channel product modulators are combined in the linear summer and produce a modulated output of

$$\text{summer output} = -0.22 \sin \omega_c t - 0.22 \cos \omega_c t$$
$$= 0.311 \sin(\omega_c t - 135°)$$

For the remaining quadbit codes the procedure is the same. The results are shown in Figure 1-37.

Bandwidth considerations of 16-QAM. With 16-QAM, because the input data are divided into four channels, the bit rate in the I, I′, Q, or Q′ channel is equal to one-fourth of the binary input data rate ($f_b/4$). (The bit splitter stretches the I, I′, Q, and Q′ bits to four times their input bit length.) Also, because the I, I′, Q, and Q′ bits are outputted simultaneously and in parallel, the 2-to-4-level converters see a change in their inputs and outputs at a rate equal to one-fourth of the input data rate.

Figure 1-38 shows the bit timing relationship between the binary input data; the I, I′, Q, and Q′ channel data; and the I PAM signal. It can be seen that the highest fundamental frequency in the I, I′, Q, or Q′ channel is equal to one-eighth of the bit rate of the binary input data (one cycle in the I, I′, Q, or Q′ channel takes the same amount of time as 8 input bits). Also, the highest fundamental frequency of either PAM signal is equal to one-eighth of the binary input bit rate.

With a 16-QAM modulator, there is one change in the output signal (either its phase, amplitude, or both) for every 4 input data bits. Consequently, the baud equals $f_b/4$, the same as the minimum bandwidth.

Again, the balanced modulators are product modulators and their outputs can be represented mathematically as

$$\text{output} = (X \sin \omega_a t)(\sin \omega_c t) \tag{1-13}$$

where

$$\omega_a t = 2\pi \frac{f_b}{8} t \quad \text{and} \quad \omega_c t = 2\pi f_c t$$

modulating signal phase   carrier phase

Binary input				16-QAM output
Q	Q′	I	I′	
0	0	0	0	0.311 V −135°
0	0	0	1	0.850 V −165°
0	0	1	0	0.311 V −45°
0	0	1	1	0.850 V −15°
0	1	0	0	0.850 V −105°
0	1	0	1	1.161 V −135°
0	1	1	0	0.850 V −75°
0	1	1	1	1.161 V −45°
1	0	0	0	0.311 V 135°
1	0	0	1	0.850 V 165°
1	0	1	0	0.311 V 45°
1	0	1	1	0.850 V 15°
1	1	0	0	0.850 V 105°
1	1	0	1	1.161 V 135°
1	1	1	0	0.850 V 75°
1	1	1	1	1.161 V 45°

(a)

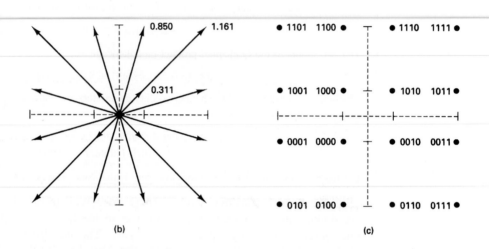

(b)   (c)

FIGURE 1-37 16-QAM modulator: (a) truth table; (b) phasor diagram; (c) constellation diagram

and $\qquad\qquad X = \pm 0.22 \quad \text{or} \quad \pm 0.821$

Thus, $\qquad\qquad \text{output} = \left(X \sin 2\,\pi \frac{f_b}{8}\,t \right)(\sin 2\pi f_c t)$

$$= \frac{X}{2} \cos 2\pi \left(f_c - \frac{f_b}{8} \right)t - \frac{X}{2} \cos 2\pi \left(f_c + \frac{f_b}{8} \right)t$$

The output frequency spectrum extends from $f_c + f_b/8$ to $f_c - f_b/8$ and the minimum bandwidth (f_N) is

$$\left(f_c + \frac{f_b}{8} \right) - \left(f_c - \frac{f_b}{8} \right) = \frac{2f_b}{8} = \frac{f_b}{4}$$

Example 1-9

For a 16-QAM modulator with an input data rate (f_b) equal to 10 Mbps and a carrier frequency of 70 MHz, determine the minimum double-sided Nyquist frequency (f_N) and the baud. Also, compare the results with those achieved with the BPSK, QPSK, and 8-PSK modulators in Examples 1-2, 1-4, and 1-6. Use the 16-QAM block diagram shown in Figure 1-35 as the modulator model.

FIGURE 1-38 Bandwidth considerations of a 16-QAM modulator

Solution The bit rate in the I, I′, Q, and Q′ channels is equal to one-fourth of the input bit rate or

$$f_{bI} = f_{bI'} = f_{bQ} = f_{bQ'} = \frac{f_b}{4} = \frac{10 \text{ Mbps}}{4} = 2.5 \text{ Mbps}$$

Therefore, the fastest rate of change and highest fundamental frequency presented to either balanced modulator is

$$f_a = \frac{f_{bI}}{2} \quad \text{or} \quad \frac{f_{bI'}}{2} \quad \text{or} \quad \frac{f_{bQ}}{2} \quad \text{or} \quad \frac{f_{bQ'}}{2} = \frac{2.5 \text{ Mbps}}{2} = 1.25 \text{ MHz}$$

The output wave from the balanced modulator is

$$(\sin 2\pi f_a t)(\sin 2\pi f_c t)$$

$$\frac{1}{2} \cos 2\pi (f_c - f_a)t - \frac{1}{2} \cos 2\pi (f_c + f_a)t$$

$$\frac{1}{2} \cos 2\pi [(70 - 1.25) \text{ MHz}]t - \frac{1}{2} \cos 2\pi [(70 + 1.25) \text{ MHz}]t$$

$$\frac{1}{2} \cos 2\pi (68.75 \text{ MHz})t - \frac{1}{2} \cos 2\pi (71.25 \text{ MHz})t$$

Quadrature Amplitude Modulation

The minimum Nyquist bandwidth is

$$f_N = (71.25 - 68.75) \text{ MHz} = 2.5 \text{ MHz}$$

The symbol rate equals the bandwidth; thus,

$$\text{symbol rate} = 2.5 \text{ megabaud}$$

The output spectrum is as follows:

(Suppressed)

$$f_N = 2.5 \text{ MHz}$$

For the same input bit rate, the minimum bandwidth required to pass the output of a 16-QAM modulator is equal to one-fourth that of the BPSK modulator, one-half that of QPSK, and 25% less than with 8-PSK. For each modulation technique, the baud is also reduced by the same proportions.

BANDWIDTH EFFICIENCY

Bandwidth efficiency (or *information density* as it is sometimes called) is often used to compare the performance of one digital modulation technique to another. In essence, it is the ratio of the transmission bit rate to the minimum bandwidth required for a particular modulation scheme. Bandwidth efficiency generally is normalized to a 1-Hz bandwidth and, thus, indicates the number of bits that can be propagated through a medium for each hertz of bandwidth. Mathematically, bandwidth efficiency is

$$\text{BW efficiency} = \frac{\text{transmission rate (bps)}}{\text{minimum bandwidth (Hz)}} \qquad (1\text{-}14)$$

$$= \frac{\text{bits/second}}{\text{hertz}} = \frac{\text{bits/second}}{\text{cycles/second}} = \frac{\text{bits}}{\text{cycle}}$$

Example 1-10

Determine the bandwidth efficiencies for the following modulation schemes: BPSK, QPSK, 8-PSK, and 16-QAM.

Solution Recall from Examples 1-2, 1-4, 1-6, and 1-9 the minimum bandwidths required to propagate a 10-Mbps transmission rate with the following modulation schemes:

Modulation Scheme	Minimum Bandwidth (MHz)
BPSK	10
QPSK	5
8-PSK	3.33
16-QAM	2.5

Substituting into Equation 1-14, the bandwidth efficiencies are determined as follows:

$$\text{BPSK:} \quad \text{BW efficiency} = \frac{10 \text{ Mbps}}{10 \text{ MHz}} = \frac{1 \text{ bps}}{\text{Hz}} = \frac{1 \text{ bit}}{\text{cycle}}$$

$$\text{QPSK:} \quad \text{BW efficiency} = \frac{10 \text{ Mbps}}{5 \text{ MHz}} = \frac{2 \text{ bps}}{\text{Hz}} = \frac{2 \text{ bits}}{\text{cycle}}$$

TABLE 1-1 Digital Modulation Summary

Modulation	Encoding	Bandwidth (Hz)	Baud	Bandwidth Efficiency (bps/Hz)
FSK	Single bit	$\geq f_b$	f_b	≤ 1
BPSK	Single bit	f_b	f_b	1
QPSK	Dibit	$f_b/2$	$f_b/2$	2
8-PSK	Tribit	$f_b/3$	$f_b/3$	3
8-QAM	Tribit	$f_b/3$	$f_b/3$	3
16-PSK	Quadbit	$f_b/4$	$f_b/4$	4
16-QAM	Quadbit	$f_b/4$	$f_b/4$	4

$$8\text{-PSK:} \quad \text{BW efficiency} = \frac{10 \text{ Mbps}}{3.33 \text{ MHz}} = \frac{3 \text{ bps}}{\text{Hz}} = \frac{3 \text{ bits}}{\text{cycle}}$$

$$16\text{-QAM:} \quad \text{BW efficiency} = \frac{10 \text{ Mbps}}{2.5 \text{ MHz}} = \frac{4 \text{ bps}}{\text{Hz}} = \frac{4 \text{ bits}}{\text{cycle}}$$

The results indicate that BPSK is the least efficient and 16-QAM is the most efficient. 16-QAM requires one-fourth as much bandwidth as BPSK for the same input bit rate.

The various forms of FSK, PSK, and QAM are summarized in Table 1-1.

CARRIER RECOVERY

Carrier recovery is the process of extracting a phase-coherent reference carrier from a receiver signal. This is sometimes called *phase referencing.*

In the phase modulation techniques described thus far, the binary data were encoded as a precise phase of the transmitted carrier. (This is referred to as *absolute phase encoding.*) Depending on the encoding method, the angular separation between adjacent phasors varied between 30° and 180°. To correctly demodulate the data, a phase-coherent carrier was recovered and compared with the received carrier in a product detector. To determine the absolute phase of the received carrier, it is necessary to produce a carrier at the receiver that is phase coherent with the transmit reference oscillator. This is the function of the carrier recovery circuit.

With PSK and QAM, the carrier is suppressed in the balanced modulators and, therefore, is not transmitted. Consequently, at the receiver the carrier cannot simply be tracked with a standard phase-locked loop. With suppressed-carrier systems, such as PSK and QAM, sophisticated methods of carrier recovery are required such as a *squaring loop,* a *Costas loop,* or a *remodulator.*

Squaring Loop

A common method of achieving carrier recovery for BPSK is the *squaring loop.* Figure 1-39 shows the block diagram of a squaring loop. The received BPSK waveform is filtered and then squared. The filtering reduces the spectral width of the received noise. The squaring circuit removes the modulation and generates the second harmonic of the carrier frequency. This harmonic is phase tracked by the PLL. The VCO output frequency from the PLL then is divided by 2 and used as the phase reference for the product detectors.

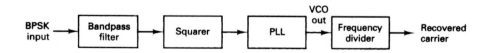

FIGURE 1-39 Squaring loop carrier recovery circuit for a BPSK receiver

FIGURE 1-40 Costas loop carrier recovery circuit

With BPSK, only two output phases are possible: $+\sin \omega_c t$ and $-\sin \omega_c t$. Mathematically, the operation of the squaring circuit can be described as follows. For a receive signal of $+\sin \omega_c t$ the output of the squaring circuit is

$$\text{output} = (+\sin \omega_c t)(+\sin \omega_c t) = +\sin^2 \omega_c t$$

$$= \frac{1}{2}(1 - \cos 2\omega_c t) = \frac{1}{2} - \frac{1}{2}\cos 2\omega_c t$$

For a received signal of $-\sin \omega_c t$ the output of the squaring circuit is

$$\text{output} = (-\sin \omega_c t)(-\sin \omega_c t) = +\sin^2 \omega_c t$$

$$= \frac{1}{2}(1 - \cos 2\omega_c t) = \frac{1}{2} - \frac{1}{2}\cos 2\omega_c t$$

It can be seen that in both cases the output from the squaring circuit contained a constant voltage (+1/2 V) and a signal at twice the carrier frequency ($\cos 2\omega_c t$). The constant voltage is removed by filtering, leaving only $\cos 2\omega_c t$.

Costas Loop

A second method of carrier recovery is the Costas, or quadrature, loop shown in Figure 1-40. The Costas loop produces the same results as a squaring circuit followed by an ordinary PLL in place of the BPF. This recovery scheme uses two parallel tracking loops (I and Q) simultaneously to derive the product of the I and Q components of the signal that drives the VCO. The in-phase (I) loop uses the VCO as in a PLL, and the quadrature (Q) loop uses a 90° shifted VCO signal. Once the frequency of the VCO is equal to the suppressed-carrier frequency, the product of the I and Q signals will produce an error voltage proportional to any phase error in the VCO. The error voltage controls the phase and, thus, the frequency of the VCO.

FIGURE 1-41 Remodulator loop carrier recovery circuit

Remodulator

A third method of achieving recovery of a phase and frequency coherent carrier is the remodulator, shown in Figure 1-41. The remodulator produces a loop error voltage that is proportional to twice the phase error between the incoming signal and the VCO signal. The remodulator has a faster acquisition time than either the squaring or the Costas loops.

Carrier recovery circuits for higher-than-binary encoding techniques are similar to BPSK except that circuits that raise the receive signal to the fourth, eighth, and higher powers are used.

DIFFERENTIAL PHASE SHIFT KEYING

Differential phase shift keying (DPSK) is an alternative form of digital modulation where the binary input information is contained in the difference between two successive signaling elements rather than the absolute phase. With DPSK it is not necessary to recover a phase-coherent carrier. Instead, a received signaling element is delayed by one signaling element time slot and then compared to the next received signaling element. The difference in the phase of the two signaling elements determines the logic condition of the data.

Differential BPSK

DBPSK transmitter. Figure 1-42a shows a simplified block diagram of a *differential binary phase shift keying* (DBPSK) transmitter. An incoming information bit is XNORed with the preceding bit prior to entering the BPSK modulator (balanced modulator). For the first data bit, there is no preceding bit with which to compare it. Therefore, an initial reference bit is assumed. Figure 1-42b shows the relationship between the input data, the XNOR output data, and the phase at the output of the balanced modulator. If the initial reference bit is assumed a logic 1, the output from the XNOR circuit is simply the complement of that shown.

FIGURE 1-42 DBPSK modulator: (a) block diagram; (b) timing diagram

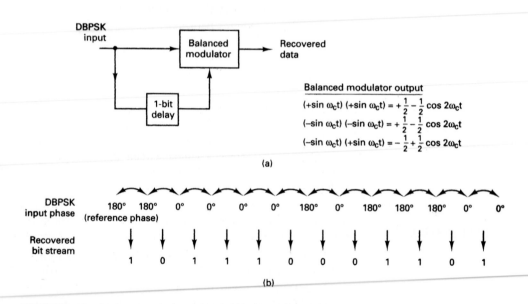

FIGURE 1-43 DBPSK demodulator: (a) block diagram; (b) timing sequence

In Figure 1-42b the first data bit is XNORed with the reference bit. If they are the same, the XNOR output is a logic 1; if they are different, the XNOR output is a logic 0. The balanced modulator operates the same as a conventional BPSK modulator; a logic 1 produces $+\sin \omega_c t$ at the output and a logic 0 produces $-\sin \omega_c t$ at the output.

DBPSK receiver. Figure 1-43 shows the block diagram and timing sequence for a DBPSK receiver. The received signal is delayed by one bit time, then compared with the next signaling element in the balanced modulator. If they are the same, a logic 1 (+ voltage) is generated. If they are different, a logic 0 (− voltage) is generated. If the reference phase is incorrectly assumed, only the first demodulated bit is in error. Differential encoding can be implemented with higher-than-binary digital modulation schemes, although the differential algorithms are much more complicated than for DBPSK.

FIGURE 1-44   (a) Clock recovery circuit; (b) timing diagram

The primary advantage of DBPSK is the simplicity with which it can be implemented. With DBPSK, no carrier recovery circuit is needed. A disadvantage of DBPSK is that it requires between 1 dB and 3 dB more signal-to-noise ratio to achieve the same bit error rate as that of absolute PSK.

CLOCK RECOVERY

As with any digital system, digital radio requires precise timing or clock synchronization between the transmit and the receive circuitry. Because of this, it is necessary to regenerate clocks at the receiver that are synchronous with those at the transmitter.

Figure 1-44a shows a simple circuit that is commonly used to recover clocking information from the received data. The recovered data are delayed by one-half a bit time and then compared with the original data in an XOR circuit. The frequency of the clock that is recovered with this method is equal to the received data rate (f_b). Figure 1-44b shows the relationship between the data and the recovered clock timing. From Figure 1-44b it can be seen that as long as the receive data contains a substantial number of transitions (1/0 sequences), the recovered clock is maintained. If the receive data were to undergo an extended period of successive 1s or 0s, the recovered clock would be lost. To prevent this from occurring, the data are scrambled at the transmit end and descrambled at the receive end. Scrambling introduces transitions (pulses) into the binary signal using a prescribed algorithm, and the descrambler uses the same algorithm to remove the transitions.

PROBABILITY OF ERROR AND BIT ERROR RATE

Probability of error $P(e)$ and *bit error rate* (BER) are often used interchangeably, although in practice they do have slightly different meanings. $P(e)$ is a theoretical (mathematical) expectation of the bit error rate for a given system. BER is an empirical (historical) record of a system's actual bit error performance. For example, if a system has a $P(e)$ of 10^{-5}, this means that mathematically, you can expect one bit error in every 100,000 bits transmitted ($1/10^5 = 1/100,000$). If a system has a BER of 10^{-5}, this means that in the past there was one bit error for every 100,000 bits transmitted. A bit error rate is measured, then compared to the expected probability of error to evaluate a system's performance.

Probability of error is a function of the *carrier-to-noise power ratio* (or more specifically, the average *energy per bit-to-noise power density ratio*) and the number of possible encoding conditions used (*M*-ary). Carrier-to-noise power ratio is the ratio of the average carrier power (the combined power of the carrier and its associated sidebands) to the *thermal noise power.* Carrier power can be stated in watts or dBm, where

$$C_{(dBm)} = 10 \log \frac{C_{(watts)}}{0.001} \tag{1-15}$$

Thermal noise power is expressed mathematically as

$$N = KTB \quad \text{(watts)} \tag{1-16a}$$

where N = thermal noise power (W)
   K = Boltzmann's proportionality constant (1.38×10^{-23} J/K)
   T = temperature (kelvin: 0 K = $-273°$ C, room temperature = 290 K)
   B = bandwidth (Hz)

Stated in dBm, $$N_{(dBm)} = 10 \log \frac{KTB}{0.001} \tag{1-16b}$$

Mathematically, the carrier-to-noise power ratio is

$$\frac{C}{N} = \frac{C}{KTB} \quad \text{(unitless ratio)} \tag{1-17a}$$

where C = carrier power (W)
   N = noise power (W)

Stated in dB, $$\frac{C}{N} \text{(dB)} = 10 \log \frac{C}{N} \tag{1-17b}$$

$$= C_{(dBm)} - N_{(dBm)}$$

Energy per bit is simply the energy of a single bit of information. Mathematically, energy per bit is

$$E_b = CT_b \quad \text{(J/bit)} \tag{1-18a}$$

where E_b = energy of a single bit (J/bit)
   T_b = time of a single bit (s)
   C = carrier power (W)

Stated in dBJ, $$E_{b(dBJ)} = 10 \log E_b \tag{1-18b}$$

and because $T_b = 1/f_b$, where f_b is the bit rate in bits per second, E_b can be rewritten as

$$E_b = \frac{C}{f_b} \quad \text{(J/bit)} \tag{1-18c}$$

Stated in dBJ, $$E_{b(dBJ)} = 10 \log \frac{C}{f_b} \tag{1-18d}$$

$$= 10 \log C - 10 \log f_b \tag{1-18e}$$

Noise power density is the thermal noise power normalized to a 1-Hz bandwidth (i.e., the noise power present in a 1-Hz bandwidth). Mathematically, noise power density is

$$N_0 = \frac{N}{B} \quad \text{(W/Hz)} \tag{1-19a}$$

where N_0 = noise power density (W/Hz)
   N = thermal noise power (W)
   B = bandwidth (Hz)

Stated in dBm,
$$N_{0(\text{dBm})} = 10 \log \frac{N}{0.001} - 10 \log B \qquad (1\text{-}19b)$$

$$= N_{(\text{dBm})} - 10 \log B \qquad (1\text{-}19c)$$

Combining Equations 1-16a and 1-19a yields

$$N_0 = \frac{KTB}{B} = KT \quad (\text{W/Hz}) \qquad (1\text{-}19d)$$

Stated in dBm,
$$N_{0(\text{dBm})} = 10 \log \frac{K}{0.001} + 10 \log T \qquad (1\text{-}19e)$$

Energy per bit-to-noise power density ratio is used to compare two or more digital modulation systems that use different transmission rates (bit rates), modulation schemes (FSK, PSK, QAM), or encoding techniques (*M*-ary). The energy per bit-to-noise power density ratio is simply the ratio of the energy of a single bit to the noise power present in 1 Hz of bandwidth. Thus, E_b/N_0 normalizes all multiphase modulation schemes to a common noise bandwidth allowing for a simpler and more accurate comparison of their error performance. Mathematically, E_b/N_0 is

$$\frac{E_b}{N_0} = \frac{C/f_b}{N/B} = \frac{CB}{Nf_b} \qquad (1\text{-}20a)$$

where $E_b N_0$ is the energy per bit-to-noise power density ratio. Rearranging Equation 1-20a yields the following expression:

$$\frac{E_b}{N_0} = \frac{C}{N} \times \frac{B}{f_b} \qquad (1\text{-}20b)$$

where E_b/N_0 = energy per bit-to-noise power density ratio
          C/N = carrier-to-noise power ratio
          B/f_b = noise bandwidth-to-bit rate ratio

Stated in dB,
$$\frac{E_b}{N_0}(\text{dB}) = 10 \log \frac{C}{N} + 10 \log \frac{B}{f_b} \qquad (1\text{-}20c)$$

or
$$= 10 \log E_b - 10 \log N_0 \qquad (1\text{-}20d)$$

From Equation 1-20b it can be seen that the E_b/N_0 ratio is simply the product of the carrier-to-noise power ratio and the noise bandwidth-to-bit rate ratio. Also, from Equation 1-20b, it can be seen that when the bandwidth equals the bit rate, $E_b/N_0 = C/N$.

In general, the minimum carrier-to-noise power ratio required for QAM systems is less than that required for comparable PSK systems, Also, the higher the level of encoding used (the higher the value of *M*), the higher the minimum carrier-to-noise power ratio. In Chapter 7, several examples are shown for determining the minimum carrier-to-noise power and energy per bit-to-noise density ratios for a give *M*-ary system and desired $P(e)$.

Example 1-11

For a QPSK system and the given parameters, determine

(a) Carrier power in dBm.
(b) Noise power in dBm.
(c) Noise power density in dBm.
(d) Energy per bit in dBJ.
(e) Carrier-to-noise power ratio in dB.
(f) E_b/N_0 ratio.

$$C = 10^{-12} \text{ W} \qquad f_b = 60 \text{ kbps}$$
$$N = 1.2 \times 10^{-14} \text{ W} \qquad B = 120 \text{ kHz}$$

Solution   (a) The carrier power in dBm is determined by substituting into Equation 1-15.

$$C = 10 \log \frac{10^{-12}}{0.001} = -90 \text{ dBm}$$

(b) The noise power in dBm is determined by substituting into Equation 1-16b.

$$N = 10 \log \frac{1.2 \times 10^{-14}}{0.001} = -109.2 \text{ dBm}$$

(c) The noise power density is determined by substituting into Equation 1-19c.

$$N_0 = -109.2 \text{ dBm} - 10 \log 120 \text{ kHz} = -160 \text{ dBm}$$

(d) The energy per bit is determined by substituting into Equation 1-18d.

$$E_b = 10 \log \frac{10^{-12}}{60 \text{ kbps}} = -167.8 \text{ dBJ}$$

(e) The carrier-to-noise power ratio is determined by substituting into Equation 1-17b.

$$\frac{C}{N} = 10 \log \frac{10^{-12}}{1.2 \times 10^{-14}} = 19.2 \text{ dB}$$

(f) The energy per bit-to-noise density ratio is determined by substituting into Equation 1-20c.

$$\frac{E_b}{N_0} = 19.2 + 10 \log \frac{120 \text{ kHz}}{60 \text{ kbps}} = 22.2 \text{ dB}$$

PSK Error Performance

The bit error performance for the various multiphase digital modulation systems is directly related to the distance between points on a signal state-space diagram. For example, on the signal state-space diagram for BPSK shown in Figure 1-45a, it can be seen that the two signal points (logic 1 and logic 0) have maximum separation (d) for a given power level (D). In essence, one BPSK signal state is the exact negative of the other. As the figure shows, a noise vector (V_N), when combined with the signal vector (V_S), effectively shifts the phase of the signaling element (V_{SE}) alpha degrees. If the phase shift exceeds $\pm 90°$, the signal element is shifted beyond the threshold points into the error region. For BPSK, it would require a noise vector of sufficient amplitude and phase to produce more than a $\pm 90°$ phase shift in the signaling element to produce an error. For PSK systems, the general formula for the threshold points is

$$TP = \pm \frac{\pi}{M} \tag{1-21}$$

where M is the number of signal states.

The phase relationship between signaling elements for BPSK (i.e., 180° out of phase) is the optimum signaling format, referred to as *antipodal signaling,* and occurs only when two binary signal levels are allowed and when one signal is the exact negative of the other. Because no other bit-by-bit signaling scheme is any better, antipodal performance is often used as a reference for comparison.

The error performance of the other multiphase PSK systems can be compared to that of BPSK simply by determining the relative decrease in error distance between points on a signal state-space diagram. For PSK, the general formula for the maximum distance between signaling points is given by

FIGURE 1-45 PSK error region: (a) BPSK; (b) QPSK

$$\sin \theta = \sin \frac{360°}{2M} = \frac{d/2}{D} \tag{1-22}$$

where d = error distance
           M = number of phases
           D = peak signal amplitude

Rearranging Equation 1-22 and solving for d yields

$$d = \left(2 \sin \frac{180°}{M}\right) \times D \tag{1-23}$$

Figure 1-45b shows the signal state-space diagram for QPSK. From Figure 1-45b and Equation 1-22 it can be seen that QPSK can tolerate only a ±45° phase shift. From Equation 1-21, the maximum phase shift for 8-PSK and 16-PSK is ±22.5° and ±11.5°,

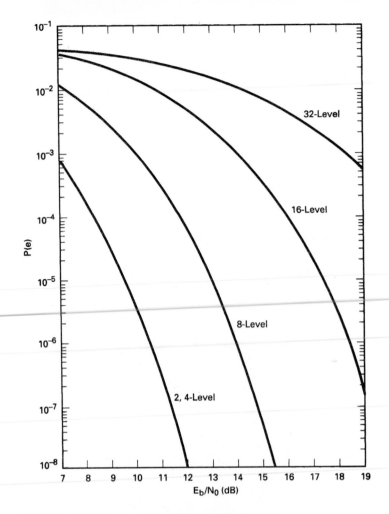

FIGURE 1-46 Error rates of PSK modulation systems

respectively. Consequently, the higher levels of modulation (i.e., the greater the value of M) require a greater energy per bit-to-noise power density ratio to reduce the effect of noise interference. Hence, the higher the level of modulation, the smaller the angular separation between signal points and the smaller the error distance.

The general expression for the bit-error probability of an M-phase PSK system is

$$P(e) = \frac{1}{\log_2 M} \text{ erf } (z) \tag{1-24}$$

where   erf = error function

$$z = \sin(\pi/M)\left(\sqrt{\log_2 M}\right)\left(\sqrt{E_b/N_0}\right)$$

By substituting into Equation 1-24 it can be shown that QPSK provides the same error performance as BPSK. This is because the 3-dB reduction in error distance for QPSK is offset by the 3-dB decrease in its bandwidth (in addition to the error distance, the relative widths of the noise bandwidths must also be considered). Thus, both systems provide optimum performance. Figure 1-46 shows the error performance for 2-, 4-, 8-, 16-, and 32-PSK systems as a function of E_b/N_0.

Example 1-12

Determine the minimum bandwidth required to achieve a $P(e)$ of 10^{-7} for an 8-PSK system operating at 10 Mbps with a carrier-to-noise power ratio of 11.7 dB.

Solution From Figure 1-46, the minimum E_b/N_0 ratio to achieve a $P(e)$ of 10^{-7} for an 8-PSK system is 14.7 dB. The minimum bandwidth is found by rearranging Equation 1-20b.

$$\frac{B}{f_b} = \frac{E_b}{N_0} - \frac{C}{N}$$

$$= 14.7 \text{ dB} - 11.7 \text{ dB} = 3 \text{ dB}$$

$$\frac{B}{f_b} = \text{antilog } 3 = 2$$

$$B = 2 \times 10 \text{ Mbps} = 20 \text{ MHz}$$

QAM Error Performance

For a large number of signal points (i.e., M-ary systems greater than 4), QAM outperforms PSK. This is because the distance between signaling points in a PSK system is smaller than the distance between points in a comparable QAM system. The general expression for the distance between adjacent signaling points for a QAM system with L levels on each axis is

$$d = \frac{\sqrt{2}}{L-1} \times D \tag{1-25}$$

where d = error distance
L = number of levels on each axis
D = peak signal amplitude

In comparing Equation 1-23 to Equation 1-25, it can be seen that QAM systems have an advantage over PSK systems with the same peak signal power level.

The general expression for the bit error probability of an L-level QAM system is

$$P(e) = \frac{1}{\log_2 L}\left(\frac{L-1}{L}\right)\text{erfc}(z) \tag{1-26}$$

where $\text{erfc}(z)$ is the complementary error function.

$$z = \frac{\sqrt{\log_2 L}}{L-1}\sqrt{\frac{E_b}{N_0}}$$

Figure 1-47 shows the error performance for 4-, 16-, 32-, and 64-QAM systems as a function of E_b/N_0.

Table 1-2 lists the minimum carrier-to-noise power ratios and energy per bit-to-noise power density ratios required for a probability of error 10^{-6} for several PSK and QAM modulation schemes.

Example 1-13

Which system requires the highest E_b/N_0 ratio for a probability of error of 10^{-6}, a four-level QAM system or an 8-PSK system?

Solution From Figure 1-47, the minimum E_b/N_0 ratio required for a four-level QAM system is 10.6 dB. From Figure 1-46, the minimum E_b/N_0 ratio required for an 8-PSK system is 14 dB. Therefore, to achieve a $P(e)$ of 10^{-6}, a four-level QAM system would require 3.4-dB less E_b/N_0 ratio.

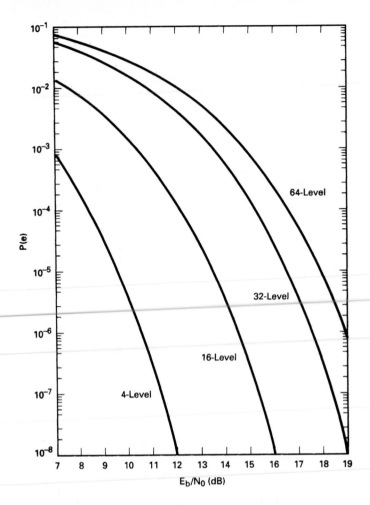

FIGURE 1-47 Error rates of QAM modulation systems

TABLE 1-2 Performance Comparison of Various Digital
Modulation Schemes (BER = 10^{-6})

Modulation Technique	C/N Ratio (dB)	E_b/N_0 Ratio (dB)
BPSK	10.6	10.6
QPSK	13.6	10.6
4-QAM	13.6	10.6
8-QAM	17.6	10.6
8-PSK	18.5	14
16-PSK	24.3	18.3
16-QAM	20.5	14.5
32-QAM	24.4	17.4
64-QAM	26.6	18.8

FSK Error Performance

The error probability for FSK systems is evaluated in a somewhat different manner than PSK and QAM. There are essentially only two types of FSK systems: noncoherent (asynchronous) and coherent (synchronous). With noncoherent FSK, the transmitter and receiver are not frequency or phase synchronized. With coherent FSK, local receiver

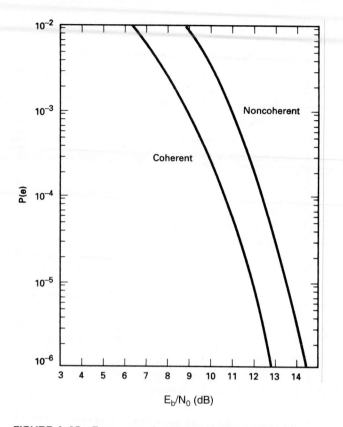

FIGURE 1-48 Error rates for FSK modulation systems

reference signals are in frequency and phase lock with the transmitted signals. The probability of error for noncoherent FSK is

$$P(e) = \frac{1}{2} \exp\left(-\frac{E_b}{2N_0}\right) \tag{1-27}$$

The probability of error for coherent FSK is

$$P(e) = \text{erfc} \sqrt{\frac{E_b}{N_0}} \tag{1-28}$$

Figure 1-48 shows probability of error curves for both coherent and noncoherent FSK for several values of E_b/N_0. From Equations 1-27 and 1-28 it can be determined that the probability of error for noncoherent FSK is greater than that of coherent FSK for equal energy per bit-to-noise power density ratios.

QUESTIONS

1-1. Explain *digital transmission* and *digital radio*.

1-2. Define *information capacity*.

1-3. What are the three most predominant modulation schemes used in digital radio systems?

1-4. Explain the relationship between bits per second and baud for an FSK system.

1-5. Define the following terms for FSK modulation: frequency deviation, modulation index, and deviation ratio.

1-6. Explain the relationship between (a) the minimum bandwidth required for an FSK system and the bit rate, and (b) the mark and space frequencies.

1-7. What is the difference between standard FSK and MSK? What is the advantage of MSK?

1-8. Define *PSK*.

1-9. Explain the relationship between bits per second and baud for a BPSK system.

1-10. What is a constellation diagram, and how is it used with PSK?

1-11. Explain the relationship between the minimum bandwidth required for a BPSK system and the bit rate.

1-12. Explain *M-ary*.

1-13. Explain the relationship between bits per second and baud for a QPSK system.

1-14. Explain the significance of the I and Q channels in a QPSK modulator.

1-15. Define *dibit*.

1-16. Explain the relationship between the minimum bandwidth required for a QPSK system and the bit rate.

1-17. What is a coherent demodulator?

1-18. What advantage does OQPSK have over conventional QPSK? What is a disadvantage of OQPSK?

1-19. Explain the relationship between bits per second and baud for an 8-PSK system.

1-20. Define *tribit*.

1-21. Explain the relationship between the minimum bandwidth required for an 8-PSK system and the bit rate.

1-22. Explain the relationship between bits per second and baud for a 16-PSK system.

1-23. Define *quadbit*.

1-24. Define *QAM*.

1-25. Explain the relationship between the minimum bandwidth required for a 16-QAM system and the bit rate.

1-26. What is the difference between PSK and QAM?

1-27. Define *bandwidth efficiency*.

1-28. Define *carrier recovery*.

1-29. Explain the differences between absolute PSK and differential PSK.

1-30. What is the purpose of a clock recovery circuit? When is it used?

1-31. What is the difference between probability of error and bit error rate?

PROBLEMS

1-1. Determine the bandwidth and baud for an FSK signal with a mark frequency of 32 kHz, a space frequency of 24 kHz, and a bit rate of 4 kbps.

1-2. Determine the maximum bit rate for an FSK signal with a mark frequency of 48 kHz, a space frequency of 52 kHz, and an available bandwidth of 10 kHz.

1-3. Determine the bandwidth and baud for an FSK signal with a mark frequency of 99 kHz, a space frequency of 101 kHz, and a bit rate of 10 kbps.

1-4. Determine the maximum bit rate for an FSK signal with a mark frequency of 102 kHz, a space frequency of 104 kHz, and an available bandwidth of 8 kHz.

1-5. Determine the minimum bandwidth and baud for a BPSK modulator with a carrier frequency of 40 MHz, and an input bit rate of 500 kbps. Sketch the output spectrum.

1-6. For the QPSK modulator shown in Figure 1-18, change the +90° phase-shift network to −90° and sketch the new constellation diagram.

1-7. For the QPSK demodulator shown in Figure 1-22, determine the I and Q bits for an input signal of $\sin \omega_c t - \cos \omega_c t$.

1-8. For an 8-PSK modulator with an input data rate (f_b) equal to 20 Mbps and a carrier frequency of 100 MHz, determine the minimum double-sided Nyquist bandwidth (f_N) and the baud. Sketch the output spectrum.

1-9. For the 8-PSK modulator shown in Figure 1-24, change the reference oscillator to cos $\omega_c t$ and sketch the new constellation diagram.

1-10. For a 16-QAM modulator with an input bit rate (f_b) equal to 20 Mbps and a carrier frequency of 100 MHz, determine the minimum double-sided Nyquist bandwidth (f_N) and the baud. Sketch the output spectrum.

1-11. For the 16-QAM modulator shown in Figure 1-35, change the reference oscillator to cos $\omega_c t$ and determine the output expressions for the following I, I', Q, and Q' input conditions: 0000, 1111, 1010, and 0101.

1-12. Determine the bandwidth efficiency for the following modulators.
(a) QPSK, f_b = 10 Mbps
(b) 8-PSK, f_b = 21 Mbps
(c) 16-QAM, f_b = 20 Mbps

1-13. For the DBPSK modulator shown in Figure 1-42, determine the output phase sequence for the following input bit sequence: 00110011010101 (assume that the reference bit = 1).

1-14. For a QPSK system and the given parameters, determine
(a) Carrier power in dBm.
(b) Noise power in dBm.
(c) Noise power density in dBm.
(d) Energy per bit in dBJ.
(e) Carrier-to-noise power ratio.
(f) E_b/N_0 ratio.

$$C = 10^{-13}\text{W} \qquad f_b = 30 \text{ kbps}$$
$$N = 0.06 \times 10^{-15} \text{ W} \qquad B = 60 \text{ kHz}$$

1-15. Determine the minimum bandwidth required to achieve a $P(e)$ of 10^{-6} for an 8-PSK system operating at 20 Mbps with a carrier-to-noise power ratio of 11 dB.

1-16. Determine the minimum bandwidth and baud for a BPSK modulator with a carrier frequency of 80 MHz and an input bit rate f_b = 1 Mbps. Sketch the output spectrum.

1-17. For the QPSK modulator shown in Figure 1-18, change the reference oscillator to cos $\omega_c t$ and sketch the new constellation diagram.

1-18. For the QPSK demodulator shown in Figure 1-22, determine the I and Q bits for an input signal $-\sin \omega_c t + \cos \omega_c t$.

1-19. For an 8-PSK modulator with an input bit rate f_b = 10 Mbps and a carrier frequency f_c = 80 MHz, determine the minimum Nyquist bandwidth and the baud. Sketch the output spectrum.

1-20. For the 8-PSK modulator shown in Figure 1-24, change the +90° phase-shift network to a −90° phase-shifter and sketch the new constellation diagram.

1-21. For a 16-QAM modulator with an input bit rate f_b = 10 Mbps and a carrier frequency f_c = 60 MHz, determine the minimum double-sided Nyquist frequency and the baud. Sketch the output spectrum.

1-22. For the 16-QAM modulator shown in Figure 1-35, change the 90° phase-shift network to a −90° phase shifter and determine the output expressions for the following I, I', Q, and Q' input conditions: 0000, 1111, 1010, and 0101.

1-23. Determine the bandwidth efficiency for the following modulators:
(a) QPSK, f_b = 20 Mbps.
(b) 8-PSK, f_b = 28 Mbps.
(c) 16-PSK, f_b = 40 Mbps.

1-24. For the DBPSK modulator shown in Figure 1-42, determine the output phase sequence for the following input bit sequence: 11001100101010 (assume that the reference bit is a logic 1).

CHAPTER 2

Data Communications

INTRODUCTION

In the *data communications* world, *data* generally are defined as information that is stored in digital form. The word *data* is plural; a single unit of data is called a *datum*. *Data communications* is the process of transferring digital *information* (usually in binary form) between two or more points. Information is defined as knowledge or intelligence. Information that has been processed, organized, and stored is called data. Data can be alphabetic, numeric, or symbolic in nature and be comprised of any one or a combination of the following: binary-coded alpha/numeric symbols, microprocessor op-codes, control codes, user addresses, program data, or data base information. At both the source and destination, data are in digital form. However, during transmission, data may be in digital or analog form.

A data communications network can be as simple as two personal computers connected together through a public telecommunications network, or it can comprise a complex network of one or more mainframe computers and hundreds (or even thousands) of remote terminals, personal computers, and work stations. Today, data communications networks are used to interconnect virtually all kinds of digital computing equipment such as automatic teller machines (ATMs) to bank computers; personal computers to information highways, such as the Internet; and work stations to mainframe computers. Data communications networks are also used for airline and hotel reservation systems and for mass media and news networks such as the Associated Press (AP) or United Press International (UPI). The list of applications for data communications networks goes on almost indefinitely.

HISTORY OF DATA COMMUNICATIONS

It is highly likely that data communications began long before recorded time in the form of smoke signals or tom-tom drums, although it is improbable that these signals were binary coded. If we limit the scope of data communications to methods that use electrical signals to transmit binary-coded information, then data communications began in 1837 with the invention of the *telegraph* and the development of the *Morse code* by Samuel F. B. Morse. With telegraph, dots and dashes (analogous to binary 1s and 0s) are transmitted across a wire using electromechanical induction. Various combinations of these dots and dashes were used to represent binary codes for letters, numbers, and punctuation. Actually, the first telegraph was invented in England by Sir Charles Wheatstone and Sir William Cooke, but their contraption required six different wires for a single telegraph line. In 1840, Morse secured an American patent for the telegraph and in 1844 the first telegraph line was established between Baltimore and Washington, D.C. In 1849, the first slow-speed telegraph printer was invented, but it was not until 1860 that high-speed (15 bps) printers were available. In 1850, the Western Union Telegraph Company was formed in Rochester, New York, for the purpose of carrying coded messages from one person to another.

In 1874, Emile Baudot invented a telegraph *multiplexer,* which allowed signals from up to six different telegraph machines to be transmitted simultaneously over a single wire. The telephone was invented in 1876 by Alexander Graham Bell and, consequently, very little new evolved in telegraph until 1899, when Marconi succeeded in sending radio telegraph messages. Telegraph was the only means of sending information across large spans of water until 1920, when the first commercial radio stations were installed.

Bell Laboratories developed the first special-purpose computer in 1940 using electromechanical relays. The first general-purpose computer was an automatic sequence-controlled calculator developed jointly by Harvard University and International Business Machines Corporation (IBM). The UNIVAC computer, built in 1951 by Remington Rand Corporation (now Sperry Rand), was the first mass-produced electronic computer. Since 1951, the number of mainframe computers, small business computers, personal computers, and computer terminals has increased exponentially, creating a situation where more and more people have the need to exchange digital information with each other. Consequently, the need for data communications has also increased exponentially.

Until 1968, the AT&T operating tariff allowed only equipment furnished by AT&T to be connected to AT&T lines. In 1968, a landmark Supreme Court decision, the Carterfone decision, allowed non-Bell companies to interconnect to the vast AT&T communications network. This decision started the *interconnect industry,* which has led to competitive data communications offerings by a large number of independent companies.

STANDARDS ORGANIZATIONS FOR DATA COMMUNICATIONS

During the past decade, the data communications industry has grown at an astronomical rate. Consequently, the need to provide communications between dissimilar computer systems has also increased. Thus, to ensure an orderly transfer of information between two or more data communications systems using different equipment with different needs, a consortium of organizations, manufacturers, and users meet on a regular basis to establish guidelines and standards. It is the intent that all data communications users comply with these standards. Several of the organizations are described below.

International Standards Organization (ISO). The ISO is the international organization for standardization. The ISO creates the sets of rules and standards for graphics, document exchange, and related technologies. The ISO is responsible for endorsing and coordinating the work of the other standards organizations.

Consultative Committee for International Telephony and Telegraphy (CCITT). The membership of the CCITT consists of government authorities and representatives from many countries. The CCITT is now the standards organization for the United Nations and develops the recommended sets of rules and standards for telephone and telegraph communications. The CCITT has developed three sets of specifications: the V series for modem interfacing, the X series for data communications, and the I and Q series for Integrated Services Digital Network (ISDN).

American National Standards Institute (ANSI). ANSI is the official standards agency for the United States and is the U.S. voting representative for ISO.

Institute of Electrical and Electronics Engineers (IEEE). The IEEE is a U.S. professional organization of electronics, computer, and communications engineers.

Electronic Industries Association (EIA). The EIA is a U.S. organization that establishes and recommends industrial standards. The EIA is responsible for developing the RS (recommended standard) series of standards for data and telecommunications.

Standards Council of Canada (SCC). The SCC is the official standards agency for Canada with similar responsibilities to those of ANSI.

DATA COMMUNICATIONS CIRCUITS

Figure 2-1 shows a simplified block diagram of a data communications network. As the figure shows, there is a source of digital information (primary station), a transmission medium (facility), and a destination (*secondary* station). The *primary* (or host) location is very often a mainframe computer with its own set of local terminals and peripheral equipment. For simplicity, there is only one secondary (or remote) station shown on the figure. The secondary stations are the users of the network. How many secondary stations there are and how they are interconnected to each other and the host station vary considerably depending on the system and its applications. There are many different types of transmission media, including free-space radio transmission (terrestrial and satellite microwave), metallic cable facilities (both digital and analog systems), and optical fiber cables (light wave propagation).

Data terminal equipment (DTE) is a general term that describes the interface equipment used at the stations to adapt the digital signals from the computers and terminals to a form more suitable for transmission. Essentially, any piece of equipment between the mainframe computer and the modem or the station equipment and its modem

FIGURE 2-1   Simplified block diagram of a data communications network

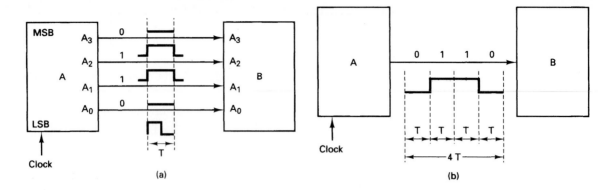

FIGURE 2-2 Data transmission: (a) parallel; (b) serial

is classified as data terminal equipment. *Data communications equipment* (DCE) is a general term that describes the equipment that converts digital signals to analog signals and interfaces the data terminal equipment to the analog transmission medium. In essence, a DCE is a *modem* (*mod*ulator/*dem*odulator). A modem converts binary digital signals to analog signals such as FSK, PSK, and QAM, and vice versa.

Serial and Parallel Data Transmission

Binary information can be transmitted either in parallel or serially. Figure 2-2a shows how the binary code 0110 is transmitted from location A to location B in parallel. As the figure shows, each bit position (A_0 to A_3) has its own transmission line. Consequently, all 4 bits can be transmitted simultaneously during the time of a single clock pulse (T). This type of transmission is called *parallel-by-bit* or *serial-by-character.*

Figure 2-2b shows how the same binary code is transmitted serially. As the figure shows, there is a single transmission line and, thus, only one bit can be transmitted at a time. Consequently, it requires four clock pulses ($4T$) to transmit the entire word. This type of transmission is often called *serial-by-bit.*

Obviously, the principal trade-off between parallel and serial transmission is speed versus simplicity. Data transmission can be accomplished much more quickly using parallel transmission. However, parallel transmission requires more lines between the source and destination. As a general rule, parallel transmission is used for short-distance communications, and within a computer, and serial transmission is used for long-distance communications.

Configurations

Data communications circuits can be categorized generally as either two-point or multipoint. A *two-point* configuration involves only two locations or stations, whereas a *multipoint* configuration involves three or more stations. A two-point circuit can involve the transfer of information between a mainframe computer and a remote computer terminal, two mainframe computers, or two remote computer terminals. A multipoint circuit is generally used to interconnect a single mainframe computer (*host*) to many remote computer terminals, although any combination of three or more computers or computer terminals constitutes a multipoint circuit.

Topologies

The topology or architecture of a data communications circuit identifies how the various locations within the network are interconnected. The most common topologies used are the *point to point,* the *star,* the *bus* or *multidrop,* the *ring* or *loop,* and the *mesh.* These are multipoint configurations except the point to point. Figure 2-3 shows the various circuit configurations and topologies used for data communications networks.

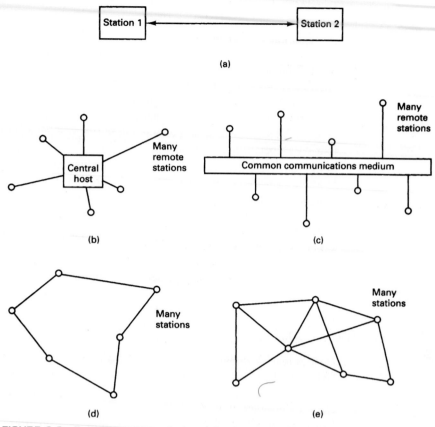

FIGURE 2-3 Data network topologies: (a) point to point; (b) star; (c) bus or multidrop; (d) ring or loop; (e) mesh

Transmission Modes

Essentially, there are four modes of transmission for data communications circuits: *simplex, half duplex, full duplex,* and *full/full duplex.*

Simplex. With simplex operation, data transmission is unidirectional; information can be sent only in one direction. Simplex lines are also called *receive-only, transmit-only,* or *one-way-only* lines. Commercial television and radio systems are examples of simplex transmission.

Half duplex (HDX). In the half-duplex mode, data transmission is possible in both directions, but not at the same time. Half-duplex lines are also called two-way alternate or either-way lines. Citizens band (CB) radio is an example of half-duplex transmission.

Full duplex (FDX). In the full-duplex mode, transmissions are possible in both directions simultaneously, but they must be between the same two stations. Full-duplex lines are also called two-way-simultaneous, *duplex,* or both-way lines. A standard telephone system is an example of full-duplex transmission.

Full/full duplex (F/FDX). In the F/FDX mode, transmission is possible in both directions at the same time but not between the same two stations (i.e., one station is transmitting to a second station and receiving from a third station at the same time). F/FDX is possible only on multipoint circuits. The U.S. postal system is an example of full/full duplex transmission.

Two-Wire Versus Four-Wire Operation

Two-wire, as the name implies, involves a transmission medium that either uses two wires (a signal and a reference lead) or a configuration that is equivalent to having only two wires. With two-wire operation, simplex, half-, or full-duplex transmission is possible. For full-duplex operation, the signals propagating in opposite directions must occupy different bandwidths; otherwise, they will mix linearly and interfere with each other.

Four-wire, as the name implies, involves a transmission medium that uses four wires (two are used for signals that are propagating in opposite directions and two are used for reference leads) or a configuration that is equivalent to having four wires. With four-wire operation, the signals propagating in opposite directions are physically separated and, therefore, can occupy the same bandwidths without interfering with each other. Four-wire operation provides more isolation and is preferred over two-wire, although four-wire requires twice as many wires and, consequently, twice the cost.

A transmitter and its associated receiver are equivalent to a two-wire circuit. A transmitter and a receiver for both directions of propagation is equivalent to a four-wire circuit. With full-duplex transmission over a two-wire line, the available bandwidth must be divided in half, thus, reducing the information capacity in either direction to one-half of the half-duplex value. Consequently, full-duplex operation over two-wire lines requires twice as much time to transfer the same amount of information.

DATA COMMUNICATIONS CODES

Data communications codes are prescribed bit sequences used for encoding characters and symbols. Consequently, data communications codes are often called *character sets, character codes, symbol codes,* or *character languages.* In essence, there are only three types of characters used in data communications codes: *data link control characters,* which are used to facilitate the orderly flow of data from a source to a destination; *graphic control characters,* which involve the syntax or presentation of the data at the receive terminal; and *alpha/numeric* characters, which are used to represent the various symbols used for letters, numbers, and punctuation in the English language.

The first data communications code that saw widespread usage was the Morse code. The Morse code used three unequal-length symbols (dot, dash, and space) to encode alpha/numeric characters, punctuation marks, and an interrogation word.

The Morse code is inadequate for use in modern digital computer equipment because all characters do not have the same number of symbols or take the same length of time to send, and each Morse code operator transmits code at a different rate. Also, with Morse code, there is an insufficient selection of graphic and data link control characters to facilitate the transmission and presentation of the data typically used in contemporary computer applications.

The three most common character sets presently used for character encoding are the Baudot code, the American Standard Code for Information Interchange (ASCII), and the Extended Binary-Coded Decimal Interchange Code (EBCDIC).

Baudot Code

The *Baudot code* (sometimes called the *Telex code*) was the first fixed-length character code. The Baudot code was developed by a French postal engineer, Thomas Murray, in 1875 and named after Emile Baudot, an early pioneer in telegraph printing. The Baudot code is a 5-bit character code that is used primarily for low-speed teletype equipment such as the TWX/Telex system. With a 5-bit code there are only 2^5 or 32 combinations possible, which is insufficient to represent the 26 letters of the alphabet, the 10 digits, and the various punctuation marks and control characters. Therefore, the Baudot code uses *figure* shift and *letter* shift characters to expand its capabilities to 58 characters. The latest version of the Baudot code is recommended by the CCITT as the International Alphabet

TABLE 2-1 Baudot Code

Character Shift		Binary Code				
Letter	Figure	Bit: 4	3	2	1	0
A	—	1	1	0	0	0
B	?	1	0	0	1	1
C	:	0	1	1	1	0
D	$	1	0	0	1	0
E	3	1	0	0	0	0
F	!	1	0	1	1	0
G	&	0	1	0	1	1
H	#	0	0	1	0	1
I	8	0	1	1	0	0
J	'	1	1	0	1	0
K	(	1	1	1	1	0
L	)	0	1	0	0	1
M	.	0	0	1	1	1
N	,	0	0	1	1	0
O	9	0	0	0	1	1
P	0	0	1	1	0	1
Q	1	1	1	1	0	1
R	4	0	1	0	1	0
S	bel	1	0	1	0	0
T	5	0	0	0	0	1
U	7	1	1	1	0	0
V	;	0	1	1	1	1
W	2	1	1	0	0	1
X	/	1	0	1	1	1
Y	6	1	0	1	0	1
Z	"	1	0	0	0	1
Figure shift		1	1	1	1	1
Letter shift		1	1	0	1	1
Space		0	0	1	0	0
Line feed (LF)		0	1	0	0	0
Blank (null)		0	0	0	0	0

No. 2. The Baudot code is still used by Western Union Company for the TWX and Telex teletype systems. The AP and UPI news services for years used the Baudot code for sending news information around the world. The most recent version of the Baudot code is shown in Table 2-1.

ASCII Code

In 1963, in an effort to standardize data communications codes, the United States adopted the Bell System model 33 teletype code as the United States of America Standard Code for Information Interchange (USASCII), better known simply as ASCII-63. Since its adoption, ASCII has generically progressed through the 1965, 1967, and 1977 versions, with the 1977 version being recommended by the CCITT as the International Alphabet No. 5. ASCII is a 7-bit character set, which has 2^7 or 128 combinations. With ASCII, the least significant bit (LSB) is designated b_0 and the most significant bit (MSB) is designated b_6. b_7 is not part of the ASCII code but is generally reserved for the parity bit, which is explained later in this chapter. Actually, with any character set, all bits are equally significant because the code does not represent a weighted binary number. It is common with character codes to refer to bits by their order; b_0 is the zero-order bit, b_1 is the first-order bit, b_7 is the seventh-order bit, and so on. With serial transmission, the bit transmitted first is called the LSB. With ASCII, the low-order bit (b_0) is the LSB and is transmitted first. ASCII is probably the code most often used today. The 1977 version of the ASCII code is shown in Table 2-2.

TABLE 2-2 ASCII-77 Code—Odd Parity

	Binary Code										Binary Code								
Bit:	7	6	5	4	3	2	1	0	Hex	Bit:	7	6	5	4	3	2	1	0	Hex
NUL	1	0	0	0	0	0	0	0	00	@	0	1	0	0	0	0	0	0	40
SOH	0	0	0	0	0	0	0	1	01	A	1	1	0	0	0	0	0	1	41
STX	0	0	0	0	0	0	1	0	02	B	1	1	0	0	0	0	1	0	42
ETX	1	0	0	0	0	0	1	1	03	C	0	1	0	0	0	0	1	1	43
EOT	0	0	0	0	0	1	0	0	04	D	1	1	0	0	0	1	0	0	44
ENQ	1	0	0	0	0	1	0	1	05	E	0	1	0	0	0	1	0	1	45
ACK	1	0	0	0	0	1	1	0	06	F	0	1	0	0	0	1	1	0	46
BEL	0	0	0	0	0	1	1	1	07	G	1	1	0	0	0	1	1	1	47
BS	0	0	0	0	1	0	0	0	08	H	1	1	0	0	1	0	0	0	48
HT	1	0	0	0	1	0	0	1	09	I	0	1	0	0	1	0	0	1	49
NL	1	0	0	0	1	0	1	0	0A	J	0	1	0	0	1	0	1	0	4A
VT	0	0	0	0	1	0	1	1	0B	K	1	1	0	0	1	0	1	1	4B
FF	1	0	0	0	1	1	0	0	0C	L	0	1	0	0	1	1	0	0	4C
CR	0	0	0	0	1	1	0	1	0D	M	1	1	0	0	1	1	0	1	4D
SO	0	0	0	0	1	1	1	0	0E	N	1	1	0	0	1	1	1	0	4E
SI	1	0	0	0	1	1	1	1	0F	O	0	1	0	0	1	1	1	1	4F
DLE	0	0	0	1	0	0	0	0	10	P	1	1	0	1	0	0	0	0	50
DC1	0	0	0	1	0	0	0	1	11	Q	0	1	0	1	0	0	0	1	51
DC2	1	0	0	1	0	0	1	0	12	R	0	1	0	1	0	0	1	0	52
DC3	0	0	0	1	0	0	1	1	13	S	1	1	0	1	0	0	1	1	53
DC4	1	0	0	1	0	1	0	0	14	T	0	1	0	1	0	1	0	0	54
NAK	0	0	0	1	0	1	0	1	15	U	1	1	0	1	0	1	0	1	55
SYN	0	0	0	1	0	1	1	0	16	V	1	1	0	1	0	1	1	0	56
ETB	1	0	0	1	0	1	1	1	17	W	0	1	0	1	0	1	1	1	57
CAN	1	0	0	1	1	0	0	0	18	X	0	1	0	1	1	0	0	0	58
EM	0	0	0	1	1	0	0	1	19	Y	1	1	0	1	1	0	0	1	59
SUB	0	0	0	1	1	0	1	0	1A	Z	1	1	0	1	1	0	1	0	5A
ESC	1	0	0	1	1	0	1	1	1B	[	0	1	0	1	1	0	1	1	5B
FS	0	0	0	1	1	1	0	0	1C	\	1	1	0	1	1	1	0	0	5C
GS	1	0	0	1	1	1	0	1	1D	]	0	1	0	1	1	1	0	1	5D
RS	1	0	0	1	1	1	1	0	1E	∧	0	1	0	1	1	1	1	0	5E
US	0	0	0	1	1	1	1	1	1F	-	1	1	0	1	1	1	1	1	5F
SP	0	0	1	0	0	0	0	0	20	`	1	1	1	0	0	0	0	0	60
!	1	0	1	0	0	0	0	1	21	a	0	1	1	0	0	0	0	1	61
"	1	0	1	0	0	0	1	0	22	b	0	1	1	0	0	0	1	0	62
#	0	0	1	0	0	0	1	1	23	c	1	1	1	0	0	0	1	1	63
$	1	0	1	0	0	1	0	0	24	d	0	1	1	0	0	1	0	0	64
%	0	0	1	0	0	1	0	1	25	e	1	1	1	0	0	1	0	1	65
&	0	0	1	0	0	1	1	0	26	f	1	1	1	0	0	1	1	0	66
'	1	0	1	0	0	1	1	1	27	g	0	1	1	0	0	1	1	1	67
(	1	0	1	0	1	0	0	0	28	h	0	1	1	0	1	0	0	0	68
)	0	0	1	0	1	0	0	1	29	i	1	1	1	0	1	0	0	1	69
*	0	0	1	0	1	0	1	0	2A	j	1	1	1	0	1	0	1	0	6A
+	1	0	1	0	1	0	1	1	2B	k	0	1	1	0	1	0	1	1	6B
,	0	0	1	0	1	1	0	0	2C	l	1	1	1	0	1	1	0	0	6C
-	1	0	1	0	1	1	0	1	2D	m	0	1	1	0	1	1	0	1	6D
.	1	0	1	0	1	1	1	0	2E	n	0	1	1	0	1	1	1	0	6E
/	0	0	1	0	1	1	1	1	2F	o	1	1	1	0	1	1	1	1	6F
0	1	0	1	1	0	0	0	0	30	p	0	1	1	1	0	0	0	0	70
1	0	0	1	1	0	0	0	1	31	q	1	1	1	1	0	0	0	1	71
2	0	0	1	1	0	0	1	0	32	r	1	1	1	1	0	0	1	0	72
3	1	0	1	1	0	0	1	1	33	s	0	1	1	1	0	0	1	1	73
4	0	0	1	1	0	1	0	0	34	t	0	1	1	1	0	1	0	0	74
5	1	0	1	1	0	1	0	1	35	u	0	1	1	1	0	1	0	1	75
6	1	0	1	1	0	1	1	0	36	v	0	1	1	1	0	1	1	0	76
7	0	0	1	1	0	1	1	1	37	w	1	1	1	1	0	1	1	1	77
8	0	0	1	1	1	0	0	0	38	x	1	1	1	1	1	0	0	0	78

(Continued)

TABLE 2-2 [Continued]

			Binary Code											Binary Code					
Bit:	7	6	5	4	3	2	1	0	Hex	Bit:	7	6	5	4	3	2	1	0	Hex
9	1	0	1	1	1	0	0	1	39	y	0	1	1	1	1	0	0	1	79
:	1	0	1	1	1	0	1	0	3A	z	0	1	1	1	1	0	1	0	7A
;	0	0	1	1	1	0	1	1	3B	{	1	1	1	1	1	0	1	1	7B
<	1	0	1	1	1	1	0	0	3C	|	0	1	1	1	1	1	0	0	7C
=	0	0	1	1	1	1	0	1	3D	}	1	1	1	1	1	1	0	1	7D
>	0	0	1	1	1	1	1	0	3E	~	1	1	1	1	1	1	1	0	7E
?	1	0	1	1	1	1	1	1	3F	DEL	0	1	1	1	1	1	1	1	7F

NUL = null	VT = vertical tab	SYN = synchronous
SOH = start of heading	FF = form feed	ETB = end of transmission block
STX = start of text	CR = carriage return	CAN = cancel
ETX = end of text	SO = shift-out	SUB = substitute
EOT = end of transmission	SI = shift-in	ESC = escape
ENQ = enquiry	DLE = data link escape	FS = field separator
ACK = acknowledge	DC1 = device control 1	GS = group separator
BEL = bell	DC2 = device control 2	RS = record separator
BS = back space	DC3 = device control 3	US = unit separator
HT = horizontal tab	DC4 = device control 4	SP = space
NL = new line	NAK = negative acknowledge	DEL = delete

Start margin	Data character	Check characters	Stop characters	Stop margin

(a)   (b)

FIGURE 2-4 (a) Bar code; (b) bar code structure

EBCDIC Code

EBCDIC is an 8-bit character code developed by IBM. With 8 bits, 2^8 or 256 combinations are possible, making EBCDIC the most powerful character set. Note that with EBCDIC the LSB is designated b_7 and the MSB is designated b_0. Therefore, with EBCDIC, the high-order bit (b_7) is transmitted first and the low-order bit (b_0) is transmitted last. The EBCDIC code does not facilitate the use of a parity bit.

Bar Codes

Bar codes are those omnipresent black and white striped stickers that seem to be showing up on almost every consumer item found in nearly every store in the United States and most of the rest of the modern world. The bar code is a series of black bars separated by white spaces. The widths of the bars along with their reflective abilities represent binary 1s and 0s that identify the cost of the item. In addition, bar codes may contain information regarding inventory management and control, security access, shipping and receiving, production counting, document and order processing, automatic billing, and many other applications. A typical bar code is shown in Figure 2-4a.

Data Communications Codes

Figure 2-4b shows the layout of the fields found on a typical bar code. The start field consists of a unique sequence of bars and spaces used to identify the beginning of the data field. The data characters correspond to the bar code symbology or format used. Serial data encoded in the data character field are extracted from the card with an optical scanner. The scanner reproduces logic conditions that correspond to the difference in reflectivity of the printed bars and underlying white spaces. To read the information, simply scan over the printed bar with a smooth, uniform motion. A photodetector in the scanner senses the reflected light and converts it to electrical signals (1s and 0s) for decoding.

There are numerous bar code formats available using codes that vary from numeric symbols only to the full ASCII code. One of the most common codes was developed in

TABLE 2-3 Code 39 Character Set

Character	Binary Word	Bars	Spaces	Check Character Value
0	000110100	00110	0100	0
1	100100001	10001	0100	1
2	001100001	01001	0100	2
3	101100000	11000	0100	3
4	000110001	00101	0100	4
5	100110000	10100	0100	5
6	001110000	01100	0100	6
7	000100101	00011	0100	7
8	100100100	10010	0100	8
9	001100100	01010	0100	9
A	100001001	10001	0010	10
B	001001001	01001	0010	11
C	101001000	11000	0010	12
D	000011001	00101	0010	13
E	100011000	10100	0010	14
F	001011000	01100	0010	15
G	000001101	00011	0010	16
H	100001100	10010	0010	17
I	001001100	01010	0010	18
J	000011100	00110	0010	19
K	100000011	10001	0001	20
L	001000011	01001	0001	21
M	101000010	11000	0001	22
N	000010011	00101	0001	23
O	100010010	10100	0001	24
P	001010010	01100	0001	25
Q	000000111	00011	0001	26
R	100000110	10010	0001	27
S	001000110	01010	0001	28
T	000010110	00110	0001	29
U	110000001	10001	1000	30
V	011000001	01001	1000	31
W	111000000	11000	1000	32
X	010010001	00101	1000	33
Y	110010000	10100	1000	34
Z	011010000	01100	1000	35
–	010000101	00011	1000	36
.	110000100	10010	1000	37
(space)	011000100	01010	1000	38
*	010010100	00110	1000	–
$	010101000	00000	1110	39
/	010100010	00000	1101	40
+	010001010	00000	1011	41
%	000101010	00000	0111	42

1974 and is referred to as simply *Code 39*. Code 39 (also called *Code 3 of 9* or *3 of 9 Code*) uses an alpha/numeric code similar to ASCII and is shown in Table 2-3. Code 39 consists of 36 unique codes representing the ten digits and 24 uppercase letters. There are seven additional codes used for special characters, and an exclusive start/stop character coded as an asterisk (*).

Each character contains nine elements (bars and spaces). The logic condition (1 or 0) of each element is encoded by varying the width of the bar or space. A wide element, whether it is a bar or a space, represents a logic 1 and a narrow element represents a logic 0. A 3:1 width ratio is used to distinguish 1s from 0s (i.e., a bar or space representing a logic 1 is three times wider than a bar or space representing a logic 0).

Three of the nine elements in Code 39 must be logic 1s and the remaining six must be logic 0s. In addition, of the three logic 1s, two must be bars and one a space. Each character begins and ends with a black bar with alternating white bars in between. All characters are separated with an intercharacter space. Codes that use intercharacter spaces are classified as codes whose characters are separated by gaps. Gaps are generally one element wide.

The Code 39 format includes two optional check characters for error detection. Each character has a check character value assigned to it. The value of the characters within a message are summed then divided by a constant. The remainder is rounded off to one or two decimal places then converted to a Code 39 character and appended to the end of the character field. For example, if a data field contained the message "CODE 39", the check character(s) would be determined as follows:

Message	C	O	D	E	space	3	9
Check value	12	24	13	14	38	3	9

Sum of check values = 113

Dividing by constant 43 gives 113/43 = 2 remainder 27

Final message: CODE 39R

where R equals code for 27.

ERROR CONTROL

A data communications circuit can be as short as a few feet or as long as several thousand miles, and the transmission medium can be as simple as a piece of wire or as complex as a microwave, satellite, or optical fiber system. Therefore, due to the nonideal transmission characteristics that are associated with any communications system, it is inevitable that errors will occur and that it is necessary to develop and implement procedures for error control. Error control can be divided into two general categories: error detection and error correction.

Error Detection

Error detection is simply the process of monitoring the received data and determining when a transmission error has occurred. Error detection techniques do not identify which bit (or bits) is in error, only that an error has occurred. The purpose of error detection is not to prevent errors from occurring but to prevent undetected errors from occurring. How a system reacts to transmission errors is system dependent and varies considerably. The most common error detection techniques used for data communications circuits are: redundancy, echoplex, exact-count encoding, parity, checksum, vertical and longitudinal redundancy checking, and cyclic redundancy checking.

Redundancy. *Redundancy* involves transmitting each character twice. If the same character is not received twice in succession, a transmission error has occurred. The same concept can be used for messages. If the same sequence of characters is not received twice in succession, in exactly the same order, a transmission error has occurred.

Echoplex. Echoplex is a relatively simple type of error detection scheme that is used almost exclusively in data communications systems where human operators are used to enter data manually from a keyboard. Echoplex requires full-duplex operation where each character is transmitted immediately after it has been typed into the transmit terminal. At the receive terminal, once a character has been received, it is immediately transmitted back to the originating terminal where it appears on that terminal's screen. When the character appears on the screen, the operator has verification that that character has been received at the destination terminal. If a transmission error has occurred, the wrong character will be displayed on the transmit terminal's screen. When this occurs, the operator can send a backspace and remove the erroneous character then retype the correct character.

Echoplex is a simple concept requiring relatively simple circuitry. One disadvantage of echoplex, however, occurs when a transmitted character has been received correctly, then a transmission error occurs while it is being sent back to the originator. This would necessitate an unnecessary retransmission. Another disadvantage of echoplex is it relies on human operators to detect and correct transmission errors. Echoplex also requires a full-duplex circuit when useful information is actually only being sent in one direction.

Exact-count encoding. With *exact-count encoding,* the number of 1s in each character is the same. An example of an exact-count encoding scheme is the ARQ code shown in Table 2-4. With the ARQ code, each character has three 1s in it, and, therefore, a simple count of the number of 1s received in each character can determine if a transmission error has occurred.

Parity. *Parity* is probably the simplest error detection scheme used for data communications systems and is used with both vertical and horizontal redundancy checking. With parity, a single bit (called a *parity bit*) is added to each character to force the total number of 1s in the character, including the parity bit, to be either an odd number (odd parity) or an even number (even parity). For example, the ASCII code for the letter "C" is 43 hex or P1000011 binary, with the P bit representing the parity bit. There are three 1s in the code, not counting the parity bit. If odd parity is used, the P bit is made a 0, keeping the total number of 1s at three, an odd number. If even parity is used, the P bit is made a 1 and the total number of 1s is four, an even number.

Taking a closer look at parity, it can be seen that the parity bit is independent of the number of 0s in the code and unaffected by pairs of 1s. For the letter "C," if all the 0 bits are dropped, the code is P1————11. For odd parity, the P bit is still a 0 and for even parity, the P bit is still a 1. If pairs of 1s are also excluded, the code is either P1————, P————1, or P————1—. Again, for odd parity the P bit is a 0, and for even parity the P bit is a 1.

The definition of parity is *equivalence* or *equality.* A logic gate that will determine when all its inputs are equal is the XOR gate. With an XOR gate, if all the inputs are equal (either all 0s or all 1s), the output is a 0. If all inputs are not equal, the output is a 1. Figure 2-5 shows two circuits that are commonly used to generate a parity bit. Essentially, both circuits go through a comparison process eliminating 0s and pairs of 1s. The circuit shown in Figure 2-5a uses *sequential (serial)* comparison, whereas the circuit shown in Figure 2-5b uses *combinational (parallel)* comparison. With the sequential parity generator b_0 is XORed with b_1, the result is XORed with b_2, and so on. The result of the last XOR operation is compared with a *bias* bit. If even parity is desired, the bias bit is made a logic 0. If odd parity is desired, the bias bit is made a logic 1. The output of the circuit is the parity bit, which is appended to the character code. With the parallel parity generator, comparisons are made in layers or levels. Pairs of bits (b_0 and

TABLE 2-4 ARQ Exact-Count Code

	Binary Code							Character	
Bit:	1	2	3	4	5	6	7	Letter	Figure
	0	0	0	1	1	1	0	Letter shift	
	0	1	0	0	1	1	0	Figure shift	
	0	0	1	1	0	1	0	A	-
	0	0	1	1	0	0	1	B	?
	1	0	0	1	1	0	0	C	:
	0	0	1	1	1	0	0	D	(WRU)
	0	1	1	1	0	0	0	E	3
	0	0	1	0	0	1	1	F	%
	1	1	0	0	0	0	1	G	@
	1	0	1	0	0	1	0	H	£
	1	1	1	0	0	0	0	I	8
	0	1	0	0	0	1	1	J	(bell)
	0	0	0	1	0	1	1	K	(
	1	1	0	0	0	1	0	L	)
	1	0	1	0	0	0	1	M	.
	1	0	1	0	1	0	0	N	'
	1	0	0	0	1	1	0	O	9
	1	0	0	1	0	1	0	P	0
	0	0	0	1	1	0	1	Q	1
	1	1	0	0	1	0	0	R	4
	0	1	0	1	0	1	0	S	'
	1	0	0	0	1	0	1	T	5
	0	1	1	0	0	1	0	U	7
	1	0	0	1	0	0	1	V	=
	0	1	0	0	1	0	1	W	2
	0	0	1	0	1	1	0	X	/
	0	0	1	0	1	0	1	Y	6
	0	1	1	0	0	0	1	Z	+
	0	0	0	0	1	1	1	(blank)	
	1	1	0	1	0	0	0	(space)	
	1	0	1	1	0	0	0	(line feed)	
	1	0	0	0	0	1	1	(carriage return)	

b_1, b_2 and b_3, etc.) are XORed. The results of the first-level XOR gates are then XORed together. The process continues until only one bit is left, which is XORed with the bias bit. Again, if even parity is desired, the bias bit is made a logic 0 and if odd parity is desired, the bias bit is made a logic 1.

The circuits shown in Figure 2-5 can also be used for the parity checker in the receiver. A parity checker uses the same procedure as a parity generator except that the logic condition of the final comparison is used to determine if a parity violation has occurred (for odd parity a 1 indicates an error and a 0 indicates no error; for even parity, a 1 indicates an error and a 0 indicates no error).

The primary advantage of parity is its simplicity. The disadvantage is that when an even number of bits are received in error, the parity checker will not detect it (i.e., if the logic conditions of 2 bits are changed, the parity remains the same). Consequently, parity, over a long period of time, will detect only 50% of the transmission errors (this assumes an equal probability that an even or an odd number of bits could be in error).

Checksum. *Checksum* is an extremely simple method of error detection. A checksum is simply the least significant byte of the arithmetic sum of the binary data being transmitted. While data are being transmitted, each character is added (summed) with the accumulated sum of the previously transmitted characters. When the end of the

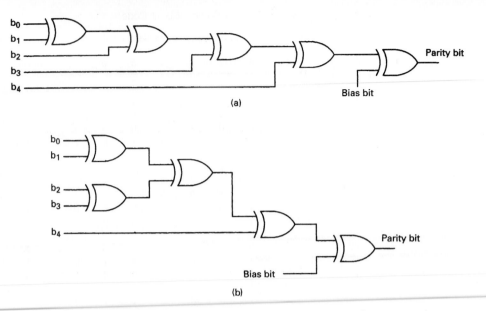

FIGURE 2-5 Parity generators: (a) serial; (b) parallel. 1 = odd parity; 2 = even parity

message is reached, the adder has accumulated the sum of all of the characters included in the message just sent. The least significant byte of the sum is appended to the end of the message and transmitted. The receive terminal replicates the summing operation and determines its own sum and checksum character. The least significant byte of the receiver's sum is compared to the checksum appended to the end of the message. If they are the same, most likely no transmission error has occurred. If they are different, a transmission error has definitely occurred. When an error is detected, a retransmission of the entire message is called for.

Vertical and horizontal redundancy checking. *Vertical redundancy checking* (VRC) is an error detection scheme that uses parity to determine if a transmission error has occurred within a character. Therefore, VRC is sometimes called *character parity*. With VRC, each character has a parity bit added to it prior to transmission. It may use even or odd parity. The example shown under the topic "Parity" involving the ASCII character "C" is an example of how VRC is used.

Horizontal or *longitudinal redundancy checking* (HRC or LRC) is an error detection scheme that uses parity to determine if a transmission error has occurred in a message and is, therefore, sometimes called *message parity*. With LRC, each bit position has a parity bit. In other words, b_0 from each character in the message is XORed with b_0 from all of the other characters in the message. Similarly, b_1, b_2, and so on, are XORed with their respective bits from all the other characters in the message. Essentially, LRC is the result of XORing the "characters" that make up a message, whereas VRC is the XORing of the bits within a single character. With LRC, only even parity is used.

The LRC bit sequence is computed in the transmitter prior to sending the data, then transmitted as though it were the last character of the message. At the receiver, the LRC is recomputed from the data and the recomputed LRC is compared with the LRC transmitted with the message. If they are the same, it is assumed that no transmission errors have occurred. If they are different, a transmission error must have occurred.

Example 2-1 shows how VRC and LRC are determined.

Example 2-1

Determine the VRC and LRC for the following ASCII-encoded message: THE CAT. Use odd parity for VRC and even parity for LRC.

Solution

Character		T	H	E	sp	C	A	T	LRC
Hex		54	48	45	20	43	41	54	2F
ASCII code									
LSB	b_0	0	0	1	0	1	1	0	1
	b_1	0	0	0	0	1	0	0	1
	b_2	1	0	1	0	0	0	1	1
	b_3	0	1	0	0	0	0	0	1
	b_4	1	0	0	0	0	0	1	0
	b_5	0	0	0	1	0	0	0	1
MSB	b_6	1	1	1	0	1	1	1	0
VRC	b_7	0	1	0	0	0	1	0	0

The LRC is 2FH or 00101111 binary. In ASCII, this is the character /.

The VRC bit for each character is computed in the vertical direction, and the LRC bits are computed in the horizontal direction. This is the same scheme that was used with early teletype paper tapes and keypunch cards and has subsequently been carried over to present-day data communications applications.

The group of characters that make up the message (i.e., THE CAT) is often called a *block* of data. Therefore, the bit sequence for the LRC is often called a *block check character* (BCC) or a *block check sequence* (BCS). BCS is more appropriate because the LRC has no function as a character (i.e., it is not an alpha/numeric, graphic, or data link control character); the LRC is simply a *sequence of bits* used for error detection.

Historically, LRC detects between 95% and 98% of all transmission errors. LRC will not detect transmission errors when an even number of characters have an error in the same bit position. For example, if b_4 in two different characters is in error, the LRC is still valid even though multiple transmission errors have occurred.

If VRC and LRC are used simultaneously, the only time an error would go undetected is when an even number of bits in an even number of characters were in error and the same bit positions in each character are in error, which is highly unlikely to happen. VRC does not identify which bit is in error in a character, and LRC does not identify which character has an error in it. However, for single bit errors, VRC used together with LRC will identify which bit is in error. Otherwise, VRC and LRC only identify that an error has occurred.

Cyclic redundancy checking. Probably the most reliable scheme for error detection is *cyclic redundancy checking* (CRC). With CRC, approximately 99.95% of all transmission errors are detected. CRC is generally used with 8-bit codes such as EBCDIC or 7-bit codes when parity is not used.

In the United States, the most common CRC code is CRC-16, which is identical to the international standard, CCITT V.41. With CRC-16, 16 bits are used for the BCS. Essentially, the CRC character is the remainder of a division process. A data message polynominal $G(x)$ is divided by a generator polynomial function $P(x)$, the quotient is discarded, and the remainder is truncated to 16 bits and added to the message as the BCS. With CRC generation, the division is not accomplished with a standard arithmetic division process. Instead of using straight subtraction, the remainder is derived from an XOR

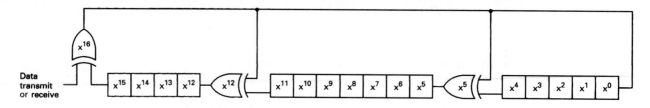

FIGURE 2-6 CRC-16 generating circuit (CCITT V.41)

operation. At the receiver, the data stream and the BCS are divided by the same generating function $P(x)$. If no transmission errors have occurred, the remainder will be zero.

The generating polynomial for CRC-16 is

$$P(x) = x^{16} + x^{12} + x^5 + x^0$$

where $x^0 = 1$.

The number of bits in the CRC code is equal to the highest exponent of the generating polynomial. The exponents identify the bit positions that contain a 1. Therefore, b_{16}, b_{12}, b_5, and b_0 are 1s and all of the other bit positions are 0s.

Figure 2-6 shows the block diagram for a circuit that will generate a CRC-16 BCS for the CCITT V.41 standard. Note that for each bit position of the generating polynomial where there is a 1 an XOR gate is placed except for x^0.

Example 2-2

Determine the BCS for the following data and CRC generating polynomials:

$$\text{data } G(x) = x^7 + x^5 + x^4 + x^2 + x^1 + x^0 \quad \text{or} \quad 10110111$$
$$\text{CRC } P(x) = x^5 + x^4 + x^1 + x^0 \quad \text{or} \quad 110011$$

Solution First $G(x)$ is multiplied by the number of bits in the CRC code, 5.

$$x^5(x^7 + x^5 + x^4 + x^2 + x^1 + x^0) = x^{12} + x^{10} + x^9 + x^7 + x^6 + x^5$$
$$= 1011011100000$$

Then divide the result by $P(x)$.

```
                          11010111
        110011 | 1011011100000
                 110011
                 111101
                 110011
                  111010
                  110011
                   100100
                   110011
                    101110
                    110011
                     111010
                     110011
                      01001  =  CRC
```

The CRC is appended to the data to give the following transmitted data stream:

$$\begin{array}{cc}
G(x) & \text{CRC} \\
10110111 & 01001
\end{array}$$

At the receiver, the transmitted data are again divided by $P(x)$.

```
                                      11010111
                     110011 | 1011011101001
                              110011
                               111101
                               110011
                                111010
                                110011
                                 100110
                                 110011
                                  101010
                                  110011
                                   110011
                                   110011
                                   000000   remainder = 0
                                            no error occurred
```

Error Correction

Essentially, there are three methods of error correction: symbol substitution, retransmission, and forward error correction.

Symbol substitution. *Symbol substitution* was designed to be used in a human environment—when there is a human being at the receive terminal to analyze the received data and make decisions on its integrity. With symbol substitution, if a character is received in error, rather than revert to a higher level of error correction or display the incorrect character, a unique character that is undefined by the character code, such as a reverse question mark (⸮), is substituted for the bad character. If the character in error cannot be discerned by the operator, retransmission is called for (i.e., symbol substitution is a form of selective retransmission). For example, if the message "Name" had an error in the first character, it would be displayed as "⸮ame." An operator can discern the correct message by inspection and retransmission is unnecessary. However, if the message "$⸮,000.00" were received, an operator could not determine the correct character, and retransmission is required.

Retransmission. *Retransmission,* as the name implies, is resending a message when it is received in error and the receive terminal automatically calls for retransmission of the entire message. Retransmission is often called ARQ, which is an old radio communications term that means *automatic request for retransmission.* ARQ is probably the most reliable method of error correction, although it is not always the most efficient. Impairments on transmission media occur in bursts. If short messages are used, the likelihood that an impairment will occur during a transmission is small. However, short messages require more acknowledgments and line turnarounds than do long messages. Acknowledgements and line turnarounds for error control are forms of *overhead* (characters other than data that must be transmitted). With long messages, less turnaround time is needed, although the likelihood that a transmission error will occur is higher than for short messages. It can be shown statistically that message blocks between 256 and 512 characters are of optimum size when using ARQ for error correction.

Forward error correction. *Forward error correction* (FEC) is the only error correction scheme that actually detects and corrects transmission errors at the receive end without calling for retransmission.

With FEC, bits are added to the message prior to transmission. A popular error-correcting code is the *Hamming code,* developed by R. W. Hamming at Bell Laboratories. The number of bits in the Hamming code is dependent on the number of bits in the data character. The number of Hamming bits that must be added to a character is determined from the following expression:

$$2^n \geq m + n + 1 \tag{2-1}$$

where n = number of Hamming bits

m = number of bits in the data character

Example 2-3

For a 12-bit data string of 101100010010, determine the number of Hamming bits required, arbitrarily place the Hamming bits into the data string, determine the condition of each Hamming bit, assume an arbitrary single-bit transmission error, and prove that the Hamming code will detect the error.

Solution   Substituting into Equation 2-1, the number of Hamming bits is

$$2^n \geq m + n + 1$$

For $n = 4$, $2^4 = 16 \geq m + n + 1 = 12 + 4 + 1 = 17$

$16 < 17$; therefore, 4 Hamming bits are insufficient.

For $n = 5$, $2^5 = 32 \geq m + n + 1 = 12 + 5 + 1 = 18$

$32 > 18$; therefore, 5 Hamming bits are sufficient to meet the criterion of Equation 2-1. Therefore, a total of $12 + 5 = 17$ bits make up the data stream.

Arbitrarily place 5 Hamming bits into the data stream:

```
17  16  15  14  13  12  11  10  9  8  7  6  5  4  3  2  1
 H   1   0   1   H   1   0   0   H  H  0  1  0  H  0  1  0
```

To determine the logic condition of the Hamming bits, express all bit positions that contain a 1 as a 5-bit binary number and XOR them together.

Bit position	Binary number
2	00010
6	00110
XOR	00100
12	01100
XOR	01000
14	01110
XOR	00110
16	10000
XOR	10110 = Hamming code

$b_{17} = 1,$ $b_{13} = 0,$ $b_9 = 1,$ $b_8 = 1,$ $b_4 = 0$

The 17-bit encoded data stream becomes

```
H           H       H H           H
1  1  0  1  0  1  0  0  1  1  0  1  0  0  0  1  0
```

Assume that during transmission, an error occurs in bit position 14. The received data stream is

$$1 \; 1 \; 0 \; 0 \; 0 \; 1 \; 0 \; 0 \; 1 \; 1 \; 0 \; 1 \; 0 \; 0 \; 0 \; 1 \; 0$$

At the receiver, to determine the bit position in error, extract the Hamming bits and XOR them with the binary code for each data bit position that contains a 1.

Bit position	Binary number
Hamming code	10110
2	00010
XOR	10100
6	00110
XOR	10010
12	01100
XOR	11110
16	10000
XOR	01110 = binary 14

Bit position 14 was received in error. To fix the error, simply complement bit 14.

The Hamming code described here will detect only single-bit errors. It cannot be used to identify multiple-bit errors or errors in the Hamming bits themselves. The Hamming code, as with all FEC codes, requires the addition of bits to the data, consequently, lengthening the transmitted message. The purpose of FEC codes is to reduce or eliminate the wasted time of retransmissions. However, the addition of the FEC bits to each message wastes transmission time in itself. Obviously, a trade-off is made between ARQ and FEC and system requirements determine which method is best suited to a particular system. FEC is often used for simplex transmissions to many receivers when acknowledgments are impractical.

SYNCHRONIZATION

Synchronize means to coincide or agree in time. In data communications, there are four types of synchronization that must be achieved: bit or clock synchronization, modem or carrier synchronization, character synchronization, and message synchronization. The clock and carrier recovery circuits discussed in Chapter 1 accomplish bit and carrier synchronization, and message synchronization is discussed in Chapter 3.

Character Synchronization
Clock synchronization ensures that the transmitter and receiver agree on a precise time slot for the occurrence of a bit. When a continuous string of data is received, it is necessary to identify which bits belong to which characters and which bit is the least significant data bit, the parity bit, and the stop bit. In essence, this is character synchronization: identifying the beginning and the end of a character code. In data communication circuits, there are two formats used to achieve character synchronization: asynchronous and synchronous.

Asynchronous data format. With *asynchronous data,* each character is framed between a *start* and a *stop* bit. Figure 2-7 shows the format used to frame a character for asynchronous data transmission. The first bit transmitted is the start bit and is always a logic 0. The character code bits are transmitted next beginning with the LSB and continuing through the MSB. The parity bit (if used) is transmitted directly after the MSB

Stop bit (1, 1.5, 2)	Parity bit		Data bits (5–7)							Start bit
1	1	1/0	b_6 MSB	b_5	b_4	b_3	b_2	b_1	b_0 LSB	0

FIGURE 2-7 Asynchronous data format

of the character. The last bit transmitted is the stop bit, which is always a logic 1. There can be either 1, 1.5, of 2 stop bits.

A logic 0 is used for the start bit because an idle condition (no data transmission) on a data communications circuit is identified by the transmission of continuous 1s (these are often called *idle line 1s*). Therefore, the start bit of the first character is identified by a high-to-low transition in the received data, and the bit that immediately follows the start bit is the LSB of the character code. All stop bits are logic 1s, which guarantees a high-to-low transition at the beginning of each character. After the start bit is detected, the data and parity bits are clocked into the receiver. If data are transmitted in real time (i.e., as an operator types data into the computer terminal), the number of idle line 1s between each character will vary. During this *dead time,* the receiver will simply wait for the occurrence of another start bit before clocking in the next character.

Example 2-4

For the following string of asynchronous ASCII-encoded data, identify each character (assume even parity and 2 stop bits).

Synchronous data format. With *synchronous data,* rather than frame each character independently with start and stop bits, a unique synchronizing character called a SYN character is transmitted at the beginning of each message. For example with ASCII code, the SYN character is 16H. The receiver disregards incoming data until it receives the SYN character, then it clocks in the next 8 bits and interprets them as a character. The character that is used to signify the end of a transmission varies with the type of protocol used and what kind of transmission it is. Message-terminating characters are discussed in Chapter 3.

With asynchronous data, it is not necessary that the transmit and receive clocks be continuously synchronized. It is only necessary that they operate at approximately the same rate and be synchronized at the beginning of each character. This was the purpose of the start bit, to establish a time reference for character synchronization. With synchronous data, the transmit and receive clocks must be synchronized because character synchronization occurs only once at the beginning of the message.

Example 2-5

For the following string of synchronous ASCII-encoded data, identify each character (assume odd parity).

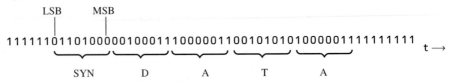

With asynchronous data, each character has 2 or 3 bits added to each character (1 start and 1 or 2 stop bits). These bits are additional overhead and, thus, reduce the efficiency of the transmission (i.e., the ratio of information bits to total transmitted bits). Synchronous data have two SYN characters (16 bits of overhead) added to each message. Therefore, asynchronous data are more efficient for short messages, and synchronous data are more efficient for long messages.

FIGURE 2-8 Multipoint data communications circuit block diagram

DATA COMMUNICATIONS HARDWARE

Figure 2-8 shows the block diagram of a multipoint data communications circuit that uses a bus topology. This arrangement is one of the most common configurations used for data communications circuits. At one station there is a mainframe computer and at each of the other two stations there is a *cluster* of computer terminals. The hardware and associated circuitry that connect the host computer to the remote computer terminals is called a *data communications link.* The station with the mainframe is called the *host* or *primary* and the other stations are called *secondaries* or simply *remotes.* An arrangement such as this is called a *centralized network;* there is one centrally located station (the host) with the responsibility of ensuring an orderly flow of data between the remote stations and itself. Data flow is controlled by an applications program that is stored at the primary station.

At the primary station there is a mainframe computer, a *line control unit* (LCU), and a *data modem* (a data modem is commonly referred to simply as a *modem*). At each secondary station there is a modem, an LCU, and terminal equipment, such as computer terminals, printers, and so on. The mainframe is the host of the network and is where the application program is stored for each circuit it serves. For simplicity, Figure 2-8 shows only one circuit served by the primary, although there can be many different circuits served by one mainframe computer. The primary station has the capability of storing, processing, or retransmitting the data it receives from the secondary stations. The primary also stores software for data base management.

The LCU at the primary station is more complicated than the LCUs at the secondary stations. The LCU at the primary station directs data traffic to and from many different circuits, which could all have different characteristics (i.e., different bit rates, character codes, data formats, etc.). The LCU at a secondary station directs data traffic between one data link and a few terminal devices, which all operate at the same speed and use the same character code. Generally speaking, if the LCU has software associated with it, it is called a *front-end processor* (FEP). The LCU at the primary station is usually an FEP.

Line Control Unit

The LCU has several important functions. The LCU at the primary station serves as an interface between the host computer and the circuits that it serves. Each circuit served is connected to a different port on the LCU. The LCU directs the flow of input and output data between the different data communications links and their respective applications program. The LCU performs parallel-to-serial and serial-to-parallel conversion of data. The mux interface channel between the mainframe computer and the LCU transfers data in parallel. Data transfers between the modem and the LCU are done serially. The LCU also houses the circuitry that performs error detection and correction. Also, data link control (DLC) characters are inserted and deleted in the LCU. Data link control characters are explained in Chapter 3.

The LCU operates on the data when it is in digital form and, therefore, is called *data terminal equipment* (DTE). Within the LCU, there is a single integrated circuit that performs several of the LCU's functions. This circuit is called a UART when asynchronous transmission is used and a USRT when synchronous transmission is used.

Universal asynchronous receiver/transmitter (UART). The UART is used for asynchronous transmission of data between the DTE and the DCE. Asynchronous transmission means that an asynchronous data format is used and there is no clocking information transferred between the DTE and the DCE. The primary functions of the UART are

1. To perform serial-to-parallel and parallel-to-serial conversion of data
2. To perform error detection by inserting and checking parity bits
3. To insert and detect start and stop bits

Functionally, the UART is divided into two sections: the transmitter and the receiver. Figure 2-9a shows a simplified block diagram of a UART transmitter.

Prior to transferring data in either direction, a *control* word must be programmed into the UART control register to indicate the nature of the data, such as the number of data bits; if parity is used, and if so, whether it is even or odd; and the number of stop bits. Essentially, the start bit is the only bit that is not optional; there is always only one start bit and it must be a logic 0. Figure 2-9b shows how to program the control word for the various functions. In the UART, the control word is used to set up the data-, parity-, and stop-bit steering logic circuit.

UART Transmitter. The operation of the UART transmitter section is really quite simple. The UART sends a transmit buffer empty (TBMT) signal to the DTE to indicate that it is ready to receive data. When the DTE senses an active condition on TBMT, it sends a parallel data character to the transmit data lines (TD_0–TD_7) and strobes them into the transmit buffer register with the transmit data strobe signal ($\overline{TDS}$). The contents of the transmit buffer register are transferred to the transmit shift register when the transmit end-of-character (TEOC) signal goes active (the TEOC signal simply tells the buffer register when the shift register is empty and available to receive data). The data pass through the steering logic circuit, where they pick up the appropriate start, stop, and parity bits. After data have been loaded into the transmit shift register, they are serially outputted on the transmit serial output (TSO) pin with a bit rate equal to the transmit clock (TCP) frequency. While the data in the transmit shift register are sequentially clocked out, the DTE loads the next character into the buffer register. The process continues until the DTE has transferred all its data. The preceding sequence is shown in Figure 2-10.

NPB	1 = no parity bit (RPE disabled)	POE	1 = parity even	NSB	1 = 2 stop bits
	0 = parity bit		0 = parity odd		0 = 1 stop bits

NDB2	NDB1	Bits/word
0	0	5
0	1	6
1	0	7
1	1	8

<u>Note</u>: When NDB2/NDB1 = 11 and NSB = 1, 1.5 stop bits

(b)

FIGURE 2-9 UART transmitter: (a) simplified block diagram; (b) control word

UART Receiver. A simplified block diagram of a UART receiver is shown in Figure 2-11. The number of stop bits, data bits, and the parity-bit information for the UART receiver are determined by the same control word that is used by the transmitter (i.e., the type of parity, the number of stop bits, and the number of data bits used for the UART receiver must be the same as that used for the UART transmitter).

The UART receiver ignores idle time line 1s. When a valid start bit is detected by the start bit verification circuit, the data character is serially clocked into the receive shift register. If parity is used, the parity bit is checked in the parity check circuit. After one

Data Communications Hardware

73

FIGURE 2-10   Timing diagram: UART transmitter

FIGURE 2-11   Simplified block diagram of a UART receiver

complete data character is loaded into the shift register, the character is transferred in parallel into the buffer register and the receive data available (RDA) flag is set in the status word register. To read the status register, the DTE monitors status word enable ($\overline{\text{SWE}}$) and if it is active, reads the character from the buffer register by placing an active condition on the receive data enable (RDE) pin. After reading the data, the DTE places an active signal on the receive data available reset ($\overline{\text{RDAR}}$) pin, which resets the RDA pin. Meanwhile, the next character is received and clocked into the receive shift register and the process is repeated until all the data have been received. The preceding sequence is shown in Figure 2-12.

The status word register is also used for diagnostic information. The receive parity error (RPE) flag is set when a received character has a parity error in it. The receive framing error (RFE) flag is set when a character is received without any or an improper number of stop bits. The receive overrun (ROR) flag is set when a character in the buffer register is written over with another character (i.e., the DTE failed to service an active condition on RDA before the next character was received by the shift register).

The receive clock for the UART (RCP) is 16 times higher than the receive data rate. This allows the start-bit verification circuit to determine if a high-to-low transition in the received data is actually a valid start bit and not simply a negative-going noise spike. Figure 2-13 shows how this is accomplished. The incoming idle line 1s (continuous high condition) are sampled at a rate 16 times the actual bit rate. This assures that a high-to-low transition is detected with 1/16 of a bit time after it occurs. Once a low is detected, the verification circuit counts off seven clock pulses, then resamples the data. If it is still low, it is assumed that a valid start bit has been detected. If it has reverted to the high condition, it is assumed that the high-to-low transition was simply a noise pulse and, therefore, is ignored. Once a valid start bit has been detected and verified, the verification circuit samples the incoming data once every 16 clock cycles, which is equal to the data rate. Sampling at 16 times the bit rate also establishes the sample time to within 1/16 of a bit time from the center of a bit.

Universal synchronous receiver/transmitter (USRT). The USRT is used for synchronous data transmission between the DTE and the DCE. Synchronous transmission means that there is clocking information transferred between the USRT and the modem and each transmission begins with a unique SYN character. The primary functions of the USRT are

1. To perform serial-to-parallel and parallel-to-serial conversion of data
2. To perform error detection by inserting and checking parity bits
3. To insert and detect SYN characters

The block diagram of the USRT is shown in Figure 2-14a. The USRT operates very similarly to the UART, and, therefore, only the differences are explained. With the USRT, start and stop bits are not allowed. Instead, unique SYN characters are loaded into the transmit and receive SYN registers prior to transferring data. The programming information for the control word is shown in Figure 2-14b.

USRT Transmitter. The transmit clock signal (TCP) is set at the desired bit rate and the desired SYN character is loaded from the parallel input pins (DB_0–DB_7) into the transmit SYN register by pulsing transmit SYN strobe (TSS). Data are loaded into the transmit data register from DB_0–DB_7 by pulsing the transmit data strobe (TDS). The next character transmitted is extracted from the transmit data register provided that the TDS pulse occurs during the presently transmitted character. If TDS is not pulsed, the next transmitted character is extracted from the transmit SYN register and the SYN character transmitted (SCT) signal is set. The transmit buffer empty (TBMT) signal is used to

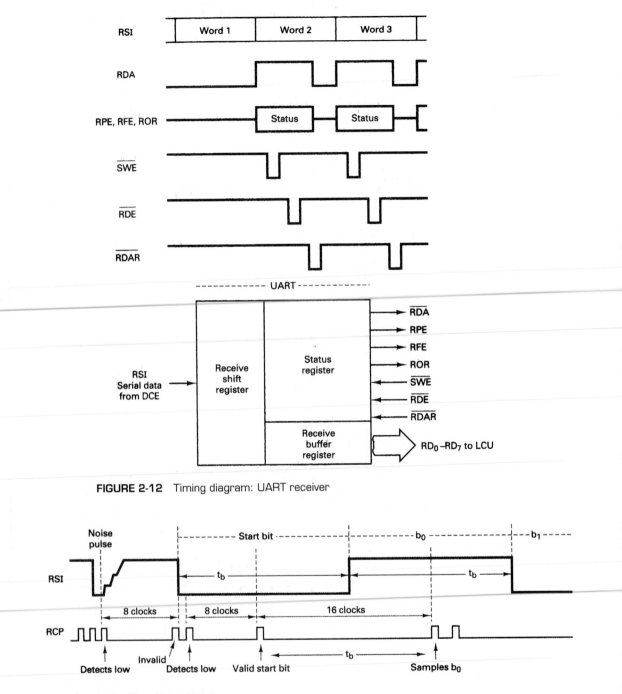

FIGURE 2-12 Timing diagram: UART receiver

FIGURE 2-13 Start-bit verification

request the next character from the DTE. The serial output data appears on the transmit serial output (TSO) pin.

USRT Receiver. The receive clock signal (RCP) is set at the desired bit rate and the desired SYN character is loaded into the receive SYN register from DB_0–DB_7 by pulsing receive SYN strobe (RSS). On a high-to-low transition of the receiver rest input (RR), the receiver is placed in the search (bit phase) mode. In the search mode, serially received data are examined on a bit-by-bit basis until a SYN character is found. After

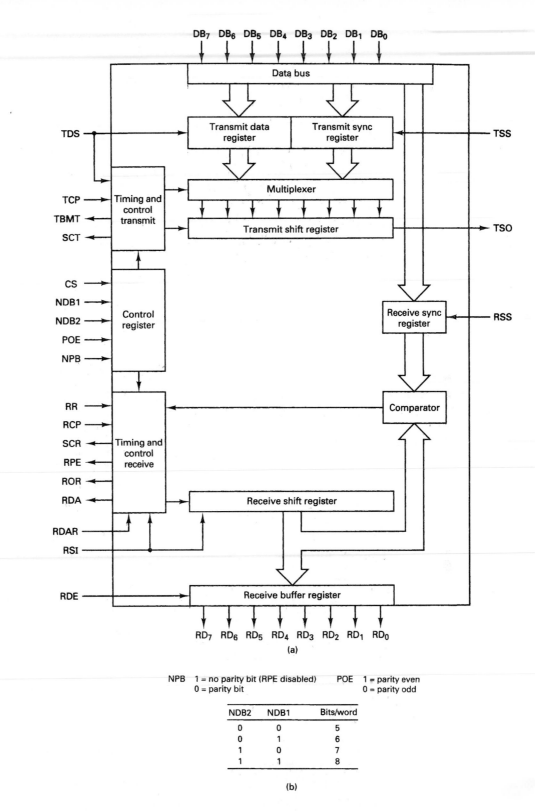

DB₇ DB₆ DB₅ DB₄ DB₃ DB₂ DB₁ DB₀

Data bus

TDS

Transmit data register   Transmit sync register   TSS

Multiplexer

Timing and control transmit

TCP
TBMT
SCT

Transmit shift register   TSO

CS
NDB1
NDB2
POE
NPB

Control register

Receive sync register   RSS

RR
RCP
SCR
RPE
ROR
RDA

Timing and control receive

Comparator

Receive shift register

RDAR
RSI

RDE

Receive buffer register

RD₇ RD₆ RD₅ RD₄ RD₃ RD₂ RD₁ RD₀

(a)

NPB   1 = no parity bit (RPE disabled)   POE   1 = parity even
       0 = parity bit   0 = parity odd

NDB2	NDB1	Bits/word
0	0	5
0	1	6
1	0	7
1	1	8

(b)

FIGURE 2-14 USRT transceiver: (a) block diagram; (b) control word each bit is clocked into the receive shift register, its contents are compared to the contents of the receive SYN register. If they are identical, a SYN character has been found and the SYN character receive (SCR) output is set. This character is transferred into the receive buffer register and the receiver is placed into the character mode. In the character mode, receive data are examined on a character-by-character basis and receiver flags for receive data available (RDA), receiver overrun (ROR), receive parity error (RPE), and SYN character received are provided to the status word register. Parallel receive data are outputted to the DTE on RD_0–RD_7.

SERIAL INTERFACES

To ensure an orderly flow of data between the line control unit and the modem, a *serial interface* is placed between them. This interface coordinates the flow of data, control signals, and timing information between the DTE and the DCE.

Before serial interfaces were standardized, every company that manufactured data communications equipment used a different interface configuration. More specifically, the cabling arrangement between the DTE and the DCE, the type and size of the connectors used, and the voltage levels varied considerably from vender to vender. To interconnect equipment manufactured by different companies, special level converters, cables, and connectors had to be built.

In 1962 the Electronic Industries Association (EIA), in an effort to standardize interface equipment between data terminal equipment and data communications equipment, agreed on a set of standards called the RS-232 specifications. In 1969, the third revision, RS-232C was published and remained the industrial standard until 1987 when RS-232D was introduced. The RS-232D version of the interface is compatible with the C version. The primary difference between the two versions are the addition of three test circuits in the D version.

The RS-232 specifications identify the mechanical, electrical, functional, and procedural description for the interface between the DTE and DCE. The RS-232 interface is similar to the combined CCITT standards V.28 (electrical specifications) and V.24 (functional description) and is designed for serial transmission of data up to 20 kbps for a distance of approximately 50 ft.

RS-232 Interface

The RS-232 interface specifies a 25-wire cable with a DB25P/DB25S-compatible connector. Figure 2-15 shows the electrical characteristics of the RS-232 interface. The terminal load capacitance of the cable is specified as 2500 pF, which includes cable capacitance. The impedance at the terminating end must be between 3000 Ω and 7000 Ω, and the output impedance is specified as greater than 300 Ω. With these electrical specifications and for a maximum bit rate of 20,000 bps, the nominal maximum length of the RS-232 interface is approximately 50 ft.

Although the RS-232 interface is simply a cable and two connectors, the standard also specifies limitations on the voltage levels that the DTE and DCE can output onto or receive from the cable. In both the DTE and DCE, there are circuits that convert their internal logic levels to RS-232 values. For example, a DTE uses TTL logic and is interfaced to a DCE that uses ECL logic; they are not compatible. Voltage-leveling circuits convert the internal voltage values of the DTE and DCE to RS-232 values. If both the DCE and DTE output and input RS-232 levels, they are electrically compatible regardless of which logic family they use internally. A leveler is called a *driver* if it outputs a signal voltage to the cable and a *terminator* if it accepts a signal voltage from the cable. Table 2-5 lists the voltage limits for both drivers and terminators. Note that the data lines use negative logic and the control lines use positive logic.

FIGURE 2-15 RS-232 electrical specifications

TABLE 2-5 RS232 Voltage Specifications (V dc)

	Data Pins		Control Pins	
	Logic 1	Logic 0	Enable "On"	Disable "Off"
Driver	−5 to −15	+5 to +15	+5 to +15	−5 to −15
Terminator	−3 to −25	+3 to +25	+3 to +25	−3 to −25

From Table 2-5 it can be seen that the limits for a driver are more inclusive than those for a terminator. The driver can output any voltage between +5 V and +15 V or −5 V and −15 V dc, and a terminator will accept any voltage between +3 V and +25 V and −3 V and −25 V dc. The difference in the voltage levels between a driver and a terminator is called *noise margin.* The noise margin reduces the susceptibility of the interface to noise transients on the cable. Typical voltages used for data and control signals are ±7 V dc and ±10 V dc.

The pins on the RS-232 interface cable are functionally categorized as either ground, data, control (handshaking), or timing pins. All the pins are unidirectional (signals are propagated only from the DTE to the DCE, or vice versa). Table 2-6 lists the 25 pins of the RS-232 interface, their designations, and the direction of signal propagation (i.e., either toward the DTE or toward the DCE). The RS-232 specifications designate the ground, data, control, and timing pins as A, B, C, and D, respectively. These are nondescriptive designations. It is more practical and useful to use acronyms to designate the pins that reflect the pin functions. Table 2-6 lists the CCITT and EIA designations and the nomenclature more commonly used by industry in the United States.

EIA RS-232 pin functions. Twenty of the 25 pins of the RS-232 interface are designated for specific purposes or functions. Pins 9, 10, 11, and 18 are unassigned; pins 1 and 7 are grounds; pins 2, 3, 14, and 16 are data pins; pins 15, 17, and 24 are timing pins; and all the other assigned pins are reserved for control or handshaking signals. There are two full-duplex data channels available with the RS-232 interface; one channel is for primary data (actual information) and the second channel is for secondary data (diagnostic information and handshaking signals). The functions of the 25 pins are summarized below.

Pin 1. Protective ground. This pin is frame ground and is used for protection against electrical shock. Pin 1 should be connected to the third-wire ground of the ac

TABLE 2-6 EIA RS-232 Pin Designations

Pin Number	EIA Nomenclature	Common Acronyms	Direction
1	Protective ground (AA)	GWG	None
2	Transmitted data (BA)	TD, SD	DTE to DCE
3	Received data (BB)	RD	DCE to DTE
4	Request to send (CA)	RS, RTS	DTE to DCE
5	Clear to send (CB)	CS, CTS	DCE to DTE
6	Data set ready (CC)	DSR, MR	DCE to DTE
7	Signal ground (AB)	GND	None
8	Received line signal detect (CF)	RLSD, CD	DCE to DTE
9	Unassigned		
10	Unassigned		
11	Unassigned		
12	Secondary received line signal detect (SCF)	SRLSD	DCE to DTE
13	Secondary clear to send (SCB)	SCS	DCE to DTE
14	Secondary transmitted data (SBA)	STD	DTE to DCE
15	Transmission signal element timing (DB)	SCT	DCE to DTE
16	Secondary received data (SBB)	SRD	DCE to DTE
17	Receiver signal element timing (DD)	SCR	DCE to DTE
18	Local loopback	LL	DTE to DCE
19	Secondary request to send (SCA)	SRS	DTE to DCE
20	Data terminal ready (CD)	DTR	DTE or DCE
21	Signal quality detector (CG), or	SQD	DCE to DTE
	Remote loopback	RL	DTE to DCE
22	Ring indicator (CE)	RI	DCE to DTE
23	Data signal rate selector (CH)	DSRS	DTE to DCE
24	Transmit signal element timing (DA)	SCTE	DTE to DCE
25	Test mode	TM	DCE to DTE

electrical system at one end of the cable (either at the DTE or the DCE, but not at both ends).

Pin 2. Transmit data (TD). Serial data on the primary channel from the DTE to the DCE are transmitted on this pin. TD is enabled by an active condition on the CS pin.

Pin 3. Received data (RD). Serial data on the primary channel are transferred from the DCE to the DTE on this pin. RD is enabled by an active condition on the RLSD pin.

Pin 4. Request to send (RS). The DTE bids for the primary communications channel from the DCE on this pin. An active condition on RS turns on the modem's analog carrier. The analog carrier is modulated by a unique bit pattern called a training sequence that is used to initialize the communications channel and synchronize the receive modem. RS cannot go active unless pin 6 (DSR) is active.

Pin 5. Clear to send (CS). This signal is a handshake from the DCE to the DTE in response to an active condition on request to send. CS enables the TD pin.

Pin 6. Data set ready (DSR). On this pin the DCE indicates the availability of the communications channel. DSR is active as long as the DCE is connected to the communications channel (i.e., the modem or the communications channel is not being tested or is not in the voice mode).

Pin 7. Signal ground. The pin is the signal reference for all the data, control, and timing pins. Usually, this pin is strapped to frame ground (pin 1).

Pin 8. Receive line signal detect (RLSD). The DCE uses this pin to signal the DTE when the DCE is receiving an analog carrier on the primary data channel. RLSD enables the RD pin.

Pin 9. Unassigned.

Chapter 2   **Data Communications**

Pin 10. Unassigned.

Pin 11. Equalizer mode (non-EIA). This circuit is used by the data set to notify the DTE when the data set begins self-adjusting because error performance is poor. When RLSD is on and this circuit is off, the data set is retraining and the probability of error in the data on RD is high. When RLSD is on and this circuit is on, the modem is trained and the probability of error on RD is small.

Pin 12. Secondary receive line signal detect (SRLSD). This pin is active when the DCE is receiving an analog carrier on the secondary channel. SRLSD enables the SRD pin.

Pin 13. Secondary clear to send (SCS). This pin is used by the DCE to send a handshake to the DTE in response to an active condition on the secondary request to send pin. SCS enables the STD pin.

Pin 14. Secondary transmit data (STD). Diagnostic data are transferred from the DTE to the DCE on this pin. STD is enabled by an active condition on the SCS pin.

New synch (non-EIA). The use of this circuit is optional and is intended for use with a data set at the primary of a multipoint dedicated network. When the primary is in a polling operation, rapid resynchronization of the receiver to many remote transmitters is required. The receiver clock normally maintains the timing information of the previous message for some interval after the message has ended. This may interfere with resynchronization on the receipt of the next message. An on condition should be applied to this circuit by the DTE for at least 1 ms but no longer than the intermessage interval to squelch the existing timing information in the modem after the message has been received.

Pin 15. Transmission signal element timing (SCT). Transmit clocking signals are sent from the DCE to the DTE on this pin.

Pin 16. Secondary received data (SRD). Diagnostic data are transferred from the DCE to the DTE on this pin. SRD is enabled by an active condition on the SCS pin.

Pin 17. Receive signal element timing (SCR). Receive clocking signals are sent from the DCE to the DTE on this pin. The clock frequency is equal to the bit rate of the primary data channel.

Pin 18. Local loopback (LL). Control signal from the DTE to the DCE placing the DCE (modem) into a loopback condition. A local loopback disconnects the transmitted analog signal from the communications line and connects it directly to the receiver, which enables the local terminal to perform troubleshooting tests on the modem.

Pin 19. Secondary request to send (SRS). The DTE bids for the secondary communications channel from the DCE on this pin.

Pin 20. Data terminal ready (DTR). The DTE sends information to the DCE on this pin concerning the availability of the data terminal equipment (i.e., access to the mainframe at the primary station or status of the computer terminal at the secondary station). DTR is used primarily with dial-up data communications circuits to handshake with RI.

Pin 21. Signal quality detector (SQD). The DCE sends signals to the DTE on this pin that reflect the quality of the received analog carrier.

Remote loopback (RL). Control signal from the DTE to the DCE that places the DCE (modem) into a remote loopback condition. A remote loopback connects the receive data pin on the modem to its transmit data pin allowing the distant end terminal to perform troubleshooting tests on the modem.

Pin 22. Ring indicator (RI). This pin is used with dial-up lines for the DCE to signal the DTE that there is an incoming call.

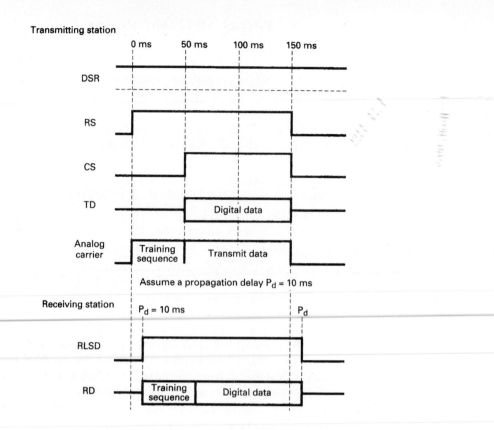

Transmitting station

0 ms   50 ms   100 ms   150 ms

DSR

RS

CS

TD — Digital data

Analog carrier — Training sequence | Transmit data

Assume a propagation delay $P_d = 10$ ms

Receiving station $P_d = 10$ ms P_d

RLSD

RD — Training sequence | Digital data

FIGURE 2-16 Timing diagram: basic operation of the RS-232 interface

Pin 23. Data signal rate selector (DSRS). The DTE uses this pin to select the transmission bit rate (clock frequency) of the DCE.

Pin 24. Transmit signal element timing (SCTE). Transmit clocking signals are sent from the DTE to the DCE on this pin when the master clock oscillator is located in the DTE.

Pin 25. Test mode (TM). Control signal from the DCE to the DTE that is enabled whenever either a local or remote loopback test is being performed.

Pins 1 through 8 are used with both asynchronous and synchronous modems. Pins 15, 17, and 24 are used for only synchronous modems. Pins 12, 13, 14, 16, and 19 are used only when the DCE is equipped with a secondary channel. Pins 19 and 22 are used exclusively for dial-up telephone connections.

The basic operation of the RS-232 interface is shown in Figure 2-16 and described as follows. When the DTE has primary data to send, it enables request to send ($t = 0$ ms). After a predetermined time delay (50 ms), CS goes active. During the RS/CS delay, the modem is outputting an analog carrier that is modulated by a unique bit pattern called a *training sequence.* The training sequence is used to initialize the communications line and synchronize the carrier and clock recovery circuits in the receive modem. After the RS/CS delay, TD is enabled and the DTE begins to transmit data. After the receive DTE detects an analog carrier, RD is enabled. When the transmission is complete ($t = 150$ ms), RS goes low turning off the analog carrier and shutting off CS.

RS-449 and RS-530 Interface Standards

Contemporary data rates have exceeded the capabilities of the RS-232 interface. Therefore, in 1977 the EIA introduced the RS-449 specification with the intention of

TABLE 2-7 RS-530 Pin Designations

Signal Name	Pin Number(s)
Shield	1
Transmitted data[a]	2, 14
Received data[a]	3, 16
Request to send[a]	4, 19
Clear to send[a]	5, 13
DCE ready[a]	6, 22
DTE ready[a]	20, 23
Signal ground	7
Received line signal detect[a]	8, 10
Transmit signal element timing (DCE source)[a]	15, 12
Receiver signal element timing (DCE source)[a]	17, 9
Local loopback[b]	18
Remote loopback[b]	21
Transmit signal element timing (DTE source)[a]	24, 11
Test mode[b]	25

[a]Category I circuits (RS-422A)

[b]Category II circuits (RS-423A)

replacing the RS-232 interface. The RS-449 interface uses a 37-pin connector that provides more functions, faster data transmission rates, and greater distance capabilities. However, the industry never embraced the RS-449 standard and it came and went virtually unnoticed by most of the data communications industry. Consequently, in 1987 the EIA introduced the RS-530 standard, which was intended to operate at data rates from 20 kbps to 2 Mbps using the same 25-pin, DB-25 connector used by the RS-232 interface. Table 2-7 lists the 25 pins for the RS-530 interface and their designations.

The RS-530 interface, however, does not include electrical specifications. Instead the electrical specifications used with the RS-530 are specified by either the RS-442A or RS-423A standard. The RS-422A standard specifies a balanced interface cable that will operate at bit rates up to 10 Mbps and span distances up to 1200 m. This does not mean, however, that 10 Mbps can be transmitted 1200 m. At 10 Mbps the maximum distance is approximately 15 m, and 90 kbps is the maximum bit rate that can be transmitted 1200 m. The RS-423A standard specifies an unbalanced interface cable that will operate at a maximum line speed of 100 kbps and span a maximum distance of 90 m.

Figure 2-17 shows the *balanced* digital interface circuit for the RS-422A, and Figure 2-18 shows the *unbalanced* digital interface circuit for the RS-423A.

A balanced interface, such as the RS-422A, transfers information to a *balanced transmission line*. With a balanced transmission line, both conductors carry current except the current in the two wires travel in opposite directions. With a bidirectional *unbalanced* line, one wire is at ground potential and the currents in the two wires may be different. Currents that flow in opposite directions in a balanced wire pair are called *metallic circuit* currents. Currents that flow in the same direction are called *longitudinal* currents. A balanced pair has the advantage that most noise interference is induced equally in both wires, producing longitudinal currents that cancel in the load. Figure 2-19 shows the results of metallic and longitudinal currents on a balanced transmission line. It can be seen that longitudinal currents (generally produced by static interference) cancel in the load. Balanced transmission lines can be connected to unbalanced loads, and vice versa, with special transformers called *baluns* (*bal*anced to *un*balanced).

The RS-232 and RS-530 standards provide specifications for answering calls, but not for dialing. The EIA has a different standard, RS-366, for automatic calling units. The principal use of RS-366 is for dial backup of private-line data circuits and for automatic dialing of remote terminals.

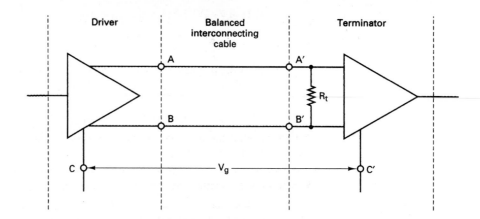

FIGURE 2-17 RS-422A interface circuit, R_t, optional cable termination resistance; V_g, ground potential difference; A, B, driver interface points; A', B', terminator interface points; C, driver circuit ground; C', terminator circuit ground; A-B, balanced driver output; A'-B', balanced terminator input

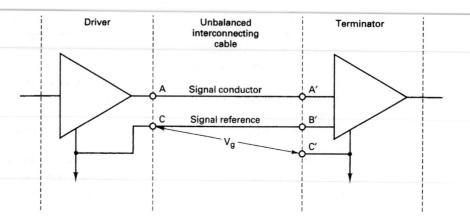

FIGURE 2-18 RS-423A interface circuit. A, C, driver interface; A', B', terminator interface; V_g, ground potential difference; C, driver circuit ground; C', terminator circuit ground

FIGURE 2-19 Results of metallic and longitudinal currents on a balanced transmission line: (a) metallic currents due to signal voltages; (b) longitudinal currents due to noise voltages

TABLE 2-8 CCITT X.21 Pin Designations

Interchange Circuit	Name	Direction
G	Signal ground	*
GA	DTE common return	DTE to DCE
T	Transmit	DTE to DCE
R	Receive	DCE to DTE
C	Control	DTE to DCE
I	Indication	DCE to DTE
S	Signal element timing	DCE to DTE
B	Byte timing	DCE to DTE

*See X.24 Recommendations

CCITT X.21

In 1976, the CCITT introduced the X.21 recommendation, which includes the specifications for placing and receiving calls and for sending and receiving data using full-duplex synchronous transmission. The X.21 recommendation presumes a direct digital connection to a digital telephone network. Thus, all data transmissions must be synchronous, and the data communications equipment will need to provide both bit and character synchronization. The minimum data rate for X.21 will probably be 64 kbps because this is the bit rate currently used to encode voice in digital form on the telephone network.

The X.21 specifies only six signals, which are listed in Table 2-8. Data are transmitted toward the modem on the transmit line, and the modem returns data on the receive line. The control and indication lines are control channels for the two transmission directions. The signal element timing line carries the bit timing signal (clock) and the byte timing line carries the character synchronization information. The electrical specifications for X.21 are listed either in recommendation X.26 (balanced) or recommendation X.27 (unbalanced).

The major advantage of the X.21 standard over the RS-232 and RS-530 standards is that X.21 signals are encoded in serial digital form, which sets the stage for providing special new services in computer communications.

PARALLEL INTERFACES

Parallel interfaces transfer data between two devices 8 or more bits at a time. That is, one entire data word is transmitted (received) at a time as opposed to one bit at a time as with serial interfaces. Parallel transmission is sometimes referred to as *serial-by-word* transmission. One obvious advantage of parallel transmission is data are transmitted much faster than with serial transmission. This, of course, is because there is a transmission path for each bit of the word. For example, a system utilizing 8-bit words would have eight separate communications channels between the transmitter and receiver. Another advantage of parallel transmission is most computer terminals and peripheral equipment process data internally in parallel. Therefore, with parallel interfaces there is no need to convert data from parallel to serial or vice versa. A disadvantage of parallel transmission is higher costs for transmission lines, especially when there are long distances between the transmitter and receiver. Therefore, parallel interfaces are commonly used to transfer data between two or more devices that are located in close proximity to each other, such as a computer and a printer.

Centronics Parallel Interface

The *Centronics parallel interface* was originally designed to be used for transferring data between a microcomputer and a printer. Centronics was one of the original companies to

FIGURE 2-20   Printer interface and pin alignment

TABLE 2-9   Centronics Printer Interface Lines

Pin Number	Return Pin	Signal	Abbreviation	Active	Type	Direction
1	19	Strobe	$\overline{STB}$	Low	Control	To printer
2	20	Data bit 0	d_0		Data	To printer
3	21	Data bit 1	d_1		Data	To printer
4	22	Data bit 2	d_2		Data	To printer
5	23	Data bit 3	d_3		Data	To printer
6	24	Data bit 4	d_4		Data	To printer
7	25	Data bit 5	d_5		Data	To printer
8	26	Data bit 6	d_6		Data	To printer
9	27	Data bit 7	$\overline{d_7}$		Data	To printer
10	28	Acknowledge	$\overline{ACK}$	Low	Status	To computer
11	29	Busy	BUSY	High	Status	To computer
12		Paper out	PO	High	Status	To computer
13		Select	SLCT	High	Status	To computer
14		Auto feed	$\overline{AF}$	Low	Control	To printer
15		Unused	—	—	—	—
16		Signal ground	SG	—	—	—
17		Frame ground	FG	—	—	—
18		+5 V	—	—	—	—
31	30	Prime	$\overline{PRIME}$	Low	Control	To printer
32		Error	$\overline{ERROR}$	Low	Status	To computer
33		Signal ground	SG	—	—	—
34		Unused	—	—	—	—
35		Unused	—	—	—	—
36		Select in	$\overline{SLCTIN}$	Low	Control	To printer

design printers especially for desktop computers. Before the advent of the Centronics interface, most printers used 20-mA loops for RS-232 interfaces. Centronics simplified the interface by designing an interface that accepted data in the same format used internally by most computers (i.e., 8-bit words transferred in parallel using TTL logic). The Centronics parallel interface soon became the de facto standard and, today, is the most common interface used for interfacing personal computers to printers and other peripheral devices. Printers manufactured by companies other than Centronics sometimes use different names for some of the control lines and the minimum timing of some of the control signals may vary slightly. However, it is safe to say that almost any printer with a Centronics port will work with almost any computer with a Centronics port.

Figure 2-20 shows a Centronics printer interface and pin alignment. The connector is a 36-pin Amphenol connector, which is sometimes called a *champ connector*. When interfacing an IBM-compatible personal computer to a Centronics printer, the Centronics interface uses a DB-25 connector at the computer end and several of the interface lines are omitted. Table 2-9 lists the pin assignments, names, abbreviations, active conditions, types, and directions of propagation for signals on the Centronics printer interface. The pins are divided into three categories: data, control, and status. Also note that all the data

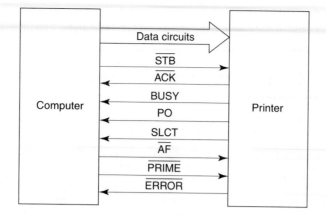

FIGURE 2-21   Control, data, and status lines for Centronics parallel interface

lines and several of the control and status lines have unique return lines. In addition there are several ground pins and one +5 V dc line. Figure 2-21 shows how the data, control, and status lines interface a computer to a printer using the Centronics parallel interface.

Data lines.   Pins 2 through 9 of the Centronics parallel interface are eight parallel data circuits that may be labeled d_0–d_7 or d_1–d_8 with either d_0 or d_1 as the least significant bit. All of the data lines are unidirectional (computer to printer) and each line has a dedicated return line. Characters are transmitted from the computer to the printer in the form of either 7-bit ASCII (possibly including an eighth bit, the parity bit) or in the form of 8-bit extended ASCII or EBCDIC characters.

Control lines.   The Centronics interface utilizes four unidirectional control lines that convey control information from the computer to the printer. The first control signal, the *strobe* ($\overline{STB}$) line, is a negative-edge-triggered signal outputted by the computer that directs the printer to accept data from the interface's data lines. The strobe signal is used for handshaking between the computer and printer.

The *auto feed* ($\overline{AF}$) control line is an active-low signal that dictates whether the printer automatically performs a line feed function after it receives a carriage return character from the computer. Normally, the carriage return character only causes the print head to return to the left side of the paper, and a separate line feed character causes the paper to advance to the next line. The auto feed line allows one signal to perform both functions. If the computer holds $\overline{AF}$ low, the printer responds to the carriage return character by performing a carriage return and a line feed.

The *prime* ($\overline{PRIME}$) control line (sometimes called *initialize*) is an active-low signal outputted by the computer to clear the printer's memory, including the printer programming and the print buffer. After detecting an active condition on the prime line, the printer returns to the condition it was in when it was first turned on. The prime control line may be used to abort a printing job while it is still in progress.

The fourth control line is called *select* ($\overline{SLCTIN}$). The select control line is seldom used. When used, the printer must see a low signal on the $\overline{SLCTIN}$ line before it will accept data from the computer. Many printers have an internal override switch that permanently places a ground on the $\overline{SLCTIN}$ line.

Status lines.   All of the status lines are unidirectional and convey information from the printer to the computer. The status lines are used by the printer to tell the computer what the printer is doing. For example, the *acknowledge* ($\overline{ACK}$) status line is an active-low response made by the printer after receiving an active $\overline{STB}$ signal from the computer. The printer uses $\overline{\text{ACK}}$ to signal the computer that it has processed the last byte of data that it received over the interface data lines and that the printer is ready for another character.

The *busy* status line is an active-high control signal that goes high anytime the printer is busy and unable to accept data from the computer. There are four conditions that can cause the printer to be busy:

1. The printer is inputting data from the data lines or the printer's data buffer is full and unable to accept any more data.
2. The printer is printing or otherwise processing data.
3. The printer is turned off or otherwise *off line*. Many printers have an off-line switch that prevents them from receiving or printing data.
4. The printer's $\overline{\text{ERROR}}$ line is low.

The *paper out* (PO) control line is self-explanatory; it goes active whenever the printer is out of paper. Whenever PO is activated, the $\overline{\text{ERROR}}$ line is also activated.

The *select* (SLCT) control line is an active-high status line that simply indicates whether the printer is selected or not. The printer holds SLCT high whenever it is on line and low whenever it is off line. The $\overline{\text{ERROR}}$ status line is an active-low signal that is used to indicate that there is a problem with the printer. The printer holds $\overline{\text{ERROR}}$ high during normal operation. The following conditions can cause $\overline{\text{ERROR}}$ to go active:

1. The printer is off line.
2. The printer is out of paper.
3. There is some other undefined problem with the printer preventing it from operating properly.

Miscellaneous lines. Pins 20 through 27 on the Centronics parallel interface are return signal lines for data pins d_0 through d_7, respectively. Pins 19, 28, 29, and 30 are the return paths for the $\overline{\text{STB}}$, $\overline{\text{ACK}}$, BUSY, and $\overline{\text{PRIME}}$ lines. Pins 16 and 33 are signal ground lines that serve as a common return path for lines that do not have their own dedicated return lines. Pin 17 is frame ground (FG), which electrically connects the chassis of the computer and the printer to reduce the possibility of electrical shock. Pin 18 is used to provide the +5 V dc power supply from the computer to the printer. The +5 V dc is used to power the printer's status circuits when the printer is turned off, but it is not designed to provide power for the printer's overall operation. Pin 18 is generally not used.

Interfacing. The Centronics interface was originally designated to use a 36-pin connector. The earliest personal computers, however, used 25-pin DB connectors for their printer port. Consequently, eleven pins had to be omitted from the interface. Today, printer cables generally come with an Amphenol 36-pin connector on the printer end of the cable and the DB-25 connector on the computer end.

Table 2-10 shows the pin assignments for both the Amphenol 36-pin connector and the adapted DB-25 connector. As the table shows, the unused Centronics pins have been omitted and only four of the individual return paths (grounds) for data signals are used. Also, signal and frame ground, the acknowledge signal return path, and the +5 V dc supply are not connected. Because printers are relatively slow devices, the personal computer version of the Centronics interface is more than adequate for sending data to a printer.

IEEE 488 Bus

The IEEE 488 bus uses eight bidirectional data lines connected in parallel to interface up to 15 remote devices (usually computer-controlled pieces of test equipment). Because the various pieces of equipment interfaced with the IEEE 488 are located in proximity with

TABLE 2-10 Connecting a Centronics Cable to a DB-25 Connector

Amphenol Connector	Signal	DB-25 Connector
1	Strobe	1
2	Data bit 0	2
3	Data bit 1	3
4	Data bit 2	4
5	Data bit 3	5
6	Data bit 4	6
7	Data bit 5	7
8	Data bit 6	8
9	Data bit 7	9
10	Acknowledge	10
11	Busy	11
12	Paper out	12
13	Select	13
14	Auto feed	14
15	Unused	Not connected
16	Signal ground	Not connected
17	Frame ground	Not connected
18	+5 V	Not connected
19	Strobe return	19
20	Data bit 0 return	Not connected
21	Data bit 1 return	20
22	Data bit 2 return	Not connected
23	Data bit 3 return	21
24	Data bit 4 return	Not connected
25	Data bit 5 return	22
26	Data bit 6 return	Not connected
27	Data bit 7 return	23
28	Acknowledge return	Not connected
29	Busy return	24
30	Prime return	25
31	Prime	16
32	Error	15
33	Signal ground	18
34	Unused	Not connected
35	Unused	Not connected
36	Select in	17

TABLE 2-11 IEEE 488 Bus Characteristics

Logic levels	TTL
Data lines	8, bidirectional
Maximum number of devices	15
Distance between adjacent devices	2 m maximum
Maximum total length	20 m
Connector	24-pin ribbon
Maximum speed with open-collector drivers	250 kbps
Maximum speed with tristate drivers	1 Mbps

each other, the interface was designed for a maximum distance between adjacent devices of less than 7 ft, and the maximum length of the entire bus is about 65 ft. Devices are connected to the bus by a 24-pin ribbon connector. Table 2-11 summarizes the characteristics of the IEEE 488 bus.

With the IEEE 488 bus, the *controller* determines which device can transmit data and which devices are receivers. The controller selects a single device to send data over the bus. The selected device is called the talker and there can be only one talker at a time. Any number of receivers (called listeners) can be selected at a time. Devices not

TABLE 2-12   IEEE 488 Devices

Device	Function
Controller	In charge of bus. Specifies which devices are programmed as the talker, as listeners, or are in the standby mode. There can be only one controller at a time.
Talker	Sends data over the bus to the listeners. There can be only one talker at a time.
Listeners	Receive data from the talker. There can be many listeners.
Standby	All devices that are not programmed as a controller, talker, or listener are in the standby mode.

programmed as talkers, listeners, or controllers are placed in the *standby mode*. The characteristics of the four types of devices are summarized in Table 2-12. The controller can change the function of the devices under its supervision. For example, the talker can be reprogrammed as a listener and a different device designated as the new talker. The controller can even relinquish control of the bus and designate another device as the controller. In this case, the former controller becomes either a talker, a listener, or placed in the standby mode.

Operating modes.   The IEEE bus has only two modes of operation: *command* and *data*. The interface is switched between the two modes by the controller using the *attention* ($\overline{\text{ATN}}$) bus management control line. When the controller puts $\overline{\text{ATN}}$ low, all devices connected to the interface switch to the command mode. When the controller makes $\overline{\text{ATN}}$ high, all devices are switched to the data mode.

When in the command mode, the controller can program other devices connected to the interface. For example, the controller could use the command mode to program the frequency of a function generator or the voltage range for a digital voltmeter. The controller could also program a device to operate as either a talker or listener. Each device connected to the interface has a unique address. In the command mode, the controller directs commands to a specific device by sending that device's address over the data bus. When in the command mode, all information that passes over the data bus is either a command or an address. When in the data mode, the only information allowed to pass over the data bus is data sent from the talker to the listener(s).

IEEE 488 interface lines.   Table 2-13 lists the pin assignments for the IEEE 488 interface. In essence, there are three groups of circuits (lines): data circuits, handshake circuits (sometimes called *byte transfer lines*), and interface management circuits.

Data Circuits.   There are eight bidirectional data lines numbered DI01 through DI08 with DI08 being the most significant. The purpose of the data lines is to carry 8-bit parallel data from the talker to the listener(s) or to carry addresses and commands from the controller to the other devices connected to the interface.

Handshake Circuits.   The IEEE 448 bus uses three handshaking circuits: not ready for data ($\overline{\text{NRFD}}$), data not accepted ($\overline{\text{NDAC}}$, and data valid ($\overline{\text{DAV}}$). The function of the handshaking circuits is to coordinate the transfer of data from the talker to the listener(s). $\overline{\text{NRFD}}$ is an active-low control signal that the listener outputs when it is not ready to accept data from the data circuits. The $\overline{\text{NRFD}}$ output pins of the devices are wire-ORed together so that any listener connected to the bus can pull the $\overline{\text{NRFD}}$ line low. If there is more than one listener, the wire-OR configuration ensures that the $\overline{\text{NRFD}}$ line remains low as long as the slowest listener is not ready to receive data.

The not data accepted ($\overline{\text{NDAC}}$) circuit is an active-low signal that is controlled by the listener(s). $\overline{\text{NDAC}}$ signals the talker that the listeners have not accepted data yet and that the talker should continue holding the data on the bus. $\overline{\text{NDAC}}$ is also wire-ORed to all the devices on the interface so that any listener can hold the line low until the slowest listener has accepted the data from the interface bus.

TABLE 2-13 Pin Assignment of the IEE 488 Interface

Pin	Line Name	Abbreviation	Type
1	Data bit 1 (LSB)	DI01	Data
2	Data bit 2	DI02	Data
3	Data bit 3	DI03	Data
4	Data bit 4	DI04	Data
5	End or identify	$\overline{\text{EOI}}$	Interface mgt.
6	Data available	$\overline{\text{DAV}}$	Handshake
7	Not ready for data	$\overline{\text{NRFD}}$	Handshake
8	Not data accepted	$\overline{\text{NDAC}}$	Handshake
9	Interface clear	$\overline{\text{IFC}}$	Interface mgt.
10	Service request	$\overline{\text{SRQ}}$	Interface mgt.
11	Attention	$\overline{\text{ATN}}$	Interface mgt.
12	Shield (earth ground)		
13	Data bit 5	DI05	Data
14	Data bit 6	DI06	Data
15	Data bit 7	DI07	Data
16	Data bit 8 (MSB)	DI08	Data
17	Remote enable	$\overline{\text{REN}}$	Interface mgt.
18	Ground return for DAV		
19	Ground return for NRFD		
20	Ground return for NDAC		
21	Ground return for IFC		
22	Ground return for SRQ		
23	Ground return for ATN		
24	Signal ground		

The data available ($\overline{\text{DAV}}$) line is an active-low control line used by the talker in the data mode or by the controller in the command mode to signal the other devices on the bus that there is either a data byte, address, or command to be read from the data bus.

Interface Management Circuits. The IEEE 488 bus has five interface management circuits that control certain operations of the devices connected to the interface and manage the flow of information among those devices.

1. *Attention ($\overline{\text{ATN}}$).* The controller uses $\overline{\text{ATN}}$ to switch the bus between the data and command modes. When $\overline{\text{ATN}}$ is high, the interface is in the data mode, and the talker can send data over the data bus to the listeners. When $\overline{\text{ATN}}$ is low, the IEEE interface is in the command mode, at which time the controller can send only addresses and commands over the data bus.

2. *Interface clear ($\overline{\text{IFC}}$).* When the controller activates $\overline{\text{IFC}}$, all devices connected to the interface suspend operations and the bus is placed in the idle state, at which time no communications can take place. $\overline{\text{IFC}}$ functions similar to a reset line.

3. *Remote enable ($\overline{\text{REN}}$).* $\overline{\text{REN}}$ is an active-low signal used by the controller to switch the devices connected to the interface between local and remote operation. When $\overline{\text{REN}}$ is activated, all devices are placed into remote operation and operate under the command of the controller. When $\overline{\text{REN}}$ is high (inactive) all devices (usually pieces of test equipment) are under local control and respond only to the control knobs on their own front panels, thus, allowing operators to control them directly without having to program them through a computer.

4. *Service request ($\overline{\text{SRQ}}$).* Any device connected to the interface can activate $\overline{\text{SRQ}}$ to interrupt the normal operation of the interface and signal the controller that it requires attention. When the controller senses an active $\overline{\text{SRQ}}$ signal, it determines which device requested the service and why by placing the interface

in the command mode and polling each device individually. When the controller addresses the device that activated the $\overline{\text{SRQ}}$, that device responds by sending codes over the data bus that disclose the action that the controller should take.

5. *End or identify ($\overline{\text{EOI}}$).* The $\overline{\text{EOI}}$ circuit has two purposes. When in the data mode, the talker has control of $\overline{\text{EOI}}$ and activates it when it sends its last byte of data in a particular message. When in the command mode, the controller can activate $\overline{\text{EOI}}$ to perform a group poll to obtain information from several devices at the same time.

THE TELEPHONE NETWORK

In its simplest form, data communication is the transmittal of digital information between two DTEs. The DTEs may be separated by a few feet or several thousand miles. At the present time, there is an insufficient number of transmission media to carry digital information from source to destination in digital form. Therefore, the most convenient alternative is to use the existing public telephone network (PTN) as the transmission medium for data communications circuits. Unfortunately, the PTN was designed (and most of it constructed) long before the advent of large-scale data communications. The PTN was intended to be used for transferring voice telephone communications signals, not digital data. Therefore, to use the PTN for data communications, the data must be converted to a form more suitable for transmission over analog carrier systems.

The following explanation is limited to telecommunications using the PTN. *Telco* includes all of the telephone companies that make up the PTN. Telco offers two general categories of service: *direct distance dialing* (DDD) and *private line*. DDD originally included only those switches and facilities required to complete a long-distance telephone call without the assistance of a Telco operator. The DDD now includes the entire public switched network; that is, any service associated with a telephone number. Private-line services are dedicated to a single user.

DDD Network

The DDD network, commonly referred to as the *dial-up* or *switched network,* imposes several limitations that must be overcome before it can be used for data communications. A basic understanding of the electrical operation of the telephone network would be helpful. The DDD network can be divided into four main sections: instruments, dial switches, local loops, and trunk circuits. An *instrument* is the device used to originate and receive signals, such as a telephone set (telset). The instrument is often referred to as *station equipment* and the location of the instrument as the *station*. A *dial switch* is a programmed matrix that provides a temporary signal path. A *local loop* is the dedicated transmission path between an instrument and the nearest dial switch. A *trunk circuit* is a transmission path between two dial switches. The dial switches are located in Telco central offices and are categorized as local, tandem, or toll. A *local* dial switch serves a limited area. The size of the area is determined by how many telephone numbers are required or desired in a given geographical area. Telco designates these areas as branch area exchanges. A branch exchange is a dial switch. The *subscriber* is the operator or user of the instrument: if you have a home telephone, you are a subscriber. A subscriber is the customer of Telco: the person placing the call. Telco refers to this person as either the talker or the listener, depending on their role at a particular time during a conversation.

A telephone number consists of seven digits. The first three digits make up the prefix and the last four constitute the extension number. Each prefix can accommodate 10,000 telephone numbers (0000 to 9999). The capacity of a dial switch is determined by how many prefixes it serves. The local dial switch provides a two-wire cable (local loop) for each telephone number if serves (Figure 2-22). One wire is designated the *tip* and the

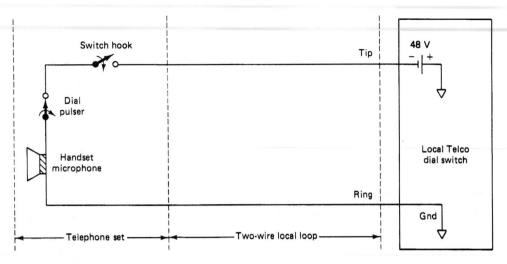

FIGURE 2-22 Simplified two-wire loop showing telset hookup to a local dial switch (loop start operation)

other the *ring*. The station end of the loop is terminated in a telephone set. The dial switch applies −48 V dc on the tip and a ground on the ring of each loop. This dc voltage is used for supervisory signaling and to provide a talk battery for the telset microphone. On-hook, off-hook, and dial pulsing are examples of supervisory signaling.

When a subscriber goes off-hook (lifts the handset off the teleset cradle), a switch hook is released, completing a dc short between the tip and the ring of the loop through the telset microphone. The dial switch senses a dc current in the loop and recognizes this as an off-hook condition. This procedure is referred to as a *loop start operation:* the loop is completed to indicate an off-hook condition. The dial switch responds with an audible dial tone. On hearing the dial tone, the subscriber dials the destination telephone number. The originating and destination telephone numbers are referred to as the *calling* and the *called numbers,* respectively.

Dialing is accomplished with switch closures (dial pulses) or touch-tone signaling. Dial pulsing is the interruption of the dc loop current by a telset dialing mechanism. Eight tone oscillators are contained in each telset equipped with a touch-tone pad. In touch-tone signaling, depending on the digit depressed, the telset outputs two of the eight tone frequencies.

After the entire called number has been dialed, the dial switch searches for a signal path through the switching matrix to the loop associated with the number called. Once the dial switch identifies a signal path and locates the destination loop, it tests the loop for an off-hook (busy) condition. If the destination loop is busy, the dial switch signals the calling loop with a busy signal. A station busy signal is a 60-ppm buzz. If the destination loop is on-hook (idle), the dial switch applies a 20-Hz 110-V ac ringing signal to it. A typical ringing cycle is 2 seconds on, 4 seconds off. When the destination telephone is answered (goes off-hook), the dial switch terminates the ringing signal and completes the transmission path between the two loops through the matrix. The signal path through the dial switch will be maintained as long as both loops remain closed. When either instrument goes on-hook, the signal path is interrupted.

What if the calling and the called telephone numbers are not served by the same dial switch? Generally, a community is served by only one local telephone company. The community is divided into zones; each zone is served by a different dial switch. The number of zones established in a given community is determined by the number of stations served and their density. If a subscriber in one zone wishes to call a station in

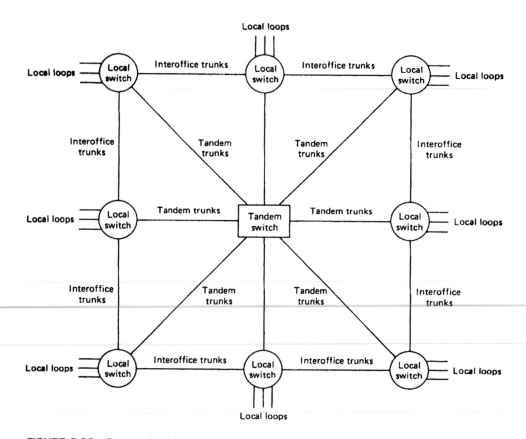

FIGURE 2-23 Community telephone system showing the use of a tandem switch to facilitate interzone calling

another zone, a minimum of two dial switches are required. The calling station receives off-hook supervision and dial pulses are outputted as previously described. The dial switch in the calling zone recognizes that the prefix of the destination telephone number is served by a different dial switch. There are two ways that the serving dial switch can complete the call. It can locate a direct trunk (interoffice) circuit to the dial switch in the destination zone or it can route the call through a tandem switch. A *tandem switch* is a switcher's switch. It is a switching matrix used to interconnect dial switches. Trunk circuits that terminate in tandem switches are called *tandem trunks*. Normally, direct trunk circuits are provided only between adjacent zones. If a call must pass through more than one zone, a tandem switch must be used (Figure 2-23). If no direct trunks between the originating and the terminating dial switches exist and a common tandem switch is not available, the call is classified as a *toll call* and cannot be completed as dialed. Toll calls involve an additional charge and the dialed number must be preceded by a "1."

The telephone number prefix identifies which particular dial switch serves a station. With three digits, 1000 (000 to 999) prefixes can be generated for dial switches. A single metropolitan exchange alone may serve 20 to 30 prefixes. In the United States, there are over 20,000 local dial switches. It is obvious that further encoding is required to differentiate between the same prefix and extension in two different parts of the country. In the United States, an additional three-digit area code is assigned to each telephone number. The area code precedes the prefix but needs to be included only when calls are destined outside the area of the originating station. When a dialed telephone number is preceded by a "1," it is routed from the local dial switch to a toll switch by way of a *toll-connecting trunk*. Telco's present toll-switching plan includes five ranks or classes of

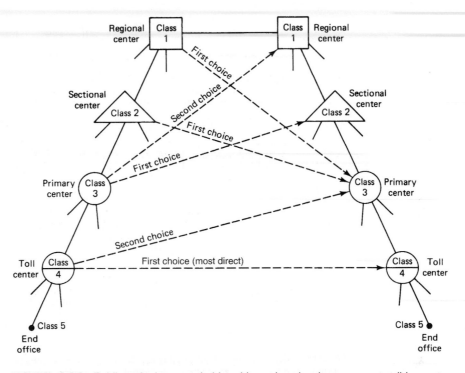

FIGURE 2-24 Public telephone switching hierarchy showing some possible route choices to complete a toll call between two end offices

switching centers. From highest to lowest classification, they are the regional center, sectional center, primary center, toll center, and end office. Local dial switches are classified as end (central) offices. All toll switches are capable of functioning as tandem switches to other toll switches.

The Telco switching plan includes a switching hierarchy that allows a certain degree of route selection when establishing a long-distance call (Figure 2-24). The choice is not offered the subscriber, but rather, the toll switches, using software translation, select the best route available at the time the call is made. The best route is not necessarily the shortest route. It is the route requiring the fewest number of dial switches. If a call cannot be completed because the necessary trunk circuits are not available, the local dial switch signals the calling station with an equipment busy signal. An equipment busy signal is similar to a station busy signal except that it repeats at a 120-ppm rate. The worst-case condition encountered when completing a long-distance call is when seven tandem toll (intertoll) trunks are required. Based on Telco statistics, the probability of this occurring is 1 in 100,000. Because software translations in the automatic switching machines permit the use of alternate routes, and each route includes many different trunk circuits, the probability of using the same facilities on identical calls is unlikely. This is an obvious disadvantage when using the PTN for data transmission because inconsistencies in the transmission parameters are introduced from call to call. Telco guarantees the transmission parameters of each local loop and trunk circuit to exceed the minimum requirements of a basic voice-grade (VG) communications channel. However, two to nine separate facilities in tandem may be required to complete a telephone call (see Figure 2-25). Because transmission impairments are additive, it is quite possible that the overall transmission parameters of a telephone connection, established through the public switched network, may be substandard. Because transmission paths vary from call to call, it is difficult to compensate for line impairments. Subscribers to the DDD network lease a dedicated loop from their station to the nearest Telco dial switch. Any additional

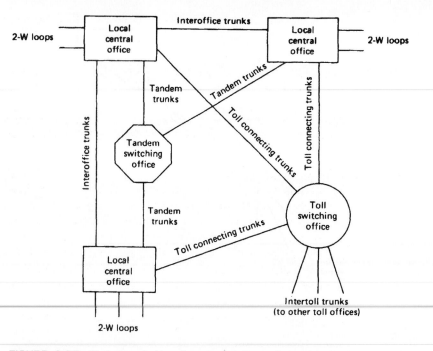

FIGURE 2-25 Typical switching layout showing relationship between local, tandem, and toll switches in the public telephone network

facilities required for the subscribers to complete a call are theirs only temporarily. The subscriber uses these facilities only for the duration of the call and then they are made available for other users of the network. These temporary facilities are called *common usage trunks*—they are shared by all of the subscribers of the network.

The switching transients associated with the dial switches are another disadvantage of using the public switched network for data transmission. The older dial switches were electromechanical machines. Mechanical relay contacts were used to establish a signal path. The contact closures in the switching machines induced static interference that bled into adjacent signal paths. The static electricity caused impulse noise that produced transmission errors in the data signals. Telco is rapidly converting to *Electronic Switching Systems* (ESS). ESS machines are by no means perfectly quiet, but they are a tremendous improvement over the older electromechanical machines.

In order for a toll call to be completed, the dialed phone number must be transferred from switch to switch. Ultimately, the switching matrix at the destination end office requires the prefix and extension numbers to establish the final connection. The transmission paths between switching machines are very often carrier systems: microwave links, coaxial cables, or digital T-carriers. Microwave links and coaxial cables use analog carriers and are ac coupled. Therefore, the traditional dc supervisory and dial pulsing techniques cannot be used. An alternate method of transferring supervisory signals using a *single-frequency* (SF) *tone* has been devised. An idle trunk circuit has a 2600-Hz SF tone present in both directions. An off-hook indication at either end is indicated by the removal of the SF tone. The receiving switch acknowledges the off-hook indication by removing the SF in the opposite direction. Two methods are available for dial pulsing. The SF tone can be pulsed on and off to represent the dialed number, or a signaling method called *multifrequency* (MF) *signaling* can be used. MF is a 2-of-6 code similar to touch tone. However, the MF tone frequencies are higher and are transmitted at a faster rate. Touch tone and MF are not compatible. Digital T-carriers use a completely different method for transferring supervisory information.

FIGURE 2-26 Simplified private-line circuit layout showing dedicated loops and trunks with hard-wired cross-connects in each Telco office (two-point circuit)

Private-Line Service

In addition to subscriptions to the public switched telephone network, Telco offers a comprehensive assortment of private-line services. Private-line subscribers lease those facilities required for a complete circuit. These facilities are hard-wired together in the Telco offices and are available only to one subscriber. Private-line circuits are *dedicated, private, leased* facilities. A dedicated circuit can be designed to meet voice-grade requirements from station to station—the end-to-end transmission parameters are fixed at the time the circuit is installed and will remain relatively constant. Circuit impairments will also remain relatively constant and can be compensated for by the subscriber. Private-line circuits afford several advantages over conventional dial-up circuits:

1. Availability
2. Improved performance
3. Greater reliability
4. Lower cost

Because private-line circuits are leased on a 24-hour basis, they are always available to the subscriber. Because the transmission parameters on a private-line circuit are guaranteed end to end, the overall performance is improved and a more reliable communications link is established. Heavy-usage private-line circuits are more economical than dial-ups. However, dial-ups are more cost effective for a person using the lines only a small percentage of the time.

Private-line circuit arrangements differ from dial-ups only in the fact that their circuits are permanently connected and dial switches and common-usage trunks are unnecessary. The terms "local loop" and "trunk" have a slightly different meaning to private-line subscribers. On a private-line circuit, a local loop is a transmission path between an instrument and the nearest Telco office; a trunk circuit is a transmission path between two Telco offices (see Figure 2-26). The only change in the definition is the substitution of "Telco office" for "dial switch."

Examples of private-line offerings are

1. Foreign exchange (FX)
2. Full data (FD)
3. Full period (FP)
4. Digital data service (DDS)

FX circuits differ from conventional DDD subscriptions only in the fact that subscribers, instead of leasing a dedicated loop to the nearest dial switch, lease a loop to a dial switch of their choice. This facilitates toll-free interzone calling to specific zones. FD circuits are four-wire, dedicated data circuits capable of full-duplex operation at a data rate of 9600 bps (bits per second). A local bank's system of automatic teller machines is an example of an FD circuit. FP circuits are four-wire, dedicated voice circuits. The hoot-and-holler (yell-down) circuits used by auto dismantlers (previously called "junkyards") to locate used auto parts is an example of an FP circuit.

FIGURE 2-27 Electrical characteristics of a transmission line

THE TELEPHONE CIRCUIT

A *telephone circuit* consists of two or more facilities, interconnected in tandem, to provide a transmission path between a source and a destination. The interconnects may be temporary, as in a dial-up circuit, or permanent private-line circuits. The facilities may be cable pairs or carrier systems, and the information may be transferred on a coaxial, metallic, microwave, optic fiber, or satellite communications system. The information transferred is called the *message* and the circuit used is called the *message channel.* Telco offers a wide assortment of message channels ranging from a basic 4-kHz voice-band circuit to wideband (30-MHz) microwave channels that are capable of transferring high-resolution video signals. The following discussion will be limited to a basic voice-band circuit. In Telco terminology, the word *message* originally denoted speech information. This definition has been extended to include any standard voice frequency signal. Thus, a message channel may include the transmission of speech, supervisory signaling, or voice-band data.

The Local Loop

The local loop is the only Telco facility required by all voice-band data circuits. It is the primary cause of attenuation distortion and phase distortion. A local loop is a metallic transmission line (cable pair), consisting of two insulated conductors twisted together. The insulating material may be wood pulp or polyethylene plastic; the wire conductor is usually copper and, in some instances, aluminum. Wire pairs are stranded together into units. Adjacent wire pairs within a unit are twisted with different pitch (twist length). This reduces the undesired effects of inductive coupling between pairs and helps to eliminate cross talk. Units are cabled together into cores and then placed inside a plastic sheath. Depending on the insulating material used, sheaths contain between 6 and 900 pairs of wire. Sheaths are connected together and strung between distribution frames within Telco central offices and junction boxes located in manholes, back alleys, or telephone equipment rooms within large building complexes. The length of a subscriber loop depends on the station location relative to a local central telephone office.

The transmission characteristics of a cable pair depend on the wire diameter, conductor spacing, dielectric constant of the insulator, and the conductivity of the wire. These physical properties, in turn, determine the inductance, resistance, capacitance, and conductance of the line. The resistance and inductance are distributed along the length of the wire, whereas the conductance and capacitance exist between the two wires. If the insulation is good, the effect of conductance is generally negligible.

The electrical characteristics of a cable (Figure 2-27) are uniformly distributed along its length and are appropriately referred to as *distributed parameters.* Because it is cumbersome working with distributed parameters, it is common practice to lump them into discrete values per unit length (i.e., millihenrys per 1000 ft). The amount of attenuation and phase delay experienced by a signal propagating down a line is a function of the *frequency* of the signal and the *electrical characteristics* of the cable pair. Figure 2-28 illustrates the effect of frequency on attenuation for a given length of line. On this unloaded wire, a 3000-Hz signal suffers 6 dB more attenuation than a 500-Hz signal on the same line. The cable acts as a low-pass filter for the signal. Extensive studies of attenuation on cable pairs have shown that a reduction in attenuation can be achieved

FIGURE 2-28 Frequency versus attenuation for 12,000 ft of 26-gauge wire

if inductors are added in series with the wire. This is called *loading*. Loaded cable is identified by the addition of the letters H, D, or B and an inductance value to the wire gauge number. H, D, and B indicate that the loading coils are separated by 6000 ft, 4500 ft, and 3000 ft, respectively. Generally, the amount of series inductance added is either 44 mH, 88 mH, or 135 mH. A cable pair with the designation 26H88 is made of 26-gauge wire with 88 mH of series inductance added every 6000 ft. If a loaded cable is used, a 3000-Hz signal will suffer only 1.5 dB more loss than a 500-Hz signal. Note that the loss-versus-frequency characteristics for a loaded cable are relatively flat up to approximately 2000 Hz.

The low-pass filter characteristics of a cable also affect the phase distortion-versus-frequency characteristics of a signal. The amount of *phase distortion* is proportional to the *length* and *gauge* of the wire. Loading a cable also affects the phase characteristics of a line. The telephone company must often add gain and delay equalizers to a circuit in order to achieve the minimum requirements. Equalizers introduce discontinuities or ripples in the bandpass characteristics of a circuit. Automatic equalizers in modems are sensitive to this condition and, very often, an overequalized circuit causes as many problems to a data signal as an underequalized circuit.

Transmission Parameters

Transmission parameters are divided into three broad categories:

1. Bandwidth parameters, which include
   (a) Attenuation distortion
   (b) Envelope delay distortion
2. Interface parameters, which include
   (a) Terminal impedance
   (b) In-band and out-of-band signal power
   (c) Test signal power
   (d) Ground isolation

3. Facility parameters, which include
   (a) Noise measurements
   (b) Frequency and phase distortion
   (c) Amplitude distortion
   (d) Nonlinear distortion

Bandwidth parameters. The only transmission parameters with limits specified by the Federal Communications Commission (FCC) are attenuation distortion and envelope delay. *Attenuation distortion* is the difference in circuit gain experienced at a particular frequency with respect to the circuit gain of a reference frequency. This characteristic is also called *frequency response, differential gain,* and *1004-Hz deviation. Envelope delay* is an indirect method of evaluating the phase delay characteristics of a circuit. FCC tariff number 260 specifies the limits for attenuation distortion and envelope delay distortion. The limits are prescribed by line conditioning requirements. Through line conditioning, the attenuation and delay characteristics of a circuit are artificially altered to meet prescribed limits. Line conditioning is available only to private-line subscribers for an additional monthly charge. The basic voice-band, 3002 channel satisfies the minimum line-conditioning requirements.

Telco offers two types of line conditioning, C type and D type. *C-type conditioning* specifies the maximum limits for attenuation distortion and envelope delay distortion. *D-type conditioning* sets the minimum requirement for signal-to-noise ratio (S/N) and deals with nonlinear distortion.

D-type conditioning is referred to as high-performance conditioning and has two categories, D1 and D2. Limits imposed by D1 and D2 conditioning are identical. D1 conditioning is available for two-point circuits, and D2 conditioning is available for multipoint arrangements. D-type conditioned circuits must meet the following specifications:

1. Signal-to-C-notched noise: $\geq$ 28 dB
2. Nonlinear distortion
   (a) Signal-to-second order: $\geq$ 35 dB
   (b) Signal-to-third order: $\geq$ 40 dB

D-type conditioning is mandatory when the data transmission rate is 9600 bps. If a facility is assigned by Telco for use as a 9600-bps circuit, and it does not meet the minimum requirements of D-type conditioning, it is so identified by Telco data technical support personnel and never considered for that purpose again. A different facility is sought. A circuit cannot be upgraded to meet D-type conditioning requirements by adding corrective devices.

C-type conditioning pertains to line impairments for which compensation can be made, to a certain degree, by filters and equalizers. This is accomplished with Telco-provided equipment. When a circuit is turned up for service with a particular C-type conditioning, it must meet the minimum requirements for that type of conditioning. The subscriber may include devices within the station equipment that compensate for minor long-term variations in the bandwidth requirements.

There are five classifications of C-type conditioning.

1. C1 and C2 pertain to two-point and multipoint circuits.
2. C4 pertains to two-point circuits and multipoint arrangements that have a maximum of four station locations.
3. C5 specifications pertain only to two-point circuits.
4. C3 conditioning is for access lines and trunk circuits associated with private-switched networks.

Private-switched networks are telephone systems dedicated to a single customer, usually with a large number of stations. An example is a large corporation with offices and

TABLE 2-14 C-Type Bandwidth Parameter Limits

Channel Conditioning	Attenuation Distortion (Frequency Response) Relative to 1004 Hz		Envelope Delay Distortion	
	Frequency Range (Hz)	Variation (dB)	Frequency Range (Hz)	Variation (μs)
Basic	500–2500	+2 to −8	800–2600	1750
	300–3000	+3 to −12		
C1	1000–2400	+1 to −3	1000–2400	1000
	300–2700	+2 to −6	800–2600	1750
	300–3000	+3 to −12		
C2	500–2800	+1 to −3	1000–2600	500
	300–3000	+2 to −6	600–2600	1500
			500–2800	3000
C3 (access line)	500–2800	+.5 to −1.5	1000–2600	110
	300–3000	+.8 to −3	600–2600	300
			500–2800	650
C3 (trunk)	500–2800	+.5 to −1	1000–2600	80
	300–3000	−.8 to −2	600–2600	260
			500–2800	500
C4	500–3000	+2 to −3	1000–2600	300
	300–3200	+2 to −6	800–2800	500
			600–3000	1500
			500–3000	3000
C5	500–2800	+.5 to −1.5	1000–2600	100
	300–3000	+1 to −3	600–2600	300
			500–2800	600

complexes at different geographical locations with an on-premises private branch exchange (PBX) at each location. A PBX is a low-capacity dial switch where the subscribers are generally limited to stations within the same building complex. Common-usage access lines and trunk circuits are required to interconnect the PBXs. They are common only to the subscribers of the private network and not to the entire public telephone network.

Table 2-14 shows the various limits prescribed by the different types of C-type conditioning on attenuation distortion and envelope delay. Figures 2-29 through 2-33 show a graphic presentation of several of the bandwidth parameter limits.

Attenuation Distortion and C-Type Conditioning. The attenuation distortion limits for a basic 3002 channel require the circuit gain at any frequency between 500 Hz and 2500 Hz to be not greater than 2 dB above the circuit gain at 1004 Hz and not more than 3 dB below the circuit gain at 1004 Hz (Figure 2-29). For attenuation distortion, the circuit gain at 1004 Hz is always used as the reference. Also, within the frequency bands from 300 Hz to 499 Hz and from 2501 Hz to 3000 Hz, the circuit gain cannot be greater than 3 dB above or more than 12 dB below the gain at 1004 Hz.

Example 2-6

A 1004-Hz test tone is transmitted at 0 dBm and received at −16 dBm. The circuit gain is −16 dB (this is actually a loss of 16 dB: negative dB values are negative gains, or losses). Frequencies from 500 Hz to 2500 Hz must be received at a minimum level of −24 dBm and at a maximum level of −14 dBm. Frequencies within the bands of 300 Hz to 499 Hz and 2501 Hz to 3000 Hz must be received at signal strength levels between −13 dBm and −28 dBm, inclusive. If the same transmission levels were applied to a circuit with C2 conditioning, frequencies between 500 Hz and 2800 Hz must be received at signal levels ranging from −15 dBm to −19 dBm. Frequencies within the bands of 300 Hz to 499 Hz and 2801 Hz to 3000 Hz must be received at signal levels ranging from −14 dBm to −22 dBm. Table 2-14 shows that the higher the classification of conditioning imposed on a circuit, the flatter the frequency response, therefore, a better-quality circuit.

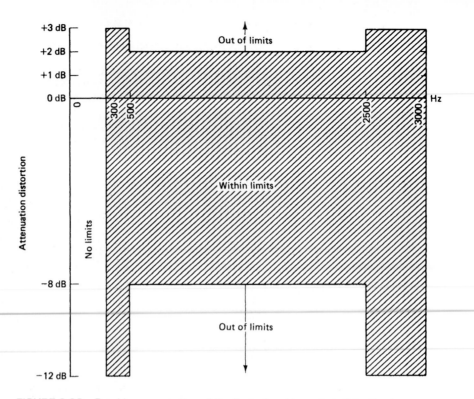

FIGURE 2-29 Graphic presentation of the limits for attenuation distortion in a basic 3002 channel

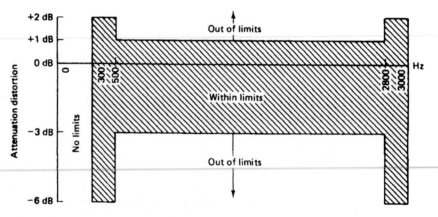

FIGURE 2-30 Graphic presentation of the limits for attenuation distortion on a channel with C2 conditioning

Envelope Delay.   A linear phase-versus-frequency relationship is a requirement for error-free data transmission. This relationship is difficult to measure because of the difficulty in establishing a phase reference. Envelope delay is an alternate method of evaluating the phase-versus-frequency relationship of a circuit.

The time delay encountered by a signal as it propagates from source to destination is called *propagation time* or *phase delay.* All frequencies in the usable voice band (300 Hz to 3000 Hz) do not experience the same time delay in a circuit. Therefore, a complex frequency spectrum, such as the output from a modem, does not possess the same phase-versus-frequency characteristics when it is received as when it was transmitted.

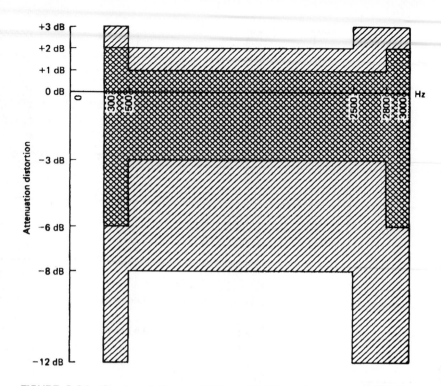

FIGURE 2-31 Overlay of Figures 2-29 and 2-30 to demonstrate the more stringent requirements imposed by C2 conditioning

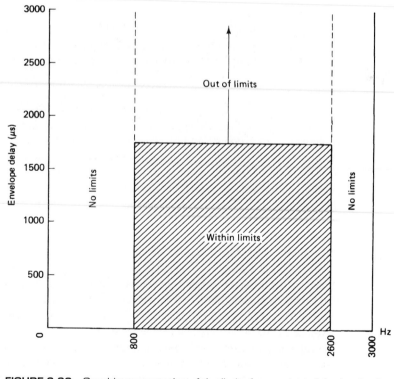

FIGURE 2-32 Graphic presentation of the limits for envelope delay in a basic 3002 channel

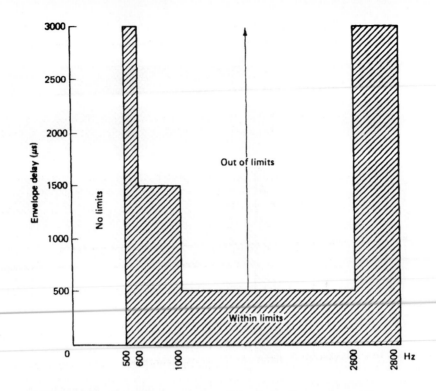

FIGURE 2-33 Graphic presentation of the limits for envelope delay on a channel with C2 conditioning

This condition represents a possible impairment to a data signal. The *absolute phase delay* is the actual time required for a particular frequency to be propagated from source to destination. The difference between the absolute delays of different frequencies is phase distortion. A graph of phase delay versus frequency for a typical circuit is nonlinear.

By definition, envelope delay is the first derivative of phase with respect to frequency:

$$\text{envelope delay} = \frac{d\phi(\omega)}{d\omega}$$

In actuality, envelope delay only closely approximates $d\phi(\omega)/d\omega$. Envelope delay measurements do not evaluate true phase-versus-frequency characteristics, but rather, the phase of a wave that is the resultant of a narrow band of frequencies. It is a common misconception to confuse true phase distortion (also called delay distortion) with envelope delay distortion (EDD). *Envelope delay* is the time required to propagate a change in an AM envelope through a transmission medium. To measure envelope delay, a narrowband amplitude-modulated carrier, whose frequency is varied over the usable voice band, is transmitted. (The AM modulation rate is typically between 25 Hz and 100 Hz.) At the receiver, phase variations of the low-frequency envelopes are measured. The phase difference at the different carrier frequencies is *envelope delay distortion*. The carrier frequency that produces the minimum envelope delay is established as the reference and is normalized to zero. Therefore, EDD measurements yield only positive values and indicate the relative envelope delays of the various carrier frequencies with respect to the reference frequency. The reference frequency of a typical voice-band circuit is approximately 1800 Hz.

EDD measurements do not yield true phase delays, nor do they determine the relative relationships between true phase delays. EDD measurements are used to determine a close approximation of the relative phase delay characteristics of a circuit.

The EDD limit of a basic 3002 channel is 1750 μs between 800 Hz and 2600 Hz, as shown on Table 2-14. This indicates that the maximum difference in envelope delay between any two carrier frequencies in this range cannot exceed 1750 μs.

Example 2-7

An EDD test on a basic 3002 channel indicated that an 1800-Hz carrier experienced the minimum absolute delay of 400 μs. Therefore, it is the reference. The absolute envelope delay experienced by any frequency within the 800-Hz to 2600-Hz band cannot exceed 2150 (400 + 1750) μs.

The absolute time delay encountered by a signal between any two points in the continental United States will never exceed 100 ms. This is not sufficient to cause any problems. Consequently, relative rather than absolute values of envelope delay are measured. For the previous example, as long as EDD tests yielded relative values less than +1750 μs, the circuit is within limits.

Interface parameters. The two primary considerations of the interface parameters are

1. Electrical protection of the telephone network and its personnel
2. Standardization of design arrangements

These considerations are summarized below. Station equipment impedances should be 600 Ω resistive over the usable voice band, and the station equipment should be isolated from ground by a minimum of 20 MΩ dc and 50 kΩ ac. The basic voice-grade telephone circuit is a 3002 channel; it has a usable bandwidth of 300 Hz to 3000 Hz. The circuit gain at 3000 Hz is 3 dB below the specified in-band signal power. The gain at 4 kHz must be at least 15 dB below the gain at 3 kHz. The maximum transmitted signal power for a private-line circuit is 0 dBm. The transmitted signal power for dial-up circuits is established for each loop so that the signal is received at the central Telco office at −12 dBm.

Facility parameters. Facility parameters represent potential impairments to a data signal. These impairments are caused by Telco equipment and the limits specified pertain to all voice-band circuits regardless of conditioning.

1004-Hz Variation. Telco has established 1004 Hz as the standard test-tone frequency. The frequency 1004 Hz was selected because of its relative location in the passband of a standard voice-band circuit. The purpose of this test tone is to simulate the combined signal power of a standard voice-band transmission. The 1004-Hz channel loss for a private-line circuit is 16 dB. A 1004-Hz test tone applied to the transmit local loop at 0 dBm should appear at the output of the destination loop at −16 dBm. Long-term variations in the gain of the transmission facilities should not exceed ±4 dB; the received signal power must be within the limits of −12 dBm to −20 dBm.

Noise. Noise can be generally defined as any undesired energy present in the usable passband of a communication channel. The noise is either correlated or uncorrelated. *Correlation* implies a relationship between the signal and the noise. Uncorrelated noise is energy present in the absence of a signal such as thermal noise. Correlated noise is unwanted energy that is present as a direct result of the signal, such as nonlinear distortion.

Noise Weighting. Signal interference by noise is categorized in terms of annoyance or intelligibility. Noise may be annoying to the listener but not to the degree that the conversation cannot be understood. Western Electric Company conducted experiments in which groups of listeners were asked to rate the annoyance caused by 14 different audible frequencies between 180 Hz and 3500 Hz. These frequencies were presented to the listeners on a standard 500-type telephone (the old black dialer that Grandma had). The

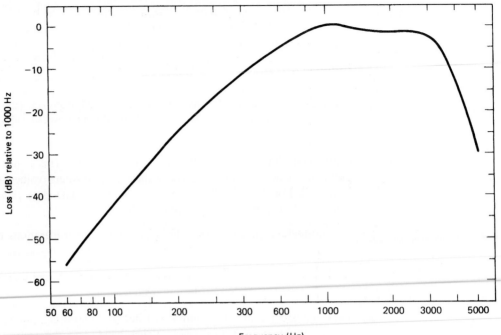

FIGURE 2-34 C-message weighting curve

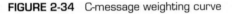

listeners first compared the annoyance of each frequency to the annoyance of a reference frequency of 1000 Hz in the absence of speech power. Then the same experiments were repeated with speech present. The results of the two tests were averaged and smoothed to produce the *C-message weighting curve.* This curve is shown in Figure 2-34.

C-message noise is significant because it indicates the passband characteristics that should be considered when conducting noise tests on voice-band communications circuits. The frequencies from 600 Hz to 3000 Hz proved to be the most annoying and, as the frequency decreased below 600 Hz, the annoyance factor also decreased. Because of these results, C-message filters were developed that have a response similar to the C-message weighting curve. These filters increase the attenuation of the noise power at frequencies below 600 Hz and above 3000 Hz, but they have a relatively flat response to noise power within the 600-Hz to 3000-Hz passband. This response makes the measured strength of the noise frequencies proportional to the amount of annoyance they produce. These filters are inserted in noise-measuring sets at a point just before where the noise power is measured. The noise-measuring set then evaluates the noise in a manner similar to the human ear. The human ear cannot appreciate the true rms power of sound if the duration of the sound is 200 ms or less. Therefore, a noise-measuring set for voice circuits includes a 200-ms time constant that prevents them from reacting to short bursts of noise power. What significance does C-message weighting have on data circuits? Typical voice-band data modems exhibit an output frequency spectrum that concentrates most of the transmitted signal power in the 600-Hz to 3000-Hz band. Because a C-message filter has a relatively flat frequency response over this range, noise measurements with this type of filter are valid for data applications also.

C-Message Noise. C-message noise measurements determine the average continuous rms noise power. This noise is commonly referred to as background, white, thermal, or Gaussian noise. This noise is inherently present in a circuit due to the electrical makeup of the circuit. Because white noise is additive, its magnitude is dependent, in part, on the electrical length of the circuit. C-message noise measurements

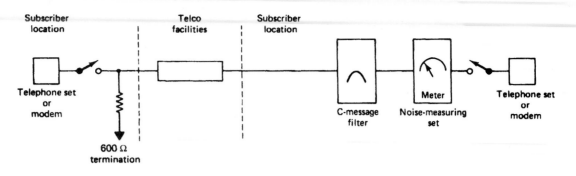

FIGURE 2-35 Terminated C-message noise test

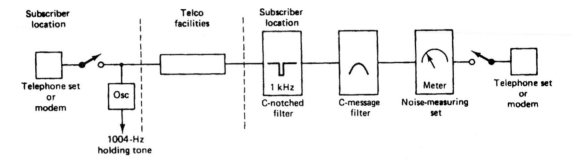

FIGURE 2-36 C-notched noise test

are the terminated rms power readings at the receive end of a circuit with the transmit end terminated in the characteristic impedance of the telephone line (see Figure 2-35). There is a disadvantage in measuring noise this way. The overall circuit characteristics, in the absence of a signal, are not necessarily the same as when a signal is present. The use of companders and automatic gain devices in the circuit causes this difference. Companders are devices that exhibit frequency-dependent gain characteristics (companders are explained in detail in Chapter 4). For this reason C-notched noise measurements were developed.

C-notched noise measurements differ from standard C-message noise measurements only in the fact that a holding tone (usually, 1004 Hz or 2804 Hz) is applied to the transmit end of the circuit during the test. The holding tone ensures that the circuit operation simulates a loaded voice or data transmission. "Loaded" is a communications term that indicates the presence of a signal power comparable to the power of an actual message transmission. The holding tone is filtered (notched out) in the noise-measuring set prior to the C-message filter. The bandpass characteristics of the notch filter are such that only the holding tone is removed. The noise power in the usable passband is measured with a standard C-message noise-measuring set. This test (Figure 2-36) assures that the noise readings obtained actually reflect the loaded circuit characteristics of a normal voice-band transmission.

The physical makeup of a private-line data circuit may require the use of several trunk circuits in tandem. Each individual trunk may be an analog, digital, companded, or a noncompanded facility. Various combinations of these facilities may be used to configure a circuit. Telco has established realistic C-notched noise requirements for each type of facility for various trunk lengths. These requirements assist Telco in evaluating the performance of a facility and in expediting trouble-isolation procedures. A subscriber to the telephone network need only be concerned with the overall (end-to-end) C-notched noise requirement. Standard private-line data circuits, operating at less than 9600 bps,

The Telephone Circuit

FIGURE 2-37 C-notched and impulse noise

require a minimum signal-to-C-notched noise ratio of 24 dB. Data circuits operating at 9600 bps require a high-performance line with a minimum signal-to-C-notched noise ratio of 28 dB.

Impulse Noise. *Impulse noise* is characterized by high-amplitude peaks (impulses) of short duration in the total noise spectrum. The significance of impulse noise hits on data transmission has been a controversial topic. Telco has accepted the fact that the absolute magnitude of the impulse hit is not as important as the magnitude of the hit relative to the signal amplitude. Empirically, it has been determined that an impulse hit will not produce transmission errors in a data signal unless it comes within 6 dB of the signal level (see Figure 2-37). Hit counters are designed to register a maximum of seven counts per second. This produces a "dead" time of 143 ms between counts when additional impulse hits are not registered. Contemporary high-speed data formats transfer data in block form and whether one hit or many occur during a single block is unimportant. Any error within a block necessitates retransmission of the entire block. Counting additional impulses during the time of a single block does not correlate well with data transmission performance.

Impulse tests are performed by placing a 2804-Hz holding tone on the circuit to ensure loaded circuit characteristics. The counter records the number of hits in a prescribed time interval (usually 15 minutes). An impulse hit is typically less than 4 ms and never more than 10 ms in duration. Telco's limit for recordable impulse hits in 15 within a 15-minute time interval. This does not limit the number of hits to one per minute but rather limits the average to one per minute.

Gain Hits and Dropouts. A *gain hit* is a sudden, random change in the gain of a circuit. Gain hits are classified as temporary variations in the gain exceeding ±3 dB, lasting more than 4 ms, and returning to the original value within 200 ms. The primary cause of a gain hit is that of transients caused by switching radio facilities in the normal course of a day. Atmospheric fades produce the necessity for switching radio facilities. A

FIGURE 2-38 Gain hits and dropouts

Phase jitter
continuous changes < 10 p-p

Phase hit
rapid changes > 20 p-p

FIGURE 2-39 Phase distortion

dropout is a decrease in circuit gain of more than 12 dB that lasts longer than 4 ms. Dropouts are characteristics of a temporary open-circuit condition and are caused by deep radio fades or Telco maintenance activities. Dropouts occur at a rate of approximately one per hour. Gain hits and dropouts (see Figure 2-38) are detected by monitoring the receive level of a 1004-Hz test tone.

Phase Hits.   *Phase hits* (see Figure 2-39) are sudden, random changes in the phase of a transmitted signal. Phase hits are classified as temporary variations in the phase of a signal that last longer than 4 ms. Generally, phase hits are not recorded unless they exceed ±20° peak. Phase hits, as gain hits, are caused by transients produced when radio facilities are switched.

Phase Jitter.   *Phase jitter* (see Figure 2-39) is a form of incidental phase modulation—a continuous, uncontrolled variation in the zero crossings of a signal. Generally, a phase jitter occurs at less than a 300-Hz rate, and its primary cause is a low-frequency ac ripple in Telco power plant supplies. The number of power supplies required in a circuit is directly proportional to the number of trunk circuits and Telco offices that make up a message channel. Each trunk facility has a separate phase jitter specification. The maximum end-to-end phase jitter allowed is 10° peak-to-peak regardless of the number of radio links, cable facilities, or digital carrier spans used in the circuit. Limiting the number of trunk circuits is a primary design consideration for a data circuit. Phase jitters is measured by observing the zero crossings of a 1004-Hz test tone.

Single-Frequency Interference.   *Single-frequency interference* is the presence of one or more continuous, unwanted tones within a message channel. The tones are called spurious tones and are often caused by cross talk or cross modulation between different channels in a carrier system. Spurious tones are measured by terminating the transmit end

| 300 Hz | 704 Hz | 1408 Hz | 2112 Hz | 3000 Hz |
| | Fundamental | Second harmonic | Third harmonic | |

FIGURE 2-40 Harmonic distortion

of a circuit, then searching through the channel spectrum with a frequency-selective voltmeter or observing the channel passband with a spectrum analyzer. Spurious tones can produce the same undesired circuit behavior as white noise.

Frequency Shifts. Analog carrier systems used by the telephone companies operate single-sideband suppressed carrier (SSBSC) and, therefore, require coherent demodulation. In *coherent demodulation,* the frequency of the suppressed carrier must be recovered and reproduced exactly by the receiver. If this is not done, the demodulated signal will be offset in frequency by the difference between the transmit and the receive carrier frequencies. Frequency shift is measured by transmitting a 1004-Hz test tone and, then, measuring the frequency of the tone at the receiver.

Phase Intercept Distortion. *Phase intercept distortion* occurs in coherent SSBSC systems when the received carrier is not reinserted with the exact phase relationship to the received signal as the transmit carrier possessed. This impairment causes a constant phase shift to all frequencies. This impairment is of little concern with data modems that use frequency shift keying, differential phase shift keying, or quadrature amplitude modulation. Because these are the more common methods of modulation, the telephone company has not set any limits on phase intercept distortion.

Nonlinear Distortion. Nonlinear distortion is an example of correlated noise. The noise caused by nonlinear distortion is in the form of additional tones present because of the nonlinear amplification of a signal—no signal, no noise! Nonlinear distortion produces distorted sine waves. Two classifications of nonlinear distortion are

1. *Harmonic distortion*—unwanted multiples of the transmitted frequencies
2. *Intermodulation distortion*—cross products (sums and differences) of the input frequencies

Harmonic and intermodulation distortion, if of sufficient amplitude, can cause a data signal to be destroyed. The degree of circuit nonlinearity can be measured using either harmonic or intermodulation distortion tests.

Harmonic distortion is measured by applying a single-frequency test tone to a data channel. At the receive end, the power of the fundamental, second, and third harmonic frequencies is measured. Harmonic distortion is classified as second, third, *n*th order or as total harmonic distortion. Generally, harmonics above the third extend beyond the passband of a voice-band channel and are of insufficient amplitude to be important. The actual amount of nonlinearity in a circuit is determined by comparing the power of the fundamental to the combined powers of the second and third harmonics. Harmonic distortion tests use a single-frequency (704-Hz) source (see Figure 2-40); therefore, no cross-product frequencies are produced.

Although simple harmonic distortion tests provide an accurate measurement of the nonlinear characteristics of an analog message channel, they are inadequate for digital (T-carrier) facilities. For this reason, a more refined method was developed that uses a multifrequency test tone signal. Four test frequencies are used (see Figure 2-41): two designated the A band (A1 = 856 Hz, A2 = 863 Hz), and two designated the B band

FIGURE 2-41 Nonlinear distortion

(B1 = 1374 Hz, B2 = 1385 Hz). The four frequencies are transmitted with equal power, and the total combined power is equal to that of a composite data signal. The nonlinear amplification of the circuit produces multiples of each frequency and also their cross products. For reasons beyond the scope of this text, the following second- and third-order products were selected for measurement: B + A, B − A, and 2B − A. The combined signal power of the four A and B band frequencies is compared with the second-order products and, then, compared with the third-order products. Harmonic and intermodulation distortion tests do not directly determine the amount of interference caused by nonlinear circuit gain. They serve as a figure of merit only when evaluating circuit parameters.

Peak-to-Average Ratio. The difficulties encountered in measuring true phase distortion or envelope delay distortion led to the development of peak-to-average (PAR) tests. A signal containing a series of distinctly shaped pulses with a high peak-to-average ratio (hence, the name) is transmitted. Delay distortion in a circuit has a tendency to spread the pulses and reduce the peak-to-average ratio. The received peak-to-average ratio is converted to a number between 0 and 100. The higher the number, the less the phase distortion. Peak-to-average tests do not indicate the exact amount of phase distortion present in a circuit; they only provide a figure of merit that can indicate the presence of a problem. Peak-to-average tests are less sensitive to attenuation distortion than envelope delay distortion tests and are easier to accomplish.

Tables 2-15 and 2-16 summarize the interface parameter limits and facility parameter limits discussed in this chapter.

Abbreviations associated with signal and noise level measurements

1. *dB (decibel).* Experiments indicate that a listener cannot give a reliable estimate of the loudness of a sound, but he can distinguish the difference in loudness between two sounds. The ear's sensitivity to a change in sound power follows a logarithmic rather than linear scale, and the dB has become the unit of this change.

$$dB = 20 \log \frac{V_1}{V_2} \qquad dB = 20 \log \frac{I_1}{I_2} \qquad dB = 10 \log \frac{P_1}{P_2}$$

If the larger value is assigned to the numerator, the dB value will be positive. dB yields a relative value—the relative size of the numerator compared to the denominator.

2. *dBm*
   (a) dBm is the dB in reference to 1 mW.
   (b) dBm is a measure of absolute power.
   (c) A 10 dBm signal is equal to 10 mW.
   (d) A 20 dBm signal is equal to 100 mW.

TABLE 2-15 Summary of Interface Parameter Limits

Parameter	Limit
1. Recommended impedance of terminal equipment	600 Ω resistive ± 10%
2. Recommended isolation to ground of terminal equipment	At least 20 MΩ dc
	At least 50 kΩ ac
	At least 1500 V rms breakdown voltage at 60 Hz
3. Data transmit signal power	0 dBm (3-s average)
4. In-band transmitted signal power	2450-Hz to 2750-Hz band should not exceed signal power in 800-Hz to 2450-Hz band
5. Out-of-band transmitted signal power *Above voice band:*	
(a) 3995 Hz–4005 Hz	At least 18 dB below maximum allowed in-band signal power
(b) 4 kHz–10 kHz band	Less than −16 dBm
(c) 10 kHz–25 kHz band	Less than −24 dBm
(d) 25 kHz–40 kHz band	Less than −36 dBm
(e) Above 40 kHz	Less than −50 dBm

Below voice band:

(f) Rms current per conductor as specified by Telco, but never greater than 0.35 A.

(g) Magnitude of peak conductor-to-ground voltage not to exceed 70 V.

(h) Conductor-to-conductor voltage shall be such that conductor-to-ground voltage is not exceeded. For an underground signal source, the conductor-to-conductor limit is the same as the conductor-to-ground limit.

(i) Total weighted rms voltage in band from 50 Hz to 300 Hz, not to exceed 100 V. Weighting factors for each frequency component (f) are: $f^2/10^4$ for f between 50 Hz and 100 Hz, and $f^{3.3}/10^{6.6}$ for f between 101 Hz and 300 Hz.

6. Maximum test signal power: same as transmitted data power.

3. *TLP (transmission level point).* Knowing the signal power at any point in a system is relatively worthless. A signal at a particular point can be 10 dBm. Is this good or bad? This could be answered if it is known what the signal strength should be at that point. The TLP does just that. The reference for TLP is 0 dBm. A −15 dBm TLP indicates that, at this specified point, the signal should be −15 dBm. A 0 TLP is a TLP where the signal power should be 0 dBm. The TLP says nothing about the signal itself.

4. *dBmO.* dBmO is a power measurement adjusted to 0 dBm that indicates what the power would be if it were measured at 0 TLP. This value compares the actual signal at a point to what that signal should be at that point (TLP). A +4-dBm signal measured at a −16 dBm TLP is +20 dBmO. It is 20 dB stronger than the reference. A −2-dBm signal measured at a −10 dBm TLP is equal to +8 dBmO.

5. *rn (reference noise).* This value is the dB value used as noise reference. This value is *always* −90 dBm or 1 pW. This value is taken as the reference because the signal value at any point should never be less than this.

6. *dBrnc.* This is the dB value of noise with respect to reference noise with C-message weighting. The larger this value is, the worse the condition because of a larger amount of noise.

7. *dBrncO.* This is the amount of noise corrected to 0 TLP. The amount of noise at a point does not really indicate how detrimental its effect is on a given signal. 0.3 dBm of noise with a 20 dBm signal is insignificant; however, the same amount of noise with a 0.3 dBm signal strength may completely obscure the

TABLE 2-16 Summary of Facility Parameter Limits

Parameter	Limit
1. 1004-Hz loss variation	Not more than ±4 dB long-term
2. C-message noise	Maximum rms noise at modem receiver (nominal −16 dBm point)

Facility miles	dBm	dBrncO
0–50	−61	32
51–100	−59	34
101–400	−58	35
401–1000	−55	38
1001–1500	−54	39
1501–2500	−52	41
2501–4000	−50	43
4001–8000	−47	46
8001–16000	−44	49

Parameter	Limit
3. C-notched noise	(minimum values)
(a) Standard voice-band channel	24-dB signal-to-C-notched noise
(b) High-performance line	28-dB signal-to-C-notched noise
4. Single-frequency interference	At least 3 dB below C-message noise limits
5. Impulse noise	

Threshold with respect to 1004-Hz holding tone	Maximum counts above threshold allowed in 15 minutes
0 dB	15
+4 dB	9
+8 dB	5

Parameter	Limit
6. Frequency shift	±5 Hz end to end
7. Phase intercept distortion	No limits
8. Phase jitter	No more than 10° peak to peak (end-to-end requirement)
9. Nonlinear distortion (D-conditioned circuits only)	
Signal-to-second order	At least 35 dB
Signal-to-third order	At least 40 dB
10. Peak-average ratio	Reading of 50 minimum end to end with standard PAR meter
11. Phase hits	8 or less in any 15-minute period greater than ±20° peak
12. Gain hits	8 or less in any 15-minute period greater than ±3 dB
13. Dropouts	2 or less in any 15-minute period greater than 12 dB

signal. Noise of 34 dBrncO at +7 dBm TLP yields a value of 27 dBrncO. dBrncO relates noise power reading (dBrnc) to 0 TLP. This unit establishes a common reference point throughout the system.

8. *DLP (data level point).* This parameter is equivalent to the TLP as far as its function is concerned. It is used as a reference for data transmission. TLP is used as a reference for voice transmission. Whatever the TLP is, the DLP is always 13 dB below that value for the same point. If the TLP is −12 dBm, the DLP is −25 dBm for that same point. For example,

Noise = 72 dBm (noise, in all cases, will mean C-message noise)
Signal = −27 dBm at −24 dBm TLP
Find:

Signal	_____ dBmO	answer	−3
Noise	_____ dBrnc	answer	+18
Noise	_____ dBrncO	answer	+42
S/N	_____ dB	answer	+45

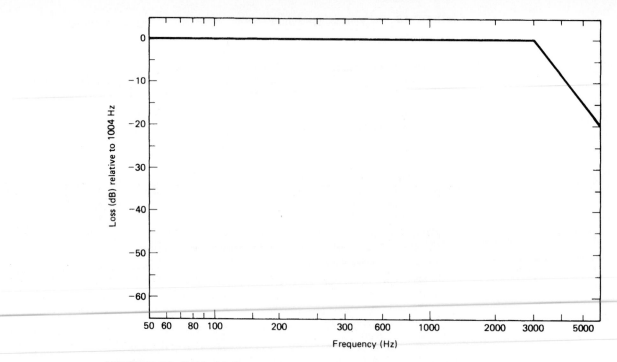

FIGURE 2-42   3-kHz flat filter

9. *dBrn.* This value is used only when there is excessive low-frequency noise and that noise is exceeding the levels specified in the interface parameters. Its value is measured with a device that has a 3-kHz flat filter (instead of a C-message filter) (see Figure 2-42). in normal circuits, dBrn is typically 1.5 dB above what would be read with a C-message filter.

DATA MODEMS

The primary purpose of the data modem is to interface the digital terminal equipment to an analog communications channel. The data modem is also called a DCE, a *dataset,* a *dataphone,* or simply a *modem.* At the transmit end, the modem converts digital pulses from the serial interface to analog signals, and at the receive end, the modem converts analog signals to digital pulses.

FIGURE 2-43 Output spectrum for a 103 modem. Carrier frequency: low band = 1170, high band = 2125; input data = 300 bps alternating 1/0 sequence

Modems are generally classified as either asynchronous or synchronous and use either FSK, PSK, or QAM modulation. With synchronous modems, clocking information is recovered in the receive modem; with asynchronous modems, it is not. Asynchronous modems use FSK modulation and are restricted to low-speed applications (below 2000 bps). Synchronous modems use PSK and QAM modulation and are used for medium-speed (2400 bps to 4800 bps) and high-speed (9600 bps) applications.

Asynchronous Modems

Asynchronous modems are used primarily for low-speed dial-up circuits. There are several standard modem designs commonly used for asynchronous data transmission. For half-duplex operation using the two-wire DDD network or full-duplex operation with four-wire private-line circuit, the Western Electric 202T/S or equivalent is a popular modem. The 202T is a four-wire full-duplex modem and the 202S is a two-wire, half-duplex modem.

The 202T modem is an asynchronous transceiver utilizing frequency shift keying. It uses a 1700-Hz carrier that can be shifted at a maximum rate of 1200 times a second. When a logic 1 (mark) is applied to the modulator, the carrier is shifted down 500 Hz, to 1200 Hz. When a logic 0 (space) is applied, the carrier is shifted up 500 Hz, to 2200 Hz. Consequently, as the data input signal alternates between 1 and 0, the carrier is shifted back and forth between 1200 and 2200 Hz, respectively. This process can be related to conventional frequency modulation. The difference between the mark and space frequencies (1200 Hz to 2200 Hz) is the peak-to-peak frequency deviation, and the rate of change of the digital input signal (bit rate) is equal to twice the frequency of the modulating signal. Therefore, for the worst-case situation, the 1700-Hz carrier is frequency modulated by a 1200-Hz square wave.

To operate full duplex with a two-wire dial-up circuit, it is necessary to divide the usable bandwidth of a voice-band circuit in half, creating two equal-capacity data channels. A popular modem that does this is the Western Electric 103 or equivalent. The 103 modem is capable of full-duplex operation over a two-wire line at bit rates up to 300 bps. With the 103 modem, there are two data channels each with separate mark and space frequencies. One channel is the *low-band channel* and occupies a passband from 300 Hz to 1650 Hz. The second channel is the *high-band channel* and occupies a passband from 1650 Hz to 3000 Hz. The mark and space frequencies for the low-band channel are 1270 Hz and 1070 Hz, respectively. The mark and space frequencies for the high-band channel are 2225 Hz and 2025 Hz, respectively. The frequency spectrum for a 103 modem is shown in Figure 2-43. The high- and low-band data channels occupy different frequency bands and, therefore, can use the same two-wire facility without interfering with each other. This is called *frequency-division multiplexing* and is explained in detail in Chapter 6.

The low-band channel is commonly called the *originate channel* and the high-band channel is called the *answer channel*. It is standard procedure on a dial-up circuit for the station that originates the call to transmit on the low-band frequencies and receive on the high-band frequencies, and the station that answers the call to transmit on the high-band frequencies and receive on the low-band frequencies.

Synchronous Modems

Synchronous modems are used for medium- and high-speed data transmission and use either PSK or QAM modulation. With synchronous modems the transmit clock, together with the data, digitally modulate an analog carrier. The modulated carrier is transmitted to the receive modem, where a coherent carrier is recovered and used to demodulate the data. The transmit clock is recovered from the data and used to clock the received data into the DTE. Because of the clock and carrier recovery circuits, a synchronous modem is more complicated and, thus, more expensive than its asynchronous counterpart.

PSK modulation is used for medium-speed (2400 bps to 4800 bps) synchronous modems. More specifically, QPSK is used with 2400-bps modems and 8-PSK is used with 4800-bps modems. QPSK has a bandwidth efficiency of 2 bps/Hz; therefore, the baud rate and minimum bandwidth for a 2400-bps synchronous modem are 1200 baud and 1200 Hz. The standard 2400-bps synchronous modem is the Western Electric 201C or equivalent. The 201C uses a 1600-Hz carrier and has an output spectrum that extends from 1000 Hz to 2200 Hz. 8-PSK has a bandwidth efficiency of 3 bps/Hz; therefore, the baud rate and minimum bandwidth for 4800-bps synchronous modems are 1600 baud and 1600 Hz. The standard 4800-bps synchronous modem is the Western Electric 208A or equivalent. The 208A also uses a 1600-Hz carrier but has an output spectrum that extends from 800 Hz to 2400 Hz. Both the 201C and 208A are full-duplex modems designed to be used with four-wire private-line circuits. The 201C and 208A can operate over two-wire dial-up circuits but only in the simplex mode. There are half-duplex two-wire versions of both models: the 201B and 208B.

High-speed synchronous modems operate at 9600 bps and use 16-QAM modulation. 16-QAM has a bandwidth efficiency of 4 bps/Hz; therefore, the baud rate and minimum bandwidth for 9600-bps synchronous modems are 2400 baud and 2400 Hz. The standard 9600-bps modem is the Western Electric 209A or equivalent. The 209A uses a 1650-Hz carrier and has an output spectrum that extends from 450 Hz to 2850 Hz. The Western Electric 209A is a four-wire synchronous modem designed to be used on full-duplex private-line circuits. The 209B is the two-wire version designed for half-duplex dial-up circuits.

Normally, an asynchronous data format is used with asynchronous modems and a synchronous data format is used with synchronous modems. However, asynchronous data are occasionally used with synchronous modems; this is called *isochronous transmission*. Synchronous data are never used with asynchronous modems.

Table 2-17 summarizes the standard Western Electric modems.

Modem Synchronization

During the RTS/CTS delay, the transmit modem outputs a special, internally generated bit pattern called the *training sequence*. This bit pattern is used to synchronize (train) the receive modem. Depending on the type of modulation, transmission bit rate, and the complexity of the modem, the training sequence accomplishes one or more of the following functions in the receive modem:

TABLE 2-17 Modem Summary

Western Electric Designation	Line Facility	Operating Mode	Synchronization	Type of Modulation	Maximum Data Rate (bps)
103	Dial-up	FDX	Asynchronous	FSK	300
113A	Dial-up	Simplex	Asynchronous	FSK	300
113B	Dial-up	Simplex	Asynchronous	FSK	300
201B	Dial-up	HDX	Synchronous	QPSK	2400
201C	Private	HDX/FDX	Synchronous	QPSK	2400
202S	Dial-up	HDX	Asynchronous	FSK	1200
202T	Private	HDX/FDX	Asynchronous	FSK	1200 (basic) 1800 (C1 conditioning)
208A	Private	HDX/FDX	Synchronous	8-PSK	4800
208B	Dial-up	HDX	Synchronous	8-PSK	4800
209A	Private	HDX/FDX	Synchronous	16-QAM	9600 (D1 conditioning)
209B	Dial-up	HDX	Synchronous	16-QAM	9600

1. Verify continuity (activate RLSD).
2. Initialize the descrambler circuits. (These circuits are used for clock recovery—explained later in this section.)
3. Initialize the automatic equalizer. (These circuits compensate for telephone line impairments—explained later in this section.)
4. Synchronize the transmitter and receiver carrier oscillators.
5. Synchronize the transmitter and receiver clock oscillators.
6. Disable any echo suppressors in the circuit.
7. Establish the gain of any AGC amplifiers in the circuit.

Low-Speed Modems

Because low-speed modems are generally asynchronous and use noncoherent FSK, the transmit carrier and clock frequencies need not be recovered by the receive modem. Therefore, scrambler and descrambler circuits are unnecessary. The pre- and post-equalization circuits, if used, are generally manual and do not require initialization. The special bit pattern transmitted during the RTS/CTS delay is usually a constant string of 1s (idle line 1s) and is used to verify continuity, set the gain of the AGC amplifiers, and disable any echo suppressors in dial-up applications.

Medium- and High-Speed Modems

Medium- and high-speed modems are used where transmission rates of 2400 bps or more are required. In order to transmit at these higher bit rates, PSK or QAM modulation is used, which requires the receiver carrier oscillators to be at least frequency coherent (and possibly phase coherent). Because these modems are synchronous, clock timing recovery by the receive modem must be achieved. These modems contain *scrambler* and *descrambler circuits* and *adaptive (automatic) equalizers*.

Training. The type of modulation and encoding technique used determines the number of bits required and, therefore, the duration of the training sequence. The 208 modem is a synchronous, 4800-bps modem that uses 8-DPSK. The training sequence for this modem is shown in Figure 2-44. Each symbol represents 3 bits (1 tribit) and is 0.625 ms in duration. The four-phase idle code sequences through four of the eight possible phase shifts. This allows the receiver to recover the carrier and the clock timing information rapidly. The four-phase test word allows the adaptive equalizer in the receive

4-Phase idle code (13 symbols)	4-Phase test word (52 symbols)	8-Phase initialization period (13 symbols)	Customer data

RTS On   ——Time——▶   CTS On

FIGURE 2-44   Training sequence for a 208 modem

FIGURE 2-45   Clock recovery circuit for QPSK demodulator

FIGURE 2-46   Clock recovery from I (or Q) channel of a QPSK demodulator

modem to adjust to its final setting. The eight-phase initialization period prepares the descrambler circuits for eight-phase operation. The entire training sequence (234 bits) requires 48.75 ms for transmission.

Clock recovery. Although timing (clock) synchronization is first established during the training sequence, it must be maintained for the duration of the transmission. The clocking information can be extracted from either the I or the Q channel, or from the output of the bit combiner. If an alternating 1/0 pattern is assumed at the output of the LPF (Figure 2-45) a clock frequency at the bit rate of the I (or Q) channel can be recovered. The waveforms associated with Figure 2-45 are shown in Figure 2-46.

This clocking information is used to phase-lock loop the receive clock oscillator onto the transmitter clock frequency. To recover clocking information by this method successfully, there must be sufficient transitions in the received data stream. That these transitions will automatically occur cannot be assumed. In a QPSK system, an alternating

FIGURE 2-47 Scrambler and descrambler circuits

1/0 pattern applied to the transmit modulator produces a sequence of all 1s in the I or Q channel, and a sequence of all 0s in the opposite channel. A prolonged sequence of all 1s or all 0s applied to the transmit modulator would not provide any transitions in either the I, Q, or the composite received data stream. Restrictions could be placed on the customer's protocol and message format to prevent an undesirable bit sequence from occurring, but this is a poor solution to the problem.

Scramblers and descramblers. A better method is to scramble the customer's data before it modulates the carrier. The receiver circuitry must contain the corresponding descrambling algorithm to recover the original bit sequence before data are sent to the DTE. The purpose of a scrambler is not simply to randomize the transmitted bit sequence but to detect the occurrence of an undesirable bit sequence and convert it to a more acceptable pattern.

A block diagram of a scrambler and descrambler circuit is shown in Figure 2-47. These circuits are incomplete because an additional gate would be required to detect a varying sequence that would create an all 1 or all 0 sequence in a modulator channel after the bits were split.

The scrambler circuit is inserted prior to the bit splitter in the QPSK modulator and the descrambler is inserted after the bit combiner in the QPSK demodulator. In general, the output of the scrambler or descrambler OR gate is A B C D + A' B' C' D'.

$$f_m = f_d \oplus (\text{A B C D} + \text{A'B'C'D'}) \quad \text{top XOR gate}$$
$$f_r = f_m \oplus (\text{A B C D} + \text{A'B'C'D'}) \quad \text{bottom XOR gate}$$

Substituting for f_m in the second equation, we have

$$f_r = f_d \oplus (\text{A B C D} + \text{A'B'C'D'}) \oplus (\text{A B C D} + \text{A'B'C'D'})$$

Data Modems

Because any identity XORed with itself yields 0,

$$f_r = f_d \oplus 0$$
$$f_r = f_d$$

This simply shows that the original transmitted data (f_d) will be fully recovered by the receiver.

The output of either OR gate will be a 1 if the 4-bit register contains either all 1s or all 0s. Neither of these is a desirable sequence. If the OR gate output is a 1, f_m will be the complement (opposite) of f_d, or f_r will be complement of f_m. The intent is to create transitions in a prolonged bit stream of either all 1s or all 0s. If the output of the OR gate is a 0, neither of these undesired conditions exists and $f_m = f_d$ or $f_r = f_m$: the data pass through the XOR gate unchanged. If the other logic gates (AND, OR, NAND, NOR) were used either alone or in combination in place of the XOR gates, the necessary transitions could be created in the scrambler circuit, but the original data could not be recovered in the descrambler circuit. If a long string of all 1s or all 0s is applied to the scrambler circuit, this circuit will introduce transitions. However, there may be times when the scrambler creates an undesired sequence. The XOR output is always either a 1 or a 0. No matter what the output of the OR gate, a value of f_d may be found to produce a 1 or a 0 at the XOR output. If either value for f_d was equiprobable, the scrambler circuit would be unnecessary. If the 4-bit register contains all 1s, if $f_d = 1$, we would like to see it inverted. However, if $f_d = 0$, we would prefer to pass it through the XOR gate unchanged. The scrambler circuit for this situation inverts the 0 and extends the output string of 1s. It is beyond the intended scope of this book to delve deeply into all parameters involved in scrambler design. Let it be enough to say that scramblers will cure more problems than they create.

Equalizers.   *Equalization* is the compensation for the phase delay distortion and amplitude distortion of a telephone line. One form of equalization is C-type conditioning. Additional equalization may be performed by the modems. *Compromise equalizers* are contained in the transmit section of the modem and they provide *preequalization*. They shape the transmitted signal by altering its delay and gain characteristics before it reaches the telephone line. It is an attempt to compensate for impairments anticipated in the bandwidth parameters of the line. When a modem is installed, the compromise equalizers are manually adjusted to provide the best *bit error rate* (BER). Typically, compromise equalizer settings affect

1. Amplitude only
2. Delay only
3. Amplitude and delay
4. Neither amplitude nor delay

The settings above may be applied to either the high- or low-voice-band frequencies or symmetrically to both at the same time. Once a compromise equalizer setting has been selected, it can only be changed manually. The setting that achieves the best BER is dependent on the electrical length of the circuit and the type of facilities that make it up. *Adaptive equalizers* are located in the receiver section of the modem and provide *postequalization* to the received analog signal. Adaptive equalizers automatically adjust their gain and delay characteristics to compensate for telephone-line impairments. An adaptive equalizer may determine the quality of the received signal within its own circuitry or it may acquire this information from the demodulator or descrambler circuits. Whichever the case, the adaptive equalizer may continuously vary its settings to achieve the best overall bandwidth characteristics for the circuit.

TABLE 2-18 AT Command Set (Partial List)

Character(s)	Command
AT	Attention
A	Answer an incoming call
DT	Dial using DTMF tones
DP	Dial using pulse dialing
E0	Do not echo transmitted data to terminal screen
E1	Echo transmitted data to terminal screen
F0	Half-duplex communications
F1	Full-duplex communications
H	Go on-hook (hang up)
O	Switch from command to on-line mode
Z	Reset modem
+++	Escape code; switch from on-line to command mode

Modem Control—The AT Command Set

First generation modems are often called *dumb modems* because they consisted of little more than a modulator and demodulator. Modems were originally designed to be used primarily on private-line data circuits, which made it awkward to use them on dial-up telephone circuits. Operators at both ends of the circuit were required to perform almost all the functions necessary to initiate, complete, and terminate a call. *Intelligent (smart)* modems were introduced in the early 1970s. Smart modems have built in microprocessors that performed routine functions such as automatic answering, call initiating and dialing, busy signal recognition, and error correction. Smart modems are often controlled by other larger computers through a system of commands. The most common system of modem commands is the *AT command set,* which is also known as the *Hayes command set.* Hayes Microcomputer Products originally developed the AT command set for its own line of modems, but other manufacturers soon adopted the system and it rapidly became the de facto standard in the United States. Table 2-18 lists some of the most common AT commands.

AT command mode. All modem commands in the AT command set begin with the ASCII characters AT (ATtention). Whenever a modem is not communicating directly with another modem, it is in the *command mode.* In the command mode, the modem monitors information sent to it through the DTE by the local terminal looking for the ASCII characters AT. After detecting the AT sequence, the modem interprets the characters that immediately follow the AT as commands. For example, the ASCII character T is the command to use tones rather than dial pulses, and the ASCII character D is the command to dial. For example to dial the telephone number 1-(602)461-7777 the character sequence would be: ATDT16024617777.

AT on-line mode. Once communications have been established with a remote modem, the local modem switches to the *on-line mode.* In the on-line mode, a modem becomes transparent and interprets characters received from the DTE, including AT characters, as data. The local modem simply accepts the characters and allows them to modulate its carrier before sending them to a remote location. The local terminal can switch the modem from the on-line mode to the command mode, by momentarily pausing the transmission of data, sending three consecutive plus signs (+++), then pausing again. This sequence is called an *escape code.* In response to the escape code, the modem switches to the command mode and begins monitoring data for the ASCII AT command code.

CCITT Modem Recommendations

The CCITT, which is part of the International Telecommunications Union, sets data transmission standards outside of the United States. CCITT standards V.21, V.23, and

TABLE 2-19 CCITT Modem Recommendations

Recommendations	Description
V.21	0 bps to 200 (300) bps (similar to Bell 103); defined for FDX-switched network operation
V.22	1200-bps, FDX-switched and leased-line network operation
V.22bis	1200/2400-bps, FDX-switched and leased-line network operation
V.23	600/1200-bps (similar to Bell 202); defined for HDX-switched network operation; optional 75-bps reverse channel
V.24	Definition of interchange circuits (similar to EIA RS-232)
V.25	Automatic calling units (similar to Bell 801)
V.25bis	Serial interface autocalling
V.26	2400 bps (identical to Bell 201B); defined for four-wire leased circuits
V.26bis	2400/1200 bps (similar to Bell 201C); defined for switched network operation
V.26ter	2400 bps over the switched network using echo cancelling
V.27	4800 bps (similar to Bell 208A); defined for leased circuits using manual equalizers
V.27bis	4800/2400 bps with autoequalizers for leased lines
V.27ter	4800/2400 bps for use on switched lines
V.28	Electrical characteristics for interchange circuits (similar to RS-232)
V.29	9600-bps FDX (similar to Bell 209); defined for leased circuits
V.32	9600-bps FDX for switched- or leased-line circuits using echo cancelling
V.32bis	14,400-bps FDX for switched- or leased-line circuits using echo cancelling
V.33	14,400-bps FDX for leased lines
V.42	Error-correction procedures for DCEs using asynchronous to synchronous conversion
V.42bis	An extension of V.42 that defines data compression for use with V.42
V.34	(V.FAST) ITU-TS 28,800 bps standard

V.26 describe modems similar to the Bell System 103, 202, and 201, respectively. V.22 describes modem specifications similar to the Bell System 212A, and V.29 outlines specifications similar to the Bell System 209A. Table 2-19 lists some of the other CCITT recommendations.

QUESTIONS

2-1. Define *data communications*.

2-2. What was the significance of the Carterfone decision?

2-3. Explain the difference between a two-point and a multipoint circuit.

2-4. What is a data communications topology?

2-5. Define the four transmission modes for data communications circuits.

2-6. Which of the four transmission modes can be used only with multipoint circuits?

2-7. Explain the differences between two-wire and four-wire circuits.

2-8. What is a data communications code? What are some of the other names for data communications codes?

2-9. What are the three types of characters used in data communications codes?

2-10. Which data communications code is the most powerful? Why?

2-11. What are the two general categories of error control? What is the difference between them?

2-12. Explain the following error detection techniques: redundancy, exact-count encoding, parity, vertical redundancy checking, longitudinal redundancy checking, and cyclic redundancy checking.

2-13. Which error detection technique is the simplest?

2-14. Which error detection technique is the most reliable?

2-15. Explain the following error correction techniques: symbol substitution, retransmission, and forward error correction.

2-16. Which error correction technique is designed to be used in a human environment?

2-17. Which error correction technique is the most reliable?

2-18. Define *character synchronization.*

2-19. Describe the asynchronous data format.

2-20. Describe the synchronous data format.

2-21. Which data format is best suited to long messages? Why?

2-22. What is a cluster?

2-23. Describe the functions of a control unit.

2-24. What is the purpose of the data modem?

2-25. What are the primary functions of the UART?

2-26. What is the maximum number of bits that can make up a single character with a UART?

2-27. What do the status signals RPE, RFE, and ROR indicate?

2-28. Why does the receive clock for a UART operate 16 times faster than the receive bit rate?

2-29. What are the major differences between a UART and a USRT?

2-30. What is the purpose of the serial interface?

2-31. What is the most prominent serial interface in the United States?

2-32. Why did the EIA establish the RS-232 interface?

2-33. What is the nominal maximum length for the RS-232 interface?

2-34. What are the four general classifications of pins on the RS-232 interface?

2-35. What is the maximum positive voltage that a driver will output?

2-36. Which classification of pins uses negative logic?

2-37. What is the primary difference between the RS-449A interface and the RS-232 interface?

2-38. Higher bit rates are possible with a *(balanced, unbalanced)* interface cable.

2-39. Who provides the most commonly used transmission medium for data communications circuits? Why?

2-40. Explain the differences between DDD circuits and private-line circuits.

2-41. Define the following terms: local loop, trunk, common usage, and dial switch.

2-42. What is a DCE?

2-43. What is the primary difference between a synchronous and an asynchronous modem?

2-44. What is necessary for full-duplex operation using a two-wire circuit?

2-45. What do *originate* and *answer mode* mean?

2-46. What modulation scheme is used for low-speed applications? For medium-speed applications? For high-speed applications?

2-47. Why are synchronous modems required for medium- and high-speed applications?

2-48. Higher frequencies generally suffer greater attenuation than lower frequencies when traveling through a given cable of a fixed length. (T, F)

2-49. A loaded telephone cable identification number indicates three characteristics of that cable. What are they?

2-50. A metallic cable acts as what type of filter?

2-51. A cable is loaded by adding _____ in series with the wire.

2-52. 1004-Hz deviation is another name for envelope delay. (T, F)

2-53. Dial-up lines may be conditioned. (T, F)

2-54. What type of line has minimum conditioning?

2-55. D-type conditioning may be achieved by adding inductors in series to the line. (T, F)

2-56. D-type conditioning is mandatory if the transmission rate is _____ bps.

2-57. Which frequency is used as the reference for attenuation distortion measurements when determining the type of conditioning?

2-58. Which frequency is used as the reference for envelope delay measurements when determining the type of conditioning?

2-59. All frequencies take the same time to propagate down a particular cable of fixed length. (T, F)

2-60. In determining the amount of phase distortion, (*relative, absolute*) phase delay is the more important parameter.

2-61. A C4 conditioned line must meet (*more, less*) stringent requirements than a C2 conditioned line.

2-62. Phase distortion is caused by the fact that it takes different frequencies different times to propagate down a line.   (T, F)

2-63. Phase distortion is synonymous with delay distortion.   (T, F)

2-64. Delay distortion is synonymous with EDD.   (T, F)

2-65. The maximum allowed transmitted signal power for a dial-up circuit is always 2 mW.   (T, F)

2-66. The maximum allowed transmitted signal power for a private-line circuit is _____ mW.

2-67. All voice-band frequencies suffer the same attenuation when passing through a C-message filter.   (T, F)

2-68. C-message filters are used in circuits to improve the signal-to-noise ratio.   (T, F)

2-69. What is the difference in measuring C-message noise and C-notched noise?

2-70. For a private line, what is the minimum signal-to-C-notched noise for
   (a) Transmission at less than 9600 bps?
   (b) 9600-bps transmission?

2-71. Empirical determinations are the results of mathematical proofs of theory.   (T, F)

2-72. Three impulse hits on a message block would necessitate a different action than a single impulse hit on the same block.   (T, F)

2-73. What is the difference between a gain hit and an impulse hit?

2-74. Name two types of nonlinear distortion.

2-75. What unit of measurement indicates the actual signal strength relative to what the signal strength should be?

2-76. What is the magnitude of noise, in dBm, that is used as the reference?

2-77. What is the unit of noise measurement that is corrected to 0 TLP?

2-78. Data transmission relates a signal strength to a DLP that is always _____ dB below the TLP?

2-79. What is the noise unit that is used to measure low-frequency noise?

PROBLEMS

2-1. Determine the LRC and VRC for the following message (use even parity for LRC and odd parity for VRC).

$$\text{D A T A sp C O M M U N I C A T I O N S}$$

2-2. Determine the BCS for the following data- and CRC-generating polynomials.

$$G(x) = x^7 + x^4 + x^2 + x^0 = 1\,0\,0\,1\,0\,1\,0\,1$$
$$P(x) = x^5 + x^4 + x^1 + x^0 = 1\,1\,0\,0\,1\,1$$

2-3. How many Hamming bits are required for a single ASCII character?

2-4. Determine the Hamming bits for the ASCII character "B." Insert the Hamming bits into every other location starting at the left.

2-5. Determine the LRC and VRC for the following message (use even parity for LRC and odd parity for VRC).

$$
\begin{array}{llllllllllllllllll}
\text{P} & \text{S} & \text{S} & & & & & & & & & & & & \text{E} & \text{B} & \text{P} \\
\text{A} & \text{Y} & \text{Y} & \text{T} & \text{A} & \text{S} & \text{C} & \text{I} & \text{I} & \text{sp} & \text{C} & \text{O} & \text{D} & \text{E} & \text{T} & \text{C} & \text{A} \\
\text{D} & \text{N} & \text{N} & \text{X} & & & & & & & & & & & \text{X} & \text{C} & \text{D}
\end{array}
$$

2-6. Determine the BSC for the following data- and CRC-generating polynomials:

$$G(x) = x^8 + x^5 + x^2 + x^0$$
$$P(x) = x^5 + x^4 + x^1 + x^0$$

2-7. How many Hamming bits are required for an ASCII character (1 start bit, 7 data bits, 1 parity bit, and 2 stop bits; 11 total bits)?

2-8. Determine the Hamming bits for the ASCII character C (use odd parity and two stop bits). Insert the Hamming bits into every other location starting at the right.

2-9. A cable is identified as 16D44. This indicates that _____-mH inductors have been added in series every _____ feet to a _____-gauge wire.

2-10. A 1800-Hz signal takes 2 ms to propagate down a line. A 600-Hz signal takes 2.5 ms to travel down the same line. What is the absolute phase delay of the 600-Hz signal? What is the relative phase delay of this same signal?

2-11. A line has C4 conditioning. A 1004-Hz signal is received at −10 dBm and the propagation delay for a 1800-Hz signal is 5 ms. A signal frequency of 400 Hz can take no more than _____ ms to travel down this line and its received signal strength must be between _____ dBm and _____ dBm.

2-12. Draw a graphic representation for attenuation distortion and envelope delay distortion for a channel with C4 conditioning.

2-13. Frequencies of 250 Hz and 1 kHz are applied to a C-message filter. Their difference in amplitude would be *(greater, the same, less)* at the output than at the input.

2-14. Dedicated lines are used to transmit data at 4800 bps. The received signal level is 500 μW. What is the maximum amount of C-notched noise allowed to satisfy D-type conditioning?

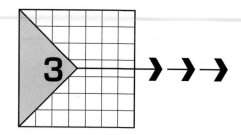

C H A P T E R 3

Data Communications Protocols and Network Configurations

INTRODUCTION

The primary goal of *network architecture* is to give the users of the network the tools necessary for setting up the network and for performing flow control. A network architecture outlines the way in which a data communications network is arranged or structured and generally includes the concept of *levels* or *layers* within the architecture. Each layer within the network consists of specific *protocols* or rules for communicating that perform a given set of functions.

Protocols are arrangements between people or processes. In essence, a protocol is a set of customs or regulations dealing with formality or precedence, such as diplomatic or military protocol. A *data communications network protocol* is a set of rules governing the orderly exchange of data.

As stated previously, the function of a line control unit is to control the flow of data between the applications program and the remote terminals. Therefore, there must be a set of rules that govern how an LCU reacts to or initiates different types of transmissions. This set of rules is called a *data link protocol*. Essentially, a data link protocol is a set of procedures, including precise character sequences, that ensure an orderly exchange of data between two LCUs.

In a data communications circuit, the station that is presently transmitting is called the *master* and the receiving station is called the *slave*. In a centralized network, the primary station controls when each secondary station can transmit. When a secondary station is transmitting, it is the master and the primary station is now the slave. The role of master is temporary and which station is master is delegated by the primary. Initially, the primary is master. The primary station solicits each secondary station, in turn, by *polling* it. A poll is an invitation from the primary to a secondary to transmit a message. Secondaries cannot poll a primary. When a primary polls a secondary, the primary is initiating a *line turnaround;* the polled secondary has been designated the master and must respond. If the primary *selects* a secondary, the secondary is identified as a receiver. A selection is an interrogation by the primary of a secondary to determine the secondary's status (i.e., ready to receive or not ready to receive a message). Secondary stations cannot select the primary. Transmissions from the primary go to all the secondaries; it is up to the secondary stations to individually decode each transmission and determine if it is intended for them. When a secondary transmits, it sends only to the primary.

Data link protocols are generally categorized as either asynchronous or synchronous. As a rule, asynchronous protocols use an asynchronous data format and asynchronous modems, whereas synchronous protocols use a synchronous data format and synchronous modems.

OPEN SYSTEMS INTERCONNECTION

The term *open systems interconnection* (OSI) is the name for a set of standards for communications among computers. The primary purpose of OSI standards is to serve as a structural guideline for exchanging information between computers, terminals, and networks. The OSI is endorsed by both the ISO and CCITT, which have worked together to establish a set of ISO standards and CCITT recommendations that are essentially identical. In 1983, the ISO and CCITT adopted a seven-layer communication architecture reference model. Each layer consists of specific protocols for communicating.

The ISO Protocol Hierarchy

The ISO–Open Systems Interconnection Seven-Layer Model is shown in Figure 3-1. This hierarchy was developed to facilitate the intercommunications of data processing equipment by separating network responsibilities into seven distinct layers. The basic concept of layering responsibilities is that each layer adds value to services provided by the sets of lower layers. In this way, the highest level is offered the full set of services needed to run a distributed data application.

There are several advantages to using a layered architecture for the OSI model. The different layers allow different computers to communicate at different levels. In addition,

FIGURE 3-1 ISO international protocol hierarchy. AH, applications header; PH, presentation header; SH, session header; TH, transport header; NH, network header; LH, link header; PH, physical header as technological advances occur, it is easier to modify one layer's protocol without having to modify all of the other layers. Each layer is essentially independent of every other layer. Therefore, many of the functions found in the lower layers have been removed entirely from software tasks and replaced with hardware. Some examples of these functions are shown in Figure 3-1. The primary disadvantage of the seven-layer architecture is the tremendous amount of overhead required in adding headers to the information being transmitted through the various layers. In fact, if all seven levels are addressed, less than 15% of the transmitted message is source information; the rest is overhead. The result of adding headers to each layer is illustrated in Figure 3-1.

Levels 4, 5, 6, and 7 allow for two host computers to communicate directly. The three bottom layers are concerned with the actual mechanics of moving data (at the bit level) from one machine to another. The basic services provided by each layer of the hierarchy are summarized below.

1. *Physical layer.* The physical layer is the lowest level of the hierarchy and specifies the physical, electrical, functional, and procedural standards for accessing the data communications network. Definitions such as maximum and minimum voltage levels and circuit impedances are made at the physical layer. The specifications outlined by the physical layer are similar to those specified by the EIA RS-232 serial interface standard.

2. *Data link layer.* The data link layer is responsible for communications between primary and secondary nodes within the network. The data link layer provides a means to activate, maintain, and deactivate the data link. The data link layer provides the final framing of the information envelope, facilitates the orderly flow of data between nodes, and allows for error detection and correction. Examples of data link protocols are IBM's bisynchronous communications (Bisync) and synchronous data link control (SDLC).

3. *Network layer.* The network layer determines which network configuration (dial-up, leased, or packet) is most appropriate for the function provided by the network. The network layer also defines the mechanism in which messages are broken into data packets and routed from a sending node to a receiving node within a communications network.

4. *Transport layer.* The transport layer controls the end-to-end integrity of the message, which includes message routing, segmenting, and error recovery. The transport layer is the highest layer in terms of communications. Layers above the transport layer are not concerned with technological aspects of the network. The upper three layers address the applications aspects of the network, where the lower three layers address the message transfer. Thus, the transport layer acts as the interface between the network and the session layers.

5. *Session layer.* The session layer is responsible for network availability (i.e., buffer storage and processor capacity). Session responsibilities include network log-on and log-off procedures and user authentication. A session is a temporary condition that exists when data are actually in the process of being transferred and does not include procedures such as call establishment, setup, or disconnect procedures. The session layer determines the type of dialogue available (i.e., simplex, half duplex, or full duplex).

6. *Presentation layer.* The presentation layer addresses any code or syntax conversion necessary to present the data to the network in a common format for communications. Presentation functions include data file formatting, encoding (ASCII, EBCDIC, etc.), encryption and decryption of messages, dialogue procedures, data compression, synchronization, interruption, and termination. The presentation layer performs code and character set translation and determines the display mechanism for messages.

7. *Applications layer.* The application layer is the highest layer in the hierarchy and is analogous to the general manager of the network. The application layer controls the sequence of activities within an application and also the sequence of events between the computer application and the user of another application. The application layer communicates directly with the user's application program.

DATA TRANSMISSION MODES

Data transmission modes describe how human-operated terminals transmit alpha/numeric data characters to host computers. Basically, there are only two transmission modes available: character and block.

Character Mode

When operating in the character mode, character codes are transmitted to the host computer immediately after a key has been depressed by an operator. The character is sent asynchronously because transmissions are not synchronized with the speed of the operators keystrokes. When an operator is not typing, the terminal is in the *idle state*. Data characters transmitted from the host to the remote terminal are displayed on the screen at the current position of the cursor. Nondata characters (such as Bel, CR, LF, etc.) are acted on accordingly.

Block Mode

In the block mode of data transmission, characters are not transmitted immediately as they are typed. Instead, the operator enters characters into their terminals where they are stored in buffers and displayed on the screen. When the operator is ready to transmit the information displayed on the screen, they depress the ENTER or RETURN key, which transmits all of the data characters entered into the local terminal. The assortment of characters transmitted as a group is called a *block* of data. The format used within the block depends on the system protocol selected. Most modern, smart terminals are capable of operating in either the character or block mode. The character mode of transmission is more common when terminals are communicating directly to the host through a direct communications connection, such as a dial-up telephone line. The block mode of transmission is more appropriate for multidrop data communications circuits operating in a polling environment.

ASYNCHRONOUS PROTOCOLS

Two of the most commonly used asynchronous data protocols are Western Electric's *selective calling system* (8A1/8B1) and IBM's *asynchronous data link protocol* (83B). In essence, these two protocols are the same set of procedures.

Asynchronous protocols are *character oriented*. That is, unique data link control characters such as end of transmission (EOT) and start of text (STX), no matter where they occur in a transmission, warrant the same action or perform the same function. For example, the end-of-transmission character used with ASCII is 04H. No matter when 04H is received by a secondary, the LCU is cleared and placed in the line monitor mode. Consequently, care must be taken to ensure that the bit sequences for data link control characters do not occur within a message unless they are intended to perform their designated data link functions. Vertical redundancy checking (parity) is the only type of error detection used with asynchronous protocols, and symbol substitution and ARQ (retransmission) are used for error correction. With asynchronous protocols, each secondary station is generally limited to a single terminal/printer pair. This station arrangement is called a *stand alone*. With the stand-alone configuration, all messages transmitted from or received on the terminal CRT are also written on the printer. Thus, the printer simply generates a hard copy of all transmissions.

In addition to the line monitoring mode, a remote station can be in any one of three operating modes: *transmit, receive,* and *local.* A secondary station is in the transmit mode whenever it has been designed master. In the transmit mode, the secondary can send formatted messages or acknowledgments. A secondary is in the receive mode whenever it has been selected by the primary. In the receive mode, the secondary can receive formatted messages from the primary. For a terminal operator to enter information into his or her computer terminal, the terminal must be in the local mode. A terminal can be placed in the local mode through software commands sent from the primary or the operator can do it manually from the keyboard.

The polling sequence for most asynchronous protocols is quite simple and usually encompasses sending one or two data link control characters, then a *station polling address.* A typical polling sequence is

```
E  D
O  C  A
T  3
```

The EOT character is the *clearing* character and always precedes the polling sequence. EOT places all the secondaries in the line monitor mode. When in the line monitor mode, a secondary station listens to the line for its polling or selection address. When DC3 immediately follows EOT, it indicates that the next character is a station polling address. For this example, the station polling address is the single ASCII character "A." Station "A" has been designated the master and must respond with either a formatted message or an acknowledgment. There are two acknowledgment sequences that may be transmitted in response to a poll. They are listed below together with their functions.

Acknowledgment	Function
A \ C K	No message to transmit, ready to receive
\ \	No message to transmit, not ready to receive

The selection sequence, which is very similar to the polling sequence, is

```
E
O  X  Y
T
```

Again, the EOT character is transmitted first to ensure that all the secondary stations are in the line monitor mode. Following the EOT is a two-character selection address "XY." Station XY has been selected by the primary and designated as a receiver. Once selected, a secondary station must respond with one of three acknowledgment sequences indicating its status. They are listed below together with their functions.

Acknowledgment	Function
A \ C K	Ready to receive
\ \	Not ready to receive, terminal in local, or printer out of paper
* *	Not ready to receive, have a formatted message to transmit

More than one station can be selected simultaneously with *group* or *broadcast* addresses. Group addresses are used when the primary desires to select more than one but not all of the remote stations. There is a single broadcast address that is used to select simultaneously all the remote stations. With asynchronous protocols, acknowledgment procedures for group and broadcast selections are somewhat involved and for this reason are seldom used.

Messages transmitted from the primary and secondary use exactly the same data format. The format is as follows:

```
S                        E
T  message data  0
X                        T
```

The preceding format is used by the secondary to transmit data to the primary in response to a poll. The STX and EOT characters frame the message. STX precedes the data and indicates that the message begins with the character that immediately follows it. The EOT character signals the end of the message and relinquishes the role of master to the primary. The same format is used when the primary transmits a message except that the STX and EOT characters have an additional function. The STX is a *blinding* character. Upon receipt of the STX character, all previously unselected stations are "blinded," which means that they ignore all transmissions except EOT. Consequently, the subsequent message transmitted by the primary is received only by the previously selected station. The unselected secondaries remain blinded until they receive an EOT character, at which time they will return to the line monitor mode and again listen to the line for their polling or selection addresses. STX and EOT are not part of the message; they are data link control characters and are inserted and deleted by the LCU.

Sometimes it is necessary or desirable to transmit coded data in addition to the message that are used only for data link management, such as date, time of message, message number, message priority, routing information, and so on. This bookkeeping information is not part of the message; it is overhead and is transmitted as *heading* information. To identify the heading, the message begins with a start-of-heading character (SOH). SOH is transmitted first, followed by the heading information, STX, then the message. The entire sequence is terminated with an EOT character. When a heading is included, STX terminates the heading and also indicates the beginning of the message. The format for transmitting heading information together with message data is

```
S              S                   E
0  heading  T  message data  0
H              X                   T
```

SYNCHRONOUS PROTOCOLS

With synchronous protocols, a secondary station can have more than a single terminal/printer pair. The group of devices is commonly called a *cluster.* A single LCU can serve a cluster with as many as 50 devices (terminals and printers). Synchronous protocols can be either character or bit oriented. The most commonly used character-oriented synchronous protocol is IBM's 3270 binary synchronous communications (BSC or bisync), and the most popular bit-oriented protocol (BOP) is IBM's synchronous data link control (SDLC).

IBM's Bisync Protocol

With bisync, each transmission is preceded by a unique SYN character: 16H for ASCII and 32H for EBCDIC. The SYN character places the receive USRT in the character or byte mode and prepares it to receive data in 8-bit groupings. With bisync, SYN characters are always transmitted in pairs (hence, the name "bisync"). Figure 3-2 shows the logic

FIGURE 3-2 Bisync detector circuit

diagram for an even parity ASCII SYN character detection circuit. Received data are shifted serially through the detection circuit and monitored in groups of 16 bits looking for the occurrence of two successive SYN characters. When two successive SYN characters are detected the SYNC output signal goes active.

If 8 successive bits are received in the middle of a message that are equivalent to a SYN character, they are ignored. For example, the characters "A" and "b" have the following hex and binary codes:

```
A = 41H = 0 1 0 0 0 0 0 1
b = 62H = 0 1 1 0 0 0 1 0
```

If the ASCII characters A and b occur successively during a message or heading, the following bit sequence occurs:

As you can see, it appears that a SYN character has been transmitted when actually it has not. To avoid this situation, SYN characters are always transmitted in pairs, and consequently, if only one is received, it is ignored. The likelihood of two false SYN characters occurring one immediately after the other is remote.

With synchronous protocols, the concepts of polling, selecting, and acknowledging are identical to those used with asynchronous protocols except, with bisync, group, and broadcast selections are not allowed. There are two polling formats used with bisync: general and specific. The format for a general poll is

```
P S S E P S S S     E P
A Y Y O A Y Y P P " " N A
D N N T D N N A A     Q D
```

The PAD character at the beginning of the sequence is called a *leading* pad and is either a 55H or an AAH (01010101 or 10101010 binary). As you can see, a leading pad is simply a string of alternating 1s and 0s. The purpose of the leading pad is to ensure that transitions occur in the data prior to the actual message. The transitions are needed for clock recovery in the receive modem to maintain bit synchronization. Next, there are two SYN characters to establish character synchronization. The EOT character is again used as a clearing character and places all the secondary stations into the line monitor mode. The PAD character immediately following the second SYN character is simply a string of successive logic 1s that is used for a time fill, giving each of the secondary stations time to clear. The number of 1s transmitted during this time fill may not be a multiple of 8 bits. Consequently, the two SYN characters are repeated to reestablish character synchronization. The SPA is not an ASCII or EBCDIC character. The letters SPA stand for *station polling address*. Each secondary station has a unique SPA. Two SPAs are transmitted for the purpose of error detection (redundancy). A secondary will not respond to a poll unless its SPA appears twice. The two quotation marks signify that the poll is for any device at that station that is in the send mode. If two or more devices are in the send mode when a general poll is received, the LCU determines which device's message is transmitted. The enquiry (ENQ) character is sometimes called a *format* or *line turnaround character* because it completes the polling format and initiates a line turnaround (i.e., the secondary station identified by the SPA is designated master and must respond).

The PAD character at the end of the polling sequence is called a *trailing* pad and is simply a 7FH (DEL or delete character). The purpose of the trailing pad is to ensure that the RLSD signal in the receive modem is held active long enough for the entire received message to be demodulated. If the carrier were shut off immediately at the end of the message, RLSD would go inactive and disable the receive data pin. If the last character of the message were not completely demodulated, the end of it would be cut off.

The format for a specific poll is

```
P  S  S  E  P  S  S  S        E  P
A  Y  Y  O  A  Y  Y  P  P  D  D  N  A
D  N  N  T  D  N  N  A  A  A  A  Q  D
```

The character sequence for a specific poll is similar to that of a general poll except that the two DAs (*device addresses*) are substituted for the two quotation marks. With a specific poll, both the station and device addresses are included. Therefore, a specific poll is an invitation for a specific device at a given station to transmit its message. Again, two DAs are transmitted for redundancy error detection.

The character sequence for a selection is

```
P  S  S  E  P  S  S  S        E  P
A  Y  Y  O  A  Y  Y  S  S  D  D  N  A
D  N  N  T  D  N  N  A  A  A  A  Q  D
```

The sequence for a selection is similar to that of a specific poll except that two SSA characters are substituted for the two SPAs. SSA stands for "station select address." All selections are specific; they are for a specific device (device DA). Table 3-1 lists the SPAs, SSAs, and DAs for a network that can have a maximum of 32 stations and the LCU at each station can serve a 32-device cluster.

Example 3-1

Determine the character sequences for

(a) A general poll for station 8.
(b) A specific poll for device 6 at station 8.
(c) A selection of device 6 at station 8.

Solution (a) From Table 3-1 the SPA for station 8 is H; therefore, the sequence for a general poll is

TABLE 3-1 Station and Device Addresses

Station or Device Number	SPA	SSA	DA	Station or Device Number	SPA	SSA	DA
0	sp	-	sp	16	&	0	&
1	A	/.	A	17	J	1	J
2	B	S	B	18	K	2	K
3	C	T	C	19	L	3	L
4	D	U	D	20	M	4	M
5	E	V	E	21	N	5	N
6	F	W	F	22	O	6	O
7	G	X	G	23	P	7	P
8	H	Y	H	24	Q	8	Q
9	I	Z	I	25	R	9	R
10	[	|	[	26	]	:	]
11	.	,	.	27	$	#	$
12	<	%	<	28	*	@	*
13	(	—	(	29	)	'	)
14	+	>	+	30	;	=	;
15	!	?	!	31	∧	"	∧

```
P S S E P S S             E P
A Y Y O A Y Y H H " " N A
D N N T D N N             Q D
```

(b) From Table 3-1 the DA for device 6 is F; therefore, the sequence for a specific poll is

```
P S S E P S S             E P
A Y Y O A Y Y H H F F N A
D N N T D N N             Q D
```

(c) From Table 3-1 the SSA for station 8 is Y; therefore, the sequence for a selection is

```
P S S E P S S             E P
A Y Y O A Y Y Y Y F F N A
D N N T D N N             Q D
```

With bisync, there are only two ways in which a secondary can respond to a poll: with a formatted message or with a *handshake*. A handshake is simply a response from the secondary that indicates it has no formatted messages to transmit (i.e., a handshake is a negative acknowledgment to a poll). The character sequence for a handshake is

```
P S S E P
A Y Y O A
D N N T D
```

A secondary can respond to a selection with either a positive or a negative acknowledgment. A positive acknowledgment to a selection indicates that the device selected is ready to receive. The character sequence for a positive acknowledgment is

```
P S S D   P
A Y Y L 0 A
D N N E   D
```

A negative acknowledgment to a selection indicates that the device selected is not ready to receive. A negative acknowledgment is called a *reverse interrupt* (RVI). The character sequence for an RVI is

```
P S S D   P
A Y Y L < A
D N N E   D
```

With bisync, formatted messages are sent from a secondary to the primary in response to a poll and sent from the primary to a secondary after the secondary has been selected. Formatted messages use the following format:

```
P S S S             S           E B P
A Y Y 0  heading  T  message  T C A
D N N H             X           X C D
```

Note: If CRC-16 is used for error detection, there are two block check characters.

Longitudinal redundancy checking (LRC) is used for error detection with ASCII-coded messages, and cyclic redundancy checking (CRC) is used for EBCDIC. The BCC is computed beginning with the first character after SOH and continues through and includes ETX. (If there is no heading, the BCC is computed beginning with the first character after STX.) With synchronous protocols, data are transmitted in blocks. Blocks of data are generally limited to 256 characters. ETX is used to terminate the last block of a message. ETB is used for multiple block messages to terminate all message blocks except the last one. The last block of a message is always terminated with ETX. All BCCs must be acknowledged by the receiving station. A positive acknowledgment indicates that the BCC was good and a negative acknowledgement means that the BCC was bad. A negative acknowledgment is an automatic request for retransmission. The character sequences for positive and negative acknowledgments are as follows:

Positive acknowledgment

```
P S S D     P       P S S D     P
A Y Y L 0  A  or  A Y Y L 1  A
D N N E     D       D N N E     D
  even-numbered       odd-numbered
     blocks              blocks
```

Negative acknowledgment

```
P S S N P
A Y Y A A
D N N K D
```

Examples of dialogue using bisync protocol

```
P S S E P S S       E P
A Y Y 0 A Y Y A A " " N A  ——————————→┐
D N N T D N N       Q D                │
```

Primary station sends a general poll for station 1.

```
            P S S E P
      ┌←———— A Y Y 0 A  ——————————┘
      │     D N N T D
```

Station 1 responds with a negative acknowledgment—no messages to transmit.

```
      ┌———— P S S E P S S       E P
      │     A Y Y 0 A Y Y B B " " N A  ——————————→┐
      │     D N N T D N N       Q D                │
```

Primary station sends a general poll for station 2.

```
            P S S       S  message  E B P
      ┌←———— A Y Y 0  heading  T  block 1  T C A  ———————
      │     D Y Y H       X           B C D
```

Station 2 responds with the first block of a multiblock message.

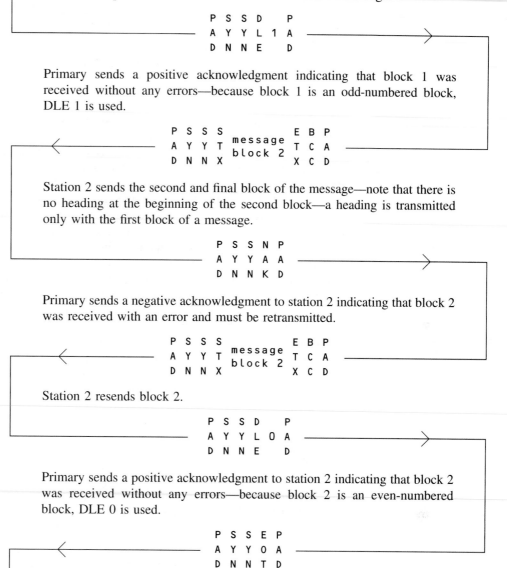

```
                    P S S D   P
                    A Y Y L 1 A  ─────────────────────────────>
                    D N N E   D
```

Primary sends a positive acknowledgment indicating that block 1 was received without any errors—because block 1 is an odd-numbered block, DLE 1 is used.

```
        P S S S           E B P
   <─── A Y Y T message  T C A ────────────
        D N N X block 2   X C D
```

Station 2 sends the second and final block of the message—note that there is no heading at the beginning of the second block—a heading is transmitted only with the first block of a message.

```
                    P S S N P
                    A Y Y A A  ─────────────────────────────>
                    D N N K D
```

Primary sends a negative acknowledgment to station 2 indicating that block 2 was received with an error and must be retransmitted.

```
        P S S S           E B P
   <─── A Y Y T message  T C A ────────────
        D N N X block 2   X C D
```

Station 2 resends block 2.

```
                    P S S D   P
                    A Y Y L 0 A  ─────────────────────────────>
                    D N N E   D
```

Primary sends a positive acknowledgment to station 2 indicating that block 2 was received without any errors—because block 2 is an even-numbered block, DLE 0 is used.

```
        P S S E P
   <─── A Y Y O A ────────────
        D N N T D
```

Secondary responds with a handshake—a secondary sends a handshake whenever it is its turn to transmit but it has nothing to say.

```
             P S S E P S S       E P
             A Y Y O A Y Y T T E E N A ─────────────>
             D N N T D N N       Q D
```

Primary selects station 3, device 5.

```
        P S S D   P
   <─── A Y Y L 0 A ────────────
        D N N E   D
```

Station 3 sends a positive acknowledgment to the selection; device 5 is ready to receive.

```
  ┌──────          P S S         S  message  E B P
  │               A Y Y O heading T  block 1 T C A ────────→
  │               D N N H         X           X C D        │
  │                                                         │
```

Primary sends a single block message to station 3.

```
  │                      P S S D   P                       │
  ┌─────────←──────────  A Y Y L 1 A ──────────────────────┘
  │                      D N N E   D
  │
```

Station 3 responds with a positive acknowledgment indicating the block of data was received without any errors.

Transparency.   It is possible that a device that is attached to one of the ports of a station LCU is not a computer terminal or a printer. For example, a microprocessor-controlled monitor system that is used to monitor environmental conditions (temperature, humidity, etc.) or a security alarm system. If so, the data transferred between it and the applications program are not ASCII- or EBCDIC-encoded characters; they are micropro-cessor op-codes or binary-encoded data. Consequently, it is possible that an 8-bit sequence could occur in the message that is equivalent to a data link control character. For example, if the binary code 00000011 (03H) occurred in a message, the LCU would misinterpret it as the ASCII code for ETX. Consequently, the receive LCU would prematurely terminate the message and interpret the next 8-bit sequence as a BCC. To prevent this from occurring, the LCU is made *transparent* to the data. With bisync, a *data link escape* character (DLE) is used to achieve transparency. To place an LCU in the transparent mode, STX is preceded by a DLE. This causes the LCU to transfer the data to the selected device without searching through the message for data link control characters. To come out of the transparent mode, DLE ETX is transmitted. To transmit a DLE as part of the text, it must be preceded by DLE (i.e., DLE DLE). Actually, there are only five characters that it is necessary to precede with DLE:

1. *DLE STX*. Places the receive LCU into the transparent mode.
2. *DLE ETX*. Used to terminate the last block of transparent text and take the LCU out of the transparent mode.
3. *DLE ETB*. Used to terminate blocks of transparent text other than the final block.
4. *DLE ITB*. Used to terminate blocks of transparent text other than the final block when ITB is used for a block terminating character.
5. *DLE SYN*. Used only with transparent messages that are more than 1 s long. With bisync, two SYN characters are inserted in the text entry 1 s to ensure that the receive LCU does not lose character synchronization. In a multipoint circuit with a polling environment, it is highly unlikely that any blocks of data would exceed 1 s in duration. SYN character insertion is used almost exclusively for two-point circuits.

Synchronous Data Link Communications

Synchronous data link communications (SDLC) is a synchronous *bit-oriented* protocol developed by IBM. A bit-oriented protocol (BOP) is a discipline for serial-by-bit information transfer over a data communication channel. With a BOP, data link control information is transferred and interpreted on a bit-by-bit basis rather than with unique data link control characters. SDLC can transfer data either simplex, half duplex, or full duplex. With a BOP, there is a single control field that performs essentially all the data link control functions. The character language used with SDLC is EBCDIC and data are transferred in groups called *frames*. Frames are generally limited to 256 characters in

F Flag 01111110	A Address	C Control	I Information	FCS Frame check sequence	F Flag 01111110
8 bits	8 bits	8 bits	Variable must be multiple of 8 bits	16 bits CRC-16	8 bits

←——— Span of CRC accumulation ———→

←——————————— Span of zero insertion ———————————→

FIGURE 3-3 SDLC frame format

length. There are two types of stations in SDLC: primary stations and secondary stations. The *primary station* controls data exchange on the communications channel and issues *commands*. The *secondary station* receives commands and returns *responses* to the primary.

There are three transmission states with SDLC: transient, idle, and active. The *transient state* exists before and after the initial transmission and after each line turnaround. An *idle state* is presumed after 15 or more consecutive 1s have been received. The *active state* exists whenever either the primary or a secondary station is transmitting information or control signals.

Figure 3-3 shows the frame format used with SDLC. The frames sent from the primary and the frames sent from a secondary use exactly the same format. There are five fields used with SDLC: the flag field, the address field, the control field, the text or information field, and the frame check field.

Information field. All information transmitted in an SDLC frame must be in the information field (I field), and the number of bits in the I field must be a multiple of 8. An I field is not allowed with all SDLC frames. The types of frames that allow an I field are discussed later.

Flag field. There are two flag fields per frame: the beginning flag and the ending flag. The flags are used for the *delimiting sequence* and to achieve character synchronization. The delimiting sequence sets the limits of the frame (i.e., when the frame begins and when it ends). The flag is used with SDLC in the same manner that SYN characters are used with bisync, to achieve character synchronization. The sequence for a flag is 7EH, 01111110 binary, or the EBCDIC character " =." There are several variations of how flags are used. They are

1. One beginning and one ending flag for each frame.

```
         beginning flag                                    ending flag
 . . .  01111110 address control text FCC 01111110 . . .
```

2. The ending flag from one frame can be used for the beginning flag for the next frame.

```
                          ←——————————————— frame N + 1 ———————————→
       ←———— frame N ————→
 . . . text FCC 01111110 address control text FCC 01111110 . . .
                        /          \
                ending flag    beginning flag
                frame N        frame N + 1
```

3. The last zero of an ending flag is also the first zero of the beginning flag of the next frame.

4. Flags are transmitted in lieu of idle line 1s.

011111101111110111111**01111110** address control text . . .

idle   line   flags   beginning flag

Address field. The address field has 8 bits; thus, 256 addresses are possible with SDLC. The address 00H (00000000) is called the *null* or *void address* and is never assigned to a secondary. The null address is used for network testing. The address FFH (11111111) is the *broadcast address* and is common to all secondaries. The remaining 254 addresses can be used as *unique* station addresses or as *group* addresses. In frames sent from the primary, the address field contains the address of the destination station (a secondary). In frames sent from a secondary, the address field contains the address of that secondary. Therefore, the address is always that of a secondary. The primary station has no address because all transmissions from secondary stations go to the primary.

Control field. The control field is an 8-bit field that identifies the type of frame it is. The control field is used for polling, confirming previously received information frames, and several other data link management functions. There are three frame formats used with SDLC: *information, supervisory,* and *unnumbered*.

Information Frame. With an information frame there must be an information field. Information frames are used for transmitting sequenced information. The bit pattern for the control field of an information frame is

Bit:	b_0	b_1	b_2	b_3	b_4	b_5	b_6	b_7
Function:	←	nr	→	P or F / $\overline{P}$ or $\overline{F}$	←	ns	→	0

An information frame is identified by a 0 in the least significant bit position (b_7 with EBCDIC code). Bits b_4, b_5, and b_6 are used for numbering transmitted frames (ns = number sent). With 3 bits, the binary numbers 000 through 111 (0–7) can be represented. The first frame transmitted is designated frame 000, the second frame 001, and so on up to frame 111 (the eighth frame); then, the count cycles back to 000 and repeats.

Bits b_0, b_1, and b_2 are used to confirm correctly received information frames (nr = number received) and to automatically request retransmission of incorrectly received information frames. The nr is the number of the next frame that the transmitting station expects to receive, or the number of the next frame that the receiving station will transmit. The nr confirms received frames through nr − 1. Frame nr − 1 is the last frame received without a transmission error. Any transmitted I frame not confirmed must be retransmitted. Together, the ns and nr bits are used for error correction (ARQ). The primary must keep track of an ns and nr for each secondary. Each secondary must keep track of only its ns and nr. After all frames have been confirmed, the primary's ns must agree with the secondary's nr, and vice versa. For the example shown next, the primary and secondary stations begin with their ns and nr counters reset to 000. The primary sends three numbered information frames (ns = 0, 1, and 2). At the same time the primary sends nr = 0 because the next frame it expects to receive is frame 0, which is the secondary's present ns. The secondary responds with two information frames (ns = 0 and 1). The secondary received all three frames from the primary without any errors, so the nr transmitted in the secondary's control field is 3 (which is the number of the next frame that the primary will send). The primary now sends information frames 3 and 4 with an nr = 2. The nr = 2 confirms the correct reception of frames 0 and 1. The secondary responds with frames ns = 2, 3, and 4 with an nr = 4. The nr = 4 confirms reception of only frame 3 from the primary (nr − 1). Consequently, the primary must retransmit frame 4. Frame 4 is retransmitted together with four additional frames (ns = 5, 6, 7, and 0). The primary's nr = 5, which confirms frames 2, 3, and 4 from the secondary. Finally, the secondary sends information frame 5 with an nr = 1. The nr = 1 confirms frames 4, 5, 6, 7, and 0 from the primary. At this point, all the frames transmitted have been confirmed except frame 5 from the secondary.

Primary's ns:	0 1 2		3 4		4 5 6 7 0	
Primary's nr:	0 0 0		2 2		5 5 5 5 5	
Secondary's ns:		0 1		2 3 4		5
Secondary's nr:		3 3		4 4 4		1

With SDLC, a station can never send more than seven numbered frames without receiving a confirmation. For example, if the primary sent eight frames (ns = 0, 1, 2, 3, 4, 5, 6, and 7) and the secondary responded with an nr = 0, it is ambiguous which frames are being confirmed. Does nr = 0 mean that all eight frames were received correctly, or that frame 0 had an error in it and all eight frames must be retransmitted? (With SDLC, all previously transmitted frames beginning with frame nr − 1 must be retransmitted.)

Bit b_3 is the *poll* (P) or *not-a-poll* ($\overline{P}$) bit when sent from the primary and the *final* (F) or *not-a-final* ($\overline{F}$) bit when sent by a secondary. In a frame sent by the primary, if the primary desires to poll the secondary, the P bit is set (1). If the primary does not wish to poll the secondary, the P bit is reset (0). A secondary cannot transmit unless it receives a frame addressed to it with the P bit set. In a frame sent from a secondary, if it is the last (final) frame of the message, the F bit is set (1). If it is not the final frame, the F bit is reset (0). With I frames, the primary can select a secondary station, send formatted information, confirm previously received I frames, and poll with a single transmission.

Example 3-2

Determine the bit pattern for the control field of a frame sent from the primary to a secondary station for the following conditions: primary is sending information frame 3, it is a poll, and the primary is confirming the correct reception of frames 2, 3, and 4 from the secondary.

Solution

$b_7 = 0$ because it is an information frame.
b_4, b_5, and b_6 are 011 (binary 3 for ns = 3).
$b_3 = 1$, it is a polling frame.
b_0, b_1, and b_2 are 101 (binary 5 for nr = 5).
control field = B6H.

b_0	b_1	b_2	b_3	b_4	b_5	b_6	b_7
1	0	1	1	0	1	1	0

Supervisory frame. An information field is not allowed with a supervisory frame. Consequently, supervisory frames cannot be used to transfer information; they are used to assist in the transfer of information. Supervisory frames are used to confirm previously received information frames, convey ready or busy conditions, and to report frame numbering errors. The bit pattern for the control field of a supervisory frame is

Bit:	b_0	b_1	b_2	b_3	b_4	b_5	b_6	b_7
Function:	←	nr	→	P or F $\overline{P}$ or $\overline{F}$	X	X	0	1

A supervisory frame is identified by a 01 in bit positions b_6 and b_7, respectively, of the control field. With the supervisory format, bit b_3 is again the poll/not-a-poll or final/not-a-final bit and b_0, b_1, and b_2 are the nr bits. However, with a supervisory format, b_4 and b_5 are used to indicate either the receive status of the station transmitting the frame or to request transmission or retransmission of sequenced information frames. With two bits, there are four combinations possible. The four combinations and their functions are as follows:

b_4	b_5	Receiver Status
0	0	Ready to receive (RR)
0	1	Ready not to receive (RNR)
1	0	Reject (REJ)
1	1	Not used with SDLC

When the primary sends a supervisory frame with the P bit set and a status of ready to receive, it is equivalent to a general poll with bisync. Supervisory frames are used by the primary for polling and for confirming previously received information frames when there is no information to send. A secondary uses the supervisory format for confirming previously received information frames and for reporting its receive status to the primary. If a secondary sends a supervisory frame with RNR status, the primary cannot send it numbered information frames until that status is cleared. RNR is cleared when a secondary sends an information frame with the F bit = 1 or an RR or REJ frame with the F bit = 0. The REJ command/response is used to confirm information frames through nr − 1 and to request retransmission of numbered information frames beginning with the frame number identified in the REJ frame. An information field is prohibited with a supervisory frame and the REJ command/response is used only with full-duplex operation.

Example 3-3

Determine the bit pattern for the control field of a supervisory frame sent from a secondary station to the primary for the following conditions: the secondary is ready to receive, it is the final frame, and the secondary station is confirming frames 3, 4, and 5.

Solution

b_6 and b_7 = 01 because it is a supervisory frame.
b_4 and b_5 = 00 (ready to receive).
b_3 = 1 (it is the final frame).
b_0, b_1 and b_2 = 110 (binary 6 for nr = 6).
control field = D1H

b_0	b_1	b_2	b_3	b_4	b_5	b_6	b_7
1	1	0	1	0	0	0	1

Unnumbered Frame. An unnumbered frame is identified by making bits b_6 and b_7 in the control field 11. The bit pattern for the control field of an unnumbered frame is

Bit:	b_0	b_1	b_2	b_3	b_4	b_5	b_6	b_7
Function:	X	X	X	P or F $\overline{P}$ or $\overline{F}$	X	X	1	1

With an unnumbered frame, bit b_3 is again either the $P/\overline{P}$ or $F/\overline{F}$ bit. Bits b_0, b_1, b_2, b_4, and b_5 are used for various unnumbered commands and responses. With 5 bits

TABLE 3-2 Unnumbered Commands and Responses

b$_0$		b$_7$	Acronym	Command	Response	I Field Prohibited	Resets ns and nr
000	P/F	0011	UI	Yes	Yes	No	No
000	F	0111	RIM	No	Yes	Yes	No
000	P	0111	SIM	Yes	No	Yes	Yes
100	P	0011	SNRM	Yes	No	Yes	Yes
000	F	1111	DM	No	Yes	Yes	No
010	P	0011	DISC	Yes	No	Yes	No
011	F	0011	UA	No	Yes	Yes	No
100	F	0111	FRMR	No	Yes	No	No
111	F	1111	BCN	No	Yes	Yes	No
110	P/F	0111	CFGR	Yes	Yes	No	No
010	F	0011	RD	No	Yes	Yes	No
101	P/F	1111	XID	Yes	Yes	No	No
001	P	0011	UP	Yes	No	Yes	No
111	P/F	0011	TEST	Yes	Yes	No	No

(The column above b$_0$ and b$_7$ is headed "Binary Configuration")

available, 32 unnumbered commands/responses are possible. The control field in an unnumbered frame sent by the primary is a command. The control field in an unnumbered frame sent by a secondary is a response. With unnumbered frames, there are no ns or nr bits. Therefore, numbered information frames cannot be sent or confirmed with the unnumbered format. Unnumbered frames are used to send network control and status information. Two examples of control functions are (1) placing secondary stations on-line and off-line and (2) LCU initialization. Table 3-2 lists several of the more commonly used unnumbered commands and responses. An information field is prohibited with all the unnumbered commands/responses except UI, FRMR, CFGR, TEST, and XID.

A secondary station must be in one of three modes: the initialization mode, the normal response mode, or the normal disconnect mode. The procedures for the *initialization mode* are system specified and vary considerably. A secondary in the *normal response mode* cannot initiate unsolicited transmissions; it can transmit only in response to a frame received with the P bit set. When in the *normal disconnect mode,* a secondary is off-line. In this mode, a secondary can receive only a TEST, XID, CFGR, SNRM, or SIM command from the primary and can respond only if the P bit is set.

The unnumbered commands and responses are summarized below.

Unnumbered information (UI). UI is a command/response that is used to send unnumbered information. Unnumbered information transmitted in the I field is not confirmed.

Set initialization mode (SIM). SIM is a command that places the secondary station into the initialization mode. The initialization procedure is system specified and varies from a simple self-test of the station controller to executing a complete IPL (initial program logic) program. SIM resets the ns and nr counters at the primary and secondary stations. A secondary is expected to respond to a SIM command with a UA response.

Request initialization mode (RIM). RIM is a response sent by a secondary station to request the primary to send an SIM command.

Set normal response mode (SNRM). SNRM is a command that places a secondary station in the normal response mode (NRM). A secondary station cannot send or receive numbered information frames unless it is in the normal response mode. Essentially, SNRM places a secondary station on-line. SNRM resets the ns and nr counters at the primary and secondary stations. UA is the normal response to an SNRM command. Unsolicited responses are not allowed when the secondary is in the NRM. A secondary remains in the NRM until it receives a DISC or SIM command.

Disconnect mode (DM). DM is a response that is sent from a secondary station if the primary attempts to send numbered information frames to it when the secondary is in the normal disconnect mode.

Request disconnect (RD). RD is a response sent when a secondary wishes to be placed in the disconnect mode.

Disconnect (DISC). DISC is a command that places a secondary station in the normal disconnect mode (NDM). A secondary cannot send or receive numbered information frames when it is in the normal disconnect mode. When in the normal disconnect mode, a secondary can receive only an SIM or SNRM command and can transmit only a DM response. The expected response to a DISC command is UA.

Unnumbered acknowledgment (UA). UA is an affirmative response that indicates compliance to a SIM, SNRM, or DISC command. UA is also used to acknowledge unnumbered information frames.

Frame reject (FRMR). FRMR is for reporting procedural errors. The FRMR sequence is a response transmitted when the secondary has received an invalid frame from the primary. A received frame may be invalid for any one of the following reasons:

1. The control field contains an invalid or unassigned command.
2. The amount of data in the information field exceeds the buffer space at the secondary.
3. An information field is received in a frame that does not allow information.
4. The nr received is incongruous with the secondary's ns. For example, if the secondary transmitted ns frames 2, 3, and 4 and then the primary responded with an nr of 7.

    A secondary cannot release itself from the FRMR condition, nor does it act on the frame that caused the condition. The secondary repeats the FRMR response until it receives one of the following *mode-setting* commands: SNRM, DISC, or SIM. The information field for a FRMR response always contains three bytes (24 bits) and has the following format:

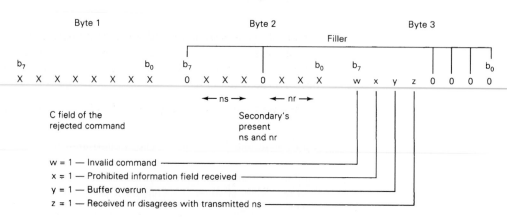

TEST. Test is a command that can be sent in any mode to solicit a TEST response. If an information field is included with the command, the secondary returns it with the response. The TEST command/response is exchanged for link testing purposes.

Exchange station identification (XID). As a command, XID solicits the identification of the secondary station. An information field can be included in the frame to

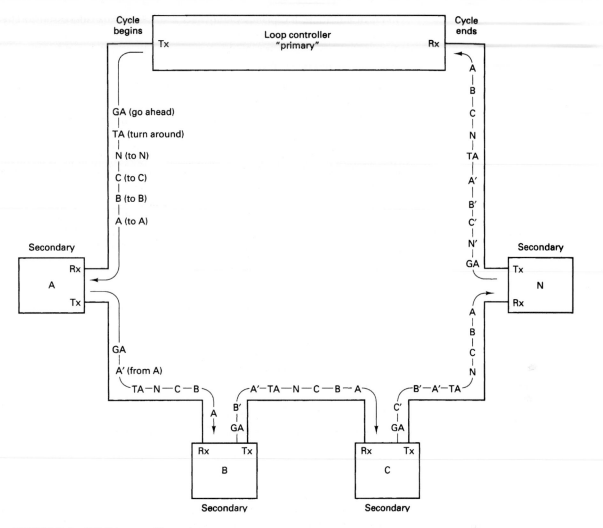

FIGURE 3-4 SDLC loop configuration

convey the identification data of either the primary or secondary station. For dial-up circuits, it is often necessary that the secondary station identify itself before the primary will exchange information frames with it, although XID is not restricted to only dial-up data circuits.

Frame check sequence field. The FCS field contains the error detection mechanism for SDLC. The FCS is equivalent to the BCC used with bisync. SDLC uses CRC-16 and the following generating polynomial:

$$x^{16} + x^{12} + x^5 + x^1$$

SDLC Loop Operation

An SDLC *loop* is operated in the half-duplex mode. The primary difference between the loop and bus configurations is that in a loop, all transmissions travel in the same direction on the communications channel. In a loop configuration, only one station transmits at a time. The primary transmits first, then each secondary station responds sequentially. In an SDLC loop, the transmit port of the primary station controller is connected to one or more secondary stations in a serial fashion; then the loop is terminated back at the receive port of the primary. Figure 3-4 shows an SDLC loop configuration.

In an SDLC loop, the primary transmits frames that are addressed to any or all of the secondary stations. Each frame transmitted by the primary contains an address of the secondary station to which that frame is directed. Each secondary station, in turn, decodes the address field of every frame, then serves as a repeater for all stations that are down-loop from it. If a secondary detects a frame with its address, it accepts the frame, then passes it onto the next down-loop station. All frames transmitted by the primary are returned to the primary. When the primary has completed transmitting, it follows the last flag with eight consecutive 0s. A flag followed by eight consecutive 0s is called a *turnaround* sequence, which signals the end of the primary's transmission. Immediately following the turnaround sequence, the primary transmits continuous 1s, which generates a *go-ahead* sequence (01111111). A secondary cannot transmit until it has received a frame addressed to it with the P bit set, a turnaround sequence, and then a go-ahead sequence. Once the primary has begun transmitting 1s, it goes into the receive mode.

The first down-loop secondary station that has received a frame addressed to it with the P bit set, changes the seventh 1 bit in the go-ahead sequence to a 0, thus, creating a flag. That flag becomes the beginning flag of the secondary's response frame or frames. After the secondary has transmitted its last frame, it again becomes a repeater for the idle line 1s from the primary. These idle line 1s again become the go-ahead sequence for the next secondary station. The next down-loop station that has received a frame addressed to it with the P bit set detects the turnaround sequence, any frames transmitted from up-loop secondaries, and then, the go-ahead sequence. Each secondary station inserts its response frames immediately after the last repeated frame. The cycle is completed when the primary receives its own turnaround sequence, a series of response frames, and then, the go-ahead sequence.

Configure command/response. The configure command/response (CFGR) is an unnumbered command/response that is used only in a loop configuration. CFGR contains a one-byte *function descriptor* (essentially a subcommand) in the information field. A CFGR command is acknowledged with a CFGR response. If the low-order bit of the function descriptor is set, a specified function is initiated. If it is reset, the specified function is cleared. There are six subcommands that can appear in the configure command's function field.

1. *Clear—00000000.* A clear subcommand causes all previously set functions to be cleared by the secondary. The secondary's response to a clear subcommand is another clear subcommand, 00000000.

2. *Beacon test (BCN)—0000000X.* The beacon test causes the secondary receiving it to turn on or turn off its carrier. If the X bit is set, the secondary suppresses transmission of the carrier. If the X bit is reset, the secondary resumes transmission of the carrier. The beacon test is used to isolate an open-loop problem. Also, whenever a secondary detects the loss of a receive carrier, it automatically begins to transmit its beacon response. The secondary will continue transmitting the beacon until the loop resumes normal status.

3. *Monitor mode—0000010X.* The monitor command causes the addressed secondary to place itself into a monitor (receive only) mode. Once in the monitor mode, a secondary cannot transmit until it receives a monitor mode clear (00000100) or a clear (00000000) subcommand.

4. *Wrap—0000100X.* The wrap command causes the secondary station to loop its transmissions directly to its receiver input. The wrap command places the secondary effectively off-line for the duration of the test. A secondary station does not send the results of a wrap test to the primary.

5. *Self-test—0000101X.* The self-test subcommand causes the addressed secondary to initiate a series of internal diagnostic tests. When the tests are completed, the secondary will respond. If the P bit in the configure command is set, the secondary will respond following completion of the self-test at its earliest opportunity. If the P bit is reset, the secondary will respond following completion of the test to the next poll-type frame it receives. All other transmissions are ignored by the secondary while it is performing the self-tests. The secondary indicates the results of the self-test by setting or resetting the low-order bit (X) of its self-test response. A 1 indicates that the tests were unsuccessful, and a 0 indicates that they were successful.

6. *Modified link test—0000110X.* If the modified link test function is set (X bit set), the secondary station will respond to a TEST command with a TEST response that has an information field containing the first byte of the TEST command information field repeated *n* times. The number *n* is system implementation dependent. If the X bit is reset, the secondary station will respond to a TEST command, with or without an information field, with a TEST response with a zero-length information field. The modified link test is an optional subcommand and is only used to provide an alternative form of link test to that previously described for the TEST command.

Transparency

The transparency mechanism used with SDLC is called *zero-bit insertion* or *zero stuffing*. The flag bit sequence (01111110) can occur in a frame where this pattern is not intended to be a flag. For example, any time that 7EH occurs in the address, control, information, or FCS field it would be interpreted as a flag and disrupt character synchronization. Therefore, 7EH must be prohibited from occurring except when it is intended to be a flag. To prevent a 7EH sequence from occurring, a zero is automatically inserted after any occurrence of five consecutive 1s except in a designated flag sequence (i.e., flags are not zero inserted). When five consecutive 1s are received and the next bit is a 0, the 0 is deleted or removed. If the next bit is a 1, it must be a valid flag. An example of zero insertion/deletion is shown below.

Original frame bits at the transmit station:

01111110	01101111	11010011	1110001100110101	01111110
flag	address	control	FCS	flag

After zero insertion but prior to transmission:

01111110	01101111	101010011	1110000100110101	01111110
flag	address	control	FCS	flag

inserted zeros

After zero deletion at the receive end:

01111110	01101111	11010011	1110001100110101	01111110
flag	address	control	FCS	flag

Message Abort

Message abort is used to prematurely terminate a frame. Generally, this is only done to accommodate high-priority messages such as emergency link recovery procedures, and so on. A message abort is any occurrence of 7 to 14 consecutive 1s. Zeros are not inserted in an abort sequence. A message abort terminates an existing frame and immediately begins the higher-priority frame. If more than 14 consecutive 1s occur in succession, it is considered an idle line condition. Therefore, 15 or more successive 1s place the circuit into the idle state.

Invert-On-Zero Encoding

A binary synchronous transmission such as SDLC is time synchronized to enable identification of sequential binary digits. Synchronous data communications assumes that bit or clock synchronization is provided by either the DCE or the DTE. With synchronous

Incoming data 1 1 0 0 0 0 0 1 0 0 0 1 1 1 0 1 1

NRZI encoded

FIGURE 3-5 NRZI encoding

transmissions, a receiver samples incoming data at the same rate that they were transmitted. Although minor variations in timing can exist, synchronous modems provide received data clock recovery and dynamically adjusted sample timing to keep sample times midway between bits. For a DTE or a DCE to recover the clock, it is necessary that transitions occur in the data. *Invert-on-zero coding* is an encoding scheme that guarantees at least one transition in the data for every 7 bits transmitted. Invert-on-zero coding is also called NRZI *(nonreturn-to-zero inverted).*

With NRZI encoding, the data are encoded in the transmitter, then decoded in the receiver. Figure 3-5 shows an example of NRZI encoding. The encoded waveform is unchanged by 1s in the NRZI encoder. However, 0s invert the encoded transmission level. Consequently, consecutive 0s generate an alternating high/low sequence. With SDLC, there can never be more than six 1s in succession (a flag). Therefore, a high-to-low transition is guaranteed to occur at least once for every 7 bits transmitted except during a message abort or an idle line condition. In a NRZI decoder, whenever a high/low transition occurs in the received data, a 0 is generated. The absence of a transition simply generates a 1. In Figure 3-5, a high level is assumed prior to encoding the incoming data.

NRZI encoding was intended to be used with asynchronous modems that do not have clock recovery capabilities. Consequently, the DTE must provide time synchronization, which is aided by using NRZI-encoded data. Synchronous modems have built in scramblers and descramblers that ensure that transitions occur in the data, and, thus, NRZI encoding is unnecessary. The NRZI encoder/decoder is placed between the DTE and the DCE.

High-Level Data Link Control

In 1975, the International Standards Organization (ISO) defined several sets of substandards that, when combined, are called *high-level data link control* (HDLC). Since HDLC is a superset of SDLC, only the added capabilities are explained.

HDLC comprises three standards (subdivisions) that, when combined, outline the frame structure, control standards, and class of operation for a bit-oriented data link control (DLC).

ISO 3309–1976(E). This standard defines the frame structure, delimiting, sequence, and transparency mechanism used with HDLC. These are essentially the same as with SDLC except that HDLC has extended addressing capabilities and checks the FCS in a slightly different manner. The delimiting sequence used with HDLC is identical to SDLC: a 01111110 sequence.

HDLC can use either the *basic* 8-bit address field or an *extended* addressing format. With extended addressing the address field may be extended recursively. If b_0 in the address byte is a logic 1, the 7 remaining bits are the secondary's address (the ISO defines the low-order bit as b_0, whereas SDLC designates the high order bit as b_0). If b_0 is a logic 0, the next byte is also part of the address. If b_0 of the second byte is a 0, a third address byte follows, and so on, until an address byte with a logic 1 for the low-order bit is encountered. Essentially, there are 7 bits unavailable in each address byte for address encoding. An example of a three-byte extended addressing scheme is shown, b_0 in the first two bytes of the address field are 0s, indicating that additional address bytes follow and b_0 in the third address byte is a logic 1, which terminates the address field.

```
                  b₀ = 0        b₀ = 0        b₀ = 1
                  |             |             |
   01111110    0XXXXXXX     0XXXXXXX     1XXXXXXX    . . .
     flag                three-byte address field        control field, etc.
```

HDLC uses CRC-16 with a generating polynomial specified by CCITT V.41. At the transmit station, the CRC is computed such that if it is included in the FCS computation at the receive end, the remainder for an errorless transmission is always F0BBH.

ISO 4335–1979(E).   This standard defines the elements of procedure for HDLC. The control field, information field, and supervisory format have increased capabilities over SDLC.

Control Field.   With HDLC, the control field can be extended to 16 bits. Seven bits are for the ns and 7 bits are for the nr. Therefore, with the extended control format, there can be a maximum of 127 outstanding (unconfirmed) frames at any given time.

Information Field.   HDLC permits any number of bits in the information field of an information command or response (SDLC is limited to 8-bit bytes). With HDLC any number of bits may be used for a character in the I field as long as all characters have the same number of bits.

Supervisory Format.   With HDLC, the supervisory format includes a fourth status condition: selective reject (SREJ). SREJ is identified by a 11 in bit position b_4 and b_5 of a supervisory control field. With a SREJ, a single frame can be rejected. An SREJ calls for the retransmission of only the frame identified by nr, whereas an REJ calls for the retransmission of all frames beginning with nr. For example, the primary sends I frames ns = 2, 3, 4, and 5. Frame 3 was received in error. An REJ would call for a retransmission of frames 3, 4, and 5; an SREJ would call for the retransmission of only frame 3. SREJ can be used to call for the retransmission of any number of frames except that only one is identified at a time.

Operational Modes.   HDLC has two operational modes not specified in SDLC: asynchronous response mode and asynchronous disconnect mode.

1. *Asynchronous response mode (ARM).* With the ARM, secondary stations are allowed to send unsolicited responses. To transmit, a secondary does not need to have received a frame from the primary with the P bit set. However, if a secondary receives a frame with the P bit set, it must respond with a frame with the F bit set.
2. *Asynchronous disconnect mode (ADM).* An ADM is identical to the normal disconnect mode except that the secondary can initiate a DM or RIM response at any time.

ISO 7809–1985(E).   This standard combines previous standards 6159(E) (unbalanced) and 6256(E) (balanced) and outlines the class of operation necessary to establish the link-level protocol.

Unbalanced Operation. This class of operation is logically equivalent to a multipoint private-line circuit with a polling environment. There is a single primary station responsible for central control of the network. Data transmission may be either half or full duplex.

Balanced Operation. This class of operation is logically equivalent to a two-point private line circuit. Each station has equal data link responsibilities, and channel access is through contention using the asynchronous response mode. Data transmission may be half or full duplex.

PUBLIC DATA NETWORK

A *public data network* (PDN) is a switched data communications network similar to the public telephone network except that a PDN is designed for transferring data only. Public data networks combine the concepts of both *value-added networks* (VANs) and *packet-switching networks.*

Value-Added Network

A value-added network "adds value" to the services or facilities provided by a common carrier to provide new types of communication services. Examples of added values are error control, enhanced connection reliability, dynamic routing, failure protection, logical multiplexing, and data format conversions. A VAN comprises an organization that leases communications lines from common carriers such as AT&T and MCI and adds new types of communications services to those lines. Examples of value-added networks are GTE Telnet, DATAPAC, TRANSPAC, and Tymnet Inc.

Packet-Switching Network

Packet switching involves dividing data messages into small bundles of information and transmitting them through communications networks to their intended destinations using computer-controlled switches. Three common switching techniques are used with public data networks: *circuit switching, message switching,* and *packet switching.*

Circuit switching. Circuit switching is used for making a standard telephone call on the public telephone network. The call is established, information is transferred, and then, the call is disconnected. The time required to establish the call is called the *setup* time. Once the call has been established, the circuits interconnected by the network switches are allocated to a single user for the duration of the call. After a call has been established, information is transferred in *real time.* When a call is terminated, the circuits and switches are once again available for another user. Because there are a limited number of circuits and switching paths available, *blocking* can occur. Blocking is the inability to complete a call because there are no facilities or switching paths available between the source and destination locations. When circuit switching is used for data transfer, the terminal equipment at the source and destination must be compatible; they must use compatible modems and the same bit rate, character set, and protocol.

A circuit switch is a *transparent* switch. The switch is transparent to the data; it does nothing more than interconnect the source and destination terminal equipment. A circuit switch adds no value to the circuit.

Message switching. Message switching is a form of *store-and-forward* network. Data, including source and destination identification codes, are transmitted into the network and stored in a switch. Each switch within the network has message storage capabilities. The network transfers the data from switch to switch when it is convenient to do so. Consequently, data are not transferred in real time; there can be a delay at each switch. With message switching, blocking cannot occur. However, the delay time from message transmission to reception varies from call to call and can be quite long (possibly as long as 24 hours). With message switching, once the information has entered the network, it is converted to a more suitable format for transmission through the network. At the receive end, the data are converted to a format compatible with the receiving data terminal equipment. Therefore, with message switching, the source and destination data terminal equipment do not need to be compatible. Message switching is more efficient than circuit switching because data that enter the network during busy times can be held and transmitted later when the load has decreased.

A message switch is a *transactional* switch because it does more than simply transfer the data from the source to the destination. A message switch can store data or change its format and bit rate, then convert the data back to their original form or an

TABLE 3-3 Switching Technique Summary

Circuit Switching	Message Switching	Packet Switching
Dedicated transmission path	No dedicated transmission path	No dedicated transmission path
Continuous transmission of data	Transmission of messages	Transmission of packets
Operates in real time	Not real time	Near real time
Messages not stored	Messages stored	Messages held for short time
Path established for entire message	Route established for each message	Route established for each packet
Call setup delay	Message transmission delay	Packet transmission delay
Busy signal if called party busy	No busy signal	No busy signal
Blocking may occur	Blocking cannot occur	Blocking cannot occur
User responsible for message-loss protection	Network responsible for lost messages	Network may be responsible for each packet but not for entire message
No speed or code conversion	Speed and code conversion	Speed and code conversion
Fixed bandwidth transmission (i.e., fixed information capacity)	Dynamic use of bandwidth	Dynamic use of bandwidth
No overhead bits after initial setup delay	Overhead bits in each message	Overhead bits in each packet

entirely different form at the receive end. Message switching multiplexes data from different sources onto a common facility.

Packet switching. With packet switching, data are divided into smaller segments, called *packets,* prior to transmission through the network. Because a packet can be held in memory at a switch for a short period of time, packet switching is sometimes called a *hold-and-forward* network. With packet switching, a message is divided into packets and each packet can take a different path through the network. Consequently, all packets do not necessarily arrive at the receive end at the same time or in the same order in which they were transmitted. Because packets are small, the hold time is generally quite short and message transfer is near real time and blocking cannot occur. However, packet-switching networks require complex and expensive switching arrangements and complicated protocols. A packet switch is also a transactional switch. Circuit, message, and packet switching techniques are summarized in Table 3-3.

CCITT X.1 International User Class of Service

The CCITT X.1 standard divides the various classes of service into three basic modes of transmission for a public data network. The three modes are: *start/stop, synchronous,* and *packet.*

Start/stop mode. With the start/stop mode, data are transferred from the source to the network and from the network to the destination in an asynchronous data format (i.e., each character is framed within a start and stop bit). Call control signaling is done in International Alphabet No. 5 (ASCII-77). Two common protocols used for start/stop transmission are IBM's 83B protocol and AT&T's 8A1/B1 selective calling arrangement.

Synchronous mode. With the synchronous mode, data are transferred from the source to the network and from the network to the destination in a synchronous data format (i.e., each message is preceded by a unique synchronizing character). Call control signaling is identical to that used with private-line data circuits and common protocols used for synchronous transmission are IBM's 3270 bisync, Burrough's BASIC, and UNIVAC's UNISCOPE.

Packet mode. With the packet mode, data are transferred from the source to the network and from the network to the destination in a frame format. The ISO HDLC frame

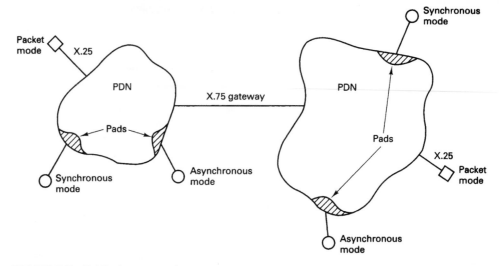

FIGURE 3-6 Public data network

format is the standard data link protocol used with the packet mode. Within the network, data are divided into smaller packets and transferred in accordance with the CCITT X.25 user-to-network interface protocol.

Figure 3-6 illustrates a typical layout for a public data network showing each of the three modes of operation. The packet assembler/disassembler (PAD) interfaces user data to X.25 format when the user's data are in either the asynchronous or synchronous mode of operation. A PAD is unnecessary when the user is operating in the packet mode. X.75 is recommended by the CCITT for the gateway protocol. A gateway is used to interface two public data networks.

CCITT X.25 USER-TO-NETWORK INTERFACE PROTOCOL

In 1976, the CCITT designated the X.25 user interface as the international standard for packet network access. Keep in mind that X.25 is strictly a *user-to-network* interface and addresses only the physical, data link, and network layers in the ISO seven layer model. X.25 uses existing standards whenever possible. For example, X.25 specifies X.21, X.26, and X.27 standards as the physical interface, which correspond to EIA RS-232, RS-423A, and RS-422A standards, respectively. X.25 defines HDLC as the international standard for the data link layer and the American National Standards Institute (ANSI) 3.66 *Advanced Data Communications Control Procedures* (ADCCP) as the U.S. standard. ANSI 3.66 and ISO HDLC were designed for private-line data circuits with a polling environment. Consequently, the addressing and control procedures outlined by them are not appropriate for packet data networks. ANSI 3.66 and HDLC were selected for the data link layer because of their frame format, delimiting sequence, transparency mechanism, and error detection method.

At the link level, the protocol specified by X.25 is a subset of HDLC, referred to as *Link Access Procedure Balanced* (LAPB). LAPB provides for two-way, full-duplex communications between DTE and DCE at the packet network gateway. Only the address of the DTE or DCE may appear in the address field of a LAPB frame. The address field refers to a link address, not a network address. The network address of the destination terminal is embedded in the packet header, which is part of the information field.

Tables 3-4 and 3-5 show the commands and responses, respectively, for an LAPB frame. During LAPB operation, most frames are commands. A response frame is compelled only when a command frame is received containing a poll (P-bit) = 1.

TABLE 3-4 LAPB Commands

Command Name	Bit Number			
	8 7 6	5	4 3 2	1
1 (information)	nr	P	ns	0
RR (receiver ready)	nr	P	0 0 0	1
RNR (receiver not ready)	nr	P	0 1 0	1
REJ (reject)	nr	P	1 0 0	1
SABM (set asynchronous balanced mode)	0 0 1	P	1 1 1	1
DISC (disconnect)	0 1 0	P	0 0 1	1

TABLE 3-5 LAPB Responses

Command Name	Bit Number			
	8 7 6	5	4 3 2	1
RR (receiver ready)	nr	F	0 0 0	1
RNR (receiver not ready)	nr	F	0 1 0	1
REJ (reject)	nr	F	1 0 0	1
UA (unnumbered acknowledgment)	0 1 1	F	0 0 1	1
DM (disconnect mode)	0 0 0	F	1 1 1	1
FRMR (frame rejected)	1 0 0	F	0 1 1	1

SABM/UA is a command/response pair used to initialize all counters and timers at the beginning of a session. Similarly, DISC/DM is a command/response pair used at the end of a session. FRMR is a response to any illegal command for which there is no indication of transmission errors according to the frame check sequence field.

Information (I) commands are used to transmit packets. Packets are never sent as responses. Packets are acknowledged using ns and nr just as they were in SDLC. RR is sent by a station when it needs to respond (acknowledge) something, but has no information packets to send. A response to an information command could be RR with F = 1. This procedure is called *checkpointing*.

REJ is another way of requesting transmission of frames. RNR is used for the flow control to indicate a busy condition and prevents further transmissions until cleared with an RR.

The network layer of X.25 specifies three switching services offered in a switched data network: permanent virtual circuit, virtual call, and datagram.

Permanent Virtual Circuit

A *permanent virtual circuit* (PVC) is logically equivalent to a two-point dedicated private-line circuit except slower. A PVC is slower because a hardwired end-to-end connection is not provided. The first time a connection is requested, the appropriate switches and circuits must be established through the network to provide the interconnection. A PVC identifies the routing between two predetermined subscribers of the network that is used for all subsequent messages. With a PVC, a source and destination address are unnecessary because the two users are fixed.

Virtual Call

A *virtual call* (VC) is logically equivalent to making a telephone call through the DDD network except no direct end-to-end connection is made. A VC is a one-to-many arrangement. Any VC subscriber can access any other VC subscriber through a network of switches and communication channels. Virtual calls are temporary virtual connections that use common usage equipment and circuits. The source must provide its address and the address of the destination before a VC can be completed.

Flag	Link address field	Link control field	Format identifier	Logical channel identifier	Packet type	Calling address length	Called address length	Called address	Calling address	0	Facilities field length	Facilities field	Protocol ID	User data	Frame check sequence	Flag
Bits: 8	8	8	4	12	8	4	4	To 60	To 60	2	6	To 512	32	To 96	16	8

FIGURE 3-7 Call request packet format

Datagram

A *datagram* (DG) is, at best, vaguely defined by X.25 and, until it is completely outlined, has very limited usefulness. With a DG, users send small packets of data into the network. Each packet is self-contained and travels through the network independent of other packets of the same message by whatever means available. The network does not acknowledge packets nor does it guarantee successful transmission. However, if a message will fit into a single packet, a DG is somewhat reliable. This is called a *single-packet-per-segment* protocol.

X.25 Packet Format

A virtual call is the most efficient service offered for a packet network. There are two packet formats used with virtual calls: a call request packet and a data transfer packet.

Call request packet. Figure 3-7 shows the field format for a call request packet. The delimiting sequence is 01111110 (an HDLC flag), and the error detection/correction mechanism is CRC-16 with ARQ. The link address field and the control field have little use and, therefore, are seldom used with packet networks. The rest of the fields are defined in sequence.

Format Identifier. The format identifier identifies whether the packet is a new call request or a previously established call. The format identifier also identifies the packet numbering sequence (either 0–7 or 0–127).

Logical Channel Identifier (LCI). The LCI is a 12-bit binary number that identifies the source and destination users for a given virtual call. After a source user has gained access to the network and has identified the destination user, they are assigned an LCI. In subsequent packets, the source and destination addresses are unnecessary; only the LCI is needed. When two users disconnect, the LCI is relinquished and can be reassigned to new users. There are 4096 LCIs available. Therefore, there may be as many as 4096 virtual calls established at any given time.

Packet Type. This field is used to identify the function and the content of the packet (i.e., new request, call clear, call reset, etc.).

Calling Address Length. This 4-bit field gives the number of digits (in binary) that appear in the calling address field. With 4 bits, up to 15 digits can be specified.

Called Address Length. This field is the same as the calling address field except that it identifies the number of digits that appear in the called address field.

Called Address. This field contains the destination address. Up to 15 BCD digits (60 bits) can be assigned to a destination user.

Calling Address. This field is the same as the called address field except that it contains up to 15 BCD digits that can be assigned to a source user.

Facilities Length Field. This field identifies (in binary) the number of 8-bit octets present in the facilities field.

Facilities Field. This field contains up to 512 bits of optional network facility information, such as reverse billing information, closed user groups, and whether it is a simplex transmit or simplex receive connection.

Flag	Link address field	Link control field	Format identifier	Logical channel identifier	Send packet sequence number P(s)	0	Receive packet sequence number P(r)	0	User data	Frame check sequence	Flag
Bits: 8	8	8	4	12	3/7	5/1	3/7	5/1	To 1024	16	8

FIGURE 3-8 Data transfer packet format

Protocol Identifier.   This 32-bit field is reserved for the subscriber to insert user-level protocol functions such as log-on procedures and user identification practices.

User Data Field.   Up to 96 bits of user data can be transmitted with a call request packet. These are unnumbered data that are not confirmed. This field is generally used for user passwords.

Data transfer packet.   Figure 3-8 shows the field format for a data transfer packet. A data transfer packet is similar to a call request packet except that a data transfer packet has considerably less overhead and can accommodate a much larger user data field. The data transfer packet contains a send and receive packet sequence field that were not included with the call request format.

The flag, link address, link control, format identifier, LCI, and FCS fields are identical to those used with the call request packet. The send and receive packet sequence fields are described as follows.

Send Packet Sequence Field.   The P(s) field is used in the same manner that the ns and nr sequences are used with SDLC and HDLC. P(s) is analogous to ns, and P(r) is analogous to nr. Each successive data transfer packet is assigned the next P(s) number in sequence. The P(s) can be a 14- or 7-bit binary number and, thus, number packets from either 0–7 or 0–127. The numbering sequence is identified in the format identifier. The send packet field always contains 8 bits and the unused bits are reset.

Receive Packet Sequence Field.   P(r) is used to confirm received packets and call for retransmission of packets received in error (ARQ). The I field in a data transfer packet can have considerably more source information than an I field in a call request packet.

The X Series of Recommended Standards

X.25 is part of the X series of CCITT-recommended standards for public data networks. The X series is classified into two categories: X.1 through X.39, which deal with services and facilities, terminals, and interfaces; and X.40 through X.199, which deal with network architecture, transmission, signaling, switching, maintenance, and administrative arrangements. Table 3-6 lists the most important X standards with their titles and descriptions.

Asynchronous Transfer Mode

Asynchronous transfer mode (ATM) is a communications standard that uses a high-speed form of packet switching network as the transmission media. ATM was developed as part of the *Broadband Integrated Services Digital Network* (BISDN), which is described later in this chapter. ATM is intended to utilize the Synchronous Optical Network (SONET), also discussed later in this chapter, to accommodate the specialized data communications needs of corporate private networks. Some experts claim that ATM may eventually replace both private leased T1 digital carrier systems and on-premise switching equipment. Conventional electronic switching (ESS) machines currently utilize a central processor to establish switching paths and route traffic through a network. ATM switches, however, will include self-routing procedures where individual *cells* containing subscriber data will route their own way through the ATM switching network in real time

TABLE 3-6 CCITT X Series Standards

X.1	International user classes of service in public data networks. Assigns numerical class designations to different terminal speeds and types.
X.2	International user services and facilities in public data networks. Specifies essential and additional services and facilities.
X.3	Packet assembly/disassembly facility (PAD) in a public data network. Describes the packet assembler/disassembler, which normally is used at a network gateway to allow connection of a start/stop terminal to a packet network.
X.20-bis	Use on public data networks of DTE designed for interfacing to asynchronous full-duplex V-series modems. Allows use of V.24/V.28 (essentially the same as EIA RS-232).
X.21-bis	Use on public data networks of DTE designed for interfacing to synchronous full-duplex V-series modems. Allows use of V.24/V.28 (essentially the same as EIA RS-232) or V.35.
X.25	Interface between DTE and DCE for terminals operating in the packet mode on public data networks. Defines the architecture of three levels of protocols existing in the serial interface cable between a packet-mode terminal and a gateway to a packet network.
X.28	DTE/DCE interface for a start/stop mode DTE accessing the PAD in a public data network situated in the same country. Defines the architecture of protocols existing in a serial interface cable between a start/stop terminal and an X.3 PAD.
X.29	Procedures for the exchange of control information and user data between a PAD and a packet mode DTE or another PAD. Defines the architecture of protocols behind the X.3 PAD, either between two PADs or between a PAD and a packet-mode terminal on the other side of the network.
X.75	Terminal and transit call control procedures and data transfer system on international circuits between packet-switched data networks. Defines the architecture of protocols between two public packet networks.
X.121	International numbering plan for public data networks. Defines a numbering plan including code assignments for each nation.

GFC (4)	VPI (4)	VPI (4)	VCI (4)	VCI (8)	VCI (4)	PT (3)	CLP (1)	HEC (8)	48–byte information field
Byte: 1		2		3		4		5	

FIGURE 3-9 ATM five-byte header field structure

using their own address instead of relying on an external process to establish the switching path (a cell is a short, fixed-length packet of data).

ATM uses *virtual channels* (VCs) and *virtual paths* (VPs) to route cells through a network. In essence, a virtual channel is merely a connection between a source and a destination location, which may entail establishing several ATM links between local switching centers. With ATM, all communications occur on the virtual channel, which preserves cell sequence. On the other hand, a virtual path is a group of virtual channels connected between two points that could comprise several ATM links.

An ATM cell contains all of the network information needed to relay individual cells from node to node over a preestablished ATM connection. Figure 3-9 shows the ATM cell structure, which is 53 bytes long, which includes a 5-byte header field and a 48-byte information field. The information field consists entirely of user data. Individual cells can be mixed together and routed to their destination through the telecommunications network. The header field is for networking purposes and contains all of the address and control information necessary for address and flow control.

ATM header field. Figure 3-10 shows the structure of the 5-byte ATM header field, which includes the following: generic flow control field, virtual path identifier, virtual channel identifier, payload type identifier, cell loss priority, and header error control.

FIGURE 3-10 ATM cell structure

Generic Flow Control Field (GFC). The GFC field uses the first 4 bits of the first byte of the header field. The GFC controls the flow of traffic across the user network interface (UNI) and into the network.

Virtual Path Identifier (VPI) and Virtual Channel Identifier (VCI). The 24 bits immediately following the GFC are used for the ATM address.

Payload Type (PT). The first 3 bits of the second half of byte 4 specify the type of message (payload) in cell. With 3 bits, there are eight different types of payloads possible. At the present time, however, types 0–3 are used for identifying the type of user data, types 4 and 5 indicate management information, and types 6 and 7 are reserved for future use.

Cell Loss Priority (CLP). The last bit of byte 4 is used to indicate whether a cell is eligible to be discarded by the network during congested traffic periods. The CLP bit is set by the user or cleared by the user. If set, the network may discard the cell during times of heavy use.

Header Error Control (HEC). The last byte of the header field is for error control and is used to detect and correct single-bit errors that occur in the header field only; the HEC does not serve as an entire cell check character. The value placed in the HEC is computed from the 4 previous bytes of the header field. The HEC provides some protection against the delivery of cells to the wrong destination address.

ATM information field. The 48-byte information field is reserved for user data. Insertion of data into the information field of a cell is a function of the upper half of layer two of the ISO-OSI seven-layer protocol hierarchy. This layer is specifically called the ATM Adaptation Layer (AAL). The AAL gives ATM the versatility necessary to facilitate, in a single format, a wide variety of different types of services ranging from continuous processes signals, such as voice transmission, to messages carrying highly fragmented bursts of data such as those produced from local area networks. Because most user data occupy more than 48 bytes, the AAL divides information into 48-byte segments and places them into a series of segments. The five types of AALs are

1. *Constant bit rate (CBR).* CBR information fields are designed to accommodate PCM-TDM traffic, which allows the ATM network to emulate voice or DSN services.
2. *Variable bit rate (VBR) timing-sensitive services.* This type of AAL is currently undefined; however, it is reserved for future data services requiring transfer of timing information between terminal points as well as data (i.e., packet video).
3. *Connection-oriented VBR data transfer.* Type 3 information fields transfer VBR data such as impulsive data generated at irregular intervals between two subscribers over a preestablished data link. The data link is established by network signaling procedures that are very similar to those used by the public-switched telephone network. This type of service is intended for large, long-duration data transfers, such as file transfers or file backups.
4. *Connectionless VBR data transfer.* This AAL type provides for transmission of VBR data that does not have a preestablished connection. Type 4 information fields are intended to be used for short, highly bursty type transmissions, such as those generated from a local area network.

TABLE 3-7 SONET Transmission Rates

Optical Carrier	Synchronous Transport Signal	Line Rate (Mbps)
OC-1*	STS-1	51.84
OC-3*	STS-3	155.52
OC-9	STS-9	466.56
OC-12*	STS-12	622.08
OC-18	STS-18	933.12
OC-24	STS-24	1244.16
OC-36	STS-36	1866.24
OC-48*	STS-48	2488.32

*Popular SONET physical layer interface

5. *Simple and efficient adaption layer (SEAL).* This is a relatively new and well-defined AAL offering designed to improve efficiency over type 3 transmissions. SEAL serves the same purpose as type 3 transmissions and assumes that higher layer processes will provide error detection and correction. The SEAL format simplifies sublayers of the AAL by filling all 48 bytes of the information field with user data.

It is hoped that incorporating high-speed ATM systems into data communications networks will encourage the installation of more optical fiber systems in the very near future. The transmission rates agreed upon by a consortium of over 120 firms, known as the ATM Forum, are 45 Mbps, 100 Mbps, and 155 Mbps, which are the same rates used by the Synchronous Optical Network (SONET) OC-3 rate. The ATM Forum was founded in 1991 by Adaptive, Cisco, Northern Telcom, and Sprint. Current ATM transmission rates go up to 622 Mbps.

Synchronous Optical Network (SONET)

The American National Standards Institute (ANSI) published a standard called Synchronous Optical Network (SONET) in 1988 and entitled it ANSI T1.105. Since then, the CCITT has incorporated the SONET standard into their Synchronous Digital Hierarchy (SDH) recommendations. SONET has since emerged as a vanguard in telecommunications technologies. SONET's major goal is to standardize optical fiber network equipment, thus, allowing for internetworking optical communications systems from a variety of different vendors. It is believed that SONET possesses sufficient flexibility to allow it to eventually be used as the underlying transport layer for BISDN and ATM cells.

SONET signal hierarchy and bit rates. SONET defined their *optical carrier hierarchy* and their equivalent electrical *synchronous transport signals* (STS) for an optical fiber-based transmission system. Table 3-7 lists the standard transmission bit rates used with SONET.

The 51.84 Mbps STS-1 rate is the fundamental line rate from which all the other SONET optical bit rates are derived. As the table shows, higher bit rates are integer multiples of the OC-1 rate. For STS-N, the only values of N allowed are 1, 3, 9, 12, 18, 24, 36, and 48. The current standard does not provide for future bit rates in excess of N = 256.

SONET frame format. The transport mechanism adopted by SONET uses a synchronous binary bit stream made up of groups of bytes organized into a frame structure, which includes user data. The basic 51.84 Mbps STS-1 frame format is shown in Figure 3-11. It can be seen that the frame format is best described as a 9 row by 90 column matrix representing individual bytes of synchronous data. Data are transmitted byte by byte beginning with byte 1, then, continuing from left to right and top to bottom for a total of 810 bytes (9×90) or 6408 bits (810×8). The transmission bit rate is

51.84 Mbps

Frame 1 | Frame 2 | Frame 3 | Frame N

STS-1

90 columns (bytes)

1 . . . 3   4   90

| 1 | 2 | 3 | 4 | 5 . . . | . . . 89 90 |
| 91 | 92 | 93 | 94 | 95 . . . | . . . 179 180 |

9 rows (bytes)

Transport overhead (TOH)

STS path overhead

Synchronous payload envelope (SPE)

9 | 720 721 722 | 723 | 724 . . . | . . . 809 810

125 µs

810 bytes/frame x 8 bits/byte x 8000 frames/sec = 51.84 Mbps

FIGURE 3-11 SONET STS-1 frame format

$$\text{bps} = \frac{\text{bits}}{\text{time}} = \frac{6480 \text{ bits}}{125 \text{ µs}} = 51.84 \text{ Mbps}$$

STS-1 frames are divided into two general areas: the *transport overhead* (TOH) and the *synchronous payload envelope* (SPE). The TOH occupies the first three columns of the 90-column matrix. The remaining 87 columns comprise the SPE. The initial SPE column is called the STS *path overhead,* which contains payload specific data, which does not change as the SPE travels through the network. The remaining 86 columns in the SPE carry the payload or network traffic.

The TOH portion of the STS-1 frame is used for alarm monitoring, bit error monitoring, and other data communications overhead necessary to ensure reliable transmission of the synchronous payload envelope between nodes within the synchronous network. The SPE is designed to transport user data through the synchronous network from source to destination. The SPE is assembled and disassembled only once on its route through the network, regardless of how many times it changes transport systems. In most cases, however, the SPE is assembled where it enters the network and disassembled where it exits.

The *payload* is the revenue-producing traffic transported through the SONET network. Once assembled, the payload can be routed through the network to its destination. STS-1 payload has the capacity to transport the various types of digital signals listed in Table 3-8.

The 86 columns of the SPE designed to carry payload are arranged in accordance with standard mapping rules, which are a function of the data service subscribing to the network (i.e., DS1, DS2, etc.). The specific arrangement used for a given service is called a *virtual tributary* (VT). SONET facilitates various size VTs. For example, VT1.5 is a frame comprised of 27 bytes formatted in 3 columns of 9 bytes each. With a 125 µs frame time (i.e., 8 kHz rate), the bytes provide a transport capacity of 1.728 Mbps, which will

TABLE 3-8 STS-1 Payload Capacity

Capacity	Signal Type	Signal Rate (Mbps)	Voice Circuits	T1s
28	DS1	1.544	24	1
21	CEPT1	2.048	30	—
14	DS1C	3.152	48	2
7	DS2	6.312	96	4
1	DS3	44.736	672	28

FIGURE 3-12 SONET STS-3 byte-interleaved multiplexing

accommodate mapping a DS1 compatible signal that has a rate of 1.544 Mbps. Twenty-eight VT1.5s may be multiplexed into the STS-1 SPE.

SONET multiplexing. SONET utilizes a multiplexing technique called byte-interleaved multiplexing to achieve higher levels of synchronous transport. By using byte-interleave multiplexing, N STS-1 circuits can be multiplexed into a single STS-N circuit. Figure 3-12 shows how three STS-1 frames are multiplexed into a single STS-3 frame. The STS-3 frame has 270 columns and 9 rows for a total byte capacity of 2430 bytes. Because the STS-3 frame is also transmitted in 125 μs, the transmission rate is three times that of a single STS-1 frame or 155.52 Mbps. Note in Figure 3-12 that the byte-interleaved process produces a matrix with multiplexed rows and columns. The first 9 columns of the STS-3 frame comprise the TOHs from the three STS-1 signals, and the remaining 261 columns are occupied by the SPEs of the three STS-1 signals.

INTEGRATED SERVICES DIGITAL NETWORK

Introduction to ISDN

The data and telephone communications industry is continually changing to meet the demands of contemporary telephone, video, and computer communications systems. Today, more and more people have a need to communicate with each other than ever before. In order to meet these needs, old standards are being updated and new standards are being developed and implemented almost on a daily basis.

The *Integrated Services Digital Network* (ISDN) is a proposed network designed by the major telephone companies in conjunction with the CCITT with the intent of providing worldwide telecommunications support of voice, data, video, and facsimile information within the same network (in essence, ISDN is the integrating of a wide range of services into a single multipurpose network). ISDN is a network that proposes to interconnect an unlimited number of independent users through a common communications network.

To date only a small number of ISDN facilities have been developed; however, the telephone industry is presently implementing an ISDN system so that in the near future, subscribers will access the ISDN system using existing public telephone and data networks. The basic principles and evolution of ISDN have been outlined by the Consultative Committee for International Telephony and Telegraphy (CCITT) in its recommendation CCITT 1.120 (1984). CCITT 1.120 lists the following principles and evolution of ISDN:

Principles of ISDN

1. The main feature of the ISDN concept is to support a wide range of voice (telephone) and nonvoice (digital data) applications in the same network using a limited number of standardized facilities.

2. ISDNs support a wide variety of applications including both switched and nonswitched (dedicated) connections. Switched connections include both circuit- and packet-switched connections and their concatenations.

3. Whenever practical, new services introduced into an ISDN should be compatible with 64 kbps switched digital connections. The 64 kbps digital connection is the basic building block of ISDN.

4. An ISDN will contain intelligence for the purpose of providing service features, maintenance, and network management functions. In other words, ISDN is expected to provide services beyond the simple setting up of switched-circuit calls.

5. A layered protocol structure should be used to specify the access procedures to an ISDN and can be mapped into the open system interconnection (OSI) model. Standards already developed for OSI-related applications can be used for ISDN, such as X.25 level 3 for access to packet-switching services.

6. It is recognized that ISDN's may be implemented in a variety of configurations according to specific national situations. This accommodates both single-source or competitive national policy.

Evolution of ISDNs

1. ISDNs will be based on the concepts developed for telephone ISDNs and may evolve by progressively incorporating additional functions and network features including those of any other dedicated networks such as circuit and packet switching for data so as to provide for existing and new services.

2. The transition from an existing network to a comprehensive ISDN may require a period of time extending over one or more decades. During this period, arrangements must be developed for the internetworking of services on ISDNs and services on other networks.

3. In the evolution towards an ISDN, digital end-to-end connectivity will be obtained via plant and equipment used in existing networks, such as digital transmission, time-division multiplex and/or space-division multiplex switching. Existing relevant recommendations for these constituent elements of an ISDN are contained in the appropriate series of recommendations of CCITT and CCIR.

4. In the early stages of the evolution of ISDNs, some interim user-network arrangements may need to be adopted in certain countries to facilitate early penetration of digital service capabilities.

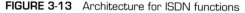

FIGURE 3-13 Architecture for ISDN functions

5. An evolving ISDN may also include at later stages switched connections at bit rates higher and lower than 64 kbps.

ISDN Architecture

A block diagram indicating the proposed architecture for ISDN functions is shown in Figure 3-13. The ISDN is designed to support an entirely new physical connection for the user, a digital subscriber loop, and a variety of transmission services.

A *common physical interface* will be defined to provide a DTE-DCE interface connection. A single interface will be used for telephones, computer terminals, and video equipment. Therefore, various protocols will be required to allow control information to be exchanged between the user's device and the ISDN. There are three basic types of channels available with ISDN. They are

B channel: 64 kbps

D channel: 16 or 64 kbps

H channel: 384, 1536, or 1920 kbps

ISDN standards specify that residential users of the network (that is, the subscribers) be provided a *basic access* consisting of three full-duplex time-division multiplexed digital channels, two operating at 64 kbps (designated the B channels, for *bearer*) and one at 16 kbps (designated the D channel, for *data*). The B and D bit rates were selected to be compatible with existing DS1–DS4 digital carrier systems. The D channel is used for carrying signaling information and for exchanging network control information. One B channel is used for digitally encoded voice and the other for applications such as data transmission, PCM-encoded digitized voice, and videotex. The 2B + D service is sometimes called the *basic rate interface* (BRI). BRI systems require bandwidths that can accommodate two 64-kbps B channels and one 16-kbps D channel plus framing, synchronization, and other overhead bits for a total bit rate of 192 kbps. The H channels are used to provide higher bit rates for special services such as fast facsimile, video, high-speed data, and high-quality audio.

There is another service called the *primary service, primary access,* or *primary rate interface* (PRI) that will provide multiple 64-kbps channels intended to be used by the

TABLE 3-9 Projected ISDN Services

Service	Transmission Rate	Channel
Telephone	64 kbps	BC
System Alarms	100 bps	D
Utility company metering	100 bps	D
Energy management	100 bps	D
Video	2.4–64 kbps	BP
Electronic mail	4.8–64 kbps	BP
Facsimile	4.8–64 kbps	BC
Slow scan television	64 kbps	BC

FIGURE 3-14 ISDN connections and reference points

higher volume subscribers to the network. In the United States, Canada, Japan, and Korea, the primary rate interface consists of twenty-three 64-kbps B channels and one 64-kbps D channel (23B + D) for a combined bit rate of 1.544 Mbps. In Europe, the primary rate interface uses thirty 64-kbps B channels and one 64-kbps D channel for a combined bit rate of 2.048 Mbps.

It is intended that ISDN provide a circuit-switched B channel with the existing telephone system, however, packet-switched B channels for data transmission at non-standard rates would have to be created.

The subscriber's loop, as with the twisted pair cable used with a common telephone, provides the physical signal path from the subscriber's equipment to the ISDN central office. The subscriber loop must be capable of supporting full-duplex digital transmission for both basic and primary data rates. Ideally, as the network grows, optical fiber cables will replace the metallic cables.

Table 3-9 lists the services proposed to be used by ISDN subscribers. BC designates a circuit-switched B channel, BP designates a packed-switched B channel, and D designates a D channel.

ISDN System Connections and Interface Units

ISDN subscriber units and interfaces are defined by their function and reference within the network. Figure 3-14 shows how users may be connected to an ISDN. As the figure shows, subscribers must access the network through one of two different types of entry devices, *terminal equipment type 1* (TE1) and *terminal equipment type 2* (TE2). TE1 equipment supports standard ISDN interfaces and, therefore, requires no protocol translation. Data enters the network and are immediately configured into ISDN protocol format. TE2 equipment is classified as non-ISDN, thus, computer terminals are connected to the system through physical interfaces such as the RS-232 and host computers with X.25. Translation between non-ISDN data protocol and ISDN protocol is performed in a device called a *terminal adapter* (TA). Terminal adapters convert the user's data into the 64 kbps ISDN channel B or the 16 kbps channel D format, and X.25 packets are converted to ISDN packet formats. If any additional signaling is required, it is added by the terminal adapter. The terminal adapters can also support traditional analog telephones and facsimile signals by using a 3.1 kHz audio service channel. The analog signals are digitized and put into ISDN format before entering the network.

User data at points designated as *reference point S (system)* are presently in ISDN format and provide the 2B + D data at 192 kbps. These reference points separate user terminal equipment from network-related system functions. *Reference point T (terminal)* locations correspond to a minimal ISDN network termination at the user's location. These reference points separate the network provider's equipment from the user's equipment. *Reference point R (rate)* provides an interface between non-ISDN compatible user equipment and the terminal adapters. *Network termination* 1 (NT1) provides the functions associated with the physical interface between the user and the common carrier and are designated by the letter T (these functions correspond to OSI layer 1). The NT1 is a boundary to the network and may be controlled by the ISDN provider. The NTI performs line maintenance functions and supports multiple channels at the physical level (e.g., 2B + D). Data from these channels are time-division multiplexed together. Network terminal 2 devices are intelligent and can perform *concentration* and switching functions (functionally up through OSI level 3). NT2 terminations can also be used to terminate several S-point connections and provide local switching functions and two-wire to four-wire and four-wire to two-wire conversions. *U-reference points* refer to interfaces between the common carrier subscriber loop and the *central office switch*. A *U loop* is the media interface point between an NT1 and the central office. Network termination 1,2 (NT12) constitutes one piece of equipment that combines the functions of NT1 and NT2. U loops are terminated at the central office by a *line termination* (LT) unit, which provides physical layer interface functions between the central office and the loop lines. The LT unit is connected to an *exchange termination* (ET) at *reference point* V. An ET routes data to an outgoing channel or central office user.

There are several types of transmission channels in addition to the B and D types described in the previous section. They include the following:

HO channel. This interface supports multiple 384-kbps HO channels. These structures are 3HO + D and 4HO + D for the 1.544-Mbps interface and 5HO + D for the 2.048 Mbps interface.

H11 channel. This interface consists of one 1.536-Mbps H11 channel (twenty-four 64-kbps channels).

H12 channel. European version of H11 that uses 30 channels for a combined data rate of 1.92 Mbps.

E channel. Packet switched using 64 kbps (similar to the standard D channel)

ISDN Protocols

Standards developed for ISDN include protocols that allow interaction between ISDN users and the network itself and also for interaction between one ISDN user and another. In addition, it is desirable to fit the new ISDN protocols into the OSI framework. Figure 3-15 shows the relationships between OSI and ISDN. In essence, ISDN is not concerned with OSI layers 4–7. These layers are for end-to-end exchange of information between the network users.

Layer 1 specifies the physical interface for both basic and primary access to the network. B and D channels are time-division multiplexed onto the same interface,

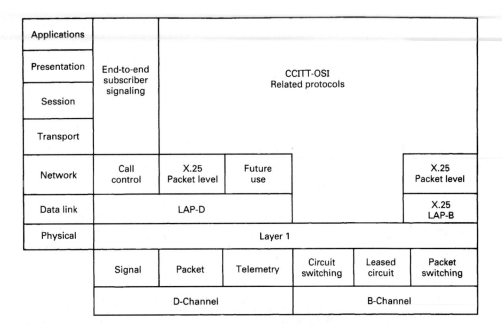

Applications	End-to-end subscriber signaling	CCITT-OSI Related protocols				
Presentation						
Session						
Transport						
Network	Call control	X.25 Packet level	Future use			X.25 Packet level
Data link	LAP-D					X.25 LAP-B
Physical	Layer 1					
	Signal	Packet	Telemetry	Circuit switching	Leased circuit	Packet switching
	D-Channel			B-Channel		

FIGURE 3-15 Structured relationships between OSI and ISDN user network

consequently, the same standards apply to both types of channels. However, the protocols of layers 2 and 3 differ for the two channels. The protocol used by ISDN for the data link layer is very similar to the HDLC format discussed earlier in this chapter and is called *Link Access Protocol for D-Channels* (LAP-D) and *Link Access Protocol for B-Channels* (LAP-B). CCITT standards Q920 and Q921 give the details of these specifications.

LAP-D services.   All data transmissions on the LAP-D channel are between the subscriber equipment and an ISDN switching element. LAP-D provides two types of services: *unacknowledged* and *acknowledged information transfer.* The unacknowledged information transfer provides for the transfer of data frames with no acknowledgment. This service supports both point-to-point or broadcast transmission but does not guarantee successful transmission of data, nor does it inform the sender if the transmission fails. Unacknowledged information transfer does not provide any type of data flow control or error control mechanism. Error detection is used to detect and discard any damaged frames. Transmission of unacknowledged information transfer simply provides a means of transferring data quickly and is useful for services such as sending alarm messages.

The acknowledged information transfer service is much more commonly used. This service is similar to the services offered by LAP-B. With acknowledged information transfer, a logical connection is established between two subscribers prior to the transfer of any data. Then data are transferred in sequentially numbered frames that are acknowledged either individually or in groups. Both error and flow control are included in this service. This type of service is sometimes referred to as multiple-frame operation.

LAP-D format.   With LAP-D protocol, subscriber information as well as protocol control information and parameters are transmitted in frames. The basic LAP-D frame is identical to that of HDLC except for the address field. The LAP-D frame format is shown in Figure 3-16. As shown, the frame begins with the transmission of a flag field, followed by the address field. The flag field delimits the frame at both ends with a hex 7E (binary 01111110). LAP-D has to contend with two types of multiplexing: subscriber site multiplexing where there may be multiple devices sharing the same physical interface and

Beginning flag	Address field		Control field	Information field	Frame check sequence	Ending flag
7E 01111110	C/R SAPI 0 X XXXXXX	TEI 1 XXXXXXX	Control word	Data	CRC-16	7E 01111110
1-byte	1-byte	1-byte	1-2 bytes	1-128 or 0-260 bytes	2-bytes	1-byte

SAPI = Service point identifier
TEI = Terminal endpoint identifier
CRC = Cyclic redundancy check
C/R = Command/response

FIGURE 3-16 ISDN LAP-D format

TABLE 3-10 TEI Assignments

TEI	User Type
0-63	Nonautomatic TEI assignment subscriber equipment
64-126	Automatic TEI assignment subscriber equipment
127	Used during automatic TEI assignment

TABLE 3-11 SAPI Assignments

SAPI	Related Layer 3 or Management Function
0	Call control procedures
1	Reserved for packet-mode transmissions using I.451 call control procedures
16	Packet-mode transmissions using X.25 level 3
63	Layer 2 management and control procedures
all others	Reserved for future uses

within each user device where there may be multiple forms of traffic multiplexed together (such as packet-switched data and control signalling).

To accommodate the two forms of multiplexing, LAP-D uses a two-part address field that consists of a *terminal endpoint identifier* (TEI) and a *service point identifier* (SAPI). Typically each subscriber is assigned a unique TEI. It is also possible for a single device to have more than one TEI, such as for a terminal concentrator. TEI assignments can be made automatically when the equipment is first turned up, or manually by the subscriber. The SAPI identifies a layer 3 subscriber of LAP-D. Only four SAPI identifiers are currently in use. A SAPI of 0 is used for call control procedures for managing B channel circuits, a SAPI of 1 is used for packet-mode transmissions using I.451 control procedures (such as subscriber-to-subscriber signaling), a SAPI of 16 is reserved for packet-mode transmissions on the D channel using X.25 level 3, and a SAPI of 63 is used for the exchange of layer 2 management and control information. The TEI and SAPI assignments are given in Tables 3-10 and 3-11, respectively. The TEI and SAPI can be used together to uniquely identify a logical connection. When used in this manner, the combination of TEI and SAPI is referred to as a *data link connection identifier* (DLCI).

An additional bit, called the *command/response* (C/R) bit, is used to identify the frame as a command (logic 0 for traffic from terminals and logic 1 for traffic from the network) or a response message (opposite logic condition).

The control field identifies the type of frame and keeps track of the frame sequence the same as with SDLC and HDLC. Information, supervisory, and unnumbered control fields are also the same as with SDLC and HDLC with these exceptions. The set normal response unnumbered frame is replaced with a set asynchronous balanced mode extended frame, which functions in a similar manner and establishes a data link for acknowledged data transfers of information frames. An additional unnumbered frame, *transfer ID* (XID), is also included to allow stations to identify themselves for line management purposes.

The information field is allowed only with information frames and certain special unnumbered frames. The information field can contain any sequence of bits so long as they consist of an integral multiple of eight (octets). The information field is variable within system-defined specifications; however, for both control signaling and packet information, the maximum length is 260 octets.

The frame check sequence (FCS) is a CRC-CCITT code used for error-detection of all bits within the frame except the flags.

LAP-B frames are similar to LAP-D although XID and unnumbered information (UI) frames are not used. Also, with LAP-B the frames are limited to 14-bit modulo 8 numbers (0–7) where LAP-D uses 7-bit modulo 128 numbers (0–127).

Broadband ISDN (BISDN)

Broadband ISDN (BISDN) is defined by the CCITT as a service that provides transmission channels capable of supporting transmission rates greater than the primary data rate. With BISDN, services requiring data rates of a magnitude beyond those provided by ISDN, such as video transmission, will become available. With the advent of BISDN, the original concept of ISDN is being referred to as *narrowband* ISDN.

In 1988, the CCITT first recommended as part of its I-series recommendations relating to BISDN: I.113, *Vocabulary of terms for broadband aspects of ISDN,* and I.121, *Broadband aspects of ISDN.* These two documents are a consensus concerning the aspects of the future of BISDN. They outline preliminary descriptions of future standards and development work.

The new BISDN standards are based upon the concept of an *asynchronous transfer mode* (ATM), which will incorporate optical fiber cable as the transmission medium for data transmission. The BISDN specifications set a maximum length of 1 km per cable length but is making provisions for repeated interface extensions. The expected data rates on the optical fiber cables will be either 11 Mbps, 155 Mbps, or 600 Mbps, depending on the specific application and the location of the fiber cable within the network.

CCITT classifies the services that could be provided by BISDN as interactive and distribution services. *Interactive services* include those in which there is a two-way exchange of information (excluding control signaling) between two subscribers or between a subscriber and a service provider. *Distribution services* are those in which information transfer is primarily from service provider to subscriber. On the other hand, *conversational services* will provide a means for bidirectional end-to-end data transmission, in real time, between two subscribers or between a subscriber and a service provider.

The authors of BISDN composed specifications that require the new services meet both existing ISDN interface specifications and the new BISDN needs. A standard ISDN terminal and a *broadband terminal interface* (BTI) will be serviced by the *subscriber's premise network* (SPN), which will multiplex incoming data and transfer them to the *broadband node.* The broadband node is called a *broadband network termination* (BNT), which codes the data information into smaller packets used by the BISDN network. Data transmission within the BISDN network can be asymmetric (that is, access on to and off of the network may be accomplished at different transmission rates, depending on system requirements).

Asynchronous transfer mode. The asynchronous transfer mode (ATM) is a means by which data can enter and exit the BISDN network in an asynchronous (time independent) fashion. ATM uses labeled channels that are transferable at fixed data rates. The data rates can be anywhere from 16 kbps up to the maximum rate of the system.

Virtual channel identifier	Header error detection character	Undefined	Channel data

FIGURE 3-17 ATM cell header format

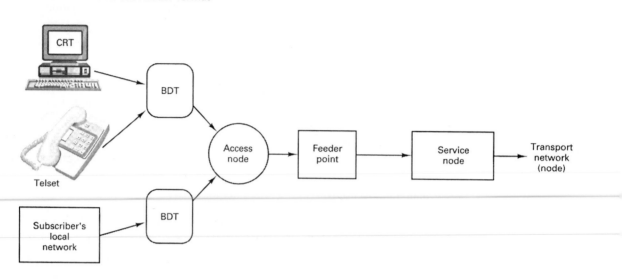

FIGURE 3-18 BISDN access

Once data has entered the network, they are transferred into fixed time slots called *cells*. A cell is identified by a *label* in the *cell header*. The format for a cell header is shown in Figure 3-17. The *virtual channel identifier* indicates the node source and packet destination. The channel is virtual, rather than specific, which allows the actual physical routing of the packet and network entry and exit times to be determined by network availability and access rights. Immediately after the virtual channel identifier, is the *header error detection character,* which may be a CRC character or any other form of error detection. The CRC is for the header label only and separate error detection methods are used for the actual data field. The next section of the header cell is unidentified and is reserved for future use.

BISDN configuration. Figure 3-18 shows how access to the BISDN network is accomplished. Each peripheral device is interfaced to the *access node* of a BISDN network through a *broadband distant terminal* (BDT). The BDT is responsible for the electrical to optical conversion, multiplexing of peripherals, and maintenance of the subscriber's local system. Access nodes concentrate several BDTs into high-speed optical fiber lines directed through a *feeder point* into a *service node*. Most of the control functions for system access are managed by the service node, such as call processing, administrative functions, and switching and maintenance functions. The functional modules are interconnected in a star configuration and include switching, administrative, gateway, and maintenance modules. The interconnection of the function modules is shown in Figure 3-19. The central control hub acts as the end user interface for control signaling and data traffic maintenance. In essence, it oversees the operation of the modules.

Subscriber terminals near the central office may bypass the access nodes entirely and be directly connected to the BISDN network through a service node. BISDN networks that use optical fiber cables can utilize much wider bandwidths and, consequently, have higher transmission rates and offer more channel-handling capacity than ISDN systems.

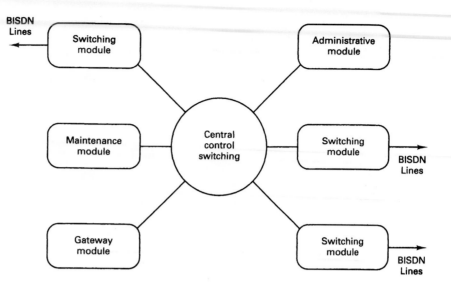

FIGURE 3-19   BISDN functional module interconnections

Broadband channel rates.   The CCITT has published preliminary definitions of new broadband channel rates that will be added to the existing ISDN narrowband channel rates. The new channel rates are

1. H21: 32.768 Mbps
2. H22: 43 to 45 Mbps
3. H4: 132 to 138.24 Mbps

The H21 and H22 data rates are intended to be used for full-motion video transmission for video conferencing, video telephone, and video messaging. The H4 data rate is intended for bulk data transfer of text, facsimile, and enhanced video information. The H21 data rate is equivalent to 512 64-kbps channels. The H22 and H4 data rates must be multiples of the basic 64 kbps transmission rate.

LOCAL AREA NETWORKS

Studies have indicated that most (80%) of the communications among data terminals and other data equipment occurs within a relatively small local environment. A *local area network* (LAN) provides the most economical and effective means of handling local data communication needs. A local area network is typically a privately owned data communications system in which the users share resources, including software. LANs provide two-way communications between a large variety of data communications terminals within a limited geographical area such as within the same room, building, or building complex. Most LANs link equipment together that are within a few miles of each other.

Figure 3-20 shows how several PCs could be connected to a LAN to share common resources such as a modem, printer, or server. The server may be a more powerful computer than the other PCs sharing the network or it may simply have more disk storage space. The server "serves" information to the other PCs on the network in the form of software and data-information files. A PC server is analogous to a mainframe computer, except on a much smaller scale.

LANs allow for a room full or more of computers to share common resources such as printers and modems. The average PC uses these devices only a small percentage of the time, so there is no need to dedicate individual printers and modems to each PC. To

FIGURE 3-20 Typical local area network component configuration

print a document or file, a PC simply sends the information over the network to the server. The server organizes and prioritizes the documents, then sends them, one document at a time, to the common usage printer. Meanwhile, the PCs are free to continue performing other useful tasks. When a PC needs a modem, the network establishes a *virtual connection* between the modem and the PC. The network is transparent to the virtual connection, which allows the PC to communicate with the modem as if they were connected directly to each other.

LANS allow people to send and receive messages and documents through the network much quicker than they could be sent through a paper mail system. *Electronic mail* is a communications system that allows users to send messages to each other through their computers. Electronic mail enables any PC on the network to send or receive information from any other PC on the network as long as the PCs and the server use the same or compatible software. Electronic mail can also be used to interconnect users on different networks in different cities, states, countries or even continents. To send an electronic mail message, a user at one PC sends its address and message along with the destination address to the server. The server effectively "relays" the message to the destination PC if they are subscribers to the same network. If the destination PC is busy or not available for whatever reason, the server stores the message and resends it later. The server is the only computer that has to keep track of the location and address of all the other PCs on the network. To send electronic mail to subscribers of other networks, the server relays the message to the server on the destination user's network, which in turn relays the mail to the destination PC. Electronic mail can be used to send text information (letters) as well as program files, graphics, audio, and even video. This is referred to as multimedia communications.

LANs are used extensively to interconnect a wide range of data services including the following:

Data terminals
Laser printers
Graphic plotters
Large volume disk and tape storage devices
Facsimile machines
Personal computers
Mainframe computers

Data modems
Databases
Word processors
Public-switched telephone networks
Digital carrier systems (T-carriers)
Electronic mail servers

Local Area Network System Considerations

The capabilities of a local area network are established primarily by three factors: *topology, transmission medium,* and *access control protocol.* Together, these three factors determine the type of data, rate of transmission, efficiency, and applications that a network can effectively support.

LAN topologies. The topology or physical architecture of a LAN identifies how the stations (terminals, printers, modems, etc.) are interconnected. The transmission media used with LANs include metallic *twisted-wire pairs, coaxial cable,* and *optical fiber cables.* Presently, most LANs use coaxial cable, however optical fiber cable systems are being installed in many new networks. Fiber systems can operate at higher transmission bit rates and have a larger capacity to transfer information than coaxial cables.

The most common LAN topologies are the star, bus, bus tree, and ring, which are illustrated in Figure 3-21.

Star Topology. The preeminent feature of the star topology is that each station is radially linked to a *central node* through a direct point-to-point connection as shown in Figure 3-21a. With a star configuration, a transmission from one station enters the central node where it is retransmitted on all of the outgoing links. Therefore, although the circuit arrangement physically resembles a star, it is logically configured as a bus (i.e., transmissions from any station are received by all other stations).

Central nodes offer a convenient location for system or station troubleshooting because all traffic between outlying nodes must flow through the central node. The central node is sometimes referred to as *central control, star coupler,* or *central switch* and typically is a computer. The star configuration is best adapted to applications where most of the communications occur between the central node and outlying nodes. The star arrangement is also well suited to systems where there is a large demand to communicate with only a few of the remote terminals. Time-sharing systems are generally configured with a star topology. A star configuration is also well suited for word-processing and data-base management applications.

Star couplers can be implemented either passively or actively. When passive couplers are used with a metallic transmission medium, transformers in the coupler provide an electromagnetic linkage through the coupler, which passes incoming signals on to outgoing links. If optical fiber cables are used for the transmission media, coupling can be achieved by fusing fibers together. With active couplers, digital circuitry in the central node acts as a repeater. Incoming data are simply regenerated and repeated on to all outgoing lines.

One disadvantage of a star topology is that the network is only as reliable as the central node. When the central node fails, the system fails. If one or more outlying node fails, however, the rest of the users can continue to use the remainder of the network. When failure of any single entity within a network is critical to the point that it will disrupt service on the entire network, that entity is referred to as a *critical resource.* Thus, the central node in a star configuration is a critical resource.

Bus Topology. In essence, the bus topology is a multipoint or multidrop circuit configuration where individual nodes are interconnected by a common, shared communications

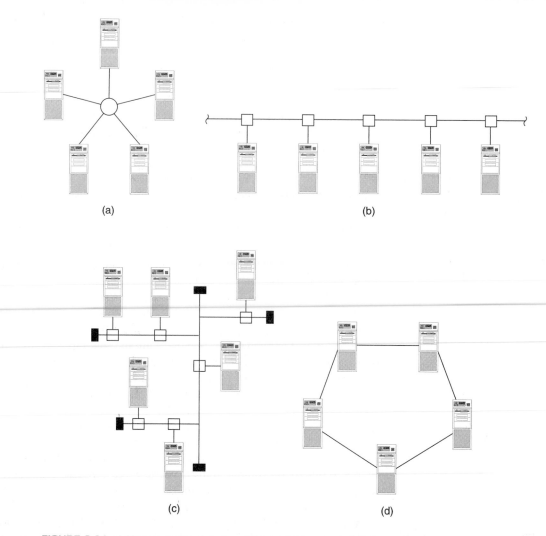

FIGURE 3-21 LAN topologies: (a) star; (b) bus; (c) bus tree; (d) ring or loop

channel as shown in Figure 3-21b. With the bus topology, all stations connect, using appropriate interfacing hardware, directly to a common linear transmission medium, generally referred to as a bus. In a bus configuration, network control is not centralized to a particular node. In fact, the most distinguishing feature of a bus LAN is that control is distributed among all the nodes connected to the LAN. Data transmissions on a bus network are usually in the form of small packets containing user addresses and data. When one station desires to transmit data to another station, it monitors the bus first to determine if it is currently being used. If no other stations are communicating over the network (i.e., the network is clear), the monitoring station can commence to transmit its data. When one station begins transmitting, all other stations become receivers. Each receiver must monitor all transmission on the network and determine which are intended for them. When a station identifies its address on a received data message, it acts upon it, otherwise, it ignores that transmission.

One advantage of a bus topology is no special routing or circuit switching is required and, therefore, it is not necessary to store and retransmit messages intended for other nodes. This advantage eliminates a considerable amount of message identification overhead and processing time. However, with heavy usage systems, there is a high likelihood that more than one station may desire to transmit at the same time. When transmissions from two or more stations occur simultaneously, a data collision occurs, disrupting data communications on the entire network. Obviously, a priority contention scheme is necessary to handle data collision. Such a priority scheme is called *carrier sense, multiple access with collision detect* (CSMA/CD) which is discussed in a later section of this chapter.

Because network control is not centralized in a bus configuration, a node failure will not disrupt data flow on the entire LAN. The critical resource in this case is not a node but instead the bus itself. A failure anywhere along the bus opens the network and, depending on the versatility of the communications channel, may disrupt communication on the entire network.

The addition of new nodes on a bus can sometimes be a problem because gaining access to the bus cable may be a cumbersome task, especially if it is enclosed within a wall, floor, or ceiling. One means of reducing installation problems is to add secondary buses to the primary communications channel. By branching off into other bases, a multiple bus structure called a *tree bus* is formed. Figure 3-21c shows a tree bus configuration.

Ring Topology. With a ring topology, adjacent stations are interconnected by repeaters in a closed-loop configuration as shown in Figure 3-21d. Each node participates as a repeater between two adjacent links within the ring. The repeaters are relatively simple devices capable of receiving data from one link and retransmitting them on a second link. Messages, usually in packet form, are propagated in the simplex mode (one-way only) from node to node around the ring until it has circled the entire loop and returned to the originating node where it is verified that the data in the returned message is identical to the data originally transmitted. Hence, the network configuration serves as an inherent error detection mechanism. The destination station(s) can acknowledge reception of the data by setting or clearing appropriate bits within the control segment of the message packet. Packets contain both source and destination address fields as well as additional network control information and user data. Each node examines incoming data packets, copying packets designated for them, and acting as a repeater for all data packets by retransmitting them (bit by bit) to the next down-line repeater. A repeater should neither alter the content of received packets nor change the transmission rate.

Virtually any physical transmission medium can be used with the ring topology. Twisted-wire pairs offer low cost but severely limited transmission rates. Coaxial cables provide greater capacity than twisted-wire pairs at practically the same cost. The highest data rates, however, are achieved with optical fiber cables, except a substantially higher installation cost.

LAN transmission formats. Two transmission techniques or formats are used with local area networks, baseband and broadband, to multiplex transmissions from a multitude of stations onto a single transmission medium.

Baseband Transmission Format. Baseband transmission formats are defined as transmission formats that use digital signaling. In addition, baseband formats use the transmission medium as a single-channel device. Only one station can transmit at a time and all stations must transmit and receive the same types of signals (encoding schemes, bit rates, etc.). Baseband transmission formats time-division multiplex signals onto the transmission medium. All stations can use the media but only one at a time. The entire frequency spectrum (bandwidth) is used by (or at least made available to) whichever station is presently transmitting. With a baseband format, transmissions are bidirectional. A signal inserted at any point on the transmission medium propagates in both directions to the ends, where it is absorbed. Digital signaling requires a bus topology because digital signals cannot be easily propagated through the splitters and joiners necessary in a tree bus topology. Because of transmission line losses, baseband LANs are limited to a distance of no more than a couple miles.

TABLE 3-12 Baseband Versus Broadband Transmission Formats

Baseband	Broadband
Uses digital signaling	Analog signaling requiring RF modems and amplifiers
Entire bandwidth used by each transmission—no FDM	FDM possible; i.e., multiple data channels (video, audio, data, etc.)
Bidirectional	Unidirectional
Bus topology	Bus or tree bus topology
Maximum length approximately 1500 m	Maximum length up to tens of kilometers
Advantages	
Less expensive	High capacity
Simpler technology	Multiple traffic types
Easier and quicker to install	More flexible circuit configurations, larger area covered
Disadvantages	
Single channel	RF modem and amplifiers required
Limited capacity	Complex installation and maintenance
Grounding problems	Double propagation delay
Limited distance	

Broadband Transmission Formats. Broadband transmission formats use the connecting media as a multichannel device. Each channel occupies a different frequency band within the total allocated bandwidth (i.e., frequency-division multiplexing). Consequently, each channel can contain different modulation and encoding schemes and operate at different transmission rates. A broadband network permits voice, digital data, and video to be transmitted simultaneously over the same transmission medium. However, broadband systems are unidirectional and require RF modems, amplifiers, and more complicated transceivers than baseband systems. For this reason baseband systems are more prevalent. Circuit components used with broadband LANs easily facilitate splitting and joining operations, consequently, both bus and tree bus topologies are allowed. Broadband systems can span much greater distances than baseband systems. Distances of up to tens of miles are possible.

The layout for a baseband system is much less complex than a broadband system and, therefore, easier and less expensive to implement. The primary disadvantages of baseband are its limited capacity and length. Broadband systems can carry a wide variety of different kinds of signals on a number of channels. By incorporating amplifiers, broadband can span much greater distances than baseband. Table 3-12 summarizes baseband and broadband transmission formats.

LAN access control methodologies. In a practical local area network, it is very likely that more than one user may wish to use the network media at any given time. For a medium to be shared by various users, a means of controlling access is necessary. Media-sharing methods are known as access methodologies. Network access methodologies describe how users access the communications channel in a local area network. The first LANs were developed by computer manufacturers; they were expensive and worked only with certain types of computers with a limited number of software programs. LANs also required a high degree of technical knowledge and expertise to install and maintain. In 1980, the IEEE, in an effort to resolve problems with local area networks, formed the 802 Local Area Network Standards Committee. In 1983, the committee established several recommended standards for LANs. The two most prominent standards are IEEE Standard 802.3, which addresses an access method for bus topologies called *carrier sense, multiple access with collision detection* (CSMA/CD), and IEEE Standard 802.5, which describes an access method for ring topologies called *token passing.*

Carrier Sense, Multiple Access with Collision Detection. CSMA/CD is an access method used primarily with LANs configured in a bus topology. CSMA/CD uses the basic philosophy that, *"If you have something to say, say it. If there's a problem, we'll work it out later."* With CSMA/CD, any station (node) can send a message to any other station (or stations) as long as the transmission medium is free of transmissions from other stations. Stations monitor (listen to) the line to determine if the line is busy. If a station has a message to transmit but the line is busy, it waits for an idle condition before transmitting its message. If two stations transmit at the same time, a *collision* occurs. When this happens, the station first sensing the collision sends a special jamming signal to all of the other stations on the network. All stations then cease transmitting (*back off*) and wait a random period of time before attempting a retransmission. The random delay time for each station is different and, therefore, allows for prioritizing the stations on the network. If successive collisions occur, the back-off period for each station is doubled.

With CSMA/CD, stations must contend for the network. A station is not guaranteed access to the network. To detect the occurrence of a collision, a station must be capable of transmitting and receiving simultaneously. CSMA/CD is used by most LANs configured in a bus topology. *Ethernet* is an example of a LAN that uses CSMA/CD and is described later in this chapter.

Another factor that could possibly cause collisions with CSMA/CD is *propagation delay*. Propagation delay is the time it takes a signal to travel from a source to a destination. Due to propagation delay, it is possible for the line to appear idle when, in fact, another station is transmitting a signal that has not yet reached the monitoring station.

Token Passing. Token passing is a network access method used primarily with LANs configured in a ring topology using either baseband or broadband transmission formats. When using *token passing* access, nodes do not contend for the right to transmit data. With token passing, a specific packet of data, called a *token,* is circulated around the ring from station to station, always in the same direction. The token is generated by a designated station known as the *active monitor.* Before a station is allowed to transmit, it must first possess the token. Each station, in turn, acquires the token and examines the data frame to determine if it is carrying a packet addressed to it. If the frame contains a packet with the receiving station's address, it copies the packet into memory, appends any messages it has to send to the token, then relinquishes the token by retransmitting all data packets and the token to the next node on the network. With token passing, each station has equal access to the transmission medium. As with CSMA/CD, each transmitted packet contains source and destination address fields. Successful delivery of a data frame is confirmed by the destination station by setting *frame status flags,* then forwarding the frame around the ring to the original transmitting station. The packet then is removed from the frame before transmitting the token. A token cannot be used twice, and there is a time limitation on how long a token can be held. This prevents one station from disrupting data transmissions on the network by holding the token until it has a packet to transmit. When a station does not possess the token, it can only receive and transfer other packets destined to other stations.

Some 16-Mbps token ring networks use a modified form of token passing methodology where the token is relinquished as soon as a data frame has been transmitted instead of waiting until the transmitted data frame has been returned. This is known as an *early token release mechanism.*

TOKEN PASSING RING

Olaf Soderblum is given credit for developing the first *token passing ring* network architecture in 1969. IBM, however, became the driving force behind the standardization and adoption of the token ring, and a prototype developed by IBM in Zurich, Switzerland,

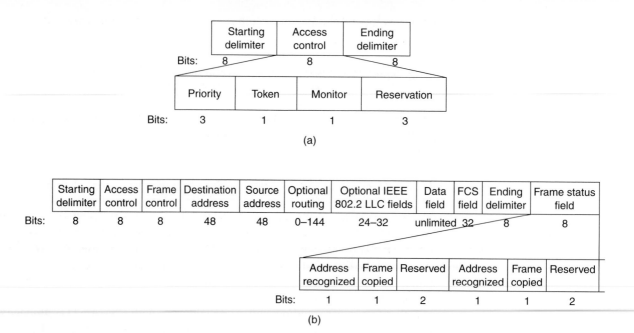

Starting delimiter	Access control	Ending delimiter
8	8	8

Priority	Token	Monitor	Reservation
3	1	1	3

(a)

Starting delimiter	Access control	Frame control	Destination address	Source address	Optional routing	Optional IEEE 802.2 LLC fields	Data field	FCS field	Ending delimiter	Frame status field
8	8	8	48	48	0–144	24–32	unlimited	32	8	8

Address recognized	Frame copied	Reserved	Address recognized	Frame copied	Reserved
1	1	2	1	1	2

(b)

FIGURE 3-22 IEEE 802.5 Token and MAC sublayer frame layout: (a) token frame layout; (b) MAC sublayer frame layout

served as a model for the IEEE Token Ring Standard 802.5. IEEE 802.5 does not include a specification for a transmission rate (bps) for token rings although IBM has specified token ring networks that operate at both 4 Mbps and 16 Mbps.

Figure 3-22a shows the token layout for the IEEE 802.5 specified frame. The token consists of three *octets* where an octet is 8 bits of data. The words octet and byte are often used interchangeably as the difference between them is rather subtle and subject to opinion. A byte is sometimes thought of as an 8-bit word that represents a particular character, number, or function, whereas an octet is merely 8 bits of data, which could represent digitized voice, video, image, or other digital information or possibly even be broken down into smaller groupings. On the other hand, a byte of data is sometimes thought of as simply any meaningful grouping of bits regardless of length. The basic functions of the fields within IEEE 802.5 token and sublayer frames are briefly summarized below.

Starting delimiter field. The starting delimiter field alerts receive stations on a token passing ring that a frame is approaching. Both the token and MAC sublayer frames begin with a starting delimiter.

Access control field. The access control field distinguishes between tokens and MAC (media access control) sublayer frames. If the token (T) bit is cleared, the received frame is a free token and the access control field is immediately followed by an ending delimiter. The receive station can obtain the token by setting the token bit. The starting delimiter field plus the access control field with the T-bit set form the first two fields of the IEEE 802.5 MAC sublayer data frame (shown in Figure 3-22b), allowing the station to append address information, data, and the remaining fields in the data frame layout, then transmit the frame onto the network.

The monitor (M) bit in the access control field is used by the station designated as the active token monitor to manage error conditions such as no token circulating and persistent busy token. The monitor station detects a lost-token condition by using a timeout greater than the time necessary for the longest frame to traverse the complete ring. If no token is detected during this time, it is assumed to be lost. To recover, the monitor station purges the ring of any residual data and releases a free token. To detect a circulating busy token, the monitor station sets a monitor bit to a logic 1 on any passing busy token. If it detects a busy token with the M-bit already set, it knows that the originating station failed to purge its packet. The monitor station then changes the busy token to a free token.

The three priority (P) bits within the access control field are used to prioritize stations waiting to transmit onto the network. There are eight levels of priority. The three reservation (R) bits are used to reserve future tokens. A station having a higher priority than the current busy token can reserve the next free token for its priority level as the busy token passes by. After the current transmitting station has completed its transmission, it issues a free token at the higher priority level. Stations with a lower priority level cannot seize the token, thus, allowing it to pass on to the requesting station of equal or higher priority.

Frame control field. If the received frame contained a set T-bit in the access control field, then the frame is the MAC sublayer data frame and the next field is the frame control field, which indicates whether the frame contains data or is a special network management frame.

Source and destination address fields. The source and destination address fields each contain six octets that identify the sending and receiving stations, respectively.

Routing information field (RIF). The routing information field is optional and used with devices called source routing bridges, which are used to link together multiple token ring LANs. The RIF can be up to 18 octets long.

IEEE 802.2 logical link control (LLC) fields. The LLC fields contain three or four optional octets for the destination service access point (DSAP) field, source service access point (SSAP) field, and control field. The DSAP and SSAP fields are used to identify the types of protocols embedded within the data field. Service access point codes are assigned by the IEEE to identify particular protocols. For example, the SAP code EO identifies a Novell protocol and a SAP code of 06 identifies a TCP/IP protocol.

Data field. The data field contains embedded upper-level protocol data if the frame is a data frame, and network management information if the frame is a network management frame. The length of the data field is unlimited as long as the transmitting station does not exceed the timing limit that a station can possess a token. For example, a 10 ms time limit places a practical limit on the length of the data field in a 4-Mbps token ring network of approximately 4500 bytes and of 16,000 to 18,000 bytes on a 16-Mbps network.

Frame check sequence (FCS) field. IEEE 802.5 specifies a 32-bit cyclic redundancy check identical to that used with IEEE 802.3.

Ending delimiter field. The ending delimiter field notifies the receiving station when the end of a frame has arrived and also whether or not the frame is an intermediate frame with more related data immediately following. The ending delimiter can also indicate that a station other than the source or destination stations has detected an error in a frame. When an error is detected, the frame should be ignored and returned around the ring to the source station for removal.

Frame status field. The frame status field contains 8 bits that are used to let the source station know if the frame was successfully delivered. If the destination station recognizes its address, the address recognize bits are set. If the frame was successfully copied into the destination station's memory, the frame copied bits are set. There are two address recognize and frame copied bits for redundancy because this field is not checked by the FCS field.

In addition to the functions described in the previous sections, the station designated as the active monitor for the network must perform the following tasks:

Remove frames that have not been removed by the sending station.

Regenerate lost or damaged tokens.

Provide a special 24-bit buffer if the physical length of the ring is not long enough to provide enough time delay (latency) to hold the 24-bit token.

Control the master system clock.

Ensure that there is only one station designated as the active monitor.

Slotted Ring

The *slotted ring* is a variation of the token passing ring. With the slotted ring, a finite number of contiguous time slots are circulated around the ring. Each slot is of fixed size and contains positions in the slot for source and destination addresses and packet data. A *busy/not busy* bit is included at the beginning of each circulating slot to indicate whether that slot is available or not. A slot is either *full* or *empty,* depending on the logic condition of the busy/not busy bit (logic 0 = empty, logic 1 = full). If a station (node) wishes to transmit data, it must find an empty time slot. The transmitting station inserts its data into the empty slot in the appropriate place, sets the busy bit, then passes the slot on to the next station. When a station identifies its address in a received packet, it copies the data into its buffers and resets the busy bit to indicate that slot is now empty and available for subsequent nodes to use.

Token Bus

Token passing is occasionally used in a bus or tree topology. In such a configuration, stations on the bus must form a logical ring. However, because the physical layout of a bus does not conform to a ring format, some kind of orderly and logical sequence has to be devised to pass the token from node to node. The token, with its destination address, is passed around the bus in a virtual ring configuration. That is, each station receives and transmits to predetermined stations as though they were up or down link from them. Again, a control packet, known as a token, regulates the right of access. When a station receives the token, it is granted control of the transmission medium for a predetermined time slot. The station may transmit one or more packets and may poll other stations or receive packets. When a station is done with the packet or when the prescribed time is over, the station passes the token on to the next logical station. Nontoken stations are allowed on the bus; however, they can only respond to polls from other stations or requests for acknowledgment.

ETHERNET

Ethernet is a baseband data transmission system designed by Xerox Corporation in the middle 1970s. A man named Robert Metcalfe, who later become the founder of 3COM Corporation, generally is considered to be the original inventor of Ethernet. By 1980, Xerox joined forces with Intel Corporation and Digital Equipment Corporation (DEC) in an attempt to make Ethernet an industry standard. In 1981 a version of Ethernet called DIX 1.0 or Ethernet I was developed. Ethernet I was replaced in 1982 by DIX 2.0 or Ethernet II, which remains the current standard. By 1983, the consortium had developed and introduced a single-chip controller for Ethernet. Later, Mostek Corporation, working with DEC and Advanced Micro Devices, announced a two-chip set for this purpose—one chip in the local area network controller for Ethernet (LANCE) and the second as a serial interface adapter. After adding safety and signaling features, the IEEE Standards Committee adopted Ethernet and published the initial Ethernet standard known as 10BASE-5. The term 10BASE-5 refers to the specifications for the physical layer and data link layers of the ISO network hierarchy. The 10 means that this adaption of Ethernet operates at 10 Mbps, and the word BASE means the LAN carries baseband data (i.e., no carrier). The 5 indicates that the maximum end-to-end network length is 500 m unless a repeater is used to amplify the signals. Ethernet uses CSMA/CD to access the network.

The combined ANSI/IEEE 802.3 subcommittee has defined alternative transmission media to the 10BASE-5 system. Today, there are four Ethernet specifications: 10BASE-5 (Thick Ethernet), 10BASE-2 (Thinwire Ethernet), 1BASE-5 (StarLAN), and 10BASE-T (Twisted-Pair Ethernet). Currently, efforts are underway to develop methods of transporting Ethernet signals on optical fiber cables [10BASE-FL (FOIRL)—fiber optic inter-repeater link], over radio frequency broadcasts (both terrestrial and satellite), and on infrared light systems at transmission rates in excess of 100 Mbps. The 1BASE-5 Ethernet system has never received widespread acceptance by industry due to its slow transmission rate, therefore, it will not be discussed.

10BASE-5 Ethernet

10BASE-5 is the original Ethernet system that specifies a "thick" 50 Ω, double-shielded coaxial cable for a transmission medium. Hence, this version of Ethernet is sometimes called *Thicknet* or *Thick Ethernet*. Because of its inflexible nature, 10BASE-5 Ethernet is also sometimes called "frozen yellow garden hose." The 10BASE-5 system uses a multidrop bus topology as shown in Figure 3-23. The 10BASE-5 system supports up to 100 nodes per segment with a minimum node separation of 2.5 m. Three additional 500 m segments can be added, provided a repeater is used to amplify the signals and pass them from one segment to another. Thus, the maximum system length is extended to 1500 m, as shown between points A and C in Figure 3-23. Remote repeaters can be used with a maximum distance of 1000 m between them, thus, extending the maximum end-to-end length to 2.5 km. In Figure 3-23, if the center and right segments were interchanged, there would be a 2.5 km separation between points A and B. However, there must always be only one signal path between any two stations. 10BASE-5 Ethernet uses a device called *media access unit* (MAU) to connect terminals to the cable. Each connection is called a *tap* and the cable that connects a MAU to its terminal is called a *drop*. Within each MAU, a transceiver transfers the electrical signals between the drop and the coaxial transmission medium.

The baseband protocol for 10BASE-5 supports a 10-Mbps transmission rate that uses a signaling technique known as *Manchester encoding*. Manchester encoding is used when a system clock is not provided on a separate line. With Manchester encoding, each bit cell is divided into two parts: the first half contains the complement of the bit value and the second half contains the actual bit value. Thus, a low-to-high transition in the middle of a bit cell represents a logic 1 and a high-to-low transition represents a logic 0. The Manchester encoding format is shown in Figure 3-24. This coding format ensures that a signal transition occurs in every bit cell, enhancing clock recovery. This technique of recovering a clock from the serial data stream is sometimes called *self-clocking*. The Manchester format also ensures that the encoded bit stream will be high 50% of the time and low 50% of the time, thus, reducing the charge developed across the inherent capacitance of the transmission.

10BASE-2 Ethernet

10BASE-5 Ethernet uses 50 Ω RG-11 coaxial cable, which is thick enough to give it a high noise immunity, thus, making it well suited to laboratory and industrial applications. The RG-11 cable is expensive to install. Consequently, the initial costs of implementing a 10BASE-5 Ethernet system are too high for many small businesses. In an effort to reduce the cost, International Computer Ltd., Hewlett-Packard, and 3COM Corporation developed an Ethernet variation that uses thinner, less expensive 50 Ω RG-58 coaxial cable. RG-58 is similar to the cable used to carry television signals. It is less expensive to purchase and to install than RG-11. In 1985, the IEEE 803.2 Standards Committee

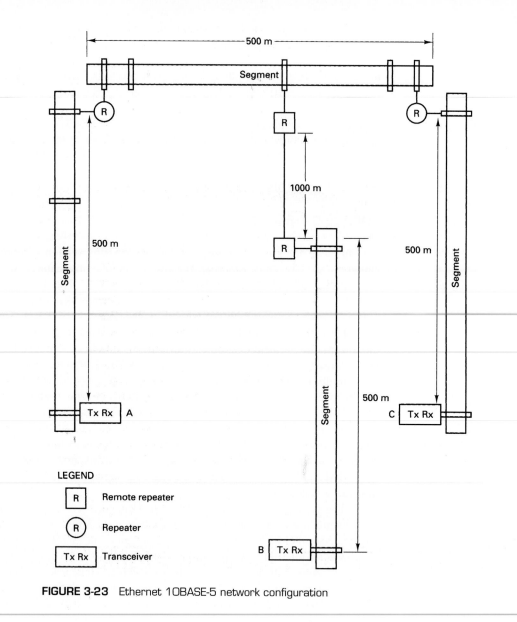

FIGURE 3-23 Ethernet 10BASE-5 network configuration

FIGURE 3-24 Manchester code

adopted the new version of Ethernet and gave it the name 10BASE-2. 10BASE-2 Ethernet is sometimes referred to as *CheaperNet* or *Thinwire Ethernet*. 10BASE-2 Ethernet allows a maximum segment length of 185 m with a maximum of 30 nodes per segment, which is sufficient for most office applications. 10BASE-2 Ethernet also eliminates the MAU. The transceiver is located inside the terminal and a simple BNC-T connector connects the Ethernet network interface card (NIC) directly to the coaxial cable. This eliminates the expensive transceiver cable and the need to tap or drill into the coaxial cable. CheaperNet is most popular in PC-based LAN applications.

10BASE-T Ethernet

10BASE-T Ethernet is another popular Ethernet transmission standard commonly used with PC-based LAN environments, utilizing a star topology. The "T" stands for *unshielded twisted-pair wire,* or simply UTP. The 10-BASE-T system was developed to allow Ethernet to utilize existing voice-grade telephone wiring to carry Ethernet signals. Standard modular RJ45 and RJ11 telephone jacks and four-pair UTP telephone wire are specified in the standard for interconnecting nodes to the LAN. The RJ45 connector plugs directly into the *network interface card* located in the PC. 10BASE-T operates at a transmission rate of 10 Mbps and uses the standard CSMA/CD protocol; however, it uses a *concentrator* to distribute the transmission media to the end-users, essentially converting a number of point-to-point connections into a single LAN. The concentrator is basically an intelligent "hub" or multipoint repeater that expands the 10BASE-5 star topology.

Nodes are added to the network through a port. When a node is turned on, its transceiver sends a DC current over the twisted pair to the hub. The hub senses the current and enables the port, thus, connecting the node to the network. The port remains connected as long as the node continues to supply DC current to the hub. If the node is turned off, or, if an open or short circuit condition arises in the twisted pair between the node and the hub, the DC current stops and the hub disconnects the port while the remainder of the LAN continues to operate status quo.

Ethernet Data Format

In actuality, Ethernet II and IEEE standard 802.3 are not identical, although the term Ethernet is generally used to refer to any IEEE 802.3-compliant network. Ethernet and IEEE 802.3 both specify that data are transmitted from one station to another in blocks called frames. The frame formats for both the IEEE 802.3 standard and Ethernet are shown in Figure 3-25 and described as follows.

Ethernet II frame layout

Preamble. The preamble consists of 8 bytes (64 bits) of alternating 1s and 0s. The purpose of the preamble is to establish clock synchronization. The last 2 bits of the preamble are reserved for the start frame delimiter.

Preamble	Destination address	Source address	Type	Data unit	Frame check sequence
Bytes: 8	6	6	2	46–1500	4

(a)

Preamble	Start frame delimiter	Destination address	Source address	Length	Logical link control IEEE 802.2 data	Frame check sequence	End of frame delimiter
Bytes: 7	1	2–6	2–6	2	46–1500	4	9.6 μs

(b)

FIGURE 3-25 (a) Ethernet frame layout; (b) IEEE 802.3 frame layout

Start frame delimiter. The start frame delimiter is simply a series of two logic 1s appended to the end of the preamble whose purpose is to mark the end of the preamble and the beginning of the data frame.

Destination address. The source and destination addresses and the field type make up the frame header. The destination address consists of 6 bytes (48 bits) and is the address of the node or nodes that have been designated to receive the frame. The address can be a unique, group, or broadcast address and is determined by the following bit combinations:

bit 0=0. If bit 0 is a 0, the address is interpreted as a unique address intended for only one station.

bit 0=1. If bit 0 is a 1, the address is interpreted as a multicast (group) address. All stations that have been preassigned with this group address will accept the frame.

bit 0–47. If all bits in the destination field are 1s, this identifies a broadcast address and all nodes have been identified as receivers of this frame.

Source address. The source address consists of 6 bytes (48 bits) that correspond to the address of the station sending the frame.

Type field. Ethernet does not use the 16-bit type field. It is placed in the frame so it can be used for higher layers of the OSI protocol hierarchy.

Data field. The data field contains the information and can be between 46 bytes and 1500 bytes long. The data field is transparent. Data link control characters and zero-bit stuffing are not used. Transparency is achieved by counting back from the FCS character.

Frame check sequence field. The CRC field contains 32 bits for error detection and is computed from the header and data fields.

IEEE 802.3 standard frame layout

Preamble. The preamble consists of 7 bytes to establish clock synchronization. The last byte of the preamble is used for the start frame delimiter.

Start frame delimiter. The start frame delimiter is simply a series of two logic 1s appended to the end of the preamble whose purpose is to mark the end of the preamble and the beginning of the data frame.

Destination and source addresses. The destination and source addresses are defined the same as with Ethernet II.

Length field. The 2-byte length field in the IEEE 802.3 frame replaces the type field in the Ethernet frame. The length field indicates the length of the variable-length logical link control (LLC) data field, which contains all upper-layered embedded protocols.

Logical link control (LLC). The LLC field contains the information and can be between 46 bytes and 1500 bytes long. The LLC field defined in IEEE 802.3 is identical to the LLC field defined for token ring networks.

Frame check sequence field. The CRC field is defined the same as with Ethernet II.

End of frame delimiter. The end frame delimiter is a period of time (9.6 μs) in which no bits are transmitted. With Manchester encoding, a void in transitions longer than 1-bit time indicates the end of the frame.

System Operation

Transmission. The data link control for Ethernet is CSMA/CD. Stations acquire access to the transmission system through contention. They are not polled, nor do they have specific time slots for transmission. A station wishing to transmit first determines if another station is currently using the transmission system. The controller accomplishes this through the transceiver by sensing the presence of a carrier on the line. The controller may be a hardware or a software function, depending on the complexity of the station.

The presence of a carrier is denoted by the signal transitions on the line produced by the Manchester code. If a carrier is detected, the station defers transmission until the line is quiet. After the required delay, the station sends digital data to the controller. The controller converts these data to Manchester code, inserts the CRC, adds the preamble, and places the packet on-line. The transmission of the entire packet is not yet assured. A different station may also have detected the quiet line and started to transmit its own packet. The first station monitors the line for a period called the *collision window* or the *collision interval*. This interval is a function of the end-to-end propagation delay of the line. This delay, including the delay caused by any repeaters, measured in distance, cannot exceed 2.5 km. If a data collision has not occurred in this interval, the station is said to have line acquisition and will continue to transmit the entire packet. Should a collision be detected, both of the transmitting stations will immediately abort their transmissions for a random period of time and then attempt retransmission. A data collision may be detected by the transceiver by comparing the received signal with the transmitted signal. To make this comparison, a station must still be transmitting its packet while a previously transmitted signal has propagated to the end of the line and back. This dictates that a packet be of some minimum size. If a collision is detected, it is the controller that must take the necessary action. The controller-transceiver interface contains a line for notification of Collision Presence (10-MHz square wave). The remaining three lines of this interface are the Transmit Data, Receive Data, and power for the transceiver. Because a collision is manifested in some form of phase violation, the controller alone may detect a collision. In Ethernet, data collision is detected mainly by the transceiver. When feasible, this is supplemented by a collision detection facility in the controller. To ensure that all stations are aware of the collision, a *collision enforcement consensus procedure* is invoked. When the controller detects a collision, it transmits four to six bytes of random data. These bytes are called the *jam sequence*. If a collision has occurred, the station's random waiting time before retransmission is determined from a *binary exponential back-off algorithm*. The time slot is usually set to be slightly longer than the round-trip transmission time of the channel. The time of the wait delay is randomly selected from this interval.

Example 3-4

Transmission time slot = time of 512 bits

$$\text{Maximum time of the interval} = \frac{512 \text{ bits}}{10 \text{ Mbps}} = 51.2 \text{ } \mu s$$

$$\text{Time delay interval} = 0 \text{ to } 51.2 \text{ } \mu s$$

For each succeeding collision encountered by the same packet, the time interval is doubled until a maximum interval is reached. The maximum interval is given as $2^{10} \times$ transmission time slot. After 15 unsuccessful attempts at transmitting a packet have been made, no further attempts are made and the error is reported to the station. This is the major drawback of Ethernet—it cannot guarantee packet delivery at a time of heavy transmission load.

Reception. The line is monitored until the station's address is detected. The controller strips the preamble, checks the CRC, and converts the Manchester code back to digital format. If the packet contains any errors, it is discarded. The end of the packet is recognized by the absence of a carrier on the transmission line. This means that no transitions were detected for the period of 75 ns to 125 ns since the center of the last bit cell. The decoding is accomplished through a phase-locked loop. The phase-locked loop is initialized by the known pattern of the preamble.

TABLE 3-13 Comparison of IEEE Standard 802.3 Physical Specifications for Ethernet 10BASE-5, 10BASE-2, and 10BASE-T

	10BASE-5 (Ethernet)	10BASE-2 (CheapNet)	10BASE-T (UTP)
Access control	CSMA/CD	CSMA/CD	CSMA/CD
Topology	Bus	Bus	Star
Message protocol	Variable packet size	Variable packet size	Variable packet size
Signaling rate	10 Mbps	10 Mbps	10 Mbps
Signaling type	Baseband	Baseband	Baseband
Cable type	IEEE 802.3 thick double-shielded coax	RG-58 coax	UTP level 3 or level 4 telephone cable
Cable impedance	50 Ω	50 Ω	NA
Minimum node separation	2.5 m	0.5 m	NA
Maximum segment length	500 m	185 m	100 m (PC to hub)
Maximum nodes per segment	100	30	1024 (per network)
Maximum number of segments	5	2	NA
Maximum station separation	2500 m	925 m	NA

Table 3-13 shows a comparison of IEEE standard 802.3 and Ethernet 10BASE-5, 10BASE-2, and 10BASE-T physical specifications.

FIBER DISTRIBUTED DATA INTERFACE

First-generation LAN standards, such as Ethernet and token ring, do not have the bandwidth necessary to handle the high transmission rates required to communicate multiplexed high-capacity systems carrying digitized sound, still pictures, and compressed video, especially over long distances. Consequently, in 1984 the American National Standards Institute (ANSI) published a set of standards (X3T9.5) called *Fiber Data Distributed Interface* (FDDI). FDDI specifies standards for a ring topology using optical fiber cables with transmission rates up to 100 Mbps that allow for distances up to 2 km between stations. FDDI is not an IEEE standard, however, it does support IEEE 802.2 logical link control protocols, offering a transparent interoperability to layers 3 through 7 of IEEE-compliant protocols.

In addition to wider bandwidths and higher operating speeds, FDDI also has a higher degree of reliability and security than Ethernet and token rings. The higher degree of reliability can be attributed to the transmission medium. Optical fibers are immune to both electromagnetic interference (EMI) and radio frequency interference (RFI). FDDI's physical topology lends itself to a more reliable system because FDDI is comprised of two separate rings: a primary and a backup ring. The topology used with FDDI is a double (dual-counter rotating) ring configuration as shown in Figure 3-26. One of the rings is designated the *primary ring* and the other the *secondary ring*. Data propagates around the two rings in opposite directions. Under normal operating conditions, only the primary ring carries data; the secondary ring is reserved as a backup and used only if the primary ring fails. As with the IEEE 802 standard, FDDI uses token passing for its access method. There are several differences between the two, however, that are intended to allow FDDI to take advantage of its high-speed ring to maximize efficiency.

FDDI Nodes

FDDI LANs can have up to 500 nodes separated by 2 km, and the entire media can extend for a total distance of up to 200 km (125 miles), if repeaters are used at least every 2 km. FDDI can use two types of nodes: *single attach* and *dual attach,* as shown in

Dual-attach stations

Node 2

Primary ring–clockwise direction of propagation

Node 1

Node 3

Secondary ring– counter clockwise direction of propagation

Concentrator

Node 4   Node 5   Node 6   Node 7

Single-attach stations

FIGURE 3-26   FDDI LAN circuit configuration

Figure 3-26. As shown in the figure, dual-attach nodes are stations that are connected to both the primary and the secondary rings of the FDDI LAN. Single-attach nodes are connected to the primary ring only through an access device similar to an Ethernet hub called a *concentrator.* Single-attach stations can not use the secondary ring as a backup if the primary ring fails. Thus, if the connection between the concentrator and the primary ring fails or is broken, all single-attach stations are disconnected from the network. Dual-attach stations must have two optical transmitters and two optical receivers, which obviously makes them more expensive. Consequently, in many FDDI networks only the most critical nodes, such as the network server, are dual attached.

As with Ethernet and token ring hubs, FDDI concentrators are able to sense when one of the single-attach nodes has the power shut off or is disconnected. When this happens, the concentrator disconnects the disabled node from the network. The concentrator also has the ability to completely bypass defective single-attach nodes to restore continuity to the remainder of the primary ring.

Figure 3-27 illustrates self-healing feature of an FDDI network. Whenever there is a break in the cable, the dual-attach nodes on either side of the break connect the primary and secondary rings to form a single, longer ring. The ability of an FDDI network to reconfigure around cable and circuit defects by establishing what is called a *ring-wrap,* makes it more reliable than either Ethernet or token ring networks.

FDDI uses a modified form of token passing for its access methodology. The FDDI methodology is different from IEEE standard 802.5 in two aspects. First, due to the greater lengths possible with FDDI LANs, it is impractical to convert free tokens to busy tokens and allow one station to monopolize the network until it receives confirmation that its last message was successfully received by the destination station. Instead of simply changing the logic condition of the T-bit in the access control byte, FDDI physically removes the token from the ring and transmits a full data frame. After completing transmission, a new token is released. Collisions are avoided as only one station can possess the free token at a time.

The second aspect that is different with FDDI is that numerous successive messages can be sent by a single station before it must relinquish the token. Recall that IEEE 802.5

FIGURE 3-27 FDDI self-healing feature

Preamble	Starting delimiter	Frame control	Ending delimiter
Bytes: 8	1	1	1

(a)

Preamble	Starting delimiter	Frame control	Destination address	Source address	DATA up to	Frame check sequence	Ending delimiter	Frame status
Bytes: 8	1	1	6	6	4500	4 (32 bit CRC)	.5 (4 bits)	1.5 (12 bits)

(b)

FIGURE 3-28 Token and data frame layouts: (a) FDDI token layout; (b) FDDI data frame structure

allows only one message per token per user. Frames transmitted in a continuous stream are called synchronous frames and are prioritized according to a methodology known as *synchronous bandwidth allocation* (SBA). Figure 3-28 shows the layout for an FDDI token and an FDDI data frame structure.

FDDI Network Using Twisted-Pair Metallic Transmission Lines

FDDI was originally designed to be used with an optical fiber transmission line rather than copper wires. Optical fiber cables can support higher data transmission rates, are much more immune to noise interference, and do not radiate electromagnetic energy as do their metallic counterparts. However, the transducers used with optical fiber cables that convert light energy to electrical energy (photodetectors) and vice versa (light emitting diodes) are relatively expensive and can add several hundred dollars to the cost of each node in the FDDI network.

To reduce the initial cost of an FDDI network, ANSI published a version of the FDDI standard that specifies twisted-pair metallic wire rather than an optical fiber cable. The standard specifies a transmission rate of 100 Mbps using the same protocol as the optical fiber version of FDDI. Because most standard telephone cable can not support a 100 Mbps data rate, special *data-grade* cable must be installed. Even with the more expensive cable, however, metallic FDDI networks are still less expensive than optical cable systems.

Fibre Channel

Although high-speed network standards, such as FDDI, provide relatively inexpensive, reliable digital communications at data rates up to 100 Mbps, many commercial, educational, industrial, and scientific environments are still investigating systems that support even higher data rates. Hewlett-Packard Co., IBM, and Sun Microsystems Computer Corp. recently announced the *Fibre Channel Systems Initiative* as an incentive to accelerate development of an affordable, high-speed interconnection standard for workstations and peripherals using optical fiber communications channels. The ANSI X3T9.3 *Fibre Channel Standard* is designed to facilitate data transmission rates in excess of 1 Gbps for distances up to 10 km using an optical fiber transmission medium.

The Fibre data channel specifies a matrix of switches, called a *fabric,* that performs network switching functions that are similar to those used with a standard telephone system. Computer systems attach to the fabric using dedicated transmit and receive lines designed to function as point-to-point, bidirectional serial communications channels. Network switches are capable of routing incoming data signals to any output port.

100BASE-T Ethernet

The 100BASE-T Ethernet includes a family of fast Ethernet standards offering 100 Mbps data transmission rates using CSMA/CD access methodology. Proposed IEEE Standard 802.3u details operation of the 100BASE-T network. There are three media-specific physical layer standards for 100BASE-T: 100BASE-TX, 100BASE-T4, and 100BASE-FX.

1. 100BASE-TX is the most common of the three standards and the one with the most technology available. The 100BASE-TX specifies 100 Mbps data transmission rates over two pair of Category 5 UTP (unshielded twisted pair) or two pair of Type 1 STP (shielded twisted pair).
2. 100BASE-T4 is a physical layer standard specifying 100 Mbps data rates over four pair of Category 3, 4, or 5 UTP.
3. 100BASE-FX is a physical layer standard specifying 100 Mbps data rates over optical fiber cables.

QUESTIONS

3-1. Define data communications protocol.

3-2. What is a master station? A slave station?

3-3. Define *polling* and *selecting.*

3-4. What is the difference between a synchronous and an asynchronous protocol?

3-5. What is the difference between a character-oriented protocol and a bit-oriented protocol?

3-6. Define the three operating modes used with data communications circuits.

3-7. What is the function of the clearing character?

3-8. What is a unique address? A group address? A broadcast address?

3-9. What does a negative acknowledgment to a poll indicate?

3-10. What is the purpose of a heading?

3-11. Why is IBM's 3270 synchronous protocol called bisync?

3-12. Why are SYN characters always transmitted in pairs?

3-13. What is an SPA? An SSA? A DA?

3-14. What is the purpose of a leading pad? A trailing pad?

3-15. What is the difference between a general poll and a specific poll?

3-16. What is a handshake?

3-17. (Primary, secondary) stations transmit polls.

3-18. What does a negative acknowledgment to a poll indicate?

3-19. What is a positive acknowledgment to a poll?

3-20. What is the difference between ETX, ETB, and ITB?

3-21. What character is used to terminate a heading and begin a block of text?

3-22. What is transparency? When is it necessary? Why?

3-23. What is the difference between a command and a response with SDLC?

3-24. What are the three transmission states used with SDLC? Explain them.

3-25. What are the five fields used with an SDLC frame? Briefly explain each.

3-26. What is the delimiting sequence used with SDLC?

3-27. What is the null address in SDLC? When is it used?

3-28. What are the three frame formats used with SDLC? Explain what each format is used for.

3-29. How is an information frame identified in SDLC? A supervisory frame? An unnumbered frame?

3-30. What are the purposes of the nr and ns sequences in SDLC?

3-31. With SDLC, when is the P bit set? The F bit?

3-32. What is the maximum number of unconfirmed frames that can be outstanding at any one time with SDLC? Why?

3-33. With SDLC, which frame formats can have an information field?

3-34. With SDLC, which frame formats can be used to confirm previously received frames?

3-35. What command/response is used for reporting procedural errors with SDLC?

3-36. Explain the three modes in SDLC that a secondary station can be in.

3-37. When is the configure command/response used with SDLC?

3-38. What is a go-ahead sequence? A turnaround sequence?

3-39. What is the transparency mechanism used with SDLC?

3-40. What is a message abort? When is it transmitted?

3-41. Explain invert-on-zero encoding. Why is it used?

3-42. What supervisory condition exists with HDLC that is not included with SDLC?

3-43. What is the delimiting sequence used with HDLC? The transparency mechanism?

3-44. Explain extended addressing as it is used with HDLC.

3-45. What is the difference between the basic control format and the extended control format with HDLC?

3-46. What is the difference in the information fields used with SDLC and HDLC?

3-47. What operational modes are included with HDLC that are not included with SDLC?

3-48. What is a public data network?

3-49. Describe a value-added network.

3-50. Explain the differences in circuit-, message-, and packet-switching techniques.

3-51. What is blocking? With which switching techniques is blocking possible?

3-52. What is a transparent switch? A transactional switch?

3-53. What is a packet?

3-54. What is the difference between a store-and-forward and a hold-and-forward network?

3-55. Explain the three modes of transmission for public data networks.

3-56. What is the user-to-network protocol designated by CCITT?

3-57. What is the user-to-network protocol designated by ANSI?

3-58. Which layers of the ISO protocol hierarchy are addressed by X.25?

3-59. Explain the following terms: permanent virtual circuit, virtual call, and datagram.

3-60. Why was HDLC selected as the link-level protocol for X.25?

3-61. Briefly explain the fields that make up an X.25 call request packet.

3-62. Describe a local area network.

3-63. What is the connecting medium used with local area networks?

3-64. Explain the two transmission formats used with local area networks.

3-65. Explain CSMA/CD.

3-66. Explain token passing.

3-67. Describe what an ISDN is and who proposed its concept.

3-68. What are the primary principles of ISDN?

3-69. What are the evolutions of ISDN?

3-70. Describe the proposed architecture for ISDN.

3-71. Describe an ISDN D channel. An ISDN B channel.

3-72. Describe the following ISDN terms: terminal equipment 1; terminal equipment 2; terminal adapter; reference point S; reference point T; reference point R; network termination 1; network termination 2; network termination 1,2; line termination unit; exchange termination; and reference point V.

3-73. Describe the ISDN LAP-D format.

3-74. What are the differences between the ISDN LAP-D and LAP-B formats?

3-75. What is an ISDN service point identifier and when is it used?

3-76. What is an ISDN terminal endpoint identifier and when is it used?

3-77. Describe the basic concepts of BISDN and how it differs from narrowband ISDN.

3-78. What is meant by the asynchronous transfer mode?

3-79. What are the proposed new BISDN channel data rates?

3-80. What is the transmission media used with the asynchronous transfer mode communications standard?

3-81. Describe virtual channels and virtual paths as they are used with ATM.

3-82. Identify and explain the various subfields used with an ATM header field.

3-83. Identify and explain the various subfields used within an ATM information field.

3-84. What is the primary transmission media used with SONET?

3-85. Describe the frame format used with SONET.

3-86. What multiplexing technique is used with SONET to achieve higher levels of synchronous transport?

3-87. Describe the topologies commonly used with LANs.

3-88. List and describe the transmission formats used with LANs.

3-89. List and describe the access control methodologies used with LANs.

3-90. Describe the various fields and sublayer frames used with a token passing ring network.

3-91. Describe the operation of a slotted ring LAN.

3-92. What is Ethernet?

3-93. Briefly describe the following Ethernet systems: 10BASE-5, 10BASE-2, and 10BASE-T.

3-94. Identify and explain the various sections of an Ethernet II frame layout.

PROBLEMS

3-1. Determine the hex code for the control field in an SDLC frame for the following conditions: information frame, poll, transmitting frame 4, and confirming reception of frames 2, 3, and 4.

3-2. Determine the hex code for the control field in an SDLC frame for the following conditions: supervisory frame, ready to receive, final, confirming reception of frames 6, 7, and 0.

3-3. Insert 0s into the following SDLC data stream.

111 001 000 011 111 111 100 111 110 100 111 101 011 111 111 111 001 011

3-4. Delete 0s from the following SDLC data stream.

010 111 110 100 011 011 111 011 101 110 101 111 101 011 100 011 111 00

3-5. Sketch the NRZI waveform for the following data stream (start with a high condition).

1 0 0   1 1 1   0 0 1   0 1 0

3-6. Determine the hex code for the control field in an SDLC frame for the following conditions: information frame, not a poll, transmitting frame number 5, and confirming the reception of frames 0, 1, 2, and 3.

3-7. Determine the hex code for the control field in an SDLC frame for the following conditions: supervisory frame, not ready to receive, not a final, confirming reception of frames 7, 0, 1, and 2.

3-8. Insert 0s into the following SDLC data stream.

011011111110110000111100101110001011111111011111001

3-9 Delete 0s from the following SDLC data stream.

00101111100111110111110110001000111101110101100101

3-10. Sketch the NRZI levels for the following data stream (start with a high condition).

1 1 0 1 0 0 0 1 1 0 1

C H A P T E R 4

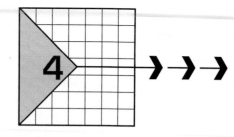

Digital Transmission

INTRODUCTION

As stated previously, digital transmission is the transmittal of digital pulses between two points in a communications system. The original source information may already be in digital form or it may be analog signals that must be converted to digital pulses prior to transmission and converted back to analog form at the receive end. With digital transmission systems, a physical facility such as a metallic wire pair, a coaxial cable, or an optical fiber link is required to interconnect the two points in the system. The pulses are contained in and propagate down the facility.

Advantages of Digital Transmission

1. The primary advantage of digital transmission is noise immunity. Analog signals are more susceptible than digital pulses to undesired amplitude, frequency, and phase variations. This is because with digital transmission, it is not necessary to evaluate these parameters as precisely as with analog transmission. Instead, the received pulses are evaluated during a sample interval, and a simple determination is made whether the pulse is above or below a certain threshold.

2. Digital pulses are better suited to processing and multiplexing than analog signals. Digital pulses can be stored easily, whereas analog signals cannot. Also, the transmission rate of a digital system can be changed easily to adapt to different environments and to interface with different types of equipment. Multiplexing is explained in detail in Chapter 5.

3. Digital systems use signal regeneration rather than signal amplification, thus, producing a more noise resistant system than their analog counterpart.

4. Digital signals are simpler to measure and evaluate. Therefore, it is easier to compare the performance of digital systems with different signaling and information capacities than it is with comparable analog systems.

5. Digital systems are better suited to evaluate error performance (i.e., error detection and correction) than analog systems.

Disadvantages of Digital Transmission

1. The transmission of digitally encoded analog signals requires more bandwidth than simply transmitting the analog signal.

2. Analog signals must be converted to digital codes prior to transmission and converted back to analog at the receiver.

3. Digital transmission requires precise time synchronization between transmitter and receiver clocks.

4. Digital transmission systems are incompatible with existing analog facilities.

PULSE MODULATION

Pulse modulation includes many different methods of converting information into pulse form for transferring pulses from a source to a destination. The four predominant methods are *pulse width modulation* (PWM), *pulse position modulation* (PPM), *pulse amplitude modulation* (PAM), and *pulse code modulation* (PCM). The four most common methods of pulse modulation are summarized below and shown in Figure 4-1.

1. PWM. This method is sometimes called pulse duration modulation (PDM) or pulse length modulation (PLM). The pulse width (active portion of the duty cycle) is proportional to the amplitude of the analog signal.

2. PPM. The position of a constant-width pulse within a prescribed time slot is varied according to the amplitude of the analog signal.

3. PAM. The amplitude of a constant-width, constant-position pulse is varied according to the amplitude of the analog signal.

4. PCM. The analog signal is sampled and converted to a fixed-length, serial binary number for transmission. The binary number varies according to the amplitude of the analog signal.

PAM is used as an intermediate form of modulation with PSK, QAM, and PCM, although it is seldom used by itself. PWM and PPM are used in special-purpose communications systems (usually for the military) but are seldom used for commercial systems. PCM is by far the most prevalent method of pulse modulation and, consequently, will be the topic of discussion for the remainder of this chapter.

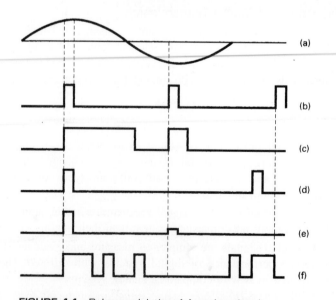

FIGURE 4-1 Pulse modulation: [a] analog signal;
[b] sample pulse; [c] PWM; [d] PPM; [e] PAM; [f] PCM

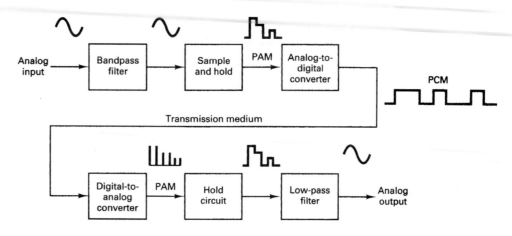

FIGURE 4-2 Simplified PCM system block diagram

PULSE CODE MODULATION

Pulse code modulation (PCM) is the only one of the digitally encoded pulse modulation techniques previously mentioned that is used in a digital transmission system. With PCM, the pulses are of fixed length and fixed amplitude. PCM is a binary system; a pulse or lack of a pulse within a prescribed time slot represents either a logic 1 or a logic 0 condition. With PWM, PPM, or PAM, a single pulse does not represent a single binary digit (bit).

Figure 4-2 shows a simplified block diagram of a single-channel, *simplex (one-way-only)* PCM system. The bandpass filter limits the input analog signal to the standard voice-band frequency range 300 Hz to 3000 Hz. The *sample-and-hold* circuit periodically samples the analog input and converts those samples to a multilevel PAM signal. The *analog-to-digital converter* (ADC) converts the PAM samples to a serial binary data stream for transmission. The transmission medium is a metallic wire or optical fiber.

At the receive end, the *digital-to-analog converter* (DAC) converts the serial binary data stream to a multilevel PAM signal. The hold circuit and low-pass filter convert the PAM signal back to its original analog form. An integrated circuit that performs the PCM encoding and decoding is called a *codec* (*co*der/*dec*oder). The codec is explained in detail in Chapter 5.

The purpose of the sample-and-hold circuit is to sample periodically the continually changing analog input signal and convert the samples to a series of constant-amplitude PAM levels. For the ADC to accurately convert a signal to a digital code, the signal must be relatively constant. If not, before the ADC can complete the conversion, the input would change. Therefore, the ADC continually would be attempting to follow the analog changes and never stabilize on any PCM code.

Figure 4-3 shows the schematic diagram of a sample-and-hold circuit. The FET acts as a simple switch. When turned on, it provides a low-impedance path to deposit the analog sample voltage on capacitor C_1. The time that Q_1 is on is called the *aperture* or *acquisition time*. Essentially, C_1 is the hold circuit. When Q_1 is off, the capacitor does not have a complete path to discharge through and, therefore, stores the sampled voltage. The *storage time* of the capacitor is called the A/D *conversion time* because it is during this time that the ADC converts the sample voltage to a digital code. The acquisition time should be very short. This assures that a minimum change occurs in the analog signal while it is being deposited across C_1. If the input to the ADC is changing while it is performing the conversion, distortion results. This distortion is called *aperture distortion*. Thus, by having a short aperture time and keeping the input to the ADC relatively

FIGURE 4-3 Sample-and-hold circuit

FIGURE 4-4 Sample-and-hold waveforms: (a) analog in; (b) sample pulse; (c) capacitor voltage

constant, the sample-and-hold circuit reduces aperture distortion. If the analog signal is sampled for a short period of time and the sample voltage is held at a constant amplitude during the A/D conversion time, this is called *flat-top sampling*. If the sample time is made longer and the analog-to-digital conversion takes place with a changing analog signal, this is called *natural sampling*. Natural sampling introduces more aperture distortion than flat-top sampling and requires a faster A/D converter.

Figure 4-4 shows the input analog signal, the sampling pulse, and the waveform developed across C_1. It is important that the output impedance of voltage follower Z_1 and the on resistance of Q_1 be as small as possible. This assures that the *RC* charging time constant of the capacitor is kept very short, allowing the capacitor to charge or discharge rapidly during the short acquisition time. The rapid drop in the capacitor voltage immediately following each sample pulse is due to the redistribution of the charge across C_1. The interelectrode capacitance between the gate and drain of the FET is placed in series with C_1 when the FET is off, thus, acting as a capacitive voltage-divider network. Also, note the gradual discharge across the capacitor during the conversion time. This is called *droop* and is caused by the capacitor discharging through its own leakage resistance and the input impedance of voltage follower Z_2. Therefore, it is important that the input impedance of Z_2 and the leakage resistance of C_1 be as high as possible. Essentially, voltage followers Z_1 and Z_2 isolate the sample-and-hold circuit (Q_1 and C_1) from the input and output circuitry.

Chapter 4   Digital Transmission

Example 4-1

For the sample-and-hold circuit shown in Figure 4-3, determine the largest-value capacitor that can be used. Use an output impedance for Z_1 of 10 Ω, an on resistance for Q_1 of 10 Ω, an acquisition time of 10 μs, a maximum peak-to-peak input voltage of 10 V, a maximum output current from Z_1 of 10 mA, and an accuracy of 1%.

Solution The expression for the current through a capacitor is

$$i = C\frac{dv}{dt}$$

Rearranging and solving for C yields

$$C = i\frac{dt}{dv}$$

where C = maximum capacitance (F)
$\quad\quad\quad\quad i$ = maximum output current from Z_1, 10 mA
$\quad\quad\quad dv$ = maximum change in voltage across C_1, which equals 10 V
$\quad\quad\quad dt$ = charge time, which equals the aperture time, 10 μs

Therefore, $$C_{max} = \frac{(10\text{ mA})(10\text{ }\mu\text{s})}{10\text{ V}} = 10\text{ nF}$$

The charge time constant for C when Q_1 is on is

$$\tau = RC$$

where τ = one charge time constant (s)
$\quad\quad\quad R$ = output impedance of Z_1 plus the on resistance of Q_1 (Ω)
$\quad\quad\quad C$ = capacitance value of C_1 (F)

Rearranging and solving for C gives us

$$C_{max} = \frac{\tau}{R}$$

The charge time of capacitor C_1 is also dependent on the accuracy desired from the device. The percent accuracy and its required RC time constant are summarized as follows:

Accuracy (%)	Charge Time
10	2.3τ
1	4.6τ
0.1	7τ
0.01	9τ

For an accuracy of 1%, $$C = \frac{10\text{ }\mu\text{s}}{4(20)} = 125\text{ nF}$$

To satisfy the output current limitations of Z_1, a maximum capacitance of 10 nF was required. To satisfy the accuracy requirements, 125 nF was required. To satisfy both requirements, the smaller-value capacitor must be used. Therefore, C_1 can be no larger than 10 nF.

Sampling Rate

The Nyquist sampling theorem establishes the *minimum sampling rate* (f_s) that can be used for a given PCM system. For a sample to be reproduced accurately at the receiver, each cycle of the analog input signal (f_a) must be sampled at least twice. Consequently, the minimum sampling rate is equal to twice the highest audio input frequency. If f_s is less than two times f_a, distortion will result. The distortion is called *aliasing* or *foldover distortion*. Mathematically, the minimum Nyquist sample rate is

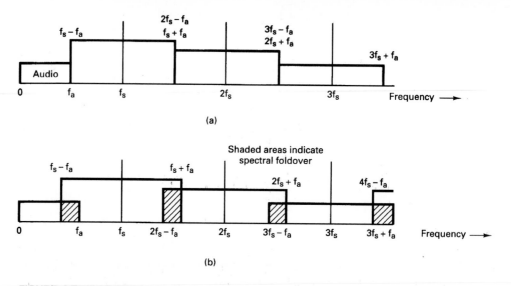

FIGURE 4-5 Output spectrum for a sample-and-hold circuit; (a) no aliasing; (b) aliasing distortion

$$f_s \geq 2f_a \qquad (4\text{-}1)$$

where f_s = minimum Nyquist sample rate (Hz)

f_a = highest frequency to be sampled (Hz)

Essentially, a sample-and-hold circuit is an AM modulator. The switch is a nonlinear device that has two inputs: the sampling pulse and the input analog signal. Consequently, *nonlinear mixing (heterodyning)* occurs between these two signals. Figure 4-5a shows the frequency-domain representation of the output spectrum from a sample-and-hold circuit. The output includes the two original inputs (the audio and the fundamental frequency of the sampling pulse), their sum and difference frequencies ($f_s \pm f_a$), all the harmonics of f_s and f_a ($2f_s$, $2f_a$, $3f_s$, $3f_a$, etc), and their associated cross products ($2f_s \pm f_a$, $3f_s \pm f_a$, etc.).

Because the sampling pulse is a repetitive waveform, it is made up of a series of harmonically related sine waves. Each of these sine waves is amplitude modulated by the analog signal and produces sum and difference frequencies symmetrical around each of the harmonics of f_s. Each sum and difference frequency generated is separated from its respective center frequency by f_a. As long as f_s is at least twice f_a, none of the side frequencies from one harmonic will spill into the sidebands of another harmonic and aliasing does not occur. Figure 4-5b shows the results when an analog input frequency greater than $f_s/2$ modulates f_s. The side frequencies from one harmonic fold over into the sideband of another harmonic. The frequency that folds over is an alias of the input signal (hence, the names "aliasing" or "foldover distortion"). If an alias side frequency from the first harmonic folds over into the audio spectrum, it cannot be removed through filtering or any other technique.

Example 4-2

For a PCM system with a maximum audio input frequency of 4 kHz, determine the minimum sample rate and the alias frequency produced if a 5-kHz audio signal were allowed to enter the sample-and-hold circuit.

Solution   Using Nyquist's sampling theorem (Equation 4-1), we have

$$f_s \geq 2f_a \quad \text{therefore,} \quad f_s \geq 8 \text{ kHz}$$

If a 5-kHz audio frequency entered the sample-and-hold circuit, the output spectrum shown in Figure 4-6 is produced. It can be seen that the 5-kHz signal produces an alias frequency of 3 kHz that has been introduced into the original audio spectrum.

FIGURE 4-6 Output spectrum for Example 4-2

TABLE 4-1 3-Bit PCM Code

Sign	Magnitude		Level	Decimal
1	1	1		+3
1	1	0		+2
1	0	1		+1
1	0	0		+0
0	0	0		−0
0	0	1		−1
0	1	0		−2
0	1	1		−3

The input bandpass filter shown in Figure 4-2 is called an *antialiasing* or *antifoldover filter.* Its upper cutoff frequency is chosen such that no frequency greater than one-half of the sampling rate is allowed to enter the sample-and-hold circuit, thus, eliminating the possibility of foldover distortion occurring.

With PCM, the analog input signal is sampled, then converted to a serial binary code. The binary code is transmitted to the receiver, where it is converted back to the original analog signal. The binary codes used for PCM are *n*-bit codes, where *n* may be any positive integer greater than 1. The codes currently used for PCM are *sign-magnitude codes,* where the *most significant bit* (MSB) is the sign bit and the remaining bits are used for magnitude. Table 4-1 shows an *n*-bit PCM code where *n* equals 3. The most significant bit is used to represent the sign of the sample (logic 1 = positive and logic 0 = negative). The two remaining bits represent the magnitude. With 2 magnitude bits, there are four codes possible for positive numbers and four possible for negative numbers. Consequently, there is a total of eight possible codes ($2^3 = 8$).

Folded Binary Code

The PCM code shown in Table 4-1 is called a *folded binary code.* Except for the sign bit, the codes on the bottom half of the table are a mirror image of the codes on the top half. (If the negative codes were folded over on top of the positive codes, they would match perfectly.) Also, with folded binary there are two codes assigned to zero volts: 100 (+0) and 000 (−0). For this example, the magnitude of the minimum step size is 1 V. Therefore, the maximum voltage that may be encoded with this scheme is +3 V (111) or −3 V (011). If the magnitude of a sample exceeds the highest quantization interval, *overload distortion* (also called *peak limiting*) occurs. Assigning PCM codes to absolute magnitudes is called *quantizing.* The magnitude of the minimum step size is called *resolution,* which is equal in magnitude to the voltage of the least significant bit (V_{lsb} or the magnitude of the minimum step size of the DAC). The resolution is the minimum voltage other than 0 V that can be decoded by the DAC at the receiver. The smaller the magnitude of the minimum step size, the better (smaller) the resolution and the more accurately the quantization interval will resemble the actual analog sample.

FIGURE 4-7 (a) Analog input signal; (b) sample pulse; (c) PAM signal; (d) PCM code

In Table 4-1, each 3-bit code has a range of input voltages that will be converted to that code. For example, any voltage between +0.5 and +1.5 will be converted to the code 101. Any voltage between +1.5 and +2.5 will be encoded as 110. Each code has a *quantization range* equal to + or − one-half the resolution except the codes for +0 V and −0 V. The 0-V codes each have an input range equal to only one-half the resolution, but because there are two 0-V codes, the range for 0 V is also + or − one-half the resolution. Consequently, the maximum input voltage to the system is equal to the voltage of the highest magnitude code plus one-half of the voltage of the least significant bit.

Figure 4-7 shows an analog input signal, the sampling pulse, the corresponding PAM signal, and the PCM code. The analog signal is sampled three times. The first sample occurs at the t_1 when the analog voltage is +2 V. The PCM code that corresponds to sample 1 is 110. Sample 2 occurs at time t_2 when the analog voltage is −1 V. The corresponding PCM code is 001. To determined the PCM code for a particular sample, simply divide the voltage of the sample by the resolution, convert it to an *n*-bit binary code, and add the sign bit to it. For sample 1, the sign bit is 1, indicating a positive voltage. The magnitude code (10) corresponds to a binary 2. Two times 1 V equals 2 V, the magnitude of the sample.

Sample 3 occurs at time t_3. The voltage at this time is +2.6 V. The folded PCM code for +2.6 V is 2.6/1 = 2.6. There is no code for this magnitude. If successive approximation ADCs are used, the magnitude of the sample is rounded off to the nearest valid code (111 or +3 V for this example). This results in an error when the code is converted back to analog by the DAC at the receive end. This error is called *quantization error* (Q_e). The quantization error is equivalent to additive noise (it alters the signal amplitude). Similar to noise, the quantization error may add to or subtract from the actual

FIGURE 4-8 Linear input-versus-output transfer curve: (a) linear transfer function; (b) quantization; (c) Q_e

signal. Consequently, quantization error is also called *quantization noise* (Q_n) and its maximum magnitude is one-half the voltage of the minimum step size ($V_{lsb}/2$). For this example, $Q_e = 1$ V/2 or 0.5 V.

Figure 4-8 shows the input-versus-output transfer function for a linear analog-to-digital converter (sometimes called a linear quantizer). As the figure shows for a linear analog input signal (i.e., a ramp), the quantized signal is a staircase. Thus, as shown in Figure 4-8c, the maximum quantization error is the same for any magnitude input signal.

Figure 4-9 shows the same analog input signal used in Figure 4-7 being sampled at a faster rate. As the figure shows, reducing the time between samples (i.e., increasing the sample rate) produces a PAM signal that more closely resembles the original analog input signal. However, it should also be noted that increasing the sample rate does not reduce the quantization error of the samples.

Dynamic Range

The number of PCM bits transmitted per sample is determined by several variables, which include maximum allowable input amplitude, resolution, and dynamic range.

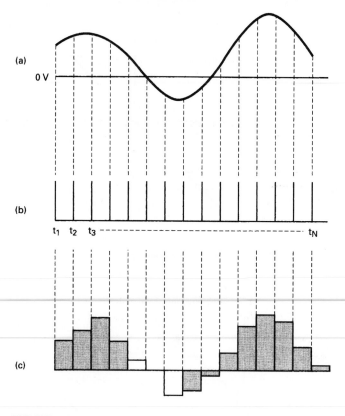

FIGURE 4-9 PAM: (a) input signal; (b) sample pulse; (c) PAM signal

Dynamic range (DR) is the ratio of the largest possible magnitude to the smallest possible magnitude that can be decoded by the DAC. Mathematically, dynamic range is

$$DR = \frac{V_{max}}{V_{min}} \qquad (4\text{-}2a)$$

where V_{min} is equal to the resolution and V_{max} is the maximum voltage magnitude that can be decoded by the DACs. Thus,

$$DR = \frac{V_{max}}{\text{resolution}}$$

For the system shown in Table 4-1,

$$DR = \frac{3 \text{ V}}{1 \text{ V}} = 3$$

It is common to represent dynamic range in decibels; therefore,

$$DR = 20 \log\frac{V_{max}}{V_{min}} = 20 \log\frac{3}{1} = 9.54 \text{ dB} \qquad (4\text{-}2b)$$

A dynamic range of 3 indicates that the ratio of the largest to the smallest decoded signal voltage is 3.

If a smaller resolution is desired, such as 0.5 V, to maintain a dynamic range of 3, the maximum allowable input voltage must be reduced by the same factor, one-half.

$$DR = \frac{1.5}{0.5} = 3$$

Therefore, V_{max} is reduced by a factor of 2 and the dynamic range is independent of resolution. If the resolution were reduced by a factor of 2 (0.25 V), to maintain the same maximum input amplitude, the dynamic range must double:

$$DR = \frac{1.5}{0.25} = 6$$

The number of bits used for a PCM code depends on the dynamic range. With a 2-bit PCM code, the minimum decodable magnitude has a binary code of 01. The maximum magnitude is 11. The ratio of the maximum binary code to the minimum binary code is 3, the same as the dynamic range. Because the minimum binary code is always 1, DR is simply the maximum binary number for a system. Consequently, to determine the number of bits required for a PCM code the following mathematical relationship is used:

$$2^n - 1 \geq DR$$

and for a minimum value of n,

$$2^n - 1 = DR \qquad (4\text{-}3a)$$

where $\quad$ n = number of PCM bits, excluding sign bit
$\qquad$ DR = absolute value of dynamic range

Why $2^n - 1$? One PCM code is used for 0 V, which is not considered for dynamic range. Therefore,

$$2^n = DR + 1 \qquad (4\text{-}3b)$$

To solve for n, convert to logs,

$$\log 2^n = \log(DR + 1) \qquad (4\text{-}3c)$$
$$n \log 2 = \log(DR + 1)$$
$$n = \frac{\log(3 + 1)}{\log 2} = \frac{0.602}{0.301} = 2$$

For a dynamic range of 3, a PCM code with 2 bits is required.

Example 4-3

A PCM system has the following parameters: a maximum analog input frequency of 4 kHz, a maximum decoded voltage at the receiver of ±2.55 V, and a minimum dynamic range of 46 dB. Determine the following: minimum sample rate, minimum number of bits used in the PCM code, resolution, and quantization error.

Solution $\quad$ Substituting into Equation 4-1, the minimum sample rate is

$$f_s = 2f_a = 2(4 \text{ kHz}) = 8 \text{ kHz}$$

To determine the absolute value of the dynamic range, substitute into Equation 4-2b:

$$46 \text{ dB} = 20 \log \frac{V_{max}}{V_{min}}$$

$$2.3 = \log \frac{V_{max}}{V_{min}}$$

$$10^{2.3} = \frac{V_{max}}{V_{min}} = DR$$

$$199.5 = DR$$

Substitute into Equation 4-3b and solve for n:

$$n = \frac{\log(199.5 + 1)}{\log 2} = 7.63$$

The closest whole number greater than 7.63 is 8; therefore, 8 bits must be used for the magnitude.

Because the input amplitude range is ±2.55 V, one additional bit, the sign bit, is required. Therefore, the total number of PCM bits is 9 and the total number of PCM codes is 2^9 or 512. (There are 255 positive codes, 255 negative codes, and 2 zero codes.)

To determine the actual dynamic range, substitute into Equation 4-3c:

$$DR = 20 \log 255 = 48.13 \text{ dB}$$

To determine the resolution, divide the maximum + or − magnitude by the number of positive or negative nonzero PCM codes.

$$\text{resolution} = \frac{V_{max}}{2^n - 1} = \frac{2.55}{2^8 - 1} = \frac{2.55}{256 - 1} = 0.01 \text{ V}$$

The maximum quantization error is

$$Q_e = \frac{\text{resolution}}{2} = \frac{0.01}{2} = 0.005 \text{ V}$$

Coding Efficiency

Coding efficiency is a numerical indication of how efficiently a PCM code is utilized. Coding efficiency is the ratio of the minimum number of bits required to achieve a certain dynamic range to the actual number of PCM bits used. Mathematically, coding efficiency is

$$\text{coding efficiency} = \frac{\substack{\text{minimum number of bits} \\ \text{(including sign bit)}}}{\substack{\text{actual number of bits} \\ \text{(including sign bit)}}} \times 100 \qquad (4\text{-}4)$$

The coding efficiency for Example 4-3 is

$$\text{coding efficiency} = \frac{8.63}{9} \times 100 = 95.89\%$$

Signal-to-Quantization Noise Ratio

The 3-bit PCM coding scheme described in the preceding section is a linear code. That is, the magnitude change between any two successive codes is the same. Consequently, the magnitude of their quantization error is also the same. The maximum quantization noise is the voltage of the least significant bit divided by 2. Therefore, the worst possible *signal voltage-to-quantization noise voltage ratio* (SQR) occurs when the input signal is at its minimum amplitude (101 or 001). Mathematically, the worst-case voltage SQR is

$$SQR = \frac{\text{minimum voltage}}{\text{quantization noise voltage}} = \frac{V_{lsb}}{V_{lsb}/2} = 2$$

For a maximum amplitude input signal of 3V (either 111 or 011), the maximum quantization noise is also the voltage of the least significant bit divided by 2. Therefore, the voltage SQR for a maximum input signal condition is

$$SQR = \frac{\text{maximum voltage}}{\text{quantization noise voltage}} = \frac{V_{max}}{V_{lsb}/2} = \frac{3}{0.5} = 6$$

From the preceding example it can be seen that even though the magnitude of error remains constant throughout the entire PCM code, the percentage of error does not; it decreases as the magnitude or the input signal increases. As a result, the SQR is not constant.

The preceding expression for SQR is for voltage and presumes the maximum quantization error and a constant-amplitude analog signal; therefore, it is of little practical use and is shown only for comparison purposes. In reality and as shown in Figure 4-7, the difference between the PAM waveform and the analog input waveform varies in

FIGURE 4-10 (a) Linear versus (b) nonlinear encoding

magnitude. Therefore, the signal-to-quantization noise ratio is not constant. Generally, the quantization error or distortion caused by digitizing an analog sample is expressed as an average signal power-to-average noise power ratio. For linear PCM codes (all quantization intervals have equal magnitudes), the signal power-to-quantizing noise power ratio (also called *signal-to-distortion ratio* or *signal-to-noise ratio*) is determined as follows:

$$\text{SQR}_{(dB)} = 10 \log \frac{v^2/R}{(q^2/12)/R}$$

where

R = resistance
v = rms signal voltage
q = quantization interval
v^2/R = average signal power
$(q^2/12)/R$ = average quantization noise power

If the resistances are assumed to be equal,

$$\text{SQR}_{(dB)} = 10 \log \frac{v^2}{q^2/12} \tag{4-5a}$$

$$= 10.8 + 20 \log \frac{v}{q} \tag{4-5b}$$

Linear Versus Nonlinear PCM Codes

Early PCM systems used *linear codes* (i.e., the magnitude change between any two successive steps is uniform). With linear encoding, the accuracy (resolution) for the higher-amplitude analog signals is the same as for the lower-amplitude signals, and the SQR for the lower-amplitude signals is less than for the higher-amplitude signals. With voice transmission, low-amplitude signals are more likely to occur than large-amplitude signals. Therefore, if there were more codes for the lower amplitudes, it would increase the accuracy where the accuracy is needed. As a result, there would be fewer codes available for the higher amplitudes, which would increase the quantization error for the larger-amplitude signals (thus, decreasing the SQR). Such a coding technique is called *nonlinear* or *nonuniform encoding*. With nonlinear encoding, the step size increases with the amplitude of the input signal. Figure 4-10 shows the step outputs from a linear and a nonlinear ADC.

Note, with nonlinear encoding, there are more codes at the bottom of the scale than there are at the top, thus, increasing the accuracy for the smaller signals. Also note that the distance between successive codes is greater for the higher-amplitude signals, thus, increasing the quantization error and reducing the SQR. Also, because the ratio of V_{max} to V_{min} is increased with nonlinear encoding, the dynamic range is larger than with a

Idle channel noise

Uniform code
with midrise
quantization

Uniform code
with midtread
quantization

Decoded noise

No decoded noise

FIGURE 4-11   Idle channel noise

uniform code. It is evident that nonlinear encoding is a compromise; SQR is sacrificed for the high-amplitude signals to achieve more accuracy for the low-amplitude signals and to achieve a larger dynamic range. It is difficult to fabricate nonlinear ADCs; consequently, alternative methods of achieving the same results have been devised and are discussed later in this chapter.

Idle Channel Noise

During times when there is no analog input signal, the only input to the PAM sampler is random, thermal noise. This noise is called *idle channel noise* and is converted to a PAM sample just as if it were a signal. Consequently, even input noise is quantized by the ADC. Figure 4-11 shows a way to reduce idle channel noise by a method called *midtread quantization*. With midtread quantizing, the first quantization interval is made larger in amplitude than the rest of the steps. Consequently, input noise can be quite large and still be quantized as a positive or negative zero code. As a result, the noise is suppressed during the encoding process.

In the PCM codes described thus far, the lowest-magnitude positive and negative codes have the same voltage range as all the other codes (+ or − one-half the resolution). This is called *midrise quantization*. Figure 4-11 contrasts the idle channel noise transmitted with a midrise PCM code to the idle channel noise transmitted when midtread quantization is used. The advantage of midtread quantization is less idle channel noise. The disadvantage is a larger possible magnitude for Q_e in the lowest quantization interval.

With a folded binary PCM code, residual noise that fluctuates slightly above and below 0 V is converted to either a + or − zero PCM code and, consequently, is eliminated. In systems that do not use the two 0-V assignments, the residual noise could cause the PCM encoder to alternate between the zero code and the minimum + or − code. Consequently, the decoder would reproduce the encoded noise. With a folded binary code, most of the residual noise is inherently eliminated by the encoder.

Coding Methods

There are several coding methods used to quantize PAM signals into 2^n levels. These methods are classified according to whether the coding operation proceeds a level at a time, a digit at a time, or a word at a time.

Level-at-a-time coding.   This type of coding compares the PAM signal to a ramp waveform while a binary counter is being advanced at a uniform rate. When the ramp

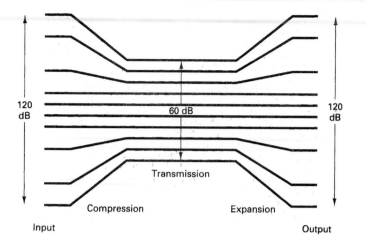

FIGURE 4-12 Basic companding process

waveform equals or exceeds the PAM sample, the counter contains the PCM code. This type of coding requires a very fast clock if the number of bits in the PCM code is large. Level-at-a-time coding also requires that 2^n sequential decisions be made for each PCM code generated. Therefore, level-at-a-time coding is generally limited to low-speed applications. Nonuniform coding is achieved by using a nonlinear function as the reference ramp.

Digit-at-a-time coding. This type of coding determines each digit of the PCM code sequentially. Digit-at-a-time coding is analogous to a balance where known reference weights are used to determine an unknown weight. Digit-at-a-time coders provide a compromise between speed and complexity. One common kind of digit-at-a-time coder, called a *feedback coder,* uses a successive approximation register (SAR). With this type of coder, the entire PCM code word is determined simultaneously.

Word-at-a-time coding. Word-at-a-time coders are flash encoders and are more complex; however, they are more suitable for high-speed applications. One common type of word-at-a-time coder uses multiple threshold circuits. Logic circuits sense the highest threshold circuit sensed by the PAM input signal and produce the approximate PCM code. This method is again impractical for large values of *n*.

Companding

Companding is the process of *compressing,* then *expanding.* With companded systems, the higher-amplitude analog signals are compressed (amplified less than the lower-amplitude signals) prior to transmission, then expanded (amplified more than the smaller-amplitude signals) at the receiver.

Figure 4-12 illustrates the process of companding. An input signal with a dynamic range of 120 dB is compressed to 60 dB for transmission, then expanded to 120 dB at the receiver. With PCM, companding may be accomplished through analog or digital techniques. Early PCM systems used analog companding, whereas more modern systems use digital companding.

Analog Companding

Historically, analog compression was implemented using specially designed diodes inserted in the analog signal path in the PCM transmitter prior to the sample-and-hold circuit. Analog expansion was also implemented with diodes that were placed just after the receive low-pass filter. Figure 4-13 shows the basic process of analog companding.

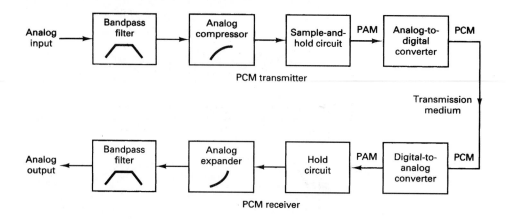

FIGURE 4-13 PCM system with analog companding

In the transmitter, the analog signal is compressed, sampled, then converted to a linear PCM code. In the receiver, the PCM code is converted to a PAM signal, filtered, then expanded back to its original input amplitude characteristics.

Different signal distributions require different companding characteristics. For instance, voice signals require relatively constant SQR performance over a wide dynamic range, which means that the distortion must be proportional to signal amplitude for any input signal level. This requires a logarithmic compression ratio. A truly logarithmic assignment code requires an infinite dynamic range and an infinite number of PCM codes, which is impossible. There are two methods of analog companding currently being used that closely approximate a logarithmic function and are often called *log-PCM* codes. They are μ-*law* and *A-law companding*.

μ-Law companding. In the United States and Japan, μ-law companding is used. The compression characteristic for μ-law is

$$V_{out} = \frac{V_{max} \times \ln(1 + \mu V_{in}/V_{max})}{\ln(1 + \mu)} \tag{4-6}$$

where V_{max} = maximum uncompressed analog input amplitude
V_{in} = amplitude of the input signal at a particular instant of time
μ = parameter used to define the amount of compression
V_{out} = compressed output amplitude

Figure 4-14 shows the compression for several values of μ. Note that the higher the μ, the more compression. Also note that for a μ = 0, the curve is linear (no compression).

The parameter μ determines the range of signal power in which the SQR is relatively constant. Voice transmission requires a minimum dynamic range of 40 dB and a 7-bit PCM code. For a relatively constant SQR and a 40-dB dynamic range, μ = 100 or larger is required. The early Bell System digital transmission systems used a 7-bit PCM code with μ = 100. The most recent digital transmission systems use 8-bit PCM codes and μ = 255.

Example 4-4

For a compressor with μ = 255, determine the gain for the following values of V_{in}: V_{max}, $0.75V_{max}$, $0.5V_{max}$, and $0.25V_{max}$.

Solution Substituting into Equation 4-6, the following gains are achieved for various input magnitudes:

FIGURE 4-14   μ-law compression characteristics

V_{in}	Gain
V_{max}	1
$0.75V_{max}$	1.26
$0.5V_{max}$	1.75
$0.25V_{max}$	3

It can be seen that as the input signal amplitude increases, the gain decreases or is compressed.

A-Law companding.   In Europe, the CCITT has established A-law companding to be used to approximate true logarithmic companding. For an intended dynamic range, A-law companding has a slightly flatter SQR than μ-law. A-law companding, however, is inferior to μ-law in terms of small-signal quality (idle channel noise). The compression characteristic for A-law companding is

$$V_{out} = V_{max} \frac{AV_{in}/V_{max}}{1 + \ln A} \qquad 0 \le \frac{V_{in}}{V_{max}} \le \frac{1}{A} \qquad (4\text{-}7a)$$

$$= V_{max} \frac{1 + \ln (AV_{in}/V_{max})}{1 + \ln A} \qquad \frac{1}{A} \le \frac{V_{in}}{V_{max}} \le 1 \qquad (4\text{-}7b)$$

Digital Companding

Digital companding involves compression at the transmit end after the input sample has been converted to a linear PCM code and expansion at the receive end prior to PCM decoding. Figure 4-15 shows the block diagram of a digitally companded PCM system.

With digital companding, the analog signal is first sampled and converted to a linear code, then the linear code is digitally compressed. At the receive end, the compressed PCM code is received, expanded, then decoded. The most recent digitally compressed PCM systems use a 12-bit linear code and an 8-bit compressed code. This companding process closely resembles a μ = 255 analog compression curve by approximating the curve with a set of eight straight line *segments* (segments 0 through 7). The slope of each successive segment is exactly one-half that of the previous segment. Figure 4-16 shows the 12-bit-to-8-bit digital compression curve for positive values only. The curve for negative values is identical except the inverse. Although there are 16 segments (eight positive and eight negative) this scheme is often called *13-segment compression*. This is

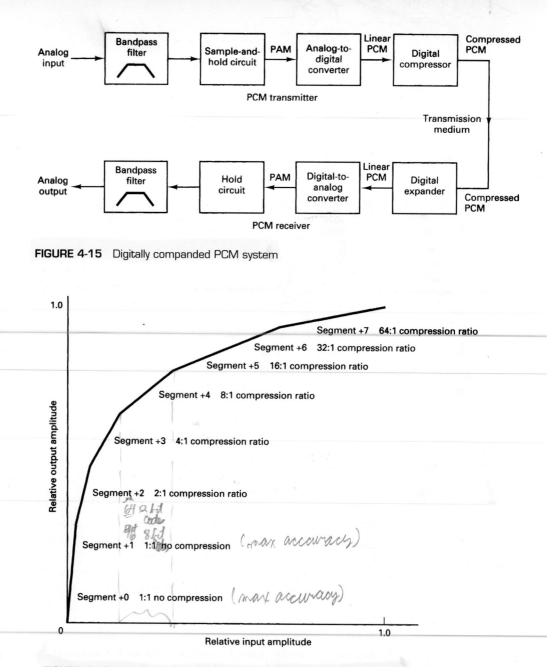

FIGURE 4-15 Digitally companded PCM system

FIGURE 4-16 µ255 compression characteristics (positive values only)

because the curve for segments +0, +1, −0, and −1 is a straight line with a constant slope and is often considered as one segment.

The digital companding algorithm for a 12-bit-linear-to-8-bit-compressed code is actually quite simple. The 8-bit compressed code is comprised of a sign bit, a 3-bit segment identifier, and a 15-bit magnitude code that identifies the *quantization interval* within the specified segment (see Figure 4-17a).

In the µ255 encoding table shown in Figure 4-17b, the bit positions designated with an X are truncated during compression and are consequently lost. Bits designated A, B, C, and D are transmitted as is. The sign bit(s) is also transmitted as is. Note that for

Sign bit 1 = + 0 = −	3-Bit segment identifier	4-Bit quantization interval A B C D
	000 to 111	0000 to 1111

(a)

at Xmtr   *at reciever*

Segment	12-Bit linear code	8-Bit compressed code	8-Bit compressed code	12-Bit recovered code	Segment
0	s0000000ABCD	s000ABCD	s000ABCD	s0000000ABCD	0
1	s0000001ABCD	s001ABCD	s001ABCD	s0000001ABCD	1
2	s000001ABCDX	s010ABCD	s010ABCD	s000001ABCD1	2
3	s00001ABCDXX	s011ABCD	s011ABCD	s00001ABCD10	3
4	s0001ABCDXXX	s100ABCD	s100ABCD	s0001ABCD100	4
5	s001ABCDXXXX	s101ABCD	s101ABCD	s001ABCD1000	5
6	s01ABCDXXXXX	s110ABCD	s110ABCD	s01ABCD10000	6
7	s1ABCDXXXXXX	s111ABCD	s111ABCD	s1ABCD100000	7

(b)   (c)

FIGURE 4-17 12-bit to 8-bit digital companding: (a) 8-bit µ255 compressed code format; (b) µ255 encoding table; (c) µ255 decoding table

segments 0 and 1, the original 12 bits are duplicated exactly at the output of the decoder (Figure 4-17c), whereas for segment 7, only the most significant 6 bits are recovered. With 11 magnitude bits, there are 2048 possible codes. There are 16 codes in segment 0 and in segment 1. In segment 2, there are 32 codes; segment 3 has 64. Each successive segment beginning with segment 3 has twice as many codes as the previous segment. In each of the eight segments, only sixteen 12-bit codes can be recovered. Consequently, in segments 0 and 1, there is no compression (of the 16 possible codes, all 16 can be recovered). In segment 2, there is a compression ratio of 2:1 (32 possible transmit codes and 16 possible recovered codes). In segment 3, there is a 4:1 compression ratio (64 possible transmit codes and 16 possible recovered codes). The compression ratio doubles with each successive segment. The compression ratio in segment 7 is 1024/16 or 64:1.

The compression process is as follows. The analog signal is sampled and converted to a linear 12-bit sign-magnitude code. The sign bit is transferred directly to the 8-bit code. The segment is determined by counting the number of leading 0s in the 11-bit magnitude portion of the code beginning with the MSB. Subtract the number of leading 0s (not to exceed 7) from 7. The result is the segment number, which is converted to a 3-bit binary number and substituted into the 8-bit code as the segment identifier. The four magnitude bits (A, B, C, and D) are the quantization interval and are substituted into the least significant 4 bits of the 8-bit compressed code.

Essentially, segments 2 through 7 are subdivided into smaller subsegments. Each segment has 16 subsegments, which correspond to the 16 conditions possible for the bits A, B, C, and D (0000-1111). In segment 2 there are two codes per subsegment. In segment 3 there are four. The number of codes per subsegment doubles with each subsequent segment. Consequently, in segment 7, each subsegment has 64 codes. Figure 4-18 shows the breakdown of segments versus subsegments for segments 2, 5, and 7. Note that in each subsegment, all 12-bit codes, once compressed and expanded, yield a single 12-bit code. This is shown in Figure 4-18.

From Figures 4-17 and 4-18, it can be seen that the most significant of the truncated bits is reinserted at the decoder as a 1. The remaining truncated bits are

Segment	12-Bit linear code		12-Bit expanded code	Subsegment	Segment	12-Bit linear code		12-Bit expanded code	Subsegment
7	s11111111111 .... s11111000000	64 : 1	s11111100000	15	5	s00111111111 .... s00111110000	16 : 1	s00111111000	15
7	s11110111111 .... s11110000000	64 : 1	s11110100000	14	5	s00111101111 .... s00111100000	16 : 1	s00111101000	14
7	s11101111111 .... s11101000000	64 : 1	s11101100000	13	5	s00111011111 .... s00111010000	16 : 1	s00111011000	13
7	s11100111111 .... s11100000000	64 : 1	s11100100000	12	5	s00111001111 .... s00111000000	16 : 1	s001110010000	12
7	s11011111111 .... s11011000000	64 : 1	s11011100000	11	5	s00110111111 .... s00110110000	16 : 1	s00110111000	11
7	s11010111111 .... s11010000000	64 : 1	s11010100000	10	5	s00110101111 .... s00110100000	16 : 1	s00110101000	10
7	s11001111111 .... s11001000000	64 : 1	s11001100000	9	5	s00110011111 .... s00110010000	16 : 1	s00110011000	9
7	s11000111111 .... s11000000000	64 : 1	s11000100000	8	5	s00110001111 .... s00110000000	16 : 1	s00110001000	8
7	s10111111111 .... s10111000000	64 : 1	s10111100000	7	5	s00101111111 .... s00101110000	16 : 1	s00101111000	7
7	s10110111111 .... s10110000000	64 : 1	s10110100000	6	5	s00101101111 .... s00101100000	16 : 1	s00101101000	6
7	s10101111111 .... s10101000000	64 : 1	s10101100000	5	5	s00101011111 .... s00101010000	16 : 1	s00101011000	5
7	s10100111111 .... s10100000000	64 : 1	s10100100000	4	5	s00101001111 .... s00101000000	16 : 1	s00101001000	4
7	s10011111111 .... s10011000000	64 : 1	s10011100000	3	5	s00100111111 .... s00100110000	16 : 1	s00100111000	3
7	s10010111111 .... s10010000000	64 : 1	s10010100000	2	5	s00100101111 .... s00100100000	16 : 1	s00100101000	2
7	s10001111111 .... s10001000000	64 : 1	s10001100000	1	5	s00100011111 .... s00100010000	16 : 1	s00100011000	1
7	s10000111111 .... s10000000000	64 : 1	s10000100000	0	5	s00100001111 .... s00100000000	16 : 1	s00100001000	0
	s1ABCD-------					s001ABCD----			
	(a)					(b)			

FIGURE 4-18 12-bit segments divided into subsegments: (a) segment 7; (b) segment 5 *(Continued)*

reinserted as 0s. This ensures that the maximum magnitude of error introduced by the compression and expansion process is minimized. Essentially, the decoder guesses what the truncated bits were prior to encoding. The most logical guess is halfway between the minimum- and maximum-magnitude codes. For example, in segment 5, the 5 least significant bits are truncated during compression. At the receiver, the decoder must determine what those bits were. The possibilities are any code between 00000 and 11111. The logical guess is 10000, approximately half the maximum magnitude. Consequently, the maximum compression error is slightly more than one-half the magnitude of that segment.

Example 4-5

Determine the 12-bit linear code, the 8-bit compressed code, and the recovered 12-bit code for a resolution of 0.01 V and analog sample voltages of

(a) 0.05 V

(b) 0.32 V

(c) 10.23 V

Segment	12-Bit linear code		12-Bit expanded code	Subsegment
2	s00000111111 .... s00000111110	} 2:1	s00000111111	15
2	s00000111101 .... s00000111100	} 2:1	s00000111101	14
2	s00000111011 .... s00000111010	} 2:1	s00000111011	13
2	s00000111001 .... s00000111000	} 2:1	s00000111001	12
2	s00000110111 .... s00000110110	} 2:1	s00000110111	11
2	s00000110101 .... s00000110100	} 2:1	s00000110101	10
2	s00000110011 .... s00000110010	} 2:1	s00000110011	9
2	s00000110001 .... s00000110000	} 2:1	s00000110001	8
2	s00000101111 .... s00000101110	} 2:1	s00000101111	7
2	s00000101101 .... s00000101100	} 2:1	s00000101101	6
2	s00000101011 .... s00000101010	} 2:1	s00000101011	5
2	s00000101001 .... s00000101000	} 2:1	s00000101001	4
2	s000000100111 .... s00000100110	} 2:1	s00000100111	3
2	s00000100101 .... s00000100100	} 2:1	s00000100101	2
2	s000000100011 .... s00000100010	} 2:1	s00000100011	1
2	s00000100001 .... s00000100000	} 2:1	s00000100001	0
	s000001ABCD-			

(c)

FIGURE 4-18 (Continued) (c) segment 2

Solution (a) To determine the 12-bit linear code for 0.05 V, simply divide the sample voltage by the resolution and convert the result to a 12-bit sign-magnitude binary number.

12-bit linear code:

$$\frac{0.05\ V}{0.01\ V} = 5 = \begin{array}{cccccccccccc} 1 & 0 & 0 & 0 & 0 & 0 & 0 & 0 & 0 & 1 & 0 & 1 \\ s & & & & & & & & & & & \end{array}$$

s ----------------magnitude----------------
(11-bit binary number)

8-bit compressed code:

$$\begin{array}{cccccccccc} 1 & 0 & 0 & 0 & 0 & 0 & 0 & 0 & 1 & 0 & 1 \\ s & & (7-7=0\ \text{or}\ 000) & & & A & B & C & D \\ 1 & & 0 & 0 & 0 & & 0 & 1 & 0 & 1 \end{array}$$

↑
sign bit   unit   quantization
(+)   identifier   interval
(segment 0)   (5)

12-bit recovered code:

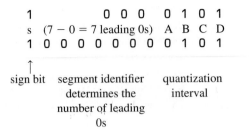

```
1              0 0 0   0 1 0 1
s   (7 − 0 = 7 leading 0s)   A  B  C  D
1  0 0 0 0 0 0 0 0 1 0 1
```

      ↑

sign bit   segment identifier   quantization
            determines the   interval
           number of leading
               0s

As you can see, the recovered 12-bit code is exactly the same as the original 12-bit linear code. This is true for all codes in segment 0 and 1. Consequently, there is no compression error in these two segments.

(b) For the 0.32-V sample,

12-bit linear code:

$$\frac{0.32 \text{ V}}{0.01 \text{ V}} = 32 = \quad \begin{array}{l} 1 \ 0 \ 0 \ 0 \ 0 \ 0 \ 1 \ 0 \ 0 \ 0 \ 0 \ 0 \\ s \ \text{--------------magnitude----------------} \end{array}$$

8-bit compressed code:

```
1 0 0 0 0 0 1     0 0 0 0 0
s   (7 − 5 = 2 or 010)   A  B  C  D  X
1       0 1 0       0 0 0 0 ↑
(+)       (segment 2)         truncated
```

12-bit recovered code:

```
1        0 1 0        0 0 0 0
s   (7 − 2 = 5 leading 0s)   A  B  C  D  X
1  0 0 0 0 0 1        0 0 0 0 1
```

               ↑   ↑
             inserted   inserted

Note the two inserted 1s in the decoded 12-bit code. The least significant bit is determined from the decoding table in Figure 4-17. The stuffed 1 in bit position 6 was dropped during the 12-bit-to-8-bit conversion. Transmission of this bit is redundant because if it were not a 1, the sample would not be in segment 2. Consequently, in all segments except 0, a 1 is automatically inserted after the reinserted zeros. For this sample, there is an error in the received voltage equal to the resolution, 0.01 V. In segment 2, for every two 12-bit codes possible, there is only one recovered 12-bit code. Thus, a coding compression of 2:1 is realized.

(c) To determine the codes for 10.23 V, the process is the same.

12-bit linear code:

```
1 1 1111 111111
↑
s    ABCD   truncated
```

8-bit compressed code:

```
1   111   1111
↑
s   segment  ABCD
```

12-bit recovered code:

```
1 1 1111 100000
↑
s ↑ ABCD    inserted
  inserted
```

The difference in the original 12-bit linear code and the recovered 12-bit code is

$$
\begin{array}{r}
111111111111 \\
-111111100000 \\
\hline
000000011111
\end{array} = 31(0.01\text{ V}) = 0.31\text{ V}
$$

Percentage Error

For comparison purposes, the following formula is used for computing the *percentage of error* introduced by digital compression:

$$\% \text{ error} = \frac{|\text{Tx voltage} - \text{Rx voltage}|}{\text{Rx voltage}} \times 100 \tag{4-8}$$

Example 4-6

The maximum percentage of error will occur for the smallest number in the lowest subsegment within any given segment. Because there is no compression error in segments 0 and 1, for segment 3 the maximum % error is computed as follows:

Transmit 12-bit code: s00001000000
Receive 12-bit code: s00001000010
Magnitude of error: 00000000010

$$
\% \text{ error} = \frac{|1000000 - 1000010|}{1000010} \times 100
$$

$$
= \frac{|64 - 66|}{66} \times 100 = 3.03\%
$$

(handwritten: Binary codes; 3.125%)

For segment 7:

Transmit 12-bit code: s10000000000
Receive 12-bit code: s10000100000
Magnitude of error: 00000100000

$$
\% \text{ error} = \frac{|10000000000 - 10000100000|}{10000100000} \times 100
$$

$$
= \frac{|1024 - 1056|}{1056} \times 100 = 3.03\%
$$

Although the magnitude of error is higher for segment 7, the percentage of error is the same. The maximum percentage of error is the same for segments 3 through 7, and consequently, the SQR degradation is the same for each segment.

Although there are several ways in which the 12-bit-to-8-bit compression and the 8-bit-to-12-bit expansion can be accomplished with hardware, the simplest and most economical method is with a look-up table in ROM (read-only memory).

Essentially every function performed by a PCM encoder and decoder is now accomplished with a single integrated-circuit chip called a *codec*. Most of the more recently developed codecs include an antialiasing (bandpass) filter, a sample-and-hold circuit, and an analog-to-digital converter in the transmit section and a digital-to-analog converter, a sample-and-hold circuit, and a bandpass filter in the receive section. The operation of a codec is explained in detail in Chapter 5.

Vocoders

The PCM coding and decoding processes described in the preceding sections were concerned primarily with reproducing waveforms as accurately as possible. The precise nature of the waveform was unimportant as long as it occupied the voice-band frequency range. When digitizing speech signals only, special voice encoders/decoders called *vocoders* are often used. To achieve acceptable speech communications, the short-term power spectrum of the speech information is all that must be preserved. The human ear is relatively insensitive to the phase relationship between individual frequency components within a voice waveform. Therefore, vocoders are designed to reproduce only the short-term power spectrum, and the decoded time waveforms often only vaguely resemble the original input signal. Vocoders cannot be used in applications where analog signals other than voice are present, such as output signals from voice-band data modems. Vocoders typically produce *unnatural* sounding speech and, therefore, are generally used for recorded information such as "wrong number" messages, encrypted voice for transmission over analog telephone circuits, computer output signals, and educational games.

The purpose of a vocoder is to encode the minimum amount of speech information necessary to reproduce a perceptible message with fewer bits than those needed by a conventional encoder/decoders. Vocoders are used primarily in limited bandwidth applications. Essentially, there are three vocoding techniques available: the *channel vocoder,* the *formant vocoder,* and the *linear predictive coder.*

Channel vocoders. The first channel vocoder was developed by Homer Dudley in 1928. Dudley's vocoder compressed conventional speech waveforms into an analog signal with a total bandwidth of approximately 300 Hz. Present-day digital vocoders operate at less than 2 kbps. Digital channel vocoders use bandpass filters to separate the speech waveform into narrower *subbands.* Each subband is full-wave rectified, filtered, then digitally encoded. The encoded signal is transmitted to the destination receiver, where it is decoded. Generally speaking, the quality of the signal at the output of a vocoder is quite poor. However, some of the more advanced channel vocoders operate at 2400 bps and can produce a highly intelligible, although slightly synthetic sounding speech.

Formant vocoders. A formant vocoder takes advantage of the fact that the short-term spectral density of typical speech signals seldom distributes uniformly across the entire voice-band spectrum (300 Hz to 3000 Hz). Instead, the spectral power of most speech energy concentrates at three or four peak frequencies called *formants.* A formant vocoder simply determines the location of these peaks and encodes and transmits only the information with the most significant short-term components. Therefore, formant vocoders can operate at lower bit rates and, thus, require narrower bandwidths. Formant vocoders sometimes have trouble tracking changes in the formants. However, once the formants have been identified, a formant vocoder can transfer intelligible speech at less than 1000 bps.

Linear predictive coders. A linear predictive coder extracts the most significant portions of speech information directly from the time waveform rather than from the frequency spectrum as with the channel and formant vocoders. A linear predictive coder produces a time-varying model of the *vocal tract excitation* and transfer function directly from the speech waveform. At the receive end, a *synthesizer* reproduces the speech by passing the specified excitation through a mathematical model of the vocal tract. Linear predictive coders provide more natural sounding speech than does either the channel or formant vocoder. Linear predictive coders typically encode and transmit speech at between 1.2 kbps and 2.4 kbps.

DELTA MODULATION PCM

Delta modulation uses a single-bit PCM code to achieve digital transmission of analog signals. With conventional PCM, each code is a binary representation of both the sign and magnitude of a particular sample. Therefore, multiple-bit codes are required to represent the many values that the sample can be. With delta modulation, rather than transmit a coded representation of the sample, only a single bit is transmitted, which simply

FIGURE 4-19   Delta modulation transmitter

FIGURE 4-20   Ideal operation of a delta modulation encoder

indicates whether that sample is larger or smaller than the previous sample. The algorithm for a delta modulation system is quite simple. If the current sample is smaller than the previous sample, a logic 0 is transmitted. If the current sample is larger than the previous sample, a logic 1 is transmitted.

Delta Modulation Transmitter

Figure 4-19 shows a block diagram of a delta modulation transmitter. The input analog is sampled and converted to a PAM signal, which is compared to the output of the DAC. The output of the DAC is a voltage equal to the regenerated magnitude of the previous sample, which was stored in the up/down-counter as a binary number. The up/down-counter is incremented or decremented depending on whether the previous sample is larger or smaller than the current sample. The up/down-counter is clocked at a rate equal to the sample rate. Therefore, the up/down-counter is updated after each comparison.

Figure 4-20 shows the ideal operation of a delta modulation encoder. Initially, the up/down-counter is zeroed and the DAC is outputting 0 V. The first sample is taken, converted to a PAM signal, and compared to zero volts. The output of the comparator is a logic 1 condition (+V), indicating that the current sample is larger in amplitude than the previous sample. On the next clock pulse, the up/down-counter is incremented to a count of 1. The DAC now outputs a voltage equal to the magnitude of the minimum step size (resolution). The steps change value at a rate equal to the clock frequency (sample rate). Consequently, with the input signal shown, the up/down-counter follows the input analog signal up until the output of the DAC exceeds the analog sample; then the up/down-counter will begin counting down until the output of the DAC drops below the sample amplitude. In the idealized situation (shown in Figure 4-20), the DAC output follows the

Delta Modulation PCM

FIGURE 4-21 Delta modulation receiver

FIGURE 4-22 Slope overload distortion   FIGURE 4-23 Granular noise

input signal. Each time the up/down-counter is incremented, a logic 1 is transmitted, and each time the up/down-counter is decremented, a logic 0 is transmitted.

Delta Modulation Receiver

Figure 4-21 shows the block diagram of a delta modulation receiver. As you can see, the receiver is almost identical to the transmitter except for the comparator. As the logic 1s and 0s are received, the up/down-counter is incremented or decremented accordingly. Consequently, the output of the DAC in the decoder is identical to the output of the DAC in the transmitter.

With delta modulation, each sample requires the transmission of only 1 bit; therefore, the bit rates associated with delta modulation are lower than conventional PCM systems. However, there are two problems associated with delta modulation that do not occur with conventional PCM: slope overload and granular noise.

Slope overload. Figure 4-22 shows what happens when the analog input signal changes at a faster rate than the DAC can keep up with. The slope of the analog signal is greater than the delta modulator can maintain. This is called *slope overload*. Increasing the clock frequency reduces the probability of slope overload occurring. Another way to prevent slope overload is to increase the magnitude of the minimum step size.

Granular noise. Figure 4-23 contrasts the original and reconstructed signals associated with a delta modulation system. It can be seen that when the original analog input signal has a relatively constant amplitude, the reconstructed signal has variations that were not present in the original signal. This is called *granular noise*. Granular noise in delta modulation is analogous to quantization noise in conventional PCM.

Granular noise can be reduced by decreasing the step size. Therefore, to reduce the granular noise, a small resolution is needed, and to reduce the possibility of slope overload occurring, a large resolution is required. Obviously, a compromise is necessary.

FIGURE 4-24   Adaptive delta modulation

Granular noise is more prevalent in analog signals that have gradual slopes and whose amplitudes vary only a small amount. Slope overload is more prevalent in analog signals that have steep slopes or whose amplitudes vary rapidly.

ADAPTIVE DELTA MODULATION PCM

Adaptive delta modulation is a delta modulation system where the step size of the DAC is automatically varied depending on the amplitude characteristics of the analog input signal. Figure 4-24 shows how an adaptive delta modulator works. When the output of the transmitter is a string of consecutive 1s or 0s, this indicates that the slope of the DAC output is less than the slope of the analog signal in either the positive or negative direction. Essentially, the DAC has lost track of exactly where the analog samples are and the possibility of slope overload occurring is high. With an adaptive delta modulator, after a predetermined number of consecutive 1s or 0s, the step size is automatically increased. After the next sample, if the DAC output amplitude is still below the sample amplitude, the next step is increased even further until eventually the DAC catches up with the analog signal. When an alternative sequence of 1s and 0s is occurring, this indicates that the possibility of granular noise occurring is high. Consequently, the DAC will automatically revert to its minimum step size and, thus, reduce the magnitude of the noise error.

A common algorithm for an adaptive delta modulator is when three consecutive 1s or 0s occur, the step size of the DAC is increased or decreased by a factor of 1.5. Various other algorithms may be used for adaptive delta modulators, depending on particular system requirements.

DIFFERENTIAL PULSE CODE MODULATION

In a typical PCM-encoded speech waveform, there are often successive samples taken in which there is little difference between the amplitudes of the two samples. This necessitates transmitting several identical PCM codes, which is redundant. Differential pulse code modulation (DPCM) is designed specifically to take advantage of the sample-to-sample redundancies in typical speech waveforms. With DPCM, the difference in the amplitude of two successive samples is transmitted rather than the actual sample. Because the range of sample differences is typically less than the range of individual samples, fewer bits are required for DPCM than conventional PCM.

Figure 4-25 shows a simplified block diagram of a DPCM transmitter. The analog input signal is bandlimited to one-half of the sample rate, then compared to the preceding accumulated signal level in the differentiator. The output of the differentiation is the

FIGURE 4-25 DPCM transmitter

FIGURE 4-26 DPCM receiver

difference between the two signals. The difference is PCM encoded and transmitted. The A/D converter operates the same as in a conventional PCM system, except that it typically uses fewer bits per sample.

Figure 4-26 shows a simplified block diagram of a DPCM receiver. Each received sample is converted back to analog, stored, and then summed with the next sample received. In the receiver shown in Figure 4-26 the integration is performed on the analog signals, although it could also be performed digitally.

PULSE TRANSMISSION

All digital carrier systems involve the transmission of pulses through a medium with a finite bandwidth. A highly selective system would require a large number of filter sections, which is impractical. Therefore, practical digital systems generally utilize filters with bandwidths that are approximately 30% or more in excess of the ideal Nyquist bandwidth. Figure 4-27a shows the typical output waveform from a *bandlimited* communications channel when a narrow pulse is applied to its input. The figure shows that bandlimiting a pulse causes the energy from the pulse to be spread over a significantly longer time in the form of *secondary lobes.* The secondary lobes are called *ringing tails.* The output frequency spectrum corresponding to a rectangular pulse is referred to as a $(\sin x)/x$ response and is given as

$$f(\omega) = (T)\frac{\sin(\omega T/2)}{\omega T/2} \tag{4-9}$$

where $\omega = 2\pi f$ (rad)
T = pulse width (s)

Figure 4-27b shows the distribution of the total spectrum power. It can be seen that approximately 90% of the signal power is contained within the first *spectral null* (i.e., $f = 1/T$). Therefore, the signal can be confined to a bandwidth $B = 1/T$ and still pass most of the energy from the original waveform. In theory, only the amplitude at the middle of

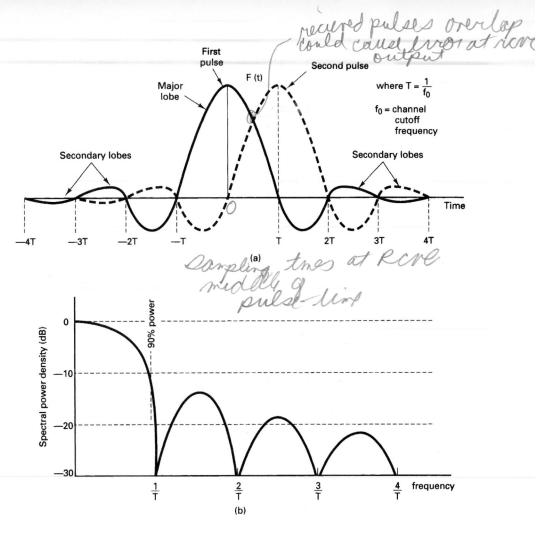

[handwritten annotations: recovered pulses overlap could cause error at rcve output; Sampling times at Rcve middle of pulse-lim]

FIGURE 4-27 Pulse response: (a) typical pulse response of a bandlimited filter; (b) spectrum of square pulse with duration $1/T$

each pulse interval needs to be preserved. Therefore, if the bandwidth is confined to $B = 1/2T$, the maximum signaling rate achievable through a low-pass filter with a specified bandwidth without causing excessive distortion is given as the Nyquist rate and is equal to twice the bandwidth. Mathematically, the Nyquist rate is

$$R = 2B \qquad (4\text{-}10)$$

where R = signaling rate = $1/T$
B = specified bandwidth

Intersymbol Interference

Figure 4-28 shows the input signal to an ideal minimum bandwidth, low-pass filter. The input signal is a random, binary nonreturn-to-zero (NRZ) sequence. Figure 4-28b shows the output of a low-pass filter that does not introduce any phase or amplitude distortion. Note that the output signal reaches its full value for each transmitted pulse at precisely the center of each sampling interval. However, if the low-pass filter is imperfect (which in reality it will be), the output response will more closely resemble that shown in Figure 4-28c. At the sampling instants (i.e., the center of the pulses), the signal does not always attain the maximum value. The ringing tails of several pulses have *overlapped*, thus, interfering with the *major pulse lobe*. Assuming no time delays through the system,

Sampling intervals

FIGURE 4-28 Pulse response: (a) NRZ input signal; (b) output from a perfect filter; (c) output from an imperfect filter

energy in the form of spurious responses from the third and fourth impulses from one pulse appears during the sampling instant ($T = 0$) of another pulse. This interference is commonly called *intersymbol interference* or simply ISI. ISI is an important consideration in the transmission of pulses over circuits with a limited bandwidth and a nonlinear phase response. Simply stated, rectangular pulses will not remain rectangular in less than an infinite bandwidth. The narrower the bandwidth, the more rounded the pulses. If the phase distortion is excessive, the pulse will *tilt* and, consequently, affect the next pulse. When pulses from more than one source are multiplexed together, the amplitude, frequency, and phase responses become even more critical. ISI causes *cross talk* between channels that occupy adjacent time slots in a time-division-multiplexed carrier system. Special filters called *equalizers* are inserted in the transmission path to "equalize" the distortion for all frequencies, creating a uniform transmission medium and reducing transmission impairments. The four primary causes of ISI are

    1. *Timing inaccuracies.* In digital transmission systems, transmitter timing inaccuracies cause intersymbol interference if the rate of transmission does not conform to the *ringing frequency* designed into the communications channel. Generally, timing inaccuracies of this type are insignificant. Because receiver clocking information is derived from

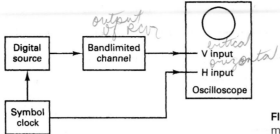

output of Rcvr

vertical

horizontal

FIGURE 4-29 Eye diagram measurement setup

the received signals, which are contaminated with noise, inaccurate sample timing is more likely to occur in receivers than in transmitters.

2. *Insufficient bandwidth.* Timing errors are less likely to occur if the transmission rate is well below the channel bandwidth (i.e., the Nyquist bandwidth is significantly below the channel bandwidth). As the bandwidth of a communications channel is reduced, the ringing frequency is reduced and intersymbol interference is more likely to occur.

3. *Amplitude distortion.* Filters are placed in a communications channel to band-limit signals and reduce or eliminate predicted noise and interference. Filters are also used to produce a specific pulse response. However, the frequency response of a channel cannot always be predicted absolutely. When the frequency characteristics of a communications channel depart from the normal or expected values, *pulse distortion* results. Pulse distortion occurs when the peaks of pulses are reduced, causing improper ringing frequencies in the time domain. Compensation for such impairments is called amplitude equalization.

4. *Phase distortion.* A pulse is simply the superposition of a series of harmonically related sine waves with specific amplitude and phase relationships. Therefore, if the relative phase relations of the individual sine waves are altered, phase distortion occurs. Phase distortion occurs when frequency components undergo different amounts of time delay while propagating through the transmission medium. Special delay equalizers are placed in the transmission path to compensate for the varying delays, thus, reducing the phase distortion. Phase equalizers can be manually adjusted or designed to automatically adjust themselves to varying transmission characteristics.

Eye Patterns

The performance of a digital transmission system depends, in part, on the ability of a repeater to regenerate the original pulses. Similarly, the quality of the regeneration process depends on the decision circuit within the repeater and the quality of the signal at the input to the decision circuit. Therefore, the performance of a digital transmission system can be measured by displaying the received signal on an oscilloscope and triggering the time base at the data rate. Thus, all waveform combinations are superimposed over adjacent signaling intervals. Such a display is called an *eye pattern* or *eye diagram*. An eye pattern is a convenient technique for determining the effects of the degradations introduced into the pulses as they travel to the regenerator. The test setup to display an eye pattern is shown in Figure 4-29. The received pulse stream is fed to the vertical input of the oscilloscope, and the symbol clock is fed to the external trigger input, while the sweep rate is set approximately equal to the symbol rate.

Figure 4-30 shows an eye pattern generated by a symmetrical waveform for *ternary* signals in which the individual pulses at the input to the regenerator have a cosine-squared shape. In an *m*-level system, there will be $m - 1$ separate eyes. The horizontal lines labeled $+1$, 0, and -1 correspond to the ideal received amplitudes. The vertical lines, separated by the signaling interval, *T*, correspond to the ideal *decision*

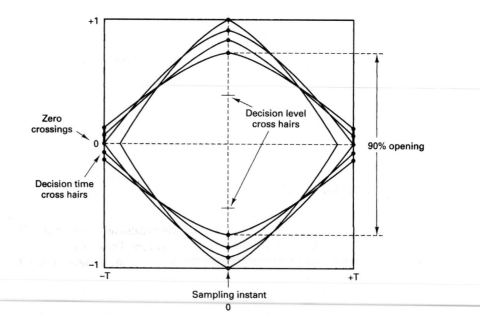

FIGURE 4-30 Eye diagram

times. The decision levels for the regenerator are represented by *crosshairs.* The vertical hairs represents the decision time, whereas the horizontal hairs represents the decision level. The eye pattern shows the quality of shaping and timing and discloses any noise and errors that might be present in the line equalization. The eye opening (the area in the middle of the eye pattern) defines a boundary within which no waveform *trajectories* can exist under any code-pattern condition. The eye opening is a function of the number of code levels and the intersymbol interference caused by the ringing tails of any preceding or succeeding pulses. To regenerate the pulse sequence without error, the eye must be open (i.e., a decision area must exist), and the decision crosshairs must be within the open area. The effect of pulse degradation is a reduction in the size of the ideal eye. In Figure 4-30 it can be seen that at the center of the eye (i.e., the sampling instant) the opening is about 90%, indicating only minor ISI degradation due to filtering imperfections. The small degradation is due to the nonideal Nyquist amplitude and phase characteristics of the transmission system. Mathematically, the ISI degradation is

$$20 \log \frac{h}{H} \tag{4-11}$$

where H = ideal vertical opening

h = degraded vertical opening

For the eye diagram shown in Figure 4-30,

$$20 \log \frac{90}{100} = 0.915 \text{ dB} \quad \text{(ISI degradation)}$$

In Figure 4-30 it can also be seen that the overlapping signal pattern does not cross the horizontal zero line at exact integer multiples of the symbol clock. This is an impairment known as *data transition jitter.* This jitter has an effect on the symbol timing (clock) recovery circuit and, if excessive, may significantly degrade the performance of cascaded regenerative sections.

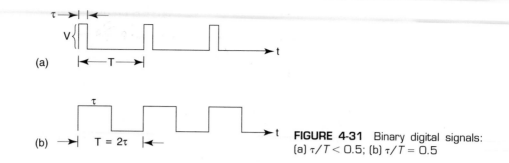

FIGURE 4-31 Binary digital signals:
(a) $\tau/T < 0.5$; (b) $\tau/T = 0.5$

SIGNAL POWER IN BINARY DIGITAL SIGNALS

Because binary digital signals can originate from literally scores of different types of data sources, it is impossible to predict which patterns or sequences of bits are most likely to occur over a given period of time in a given system. Thus, for signal analysis purposes, it is generally assumed that there is an equal probability of the occurrence of a 1 and a 0. Therefore, power can be averaged over an entire message duration and the signal can be modeled as a continuous sequence of alternating 1s and 0s as shown in Figure 4-31. Figure 4-31a shows a stream of rectangularly shaped pulses with a pulse width-to-pulse duration ratio τ/T less than 0.5, and Figure 4.31b shows a stream of square wave pulses with a τ/T ratio of 0.5.

The normalized $(R - 1)$ average power is derived for signal $f(t)$ from

$$\overline{P} = \lim_{T \to x} \frac{1}{T} \int_{-T/2}^{T/2} [f(t)]^2 \, dt \tag{4-12}$$

where T is the period of integration. If $f(t)$ is a periodic signal with period T_0, then Equation 4-12 reduces to

$$\overline{P} = \frac{1}{T_0} \int_{-T_0/2}^{T_0/2} [v(t)]^2 \, dt \tag{4-13}$$

If rectangular pulses of amplitude V with a τ/T ratio of 0.5 begin at $t = 0$, then

$$v(t) = \begin{cases} V & 0 \le t \le \tau \\ 0 & \tau < t \le T \end{cases} \tag{4-14}$$

Thus, from Equation 4-13,

$$\overline{P} = \frac{1}{T_0} \int_0^T (V)^2 \, dt = \frac{1}{T_0} V^2 t \Big|_0^\tau \tag{4-15}$$

$$= \frac{\tau}{T_0} V^2$$

and

$$P = \left(\frac{\tau}{T}\right) \frac{V^2}{R}$$

Because the effective *rms* value of a periodic wave is found from $P = (V_{rms})^2/R$, the rms voltage for a rectangular pulse is

$$V_{rms} = \sqrt{\frac{\tau}{T}} V \tag{4-16}$$

Because $P = (V_{rms})^2/R$, $P = (\sqrt{\tau/T} \, V)^2/R = (\tau V^2)/(TR)$.

With the square wave shown in Figure 4-31, $\tau/T = 0.5$, therefore, $P = V^2/2R$. Thus, the rms voltage for the square wave is the same as for sine waves, $V_{rms} = V/\sqrt{2}$.

QUESTIONS

4-1. Contrast the advantages and disadvantages of digital transmission.

4-2. What are the four most common methods of pulse modulation?

4-3. Which method listed in Question 4-2 is the only form of pulse modulation that is used in a digital transmission system? Explain.

4-4. What is the purpose of the sample-and-hold circuit?

4-5. Define *aperture* and *acquisition time*.

4-6. What is the difference between natural and flat-top sampling?

4-7. Define *droop*. What causes it?

4-8. What is the Nyquist sampling rate?

4-9. Define and state the causes of foldover distortion.

4-10. Explain the difference between a magnitude-only code and a sign-magnitude code.

4-11. Explain overload distortion.

4-12. Explain quantizing.

4-13. What is quantization range? Quantization error?

4-14. Define *dynamic range*.

4-15. Explain the relationship between dynamic range, resolution, and the number of bits in a PCM code.

4-16. Explain coding efficiency.

4-17. What is SQR? What is the relationship between SQR, resolution, dynamic range, and the number of bits in a PCM code?

4-18. Contrast linear and nonlinear PCM codes.

4-19. Explain idle channel noise.

4-20. Contrast midtread and midrise quantization.

4-21. Define *companding*.

4-22. What does the parameter μ determine?

4-23. Briefly explain the process of digital companding.

4-24. What is the effect of digital compression on SQR, resolution, quantization interval, and quantization noise?

4-25. Contrast delta modulation PCM and standard PCM.

4-26. Define *slope overload* and *granular noise*.

4-27. What is the difference between adaptive delta modulation and conventional delta modulation?

4-28. Contrast differential and conventional PCM.

PROBLEMS

4-1. Determine the Nyquist sample rate for a maximum analog input frequency of
   (a) 4 kHz
   (b) 10 kHz

4-2. For the sample-and-hold circuit shown in Figure 4-3, determine the largest-value capacitor that can be used. Use the following parameters: an output impedance for $Z_1 = 20 \, \Omega$, an on resistance of Q_1 of 20 Ω, an acquisition time of 10 μs, a maximum output current from Z_1 of 20 mA, and an accuracy of 1%.

4-3. For a sample rate of 20 kHz, determine the maximum analog input frequency.

4-4. Determine the alias frequency for a 15-kHz sample rate and an analog input frequency of 1.5 kHz.

4-5. Determine the dynamic range for a 10-bit sign-magnitude PCM code.

4-6. Determine the minimum number of bits required in a PCM code for a dynamic range of 80 dB. What is the coding efficiency?

4-7. For a resolution of 0.04 V, determine the voltages for the following linear 7-bit sign-magnitude PCM codes.
  (a) 0 1 1 0 1 0 1
  (b) 0 0 0 0 0 1 1
  (c) 1 0 0 0 0 0 1
  (d) 0 1 1 1 1 1 1
  (e) 1 0 0 0 0 0 0

4-8. Determine the SQR for a 2-v_{rms} signal and a quantization interval of 0.2 V.

4-9. Determine the resolution and quantization noise for an 8-bit linear sign-magnitude PCM code for a maximum decoded voltage of 1.27 V.

4-10. A 12-bit linear PCM code is digitally compressed into 8 bits. The resolution = 0.03 V. Determine the following for an analog input voltage of 1.465 V.
  (a) 12-bit linear PCM code
  (b) 8-bit compressed code
  (c) Decoded 12-bit code
  (d) Decoded voltage
  (e) Percentage error

4-11. For a 12-bit linear PCM code with a resolution of 0.02 V, determine the voltage range that would be converted to the following PCM codes.
  (a) 1 0 0 0 0 0 0 0 0 0 0 1
  (b) 0 0 0 0 0 0 0 0 0 0 0 0
  (c) 1 1 0 0 0 0 0 0 0 0 0 0
  (d) 0 1 0 0 0 0 0 0 0 0 0 0
  (e) 1 0 0 1 0 0 0 0 0 0 0 1
  (f) 1 0 1 0 1 0 1 0 1 0 1 0

4-12. For each of the following 12-bit linear PCM codes, determine the 8-bit compressed code to which they would be converted.
  (a) 1 0 0 0 0 0 0 0 1 0 0 0
  (b) 1 0 0 0 0 0 0 0 1 0 0 1
  (c) 1 0 0 0 0 0 0 1 0 0 0 0
  (d) 0 0 0 0 0 0 1 0 0 0 0 0
  (e) 0 1 0 0 0 0 0 0 0 0 0 0
  (f) 0 1 0 0 0 0 1 0 0 0 0 0

4-13. Determine the Nyquist sampling rate for the following maximum analog input frequencies: 2 kHz, 5 kHz, 12 kHz, and 20 kHz.

4-14. For the sample-and-hold circuit shown in Figure 4-3, determine the largest-value capacitor that can be used for the following parameters: Z_1 output impedance = 15 Ω, an on resistance of Q_1 of 15 Ω, an acquisition time of 12 μs, a maximum output current from Z_1 of 10 mA, an accuracy of 0.1%, and a maximum change in voltage dv = 10 V.

4-15. Determine the maximum analog input frequency for the following Nyquist sample rates: 2.5 kHz, 4 kHz, 9 kHz, and 11 kHz.

4-16. Determine the alias frequency for the following sample rates and analog input frequencies

f_a (kHz)	f_s (kHz)
3	4
5	8
6	8
5	7

4-17. Determine the dynamic range in dB for the following n-bit linear sign-magnitude PCM codes: n = 7, 8, 12, and 14.

4-18. Determine the minimum number of bits required for PCM codes with the following dynamic ranges, and determine the coding efficiencies: DR = 24 dB, 48 dB, and 72 dB.

4-19. For the following values of μ, V_{max}, and V_{in}; determine the compressor gain.

μ	V_{max} (V)	V_{in} (V)
255	1	0.75
100	1	0.75
255	2	0.5

4-20. For the following resolutions, determine the range of the 8-bit sign-magnitude PCM codes:

Code	Resolution (V)
10111000	0.1
00111000	0.1
11111111	0.05
00011100	0.02
00110101	0.02
11100000	0.02
00000111	0.02

4-21. Determine the SQR for the following input signal and quantization noise magnitudes:

V_s	V_n (V)
1 v_{rms}	0.01
2 v_{rms}	0.02
3 v_{rms}	0.01
4 v_{rms}	0.2

4-22. Determine the resolution and quantization noise for an 8-bit linear sign-magnitude PCM code for the following maximum decoded voltages: $V_{max} = 3.06$ V$_p$, 3.57 V$_p$, 4.08 V$_p$, and 4.59 V$_p$.

4-23. A 12-bit linear sign-magnitude PCM code is digitally compressed into 8 bits. For a resolution of 0.016 V, determine the following quantities for the indicated input voltages: 12-bit linear PCM code, 8-bit compressed code, decoded 12-bit code, decoded voltage, and percentage error. $V_{in} = -6.592$ V, $+12.992$ V, and -3.36 V.

4-24. For the 12-bit linear PCM codes given, determine the voltage range that would be converted to them.

12-Bit Linear Code	Resolution (V)
100011110010	0.12
000001000000	0.10
000111111000	0.14
111111110000	0.12

4-25. For the following 12-bit linear PCM codes, determine the 8-bit compressed code to which they would be converted.

12-Bit Linear Code
100011110010
000001000000
000111111000
111111110010
000000100000

4-26. For the following 8-bit compressed codes, determine the expanded 12-bit code.

8-Bit Code
11001010
00010010
10101010
01010101
11110000
11011011

CHAPTER 5

Multiplexing

INTRODUCTION

Multiplexing is the transmission of information (either voice or data) from more than one source to more than one destination on the same transmission medium *(facility)*. Transmissions occur on the same facility but not necessarily at the same time. The transmission medium may be a metallic wire pair, a coaxial cable, a terrestrial microwave radio system, a satellite microwave radio, or an optical fiber cable. There are several ways in which multiplexing can be achieved, although the two most common methods are *frequency-division multiplexing* (FDM) and *time-division multiplexing* (TDM).

TIME-DIVISION MULTIPLEXING

With TDM, transmissions from multiple sources occur on the same facility but not at the same time. Transmissions from various sources are *interleaved* in the time domain. The most common type of modulation used with TDM systems is PCM. With a PCM-TDM system, two or more voice-band channels are sampled, converted to PCM codes, and then time-division multiplexed onto a single metallic cable pair or an optical fiber cable.

Figure 5-1a shows a simplified block diagram of a two-channel PCM-TDM carrier system. Each channel is alternately sampled and converted to a PCM code. While the PCM code for channel 1 is being transmitted, channel 2 is sampled and converted to a PCM code. While the PCM code from channel 2 is being transmitted, the next sample is taken from channel 1 and converted to a PCM code. This process continues and samples are taken alternately from each channel, converted to PCM codes, and transmitted. The multiplexer is simply an electronic switch with two inputs and one output. Channel 1 and channel 2 are alternately selected and connected to the multiplexer output. The time it takes to transmit one sample from each channel is called the *frame time*.

The PCM code for each channel occupies a fixed time slot (epoch) within the total TDM frame. With a two-channel system, the time allocated for each channel is equal to

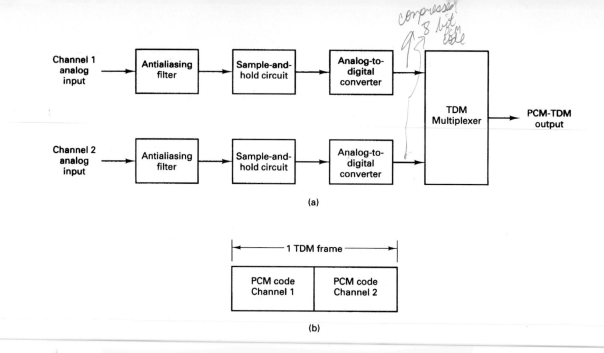

compressed 8 bit code

(a)

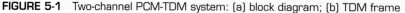

(b)

FIGURE 5-1 Two-channel PCM-TDM system: (a) block diagram; (b) TDM frame

one-half of the total frame time. A sample from each channel is taken once during each frame. Therefore, the total frame time is equal to the reciprocal of the sample rate $(1/f_s)$. Figure 5-1b shows the TDM frame allocation for a two-channel system.

T1 DIGITAL CARRIER SYSTEM

A digital carrier is a communications system that uses digital pulses to encode information rather than analog signals. Figure 5-2 shows the block diagram of the Bell System T1 digital carrier system. This system is the North American telephone standard. A T1 carrier time-division multiplexes 24 PCM encoded samples for transmission over a single metallic wire pair or optical fiber. Again, the multiplexer is simply a switch, except that now it has 24 inputs and 1 output. The 24 voice-band channels are sequentially selected and connected to the multiplexer output. Each voice-band channel occupies a 300-Hz to 3000-Hz bandwidth.

Simply time-division multiplexing 24 voice-band channels does not in itself constitute a T1 carrier. At this point, the output of the multiplexer is simply a multiplexed digital signal (DS-1). It does not actually become a T1 carrier until it is line encoded and placed on special conditioned wire pairs called *T1 lines*. This is explained in more detail later in this chapter under the heading "North American Digital Hierarchy."

With the Bell System T1 carrier system, D-type (digital) channel banks perform the sampling, encoding, and multiplexing of 24 voice-band channels. Each channel contains an 8-bit PCM code and is sampled 8000 times per second. (Each channel is sampled at the same rate but not necessarily at the same time; see Figure 5-3.) Therefore, a 64-kbps PCM encoded sample is transmitted for each voice-band channel during each frame.

$$\frac{8 \text{ bits}}{\text{sample}} \times \frac{8000 \text{ samples}}{\text{second}} = 64 \text{ kbps}$$

Within each frame an additional bit called a *framing bit* is added. The framing bit occurs at an 8000-bps rate and is recovered in the receiver circuitry and used to maintain frame and sample synchronization between the TDM transmitter and receiver. As a result, each TDM frame contains 193 bits.

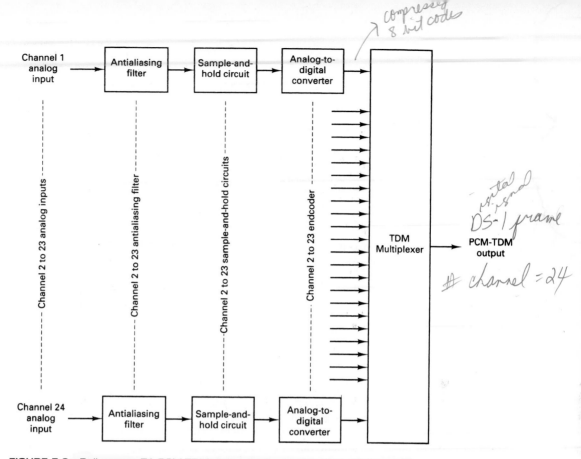

compressed 8 bit code (handwritten)

DS-1 frame (handwritten)

 # channel = 24 (handwritten)

FIGURE 5-2 Bell system T1 PCM-TDM digital carrier system block diagram

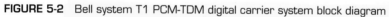

FIGURE 5-3 T1 sampling sequence

FIGURE 5-4 T1 carrier system frame and sample alignment using D1 channel banks

$$\frac{8 \text{ bits}}{\text{channel}} \times \frac{24 \text{ channels}}{\text{frame}} = \frac{192 \text{ bits}}{\text{frame}} + \frac{1 \text{ framing bit}}{\text{frame}} = \frac{193 \text{ bits}}{\text{frame}}$$

As a result, the line speed (bps) for the T1 carrier is

$$\text{line speed} = \frac{193 \text{ bits}}{\text{frame}} \times \frac{8000 \text{ frames}}{\text{second}} = 1.544 \text{ Mbps}$$

D-Type Channel Banks

The early T1 carrier systems were equipped with D1A channel banks that use a 7-bit magnitude-only PCM code with analog companding and $\mu = 100$. A later version of the D1 channel bank (D1D) used an 8-bit sign-magnitude PCM code. With D1A channel banks an eighth bit (the s bit) is added to each PCM code word for the purpose of *signaling* (supervision: on-hook, off-hook, dial pulsing, and so on). Consequently, the signaling rate for D1 channel banks is 8 kbps. Also, with D1 channel banks, the framing bit sequence is simply an alternating 1/0 pattern. Figure 5-4 shows the frame and sample alignment for the T1 carrier system using D1A channel banks.

Generically, the T1 carrier system has progressed through the D2, D3, D4, D5, and D6 channel banks. D4, D5, and D6 use a digitally companded, 8-bit sign-magnitude compressed PCM code with $\mu = 255$. In the D1 channel bank, the compression and expansion characteristics were implemented in circuitry separate from the encoder and decoder. The D2, D3, D4, and D5 channel banks incorporate the companding functions directly in the encoders and decoders. Although the D2 and D3 channel banks are functionally similar, the D3 channel banks were the first to incorporate separate customized LSI integrated circuits (codecs) for each voice-band channel. With D1, D2, and D3 channel banks, common equipment performs the encoding and decoding functions. Consequently, a single equipment malfunction constitutes a total system failure.

D1A channel banks use a magnitude-only code; consequently, an error in the most significant bit (MSB) of a channel sample always produces a decoded error equal to one-half the total quantization range (V_{max}). Because D1D, D2, D3, D4, and D5 channel banks use a sign-magnitude code, an error in the MSB (sign bit) causes a decoded error equal to twice the sample magnitude (from $+V$ to $-V$, or vice versa). The worst-case error is equal to twice the total quantization range. However, maximum amplitude samples occur rarely, and most errors with D1D, D2, D3, D4, and D5 coding are less than one-half the coding range. On the average, the error performance with a sign-magnitude code is better than with a magnitude-only code.

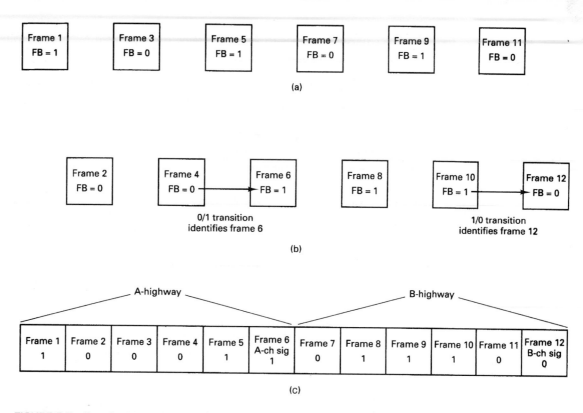

FIGURE 5-5 Framing bit sequence or the T1 superframe format using D2 or D3 channel banks: (a) frame synchronizing bits (odd-numbered frames); (b) signaling frame alignment bits (even-numbered frames); (c) composite frame alignment

Superframe Format

The 8-kbps signaling rate used with D1 channel banks is excessive for voice transmission. Therefore, with D2 and D3 channel banks, a signaling bit is substituted only into the least significant bit (LSB) of every sixth frame. Therefore, five out of every six frames have 8-bit resolution, while one out of every six frames (the signaling frame) has only 7-bit resolution. Consequently, the signaling rate on each channel is 1.333 kbps (8000 bps/6), and the effective number of bits per sample is actually 7 5/6 bits and not 8.

Because only every sixth frame includes a signaling bit, it is necessary that all the frames be numbered so that the receiver knows when to extract the signaling information. Also, because the signaling is accomplished with a 2-bit binary word, it is necessary to identify the MSB and LSB of the signaling word. Consequently, the *superframe* format shown in Figure 5-5 was devised. Within each superframe, there are 12 consecutively numbered frames (1–12). The signaling bits are substituted in frames 6 and 12, the MSB into frame 6 and the LSB into frame 12. Frames 1–6 are called the A-highway, with frame 6 designated as the A-channel signaling frame. Frames 7–12 are called the B-highway, with frame 12 designated as the B-channel signaling frame. Therefore, in addition to identifying the signaling frames, the sixth and twelfth frames must be positively identified.

To identify frames 6 and 12, a different framing bit sequence is used for the odd- and even-numbered frames. The odd frames (frames 1, 3, 5, 7, 9, and 11) have an alternating 1/0 pattern, and the even frames (frames 2, 4, 6, 8, 10, and 12) have a 0 0 1 1 1 0 repetitive pattern. As a result, the combined bit pattern for the framing bits is a 1 0 0 0 1 1 0 1 1 1 0 0 repetitive pattern. The odd-numbered frames are used for frame and sample synchronization, and the even-numbered frames are used to identify the A- and B-channel signaling frames (6 and 12). Frame 6 is identified by a 0/1 transition in the framing bit between frames 4 and 6. Frame 12 is identified by a 1/0 transition in the framing bit between frames 10 and 12.

Figure 5-6 shows the frame, sample, and signaling alignment for the T1 carrier system using D2 or D3 channel banks.

In addition to *multiframe alignment* bits and PCM sample bits, certain time slots are used to indicate alarm conditions. For example, in the case of a transmit power supply failure, a common equipment failure, or loss of multiframe alignment, the second bit in each channel is made a 0 until the alarm condition has cleared. Also, the framing bit in frame 12 is complemented whenever multiframe alignment is lost (this is assumed whenever frame alignment is lost). In addition, there are special framing conditions that must be avoided in order to maintain clock and bit synchronization at the receive demultiplexing equipment. These special conditions are explained later in this chapter.

D4 channel banks time-division multiplex 48 voice-band channels and operate at a transmission rate of 3.152 Mbps. This is slightly more than twice the line speed for 24-channel D1, D2, or D3 channel banks. This is because with D4 channel banks, rather than transmit a single framing bit with each frame, a 10-bit frame synchronization pattern is used. Consequently, the total number of bits in a D4 (DS-1C) TDM frame is

$$\frac{8 \text{ bits}}{\text{channel}} \times \frac{48 \text{ channels}}{\text{frame}} = \frac{384 \text{ bits}}{\text{frame}} + \frac{10 \text{ syn bits}}{\text{frame}} = \frac{394 \text{ bits}}{\text{frame}}$$

and the line speed is

$$\text{line speed} = \frac{394 \text{ bits}}{\text{frame}} \times \frac{8000 \text{ frames}}{\text{second}} = 3.152 \text{ Mbps}$$

The framing for the DS-1 (T1) system or the framing pattern for the DS-1C (T1C) time-division multiplexed carrier systems is added to the multiplexed digital signal at the output of the multiplexer. Figure 5-7 shows the framing bit circuitry for the 24-channel T1 carrier system using either D1, D2, or D3 channel banks (DS-1). Note that the bit rate at the output of the TDM multiplex is 1.536 Mbps and the bit rate at the output of the 193-bit shift register is 1.544 Mbps. The difference (8 kbps) is due to the addition of the framing bit in the shift register.

CCITT TIME-DIVISION MULTIPLEXED CARRIER SYSTEM

Figure 5-8 shows the frame alignment for the CCITT (Comité Consultatif International Téléphonique et Télégraphique) European standard PCM-TDM system. With the CCITT system, a 125-μs frame is divided into 32 equal time slots. Time slot 0 is used for a frame alignment pattern and for an alarm channel. Time slot 17 is used for a common signaling channel. The signaling for all the voice-band channels is accomplished on the common signaling channel. Consequently, 30 voice-band channels are time-division multiplexed into each CCITT frame.

With the CCITT standard, each time slot has 8 bits. Consequently, the total number of bits per frame is

$$\frac{8 \text{ bits}}{\text{time slot}} \times \frac{32 \text{ time slots}}{\text{frame}} = \frac{256 \text{ bits}}{\text{frame}}$$

and the line speed is

$$\text{line speed} = \frac{256 \text{ bits}}{\text{frame}} \times \frac{8000 \text{ frames}}{\text{second}} = 2.048 \text{ Mbps}$$

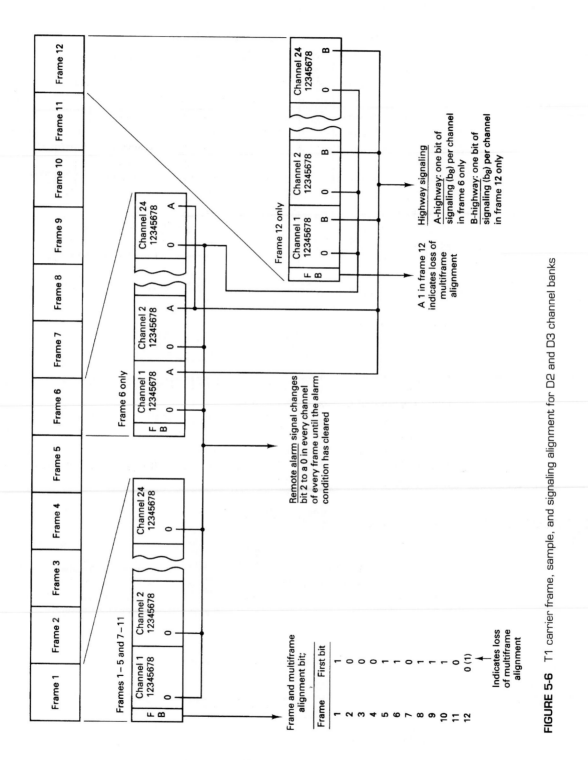

FIGURE 5-6 T1 carrier frame, sample, and signaling alignment for D2 and D3 channel banks

FIGURE 5-7 Framing bit circuitry for the DS-1 T1 carrier system

Time slot 0	Time slot 1	Time slots 2–16	Time slot 17	Time slots 18–30	Time slot 31
Framing and alarm channel	Voice channel 1	Voice channels 2–15	Common signaling channel	Voice channels 16–29	Voice channel 30
8 bits	8 bits	112 bits	8 bits	112 bits	8 bits

(a)

Time slot 17

	Bits	
Frame	1234	5678
0	0000	xyxx
1	ch 1	ch 16
2	ch 2	ch 17
3	ch 3	ch 18
4	ch 4	ch 19
5	ch 5	ch 20
6	ch 6	ch 21
7	ch 7	ch 22
8	ch 8	ch 23
9	ch 9	ch 24
10	ch 10	ch 25
11	ch 11	ch 26
12	ch 12	ch 27
13	ch 13	ch 28
14	ch 14	ch 29
15	ch 15	ch 30

16 frames equal one multiframe; 500 multiframes are transmitted each second

x = spare

y = loss of multiframe alignment if a 1

4 bits per channel are transmitted once every 16 frames, resulting in a 500-bps signaling rate for each channel

(b)

FIGURE 5-8 CCITT TDM frame alignment and common signaling channel alignment: (a) CCITT TDM frame (125 μs, 256 bits, 2.048 Mbps); (b) common signaling channel

A *codec* is a large-scale-integration (LSI) chip designed for use in the telecommunications industry for *private branch exchanges* (PBXs), central office switches, digital handsets, voice store-and-forward systems, and digital echo suppressors. Essentially, the codec is applicable for any purpose that requires the digitizing of analog signals, such as in a PCM-TDM carrier system.

Codec is a generic term that refers to the *co*ding functions performed by a device that converts analog signals to digital codes and digital codes to analog signals. Recently developed codecs are called *combo* chips because they combine codec and filter functions in the same LSI package. The input/output filter performs the following functions: bandlimiting, noise rejection, antialiasing, and reconstruction of analog audio waveforms after decoding. The codec performs the following functions: analog sampling, encoding/decoding (analog-to-digital and digital-to-analog conversions), and digital companding.

COMBO CHIPS

A combo chip can provide the analog-to-digital and the digital-to-analog conversions and the transmit and receive filtering necessary to interface a full-duplex (four-wire) voice telephone circuit to the PCM highway of a TDM carrier system. Essentially, a combo chip replaces the older codec and filter chip combination.

Table 5-1 lists several of the combo chips available and their prominent features.

General Operation

The following major functions are provided by a combo chip:

1. Bandpass filtering of the analog signals prior to encoding and after decoding
2. Encoding and decoding of voice and call progress signals
3. Encoding and decoding of signaling and supervision information
4. Digital companding

Figure 5-9 shows the block diagram of a typical combo chip.

TABLE 5-1 Features of Several Codec/Filter Combo Chips

2916 (16-Pin)	2917 (16-Pin)	2913 (20-Pin)	2914 (24-Pin)
μ-law companding only	A-law companding only	μ/A-law companding	μ/A-law companding
Master clock, 2.048 MHz only	Master clock, 2.048 MHz only	Master clock, 1.536 MHz, 1.544 MHz, or 2.048 MHz	Master clock, 1.536 MHz, 1.544 MHz, or 2.048 MHz
Fixed data rate	Fixed data rate	Fixed data rate	Fixed data rate
Variable data rate, 64 kbps–2.048 Mbps	Variable data rate, 64 kbps–4.096 Mbps	Variable data rate, 64 kbps–4.096 Mbps	Variable data rate, 64 kbps–4.096 Mbps
78-dB dynamic	78-dB dynamic range	78-dB dynamic range	78-dB dynamic range
ATT D3/4 compatible	ATT D3/4 compatible	ATT D3/4 compatible	ATT D3/4 compatible
Single-ended input	Single-ended input	Differential input	Differential input
Single-ended output	Single-ended output	Differential output	Differential output
Gain adjust transmit only	Gain adjust transmit only	Gain adjust transmit and receive	Gain adjust transmit and receive
Synchronous clocks	Synchronous clocks	Synchronous clocks	Synchronous clocks
			Asynchronous clocks
			Analog loopback
			Signaling

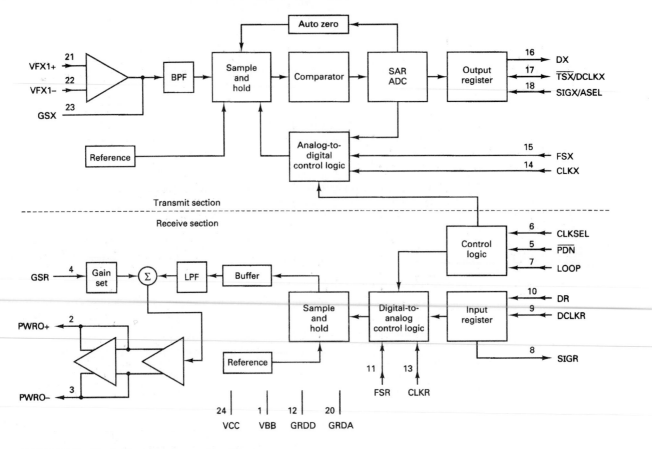

FIGURE 5-9 Block diagram of a combo chip

Fixed-Data-Rate Mode

In the *fixed-data-rate-mode,* the master *transmit* and *receive clocks* on a combo chip (CLKX and CLKR) perform the following functions:

1. Provide the master clock for the on-board switched capacitor filter
2. Provide the clock for the analog-to-digital and digital-to-analog converters
3. Determine the input and output data rates between the codec and the PCM highway

Therefore, in the fixed-data-rate mode, the transmit and receive data rates must be either 1.536 Mbps, 1.544 Mbps, or 2.048 Mbps, the same as the master clock rate.

Transmit and receive frame synchronizing pulses (FSX and FSR) are 8-kHz inputs that set the transmit and receive sampling rates and distinguish between *signaling* and *nonsignaling* frames. $\overline{\text{TSX}}$ is a *time-slot strobe buffer enable* output that is used to gate the PCM word onto the PCM highway when an external buffer is used to drive the line. $\overline{\text{TSX}}$ is also used as an external gating pulse for a time-division multiplexer (see Figure 5-10).

Data are transmitted to the PCM highway from DX on the first eight positive transitions of CLKX following the rising edge of FSX. On the receive channel, data are received from the PCM highway from DR on the first eight falling edges of CLKR after the occurrence of FSR. Therefore, the occurrence of FSX and FSR must be synchronized between codecs in a multiple-channel system to ensure that only one codec is transmitting to or receiving from the PCM highway at any given time.

(a)

FIGURE 5-10 Single-channel PCM system using a combo chip in the fixed-data-rate mode:
(a) block diagram *(Continued)*

Figure 5-10 shows the block diagram and timing sequence for a single-channel PCM system using a combo chip in the fixed-data-rate mode and operating with a master clock frequency of 1.536 MHz. In the fixed-data-rate mode, data are input and output for a single channel in short bursts. (This mode of operation is sometimes called the *burst mode.*) With only a single channel, the PCM highway is active only 1/24 of the total frame time. Additional channels can be added to the system provided that their transmissions are synchronized so that they do not occur at the same time as transmissions from any other channel.

From Figure 5-10 the following observations can be made:

1. The input and output bit rates from the codec are equal to the master clock frequency, 1.536 Mbps.
2. The codec inputs and outputs 64,000 PCM bits per second.
3. The data output (DX) and data input (DR) are enabled only 1/24 of the total frame time (125 μs).

To add channels to the system shown in Figure 5-10, the occurrence of the FSX, FSR, and $\overline{\text{TSX}}$ signals for each additional channel must be synchronized so that they follow a timely sequence and do not allow more than one codec to transmit or receive at

(b)

FIGURE 5-10 (Continued) (b) timing sequence

the same time. Figure 5-11 shows the block diagram and timing sequence for a 24-channel PCM-TDM system operating with a master clock frequency of 1.536 MHz.

Variable-Data-Rate Mode

The *variable-data-rate mode* allows for a flexible data input and output clock frequency. It provides the ability to vary the frequency of the transmit and receive bit clocks. In the variable-data-rate mode, a master clock frequency of 1.536 MHz, 1.544 MHz, or 2.048 MHz is still required for proper operation of the onboard bandpass filters and the analog-to-digital and digital-to-analog converters. However, in the variable-data-rate mode, DCLKR and DCLKX become the data clocks for the receive and transmit PCM highways, respectively. When FSX is high, data are transmitted onto the PCM highway on the next eight consecutive positive transitions of DCLKX. Similarly, while FSR is high, data from the PCM highway are clocked into the codec on the next eight consecutive negative transitions of DCLKR. This mode of operation is sometimes called the *shift register mode.*

On the transmit channel, the last transmitted PCM word is repeated in all remaining time slots in the 125-μs frame as long as DCLKX is pulsed and FSX is held active high. This feature allows the PCM word to be transmitted to the PCM highway more than once per frame. Signaling is not allowed in the variable-data-rate mode because this mode provides no means to specify a signaling frame.

Figure 5-12 (p. 241) shows the block diagram and timing sequence for a two-channel PCM-TDM system using a combo chip in the variable-data-rate mode with a master clock frequency of 1.536 MHz, a sample rate of 8 kHz, and a transmit and receive data rate of 128 kbps.

FIGURE 5-11 Twenty-four-channel PCM-TDM system using a combo chip in the fixed-data-rate mode and operating with a master clock frequency of 1.536 MHz: (a) block diagram *(Continued)*

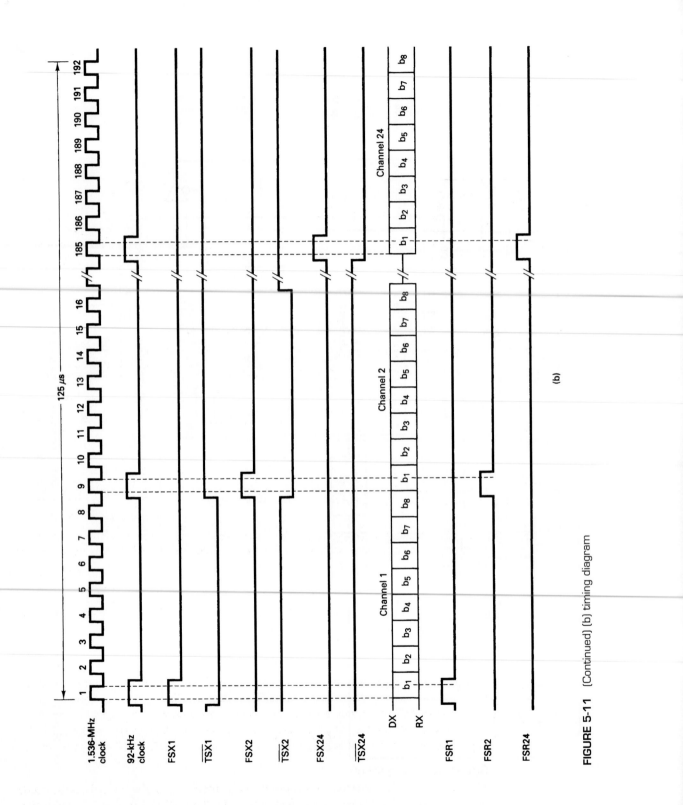

FIGURE 5-11 (Continued) (b) timing diagram

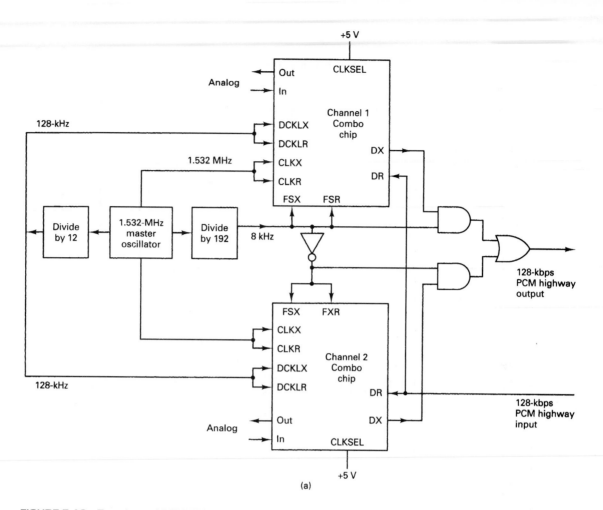

FIGURE 5-12 Two-channel PCM-TDM system using a combo chip in the variable-data-rate mode with a master clock frequency of 1.536 MHz: (a) block diagram *(Continued)*

With a sample rate of 8 kHz, the frame time is 125 μs. Therefore, one 8-bit PCM word from each channel is transmitted and/or received during each 125-μs frame. For 16 bits to occur in 125 μs, a 128-kHz transmit and receive data clock is required.

$$t_b = \frac{1 \text{ channel}}{8 \text{ bits}} \times \frac{1 \text{ frame}}{2 \text{ channels}} \times \frac{125 \mu s}{\text{frame}} = \frac{125 \text{ μs}}{16 \text{ bits}} = \frac{7.8125 \text{ μs}}{\text{bit}}$$

$$\text{bit rate} = \frac{1}{t_b} = \frac{1}{7.8125 \text{ μs}} = 128 \text{ kbps}$$

The transmit and receive enable signals (FSX and FSR) for each codec are active for one-half of the total frame time. Consequently, 8-kHz, 50% duty cycle transmit and receive data enable signals (FSX and FXR) are fed directly to one codec and fed to the other codec 180° out of phase (inverted), thereby, enabling only one codec at a time.

To expand to a four-channel system, simply increase the transmit and receive data clock rates to 256 kHz and change the enable signals to 8-kHz, 25% duty cycle pulses.

Supervisory Signaling

With a combo chip, *supervisory signaling* can be used only in the fixed-data-rate mode. A transmit signaling frame is identified by making the FSX and FSR pulses twice their normal width. During a transmit signaling frame, the signal present on input SIGX is

FIGURE 5-12 (Continued) (b) timing diagram

substituted into the least significant bit position (b_1) of the encoded PCM word. At the receive end, the signaling bit is extracted from the PCM word prior to decoding and placed on output SIGR until updated by reception of another signaling frame.

Asynchronous operation occurs when the master transmit and receive clocks are derived from separate independent sources. A combo chip can be operated in either the synchronous or asynchronous mode using separate digital-to-analog converters and voltage references in the transmit and receive channels, which allows them to be operated completely independent of each other. With either synchronous or asynchronous operation, the master clock, data clock, and time-slot strobe must be synchronized at the beginning of each frame. In the variable-data-rate mode, CLKX and DCLKX must be synchronized once per frame, but may be different frequencies.

NORTH AMERICAN DIGITAL HIERARCHY

Multiplexing signals in digital form lends itself easily to interconnecting digital transmission facilities with different transmission bit rates. Figure 5-13 shows the American Telephone and Telegraph Company's (AT&T) North American Digital Hierarchy for multiplexing digital signals with the same bit rates into a single pulse stream suitable for

FIGURE 5-13 North American Digital Hierarchy

TABLE 5-2 Summary of the North American Digital Hierarchy

Line Type	Digital Signal	Bit Rate (Mbps)	Channel Capacities	Services Offered
T1	DS-1	1.544	24	Voice-band telephone
T1C	DS-1C	3.152	48	Voice-band telephone
T2	DS-2	6.312	96	Voice-band telephone and picturephone
T3	DS-3	46.304	672	Voice-band telephone, picturephone, and broadcast-quality television
T4M	DS-4	274.176	4032	Same as T3 except more capacity
T5	DS-5	560.160	8064	Same as T4 except more capacity

transmission on the next higher level of the hierarchy. To upgrade from one level in the hierarchy to the next higher level, special devices called *muldems* (*mul*tiplexers/*dem*ultiplexers) are used. Muldems can handle bit-rate conversions in both directions. The muldem designations (M12, M23, and so on) identify the input and output digital signals associated with that muldem. For instance, an M12 muldem interfaces DS-1 and DS-2 *digital signals.* An M23 muldem interfaces DS-2 and DS-3 signals. DS-1 signals may be further multiplexed or line encoded and placed on specially conditioned lines called T1 lines. DS-2, DS-3, DS-4 and DS-5 signals may be placed on T2, T3, T4M, and T5 lines, respectively.

Digital signals are routed at central locations called *digital cross-connects.* A digital cross-connect (DSX) provides a convenient place to make patchable interconnects and to perform routine maintenance and troubleshooting. Each type of digital signal (DS-1, DS-2, and so on) has its own digital switch (DSX-1, DSX-2, and so on). The output from a digital switch may be upgraded to the next higher level or line encoded and placed on its respective T lines (T1, T2, and so on).

Table 5-2 lists the digital signals, their bit rates, channel capacities, and services offered for the line types included in the North American Digital Hierarchy.

When the bandwidth of the signals to be transmitted is such that after digital conversion it occupies the entire capacity of a digital transmission line, a single-channel terminal is provided. Examples of such single-channel terminals are picturephone, mastergroup, and commercial television terminals.

Mastergroup and Commercial Television Terminals

Figure 5-14 shows the block diagram of a mastergroup and commercial television terminal. The mastergroup terminal receives voice-band channels that have already been frequency-division multiplexed (a topic covered later in this chapter) without requiring that each voice-band channel be demultiplexed to voice frequencies. The signal processor provides frequency shifting for the mastergroup signals (shifts it from a 564-kHz to 3084-kHz bandwidth to a 0-kHz to 2520-kHz bandwidth) and dc restoration for the television signal. By shifting the mastergroup band, it is possible to sample at a 5.1-MHz rate. Sampling of the commercial television signal is at twice that rate or 10.2 MHz.

To meet the transmission requirements, a 9-bit PCM code is used to digitize each sample of the mastergroup or television signal. The digital output from the terminal is, therefore, approximately 46 Mbps for the mastergroup and twice that much (92 Mbps) for the television signal.

The digital terminal shown in Figure 5-14 has three specific functions: (1) it converts the parallel data from the output of the encoder to serial data, (2) it inserts frame synchronizing bits, and (3) it converts the serial binary signal to a form more suitable for transmission. In addition, for the commercial television terminal, the 92-Mbps digital signal must be split into two 46-Mbps digital signals because there is no 92-Mbps line speed in the digital hierarchy.

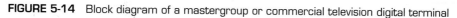

FIGURE 5-14 Block diagram of a mastergroup or commercial television digital terminal

Picturephone Terminal

Essentially, *picturephone* is a low-quality video transmission for use between nondedicated subscribers. For economic reasons it is desirable to encode a picturephone signal into the T2 capacity of 6.312 Mbps, which is substantially less than that for commercial network broadcast signals. This substantially reduces the cost and makes the service affordable. At the same time, it permits the transmission of adequate detail and contrast resolution to satisfy the average picturephone subscriber. Picturephone service is ideally suited to a differential PCM code. Differential PCM is similar to conventional PCM except that the exact magnitude of a sample is not transmitted. Instead, only the difference between that sample and the previous sample is encoded and transmitted. To encode the difference between samples requires substantially fewer bits than encoding the actual sample.

Data Terminal

The portion of communications traffic that involves data (signals other than voice) is increasing exponentially. Also, in most cases the data rates generated by each individual subscriber are substantially less than the data rate capacities of digital lines. Therefore, it seems only logical that terminals be designed that transmit data signals from several sources over the same digital line.

Data signals could be sampled directly; however, this would require excessively high sample rates, resulting in excessively high transmission bit rates, especially for sequences of data with few or no transitions. A more efficient method is one that codes the transition times. Such a method is shown in Figure 5-15. With the coding format shown, a 3-bit code is used to identify when transitions occur in the data and whether that transition is from a 1 to a 0, or vice versa. The first bit of the code is called the address bit. When this bit is a logic 1, this indicates that no transition occurred; a logic 0 indicates that a transition did occur. The second bit indicates whether the transition occurred during the first half (0) or during the second half (1) of the sample interval. The third bit indicates the sign or direction of the transition; a 1 for this bit indicates a 0-to-1 transition and a 0 indicates a 1-to-0 transition. Consequently, when there are no transitions in the data, a signal of all 1s is transmitted. Transmission of only the address bit would be sufficient; however, the sign bit provides a degree of error protection and limits error propagation (when one error leads to a second error, and so on). The efficiency of this

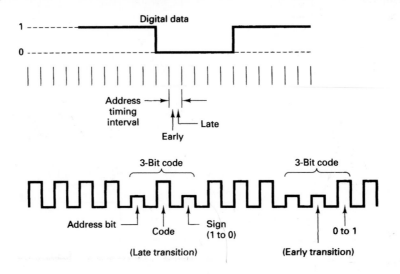

FIGURE 5-15 Data coding format

format is approximately 33%; there are 3 code bits for each data bit. The advantage of using a coded format rather than the original data is that coded data are more efficiently substituted for voice in analog systems. Without this coding format, transmitting a 250-kbps data signal, requires the same bandwidth as would be required to transmit 60 voice channels with analog multiplexing. With this coded format, a 50-kbps data signal displaces three 64-kbps PCM encoded channels, and a 250-kbps data stream displaces only 12 voice-band channels.

LINE ENCODING

Line encoding involves converting standard logic levels (TTL, CMOS, and the like) to a form more suitable to telephone line transmission. Essentially, five primary factors must be considered when selecting a line-encoding format:

1. Transmission voltages and dc component
2. Timing (clock) recovery
3. Transmission bandwidth
4. Ease of detection and decoding
5. Error detection

Transmission Voltages and DC Component

Transmission voltages or levels can be categorized as either *unipolar* (UP) or *bipolar* (BP). Unipolar transmission of binary data involves the transmission of only a single nonzero voltage level (for example, +V for logic 1 and 0 V or ground for a logic 0). In bipolar transmission, two nonzero voltage levels are involved (for example, +V for a logic 1 and −V for a logic 0).

Over a digital transmission line, it is more power efficient to encode binary data with voltages that are equal in magnitude but opposite in polarity and symmetrically balanced about 0 V. For example, assuming a 1-Ω resistance and a logic 1 level of + 5 V and a logic 0 level of 0 V, the average power required is 12.5 W (assuming an equal probability of the occurrence of a 1 or a 0). With a logic 1 level of +2.5 V and a logic 0 level of −2.5 V, the average power is only 6.25 W. Thus, by using bipolar symmetrical voltages, the average power is reduced by a factor of 50%.

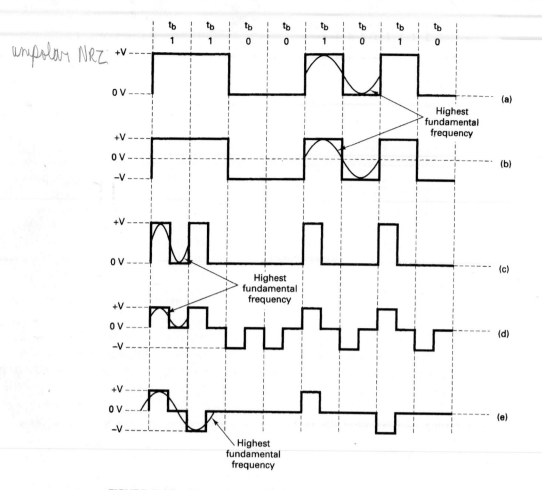

unipolar NRZ (handwritten annotation at left of graph (a))

FIGURE 5-16 Line-encoding formats: (a) UPNRZ; (b) BPNRZ; (c) UPRZ; (d) B-PRZ; (e) BPRZ-AMI

alternate mark inversion (handwritten annotation)

Duty Cycle

The *duty cycle* of a binary pulse can also be used to categorize the type of transmission. If the binary pulse is maintained for the entire bit time, this is called *nonreturn to zero* (NRZ). If the active time of the binary pulse is less than 100% of the bit time, this is called *return to zero* (RZ).

Unipolar and bipolar transmission voltages and return-to-zero and nonreturn-to-zero encoding can be combined in several ways to achieve a particular line encoding scheme. Figure 5-16 shows five line-encoding possibilities.

In Figure 5-16a, there is only one nonzero voltage level (+V = logic 1); a zero voltage simply implies a binary 0. Also, each logic 1 maintains the positive voltage for the entire bit time (100% duty cycle). Consequently, Figure 5-16a represents a unipolar nonreturn-to-zero signal (UPNRZ). In Figure 5-16b, there are two nonzero voltages (+V = logic 1 and −V = logic 0) and a 100% duty cycle is used. Figure 5-16b represents a bipolar nonreturn-to-zero signal (BPNRZ). In Figure 5-16c, only one nonzero voltage is used, but each pulse is active for only 50% of the bit time. Consequently, Figure 5-16c represents a unipolar return-to-zero signal (UPRZ). In Figure 5-16d, there are two nonzero-voltages (+V = logic 1 and −V = logic 0). Also, each pulse is active only 50% of the total bit time. Consequently, Figure 5-16d represents a bipolar return-to-zero (BPRZ) signal. In Figure 5-16e, there are again two nonzero voltage levels (−V and

FIGURE 5-17 DC wandering

+V), but here both polarities represent a logic 1 and 0 V represents a logic 0. This method of encoding is called *alternate mark inversion* (AMI). With AMI transmissions, each successive logic 1 is inverted in polarity from the previous logic 1. Because return to zero is used, this encoding technique is called *bipolar-return-to-zero alternate mark inversion* (BPRZ-AMI).

With NRZ encoding, a long string of either 1s or 0s produces a condition in which a receiver may lose its amplitude reference for optimum discrimination between received 1s and 0s. This condition is called *dc wandering*. The problem may also arise when there is a significant imbalance in the number of 1s and 0s transmitted. Figure 5-17 shows how dc wandering is produced by a long string of successive logic 1s. It can be seen that after a long string of 1s, 1-to-0 errors are more likely than 0-to-1 errors. Similarly, long strings of 0s increase the probability of a 0-to-1 error.

The method of line encoding used determines the minimum bandwidth required for transmission, how easily a clock may be extracted from it, how easily it may be decoded, the average dc level, and whether it offers a convenient means of detecting errors.

Bandwidth Considerations

To determine the minimum bandwidth required to propagate a line-encoded signal, you must determine the highest fundamental frequency associated with it (see Figure 5-16). The highest fundamental frequency is determined from the worst-case (fastest transition) binary bit sequence. With UPNRZ, the worst-case condition is an alternating 1/0 sequence; the period of the highest fundamental frequency takes the time of 2 bits and is, therefore, equal to one-half the bit rate. With BPNRZ, again the worst-case condition is an alternating 1/0 sequence, and the highest fundamental frequency is one-half of the bit rate. With UPRZ, the worst-case condition is two successive 1s. The minimum bandwidth is, therefore, equal to the bit rate. With BPRZ, the worst-case condition is either successive 1s or 0s, and the minimum bandwidth is again equal to the bit rate. With BPRZ-AMI, the worst-case condition is two or more consecutive 1s, and the minimum bandwidth is equal to one-half of the bit rate.

Clock Recovery

To recover and maintain clocking information from received data, there must be a sufficient number of transitions in the data signal. With UPNRZ and BPNRZ, a long string of consecutive 1s or 0s generates a data signal void of transitions and, therefore, is inadequate for clock synchronization. With UPRZ and BPRZ-AMI, a long string of 0s also generates a data signal void of transitions. With BPRZ, a transition occurs in each bit position regardless of whether the bit is a 1 or a 0. In the clock recovery circuit, the data are simply full-wave rectified to produce a data-independent clock equal to the receive bit rate. Therefore, BPRZ encoding is best suited for clock recovery. If long sequences of 0s are prevented from occurring, BPRZ-AMI encoding is sufficient to ensure clock synchronization.

Error Detection

With UPNRZ, BPNRZ, UPRZ, and BPRZ transmissions, there is no way to determine if the received data have errors. With BPRZ-AMI transmissions, an error in any bit will

TABLE 5-3 Line-Encoding Summary

Encoding Format	Minimum BW	Average DC	Clock Recovery	Error Detection
UPNRZ	$f_b/2$*	+V/2	Poor	No
BPNRZ	$f_b/2$*	0 V*	Poor	No
UPRZ	f_b	+V/2	Good	No
BPRZ	f_b	0 V*	Best*	No
BPRZ-AMI	$f_b/2$*	0 V*	Good	Yes*

*Denotes best performance or quality.

[handwritten: Manchester format   Fb   0   Best   None]

[handwritten: manchester]

FIGURE 5-18 Digital biphase

cause a bipolar violation (the reception of two or more consecutive 1s with the same polarity). Therefore, BPRZ-AMI has a built-in error-detection mechanism.

Ease of Detection and Decoding

Because unipolar transmission involves the transmission of only one polarity voltage, an average dc voltage is associated with the signal equal to +V/2. Assuming an equal probability of 1s and 0s occurring, bipolar transmissions have an average dc component of 0 V. A dc component is undesirable because it biases the input to a conventional threshold detector (a biased comparator) and could cause a misinterpretation of the logic condition of the received pulses. Therefore, bipolar transmission is better suited to data detection.

Table 5-3 summarizes the minimum bandwidth, average dc voltage, clock recovery, and error-detection capabilities of the line-encoding formats shown in Figure 5-16. From Table 5-3 it can be seen that BPRZ-AMI encoding has the best overall characteristics; therefore, it is the most commonly used method.

Digital Biphase, Miller, and Dicodes

Digital *biphase* (sometimes called the *Manchester code* or *diphase*) is a popular type of line encoding that produces a strong timing component for clock recovery and does not cause dc wandering. Biphase is a form of BPRZ transmission that uses one cycle of a square wave at 0° phase to represent a logic 1 and one cycle of a square wave at 180° phase to represent a logic 0. Digital biphase encoding is shown in Figure 5-18. Notice that a transition occurs in the center of every signaling element, regardless of its phase. Thus, biphase produces a strong timing component for clock recovery. In addition, assuming an equal probability of 1s and 0s, the average dc voltage is 0 V and there is no dc wandering. A disadvantage of biphase is that it contains no means of error detection.

Biphase encoding schemes have several variations including *biphase M, biphase L,* and *biphase S.* Biphase M is used for encoding SMPTE (Society of Motion Picture and Television Engineers) time-code data for recording on videotapes. Biphase M is well suited for this application because it has no dc component and the code is self-synchronizing (self-clocking). Self-synchronization is an import feature because it allows

Data   1   1   0   1   0   1   0   0   0   1   1

Biphase M

Biphase L

Biphase S

Differential
Manchester

Miller
(delay modulation)

Dicode NRZ

Dicode RZ

FIGURE 5-19 Biphase, Miller, and dicode encoding formats

TABLE 5-4 Summary of Biphase, Miller, and Dicode Encoding Formats

Biphase M (Biphase-mark)
   1 (Hi)—transition in the middle of the clock interval
   0 (Low)—no transition in the middle of the clock interval
   Note: There is always a transition at the beginning of the clock interval.
Biphase L (Biphase-level/Manchester)
   1 (Hi)—transition from high-to-low in the middle of the clock interval
   0 (Low)—transition from low-to-high in the middle of the clock interval
Biphase S (Biphase-space)
   1 (Hi)—no transition in the middle of the clock interval
   0 (Low)—transition in the middle of the clock interval
   Note: There is always a transition at the beginning of the clock interval.
Differential Manchester
   1 (Hi)—transition in the middle of the clock interval
   0 (Low)—transition at the beginning of the clock interval
Miller/delay modulation
   1 (Hi)—transition in the middle of the clock interval
   0 (Low)—no transition at the end of the clock interval unless followed by a zero
Dicode NRZ
   One-to-zero and zero-to-one data transitions change the signal polarity.
   If the data remain constant, then a zero-voltage level is output.
Dicode RZ
   One-to-zero and zero-to-one data transitions change the signal polarity in half-step voltage increments. If
   the data do not change, then a zero-voltage level is output.

clock recovery from the data stream even when the speed varies with tape speed, such as when searching through a tape in either the fast or slow modes. Biphase L is commonly called the Manchester code. Biphase L is specified in IEEE standard 802.3 for Ethernet local area networks (Chapter 3).

Miller codes are forms of *delay-modulated codes* where a logic 1 condition produces a transition in the middle of the clock pulse and a logic 0 produces no transition at the end of the clock intervals followed by a logic 0.

Dicodes are multilevel binary codes that use more than two voltage levels to represent the data. Bipolar RZ and RZ-AMI are two dicode encoding formats already discussed. Dicode NRZ and dicode RZ are two more commonly used dicode formats.

Figure 5-19 shows several variations of biphase, Miller, and dicode encoding and Table 5-4 summarizes their characteristics.

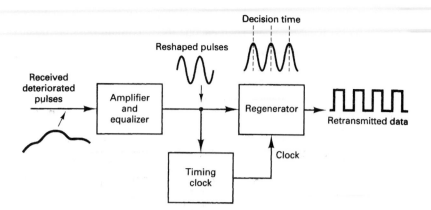

FIGURE 5-20 Regenerative repeater block diagram

T CARRIERS

T carriers are used for the transmission of PCM-encoded time-division multiplexed digital signals. In addition, T carriers utilize special line-encoded signals and metallic cables that have been conditioned to meet the relatively high bandwidths required for high-speed digital transmissions. Digital signals deteriorate as they propagate along a cable due to power loss in the metallic conductors and the low-pass filtering inherent in parallel wire transmission lines. Consequently, *regenerative repeaters* must be placed at periodic intervals. The distance between repeaters depends on the transmission bit rate and the line-encoding technique used.

Figure 5-20 shows the block diagram of a regenerative repeater. Essentially there are three functional blocks: an amplifier/equalizer, a timing circuit, and the regenerator. The amplifier/equalizer shapes the incoming digital signal and raises its power level so that a pulse/no pulse decision can be made by the regenerator circuit. The timing circuit recovers the clocking information from the received data and provides the proper timing information to the regenerator so that decisions can be made at the optimum time that minimizes the chance of an error occurring. Spacing of the repeaters is designed to maintain an adequate signal-to-noise ratio for error-free performance. The signal-to-noise ratio (S/N) at the output of a regenerator is exactly what it was at the output of the transmit terminal or at the output of the previous regenerator (that is, the S/N does not deteriorate as a digital signal propagates through a regenerator; in fact, a regenerator reconstructs the original pulses with the original S/N ratio).

T1 and T1C Carrier Systems

The T1 carrier system utilizes PCM and TDM techniques to provide short-haul transmission of 24 voice-band signals. The lengths of T1 carrier systems range from about 5 miles to 50 miles. T1 carriers use BPRZ-AMI encoding with regenerative repeaters placed every 6000 ft; 6000 ft was chosen because telephone company manholes are located at approximately 6000-ft intervals and these same manholes are used for placement of the repeaters, facilitating convenient installation, maintenance, and repair. The transmission medium for T1 carriers is either a 19-gauge or 22-gauge wire pair.

Because T1 carriers use BPRZ-AMI encoding, they are susceptible to losing synchronization on a long string of consecutive 0s. With a folded binary PCM code, the possibility of generating a long string of consecutive 0s is high (whenever a channel is idle it generates a ±0-V code, which is either seven or eight consecutive 0s). If two or more adjacent voice channels are idle, there is a high probability that a long string of consecutive 0s will be transmitted. To reduce this possibility, the PCM code is inverted prior to transmission and inverted again at the receiver prior to decoding. Consequently, the only time a long string of consecutive 0s is transmitted is when two or more adjacent voice-band channels each encode the maximum possible positive sample voltage, which is unlikely to happen.

With T1 and T1C carrier systems, provisions are taken to prevent more than 14 consecutive 0s from occurring. The transmissions from each frame are monitored for the presence of either 15 consecutive 0s or any one PCM sample (8 bits) without at least one nonzero bit. If either of these conditions occurs, a 1 is substituted into the appropriate bit position. The worst-case conditions are as follows:

	MSB	LSB	MSB	LSB	
Original DS-1 signal	1000	0000	0000	0001	14 consecutive 0s (no substitution)

	MSB	LSB	MSB	LSB	
Original DS-1 signal	1000	0000	0000	0000	15 consecutive 0s
Substituted DS-1 signal	1000	0000	0000	0010	

↑
substituted bit

A 1 is substituted into the second least significant bit. This introduces an encoding error equal to twice the amplitude resolution. This bit is selected rather than the least significance bit because, with the superframe format, during every sixth frame the LSB is the signaling bit and to alter it would alter the signaling word.

	MSB	LSB	MSB	LSB	MSB	LSB
Original DS-1 signal	1010	1000	0000	0000	0000	0001
Substituted DS-1 signal	1010	1000	0000	0010	0000	0001

↑
substituted bit

The process shown is used for T1 and T1C carrier systems. Also, if at any time 32 consecutive 0s are received, it is assumed that the system is not generating pulses and is, therefore, out of service; this is because the occurrence of 32 consecutive 0s is prohibited.

T2 Carrier System

The T2 carrier utilizes PCM to time-division multiplex 96 voice-band channels into a single 6.312-Mbps data signal for transmission up to 500 miles over a special LOCAP (low capacitance) cable. A T2 carrier is also used to carry a single picturephone signal. T2 carriers also use BPRZ-AMI encoding. However, because of the higher transmission rate, clock synchronization becomes more critical. A sequence of six consecutive 0s could be sufficient to cause loss of clock synchronization. Therefore, T2 carrier systems use an alternative method of ensuring that ample transitions occur in the data. This method is called *binary six zero substitution* (B6ZS).

With B6ZS, whenever six consecutive 0s occur, one of the following codes is substituted in its place: $0 - + 0 + -$ or $0 + - 0 - +$. The + and − represent positive and negative logic 1s. A zero simply indicates a logic 0 condition. The 6-bit code substituted for the six 0s is selected to purposely cause a bipolar violation. If the violation is caught at the receiver and the B6ZS code is detected, the original six 0s can be substituted back into the data signal. The substituted patterns cause a bipolar violation in the second and fifth bits of the substituted pattern. If DS-2 signals are multiplexed to form DS-3 signals, the B6ZS code must be detected and stripped from the DS-2 signal prior to DS-3 multiplexing. An example of B6ZS is as follows:

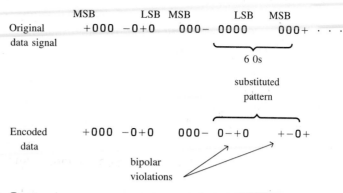

T3 Carrier System

A T3 carrier time-division multiplexes 672 PCM-encoded voice channels for transmission over a single metallic cable. The transmission rate for T3 signals is 46.304 Mbps. The encoding technique used with T3 carriers is *binary three zero substitution* (B3ZS). Substitutions are made for any occurrence of three consecutive 0s. There are four substitution patterns used: 00−, −0−, 00+, and +0+. The pattern chosen should cause a bipolar error in the third substitute bit. An example is as follows:

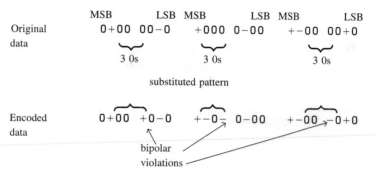

T4M Carrier System

A T4M carrier time-division multiplexes 4032 PCM-encoded voice-band channels for transmission over a single coaxial cable up to 500 miles. The transmission rate is sufficiently high that substitute patterns are impractical. Instead, T4M carriers transmit scrambled unipolar NRZ digital signals; the scrambling and descrambling functions are performed in the subscriber's terminal equipment.

T5 Carrier System

A T5 carrier system time-division multiplexes 8064 PCM-encoded voice-band channels and transmits them at a 560.16-Mbps rate over a single coaxial cable.

FRAME SYNCHRONIZATION

With TDM systems it is imperative that a frame be identified and that individual time slots (samples) within the frame also be identified. To acquire frame synchronization, a certain amount of overhead must be added to the transmission. Five methods are commonly used to establish frame synchronization: added-digit framing, robbed-digit framing, added-channel framing, statistical framing, and unique-line signal framing.

Added-Digit Framing

T1 carriers using D1, D2, or D3 channel banks use *added-digit framing*. A special *framing digit* (framing pulse) is added to each frame. Consequently, for an 8-kHz sample rate (125-μs frame), 8000 digits are added per second. With T1 carriers, an alternating 1/0 frame synchronizing pattern is used.

To acquire frame synchronization, the receive terminal searches through the incoming data until it finds the alternating 1/0 sequence used for the framing bit pattern. This encompasses testing a bit, counting off 193 bits and then testing again for the opposite condition. This process continues until an alternating 1/0 sequence is found. Initial frame synchronization depends on the total frame time, the number of bits per frame, and the period of each bit. Searching through all possible bit positions requires N tests, where N is the number of bit positions in the frame. On average, the receiving terminal dwells at a false framing position for two frame periods during a search; therefore, the maximum average synchronization time is

$$\text{synchronization time} = 2NT = 2N^2t$$

where
T = frame period of Nt
N = number of bits per frame
t = bit time

For the T1 carrier, $N = 193$, $T = 125$ µs, and $t = 0.648$ µs; therefore, a maximum of 74,498 bits must be tested and the maximum average synchronization time is 48.25 ms.

Robbed-Digit Framing

When a short frame is used, added-digit framing is very inefficient. This occurs in single-channel PCM systems such as those used in television terminals. An alternative solution is to replace the least significant bit of every nth frame with a framing bit. The parameter n is chosen as a compromise between reframe time and signal impairment. For $n = 10$, the SQR is impaired by only 1 dB. *Robbed-digit framing* does not interrupt transmission, but instead periodically replaces information bits with forced data errors to maintain clock synchronization. B6ZS and B3ZS are examples of systems that use robbed-digit techniques.

Added-Channel Framing

Essentially, *added-channel framing* is the same as added-digit framing except that digits are added in groups or words instead of as individual bits. The CCITT multiplexing scheme previously discussed uses added-channel framing. One of the 32 time slots in each frame is dedicated to a unique synchronizing sequence. The average frame synchronization time for added-channel framing is

$$\text{synchronization time (bits)} = \frac{N^2}{2(2^L - 1)}$$

where
N = number of bits per frame
L = number of bits in the frame code

For the CCITT 32-channel system, $N = 256$ and $L = 8$. Therefore, the average number of bits needed to acquire frame synchronization is 128.5. At 2.048 Mbps, the synchronization time is approximately 62.7 µs.

Statistical Framing

With *statistical framing,* it is not necessary to either rob or add digits. With the Gray code, the second bit is a 1 in the central half of the code range and 0 at the extremes. Therefore, a signal that has a centrally peaked amplitude distribution generates a high probability of a 1 in the second digit. A mastergroup signal has such a distribution. With a mastergroup encoder, the probability that the second bit will be a 1 is 95%. For any other bit, it is less than 50%. Therefore, the second bit can be used for a framing bit.

Unique-Line Code Framing

With *unique-line code framing,* the framing bit is different from the information bits. It is either made higher or lower in amplitude or of a different time duration. The earliest

FIGURE 5-21 Interleaving: (a) bit; (b) word

PCM/TDM systems used unique-line code framing. D1 channel banks used framing pulses that were twice the amplitude of normal data bits. With unique-line code framing, added-digit or added-word framing can be used or data bits can be used to simultaneously convey information and carry synchronizing signals. The advantage of unique-line code framing is that synchronization is immediate and automatic. The disadvantage is the additional processing requirements required to generate and recognize the unique framing bit.

BIT INTERLEAVING VERSUS WORD INTERLEAVING

When time-division multiplexing two or more PCM systems, it is necessary to interleave the transmissions from the various terminals in the time domain. Figure 5-21 shows two methods of interleaving PCM transmissions: *bit interleaving* and *word interleaving*.

T1 carrier systems use word interleaving; 8-bit samples from each channel are interleaved into a single 24-channel TDM frame. Higher-speed TDM systems and delta modulation systems use bit interleaving. The decision as to which type of interleaving to use is usually determined by the nature of the signals to be multiplexed.

STATISTICAL TIME-DIVISION MULTIPLEXING

Typically, transmissions over a synchronous time-division multiplexing system contain an abundance of time slots within each frame that contain no information (that is, the channels are idle). For example, TDM is commonly used to link remote data terminals or PCs to a common server or mainframe computer. A majority of the time, however, there is no data being transferred in either direction, even if all the terminals are active. The same is true for PCM TDM systems carrying voice-grade telephone conversations. Normal conversation generally involves information being transferred in only one direction at a time with significant pauses embedded in typical speech patterns. Consequently, there is a lot of time within each TDM frame wasted. There is, however, an efficient alternative to synchronous TDM called statistical TDM (sometimes called asynchronous or intelligent TDM).

XX denotes data present
−− denotes no data present

FIGURE 5-22 Comparison between synchronous and statistical TDM

A statistical TDM multiplexer exploits the natural breaks in transmissions by dynamically allocating time slots on demand. Just as with the multiplexer in a synchronous TDM system, a statistical multiplexer has a finite number of low-speed data input lines and one high-speed multiplexed data output line, and each input line has its own buffer. With the statistical multiplexer, there are n input lines, but only k time slots available within the TDM frame (where $k < n$). The multiplexer scans the input buffers, collecting data until a frame is filled, at which time the frame is transmitted. On the receive end, the same holds true; there are more output lines than time slots within the TDM frame. The demultiplexer removes the data from the time slots and distributes them to their appropriate output buffers.

Statistical TDM takes advantage of the fact that the devices attached to the inputs and outputs are not all transmitting or receiving all of the time, and the data rate on the multiplexed line is lower than the combined data rates of the attached devices. In other words, a statistical TDM multiplexer requires a lower data rate than a synchronous multiplexer needs to support the same number of input devices. Alternatively, a statistical TDM multiplexer operating at the same transmission rate as a synchronous TDM muliplexer can support more devices.

Figure 5-22 shows a comparison between statistical and synchronous TDM. Four data sources are shown (A, B, C, and D) and four time slots or epochs (t_0, t_1, t_2, and t_3). The synchronous multiplexer has an output data rate equal to four times the data rate of each of the input channels. During each frame, data are collected from all four sources and transmitted regardless of whether or not there is any input data. As the figure shows, during time slot t_0 channels C and D had no input data resulting in a transmitted TDM frame void of information in time slots C and D. With a statistical multiplexer, however, the empty time slots are not transmitted. Thus, during the first time slot, only information from channels A and B are transmitted. A disadvantage of the statistical format, however, is that the positional significance of the time slots is lost. There is no way of knowing ahead of time which channel's data will be in which time slot. Because data arrive and are distributed to receive buffers unpredictably, address information is necessary to assure proper delivery. This necessitates more overhead per time slot for statistical TDM because each slot must carry an address as well as data.

Beginning flag	Address field	Control field	Statistical TDM subframe	FCS field	Ending flag

(a)

Address field	Data field

(b)

Address field	Length field	Data field	...	Address field	Length field	Data field

(c)

FIGURE 5-23 Statistical TDM frame format: (a) overall statistical TDM frame; (b) one-source per frame; (c) multiple sources per frame

The frame format used by a statistical multiplexer has a direct impact on system performance. Obviously, it is desirable to minimize overhead to improve data throughput. Normally, a statistical TDM system will use a synchronous protocol such as HDLC. Control bits for multiplexing must be included within the HDLC frame. Figure 5-23a shows the overall frame format for a statistical TDM multiplexer. Figure 5-23b shows the frame when only one data source is transmitting. The transmitting device is identified by an address. The data field length is variable and limited only by the length of the frame. Such a scheme works well in times of light loads but rather inefficiently under heavy loads. Figure 5-23c shows one way to improve the efficiency by allowing more than one data source to be included within a single frame. With multiple sources, however, some means is necessary to specify the length of the data stream from each source. Hence, the statistical frame is comprised of sequences of data fields labeled with an address and a bit count. There are several techniques that can be used to further improve the efficiency. The address field can be shortened by using a relative addressing scheme where each address specifies the position of the current source relative to the previously transmitted source, modulo the total number of sources. With relative addressing an 8-bit address field can be replaced with a 4-bit address field.

Another method of refining the frame is to use a 2-bit label with the length field. The binary values 00, 01, 10, and 11 correspond to a data field of 1, 2, or 3 bytes and no length field is necessary. The 11 code means that a length field is included.

FREQUENCY-DIVISION MULTIPLEXING

In *frequency-division multiplexing* (FDM), multiple sources that originally occupied the same frequency spectrum are each converted to a different frequency band and transmitted simultaneously over a single transmission medium. Thus, many relatively narrowband channels can be transmitted over a single wideband transmission system.

FDM is an analog multiplexing scheme; the information entering an FDM system is analog and it remains analog throughout transmission. An example of FDM is the AM commercial broadcast band, which occupies a frequency spectrum from 535 kHz to 1605 kHz. Each station carries an intelligence signal with a bandwidth of 0 kHz to 5 kHz. If the audio from each station were transmitted with the original frequency spectrum, it would be impossible to separate one station from another. Instead, each station amplitude modulates a different carrier frequency and produces a 10-kHz double-sideband signal. Because adjacent stations' carrier frequencies are separated by 10 kHz, the total commercial AM band is divided into 107 10-kHz frequency slots stacked next to each other in the frequency domain. To receive a particular station, a receiver is simply tuned to the frequency band associated with that station's transmissions. Figure 5-24 shows how commercial AM broadcast station signals are frequency-division multiplexed and transmitted over a single transmission medium (free space).

FIGURE 5-24 Frequency-division multiplexing commercial AM broadcast band stations

There are many other applications for FDM, such as commercial FM and television broadcasting and high-volume telecommunications systems. Within any of the commercial broadcast bands, each station's transmissions are independent of all the other stations' transmissions. Consequently, the multiplexing (stacking) process is accomplished without any synchronization between stations. With a high-volume telephone communication system, many voice-band telephone channels may originate from a common source and terminate in a common destination. The source and destination terminal equipment is most likely a high-capacity *electronic switching system* (ESS). Because of the possibility of a large number of narrowband channels originating and terminating at the same location, all multiplexing and demultiplexing operations must be synchronized.

AT&T'S FDM HIERARCHY

Although AT&T is no longer the only long-distance common carrier in the United States, it still provides a vast majority of the long-distance services and, if for no other reason than its overwhelming size, has essentially become the standards organization for the telephone industry in North America.

AT&T's nationwide communications network is subdivided into two classifications: *short haul* (short distance) and *long haul* (long distance). The T1 carrier explained earlier in this chapter is an example of a short-haul communications system.

Long-Haul Communications with FDM

Figure 5-25 shows AT&T's North American FDM hierarchy for long-haul communications. Only a transmit terminal is shown, although a complete set of inverse functions must be performed at the receiving terminal.

Message Channel

The *message channel* is the basic building block of the FDM hierarchy. The basic message channel was originally intended for voice transmission, although it now includes any transmissions that utilize voice-band frequencies (0 kHz to 4 kHz), such as voice-band data circuits. The basic voice-band (VB) circuit is called a 3002 channel and is actually bandlimited to a 300-Hz to 3000-Hz band, although for practical considerations it is considered a 4-kHz channel. The basic 3002 channel can be subdivided into 24 narrower 3001 (telegraph) channels that have been frequency-division multiplexed to form a single 3002 channel.

FIGURE 5-25 AT&T's long-haul FDM hierarchy

Basic Group

A *group* is the next higher level in the FDM hierarchy above the basic message channel and is, consequently, the first multiplexing step for the message channels. A basic group is comprised of 12 voice-band channels stacked next to each other in the frequency domain. The 12-channel modulating block is called an *A-type* (analog) channel bank. The 12-channel *group* output of the A-type channel bank is the standard building block for most long-haul *broadband* communications systems. Additions and deletions in total system capacity are accomplished with a minimum of one group (12 VB channels). The A-type channel bank has progressed generically from the early A1 channel bank to the most recent A6 channel bank.

Basic Supergroup

The next higher level in the FDM hierarchy shown in Figure 5-25 is the combination of five groups into a *supergroup.* The multiplexing of five groups is accomplished in a group bank. A single supergroup can carry information from 60 VB channels or handle high-speed data up to 250 kbps.

Basic Mastergroup

The next higher level in the FDM hierarchy is the basic *mastergroup.* A mastergroup is comprised of 10 supergroups (10 supergroups of five groups each = 600 VB channels). Supergroups are combined in supergroup banks to form mastergroups. There are two categories of mastergroups (U600 and L600), which occupy different frequency bands. The type of mastergroup used depends on the system capacity and whether the transmission medium is a coaxial cable, a microwave radio, an optical fiber, or a satellite link.

Larger Groupings

Master groups can be further multiplexed in mastergroup banks to form *jumbogroups,* *multijumbogroups,* and *superjumbogroups.* A basic FDM/FM microwave radio channel carries three mastergroups (1800 VB channels), a jumbogroup has 3600 VB channels, and a superjumbogroup has three jumbogroups (10,800 VB channels).

COMPOSITE BASEBAND SIGNAL

Baseband describes the modulating signal (intelligence) in a communications system. A single message channel is baseband. A group, supergroup, or mastergroup is also baseband. The composite baseband signal is the total intelligence signal prior to modulation of the final carrier. In Figure 5-25 the output of a channel bank is baseband. Also, the output of a group or supergroup bank is baseband. The final output of the FDM multiplexer is the *composite* (total) baseband. The formation of the composite baseband signal can include channel, group, supergroup, and mastergroup banks, depending on the capacity of the system.

Formation of Groups and Supergroups

Figure 5-26a shows how a group is formed with an A-type channel bank. Each voice-band channel is bandlimited with an antialiasing filter prior to modulating the channel carrier. FDM uses single-sideband suppressed-carrier (SSBSC) modulation. The combination of the balanced modulator and the bandpass filter makes up the SSBSC modulator. A balanced modulator is a double-sideband suppressed-carrier modulator, and the bandpass filter is tuned to the difference between the carrier and the input voice-band frequencies (LSB). The ideal input frequency range for a single voice-band channel is 0 kHz to 4 kHz. The carrier frequencies for the channel banks are determined from the following expression:

$$f_c = 112 - 4n \quad \text{kHz}$$

where n is the channel number. Table 5-5 lists the carrier frequencies for channels 1 through 12. Therefore, for channel 1, a 0-kHz to 4-kHz band of frequencies modulates a 108-kHz carrier. Mathematically, the output of a channel bandpass filter is

$$f_{out} = f_c - f_m \text{ to } f_c$$

where $\quad f_c$ = channel carrier frequency ($112 - 4n$ kHz)
$\quad\quad\quad f_m$ = channel frequency spectrum (0 kHz to 4 kHz)

For channel 1, $\quad f_{out} = 108 \text{ kHz} - (0 \text{ kHz to } 4 \text{ kHz}) = 104 \text{ kHz to } 108 \text{ kHz}$

For channel 2, $\quad f_{out} = 104 \text{ kHz} - (0 \text{ kHz to } 4 \text{ kHz}) = 100 \text{ kHz to } 104 \text{ kHz}$

For channel 12, $\quad f_{out} = 64 \text{ kHz} - (0 \text{ kHz to } 4 \text{ kHz}) = 60 \text{ kHz to } 64 \text{ kHz}$

The outputs from the 12 A-type channel modulators are summed in the *linear* combiner to produce the total group spectrum shown in Figure 5-26b (60 kHz to 108 kHz). Note that the total group bandwidth is equal to 48 kHz (12 channels × 4 kHz).

Figure 5-27a (p. 693) shows how a supergroup is formed with a group bank and combining network. Five groups are combined to form a supergroup. The frequency spectrum for each group is 60 kHz to 108 kHz. Each group is mixed with a different group carrier frequency in a balanced modulator and then bandlimited with a bandpass filter tuned to the difference frequency band (LSB) to produce a SSBSC signal. The group carrier frequencies are derived from the following expression:

$$f_c = 372 + 48n \quad \text{kHz}$$

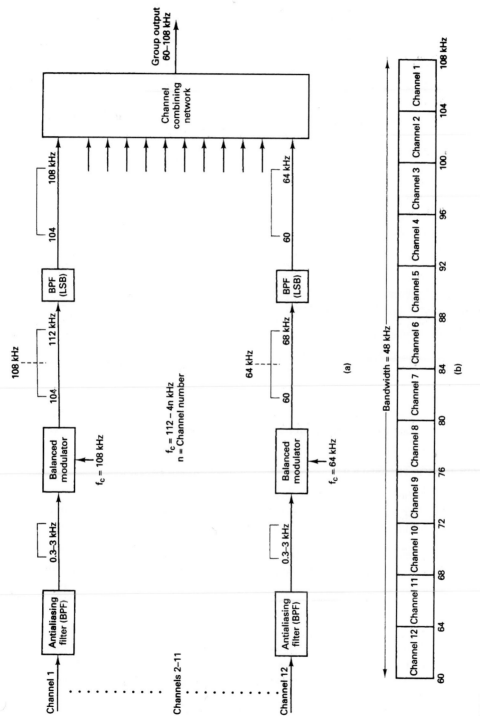

FIGURE 5-26 Formation of a group: (a) A-type channel bank block diagram; (b) output spectrum

TABLE 5-5 Channel Carrier Frequencies		**TABLE 5-6** Group Carrier Frequencies	
Channel	Carrier Frequency (kHz)	Group	Carrier Frequency (kHz)
1	108	1	420
2	104	2	468
3	100	3	516
4	96	4	564
5	92	5	612
6	88		
7	84		
8	80		
9	76		
10	72		
11	68		
12	64		

where n is the group number. Table 5-6 lists the carrier frequencies for groups 1 through 5. For group 1, a 60-kHz to 80-kHz group signal modulates a 420-kHz group carrier frequency. Mathematically, the output of a group bandpass filter is

$$f_{out} = f_c - f_g \text{ to } f_c$$

where f_c = group carrier frequency ($372 + 48n$ kHz)
  f_g = group frequency spectrum (60 kHz to 108 kHz)

For group 1, f_{out} = 420 kHz − (60 kHz to 108 kHz) = 312 kHz to 360 kHz

For group 2, f_{out} = 468 kHz − (60 kHz to 108 kHz) = 360 kHz to 408 kHz

For group 5, f_{out} = 612 kHz − (60 kHz to 108 kHz) = 504 kHz to 552 kHz

The outputs from the five group modulators are summed in the linear combiner to produce the total supergroup spectrum shown in Figure 5-27b (312 kHz to 552 kHz). Note that the total supergroup bandwidth is equal to 240 kHz (60 channels × 4 kHz).

FORMATION OF A MASTERGROUP

There are two types of mastergroups: L600 and U600 type. The L600 mastergroup is used for low-capacity microwave systems, and the U600 mastergroup may be further multiplexed and used for higher-capacity microwave radio systems.

U600 Mastergroup

Figure 5-28a (p. 264) shows how a U600 mastergroup is formed with a supergroup bank and combining network. Ten supergroups are combined to form a mastergroup. The frequency spectrum for each supergroup is 312 kHz to 552 kHz. Each supergroup is mixed with a different supergroup carrier frequency in a balanced modulator. The output is then bandlimited to the difference frequency band (LSB) to form a SSBSC signal. The 10 supergroup carrier frequencies are listed in Table 5-7 (p. 265). For supergroup 13, a 312-kHz to 552-kHz supergroup band of frequencies modulates a 1116-kHz carrier frequency. Mathematically, the output from a supergroup bandpass filter is

$$f_{out} = f_c - f_s \text{ to } f_c$$

where f_c = supergroup carrier frequency
  f_s = supergroup frequency spectrum (312 kHz to 552 kHz)

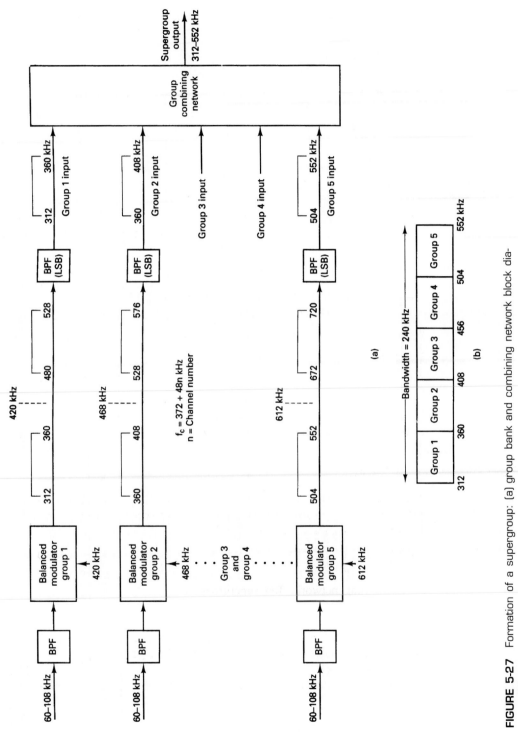

FIGURE 5-27 Formation of a supergroup: (a) group bank and combining network block diagram; (b) output spectrum

FIGURE 5-28 Formation of a U600 mastergroup: (a) supergroup bank and combining network block diagram; (b) output spectrum

TABLE 5-7 Supergroup Carrier Frequencies For a U600 Mastergroup		TABLE 5-8 Supergroup Carrier Frequencies for a L600 Mastergroup	
Supergroup	Carrier Frequency (kHz)	Supergroup	Carrier Frequency (kHz)
13	1116	1	612
14	1364	2	Direct
15	1612	3	1116
16	1860	4	1364
17	2108	5	1612
18	2356	6	1860
D25	2652	7	2108
D26	2900	8	2356
D27	3148	9	2724
D28	3396	10	3100

For supergroup 13,

$$f_{out} = 1116 \text{ kHz} - (312 \text{ kHz to } 552 \text{ kHz}) = 564 \text{ kHz to } 804 \text{ kHz}$$

For supergroup 14,

$$f_{out} = 1364 \text{ kHz} - (312 \text{ kHz to } 552 \text{ kHz}) = 812 \text{ kHz to } 1052 \text{ kHz}$$

For supergroup D28,

$$f_{out} = 3396 \text{ kHz} - (312 \text{ kHz to } 552 \text{ kHz}) = 2844 \text{ kHz to } 3084 \text{ kHz}$$

The outputs from the 10 supergroup modulators are summed in the linear summer to produce the total mastergroup spectrum shown in Figure 5-28b (564 kHz to 3084 kHz). Note that between any two adjacent supergroups there is a void band of frequencies that is not included within any supergroup band. These voids are called *guard bands*. The guard bands are necessary because the demultiplexing process is accomplished through filtering and down-converting. Without the guard bands, it would be difficult to separate one supergroup from an adjacent supergroup. The guard bands reduce the *quality factor* (Q) required to perform the necessary filtering. The guard band is 8 kHz between all supergroups except 18 and D25, where it is 56 kHz. Consequently, the bandwidth of a U600 mastergroup is 2520 kHz (564 kHz to 3084 kHz), which is greater than is necessary to stack 600 voice-band channels (600 × 4 kHz = 2400 kHz).

Guard bands were not necessary between adjacent groups because the group frequencies are sufficiently low and it is relatively easy to build bandpass filters to separate one group from another.

In the channel bank, the antialiasing filter at the channel input passes a 0.3-kHz to 3-kHz band. The separation between adjacent channel carrier frequencies is 4 kHz. Therefore, there is a 1300-Hz guard band between adjacent channels. This is shown in Figure 5-29.

L600 Mastergroup

With an L600 mastergroup, 10 supergroups are combined as with the U600 mastergroup, except that the supergroup carrier frequencies are lower. Table 5-8 lists the supergroup carrier frequencies for an L600 mastergroup. With an L600 mastergroup, the composite baseband spectrum occupies a lower-frequency band than the U-type mastergroup (Figure 5-30). An L600 mastergroup is not further multiplexed. Therefore, the maximum channel capacity for a microwave or coaxial cable system using a single L600 mastergroup is 600 voice-band channels.

FIGURE 5-29 Channel guard bands

FIGURE 5-30 L600 mastergroup

Formation of a Radio Channel

A *radio channel* comprises either a single L600 mastergroup or up to three U600 mastergroups (1800 voice-band channels). Figure 5-31a shows how an 1800-channel composite FDM baseband signal is formed for transmission over a single microwave radio channel. Mastergroup 1 is transmitted directly as is, while mastergroups 2 and 3 undergo an additional multiplexing step. The three mastergroups are summed in a mastergroup combining network to produce the output spectrum shown in Figure 5-31b. Note the 80-kHz guard band between adjacent mastergroups.

The system shown in Figure 5-31 can be increased from 1800 voice-band channels to 1860 by adding an additional supergroup (supergroup 12) directly to mastergroup 1. The additional 312-kHz to 552-kHz supergroup extends the composite output spectrum to 312 kHz to 8284 kHz.

HYBRID DATA

With *hybrid* data it is possible to combine digitally encoded signals with FDM signals and transmit them as one composite baseband signal. There are four primary types of hybrid data: data under voice (DUV), data above voice (DAV), data above video (DAVID), and data in voice (DIV).

Data Under Voice (DUV)

Figure 5-32a shows the block diagram of AT&T's 1.544-Mbps *data under FDM voice* system. With the L1800 FDM system explained earlier in this chapter, the 0 kHz to 564-kHz frequency spectrum is void of baseband signals. With FM transmission, the lower baseband frequencies realize the highest signal-to-noise ratios. Consequently, the best portion of the baseband spectrum was unused. DUV is a means of utilizing this spectrum for the transmission of digitally encoded signals. A T1 carrier system can be converted to a quasi-analog signal and then frequency-division multiplexed onto the lower portion of the FDM spectrum.

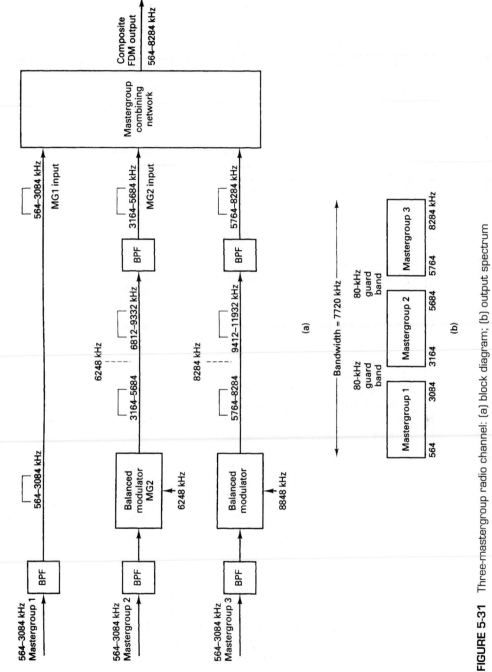

FIGURE 5-31 Three-mastergroup radio channel: (a) block diagram; (b) output spectrum

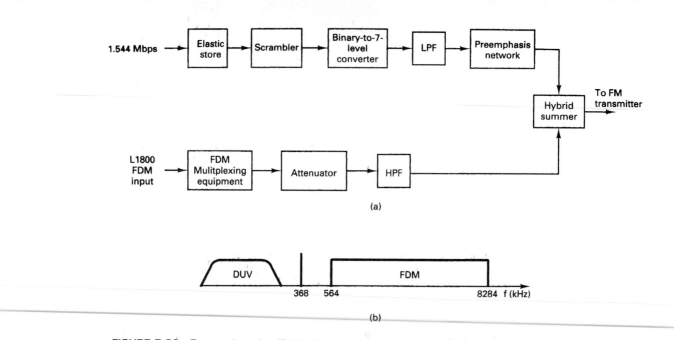

FIGURE 5-32 Data under voice (DUV): (a) block diagram; (b) frequency spectrum

In Figure 5-32a, the *elastic store* removes timing jitter from the incoming data stream. The data are then *scrambled* to suppress the discrete high-power spectral components. The advantage of scrambling is that the randomized data output spectrum is continuous and has a predictable effect on the FDM radio system. In other words, the data present a load to the system equivalent to adding additional FDM voice channels. The serial seven-level *partial response* encoder (correlative coder) compresses the data bandwidth and allows a 1.544-Mbps signal to be transmitted in a bandwidth less than 400 kHz. The low-pass filter performs the final spectral shaping of the digital information and suppresses the spectral power above 386 kHz. This prevents the DUV information from interfering with the 386-kHz pilot control tone. The DUV signal is preemphasized and combined with the L1800 baseband signal. The output spectrum is shown in Figure 5-32b.

AT&T uses DUV for *digital data service* (DDS). DDS is intended to provide a communications medium for the transfer of digital data from station to station without the use of a data modem. DDS circuits are guaranteed to average 99.5% error-free seconds at 56 kbps.

Data Above Voice (DAV)

Figure 5-33 shows the block diagram and frequency spectrum for a *data above voice* system. The advantage of DAV is for FDM systems that extend into the low end of the baseband spectrum; the low-frequency baseband does not have to be vacated for data transmission. With DAV, data PSK modulates a carrier that is then up-converted to a frequency above the FDM message. With DAV, up to 3.152 Mbps can be cost effectively transmitted using existing FDM/FM microwave systems (Chapter 6).

Data Above Video (DAVID)

Essentially, *data above video* is the same as DAV except that the lower baseband spectrum is a *vestigial sideband* video signal rather than a composite FDM signal. Figure 5-34 shows the frequency spectrum for a DAVID system.

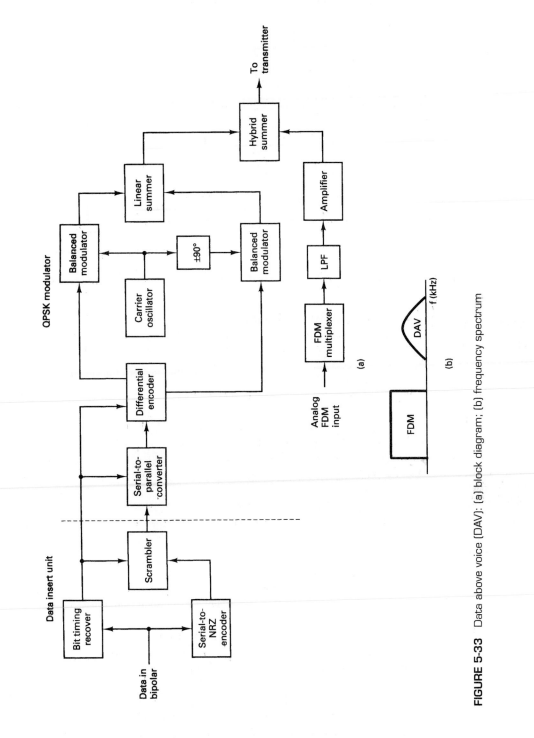

FIGURE 5-33 Data above voice (DAV): (a) block diagram; (b) frequency spectrum

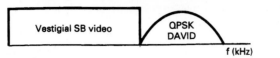

FIGURE 5-34 Data above video (DAVID)

Data In Voice (DIV)

Data in voice, developed by Fujitsu of Japan, uses an eight-level PAM-VSB modulation technique with steep filtering. It uses a highly compressed partial response encoding technique, which gives it a high bandwidth efficiency of nearly 5 bps/Hz (1.544-Mbps data are transmitted in a 344-kHz bandwidth).

QUESTIONS

5-1. Define *multiplexing.*

5-2. Describe time-division multiplexing.

5-3. Describe the Bell System T1 carrier system.

5-4. What is the purpose of the signaling bit?

5-5. What is frame synchronization? How is it achieved in a PCM/TDM system?

5-6. Describe the superframe format. Why is it used?

5-7. What is a codec? A combo chip?

5-8. What is a fixed-data-rate mode?

5-9. What is a variable-data-rate mode?

5-10. What is a DSX? What is it used for?

5-11. Explain *line coding.*

5-12. Briefly explain unipolar and bipolar transmission.

5-13. Briefly explain return-to-zero and nonreturn-to-zero transmission.

5-14. Contrast the bandwidth considerations of return-to-zero and nonreturn-to-zero transmission.

5-15. Contrast the clock recovery capabilities with return-to-zero and nonreturn-to-zero transmission.

5-16. Contrast the error detection and decoding capabilities of return-to-zero and nonreturn-to-zero transmission.

5-17. What is a regenerative repeater?

5-18. Explain B6ZS and B3ZS. When or why would you use one rather than the other?

5-19. Briefly explain the following framing techniques: added-digit framing, robbed-digit framing, added-channel framing, statistical framing, and unique-line code framing.

5-20. Contrast bit and word interleaving.

5-21. Describe frequency-division multiplexing.

5-22. Describe a message channel.

5-23. Describe the formation of a group, a supergroup, and a mastergroup.

5-24. Define *baseband* and *composite baseband.*

5-25. What is a guard band? When is a guard band used?

5-26. What are the four primary types of hybrid data network?

5-27. What is the difference between a DUV and a DAV network?

PROBLEMS

5-1. A PCM/TDM system multiplexes 24 voice-band channels. Each sample is encoded into 7 bits and a framing bit is added to each frame. The sampling rate is 9000 samples/second. BPRZ-AMI encoding is the line format. Determine

(a) Line speed in bits per second.

(b) Minimum Nyquist bandwidth.

5-2. A PCM/TDM system multiplexes 32 voice-band channels each with a bandwidth of 0 kHz to 4 kHz. Each sample is encoded with an 8-bit PCM code. UPNRZ encoding is used. Determine

(a) Minimum sample rate.

(b) Line speed in bits per second.

(c) Minimum Nyquist bandwidth.

5-3. For the following bit sequence, draw the timing diagram for UPRZ, UPNRZ, BPRZ, BPNRZ, and BPRZ-AMI encoding.

bit stream: **1 1 1 0 0 1 0 1 0 1 1 0 0**

5-4. Encode the following BPRZ-AMI data stream with B6ZS and B3ZS.

$$+-0000+-+0-00000+-00+$$

5-5. Calculate the 12 channel carrier frequencies for the U600 FDM system.

5-6. Calculate the five group carrier frequencies for the U600 FDM system.

5-7. A PCM/TDM system multiplexes 20 voice-band channels. Each sample is encoded into 8 bits and a framing bit is added to each frame. The sampling rate is 10,000 samples/second. BPRZ-AMI encoding is the line format. Determine

(a) The maximum analog input frequency.

(b) The line speed in bps.

(c) The minimum Nyquist bandwidth.

5-8. A PCM/TDM system multiplexes 30 voice-band channels each with a bandwidth of 0 kHz to 3 kHz. Each sample is encoded with a 9-bit PCM code. UPNRZ encoding is used. Determine

(a) The minimum sample rate.

(b) The line speed in bps.

(c) The minimum Nyquist bandwidth.

5-9. For the following bit sequence, draw the timing diagram for UPRZ, UPNRZ, BPRZ, BPNRZ, and BPRZ-AMI encoding.

bit stream: **1 1 0 0 0 1 0 1 0 1**

5-10. Encode the following BPRZ-AMI data stream with B6ZS and B3ZS.

$$-+000000+-000+00-$$

5-11. Calculate the frequency range for a single FDM channel at the output of the channel, group, supergroup, and mastergroup combining networks for the following assignments:

CH	GP	SG	MG
2	2	13	1
6	3	18	2
4	5	D25	2
9	4	D28	3

5-12. Determine the frequency that a single 1-kHz test tone will translate to at the output of the channel, group, supergroup, and mastergroup combining networks for the following assignments:

CH	GP	SG	MG
4	4	13	2
6	4	16	1
1	2	17	3
11	5	D26	3

5-13. Calculate the frequency range at the mastergroup combining network for the following assignments:

GP	SG	MG
3	13	2
5	D25	3
1	15	1
2	17	2

5-14. Calculate the frequency range at the mastergroup combining network for the following assignments:

SG	MG
18	2
13	3
D26	1
14	1

CHAPTER 6

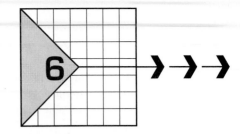

Microwave Radio Communications and System Gain

INTRODUCTION

Presently, terrestrial (earth) *microwave radio relay systems* provide less than half of the total message circuit mileage in the United States. However, at one time microwave systems carried the bulk of long-distance communications for the public telephone network, military and governmental agencies, and specialized private communications networks. There are many different types of microwave systems that operate over distances varying from 15 mi to 4000 mi in length. *Intrastate* or *feeder service* systems are generally categorized as *short haul* because they are used for relatively short distances. *Long-haul* radio systems are those used for relatively long distances, such as interstate and backbone route applications. Microwave system capacities range from less than 12 voice-band channels to more than 22,000. Early microwave radio systems carried frequency-division-multiplexed voice-band circuits and used conventional, noncoherent frequency modulation techniques. More recently developed microwave systems carry pulse-code-modulated time-division-multiplexed voice-band circuits and use more modern digital modulation techniques, such as phase shift keying and quadrature amplitude modulation. This chapter deals primarily with conventional FDM/FM microwave systems, and Chapter 8 deals with the more modern PCM/PSK techniques.

FREQUENCY VERSUS AMPLITUDE MODULATION

Frequency modulation (FM) is used in microwave radio systems rather than amplitude modulation (AM) because amplitude-modulated signals are more sensitive to amplitude nonlinearities inherent in *wideband microwave amplifiers*. Frequency-modulated signals are relatively insensitive to this type of nonlinear distortion and can be transmitted through amplifiers that have compression or amplitude nonlinearity with little penalty. In addition, FM signals are less sensitive to random noise and can be propagated with lower transmit powers.

Intermodulation noise is a major factor when designing FM radio systems. In AM systems, intermodulation noise is caused by repeater amplitude nonlinearity. In FM systems, intermodulation noise is caused primarily by transmission gain and delay distortion. Consequently, in AM systems, intermodulation noise is a function of signal amplitude, but in FM systems it is a function of signal amplitude and the magnitude of the frequency deviation. Thus, the characteristics of frequency-modulated signals are more suitable than amplitude-modulated signals for microwave transmission.

SIMPLIFIED FM MICROWAVE RADIO SYSTEM

A simplified block diagram of an FM microwave radio system is shown in Figure 6-1. The *baseband* is the composite signal that modulates the FM carrier and may comprise one or more of the following:

1. Frequency-division-multiplexed voice-band channels
2. Time-division-multiplexed voice-band channels
3. Broadcast-quality composite video or picturephone
4. Wideband data

FM Microwave Radio Transmitter

In the FM *microwave transmitter* shown in Figure 6-1a, a *preemphasis* network precedes the FM deviator. The preemphasis network provides an artificial boost in amplitude to the higher baseband frequencies. This allows the lower baseband frequencies to frequency

(a)

(b)

FIGURE 6-1 Simplified block diagram of an FM microwave radio system: (a) transmitter; (b) receiver

Chapter 6   Microwave Radio Communications and System Gain

modulate the IF carrier and the higher baseband frequencies to phase modulate it. This scheme assures a more uniform signal-to-noise ratio throughout the entire baseband spectrum. An FM deviator provides the modulation of the IF carrier that eventually becomes the main microwave carrier. Typically, IF carrier frequencies are between 60 MHz and 80 MHz, with 70 MHz the most common. *Low-index* frequency modulation is used in the FM deviator. Typically, modulation indices are kept between 0.5 and 1. This produces a *narrowband* FM signal at the output of the deviator. Consequently, the IF bandwidth resembles conventional AM and, approximately, is equal to twice the highest baseband frequency.

The IF and its associated sidebands are up-converted to the microwave region by the AM mixer, microwave oscillator, and bandpass filter. Mixing, rather than multiplying, is used to translate the IF frequencies to RF frequencies because the modulation index is unchanged by the heterodyning process. Multiplying the IF carrier would also multiply the frequency deviation and the modulation index, thus, increasing the bandwidth. Typically, frequencies above 1000 MHz (1 GHz) are considered microwave frequencies. Presently, there are microwave systems operating with carrier frequencies up to approximately 18 GHz. The most common microwave frequencies currently being used are the 2-, 4-, 6-, 12-, and 14-GHz bands. The channel-combining network provides a means of connecting more than one microwave transmitter to a single transmission line feeding the antenna.

FM Microwave Radio Receiver

In the FM microwave receiver shown in Figure 6-1b, the channel separation network provides the isolation and filtering necessary to separate individual microwave channels and direct them to their respective receivers. The bandpass filter, AM mixer, and microwave oscillator down-convert the RF microwave frequencies to IF frequencies and pass them on to the FM demodulator. The FM demodulator is a conventional, *noncoherent* FM detector (i.e., a discriminator or a PLL demodulator). At the output of the FM detector, a deemphasis network restores the baseband signal to its original amplitude versus frequency characteristics.

FM MICROWAVE RADIO REPEATERS

The permissible distance between an FM microwave transmitter and its associated microwave receiver depends on several system variables, such as transmitter output power, receiver noise threshold, terrain, atmospheric conditions, system capacity, reliability objectives, and performance expectations. Typically, this distance is between 15 mi and 40 mi. Long-haul microwave systems span distances considerably longer than this. Consequently, a single-hop microwave system, such as the one shown in Figure 6-1, is inadequate for most practical system applications. With systems that are longer than 40 mi or when geographical obstructions, such as a mountain, block the transmission path, *repeaters* are needed. A microwave repeater is a receiver and a transmitter placed back to back or in tandem with the system. A block diagram of a microwave repeater is shown in Figure 6-2. The repeater station receives a signal, amplifies and reshapes it, then retransmits the signal to the next repeater or terminal station downline from it.

Basically, there are two types of microwave repeaters: *baseband* and *IF* (Figure 6-3). IF repeaters are also called *heterodyne* repeaters. With an IF repeater (Figure 6-3a), the received RF carrier is down-converted to an IF frequency, amplified, reshaped, up-converted to an RF frequency, and then retransmitted. The signal is never demodulated below IF. Consequently, the baseband intelligence is unmodified by the repeater. With a baseband repeater (Figure 6-3b), the received RF carrier is down-converted to an IF frequency, amplified, filtered, and then further demodulated to baseband. The baseband signal, which is typically frequency-division-multiplexed voice-band channels, is further

FIGURE 6-2   Microwave repeater

(a)

(b)

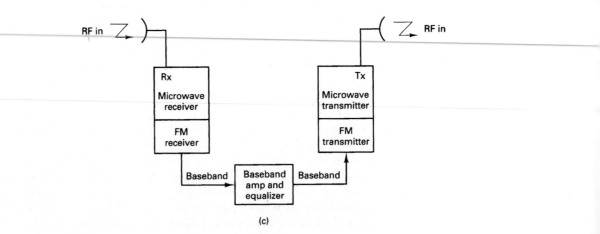

(c)

FIGURE 6-3   Microwave repeaters: (a) IF; (b) and (c) baseband demodulated to a mastergroup, supergroup, group, or even channel level. This allows the baseband signal to be reconfigured to meet the routing needs of the overall communications network. Once the baseband signal has been reconfigured, it FM modulates an IF carrier, which is up-converted to an RF carrier and then retransmitted.

Figure 6-3c shows another baseband repeater configuration. The repeater demodulates the RF to baseband, amplifies and reshapes it, then modulates the FM carrier. With this technique, the baseband is not reconfigured. Essentially, this configuration accomplishes the same thing that an IF repeater accomplishes. The difference is that in a baseband configuration, the amplifier and equalizer act on baseband frequencies rather than IF frequencies. The baseband frequencies are generally less than 9 MHz, whereas the IF frequencies are in the range 60 MHz to 80 MHz. Consequently, the filters and amplifiers necessary for baseband repeaters are simpler to design and less expensive than the ones required for IF repeaters. The disadvantage of a baseband configuration is the addition of the FM terminal equipment.

DIVERSITY

Microwave systems use *line-of-sight* transmission. There must be a direct, line-of-sight signal path between the transmit and the receive antennas. Consequently, if that signal path undergoes a severe degradation, a service interruption will occur. *Diversity* suggests that there is more than one transmission path or method of transmission available between a transmitter and a receiver. In a microwave system, the purpose of using diversity is to increase the reliability of the system by increasing its availability. When there is more than one transmission path or method of transmission available, the system can select the path or method that produces the highest-quality received signal. Generally, the highest quality is determined by evaluating the carrier-to-noise (C/N) ratio at the receiver input or by simply measuring the received carrier power. Although there are many ways of achieving diversity, the most common methods used are *frequency, space,* and *polarization.*

Frequency Diversity

Frequency diversity is simply modulating two different RF carrier frequencies with the same IF intelligence, then transmitting both RF signals to a given destination. At the destination, both carriers are demodulated, and the one that yields the better-quality IF signal is selected. Figure 6-4 shows a single-channel frequency-diversity microwave system.

In Figure 6-4a, the IF input signal is fed to a power splitter, which directs it to microwave transmitters A and B. The RF outputs from the two transmitters are combined in the channel-combining network and fed to the transmit antenna. At the receive end (Figure 6-4b), the channel separator directs the A and B RF carriers to their respective microwave receivers, where they are down-converted to IF. The quality detector circuit determines which channel, A or B, is the higher quality and directs that channel through the IF switch to be further demodulated to baseband. Many of the temporary, adverse atmospheric conditions that degrade an RF signal are frequency selective; they may degrade one frequency more than another. Therefore, over a given period of time, the IF switch may switch back and forth from receiver A to receiver B, and vice versa many times.

Space Diversity

With space diversity, the output of a transmitter is fed to two or more antennas that are physically separated by an appreciable number of wavelengths. Similarly, at the receiving end, there may be more than one antenna providing the input signal to the receiver. If multiple receiving antennas are used, they must also be separated by an appreciable number of wavelengths. Figure 6-5 shows a single-channel space-diversity microwave system.

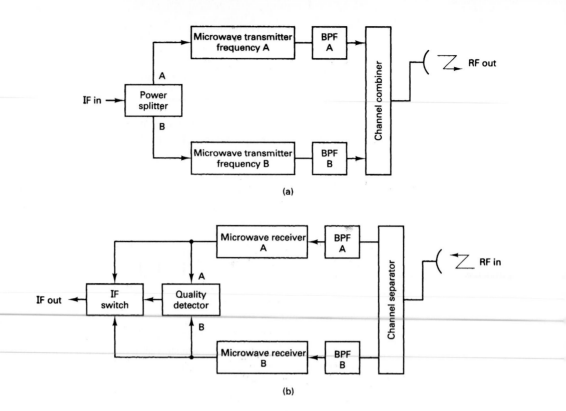

FIGURE 6-4 Frequency-diversity microwave system: (a) transmitter; (b) receiver

When space diversity is used, it is important that the electrical distance from a transmitter to each of its antennas and to a receiver from each of its antennas is an equal multiple of wavelengths long. This is to ensure that when two or more signals of the same frequency arrive at the input to a receiver, they are in phase and additive. If received out of phase, they will cancel and, consequently, result in less received signal power than if simply one antenna system were used. Adverse atmospheric conditions are often isolated to a very small geographical area. With space diversity, there is more than one transmission path between a transmitter and a receiver. When adverse atmospheric conditions exist in one of the paths, it is unlikely that the alternate path is experiencing the same degradation. Consequently, the probability of receiving an acceptable signal is higher when space diversity is used than when no diversity is used. An alternate method of space diversity uses a single transmitting antenna and two receiving antennas separated vertically. Depending on the atmospheric conditions at a particular time, one of the receiving antennas should be receiving an adequate signal. Again, there are two transmission paths that are unlikely to be affected simultaneously by fading.

Polarization Diversity

With polarization diversity, a single RF carrier is propagated with two different electromagnetic polarizations (vertical and horizontal). Electromagnetic waves of different polarizations do not necessarily experience the same transmission impairments. Polarization diversity is generally used in conjunction with space diversity. One transmit/receive antenna pair is vertically polarized and the other is horizontally polarized. It is also possible to use frequency, space, and polarization diversity simultaneously.

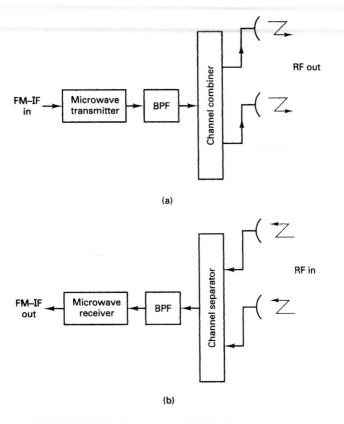

FIGURE 6-5 Space-diversity microwave system: (a) transmitter; (b) receiver

PROTECTION SWITCHING

Radio path losses vary with atmospheric conditions. Over a period of time, the atmospheric conditions between transmitting and receiving antenna can vary significantly, causing a corresponding reduction in the received signal strength of 20, 30, 40, or more dB. This reduction in signal strength is referred to as a *radio fade. Automatic gain control circuits,* built into radio receivers, can compensate for fades of 25 dB to 40 dB, depending on the system design. However, fades in excess of 40 dB cause a total loss of the received signal. When this happens, service continuity is lost. To avoid a service interruption during periods of deep fades or equipment failures, alternate facilities are temporarily made available in what is called a *protection switching* arrangement. Essentially, there are two types of protection switching arrangements: *hot standby* and *diversity.* With hot standby protection, each working radio channel has a dedicated backup or spare channel. With diversity protection, a single backup channel is made available to as many as 11 working channels. Hot standby systems offer 100% protection for each working radio channel. A diversity system offers 100% protection only to the first working channel that fails. If two radio channels fail at the same time, a service interruption will occur.

Hot Standby

Figure 6-6a shows a single-channel hot standby protection switching arrangement. At the transmitting end, the IF goes into a *head-end bridge,* which splits the signal power and directs it to the working and the spare (standby) microwave channels simultaneously.

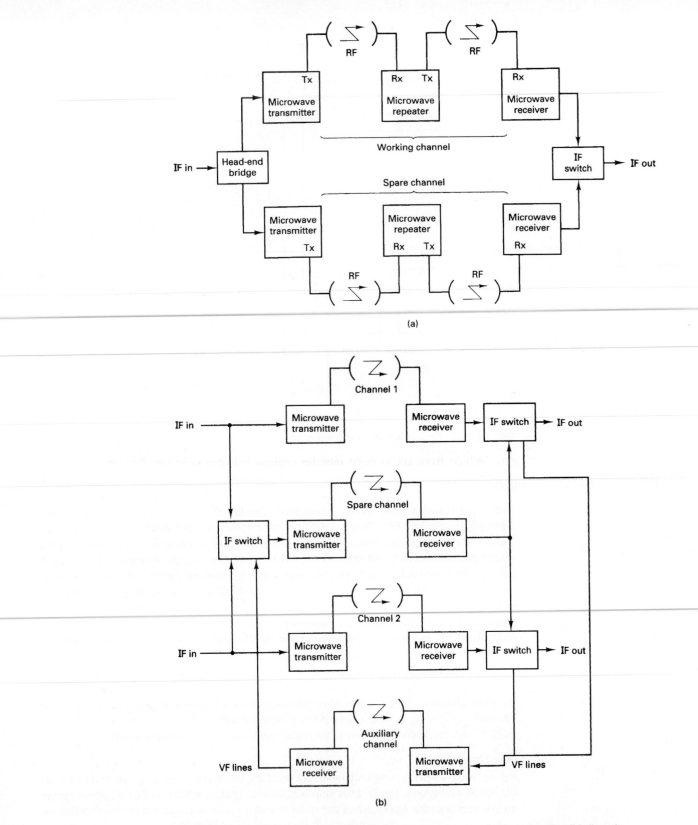

FIGURE 6-6 Microwave protection switching arrangements: (a) hot standby; (b) diversity

Consequently, both the working and standby channels are carrying the same baseband information. At the receiving end, the IF switch passes the IF signal from the working channel to the FM terminal equipment. The IF switch continuously monitors the received signal power on the working channel and, if it fails, switches to the standby channel. When the IF signal on the working channel is restored, the IF switch resumes its normal position.

Diversity

Figure 6-6b shows a diversity protection switching arrangement. This system has two working channels (channel 1 and channel 2), one spare channel, and an *auxiliary* channel. The IF switch at the receive end continuously monitors the receive signal strength of both working channels. If either one should fail, the IF switch detects a loss of carrier and sends back to the transmitting station IF switch a VF *(voice frequency)* tone-encoded signal that directs it to switch the IF signal from the failed channel onto the spare microwave channel. When the failed channel is restored, the IF switches resume their normal positions. The auxiliary channel simply provides a transmission path between the two IF switches. Typically, the auxiliary channel is a low-capacity low-power microwave radio that is designed to be used for a maintenance channel only.

Reliability

The number of repeater stations between protection switches depends on the *reliability objectives* of the system. Typically, there are between two and six repeaters between switching stations.

As you can see, diversity systems and protection switching arrangements are quite similar. The primary difference between the two is that diversity systems are permanent arrangements and are intended only to compensate for temporary, abnormal atmospheric conditions between only two selected stations in a system. Protection switching arrangements, on the other hand, compensate for both radio fades and equipment failures and may include from six to eight repeater stations between switches. Protection channels may also be used as temporary communication facilities, while routine maintenance is performed on a regular working channel. With a protection switching arrangement, all signal paths and radio equipment are protected. Diversity is used selectively, that is, only between stations that historically experience severe fading a high percentage of the time.

A statistical study of outage time (i.e., service interruptions) caused by radio fades, equipment failures, and maintenance is important in the design of a microwave radio system. From such a study, engineering decisions can be made on which type of diversity system and protection switching arrangement is best suited for a particular application.

FM MICROWAVE RADIO STATIONS

Basically, there are two types of FM microwave stations: terminals and repeaters. *Terminal stations* are points in the system where baseband signals either originate or terminate. *Repeater stations* are points in a system where baseband signals may be reconfigured or where RF carriers are simply "repeated" or amplified.

Terminal Station

Essentially, a terminal station consists of four major sections: the baseband, wire line entrance link (WLEL), FM-IF, and RF sections. Figure 6-7 shows the block diagram of the baseband, WLEL, and FM-IF sections. As mentioned previously, the baseband may be one of several different types of signals. For our example, frequency-division-multiplexed voice-band channels are used.

(a)

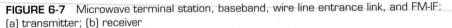

(b)

FIGURE 6-7 Microwave terminal station, baseband, wire line entrance link, and FM-IF:
(a) transmitter; (b) receiver

Wire line entrance link (WLEL). Very often in large communications networks, such as the American Telephone and Telegraph Company (AT&T), the building that houses the radio station is quite large. Consequently, it is desirable that similar equipment be physically placed at a common location (i.e., all FDM equipment in the same room). This simplifies alarm systems, providing dc power to the equipment, maintenance, and other general cabling requirements. Dissimilar equipment may be separated by a considerable distance. For example, the distance between the FDM multiplexing equipment and the FM-IF section is typically several hundred feet and in some cases several miles. For this reason a WLEL is required. A WLEL serves as the interface between the multiplex terminal equipment and the FM-IF equipment. A WLEL generally consists of an amplifier and an equalizer (which together compensate for cable transmission losses) and level-shaping devices commonly called pre- and deemphasis networks.

IF section. The FM terminal equipment shown in Figure 6-7 generates a frequency-modulated IF carrier. This is accomplished by mixing the outputs of two deviated oscillators that differ in frequency by the desired IF carrier. The oscillators are deviated in phase opposition, which reduces the magnitude of phase deviation required of a single deviator by a factor of 2, This technique also reduces the deviation linearity requirements for the oscillators and provides for the partial cancellation of unwanted modulation products. Again, the receiver is a conventional noncoherent FM detector.

RF section. A block diagram of the RF section of a microwave terminal station is shown in Figure 6-8. The IF signal enters the transmitter (Figure 6-8a) through a protection switch. The IF and compression amplifiers help keep the IF signal power constant and at approximately the required input level to the transmit modulator (*transmod*). A transmod is a balanced modulator that, when used in conjunction with a microwave generator, power amplifier, and bandpass filter, up-converts the IF carrier to an RF carrier and amplifies the RF to the desired output power. Power amplifiers for microwave radios must be capable of amplifying very high frequencies and passing very

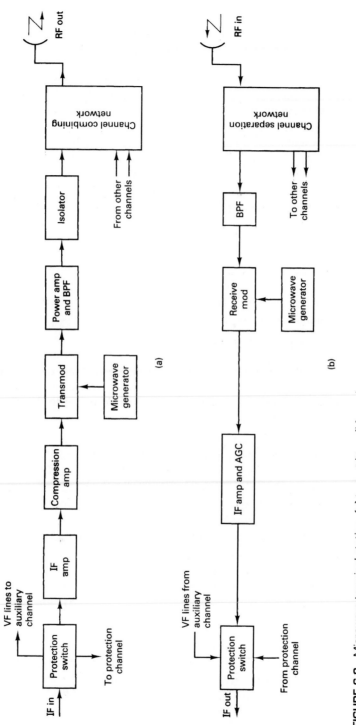

FIGURE 6-8 Microwave terminal station: (a) transmitter; (b) receiver

wide bandwidth signals. *Klystron tubes, traveling-wave tubes* (TWTs), and *IMPATT* (*imp*act/*a*valanche and *T*ransit *T*ime) diodes are several of the devices currently being used in microwave power amplifiers. Because high-gain antennas are used and the distance between microwave stations is relatively short, it is not necessary to develop a high output power from the transmitter output amplifiers. Typical gains for microwave antennas range from 10 dB to 40 dB, and typical transmitter output powers are between 0.5 W and 10 W.

A *microwave generator* provides the RF carrier input to the up-converter. It is called a microwave generator rather than an oscillator because it is difficult to construct a stable circuit that will oscillate in the gigahertz range. Instead, a crystal-controlled oscillator operating in the range 5 MHz to 25 MHz is used to provide a base frequency that is multiplied up to the desired RF carrier frequency.

An *isolator* is a unidirectional device often made from a ferrite material. The isolator is used in conjunction with a channel-combining network to prevent the output of one transmitter from interfering with the output of another transmitter.

The RF receiver (Figure 6-8b) is essentially the same as the transmitter except that it works in the opposite direction. However, one difference is the presence of an IF amplifier in the receiver. This IF amplifier has an *automatic gain control* (AGC) circuit. Also, very often, there are no RF amplifiers in the receiver. Typically, a very sensitive, low-noise balanced demodulator is used for the receive demodulator (receive mod). This eliminates the need for an RF amplifier and improves the overall signal-to-noise ratio. When RF amplifiers are required, high-quality, *low-noise amplifiers* (LNAs) are used. Examples of commonly used LNAs are tunnel diodes and parametric amplifiers.

Repeater Station

Figure 6-9 shows the block diagram of a microwave IF repeater station. The received RF signal enters the receiver through the channel separation network and bandpass filter. The receive mod down-converts the RF carrier to IF. The IF AMP/AGC and equalizer circuits amplify and reshape the IF. The equalizer compensates for *gain-versus-frequency nonlinearities* and *envelope delay distortion* introduced in the system. Again, the transmod up-converts the IF to RF for retransmission. However, in a repeater station, the method used to generate the RF microwave carrier frequencies is slightly different from the method used in a terminal station. In the IF repeater, only one microwave generator is required to supply both the transmod and the receive mod with an RF carrier signal. The microwave generator, shift oscillator, and shift modulator allow the repeater to receive one RF carrier frequency, down-convert it to IF, and then up-convert the IF to a different RF carrier frequency. It is possible for station C to receive the transmissions from both station A and station B simultaneously (this is called *multihop interference* and is shown in Figure 6-10a). This can occur only when three stations are placed in a geographical straight line in the system. To prevent this from occurring, the allocated bandwidth for the system is divided in half, creating a low-frequency and a high-frequency band. Each station, in turn, alternates from a low-band to a high-band transmit carrier frequency (Figure 6-10b). If a transmission from station A is received by station C, it will be rejected in the channel separation network and cause no interference. This arrangement is called a high/low microwave repeater system. The rules are simple: If a repeater station receives a low-band RF carrier, it retransmits a high-band RF carrier, and vice versa. The only time that multiple carriers of the same frequency can be received is when a transmission from one station is received from another station that is three hops away. This is unlikely to happen.

Another reason for using a high/low-frequency scheme is to prevent the power that "leaks" out the back and sides of a transmit antenna from interfering with the signal entering the input of a nearby receive antenna. This is called *ringaround*. All antennas, no

FIGURE 6-9 Microwave IF repeater station

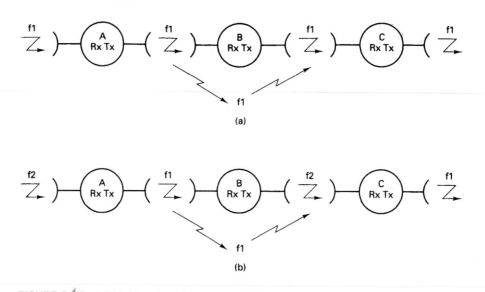

FIGURE 6-10 (a) Multihop interference and (b) high/low microwave system

matter how high their gain or how directive their radiation pattern, radiate a small percentage of their power out the back and sides; giving a finite *front-to-back* ratio for the antenna. Although the front-to-back ratio of a typical microwave antenna is quite high, the relatively small amount of power that is radiated out the back of the antenna may be quite substantial compared to the normal received carrier power in the system. If the transmit and receive carrier frequencies are different, filters in the receiver separation network will prevent ringaround from occurring.

A high/low microwave repeater station (Figure 6-10b) needs two microwave carrier supplies for the down- and up-converting process. Rather than use two microwave generators, a single generator together with a shift oscillator, a shift modulator, and a bandpass filter can generate the two required signals. One output from the microwave generator is fed directly into the transmod and another output (from the same microwave generator) is mixed with the shift oscillator signal in the shift modulator to produce a second microwave carrier frequency. The second microwave carrier frequency is offset from the first by the shift oscillator frequency. The second microwave carrier frequency is fed into the receive modulator.

Example 6-1

In Figure 6-9 the received RF carrier frequency is 6180 MHz, and the transmitted RF carrier frequency is 6000 MHz. With a 70-MHz IF frequency, a 5930-MHz microwave generator frequency, and a 180-MHz shift oscillator frequency, the output filter of the shift mod must be tuned to 6110 MHz. This is the sum of the microwave generator and the shift oscillator frequencies (5930 MHz + 180 MHz = 6110 MHz).

This process does not reduce the number of oscillators required, but it is simpler and cheaper to build one microwave generator and one relatively low-frequency shift oscillator than to build two microwave generators. This arrangement also provides a certain degree of synchronization between repeaters. The obvious disadvantage of the high/low scheme is that the number of channels available in a given bandwidth is cut in half.

Figure 6-11 shows a high/low-frequency plan with eight channels (four high-band and four low-band). Each channel occupies a 29.7-MHz bandwidth. The west terminal transmits the low-band frequencies and receives the high-band frequencies. Channels 1 and 3 (Figure 6-11a) are designated as *V channels*. This means that they are propagated with vertical polarization. Channels 2 and 4 are designated as H or horizontally polarized

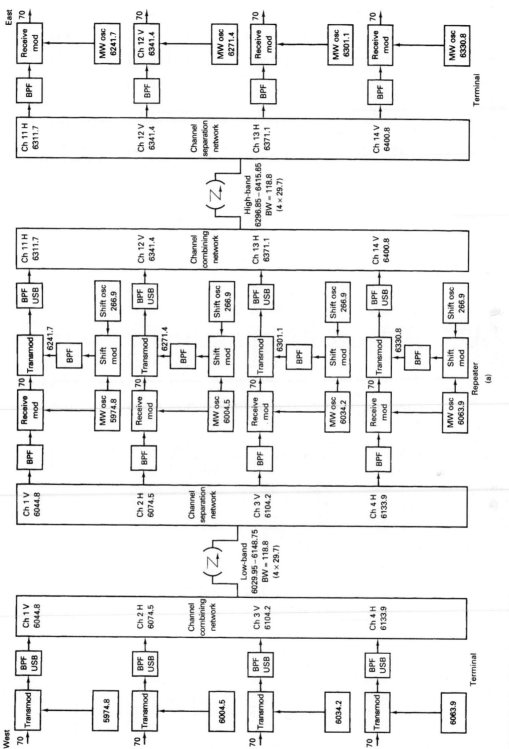

FIGURE 6-11 Eight-channel high/low frequency plan: (a) west to east *(Continued)*

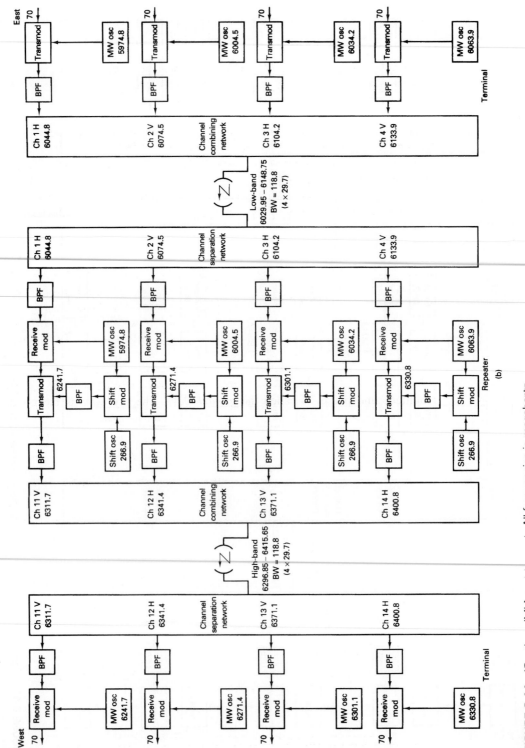

FIGURE 6-11 (Continued) (b) east to west. All frequencies in megahertz

channels. This is not a polarization diversity system. Channels 1 through 4 are totally independent of each other; they carry different baseband information. The transmission of *orthogonally* polarized carriers (90° out of phase) further enhances the isolation between the transmit and receive signals. In the west-to-east direction, the repeater receives the low-band and transmits the high-band frequencies. After channel 1 is received and down-converted to IF, it is up-converted to a different RF frequency and a different polarization for retransmission. The low-band channel 1 corresponds to the high-band channel 11, channel 2 to channel 12, and so on. The east-to-west direction (Figure 6-11b) propagates the high- and low-band carriers in the sequence opposite to the west-to-east system. The polarizations are also reversed. If some of the power from channel 1 of the west terminal were to propagate directly to the east terminal receiver, it has a different frequency and polarization than channel 11's transmissions. Consequently, it would not interfere with the reception of channel 11 (no multihop interference). Also, note that none of the transmit or receive channels at the repeater station has both the same frequency and polarization. Consequently, the interference from the transmitters to the receivers due to ringaround is insignificant.

PATH CHARACTERISTICS

The normal *propagation paths* between two radio antennas in a microwave radio system is shown in Figure 6-12. The *free-space path* is the *line-of-sight path* directly between the transmit and receive antennas (this is also called the *direct wave*). The *ground-reflected wave* is the portion of the transmit signal that is reflected off Earth's surface and captured by the receive antenna. The *surface wave* consists of the electric and magnetic fields associated with the currents induced in Earth's surface. The magnitude of the surface wave depends on the characteristics of Earth's surface and the electromagnetic polarization of the wave. The sum of these three paths (taking into account their amplitude and phase) is called the *ground wave*. The *sky wave* is the portion of the transmit signal that is returned (reflected) back to Earth's surface by the ionized layers of Earth's atmosphere.

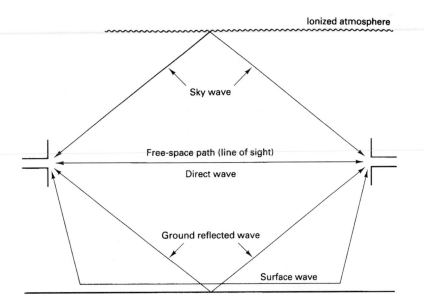

FIGURE 6-12 Propagation paths

All of the paths shown in Figure 6-12 exist in any microwave radio system, but some are negligible in certain frequency ranges. At frequencies below 1.5 MHz, the surface wave provides the primary coverage, and the sky wave helps to extend this coverage at night when the absorption of the ionosphere is at a minimum. For frequencies above about 30 MHz to 50 MHz, the free-space and ground-reflected paths are generally the only paths of importance. The surface wave can also be neglected at these frequencies, provided that the antenna heights are not too low. The sky wave is only a source of occasional long-distance interference and not a reliable signal for microwave communications purposes. In this chapter the surface and sky-wave propagations are neglected, and attention is focused on those phenomena that affect the direct and reflected waves.

SYSTEM GAIN

In its simplest form, *system gain* is the difference between the nominal output power of a transmitter and the minimum input power required by a receiver. System gain must be greater than or equal to the sum of all the gains and losses incurred by a signal as it propagates from a transmitter to a receiver. In essence, it represents the net loss of a radio system. System gain is used to predict the reliability of a system for given system parameters. Mathematically, system gain is

$$G_s = P_t - C_{min}$$

where G_s = system gain (dB)
P_t = transmitter output power (dBm)
C_{min} = minimum receiver input power for a given quality objective (dBm)

and where

$$P_t - C_{min} \geq \text{losses} - \text{gains}$$

Gains A_t = transmit antenna gain (dB) relative to an isotropic radiator
A_r = receive antenna gain (dB) relative to an isotropic radiator

Losses L_p = free-space path loss between antennas (dB)
L_f = waveguide feeder loss (dB) between the distribution network (channel combining network or channel separation network) and its respective antenna (see Table 6-1)
L_b = total coupling or branching loss (dB) in the circulators, filters, and distribution network between the output of a transmitter or the input to a receiver and its respective waveguide feed (see Table 6-1)
F_m = fade margin for a given reliability objective

Mathematically, system gain is

$$G_s = P_t - C_{min} \geq F_m + L_p + L_f + L_b - A_t - A_r \qquad (6\text{-}1)$$

where all values are expressed in dB or dBm. Because system gain is indicative of a net loss, the losses are represented with positive dB values and the gains are represented with negative dB values. Figure 6-13 shows an overall microwave system diagram and indicates where the respective losses and gains are incurred.

Free-Space Path Loss

Free-space path loss is defined as the loss incurred by an electromagnetic wave as it propagates in a straight line through a vacuum with no absorption or reflection of energy from nearby objects. The expression for free-space path loss is given as

TABLE 6-1 System Gain Parameters

| Frequency (GHz) | Feeder Loss, L_f | | Branching Loss (dB) Diversity | | Antenna Gain, A_t or A_r | |
	Type	Loss (dB/100 m)	Frequency	Space	Size (m)	Gain (dB)
1.8	Air-filled coaxial cable	5.4	5	2	1.2	25.2
					2.4	31.2
					3.0	33.2
					3.7	34.7
7.4	EWP 64 eliptical waveguide	4.7	3	2	1.5	38.8
					2.4	43.1
					3.0	44.8
					3.7	46.5
8.0	EWP 69 eliptical waveguide	6.5	3	2	2.4	43.8
					3.0	45.6
					3.7	47.3
					4.8	49.8

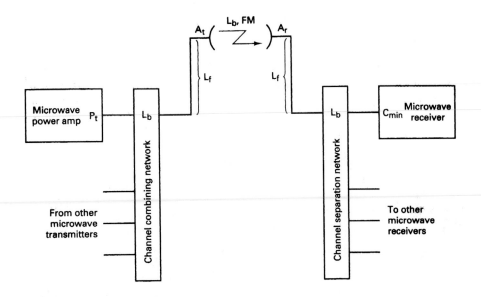

FIGURE 6-13 System gains and losses

$$L_p = \left(\frac{4\pi D}{\lambda}\right)^2 = \left(\frac{4\pi f D}{c}\right)^2$$

where L_p = free-space path loss
D = distance
f = frequency
λ = wavelength
c = velocity of light in free space (3×10^8 m/s)

Converting to dB yields

$$L_{p(dB)} = 20 \log \frac{4\pi f D}{c} = 20 \log \frac{4\pi}{c} + 20 \log f + 20 \log D$$

When the frequency is given in MHz and the distance in km,

$$L_{p(\text{dB})} = 20 \log \frac{4\pi (10)^6 (10)^3}{3 \times 10^8} + 20 \log f_{(\text{MHz})} + 20 \log D_{(\text{km})} \qquad (6\text{-}2)$$

$$= 32.4 + 20 \log f_{(\text{MHz})} + 20 \log D_{(\text{km})}$$

When the frequency is given in GHz and the distance in km,

$$L_{p(\text{dB})} = 92.4 + 20 \log f_{(\text{GHz})} + 20 \log D_{(\text{km})} \qquad (6\text{-}3)$$

Similar conversions can be made using distance in miles, frequency in kHz, and so on.

Example 6-2

For a carrier frequency of 6 GHz and a distance of 50 km, determine the free-space path loss.

Solution

$$L_p = 32.4 + 20 \log 6000 + 20 \log 50$$
$$= 32.4 + 75.6 + 34 = 142 \text{ dB}$$

or

$$L_p = 92.4 + 20 \log 6 + 20 \log 50$$
$$= 92.4 + 15.6 + 34 = 142 \text{ dB}$$

Fade Margin

Essentially, *fade margin* is a "fudge factor" included in the system gain equation that considers the nonideal and less predictable characteristics of radio-wave propagation, such as *multipath propagation (multipath loss)* and *terrain sensitivity*. These characteristics cause temporary, abnormal atmospheric conditions that alter the free-space path loss and are usually detrimental to the overall system performance. Fade margin also considers system reliability objectives. Thus, fade margin is included in the system gain equation as a loss.

Solving the Barnett–Vignant reliability equations for a specified annual system availability for an unprotected, nondiversity system yields the following expression:

$$F_m = \underbrace{30 \log D}_{\substack{\text{multipath} \\ \text{effect}}} + \underbrace{10 \log (6ABf)}_{\substack{\text{terrain} \\ \text{sensitivity}}} - \underbrace{10 \log (1 - R)}_{\substack{\text{reliability} \\ \text{objectives}}} - \underbrace{70}_{\text{constant}} \qquad (6\text{-}4)$$

where F_m = fade margin (dB)
D = distance (km)
f = frequency (GHz)
R = reliability expressed as a decimal (i.e., 99.99% = 0.9999 reliability)
$1 - R$ = reliability objective for a one-way 400-km route
A = roughness factor
= 4 over water or a very smooth terrain
= 1 over an average terrain
= 0.25 over a very rough, mountainous terrain
B = factor to convert a worst-month probability to an annual probability
= 1 to convert an annual availability to a worst-month basis
= 0.5 for hot humid areas
= 0.25 for average inland areas
= 0.125 for very dry or mountainous areas

Example 6-3

Consider a space-diversity microwave radio system operating at an RF carrier frequency of 1.8 GHz. Each station has a 2.4-m-diameter parabolic antenna that is fed by 100 m of air-filled coaxial cable. The terrain is smooth and the area has a humid climate. The distance between stations is 40 km. A reliability objective of 99.99% is desired. Determine the system gain.

Solution Substituting into Equation 6-4, we find that the fade margin is

$$F_m = 30 \log 40 + 10 \log [(6)(4)(0.5)(1.8)] - 10 \log (1 - 0.9999) - 70$$
$$= 48.06 + 13.34 - (-40) - 70$$
$$= 48.06 + 13.34 + 40 - 70 = 31.4 \text{ dB}$$

Substituting into Equation 6-3, we obtain path loss

$$L_p = 92.4 + 20 \log 1.8 + 20 \log 40$$
$$= 92.4 + 5.11 + 32.04 = 129.55 \text{ dB}$$

From Table 6-1,

$$L_b = 4 \text{ dB } (2 + 2 = 4)$$
$$L_f = 10.8 \text{ dB } (100 \text{ m} + 100 \text{ m} = 200 \text{ m})$$
$$A_t = A_r = 31.2 \text{ dB}$$

Substituting into Equation 6-1 gives us system gain

$$G_s = 31.4 + 129.55 + 10.8 + 4 - 31.2 - 31.2 = 113.35 \text{ dB}$$

The results indicate that for this system to perform at 99.99% reliability with the given terrain, distribution networks, transmission lines, and antennas, the transmitter output power must be at least 113.35 dB more than the minimum receive signal level.

Receiver Threshold

Carrier-to-noise (C/N) is probably the most important parameter considered when evaluating the performance of a microwave communications system. The minimum wideband carrier power (C_{min}) at the input to a receiver that will provide a usable baseband output is called the receiver *threshold* or, sometimes, receiver *sensitivity*. The receiver threshold is dependent on the wideband noise power present at the input of a receiver, the noise introduced within the receiver, and the noise sensitivity of the baseband detector. Before C_{min} can be calculated, the input noise power must be determined. The input noise power is expressed mathematically as

$$N = KTB$$

where N = noise power (W)
  K = Boltzmann's constant (1.38×10^{-23} J/K)
  T = equivalent noise temperature of the receiver (K) (room temperature = 290 K)
  B = noise bandwidth (Hz)

Expressed in dBm,

$$N_{(dBm)} = 10 \log \frac{KTB}{0.001} = 10 \log \frac{KT}{0.001} + 10 \log B$$

For a 1-Hz bandwidth at room temperature,

$$N = 10 \log \frac{(1.38 \times 10^{-23})(290)}{0.001} + 10 \log 1$$
$$= -174 \text{ dBm}$$

Thus,
$$N_{(dBm)} = -174 \text{ dBm} + 10 \log B \tag{6-5}$$

Example 6-4

For an equivalent noise bandwidth of 10 MHz, determine the noise power.

Solution Substituting into Equation 6-5 yields

$$N = -174 \text{ dBm} + 10 \log (10 \times 10^6)$$
$$= -174 \text{ dBm} + 70 \text{ dB} = -104 \text{ dBm}$$

If the minimum C/N requirement for a receiver with a 10-MHz noise bandwidth is 24 dB, the minimum receive carrier power is

$$C_{\min} = \frac{C}{N} + N = 24 \text{ dB} + (-104 \text{ dBm}) = -80 \text{ dBm}$$

For a system gain of 113.35 dB, it would require a minimum transmit carrier power (P_t) of

$$P_t = G_s + C_{\min} = 113.35 \text{ dB} + (-80 \text{ dBm}) = 33.35 \text{ dBm}$$

This indicates that a minimum transmit power of 33.35 dBm (2.16 W) is required to achieve a carrier-to-noise ratio of 24 dB with a system gain of 113.35 dB and a bandwidth of 10 MHz.

Carrier-to-Noise Versus Signal-to-Noise

Carrier-to-noise (C/N) is the ratio of the wideband "carrier" (actually, not just the carrier, but rather the carrier and its associated sidebands) to the wideband noise power (the noise bandwidth of the receiver). C/N can be determined at an RF or an IF point in the receiver. Essentially, C/N is a *predetection* (before the FM demodulator) signal-to-noise ratio. Signal-to-noise (S/N) is a *postdetection* (after the FM demodulator) ratio. At a baseband point in the receiver, a single voice-band channel can be separated from the rest of the baseband and measured independently. At an RF or IF point in the receiver, it is impossible to separate a single voice-band channel from the composite FM signal. For example, a typical bandwidth for a single microwave channel is 30 MHz. The bandwidth of a voice-band channel is 4 kHz. C/N is the ratio of the power of the composite RF signal to the total noise power in the 30-MHz bandwidth. S/N is the ratio of the signal power of a single voice-band channel to the noise power in a 4-kHz bandwidth.

Noise Factor and Noise Figure

Noise factor (F) and *noise figure* (NF) are figures of merit used to indicate how much the signal-to-noise ratio deteriorates as a signal passes through a circuit or series of circuits. Noise factor is simply a ratio of input signal-to-noise ratio to output signal-to-noise ratio. In other words, a ratio of ratios. Mathematically, noise factor is

$$F = \frac{\text{input signal-to-noise ratio}}{\text{output signal-to-noise ratio}} \quad \text{(unitless ratio)} \tag{6-6a}$$

Noise figure is simply the noise factor stated in dB and is a parameter commonly used to indicate the quality of a receiver. Mathematically, noise figure is

$$NF = 10 \log \frac{\text{input signal-to-noise ratio}}{\text{output signal-to-noise ratio}} \quad \text{(dB)} \tag{6-6b}$$

or
$$NF = 10 \log F$$

In essence, noise figure indicates how much the signal-to-noise ratio deteriorates as a waveform propagates from the input to the output of a circuit. For example, an amplifier with a noise figure of 6 dB means that the signal-to-noise ratio at the output is 6 dB less than it was at the input. If a circuit is perfectly noiseless and adds no additional noise to the signal, the signal-to-noise ratio at the output will equal the signal-to-noise ratio at the input. For a perfect, noiseless circuit the noise factor is 1 and the noise figure is 0 dB.

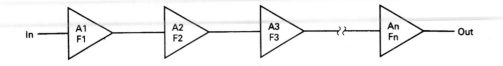

FIGURE 6-14 Total noise figure

An electronic circuit amplifies signals and noise within its passband equally well. Therefore, if the amplifier is ideal and noiseless, the input signal and noise are amplified the same, and the signal-to-noise ratio at the output will equal the signal-to-noise ratio at the input. In reality, however, amplifiers are not ideal. Therefore, the amplifier adds internally generated noise to the waveform, reducing the overall signal-to-noise ratio. The most predominant noise is thermal noise, which is generated in all electrical components. Therefore, all networks, amplifiers, and systems add noise to the signal and, thus, reduce the overall signal-to-noise ratio as the signal passes through them.

When two or more amplifiers are cascaded as shown in Figure 6-14, the total noise factor is the accumulation of the individual noise factors. *Friiss' formula* is used to calculate the total noise factor of several cascaded amplifiers. Mathematically, Friiss' formula is

$$F_T = F_1 + \frac{F_2 - 1}{A_1} + \frac{F_3 - 1}{A_1 A_2} + \frac{F_n - 1}{A_1 A_2 A_n} \qquad (6\text{-}7)$$

where F_T = total noise factor for n cascaded amplifiers
  F_1 = noise factor, amplifier 1
  F_2 = noise factor, amplifier 2
  F_3 = noise factor, amplifier 3
  F_n = noise factor, amplifier n
  A_1 = power gain, amplifier 1
  A_2 = power gain, amplifier 2
  A_n = power gain, amplifier n

Note that to use Friiss' formula, the noise figures must be converted to noise factors. The total noise figure is simply

$$\text{NF}_{T(\text{dB})} = 10 \log F_T$$

It can be seen that the noise factor of the first amplifier (NF_1) contributes the most toward the overall noise figure. The noise introduced in the first stage is amplified by each of the succeeding amplifiers. Therefore, when compared to the noise introduced in the first stage, the noise added by each succeeding amplifier is effectively reduced by a factor equal to the product of the power gains of the preceding amplifiers.

When precise noise calculations (0.1 dB or less) are necessary, it is generally more convenient to express noise figure in terms of noise temperature or equivalent noise temperature rather than as an absolute power (Chapter 8). Because noise power (N) is proportional to temperature, the noise present at the input to a device can be expressed as a function of the device's environmental temperature (T) and its equivalent noise temperature (T_e). Noise factor can be converted to a term dependent on temperature only as follows (refer to Figure 6-15).

Let

  N_d = noise power added by a single amplifier, referred to its input

Then $$N_d = KT_e B$$

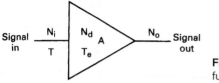

FIGURE 6-15 Noise figure as a function of temperature

where T_e is the equivalent noise temperature. Let

$$N_o = \text{total output noise power of an amplifier}$$
$$N_i = \text{total input noise power of an amplifier}$$
$$A = \text{power gain of an amplifier}$$

Therefore, N_o may be expressed as

$$N_o = AN_i + AN_d$$

and

$$N_o = AKTB + AKT_eB$$

Simplifying yields

$$N_o = AKB\,(T + T_e)$$

and the overall noise factor (F_T) equals

$$F_T = \frac{(S/N)_{in}}{(S/N)_{out}} = \frac{S/N_i}{AS/N_o} = \frac{N_o}{AN_i} = \frac{AKB\,(T + T_e)}{AKTB} \tag{6-8}$$

$$F_T = \frac{T + T_e}{T} = 1 + \frac{T_e}{T}$$

Example 6-5

In Figure 6-14, let $NF_1 = NF_2 = NF_3 = 3$ dB and $A_1 = A_2 = A_3 = 10$ dB. Solve for the total noise figure.

Solution Substituting into Equation 6-7 (*Note:* All gains and noise factors are given in absolute values) yields

$$F_T = F_1 + \frac{F_2 - 1}{A_1} + \frac{F_3 - 1}{A_1 A_2}$$

$$F_T = 2 + \frac{2 - 1}{10} + \frac{2 - 1}{10} = 2.11$$

$$NF_T = 10 \log 2.11 = 3.24 \text{ dB}$$

An overall noise figure of 3.24 dB indicates that the S/N ratio at the output of A_3 is 3.24 dB less than the S/N ratio at the input to A_1.

The noise figure of a receiver must be considered when determining C_{min}. The noise figure is included in the system gain equation as an equivalent loss. (Essentially, a gain in the total noise power is equivalent to a corresponding loss in the signal power.)

Example 6-6

Refer to Figure 6-16. For a system gain of 112 dB, a total noise figure of 6.5 dB, an input noise power of −104 dBm, and a minimum $(S/N)_{out}$ of the FM demodulator of 32 dB, determine the minimum receive carrier power and the minimum transmit power.

Solution To achieve a S/N ratio of 32 dB out of the FM demodulator, an input C/N of 15 dB is required (17 dB of improvement due to FM quieting). Solving for the receiver input carrier-to-noise ratio gives

$$\frac{C_{min}}{N} = \frac{C}{N} + NF_T = 15 \text{ dB} + 6.5 \text{ dB} = 21.5 \text{ dB}$$

FIGURE 6-16   System gain for Example 6-6

FIGURE 6-17   System gain for Example 6-7

Thus,

$$C_{min} = \frac{C_{min}}{N} + N = 21.5 \text{ dB} + (-104 \text{ dBm}) = -82.5 \text{ dBm}$$

$$P_t = G_s + C_{min} = 112 \text{ dB} + (-82.5 \text{ dBm}) = 29.5 \text{ dBm}$$

Example 6-7

For the system shown in Figure 6-17, determine the following: G_s, C_{min}/N, C_{min}, N, G_s, and P_t.

Solution   The minimum C/N at the input to the FM receiver is 23 dB.

$$\frac{C_{min}}{N} = \frac{C}{N} + NF_T = 23 \text{ dB} + 4.24 \text{ dB} = 27.24 \text{ dB}$$

Substituting into Equation 6-5 yields

$$N = -174 \text{ dBm} + 10 \log B = -174 \text{ dBm} + 68 \text{ dB} = -106 \text{ dBm}$$

$$C_{min} = \frac{C_{min}}{N} + N = 27.24 \text{ dB} + (-106 \text{ dBm}) = -78.76 \text{ dBm}$$

Substituting into Equation 6-4 gives us

$$F_m = 30 \log 50 + 10 \log [(6)(0.25)(0.125)(8)]$$
$$-10 \log (1 - 0.99999) - 70 = 32.76 \text{ dB}$$

Substituting into Equation 6-3, we have

$$L_p = 92.4 \text{ dB} + 20 \log 8 + 20 \log 50$$
$$= 92.4 \text{ dB} + 18.06 \text{ dB} + 33.98 \text{ dB} = 144.44 \text{ dB}$$

System Gain

From Table 6-1,

$$L_b = 4 \text{ dB}$$
$$L_f = 0.75 \ (6.5 \text{ dB}) = 4.875 \text{ dB}$$
$$A_t = A_r = 37.8 \text{ dB}$$

Note: The gain of an antenna increases or decreases proportional to the square of its diameter (i.e., if its diameter changes by a factor of 2, its gain changes by a factor of 4 which is 6 dB).

Substituting into Equation 6-1 yields

$$G_s = 32.76 + 144.44 + 4.875 + 4 - 37.8 - 37.8 = 110.475 \text{ dB}$$
$$P_t = G_s + C_{\min} = 110.475 \text{ dB} + (-78.76 \text{ dBm}) = 31.715 \text{ dBm}$$

QUESTIONS

6-1. What constitutes a short-haul microwave system? A long-haul microwave system?

6-2. Describe the baseband signal for a microwave system.

6-3. Why do FDM/FM microwave systems use low-index FM?

6-4. Describe a microwave repeater. Contrast baseband and IF repeaters.

6-5. Define *diversity*. Describe the three most commonly used diversity schemes.

6-6. Describe a protection switching arrangement. Contrast the two types of protection switching arrangements.

6-7. Briefly describe the four major sections of a microwave terminal station.

6-8. Define *ringaround*.

6-9. Briefly describe a high/low microwave system.

6-10. Define *system gain*.

6-11. Define the following terms: free-space path loss, branching loss, and feeder loss.

6-12. Define *fade margin*. Describe multipath losses, terrain sensitivity, and reliability objectives and how they affect fade margin.

6-13. Define *receiver threshold*.

6-14. Contrast carrier-to-noise ratio and signal-to-noise ratio.

6-15. Define *noise figure*.

PROBLEMS

6-1. Calculate the noise power at the input to a receiver that has a radio carrier frequency of 4 GHz and a bandwidth of 30 MHz (assume room temperature).

6-2. Determine the path loss for a 3.4-GHz signal propagating 20,000 m.

6-3. Determine the fade margin for a 60-km microwave hop. The RF carrier frequency is 6 GHz, the terrain is very smooth and dry, and the reliability objective is 99.95%.

6-4. Determine the noise power for a 20-MHz bandwidth at the input to a receiver with an input noise temperature of 290° C.

6-5. For a system gain of 120 dB, a minimum input C/N of 30 dB, and an input noise power of −115 dBm, determine the minimum transmit power (P_t).

6-6. Determine the amount of loss attributed to a reliability objective of 99.98%.

6-7. Determine the terrain sensitivity loss for a 4-GHz carrier that is propagating over a very dry, mountainous area.

6-8. A frequency-diversity microwave system operates at an RF carrier frequency of 7.4 GHz. The IF is a low-index frequency-modulated subcarrier. The baseband signal is the 1800-channel FDM system described in Chapter 5 (564 kHz to 8284 kHz). The antennas are 4.8-m-diameter parabolic dishes. The feeder lengths are 150 m at one station and 50 m at the other station. The reliability objective is 99.999%. The system propagates over an average terrain that has a very dry climate. The distance between stations is 50 km. The minimum carrier-to-noise ratio at the receiver input is 30 dB. Determine the following: fade margin, antenna gain, free-space path loss, total branching and feeder losses, receiver input noise power (C_{min}), minimum transmit power, and system gain.

6-9. Determine the overall noise figure for a receiver that has two RF amplifiers each with a noise figure of 6 dB and a gain of 10 dB, a mixer down-converter with a noise figure of 10 dB, and a conversion gain of −6 dB, and 40 dB of IF gain with a noise figure of 6 dB.

6-10. A microwave receiver has a total input noise power of −102 dBm and an overall noise figure of 4 dB. For a minimum C/N ratio of 20 dB at the input to the FM detector, determine the minimum receive carrier power.

6-11. Calculate the noise power at the input to a receiver for the following temperatures and bandwidths:

T (°C)	B (kHz)
0	10
20	40
200	20
500	50

6-12. Determine the path loss for the following frequencies and distances:

f (MHz)	D (km)
200	0.5
800	0.8
3000	5
5000	10
8000	25
18000	10

6-13. Determine the fade margin for a 30-km microwave hop. The RF frequency is 4 GHz, the terrain is water, and the reliability objective is 99.995%.

6-14. Determine the noise power for a 40-MHz bandwidth at the input to a receiver with an input temperature $T = 400°$ C.

6-15. For a system gain of 114 dB, a minimum input C/N = 34 dB, and an input noise power of −111 dBm, determine the minimum transmit power (P_t).

6-16. Determine the amount of loss contributed to a reliability objective of 99.9995%.

6-17. Determine the terrain sensitivity loss for a 8-GHz carrier that is propagating over a very smooth and dry terrain.

6-18. A frequency diversity microwave system operates at an RF = 7.4 GHz. The IF is a low-index frequency-modulated subcarrier. The baseband signal is a single mastergroup FDM system. The antennas are 2.4-m parabolic dishes. The feeder lengths are 120 m at one station and 80 m at the other station. The reliability objective is 99.995%. The system propagates over an average terrain that has a very dry climate. The distance between stations is 40 km. The minimum carrier-to-noise ratio at the receiver input is 28 dB. Determine the following: fade margin, antenna gain, free-space path loss, total branching and feeder losses, receiver input power (C_{min}), minimum transmit power, and system gain.

6-19. Determine the overall noise figure for a receiver that has two RF amplifiers each with a noise figure of 8 dB and a gain of 13 dB, a mixer down-converter with a noise figure of 6 dB, and a conversion gain of −6 dB, and 36 dB of IF gain with a noise figure of 10 dB.

6-20. A microwave receiver has a total input noise power of −108 dBm and an overall noise figure of 5 dB. For a minimum C/N ratio of 18 dB at the input to the FM detector, determine the minimum receive carrier power.

C H A P T E R 7 >>>>

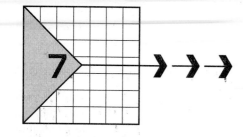

Satellite
Communications

INTRODUCTION

In the early 1960s, the American Telephone and Telegraph Company (AT&T) released studies indicating that a few powerful satellites of advanced design could handle more traffic than the entire AT&T long-distance communications network. The cost of these satellites was estimated to be only a fraction of the cost of equivalent terrestrial microwave facilities. Unfortunately, because AT&T was a utility, government regulations prevented them from developing the satellite systems. Smaller and much less lucrative corporations were left to develop the satellite systems, and AT&T continued to invest billions of dollars each year in conventional terrestrial microwave systems. Because of this, early developments in satellite technology were slow in coming.

Throughout the years the prices of most goods and services have increased substantially; however, satellite communications services have become more affordable each year. In most instances, satellite systems offer more flexibility than submarine cables, buried underground cables, line-of-sight microwave radio, tropospheric scatter radio, or optical fiber systems.

Essentially, a communications satellite is a radio repeater in the sky (*transponder*). A satellite system consists of a transponder, a ground-based station to control its operation, and a user network of earth stations that provide the facilities for transmission and reception of communications traffic through the satellite system. Satellite transmissions are categorized as either *bus* or *payload*. The bus includes control mechanisms that support the payload operation. The payload is the actual user information that is conveyed through the system. Although in recent years new data services and television broadcasting are more and more in demand, the transmission of conventional speech telephone signals (in analog or digital form) is still the bulk of the satellite payload.

HISTORY OF SATELLITES

The simplest type of satellite is a *passive reflector*, a device that simply "bounces" a signal from one place to another. The moon is a natural satellite of the earth and, consequently, in the late 1940s and early 1950s, became the first passive satellite. In 1954, the U.S. Navy successfully transmitted the first messages over this earth-to-moon-to-earth relay. In 1956, a relay service was established between Washington, D.C. and Hawaii and, until 1962, offered reliable long-distance communications. Service was limited only by the availability of the moon.

In 1957, Russia launched *Sputnik I*, the first *active* earth satellite. An active satellite is capable of receiving, amplifying, and retransmitting information to and from earth stations. *Sputnik I* transmitted telemetry information for 21 days. Later in the same year, the United States launched *Explorer I*, which transmitted telemetry information for nearly 5 months.

In 1958, NASA launched *Score*, a 150-lb conical-shaped satellite. With an on-board tape recording, *Score* rebroadcast President Eisenhower's 1958 Christmas message. *Score* was the first artificial satellite used for relaying terrestrial communications. *Score* was a *delayed repeater satellite;* it received transmissions from earth stations, stored them on magnetic tape, and rebroadcast them to ground stations farther along in its orbit.

In 1960, NASA in conjunction with Bell Telephone Laboratories and the Jet Propulsion Laboratory launched *Echo*, a 100-ft-diameter plastic balloon with an aluminum coating. *Echo* passively reflected radio signals from a large earth antenna. *Echo* was simple and reliable but required extremely high power transmitters at the earth stations. The first transatlantic transmission using a satellite was accomplished using *Echo*. Also in 1960, the Department of Defense launched *Courier*. *Courier* transmitted 3 W of power and lasted only 17 days.

In 1962, AT&T launched *Telstar I*, the first satellite to receive and transmit simultaneously. The electronic equipment in *Telstar I* was damaged by radiation from the newly discovered Van Allen belts and, consequently, lasted only a few weeks. *Telstar II* was electronically identical to *Telstar I*, but it was made more radiation resistant. *Telestar II* was successfully launched in 1963. It was used for telephone, television, facsimile, and data transmissions. The first successful transatlantic transmission of video was accomplished with *Telstar II*.

Early satellites were both of the passive and active type. Again, a passive satellite is one that simply reflects a signal back to Earth; there are no gain devices on board to amplify or repeat the signal. An active satellite is one that electronically repeats a signal back to Earth (i.e., receives, amplifies, and retransmits the signal). An advantage of passive satellites is that they do not require sophisticated electronic equipment on board, although they are not necessarily void of power. Some passive satellites require a *radio beacon transmitter* for tracking and ranging purposes. A beacon is a continuously transmitted unmodulated carrier that an earth station can lock onto and use to align its antennas or to determine the exact location of the satellite. A disadvantage of passive satellites is their inefficient use of transmitted power. With *Echo*, for example, only 1 part in every 10^{18} of the earth station transmitted power was actually returned to the earth station receiving antenna.

ORBITAL SATELLITES

The satellites mentioned thus far are called *orbital* or *nonsynchronous* satellites. Nonsynchronous satellites rotate around Earth in a low-altitude elliptical or circular pattern. If the satellite is orbiting in the same direction as Earth's rotation and at an angular velocity greater than that of Earth, the orbit is called a *prograde orbit*. If the

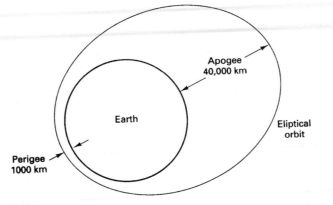

FIGURE 7-1 Soviet *Molniya* satellite orbit

satellite is orbiting in the opposite direction as Earth's rotation or in the same direction but at an angular velocity less than that of Earth, the orbit is called a *retrograde orbit*. Consequently, nonsynchronous satellites are continuously either gaining or falling back on Earth and do not remain stationary relative to any particular point on Earth. Thus, nonsynchronous satellites have to be used when available, which may be as short a period of time as 15 min per orbit. Another disadvantage of orbital satellites is the need for complicated and expensive tracking equipment at the earth stations. Each earth station must locate the satellite as it comes into view on each orbit and then lock its antenna onto the satellite and track it as it passes overhead. A major advantage of orbital satellites is that propulsion rockets are not required on board the satellites to keep them in their respective orbits.

One of the more interesting orbital satellite systems is the Soviet *Molniya* system. This is also spelled *Molnya* and *Molnia,* which means "lightning" in Russian (in colloquial Russian it means "news flash"). The Molniya satellites are used for television broadcasting and are presently the only nonsynchronous-orbit commercial satellite system in use. Molniya uses a highly elliptical orbit with *apogee* at about 40,000 km and *perigee* at about 1000 km (see Figure 7-1). The apogee is the farthest distance from Earth a satellite orbit reaches, the perigee is the minimum distance, and the *line of apsides* is the line joining the perigee and apogee through the center of Earth. With the *Molniya* system, the apogee is reached while over the northern hemisphere and the perigee while over the southern hemisphere. The size of the ellipse was chosen to make its period exactly one-half of a sidereal day (the time it takes Earth to rotate back to the same constellation). Because of its unique orbital pattern, the *Molniya* satellite is synchronous with the rotation of Earth. During its 12-h orbit, it spends about 11 h over the northern hemisphere.

GEOSTATIONARY SATELLITES

Geostationary or *geosynchronous* satellites are satellites that orbit in a circular pattern with an angular velocity equal to that of Earth. Consequently, they remain in a fixed position in respect to a given point on Earth. An obvious advantage is they are available to all the earth stations within their *shadow* 100% of the time. The shadow of a satellite includes all earth stations that have a line-of-sight path to it and lie within the radiation pattern of the satellite's antennas. An obvious disadvantage is they require sophisticated and heavy propulsion devices on board to keep them in a fixed orbit. The orbital time of a geosynchronous satellite is 24 h, the same as Earth.

Syncom I, launched in February 1963, was the first attempt to place a geosynchronous satellite into orbit. *Syncom I* was lost during orbit injection. *Syncom II* and *Syncom III* were successfully launched in February 1963 and August 1964, respectively. The *Syncom III* satellite was used to broadcast the 1964 Olympic Games from Tokyo. The *Syncom* projects demonstrated the feasibility of using geosynchronous satellites.

Since the *Syncom* projects, a number of nations and private corporations have successfully launched satellites that are currently being used to provide national as well as regional and international global communications. There are more than 200 satellite communications systems operating in the world today. They provide worldwide fixed common-carrier telephone and data circuits; point-to-point cable television (CATV); network television distribution; music broadcasting; mobile telephone service; and private networks for corporations, governmental agencies, and military applications.

In 1964 a commercial global satellite network known as *Intelsat* (International Telecommunications Satellite Organization) was established. Intelsat is owned and operated by a consortium of more than 100 countries. Intelsat is managed by the designated communications entities in their respective countries. The first Intelsat satellite was *Early Bird 1,* which was launched in 1965 and provided 480 voice channels. From 1966 to 1987, a series of satellites designated *Intelsat II, III, IV, V,* and *VI* were launched. *Intelsat VI* has a capacity of 80,000 voice channels.

ORBITAL PATTERNS

Once projected, a satellite remains in orbit because the centrifugal force caused by its rotation around Earth is counterbalanced by Earth's gravitational pull. The closer to Earth the satellite rotates, the greater the gravitational pull and the greater the velocity required to keep it from being pulled to Earth. Low-altitude satellites that orbit close to Earth (100 mi to 300 mi in height) travel at approximately 17,500 mph. At this speed, it takes approximately 1 1/2 h to rotate around the entire earth. Consequently, the time that the satellite is in line of sight of a particular earth station is only 1/4 h or less per orbit. Medium-altitude satellites (6000 mi to 12,000 mi in height) have a rotation period of 5 h to 12 h and remain in line of sight of a particular earth station for 2 h to 4 h per orbit. High-altitude, geosynchronous satellites (19,000 mi to 25,000 mi in height) travel at approximately 6879 mph and have a rotation period of 24 h, exactly the same as Earth. Consequently, they remain in a *fixed* position in respect to a given earth station and have a 24-h availability time. Figure 7-2 shows a low-, medium-, and high-altitude satellite orbit. It can be seen that three equally spaced, high-altitude geosynchronous satellites rotating around Earth above the equator can cover the entire earth except for the unpopulated areas of the north and south poles.

Figure 7-3 shows the three paths that a satellite may take as it rotates around Earth. When the satellite rotates in an orbit above the equator, it is called an *equatorial orbit.* When the satellite rotates in an orbit that takes it over the north and south poles, it is called a *polar orbit.* Any other orbital path is called an *inclined orbit.* An *ascending node* is the point where the orbit crosses the equatorial plane going from south to north, and a *descending node* is the point where the orbit crosses the equatorial plane going from north to south. The line joining the ascending and descending nodes through the center of earth is called the *line of nodes.*

It is interesting to note that 100% of Earth's surface can be covered with a single satellite in a polar orbit. The satellite is rotating around Earth in a longitudinal orbit while Earth is rotating on a latitudinal axis. Consequently, the satellite's radiation pattern is a diagonal spiral around Earth that somewhat resembles a barber pole. As a result, every location on Earth lies within the radiation pattern of the satellite twice each day.

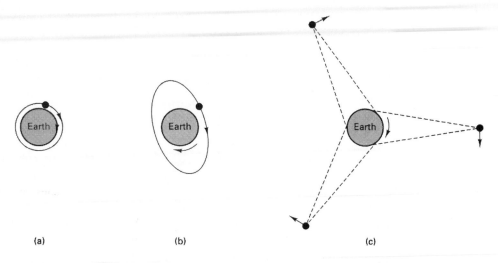

FIGURE 7-2 Satellite orbits: (a) low altitude (circular orbit, 100 mi to 300 mi); (b) medium altitude (elliptical orbit, 6000 mi to 12,000 mi); (c) high altitude (geosynchronous orbit, 19,000 mi to 25,000 mi)

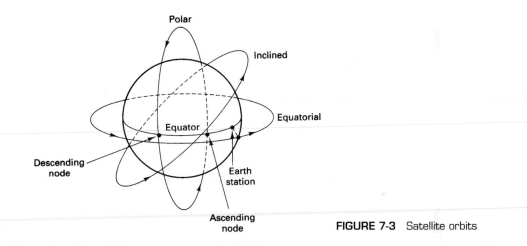

FIGURE 7-3 Satellite orbits

Summary of Geosynchronous Orbits

Advantages

1. The satellite remains almost stationary in respect to a given earth station. Consequently, expensive tracking equipment is not required at the earth stations.

2. There is no need to switch from one satellite to another as they orbit overhead. Consequently, there are no breaks in transmission because of the switching times.

3. High-altitude geosynchronous satellites can cover a much larger area of Earth than their low-altitude orbital counterparts.

4. The effects of Doppler shift are negligible.

Disadvantages

1. The higher altitudes of geosynchronous satellites introduce much longer propagation times. The round-trip propagation delay between two earth stations through a geosynchronous satellite is 500 ms to 600 ms.

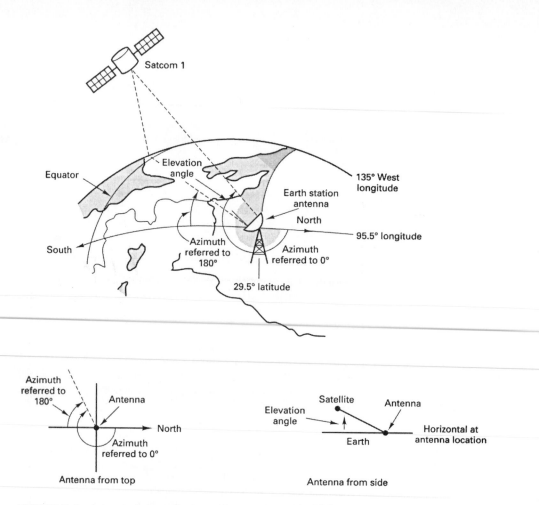

FIGURE 7-4 Azimuth and angle of elevation, "look angles"

2. Geosynchronous satellites require higher transmit powers and more sensitive receivers because of the longer distances and greater path losses.
3. High-precision spacemanship is required to place a geosynchronous satellite into orbit and to keep it there. Also, propulsion engines are required on board the satellites to keep them in their respective orbits.

LOOK ANGLES

To orient an earth station antenna toward a satellite, it is necessary to know the *elevation angle* and *azimuth* (Figure 7-4). These are called the *look angles*.

Angle of Elevation

The angle of elevation is the angle formed between the direction of travel of a wave radiated from an earth station antenna and the horizontal, or the angle subtended at the earth station antenna between the satellite and the horizontal. The smaller the angle of elevation, the greater the distance a propagated wave must pass through Earth's atmosphere. As with any wave propagated through Earth's atmosphere, it suffers absorption and may also be severely contaminated by noise. Consequently, if the angle of elevation is too small and the distance the wave is within Earth's atmosphere is too long, the wave may deteriorate to a degree that it provides inadequate transmission. Generally, 5° is considered as the minimum acceptable angle of elevation. Figure 7-5 shows how

FIGURE 7-5 Attenuation due to atmospheric absorption: (a) 6/4-GHz band; (b)14/12-GHz band

TABLE 7-1 Longitudinal Position of Several Current Synchronous Satellites Parked in an Equatorial Arc*

Satellite	Longitude (°W)
Satcom I	135
Satcom V	143
ANIK I	104
Westar I	99
Westar II	123.5
Westar III	91
Westar IV	98.5
Westar V	119.5
RCA	126
Mexico	116.5
Galaxy	74
Telstar	96

*0° Latitude

the angle of elevation affects the signal strength of a propagated wave due to normal atmospheric absorption, absorption due to thick fog, and absorption due to a heavy rain. It can be seen that the 14/12-GHz band (Figure 7-5b) is more severely affected than the 6/4-GHz band (Figure 7-5a). This is due to the smaller wavelengths associated with the higher frequencies. Also, at elevation angles less than 5°, the attenuation increases rapidly.

Azimuth

Azimuth is defined as the horizontal pointing angle of an antenna. It is usually measured in a clockwise direction in degrees from true north. The angle of elevation and the azimuth both depend on the latitude of the earth station and the longitude of both the earth station and the orbiting satellite. For a geosynchronous satellite in an equatorial orbit, the procedure is as follows: From a good map, determine the longitude and latitude of the earth station. From Table 7-1, determine the longitude of the satellite of interest. Calculate the difference, in degrees (ΔL), between the longitude of the satellite and the longitude of the earth station. Then, from Figure 7-6, determine the azimuth and elevation angle for the antenna. Figure 7-6 is for a geosynchronous satellite in an equatorial orbit.

Example 7-1

An earth station is located at Houston, Texas, which has a longitude of 95.5° W and a latitude of 29.5° N. The satellite of interest is RCA's *Satcom 1*, which has a longitude of 135° W. Determine the azimuth and elevation angle for the earth station antenna.

Solution   First determine the difference between the longitude of the earth station and the satellite.

$$\Delta L = 135° - 95.5° = 39.5°$$

Locate the intersection of ΔL and the latitude of the earth station on Figure 7-6. From the figure the angle of elevation is approximately 35°, and the azimuth is approximately 59° west of south.

ORBITAL CLASSIFICATIONS, SPACING, AND FREQUENCY ALLOCATION

There are two primary classifications for communications satellites: *spinners* and *three-axis stabilizer satellites*. Spinner satellites use the angular momentum of its spinning body to provide roll and yaw stabilization. With a three-axis stabilizer, the body

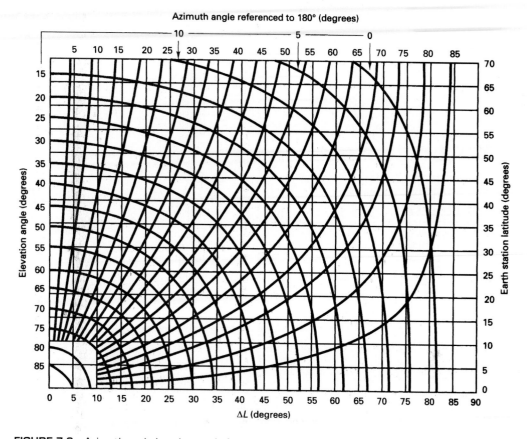

FIGURE 7-6 Azimuth and elevation angle for earth stations located in the northern hemisphere (referred to 180°)

remains fixed relative to Earth's surface while an internal subsystem provides roll and yaw stabilization. Figure 7-7 shows the two main classifications of communications satellites.

Geosynchronous satellites must share a limited space and frequency spectrum within a given arc of a geostationary orbit. Each communications satellite is assigned a longitude in the geostationary arc approximately 22,300 miles above the equator. The position in the slot depends on the communications frequency band used. Satellites operating at or near the same frequency must be sufficiently separated in space to avoid interfering with each other (Figure 7-8). There is a realistic limit to the number of satellite structures that can be stationed (*parked*) within a given area in space. The required *spatial separation* is dependent on the following variables:

1. Beamwidths and side lobe radiation of both the earth station and satellite antennas
2. RF carrier frequency
3. Encoding or modulation technique used
4. Acceptable limits of interference
5. Transmit carrier power

Generally, 3° to 6° of spatial separation is required depending on the variables stated above.

The most common carrier frequencies used for satellite communications are the 6/4- and 14/12-GHz bands. The first number is the up-link (earth station-to-transponder)

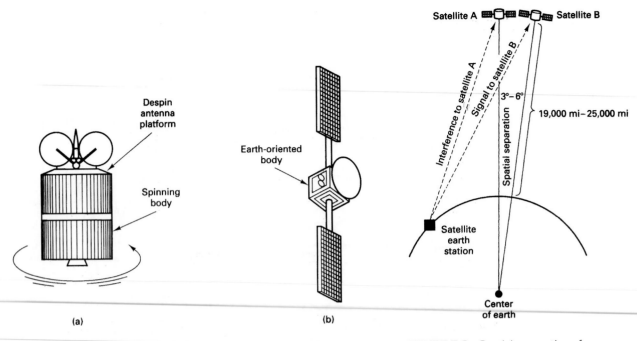

FIGURE 7-7 Satellite classes: (a) spinner; (b) three-axis stabilized

FIGURE 7-8 Spatial separation of satellites in geosynchronous orbit

frequency, and the second number is the down-link (transponder-to-earth station) frequency. Different up-link and down-link frequencies are used to prevent ringaround from occurring (Chapter 6). The higher the carrier frequency, the smaller the diameter required of an antenna for a given gain. Most domestic satellites use the 6/4-GHz band. Unfortunately, this band is also used extensively for terrestrial microwave systems. Care must be taken when designing a satellite network to avoid interference from or interference with established microwave links.

Certain positions in the geosynchronous orbit are in higher demand than the others. For example, the mid-Atlantic position, which is used to interconnect North America and Europe, is in exceptionally high demand. The mid-Pacific position is another.

The frequencies allocated by WARC (World Administrative Radio Conference) are summarized in Figure 7-9. Table 7-2 shows the bandwidths available for various services in the United States. These services include *fixed-point* (between earth stations located at fixed geographical points on earth), *broadcast* (wide-area coverage), *mobile* (ground-to-aircraft, ships, or land vehicles), and *intersatellite* (satellite-to-satellite cross-links).

RADIATION PATTERNS: FOOTPRINTS

The area of Earth covered by a satellite depends on the location of the satellite in its geosynchronous orbit, its carrier frequency, and the gain of its antennas. Satellite engineers select the antenna and carrier frequency for a particular spacecraft to concentrate the limited transmitted power on a specific area of Earth's surface. The geographical representation of a satellite antenna's radiation pattern is called a *footprint* (Figure 7-10). The contour lines represent limits of equal receive power density.

The radiation pattern from a satellite antenna may be categorized as either *spot, zonal,* or *earth* (Figure 7-11). The radiation patterns of earth coverage antennas have a beamwidth of approximately 17° and include coverage of approximately one-third of Earth's surface. Zonal coverage includes an area less than one-third of Earth's surface. Spot beams concentrate the radiated power in a very small geographic area.

FIGURE 7-9 WARC satellite frequency assignments

TABLE 7-2 Satellite Bandwidths Available in the United States

| Band | Frequency Band (GHz) | | | Bandwidth (MHz) |
	Up-link	Cross-link	Down-link	
C	5.9–6.4		3.7–4.2	500
X	7.9–8.4		7.25–7.75	500
Ku	14–14.5		11.7–12.2	500
Ka	27–30		17–20	—
	30–31		20–21	—
Q	—		40–41	1000
	—		41–43	2000
V	50–51		—	1000
(ISL)		54–58		3900
		59–64		5000

Reuse

When an allocated frequency band is filled, additional capacity can be achieved by *reuse* of the frequency spectrum. By increasing the size of an antenna (i.e., increasing the antenna gain) the beamwidth of the antenna is also reduced. Thus, different beams of the same frequency can be directed to different geographical areas of Earth. This is called frequency reuse. Another method of frequency reuse is to use dual polarization. Different information signals can be transmitted to different earth station receivers using the same band of frequencies simply by orienting their electromagnetic polarizations in an orthogonal manner (90° out of phase). Dual polarization is less effective because Earth's atmosphere has a tendency to reorient or repolarize an electromagnetic wave as it passes through. Reuse is simply another way to increase the capacity of a limited bandwidth.

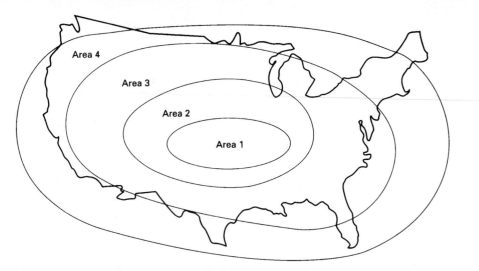

FIGURE 7-10 Satellite antenna radiation patterns ("footprints")

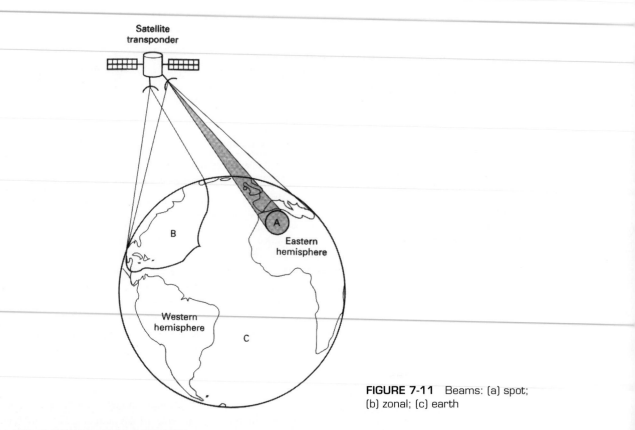

FIGURE 7-11 Beams: (a) spot; (b) zonal; (c) earth

SATELLITE SYSTEM LINK MODELS

Essentially, a satellite system consists of three basic sections: an up-link, a satellite transponder, and a down-link.

Up-Link Model

The primary component within the *up-link* section of a satellite system is the earth station transmitter. A typical earth station transmitter consists of an IF modulator, an IF-to-RF microwave up-converter, a high-power amplifier (HPA), and some means of bandlimiting

FIGURE 7-12 Satellite up-link model

FIGURE 7-13 Satellite transponder

the final output spectrum (i.e., an output bandpass filter). Figure 7-12 shows the block diagram of a satellite earth station transmitter. The IF modulator converts the input baseband signals to either an FM, a PSK, or a QAM modulated intermediate frequency. The up-converter (mixer and bandpass filter) converts the IF to an appropriate RF carrier frequency. The HPA provides adequate input sensitivity and output power to propagate the signal to the satellite transponder. HPAs commonly used are klystons and traveling-wave tubes.

Transponder

A typical *satellite transponder* consists of an input bandlimiting device (BPF), an input *low-noise amplifier* (LNA), a *frequency translator,* a low-level power amplifier, and an output bandpass filter. Figure 7-13 shows a simplified block diagram of a satellite transponder. This transponder is an RF-to-RF repeater. Other transponder configurations are IF and baseband repeaters similar to those used in microwave repeaters. In Figure 7-13, the input BPF limits the total noise applied to the input of the LNA. (A common device used as an LNA is a tunnel diode.) The output of the LNA is fed to a frequency translator (a shift oscillator and a BPF), which converts the high-band up-link frequency to the low-band down-link frequency. The low-level power amplifier, which is commonly a traveling-wave tube, amplifies the RF signal for transmission through the down-link to earth station receivers. Each RF satellite channel requires a separate transponder.

FIGURE 7-14 Satellite down-link model

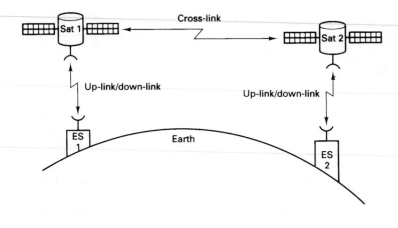

FIGURE 7-15 Intersatellite link

Down-Link Model

An earth station receiver includes an input BPF, an LNA, and an RF-to-IF down-converter. Figure 7-14 shows a block diagram of a typical earth station receiver. Again, the BPF limits the input noise power to the LNA. The LNA is a highly sensitive, low-noise device such as a tunnel diode amplifier or a parametric amplifier. The RF-to-IF down-converter is a mixer/bandpass filter combination which converts the received RF signal to an IF frequency.

Cross-Links

Occasionally, there is an application where it is necessary to communicate between satellites. This is done using *satellite cross-links* or *intersatellite links* (ISLs), shown in Figure 7-15. A disadvantage of using an ISL is that both the transmitter and receiver are *space-bound.* Consequently, both the transmitter's output power and the receiver's input sensitivity are limited.

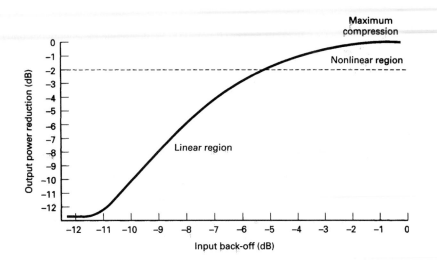

FIGURE 7-16 HPA input/output characteristic curve

SATELLITE SYSTEM PARAMETERS

Transmit Power and Bit Energy

High-power amplifiers used in earth station transmitters and the traveling-wave tubes typically used in satellite transponders are *nonlinear devices;* their gain (output power-versus-input power) is dependent on input signal level. A typical input/output power characteristic curve is shown in Figure 7-16. It can be seen that as the input power is reduced by 5 dB, the output power is reduced by only 2 dB. There is an obvious *power compression.* To reduce the amount of intermodulation distortion caused by the nonlinear amplification of the HPA, the input power must be reduced (*backed off*) by several dB. This allows the HPA to operate in a more *linear* region. The amount the output level is backed off from rated levels is equivalent to a loss and is appropriately called *back-off loss* (L_{bo}).

To operate as efficiently as possible, a power amplifier should be operated as close as possible to saturation. The *saturated output power* is designated $P_{o(\text{sat})}$ or simply P_t. The output power of a typical satellite earth station transmitter is much higher than the output power from a terrestrial microwave power amplifier. Consequently, when dealing with satellite systems, P_t is generally expressed in dBW (decibels in respect to 1 W) rather than in dBm (decibels in respect to 1 mW).

Most modern satellite systems use either phase shift keying (PSK) or quadrature amplitude modulation (QAM) rather than conventional frequency modulation (FM). With PSK and QAM, the input baseband is generally a PCM-encoded, time-division-multiplexed signal that is digital in nature. Also, with PSK and QAM, several bits may be encoded in a single transmit signaling element. Consequently, a parameter more meaningful than carrier power is *energy per bit* (E_b). Mathematically, E_b is

$$E_b = P_t T_b \qquad (7\text{-}1a)$$

where E_b = energy of a single bit (J/bit)
          P_t = total carrier power (W)
          T_b = time of a single bit (s)

or because $T_b = 1/f_b$, where f_b is the bit rate in bits per second,

$$E_b = \frac{P_t}{f_b} \qquad (7\text{-}1b)$$

Example 7-2

For a total transmit power (P_t) of 1000 W, determine the energy per bit (E_b) for a transmission rate of 50 Mbps.

Solution

$$T_b = \frac{1}{f_b} = \frac{1}{50 \times 10^6 \text{ bps}} = 0.02 \times 10^{-6} \text{ s}$$

(It appears that the units for T_b should be s/bit but the per bit is implied in the definition of T_b, time of bit.)

Substituting into Equation 7-1a yields

$$E_b = 1000 \text{ J/s } (0.02 \times 10^{-6} \text{ s/bit}) = 20 \text{ } \mu\text{J}$$

(Again the units appear to be J/bit, but the per bit is implied in the definition of E_b, energy per bit.)

$$E_b = \frac{1000 \text{ J/s}}{50 \times 10^6 \text{ bps}} = 20 \text{ } \mu\text{J}$$

Expressed as a log,

$$E_b = 10 \log (20 \times 10^{-6}) = -47 \text{ dBJ}$$

It is common to express P_t in dBW and E_b in dBW/bps. Thus,

$$P_t = 10 \log 1000 = 30 \text{ dBW}$$
$$E_b = P_t - 10 \log f_b = P_t - 10 \log (50 \times 10^6)$$
$$= 30 \text{ dBW} - 77 \text{ dB} = -47 \text{ dBW/bps}$$

or simply −47 dBW.

Effective Isotropic Radiated Power

Effective isotropic radiated power (EIRP) is defined as an equivalent transmit power and is expressed mathematically as

$$\text{EIRP} = P_r A_t$$

where   EIRP = effective isotropic radiated power (W)
P_r = total power radiated from an antenna (W)
A_t = transmit antenna gain (unitless ratio)

Expressed as a log,

$$\text{EIRP}_{(\text{dBW})} = P_{r(\text{dBW})} + A_{t(\text{dB})}$$

In respect to the transmitter output,

$$P_r = P_t - L_{\text{bo}} - L_{bf}$$

Thus $\qquad\qquad$ EIRP $= P_t - L_{\text{bo}} - L_{bf} + A_t$ $\qquad\qquad$ (7-2)

where P_t = actual power output of the transmitter (dBW)
L_{bo} = back-off losses of HPA (dB)
L_{bf} = total branching and feeder loss (dB)
A_t = transmit antenna gain (dB)

Example 7-3

For an earth station transmitter with an output power of 40 dBW (10,000 W), a back-off loss of 3 dB, a total branching and feeder loss of 3 dB, and a transmit antenna gain of 40 dB, determine the EIRP.

Solution   Substituting into Equation 7-2 yields

$$\text{EIRP} = P_t - L_{\text{bo}} - L_{bf} + A_t$$
$$= 40 \text{ dBW} - 3 \text{ dB} - 3 \text{ dB} + 40 \text{ dB} = 74 \text{ dBW}$$

Equivalent Noise Temperature

With terrestrial microwave systems, the noise introduced in a receiver or a component within a receiver was commonly specified by the parameter noise figure. In satellite communications systems, it is often necessary to differentiate or measure noise in increments as small as a tenth or a hundredth of a decibel. Noise figure, in its standard form, is inadequate for such precise calculations. Consequently, it is common to use *environmental temperature* (T) and *equivalent noise temperature* (T_e) when evaluating the performance of a satellite system. In Chapter 6 total noise power was expressed mathematically as

$$N = KTB$$

Rearranging and solving for T gives us

$$T = \frac{N}{KB}$$

where N = total noise power (W)
  K = Boltzmann's constant (J/K)
  B = bandwidth (Hz)
  T = temperature of the environment (K)

Again from Chapter 6 (Equation 6-8),

$$F = 1 + \frac{T_e}{T}$$

where T_e = equivalent noise temperature (K)
  F = noise factor
  T = temperature of the environment (K)

Rearranging Equation 6-8, we have

$$T_e = T(F - 1)$$

Typically, equivalent noise temperatures of the receivers used in satellite transponders are about 1000 K. For earth station receivers T_e values are between 20 K and 1000 K. Equivalent noise temperature is generally more useful when expressed logarithmically with the unit of dBK, as follows:

$$T_{e(dBK)} = 10 \log T_e$$

For an equivalent noise temperature of 100 K, $T_{e(dBK)}$ is

$$T_e = 10 \log 100 \quad \text{or} \quad 20 \text{ dBK}$$

Equivalent noise temperature is a hypothetical value that can be calculated but cannot be measured. Equivalent noise temperature is often used rather than noise figure because it is a more accurate method of expressing the noise contributed by a device or a receiver when evaluating its performance. Essentially, equivalent noise temperature (T_e) represents the noise power present at the input to a device plus the noise added internally by that device. This allows us to analyze the noise characteristics of a device by simply evaluating an equivalent input noise temperature. As you will see in subsequent discussions, T_e is a very useful parameter when evaluating the performance of a satellite system.

Example 7-4

Convert noise figures of 4 and 4.01 to equivalent noise temperatures. Use 300 K for the environmental temperature.

Solution Substituting into Equation 6-8 yields

$$T_e = T(F - 1)$$

For NF = 4: $T_e = 300(4 - 1) = 900 \text{ K}$

For NF = 4.01: $T_e = 300(4.01 - 1) = 903 \text{ K}$

It can be seen that the 3° difference in the equivalent temperatures is 300 times as large as the difference between the two noise figures. Consequently, equivalent noise temperature is a more accurate way of comparing the noise performances of two receivers or devices.

Noise Density

Simply stated, *noise density* (N_0) is the total noise power normalized to a 1-Hz bandwidth, or the noise power present in a 1-Hz bandwidth. Mathematically, noise density is

$$N_0 = \frac{N}{B} = \frac{KTB}{B} = KT \tag{7-3a}$$

where N_0 = noise density (W/Hz) (N_0 is generally expressed as simply watts; the per hertz is implied in the definition of N_0)
   N = total noise power (W)
   B = bandwidth (Hz)
   K = Boltzmann's constant (J/K)
   T_e = equivalent noise temperature (K)

Expressed as a log,

$$N_{0(\text{dBW/Hz})} = 10 \log N - 10 \log B \tag{7-3b}$$

$$= 10 \log K + 10 \log T_e \tag{7-3c}$$

Example 7-5

For an equivalent noise bandwidth of 10 MHz and a total noise power of 0.0276 pW, determine the noise density and equivalent noise temperature.

Solution Substituting into Equation 7-3a, we have

$$N_0 = \frac{N}{B} = \frac{276 \times 10^{-16} \text{ W}}{10 \times 10^6 \text{ Hz}} = 276 \times 10^{-23} \text{ W/Hz}$$

or simply, 276×10^{-23} W.

$$N_0 = 10 \log (276 \times 10^{-23}) = -205.6 \text{ dBW/Hz}$$

or simply -205.6 dBW. Substituting into Equation 7-3b gives us

$$N_0 = -135.6 \text{ dBW} - 70 \text{ dB} = -205.6 \text{ dBW}$$

Rearranging Equation 7-3a and solving for equivalent noise temperature yields

$$T_e = \frac{N_0}{K}$$

$$= \frac{276 \times 10^{-23} \text{ J/cycle}}{1.38 \times 10^{-23} \text{ J/K}} = 200 \text{ K/cycle}$$

$$= 10 \log 200 = 23 \text{ dBK}$$

$$= N_0 - 10 \log K$$

$$= -205.6 \text{ dBW} - (-228.6 \text{ dBWK}) = 23 \text{ dBK}$$

Carrier-to-Noise Density Ratio

C/N_0 is the average wideband carrier power-to-noise density ratio. The *wideband carrier power* is the combined power of the carrier and its associated sidebands. The noise is the thermal noise present in a normalized 1-Hz bandwidth. The carrier-to-noise density ratio may also be written as a function of noise temperature. Mathematically, C/N_0 is

$$\frac{C}{N_0} = \frac{C}{KT_e} \qquad (7\text{-}4a)$$

Expressed as a log,

$$\frac{C}{N_0}\,(\text{dB}) = C_{(\text{dBW})} - N_{0(\text{dBW})} \qquad (7\text{-}4b)$$

Energy of Bit-to-Noise Density Ratio

E_b/N_0 is one of the most important and most often used parameters when evaluating a digital radio system. The E_b/N_0 ratio is a convenient way to compare digital systems that use different transmission rates, modulation schemes, or encoding techniques. Mathematically, E_b/N_0 is

$$\frac{E_b}{N_0} = \frac{C/f_b}{N/B} = \frac{CB}{Nf_b} \qquad (7\text{-}5)$$

E_b/N_0 is a convenient term used for digital system calculations and performance comparisons, but in the real world, it is more convenient to measure the wideband carrier power-to-noise density ratio and convert it to E_b/N_0. Rearranging Equation 7-5 yields the following expression:

$$\frac{E_b}{N_0} = \frac{C}{N} \times \frac{B}{f_b}$$

The E_b/N_0 ratio is the product of the carrier-to-noise ratio (C/N) and the noise bandwidth-to-bit rate ratio (B/f_b). Expressed as a log,

$$\frac{E_b}{N_0}\,(\text{dB}) = \frac{C}{N}\,(\text{dB}) + \frac{B}{f_b}\,(\text{dB}) \qquad (7\text{-}6)$$

The energy per bit (E_b) will remain constant as long as the total wideband carrier power (C) and the transmission rate (bps) remain unchanged. Also, the noise density (N_0) will remain constant as long as the noise temperature remains constant. The following conclusion can be made: For a given carrier power, bit rate, and noise temperature, the E_b/N_0 ratio will remain constant regardless of the encoding technique, modulation scheme, or bandwidth used.

Figure 7-17 graphically illustrates the relationship between an expected probability of error $P(e)$ and the minimum C/N ratio required to achieve the $P(e)$. The C/N specified is for the minimum double-sided Nyquist bandwidth. Figure 7-18 graphically illustrates the relationship between an expected $P(e)$ and the minimum E_b/N_0 ratio required to achieve that $P(e)$.

A $P(e)$ of 10^{-5} ($1/10^5$) indicates a probability that 1 bit will be in error for every 100,000 bits transmitted. $P(e)$ is analogous to the bit error rate (BER).

Example 7-6

A coherent binary phase-shift-keyed (BPSK) transmitter operates at a bit rate of 20 Mbps. For a probability of error $P(e)$ of 10^{-4}:

(a) Determine the minimum theoretical C/N and E_b/N_0 ratios for a receiver bandwidth equal to the minimum double-sided Nyquist bandwidth.

(b) Determine the C/N if the noise is measured at a point prior to the bandpass filter, where the bandwidth is equal to twice the Nyquist bandwidth.

(c) Determine the C/N if the noise is measured at a point prior to the bandpass filter where the bandwidth is equal to three times the Nyquist bandwidth.

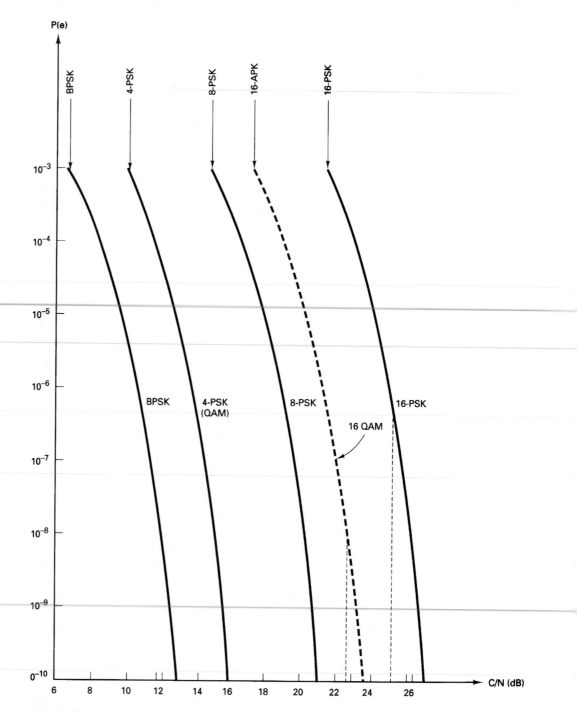

FIGURE 7-17 $P(e)$ performance of M-ary PSK, QAM, QPR, and M-ary APK coherent systems. The rms C/N is specified in the double-sided Nyquist bandwidth

Solution (a) With BPSK, the minimum bandwidth is equal to the bit rate, 20 MHz. From Figure 7-17, the minimum C/N is 8.8 dB. Substituting into Equation 7-6 gives us

$$\frac{E_b}{N_0} = \frac{C}{N} + \frac{B}{f_b}$$

$$= 8.8 \text{ dB} + 10 \log \frac{20 \times 10^6}{20 \times 10^6}$$

$$= 8.8 \text{ dB} + 0 \text{ dB} = 8.8 \text{ dB}$$

Chapter 7   Satellite Communications

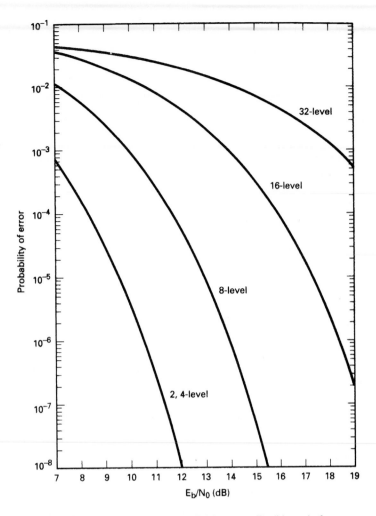

FIGURE 7-18 Probability of error $P(e)$ versus E_b/N_0 ratio for various digital modulation schemes

Note: The minimum E_b/N_0 equals the minimum C/N when the receiver noise bandwidth equals the minimum Nyquist bandwidth. The minimum E_b/N_0 of 8.8 can be verified from Figure 7-18.

What effect does increasing the noise bandwidth have on the minimum C/N and E_b/N_0 ratios? The wideband carrier power is totally independent of the noise bandwidth. Similarly, an increase in the bandwidth causes a corresponding increase in the noise power. Consequently, a decrease in C/N is realized that is directly proportional to the increase in the noise bandwidth. E_b is dependent on the wideband carrier power and the bit rate only. Therefore, E_b is unaffected by an increase in the noise bandwidth. N_0 is the noise power normalized to a 1-Hz bandwidth and, consequently, is also unaffected by an increase in the noise bandwidth.

(b) Because E_b/N_0 is independent of bandwidth, measuring the C/N at a point in the receiver where the bandwidth is equal to twice the minimum Nyquist bandwidth has absolutely no effect on E_b/N_0. Therefore, E_b/N_0 becomes the constant in Equation 7-6 and is used to solve for the new value of C/N. Rearranging Equation 7-6 and using the calculated E_b/N_0 ratio, we have

$$\frac{C}{N} = \frac{E_b}{N_0} - \frac{B}{f_b}$$

$$= 8.8 \text{ dB} - 10 \log \frac{40 \times 10^6}{20 \times 10^6}$$

$$= 8.8 \text{ dB} - 10 \log 2$$

$$= 8.8 \text{ dB} - 3 \text{ dB} = 5.8 \text{ dB}$$

(c) Measuring the C/N ratio at a point in the receiver where the bandwidth equals three times the minimum bandwidth yields the following results for C/N.

$$\frac{C}{N} = \frac{E_b}{N_0} - 10 \log \frac{60 \times 10^6}{20 \times 10^6}$$

$$= 8.8 \text{ dB} - 10 \log 3 = 4.03 \text{ dB}$$

The C/N ratios of 8.8, 5.8, and 4.03 dB indicate the C/N ratios that would be measured at the three specified points in the receiver to achieve the desired minimum E_b/N_0 and $P(e)$.

Because E_b/N_0 cannot be directly measured to determine the E_b/N_0 ratio, the wideband carrier-to-noise ratio is measured and, then, substituted into Equation 7-6. Consequently, to accurately determine the E_b/N_0 ratio, the noise bandwidth of the receiver must be known.

Example 7-7

A coherent 8-PSK transmitter operates at a bit rate of 90 Mbps. For a probability of error of 10^{-5}:

(a) Determine the minimum theoretical C/N and E_b/N_0 ratios for a receiver bandwidth equal to the minimum double-sided Nyquist bandwidth.
(b) Determine the C/N if the noise is measured at a point prior to the bandpass filter where the bandwidth is equal to twice the Nyquist bandwidth.
(c) Determine the C/N if the noise is measured at a point prior to the bandpass filter where the bandwidth is equal to three times the Nyquist bandwidth.

Solution (a) 8-PSK has a bandwidth efficiency of 3 bps/Hz and, consequently, requires a minimum bandwidth of one-third the bit rate or 30 MHz. From Figure 7-17, the minimum C/N is 18.5 dB. Substituting into Equation 7-6, we obtain

$$\frac{E_b}{N_0} = 18.5 \text{ dB} + 10 \log \frac{30 \text{ MHz}}{90 \text{ Mbps}}$$

$$= 18.5 \text{ dB} + (-4.8 \text{ dB}) = 13.7 \text{ dB}$$

(b) Rearranging Equation 7-6 and substituting for E_b/N_0 yields

$$\frac{C}{N} = 13.7 \text{ dB} - 10 \log \frac{60 \text{ MHz}}{90 \text{ Mbps}}$$

$$= 13.7 \text{ dB} - (-1.77 \text{ dB}) = 15.47 \text{ dB}$$

(c) Again, rearranging Equation 7-6 and substituting for E_b/N_0 gives us

$$\frac{C}{N} = 13.7 \text{ dB} - 10 \log \frac{90 \text{ MHz}}{90 \text{ Mbps}}$$

$$= 13.7 \text{ dB} - 0 \text{ dB} = 13.7 \text{ dB}$$

It should be evident from Examples 7-6 and 7-7 that the E_b/N_0 and C/N ratios are equal only when the noise bandwidth is equal to the bit rate. Also, as the bandwidth at the point of measurement increases, the C/N decreases.

When the modulation scheme, bit rate, bandwidth, and C/N ratios of two digital radio systems are different, it is often difficult to determine which system has the lower probability of error. Because E_b/N_0 is independent of bit rate, bandwidth, and modulation scheme, it is a convenient common denominator to use for comparing the probability of error performance of two digital radio systems.

Example 7-8

Compare the performance characteristics of the two digital systems listed below, and determine which system has the lower probability of error.

	QPSK	8-PSK
Bit rate	40 Mbps	60 Mbps
Bandwidth	1.5 × minimum	2 × minimum
C/N	10.75 dB	13.76 dB

Solution Substituting into Equation 7-6 for the QPSK system gives us

$$\frac{E_b}{N_0} = \frac{C}{N} + 10 \log \frac{B}{f_b}$$

$$= 10.75 \text{ dB} + 10 \log \frac{1.5 \times 20 \text{ MHz}}{40 \text{ Mbps}}$$

$$= 10.75 \text{ dB} + (-1.25 \text{ dB}) = 9.5 \text{ dB}$$

From Figure 7-18, the $P(e)$ is approximately 2×10^{-6}.

Substituting into Equation 7-6 for the 8-PSK system gives us

$$\frac{E_b}{N_0} = 13.76 \text{ dB} + 10 \log \frac{2 \times 20 \text{ MHz}}{60 \text{ Mbps}}$$

$$= 13.76 \text{ dB} + (-1.76 \text{ dB}) = 12 \text{ dB}$$

From Figure 7-18, the $P(e)$ is approximately 8×10^{-5}.

Although the QPSK system has lower C/N and E_b/N_0 ratios, the $P(e)$ of the QPSK system is 4 times lower (better) than the 8-PSK system.

Gain-to-Equivalent Noise Temperature Ratio

Essentially, *gain-to-equivalent noise temperature ratio* (G/T_e) is a figure of merit used to represent the quality of a satellite or an earth station receiver. The G/T_e of a receiver is the ratio of the receive antenna gain to the equivalent noise temperature (T_e) of the receiver. Because of the extremely small receive carrier powers typically experienced with satellite systems, very often an LNA is physically located at the feedpoint of the antenna. When this is the case, G/T_e is a ratio of the gain of the receiving antenna plus the gain of the LNA to the equivalent noise temperature. Mathematically, gain-to-equivalent noise temperature ratio is

$$\frac{G}{T_e} = \frac{A_r + A_{(LNA)}}{T_e} \tag{7-7}$$

Expressed in logs, we have

$$\frac{G}{T_e}(\text{dBK}^{-1}) = A_{r(dB)} + A_{(LNA)(dB)} - T_{e(dBK)} \tag{7-8}$$

G/T_e is a very useful parameter for determining the E_b/N_0 and C/N ratios at the satellite transponder and earth station receivers. G/T_e is essentially the only parameter required at a satellite or an earth station receiver when completing a link budget.

Example 7-9

For a satellite transponder with a receiver antenna gain of 22 dB, an LNA gain of 10 dB, and an equivalent noise temperature of 22 dBK, determine the G/T_e figure of merit.

Solution Substituting into Equation 7-8 yields

$$\frac{G}{T_e} = 22 \text{ dB} + 10 \text{ dB} - 22 \text{ dBK} = 10 \text{ dBK}^{-1}$$

SATELLITE SYSTEM LINK EQUATIONS

The error performance of a digital satellite system is quite predictable. Figure 7-19 shows a simplified block diagram of a digital satellite system and identifies the various gains and losses that may affect the system performance. When evaluating the performance of a digital satellite system, the up-link and down-link parameters are first considered separately, then the overall performance is determined by combining them in the appropriate manner. Keep in mind, a digital microwave or satellite radio simply means the original and demodulated baseband signals are digital in nature. The RF portion of the radio is analog; that is, FSK, PSK, QAM, or some other higher-level modulation riding on an analog microwave carrier.

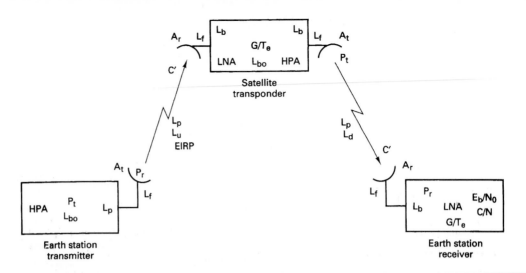

FIGURE 7-19 Overall satellite system showing the gains and losses incurred in both the up-link and down-link sections. HPA, high-power amplifier; P_t, HPA output power; L_{bo}, back-off loss; L_f, feeder loss; L_b, branching loss; A_t, transmit antenna gain; P_r, total radiated power = $P_t - L_{bo} - L_b - L_f$; EIRP, effective isotropic radiated power = $P_r A_t$; L_u, additional up-link losses due to atmosphere; L_p, path loss; A_r, receive antenna gain; G/T_e, gain-to-equivalent noise ratio; L_d, additional down-link losses due to atmosphere; LNA, low-noise amplifier; C/T_e, carrier-to-equivalent noise ratio; C/N_0, carrier-to-noise density ratio; E_b/N_0, energy of bit-to-noise density ratio; C/N, carrier-to-noise ratio

LINK EQUATIONS

The following *link equations* are used to separately analyze the up-link and the down-link sections of a single radio-frequency carrier satellite system. These equations consider only the ideal gains and losses and effects of thermal noise associated with the earth station transmitter, earth station receiver, and the satellite transponder. The nonideal aspects of the system are discussed later in this chapter.

Up-Link Equation

$$\frac{C}{N_0} = \frac{A_t P_r (L_p L_u) A_r}{K T_e} = \frac{A_t P_r (L_p L_u)}{K} \times \frac{G}{T_e}$$

where L_d and L_u are the additional up-link and down-link atmospheric losses, respectively. The up-link and down-link signals must pass through Earth's atmosphere, where they are partially absorbed by the moisture, oxygen, and particulates in the air. Depending on the elevation angle, the distance the RF signal travels through the atmosphere varies from one earth station to another. Because L_p, L_u, and L_d represent losses, they are decimal values less than 1. G/T_e is the receive antenna gain plus the gain of the LNA divided by the equivalent input noise temperature.

Expressed as a log,

$$\frac{C}{N_0} = \underbrace{10 \log A_t P_r}_{\substack{\text{EIRP} \\ \text{earth} \\ \text{station}}} - \underbrace{20 \log\left(\frac{4\pi D}{\lambda}\right)}_{\substack{\text{free-space} \\ \text{path loss}}} + \underbrace{10 \log\left(\frac{G}{T_e}\right)}_{\substack{\text{satellite} \\ G/T_e}} - \underbrace{10 \log L_u}_{\substack{\text{additional} \\ \text{atmospheric} \\ \text{losses}}} - \underbrace{10 \log K}_{\substack{\text{Boltzmann's} \\ \text{constant}}}$$

$$= \text{EIRP (dBW)} - L_p \text{ (dB)} + \frac{G}{T_e} \text{ (dBK}^{-1}\text{)} - L_u \text{ (dB)} - K \text{ (dBWK)}$$

Down-Link Equation

$$\frac{C}{N_0} = \frac{A_t P_r (L_p L_d) A_r}{K T_e} = \frac{A_t P_r (L_p L_d)}{K} \times \frac{G}{T_e}$$

Expressed as a log

$$\frac{C}{N_0} = \underbrace{10 \log A_t P_r}_{\substack{\text{EIRP} \\ \text{satellite}}} - \underbrace{20 \log\left(\frac{4\pi D}{\lambda}\right)}_{\substack{\text{free-space} \\ \text{path loss}}} + \underbrace{10 \log\left(\frac{G}{T_e}\right)}_{\substack{\text{satellite} \\ G/T_e}} - \underbrace{10 \log L_d}_{\substack{\text{additional} \\ \text{atmospheric} \\ \text{losses}}} - \underbrace{10 \log K}_{\substack{\text{Boltzmann's} \\ \text{constant}}}$$

$$= \text{EIRP (dBW)} - L_p \text{ (dB)} + \frac{G}{T_e} \text{ (dBK}^{-1}) - L_d \text{ (dB)} - K \text{ (dBWK)}$$

LINK BUDGET

Table 7-3 lists the system parameters for three typical satellite communication systems. The systems and their parameters are not necessarily for an existing or future system; they are hypothetical examples only. The system parameters are used to construct a *link budget*. A link budget identifies the system parameters and is used to determine the projected C/N and E_b/N_0 ratios at both the satellite and earth station receivers for a given modulation scheme and desired $P(e)$.

Example 7-10

Complete the link budget for a satellite system with the following parameters.

Up-link

1. Earth station transmitter output power at saturation, 2000 W	33 dBW
2. Earth station back-off loss	3 dB
3. Earth station branching and feeder losses	4 dB
4. Earth station transmit antenna gain (from Figure 7-20, 15 m at 14 GHz)	64 dB
5. Additional up-link atmospheric losses	0.6 dB
6. Free-space path loss (from Figure 7-21, at 14 GHz)	206.5 dB
7. Satellite receiver G/T_e ratio	−5.3 dBK^{-1}
8. Satellite branching and feeder losses	0 dB
9. Bit rate	120 Mbps
10. Modulation scheme	8-PSK

Down-link

1. Satellite transmitter output power at saturation, 10 W	10 dBW
2. Satellite back-off loss	0.1 dB
3. Satellite branching and feeder losses	0.5 dB
4. Satellite transmit antenna gain (from Figure 7-20, 0.37 m at 12 GHz)	30.8 dB
5. Additional down-link atmospheric losses	0.4 dB
6. Free-space path loss (from Figure 7-21, at 12 GHz)	205.6 dB
7. Earth station receive antenna gain (15 m, 12 GHz)	62 dB
8. Earth station branching and feeder losses	0 dB
9. Earth station equivalent noise temperature	270 K
10. Earth station G/T_e ratio	37.7 dBK^{-1}
11. Bit rate	120 Mbps
12. Modulation scheme	8-PSK

Solution   *Up-link budget:* Expressed as a log,

$$\text{EIRP (earth station)} = P_t + A_t - L_{\text{bo}} - L_{bf}$$
$$= 33 \text{ dBW} + 64 \text{ dB} - 3 \text{ dB} - 4 \text{ dB} = 90 \text{ dBW}$$

TABLE 7-3 System Parameters for Three Hypothetical Satellite Systems

	System A: 6/4 GHz, earth coverage QPSK modulation, 60 Mbps	System B: 14/12 GHz, earth coverage 8-PSK modulation, 90 Mbps	System C: 14/12 GHz, earth coverage 8-PSK modulation, 120 Mbps
Up-link			
Transmitter output power (saturation, dBW)	35	25	33
Earth station back-off loss (dB)	2	2	3
Earth station branching and feeder loss (dB)	3	3	4
Additional atmospheric (dB)	0.6	0.4	0.6
Earth station antenna gain (dB)	55	45	64
Free-space path loss (dB)	200	208	206.5
Satellite receive antenna gain (dB)	20	45	23.7
Satellite branching and feeder loss (dB)	1	1	0
Satellite equivalent noise temperature (K)	1000	800	800
Satellite G/T_e (dBK^{-1})	−10	16	−5.3
Down-link			
Transmitter output power (saturation, dBW)	18	20	10
Satellite back-off loss (dB)	0.5	0.2	0.1
Satellite branching and feeder loss (dB)	1	1	0.5
Additional atmospheric loss (dB)	0.8	1.4	0.4
Satellite antenna gain (dB)	16	44	30.8
Free-space path loss (dB)	197	206	205.6
Earth station receive antenna gain (dB)	51	44	62
Earth station branching and feeder loss (dB)	3	3	0
Earth station equivalent noise temperature (K)	250	1000	270
Earth station G/T_e (dBK^{-1})	27	14	37.7

Carrier power density at the satellite antenna:

$$C' = \text{EIRP (earth station)} - L_p - L_u$$
$$= 90 \text{ dBW} - 206.5 \text{ dB} - 0.6 \text{ dB} = -117.1 \text{ dBW}$$

C/N_0 at the satellite:

$$\frac{C}{N_0} = \frac{C}{KT_e} = \frac{C}{T_e} \times \frac{1}{K} \qquad \text{where } \frac{C}{T_e} = C' \times \frac{G}{T_e}$$

Thus,

$$\frac{C}{N_0} = C' \times \frac{G}{T_e} \times \frac{1}{K}$$

Expressed as a log,

$$\frac{C}{N_0} = C' + \frac{G}{T_e} - 10 \log (1.38 \times 10^{-23})$$

$$= -117.1 \text{ dBW} + (-5.3 \text{ dBK}^{-1}) - (-228.6 \text{ dBWK}) = 106.2 \text{ dB}$$

Thus,

$$\frac{E_b}{N_0} = \frac{C/f_b}{N_0} = \frac{C}{N_0} - 10 \log f_b$$

$$= 106.2 \text{ dB} - 10 \, (\log 120 \times 10^6) = 25.4 \text{ dB}$$

and for a minimum bandwidth system,

$$\frac{C}{N} = \frac{E_b}{N_0} - \frac{B}{f_b} = 25.4 - 10 \log \frac{40 \times 10^6}{120 \times 10^6} = 30.2 \text{ dB}$$

FIGURE 7-20 Antenna gain based on the gain equation for a parabolic antenna:

$$A \text{ (db)} = 10 \log \eta \ (\pi \ D/\lambda)^2$$

where D is the antenna diameter, $\lambda =$ the wavelength, and $\eta =$ the antenna efficiency. Here $\eta = 0.55$. To correct for a 100% efficient antenna, add 2.66 dB to the value.

Down-link budget: Expressed as a log,

$$\text{EIRP (satellite transponder)} = P_t + A_t - L_{bo} - L_{bf}$$
$$= 10 \text{ dBW} + 30.8 \text{ dB} - 0.1 \text{ dB} - 0.5 \text{ dB}$$
$$= 40.2 \text{ dBW}$$

Carrier power density at earth station antenna:

$$C' = \text{EIRP} - L_p - L_d$$
$$= 40.2 \text{ dBW} - 205.6 \text{ dB} - 0.4 \text{ dB} = -165.8 \text{ dBW}$$

C/N_0 at the earth station receiver:

$$\frac{C}{N_0} = \frac{C}{KT_e} = \frac{C}{T_e} \times \frac{1}{K} \qquad \text{where } \frac{C}{T_e} = C' \times \frac{G}{T_e}$$

Thus,
$$\frac{C}{N_0} = C' \times \frac{G}{T_e} \times \frac{1}{K}$$

Expressed as a log,

$$\frac{C}{N_0} = C' + \frac{G}{T_e} - 10 \log (1.38 \times 10^{-23})$$

$$= -165.8 \text{ dBW} + (37.7 \text{ dBK}^{-1}) - (-228.6 \text{ dBWK}) = 100.5 \text{ dB}$$

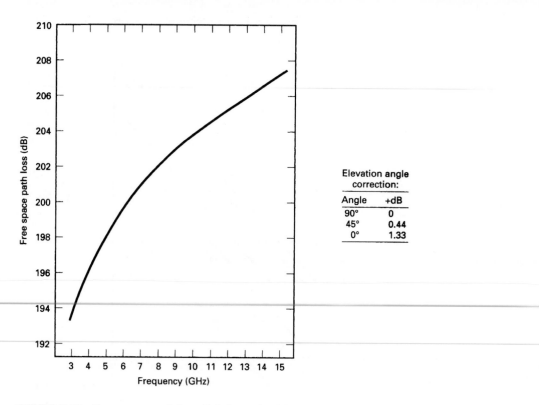

FIGURE 7-21 Free-space path loss (L_p) determined from L_p = 183.5 + 20 log f (GHz), elevation angle = 90°, and distance = 35,930 km

An alternative method of solving for C/N_0 is

$$\frac{C}{N_0} = C' + A_r - T_e - K$$

$$= -165.8 \text{ dBW} + 62 \text{ dB} - 10 \log 270 - (-228.6 \text{ dBWK})$$

$$= -165.8 \text{ dBW} + 62 \text{ dB} - 24.3 \text{ dBK}^{-1} + 228.6 \text{ dBWK} = 100.5 \text{ dB}$$

$$\frac{E_b}{N_0} = \frac{C}{N_0} - 10 \log f_b$$

$$= 100.5 \text{ dB} - 10 \log (120 \times 10^6)$$

$$= 100.5 \text{ dB} - 80.8 \text{ dB} = 19.7 \text{ dB}$$

and for a minimum bandwidth system,

$$\frac{C}{N} = \frac{E_b}{N_0} - \frac{B}{f_b} = 19.7 - 10 \log \frac{40 \times 10^6}{120 \times 10^6} = 24.5 \text{ dB}$$

With careful analysis and a little algebra, it can be shown that the overall energy of bit-to-noise density ratio (E_b/N_0), which includes the combined effects of the up-link ratio ($E_b/N_0)_u$ and the down-link ratio ($E_b/N_0)_d$, is a standard product over the sum relationship and is expressed mathematically as

$$\frac{E_b}{N_0} (\text{overall}) = \frac{(E_b/N_0)_u (E_b/N_0)_d}{(E_b/N_0)_u + (E_b/N_0)_d} \qquad (7\text{-}9)$$

where all E_b/N_0 ratios are in absolute values. For Example 7-10, the overall E_b/N_0 ratio is

$$\frac{E_b}{N_0} (\text{overall}) = \frac{(346.7)(93.3)}{346.7 + 93.3} = 73.5$$

$$= 10 \log 73.5 = 18.7 \text{ dB}$$

TABLE 7-4   Link Budget for Example 18-10

Up-link

1. Earth station transmitter output power at saturation, 2000 W	33 dBW
2. Earth station back-off loss	3 dB
3. Earth station branching and feeder losses	4 dB
4. Earth station transmit antenna gain	64 dB
5. Earth station EIRP	90 dBW
6. Additional up-link atmospheric losses	0.6 dB
7. Free-space path loss	206.5 dB
8. Carrier power density at satellite	−117.1 dBW
9. Satellite branching and feeder losses	0 dB
10. Satellite G/T_e ratio	−5.3 dBK^{-1}
11. Satellite C/T_e ratio	−122.4 dBWK^{-1}
12. Satellite C/N_0 ratio	106.2 dB
13. Satellite C/N ratio	30.2 dB
14. Satellite E_b/N_0 ratio	25.4 dB
15. Bit rate	120 Mbps
16. Modulation scheme	8-PSK

Down-link

1. Satellite transmitter output power at saturation, 10 W	10 dBW
2. Satellite back-off loss	0.1 dB
3. Satellite branching and feeder losses	0.5 dB
4. Satellite transmit antenna gain	30.8 dB
5. Satellite EIRP	40.2 dBW
6. Additional down-link atmospheric losses	0.4 dB
7. Free-space path loss	205.6 dB
8. Earth station receive antenna gain	62 dB
9. Earth station equivalent noise temperature	270 K
10. Earth station branching and feeder losses	0 dB
11. Earth station G/T_e ratio	37.7 dBK^{-1}
12. Carrier power density at earth station	−165.8 dBW
13. Earth station C/T_e ratio	−128.1 dBWK^{-1}
14. Earth station C/N_0 ratio	100.5 dB
15. Earth station C/N ratio	24.5 dB
16. Earth station E_b/N_0 ratio	19.7 dB
17. Bit rate	120 Mbps
18. Modulation scheme	8-PSK

As with all product-over-sum relationships, the smaller of the two numbers dominates. If one number is substantially smaller than the other, the overall result is approximately equal to the smaller of the two numbers.

The system parameters used for Example 7-10 were taken from system C in Table 7-3. A complete link budget for the system is shown in Table 7-4.

QUESTIONS

7-1. Briefly describe a satellite.

7-2. What is a passive satellite? An active satellite?

7-3. Contrast nonsynchronous and synchronous satellites.

7-4. Define *prograde* and *retrograde*.

7-5. Define *apogee* and *perigee*.

7-6. Briefly explain the characteristics of low-, medium-, and high-altitude satellite orbits.

7-7. Explain equatorial, polar, and inclined orbits.

7-8. Contrast the advantages and disadvantages of geosynchronous satellites.

7-9. Define *look angles, angle of elevation,* and *azimuth*.

7-10. Define *satellite spatial separation* and list its restrictions.

7-11. Describe a "footprint."

7-12. Describe spot, zonal, and earth coverage radiation patterns.

7-13. Explain *reuse.*

7-14. Briefly describe the functional characteristics of an up-link, a transponder, and a down-link model for a satellite system.

7-15. Define *back-off loss* and its relationship to saturated and transmit power.

7-16. Define *bit energy.*

7-17. Define *effective isotropic radiated power.*

7-18. Define *equivalent noise temperature.*

7-19. Define *noise density.*

7-20. Define *carrier-to-noise density ratio* and *energy of bit-to-noise density ratio.*

7-21. Define *gain-to-equivalent noise temperature ratio.*

7-22. Describe what a satellite link budget is and how it is used.

PROBLEMS

7-1. An earth station is located at Houston, Texas, which has a longitude of 99.5° and a latitude of 29.5° north. The satellite of interest is *Satcom V.* Determine the look angles for the earth station antenna.

7-2. A satellite system operates at 14-GHz up-link and 11-GHz down-link and has a projected $P(e)$ of 10^{-7}. The modulation scheme is 8-PSK, and the system will carry 120 Mbps. The equivalent noise temperature of the receiver is 400 K, and the receiver noise bandwidth is equal to the minimum Nyquist frequency. Determine the following parameters: minimum theoretical C/N ratio, minimum theoretical E_b/N_0 ratio, noise density, total receiver input noise, minimum receive carrier power, and the minimum energy per bit at the receiver input.

7-3. A satellite system operates at 6-GHz up-link and 4-GHz down-link and has a projected $P(e)$ of 10^{-6}. The modulation scheme is QPSK and the system will carry 100 Mbps. The equivalent receiver noise temperature is 290 K, and the receiver noise bandwidth is equal to the minimum Nyquist frequency. Determine the C/N ratio that would be measured at a point in the receiver prior to the BPF where the bandwidth is equal to (a) 1 1/2 times the minimum Nyquist frequency, and (b) 3 times the minimum Nyquist frequency.

7-4. Which system has the best projected BER?
(a) 8-QAM, C/N = 15 dB, $B = 2f_N$, f_b = 60 Mbps
(b) QPSK, C/N = 16 dB, $B = f_N$, f_b = 40 Mbps

7-5. An earth station satellite transmitter has an HPA with a rated saturated output power of 10,000 W. The back-off ratio is 6 dB, the branching loss is 2 dB, the feeder loss is 4 dB, and the antenna gain is 40 dB. Determine the actual radiated power and the EIRP.

7-6. Determine the total noise power for a receiver with an input bandwidth of 20 MHz and an equivalent noise temperature of 600 K.

7-7. Determine the noise density for Problem 7-6.

7-8. Determine the minimum C/N ratio required to achieve a $P(e)$ of 10^{-5} for an 8-PSK receiver with a bandwidth equal to f_N.

7-9. Determine the energy per bit-to-noise density ratio when the receiver input carrier power is -100 dBW, the receiver input noise temperature is 290 K, and a 60-Mbps transmission rate is used.

7-10. Determine the carrier-to-noise density ratio for a receiver with a -70-dBW input carrier power, an equivalent noise temperature of 180 K, and a bandwidth of 20 MHz.

7-11. Determine the minimum C/N ratio for an 8-PSK system when the transmission rate is 60 Mbps, the minimum energy of bit-to-noise density ratio is 15 dB, and the receiver bandwidth is equal to the minimum Nyquist frequency.

7-12. For an earth station receiver with an equivalent input temperature of 200 K, a noise bandwidth of 20 MHz, a receive antenna gain of 50 dB, and a carrier frequency of 12 GHz, determine the following: G/T_e, N_0, and N.

7-13. For a satellite with an up-link E_b/N_0 of 14 dB and a down-link E_b/N_0 of 18 dB, determine the overall E_b/N_0 ratio.

7-14. Complete the following link budget:

Up-link parameters
1. Earth station transmitter output power at saturation, 1 kW
2. Earth station back-off loss, 3 dB
3. Earth station total branching and feeder losses, 3 dB
4. Earth station transmit antenna gain for a 10-m parabolic dish at 14 GHz
5. Free-space path loss for 14 GHz
6. Additional up-link losses due to the earth's atmosphere, 0.8 dB
7. Satellite transponder G/Te, -4.6 dBK^{-1}
8. Transmission bit rate, 90 Mbps, 8-PSK

Down-link parameters
1. Satellite transmitter output power at saturation, 10 W
2. Satellite transmit antenna gain for a 0.5-m parabolic dish at 12 GHz
3. Satellite modulation back-off loss, 0.8 dB
4. Free-space path loss for 12 GHz
5. Additional down-link losses due to earth's atmosphere, 0.6 dB
6. Earth station receive antenna gain for a 10-m parabolic dish at 12 GHz
7. Earth station equivalent noise temperature, 200 K
8. Earth station branching and feeder losses, 0 dB
9. Transmission bit rate, 90 Mbps, 8-PSK

7-15. An earth station is located at Houston, Texas, which has a longitude of 99.5° and a latitude of 29.5° north. The satellite of interest is *Westar III*. Determine the look angles from the earth station antenna.

7-16. A satellite system operates at 14 GHz up-link and 11 GHz down-link and has a projected $P(e)$ of 1 bit error in every 1 million bits transmitted. The modulation scheme is 8-PSK, and the system will carry 90 Mbps. The equivalent noise temperature of the receiver is 350 K, and the receiver noise bandwidth is equal to the minimum Nyquist frequency. Determine the following parameters: minimum theoretical C/N ratio, minimum theoretical E_b/N_0 ratio, noise density, total receiver input noise, minimum receive carrier power, and the minimum energy per bit at the receiver input.

7-17. A satellite system operates a 6 GHz up-link and 4 GHz down-link and has a projected $P(e)$ of 1 bit error in every 100,000 bit transmitted. The modulation scheme is 4-PSK and the system will carry 80 Mbps. The equivalent receiver noise temperature is 120 K, and the receiver noise bandwidth is equal to the minimum Nyquist frequency. Determine the following:
(a) The C/N ratio that would be measured at a point in the receiver prior to the BPF where the bandwidth is equal to two times the minimum Nyquist frequency.
(b) The C/N ratio that would be measured at a point in the receiver prior to the BPF where the bandwidth is equal to three times the minimum Nyquist frequency.

7-18. Which system has the best projected BER?
(a) QPSK, C/N = 16 dB, $B = 2f_N$, $f_b = 40$ Mbps
(b) 8-PSK, C/N = 18 dB, $B = f_N$, $f_b = 60$ Mbps

7-19. An earth station satellite transmitter has an HPA with a rated saturated output power of 12,000 W. The back-off ratio of 4 dB, the branching loss is 1.5 dB, the feeder loss is 5 dB, and the antenna gain is 38 dB. Determine the actual radiated power and the EIRP.

7-20. Determine the total noise power for a receiver with an input bandwidth of 40 MHz and an equivalent noise temperature of 800 K.

7-21. Determine the noise density for Problem 7-20.

7-22. Determine the minimum C/N ratio required to achieve a $P(e)$ of 1 bit error for every 1 million bits transmitted for a QPSK receiver with a bandwidth equal to the minimum Nyquist frequency.

7-23. Determine the energy of bit-to-noise density ratio when the receiver input carrier power is -85 dBW, the receiver input noise temperature is 400 K, and a 50 Mbps transmission rate.

7-24. Determine the carrier-to-noise density ratio for a receiver with a -80 dBW carrier input power, and equivalent noise temperature of 240 K, and a bandwidth of 10 MHz.

7-25. Determine the minimum C/N ratio for a QPSK system when the transmission rate is 80 Mbps, the minimum energy of bit-to-noise density ratio is 16 dB, and the receiver bandwidth is equal to the Nyquist frequency.

7-26. For an earth station receiver with an equivalent input temperature of 400 K, a noise bandwidth of 30 MHz, a receive antenna gain of 44 dB, and a carrier frequency of 12 GHz, determine the following: G/T_e, N_0, and N.

7-27. For a satellite with an up-link E_b/N_0 of 16 dB and a down-link E_b/N_0 of 13 dB, determine the overall E_b/N_0.

7-28. Complete the following link budget:

Up-link parameters
1. Earth station output power at saturation, 12 kW
2. Earth station back-off loss, 4 dB
3. Earth station branching and feeder losses, 2 dB
4. Earth station antenna gain for a 10-m parabolic dish at 14 GHz
5. Free-space path loss for 14 GHz
6. Additional up-link losses due to Earth's atmosphere, 1 dB
7. Satellite transponder G/T_e, -3 dBk
8. Transmission bit rate, 80 Mbps
9. Modulation scheme, 4-PSK

Down-link parameters
1. Satellite transmitter output power at saturation, 5 W
2. Satellite station transmit antenna gain for a 0.5-m parabolic dish at 12 GHz
3. Satellite modulation back-off loss, 1 dB
4. Free-space path loss for 12 GHz
5. Additional down-link losses due to Earth's atmosphere, 1 dB
6. Earth station receive antenna gain for a 10-m parabolic dish at 12 GHz
7. Earth station equivalent noise temperature, 300 K
8. Transmission bit rate, 80 Mbps
9. Modulation scheme, 4-PSK

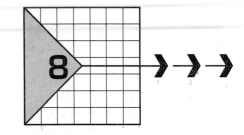
Satellite Multiple-Access Arrangements

INTRODUCTION

In Chapter 7 we analyzed the link parameters of *single-channel satellite transponders*. In this chapter, we will extend the discussion of satellite communications to systems designed for *multiple carriers*. Whenever multiple carriers are utilized in satellite communications, it is necessary that a *multiple-accessing format* be established over the system. This format allows for a distinct separation between the up-link and down-link transmissions to and from a multitude of different earth stations. Each format has its own specific characteristics, advantages, and disadvantages.

FDM/FM SATELLITE SYSTEMS

Figure 8-1a shows a single-link (two earth stations) *fixed-frequency* FDM/FM system using a single satellite transponder. With earth coverage antennas and for full-duplex operation, each link requires two RF satellite channels (i.e., four RF carrier frequencies, two up-link and two down-link). In Figure 8-1a, earth station 1 transmits on a high-band carrier (f11, f12, f13, etc.) and receives on a low-band carrier (f1, f2, f3, etc.). To avoid interfering with earth station 1, earth station 2 must transmit and receive on different RF carrier frequencies. The RF carrier frequencies are fixed and the satellite transponder is simply an RF-to-RF repeater that provides the up-link/down-link frequency translation. This arrangement is economically impractical and extremely inefficient as well. Additional earth stations can communicate through different transponders within the same satellite structure (Figure 8-1b) but each additional link requires four more RF carrier frequencies. It is unlikely that any two-point link would require the capacity available in an entire RF satellite channel. Consequently, most of the available bandwidth is wasted. Also, with this arrangement, each earth station can communicate with only one other earth station. The RF satellite channels are fixed between any two earth stations; thus, the voice-band channels from each earth station are committed to a single destination.

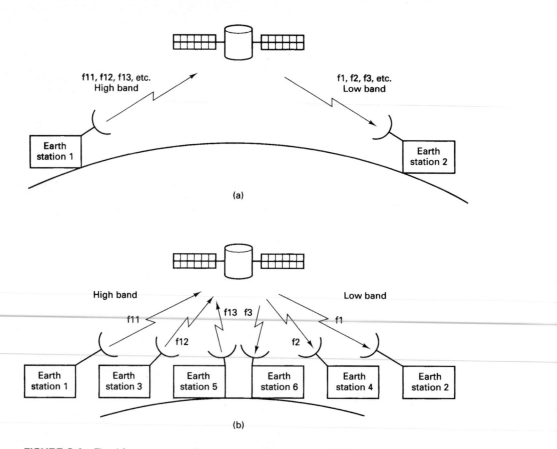

FIGURE 8-1 Fixed-frequency earth station satellite system: (a) single link; (b) multiple link

In a system where three or more earth stations wish to communicate with each other, fixed-frequency or *dedicated-channel* systems such as those shown in Figure 8-1 are inadequate; a method of *multiple accessing* is required. That is, each earth station using the satellite system has a means of communicating with each of the other earth stations in the system through a common satellite transponder. Multiple accessing is sometimes called *multiple destination* because the transmissions from each earth station are received by all the other earth stations in the system. The voice-band channels between any two earth stations may be *preassigned* (*dedicated*) or *demand-assigned* (*switched*). When preassignment is used, a given number of the available voice-band channels from each earth station are assigned a dedicated destination. With demand assignment, voice-band channels are assigned on an as-needed basis. Demand assignment provides more versatility and more efficient use of the available frequency spectrum. On the other hand, demand assignment requires a control mechanism that is common to all the earth stations to keep track of channel routing and the availability of each voice-band channel.

Remember, in an FDM/FM satellite system, each RF channel requires a separate transponder. Also, with FDM/FM transmissions, it is impossible to differentiate (separate) multiple transmissions that occupy the same bandwidth. Fixed-frequency systems may be used in a multiple-access configuration by switching the RF carriers at the satellite, reconfiguring the baseband signals with multiplexing/demultiplexing equipment on board the satellite, or by using multiple spot beam antennas (reuse). All three of these methods require relatively complicated, expensive, and heavy hardware on the spacecraft.

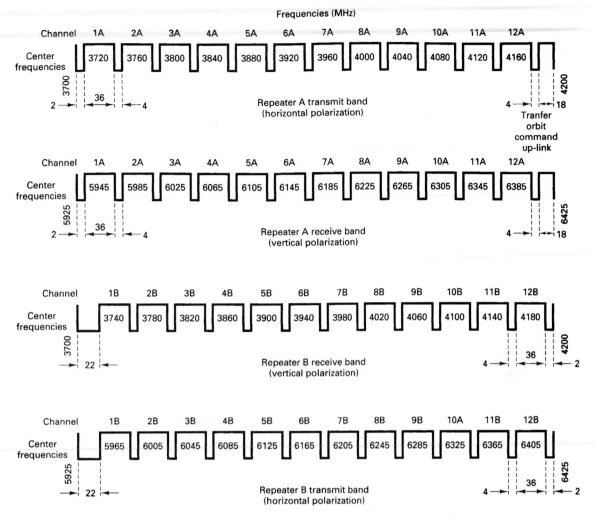

FIGURE 8-2 *Anik-E* frequency and polarization plan

Anik-E Communications Satellite

The *Anik-E* communications satellite is a domsat (domestic) satellite operated by Telsat Canada. Figure 8-2 shows the frequency and polarization plan for the *Anik-E* satellite system. There are 12 transponder channels (each approximately 36 MHz wide). However, by using horizontal polarization for one group of 12 channels (group A) and vertical polarization for another group of 12 channels (group B), a total of 24 channels can occupy a bandwidth of approximately 500 MHz. This scheme is called *frequency reuse* and is possible by using *orthogonal polarization* and spacing adjacent channels 20 MHz apart. There are 12 primary channels and 12 spare or preemptible channels.

MULTIPLE ACCESSING

Figure 8-3 illustrates the three most commonly used *multiple-accessing arrangements:* frequency-division multiple accessing (FDMA), time-division multiple accessing (TDMA), and code-division multiple (CDMA) accessing. With FDMA, each earth station's transmissions are assigned specific up-link and down-link frequency bands within

FIGURE 8-3 Multiple-accessing arrangements: (a) FDMA; (b) TDMA; (c) CDMA

an allotted satellite bandwidth; they may be *preassigned* or *demand assigned*. Consequently, FDMA transmissions are separated in the frequency domain and, therefore, must share the total available transponder bandwidth as well as the total transponder power. With TDMA, each earth station transmits a short burst of information during a specific time slot (*epoch*) within a TDMA frame. The bursts must be synchronized so that each station's burst arrives at the satellite at a different time. Consequently, TDMA transmissions are separated in the time domain, and with TDMA the entire transponder bandwidth and power are used for each transmission but for only a prescribed interval of time. With CDMA, all earth stations transmit within the same frequency band and, for all practical purposes, have no limitations on when they may transmit or on which carrier frequency. Thus, with CDMA, the entire satellite transponder bandwidth is used by all stations on a continuous basis. Signal separation is accomplished with envelope encryption/decryption techniques.

Frequency-Division Multiple Access

Frequency-division multiple access (FDMA) is a method of multiple accessing where a given RF bandwidth is divided into smaller frequency bands called *subdivisions*. Each subdivision has its own carrier frequency. A control mechanism is used to ensure that two or more earth stations do not transmit in the same subdivision at the same time. Essentially, the control mechanism designates a receive station for each of the subdivisions. In demand-assignment systems, the control mechanism is also used to establish or

FIGURE 8-4 FDMA, SPADE earth station transmitter

terminate the voice-band links between the source and destination earth stations. Consequently, any of the subdivisions may be used by any of the participating earth stations at any given time. If each subdivision carries only one 4-kHz voice-band channel, this is known as a *single-channel per carrier* (SCPC) system. When several voice-band channels are frequency-division multiplexed together to form a composite baseband signal comprised of groups, supergroups, or even mastergroups, a wider subdivision is assigned. This is referred to as *multiple-channel per carrier* (MCPC).

Carrier frequencies and bandwidths for FDM/FM satellite systems using multiple-channel-per-carrier formats are generally assigned and remained fixed for a long period of time. This is referred to as *fixed-assignment, multiple access* (FDM/FM/FAMA). An alternate channel allocation scheme is *demand-assignment, multiple access* (DAMA). Demand assignment allows all users continuous and equal access of the entire transponder bandwidth by assigning carrier frequencies on a temporary basis using a statistical assignment process. The first FDMA demand-assignment system for satellites was developed by Comsat for use on the *Intelsat* series *IVA* and *V* satellites.

SPADE DAMA satellite system.   SPADE is an acronym for *s*ingle-channel-per-carrier *P*CM multiple-*a*ccess *d*emand-assignment *e*quipment. Figures 8-4 and 8-5 show the block diagram and IF frequency assignments, respectively, for SPADE.

With SPADE, 800 PCM-encoded voice-band channels separately QPSK modulate an IF carrier signal (hence, the name *single-carrier per channel*, SCPC). Each 4-kHz voice-band channel is sampled at an 8-kHz rate and converted to an 8-bit PCM code. This produces a 64-kbps PCM code for each voice-band channel. The PCM code from each voice-band channel QPSK modulates a different IF carrier frequency. With QPSK, the minimum required bandwidth is equal to one-half the input bit rate. Consequently, the output of each QPSK modulator requires a minimum bandwidth of 32 kHz. Each channel

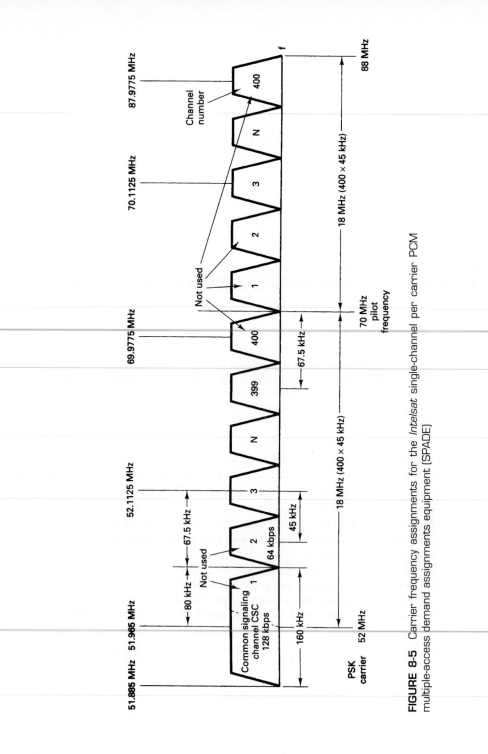

FIGURE 8-5 Carrier frequency assignments for the *Intelsat* single-channel per carrier PCM multiple-access demand assignments equipment (SPADE)

| Earth station 1 128 bits | Earth station 2 128 bits | Earth stations 3 – 49 128 bits each | Earth station 50 128 bits |

|←— 1 ms —→|←— 1 ms —→|←——————————— 47 ms ———————————→|←— 1 ms —→|

|←—————————————————————————— 50 ms —————————————————————————→|

128 bits/1ms × 1000 ms/1s = 128 kbps or 6400 bits/frame × 1 frame/50 ms = 128 kbps

FIGURE 8-6 FDMA, SPADE common signaling channel (CSC)

is allocated a 45-kHz bandwidth, allowing for a 13-kHz guard band between pairs of frequency-division-multiplexed channels. The IF carrier frequencies begin at 52.0225 MHz (low-band channel 1) and increase in 45-kHz steps to 87.9775 MHz (high-band channel 400). The entire 36-MHz band (52 MHz to 88 MHz) is divided in half, producing two 400-channel bands (a low band and a high band). For full-duplex operation, four hundred 45-kHz channels are used for one direction of transmission and 400 are used for the opposite direction. Also, channels 1, 2, and 400 from each band are left permanently vacant. This reduces the number of usable full-duplex voice-band channels to 397. The 6-GHz C-band extends from 5.725 GHz to 6.425 GHz (700 MHz). This allows for approximately nineteen 36-MHz RF channels per system. Each RF channel has a capacity of 397 full-duplex voice-band channels.

Each RF channel (Figure 8-5) has a 160-kHz *common signaling channel* (CSC). The CSC is a time-division-multiplexed transmission that is frequency-division multiplexed into the IF spectrum below the QPSK-encoded voice-band channels. Figure 8-6 shows the TDM frame structure for the CSC. The total frame time is 50 ms, which is subdivided into fifty 1-ms epochs. Each earth station transmits on the CSC channel only during its preassigned 1-ms time slot. The CSC signal is a 128-bit binary code. To transmit a 128-bit code in 1 ms, a transmission rate of 128 kbps is required. The CSC code is used for establishing and disconnecting voice-band links between two earth station users when demand-assignment channel allocation is used.

Example 8-1

For the system shown in Figure 8-7, a user earth station in New York wishes to establish a voice-band link between itself and London. New York randomly selects an idle voice-band channel. It then transmits a binary-coded message to London on the CSC channel during its respective time slot, requesting that a link be established on the randomly selected channel. London responds on the CSC channel during its time slot with a binary code, either confirming or denying the establishment of the voice-band link. The link is disconnected in a similar manner when the users are finished.

The CSC channel occupies a 160-kHz bandwidth, which includes the 45 kHz for low-band channel 1. Consequently, the CSC channel extends from 51.885 MHz to 52.045 MHz. The 128-kbps CSC binary code QPSK modulates a 51.965-MHz carrier. The minimum bandwidth required for the CSC channel is 64 kHz; this results in a 48-kHz guard band on either side of the CSC signal.

With FDMA, each earth station may transmit simultaneously within the same 36-MHz RF spectrum, but on different voice-band channels. Consequently, simultaneous transmissions of voice-band channels from all earth stations within the satellite network are interleaved in the frequency domain in the satellite transponder. Transmissions of CSC signals are interleaved in the time domain.

An obvious disadvantage of FDMA is that carriers from multiple earth stations may be present in a satellite transponder at the same time. This results in cross-modulation

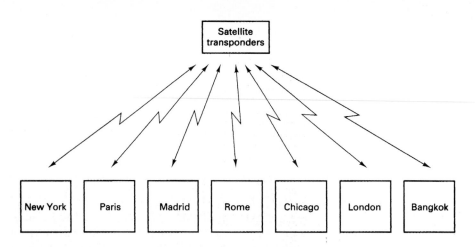

FIGURE 8-7 Diagram of the system for Example 8-1

distortion between the various earth station transmissions. This is alleviated somewhat by shutting off the IF subcarriers on all unused 45-kHz voice-band channels. Because balanced modulators are used in the generation of QPSK, carrier suppression is inherent. This also reduces the power load on a system and increases its capacity by reducing the idle channel power.

Time-Division Multiple Access

Time-division multiple access (TDMA) is the predominant multiple-access method used today. It provides the most efficient method of transmitting digitally modulated carriers (PSK). TDMA is a method of time-division multiplexing digitally modulated carriers between participating earth stations within a satellite network through a common satellite transponder. With TDMA, each earth station transmits a short *burst* of a digitally modulated carrier during a precise time slot (epoch) within a TDMA frame. Each station's burst is synchronized so that it arrives at the satellite transponder at a different time. Consequently, only one earth station's carrier is present in the transponder at any given time, thus, avoiding a collision with another station's carrier. The transponder is an RF-to-RF repeater that simply receives the earth station transmissions, amplifies them, and then, retransmits them in a down-link beam that is received by all the participating earth stations. Each earth station receives the bursts from all other earth stations and must select from them the traffic destined only for itself.

Figure 8-8 shows a basic TDMA frame. Transmissions from all earth stations are synchronized to a *reference burst*. Figure 8-8 shows the reference burst as a separate transmission, but it may be the *preamble* that precedes a reference station's transmission of data. Also, there may be more than one synchronizing reference burst.

The reference burst contains a *carrier recovery sequence* (CRS), from which all receiving stations recover a frequency and phase coherent carrier for PSK demodulation. Also included in the reference burst is a binary sequence for *bit timing recovery* (BTR, i.e., clock recovery). At the end of each reference burst, a *unique word* (UW) is transmitted. The UW sequence is used to establish a precise time reference that each of the earth stations uses to synchronize the transmission of its burst. The UW is typically a string of 20 successive binary 1s terminated with a binary 0. Each earth station receiver demodulates and integrates the UW sequence. Figure 8-9 shows the result of the integration process. The integrator and threshold detector are designed so that the threshold voltage is reached precisely when the last bit of the UW sequence is integrated. This generates a *correlation spike* at the output of the threshold detector at the exact time the UW sequence ends.

FIGURE 8-8 Basic time-division multiple-accessing (TDMA) frame

FIGURE 8-9 Unique word correlator

Each earth station synchronizes the transmission of its carrier to the occurrence of the UW correlation spike. Each station waits a different length of time before it begins transmitting. Consequently, no two stations will transmit the carrier at the same time. Note the *guard time* (GT) between transmissions from successive stations. This is analogous to a guard band in a frequency-division-multiplexed system. Each station precedes the transmission of data with a *preamble*. The preamble is logically equivalent to the reference burst. Because each station's transmissions must be received by all other earth stations, all stations must recover carrier and clocking information prior to demodulating the data. If demand assignment is used, a common signaling channel must also be included in the preamble.

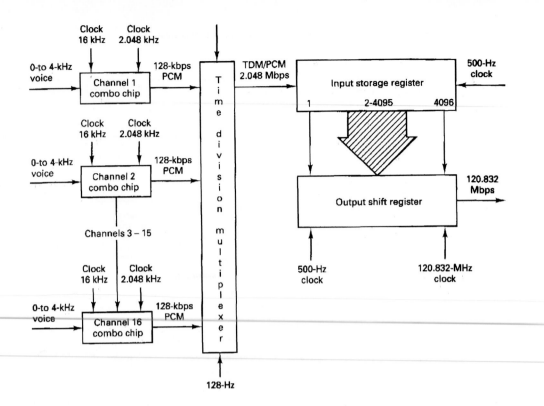

FIGURE 8-10 TDMA, CEPT primary multiplex frame transmitter

CEPT primary multiplex frame. Figures 8-10 and 8-11 show the block diagram and timing sequence, respectively, for the CEPT primary multiplex frame, (CEPT—Conference of European Postal and Telecommunications Administrations; the CEPT sets many of the European telecommunications standards). This is a commonly used TDMA frame format for digital satellite systems.

Essentially, TDMA is a *store-and-forward* system. Earth stations can transmit only during their specified time slot, although the incoming voice-band signals are continuous. Consequently, it is necessary to sample and store the voice-band signals prior to transmission. The CEPT frame is made up of 8-bit PCM encoded samples from 16 independent voice-band channels. Each channel has a separate codec that samples the incoming voice signals at a 16-kHz rate and converts those samples to 8-bit binary codes. This results in 128-kbps transmitted at a 2.048 MHz rate from each voice channel codec. The sixteen 128-kbps transmissions are time-division multiplexed into a subframe that contains one 8-bit sample from each of the 16 channels (128 bits). It requires only 62.5 μs to accumulate the 128 bits (2.048-Mbps transmission rate). The CEPT multiplex format specifies a 2-ms frame time. Consequently, each earth station can transmit only once every 2 ms and, therefore, must store the PCM-encoded samples. The 128 bits accumulated during the first sample of each voice-band channel are stored in a holding register while a second sample is taken from each channel and converted into another 128-bit *subframe*. This 128-bit sequence is stored in the holding register behind the first 128 bits. The process continues for 32 subframes (32 × 62.5 μs = 2 ms). After 2 ms, thirty-two 8-bit samples have been taken from each of 16 voice-band channels for a total of 4096 bits (32 × 8 × 16 = 4096). At this time, the 4096 bits are transferred to an output shift register for transmission. Because the total TDMA frame is 2 ms long and during this 2-ms period each of the participating earth stations must transmit at different times, the individual transmissions from each station must occur in a significantly shorter time

16 PCM samples × 8 bits/sample = 128 bits

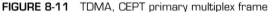

32 increments of 128 bits each (4096 bits) (62.5 μs × 32 = 2 ms)

FIGURE 8-11   TDMA, CEPT primary multiplex frame

period. In the CEPT frame, a transmission rate of 120.832 Mbps is used. This rate is the fifty-ninth multiple of 2.048 Mbps. Consequently, the actual transmission of the 4096 accumulated bits takes approximately 33.9 μs. At the earth station receivers, the 4096 bits are stored in a holding register and shifted at a 2.048-Mbps rate. Because all the clock rates (500 Hz, 16 kHz, 128 kHz, 2.048 MHz, and 120.832 MHz) are synchronized, the PCM codes are accumulated, stored, transmitted, received, and then decoded in perfect synchronization. To the users, the voice transmission appears to be a continuous process.

There are several advantages of TDMA over FDMA. The first, and probably the most significant, is that with TDMA only the carrier from one earth station is present in the satellite transponder at any given time, thus, reducing intermodulation distortion. Second, with FDMA, each earth station must be capable of transmitting and receiving on a multitude of carrier frequencies to achieve multiple-accessing capabilities. Third, TDMA is much better suited to the transmission of digital information than FDMA. Digital signals are more naturally acclimated to storage, rate conversions, and time-domain processing than their analog counterparts.

The primary disadvantage of TDMA as compared to FDMA is that in TDMA precise synchronization is required. Each earth station's transmissions must occur during an exact time slot. Also, bit and frame timing must be achieved and maintained with TDMA.

Code-Division Multiple Access (Spread-Spectrum Multiple Accessing)

With FDMA, earth stations are limited to a specific bandwidth within a satellite channel or system but have no restriction on when they can transmit. With TDMA, an earth station's transmissions are restricted to a precise time slot but have no restriction on what frequency or bandwidth it may use within a specified satellite system or channel allocation. With *code-division multiple access* (CDMA), there are no restrictions on time or bandwidth. Each earth station transmitter may transmit whenever it wishes and can use any or all of the bandwidth allocated a particular satellite system or channel. Because

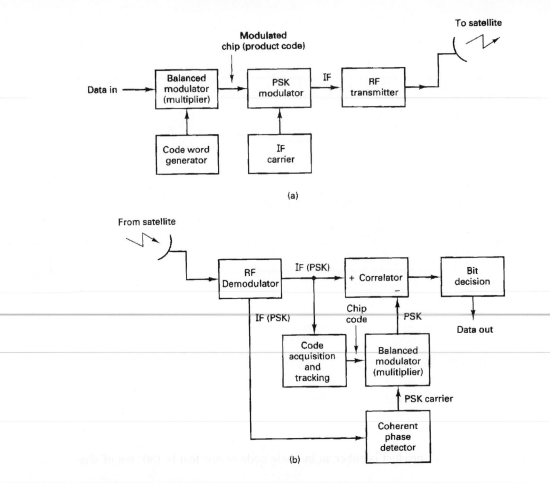

FIGURE 8-12 Code-division multiple access (CDMA): (a) encoder; (b) decoder

there is no limitation on the bandwidth, CDMA is sometimes referred to as *spread-spectrum multiple access;* transmissions can spread throughout the entire allocated bandwidth. Transmissions are separated through envelope encryption/decryption techniques. That is, each earth station's transmissions are encoded with a unique binary word called a *chip code.* Each station has a unique chip code. To receive a particular earth station's transmission, a receive station must know the chip code for that station.

Figure 8-12 shows the block diagram of a CDMA encoder and decoder. In the encoder (Figure 8-12a), the input data (which may be PCM-encoded voice-band signals or raw digital data) is multiplied by a unique chip code. The product code PSK modulates an IF carrier, which is up-converted to RF for transmission. At the receiver (Figure 8-12b), the RF is down-converted to IF. From the IF, a coherent PSK carrier is recovered. Also, the chip code is acquired and used to synchronize the receive station's code generator. Keep in mind, the receiving station knows the chip code but must generate a chip code that is synchronous in time with the receive code. The recovered synchronous chip code multiplies the recovered PSK carrier and generates a PSK modulated signal that contains the PSK carrier plus the chip code. The received IF signal that contains the chip code, the PSK carrier, and the data information is compared to the received IF signal in the *correlator.* The function of the correlator is to compare the two signals and recover the original data. Essentially, the correlator subtracts the recovered PSK carrier + chip code from the received PSK carrier + chip code + data. The resultant is the data.

FIGURE 8-13 CDMA code/data alignment: (a) correct code; (b) orthogonal code

The correlation is accomplished on the analog signals. Figure 8-13 shows how the encoding and decoding is accomplished. Figure 8-13a shows the correlation of the correctly received chip code. A +1 indicates an in-phase carrier and a −1 indicates an out-of-phase carrier. The chip code is multiplied by the data (either +1 or −1). The product is either an in-phase code or one that is 180° out of phase with the chip code. In the receiver, the recovered synchronous chip code is compared in the correlator to the received signaling elements. If the phases are the same, a +1 is produced; if they are 180° out of phase, a −1 is produced. It can be seen that if all the recovered chips correlate favorably with the incoming chip code, the output of the correlator will be a +6 (which is the case when a logic 1 is received). If all the code chips correlate 180° out of phase, a −6 is generated (which is the case when a logic 0 is received). The bit decision circuit is simply a threshold detector. Depending on whether a +6 or −6 is generated, the threshold detector will output a logic 1 or a logic 0, respectively.

As the name implies, the correlator looks for a correlation (similarity) between the incoming coded signal and the recovered chip code. When a correlation occurs, the bit decision circuit generates the corresponding logic condition.

With CDMA, all earth stations within the system may transmit on the same frequency at the same time. Consequently, an earth station receiver may be receiving coded PSK signals simultaneously from more than one transmitter. When this is the case, the job of the correlator becomes considerably more difficult. The correlator must compare the recovered chip code with the entire received spectrum and separate from it only the chip code from the desired earth station transmitter. Consequently, the chip code from one earth station must not correlate with the chip codes from any of the other earth stations.

Figure 8-13b shows how such a coding scheme is achieved. If half of the bits within a code were made the same and half were made exactly the opposite, the resultant would be zero cross correlation between chip codes. Such a code is called an *orthogonal code*. In Figure 8-13b it can be seen that when the orthogonal code is compared with the original chip code, there is no correlation (i.e., the sum of the comparison is zero). Consequently, the orthogonal code, although received simultaneously with the desired chip code, had absolutely no effect on the correlation process. For this example, the orthogonal code is received in exact time synchronization with the desired chip code; this is not always the case. For systems that do not have time-synchronous transmissions, codes must be developed where there is no correlation between one station's code and any phase of another station's code.

The primary difference between spread spectrum PSK transmitters and other types of PSK transmitters is the additional modulator where the code word is multiplied by the incoming data. Because of the pseudorandom nature of the code word, it is often referred to as *pseudorandom noise* (PRN). The PRN must have a high autocorrelation property with itself and a low correlation property with other transmitter's pseudorandom codes. The code word rate (R_{cw}) must exceed the incoming data rate (R_d) by several orders of magnitude. In addition, the code rate must be statistically independent of the data signal. When these two conditions are satisfied, the final output signal spectrum will be increased (spread) by a factor called the *processing gain.* Processing gain is expressed mathematically as

$$G = \frac{R_{cw}}{R_d} \qquad (8\text{-}1)$$

where G is processing gain and $R_{cw} \gg R_d$.

A spread-spectrum signal can not be demodulated accurately if the receiver does not possess a despreading circuit that matches the code word generator in the transmitter. Three of the most popular techniques used to produce the spreading function are: *direct sequence, frequency hopping,* and a combination of direct sequence and frequency hopping called *hybrid direct sequence frequency hopping* (hybrid-DS/FH).

Direct sequence (DS). Direct-sequence spread spectrum (DS-SS) is produced when a bipolar data-modulated signal is linearly multiplied by the spreading signal in a special balanced modulator called a *spreading correlator.* The spreading code rate $R_{cw} = 1/T_c$, where T_c is the duration of a single bipolar pulse (i.e., the chip). Chip rates are 100 to 1000 times faster than the data message, therefore, chip times are 100 to 1000 times shorter in duration than the time of a single data bit. As a result, the transmitted output frequency spectrum using spread spectrum is 100 to 1000 times wider than the bandwidth of the initial PSK data-modulated signal. The block diagram for a direct-sequence spread-spectrum system is shown in Figure 8-14. As the figure shows, the data source directly modulates the carrier signal, which is then further modulated in the spreading correlator by the spreading code word.

The spreading (chip) codes used in spread-spectrum systems are either *maximal-length sequence codes,* sometimes called *m-sequence codes,* or *Gold codes.* Gold codes are combinations of maximal-length codes invented by Magnavox Corporation in 1967 especially for multiple-access CDMA applications. There is a relatively large set of Gold codes available with minimal correlation between chip codes. For a reasonable number of satellite users, it is impossible to achieve perfectly orthogonal codes. You can only design for a minimum cross correlation among chips.

One of the advantages of CDMA was that the entire bandwidth of a satellite channel or system may be used for each transmission from every earth station. For our example, the chip rate was six times the original bit rate. Consequently, the actual transmission rate of information was one-sixth of the PSK modulation rate, and the bandwidth required is six times that required to simply transmit the original data as binary. Because of the coding inefficiency resulting from transmitting chips for bits, the advantage of more bandwidth is partially offset and is, thus, less of an advantage. Also,

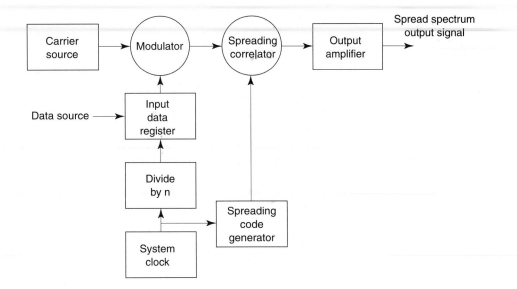

FIGURE 8-14 Simplified block diagram for a direct-sequence spread-spectrum transmitter

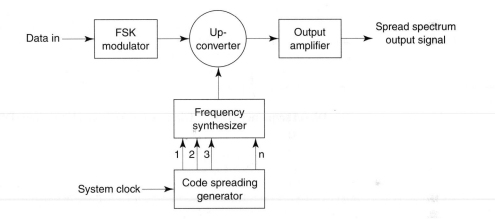

FIGURE 8-15 Simplified block diagram of a frequency-hopping spread-spectrum transmitter

if the transmission of chips from the various earth stations must be synchronized, precise timing is required for the system to work. Therefore, the disadvantage of requiring time synchronization in TDMA systems is also present with CDMA. In short, CDMA is not all that it is cracked up to be. The most significant advantage of CDMA is immunity to interference (jamming), which makes CDMA ideally suited for military applications.

Frequency-hopping spread spectrum (FH-SS).   Frequency hopping is a form of CDMA where a digital code is used to continually change the frequency of the carrier. The carrier is first modulated by the data message and, then, up-converted using a frequency-synthesized local oscillator whose output frequency is determined by an *n*-bit pseudorandom noise code produced in a spreading code generator. The simplified block diagram for a frequency-hopping spread-spectrum transmitter is shown in Figure 8-15.

With frequency hopping, the total available bandwidth is partitioned into smaller frequency bands and the total transmission time is subdivided into smaller time slots. The idea is to transmit within a limited frequency band for only a short period of time, then

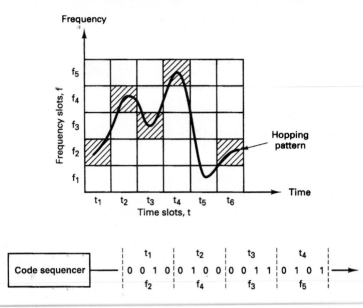

FIGURE 8-16 Frequency time-hopping matrix

switch to another frequency band, and so on. This process continues indefinitely. The frequency-hopping pattern is determined by a binary spreading code. Each station uses a different code sequence. A typical hopping pattern (frequency-time matrix) is shown in Figure 8-16.

With frequency hopping, each earth station within a CDMA network is assigned a different frequency-hopping pattern. Each transmitter switches (hops) from one frequency band to the next according to their assigned pattern. With frequency hopping, each station uses the entire RF spectrum but never occupies more than a small portion of that spectrum at any one time.

FSK is the modulation scheme most commonly used with frequency hopping. When it is a given station's turn to transmit, it sends one of the two frequencies (either mark or space) for the particular band in which it is transmitting. The number of stations in a given frequency-hopping system is limited by the number of unique hopping patterns that can be generated.

CHANNEL CAPACITY

Essentially, there are two methods used to interface terrestrial voice-band channels with satellite channels: digital noninterpolated interfaces (DNI) and digital speech interpolated interfaces (DSI).

Digital Noninterpolated Interfaces

A *digital noninterpolated interface* assigns an individual terrestrial channel (TC) to a particular satellite channel (SC) for the duration of the call. A DNI system can carry no more traffic than the number of satellite channels it has. Once a TC has been assigned an SC, the SC is unavailable to the other TCs for the duration of the call. DNI is a form of preassignment; each TC has a permanent dedicated SC.

Digital Speech Interpolated Interfaces

A *digital speech interpolated interface* assigns a terrestrial channel to a satellite channel only when speech energy is present on the TC. DSI interfaces have *speech detectors* that are similar to *echo suppressors;* they sense speech energy, then seize an SC. Whenever a speech detector senses energy on a TC, the TC is assigned to an SC. The SC assigned is randomly selected from the idle SCs. On a given TC, each time speech energy is detected, the TC could be assigned to a different SC. Therefore, a single TC can use several SCs for a single call. For demultiplexing purposes, the TC/SC assignment information must be conveyed to the receive terminal. This is done on a common signaling channel similar to the one used on the SPADE system. DSI is a form of demand assignment; SCs are randomly assigned on an as-needed basis.

With DSI it is apparent that there is a *channel compression;* there can be more TCs assigned than there are SCs. Generally, a TC:SC ratio of 2:1 is used. For a full-duplex (two-way simultaneous) communication circuit, there is speech in each direction 40% of the time, and for 20% of the time the circuit is idle in both directions. Therefore, a DSI gain of slightly more than 2 is realized. The DSI gain is affected by a phenomenon called *competitive clipping.* Competitive clipping is when speech energy is detected on a TC and there is no SC to assign it to. During the *wait* time, speech information is lost. Competitive clipping is not noticed by a subscriber if its duration is less than 50 ms.

To further enhance the channel capacity, a technique called *bit stealing* is used. With bit stealing, channels can be added to fully loaded systems by stealing bits from the in-use channels. Generally, an overload channel is generated by stealing the least significant bit from seven other satellite channels. Bit stealing results in eight channels with 7-bit resolution for the time that the *overload channel* is in use. Consequently, bit stealing results in a lower SQR than normal.

Time-Assignment Speech Interpolation

Time-assignment speech interpolation (TASI) is a form of analog channel compression that has been used for suboceanic cables for many years. TASI is very similar to DSI except that the signals interpolated are analog rather than digital. TASI also uses a 2:1 compression ratio. TASI was also the first means used to scramble voice for military security. TASI is similar to a packet data network; the voice message is chopped up into smaller segments comprised of sounds or portions of sounds. The sounds are sent through the network as separate bundles of energy, then put back together at the receive end to reform the original voice message.

SATELLITE RADIO NAVIGATION

Navigation is defined as the art or science of plotting, ascertaining, or directing the course of movements; in other words, "*knowing where you are and finding your way around.*" The most ancient and rudimentary method of navigation is known as *wandering.* Wandering is simply continuing to move about until you reach your destination, assuming of course that you have one. Wandering is a popular navigation technique used by many students during the first week of classes at all colleges and universities. Probably the earliest effective or useful means of navigation is *celestial navigation.* With celestial navigation, direction and distance are determined from precisely timed sightings of celestial bodies, including the stars and moon. This is a primitive technique that dates back thousands of years. An obvious disadvantage of celestial navigation is the fact that it works best at night, preferably with clear skies.

Another rather rudimentary method of navigation is known as *piloting.* Piloting is fixing your position and direction with respect to familiar, significant landmarks such as railroad tracks, water towers, barns, mountain peaks, and bodies of water. Piloting derived its name from early aircraft pilots who used this method of navigation. *Dead* (*ded*) *reckoning* is a navigation technique that determines position by extrapolating a series of measured velocity increments. The term "*dead*" is derived from the word *ded*uced and not from the fate of the people who used the technique. Dead reckoning was used quite successfully by Charles Lindbergh in 1927 during his historic 33-h transatlantic journey.

Although each of the navigation methods described thus far had its place in time, undoubtedly the most accurate navigation technique to date is *radio* or *electronic navigation*. With radio navigation, position is determined by measuring the travel time of an electromagnetic wave as it moves from a transmitter to a receiver. There are approximately 100 different types of domestic radio navigation systems currently being used. Some use terrestrial (land-based) broadcast transmitters and others use satellite (space-based) broadcast transmitters. The most accurate and useful radio navigation systems include:

Decca (terrestrial surface broadcast)

Omega (terrestrial surface broadcast)*

Loran (terrestrial surface broadcast)

Navy Transit GPS (low-orbit satellite broadcast)*

Navstar GPS (high-orbit satellite broadcast)*

Loran and Navstar are the two most often used radio navigation systems today.

Loran Navigation

Until recently, *Loran* (*Lo*ng *Ra*nge *N*avigation) was the most effective, reliable, and accurate means of radio navigation. Loran-A was developed during World War II, and the most recent version, Loran-C, surfaced in 1980. Today, Loran is used primarily for recreational aircraft and ships.

With Loran, receivers acquire specially coded signals from two pairs of high-powered, land-based transmitters whose locations are precisely known. The elapsed time between reception of the coded signals is precisely measured and converted in the receiver to distance using the propagation speed of electromagnetic waves. Using basic geometry and the relationship between distance (d), speed (v), and time (t) ($d = vt$), the location of the receiver can be determined with a high degree of accuracy. There is only one set of coordinates that possess a particular time (distance) relationship from four sources.

Loran is only as accurate as the preciseness of the transmission times of the coded signals. System errors are primarily due to propagation problems, such as the fact that Earth's surface is not smooth nor is it perfectly round. Atmospheric conditions and multiple transmission paths can also adversely affect the performance of Loran. However, probably the most prominent disadvantage of Loran is the fact that it does not provide continuous worldwide coverage. Land-based transmitters can only be located where there is land, which is a relatively small proportion of Earth's surface. Consequently, there are locations where Loran signals simply cannot be received (dead spots). However good or bad Loran may have been or could be is unimportant because a newer, better technique of radio navigation called GPS has emerged that utilizes satellite-based transmitters.

Navstar GPS

Navstar is an acronym for *Nav*igation *S*ystem with *T*ime *A*nd *R*anging, and GPS stands for *G*lobal *P*ositioning *S*ystem. Navstar GPS is the newest and most accurate form of radio navigation available. The United States Department of Defense (DoD) developed Navstar GPS to provide continuous, highly precise position, velocity, and time information to land, sea, air, and space-based users. In essence, Navstar GPS is a space-based navigation, three-dimensional positioning, and time-distribution system. The intent of the system is to provide navigation capabilities anywhere in the world at any time regardless of weather conditions. The Navstar Satellite System is maintained by the U.S. Air Force.

*Provides global coverage

GPS Services

GPS provides two levels of service or accuracy: standard positioning service and precise positioning service.

Standard positioning service (SPS). The *standard positioning service* is a positioning and timing service that is available to all GPS users (military, private, and commercial) on a continuous, worldwide basis with no direct charge. SPS will provide a predictable positioning accuracy that 95% of the time is to within 100 meters horizontally and 156 meters vertically with a time transfer accuracy to UTC (*Universal Transverse Mercator Grid*) within 340 nanoseconds. The accuracy of the SPS service can be downgraded during times of national emergencies. For security reasons, the accuracy of the SPS service is intentionally degraded by the DoD through the use of a technique called *selective availability*. Selective availability (SA) is accomplished by manipulating navigation message orbit data (epsilon) and/or the satellite clock frequency (dither).

Precise positioning service (PPS). The *precise positioning service* is a highly accurate military positioning, velocity, and timing service that is available on a continuous, worldwide basis to users authorized by the DoD. PPS user equipment provides a predictable positioning accuracy 95% of the time of at least 22 meters horizontally and 27.7 meters vertically and a time transfer accuracy to UTC within 200 nanoseconds. Only authorized users with cryptographic equipment and keys and specially equipped receivers can use the precise positioning service. PPS was designed primarily to be used by the U.S. and allied military, certain U.S. Government agencies, and selected civil users specifically approved by the U.S. Government.

Navstar Segments

Navstar GPS has three segments: a *space segment,* a *ground control segment,* and a *user segment.*

Satellite segment. The U.S. Air Force Space Command (AFSC) formally declared the Navstar GPS satellite system as being fully operational as of April 27, 1995. The satellite segment, sometimes called the space segment, is comprised of 24 operational satellites revolving around Earth in six orbital planes (four satellites in each plane) approximately 60° apart. Figure 8-17 shows the Navstar *satellite constellation.* GPS satellites are not geosynchronous. The satellites operate in circular orbits at an average elevation of approximately 9476 statute miles above Earth. Navstar satellites take approximately 12 h to orbit Earth at an angle of elevation of approximately 55° with respect to the equatorial plane. Therefore, their position is approximately the same at the same sidereal time each day (the satellites actually appear four minutes earlier each day).

The position of the satellites in orbit is arranged such that a minimum of five and a maximum of eight will be in view of any user at all times, thereby, ensuring continuous worldwide coverage. Information from three satellites is needed to calculate a navigational unit's horizontal location on Earth's surface (*2-dimensional reporting*), but information from four satellites enables a receiver to also determine its altitude (*3-dimensional reporting*). Three-dimensional reporting is more crucial on land because ground surfaces are not constant as is the surface of a large body of water.

Twenty-one of the 24 satellites are operational and three are reserved as spares. In the event of a satellite failure, one of the spare space vehicles can be moved into its place. Navstar satellites broadcast navigation and system data, atmospheric propagation correction data, and satellite clock bias information.

Navstar Satellite Groupings. There have been three distinct groups plus one subgroup of Navstar satellites. The groups are designated as *blocks.* The 11 block I prototype satellites were intended to be used only for system testing. Block II satellites were the first fully functional satellites that included on-board *cesium atomic clocks* for

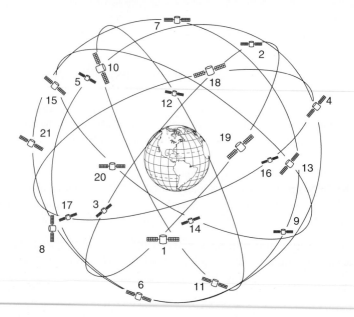

FIGURE 8-17   Navstar GPS satellite constellation

producing highly accurate timing signals. Block II satellites are capable of detecting certain error conditions, then, automatically transmitting a coded message indicating that it is out of service. Block II satellites can operate for approximately 3.5 days between receiving updates and corrections from the control segment of the system. Block IIa satellites are identical to the standard block II versions except they can operate continuously for 180 days between uploads from the ground. The latest satellites, block IIR versions, can operate for 180 days between uploads and possess autonomous navigation capabilities by generating their own navigation information. Thus, the accuracy of the system using block IIR satellites can be maintained longer between uploads.

Navstar Satellite Identification.   Each satellite has two identifying numbers. The first number is the Navstar number that identifies the specific satellite on-board hardware. The second number is the space vehicle number (SV), which is assigned according to the order of the vehicle's launch. The third number is a *psuedorandom noise* (PRN) *code* number. This is a unique integer number that is used to encrypt the signal from that satellite. Some GPS receivers identify the satellite they are receiving transmissions from by the SV numbers, others use the PRN number.

Satellite Ranging. The GPS system works by determining how long it takes a radio signal transmitted from a satellite to reach a land-based receiver and, then, using that time to calculate the distance between the satellite and the earth station receiver. Radio waves travel at approximately the speed of light, 186,000 mps. If a receiver can determine exactly when a satellite began sending a radio message and exactly when the message was received, it can determine the propagation (delay) time. From the propagation time, the receiver can determine the distance between it and the satellite using the simple mathematical relationship

$$d = v \times t$$

where d = distance between satellite and receiver
  v = velocity (186,000 mps)
  t = propagation time

FIGURE 8-18 GPS pseudorandom timing code

The trick, of course, is in determining exactly when the synchronizing signal left the satellite. To determine this, the satellite transmitter and earth station receiver produce identical synchronizing (pseudorandom) codes at exactly the same time, as shown in Figure 8-18. Each satellite continuously transmits its precise synchronizing code. After a synchronizing code is acquired, a receiver simply compares the received code to its own locally produced code to determine the propagation time. The time, difference multiplied by the velocity of the radio signal gives the distance to the satellite.

Figure 8-19 shows there are three unknown position coordinates (x, y, and z). Therefore, three equations from three satellites are required to solve for the three unknown coordinates. A fourth unknown is the error in the receiver's clock, which affects the accuracy of the time-difference measurement. To eliminate the *clock bias error* (C_b), a fourth satellite is needed to produce the fourth equation necessary to solve for four unknowns using simultaneous equations. The solutions to the simultaneous equations for determining latitude and longitude are given in Figure 8-19.

Figure 8-20 illustrates how an aircraft can determine the range (distance) it is from four different satellites by simply measuring the propagation (delay) times and multiplying them by the speed of light. Again, simultaneous equations can be used to determine the aircraft's longitude and latitude.

GPS Satellite Signals. All Navstar satellites transmit on the same two *L-band* microwave carrier frequencies: $L_1 = 1575.42$ MHz and $L_2 = 1227.6$ MHz. GPS satellites use code-division multiple accessing (spread spectrum), which allows all 24 satellites to transmit simultaneously on both carriers without interfering with each other. Three pseudorandom noise (PRN) ranging codes (chip codes) are used to modulate the L_1 and/or L_2 carriers.

1. The coarse/acquisition (C/A) code has a 1.023 MHz chip rate, a period of 1 ms, and is used primarily to acquire the P-code.
2. The precision (P) code has a 10.23 MHz rate, a period of seven days, and is the principle navigation ranging code.
3. The Y-code is used in place of the P-code whenever the *anti-spoofing* (A-S) mode of operation is activated. Anti-spoofing guards against fake transmissions of satellite data by encrypting the P-code to form the Y-code.

Due to the spread-spectrum characteristics of the modulated carriers, the Navstar system provides a large margin of resistance to interference. Each satellite transmits a navigation message containing its orbital elements, clock behavior, system time, and status messages. In addition, an almanac is also provided that gives the approximate data for each active satellite. This allows the users to find all satellites once the first one has been acquired.

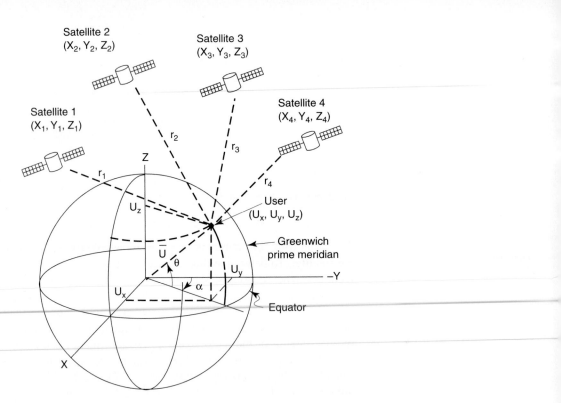

$$(X_1 - U_x)^2 + (Y_1 - U_y)^2 + (Z_1 - U_z)^2 = (r_1 - C_b)^2$$

$$(X_2 - U_x)^2 + (Y_2 - U_y)^2 + (Z_2 - U_z)^2 = (r_2 - C_b)^2$$

$$(X_3 - U_x)^2 + (Y_3 - U_y)^2 + (Z_3 - U_z)^2 = (r_3 - C_b)^2$$

$$(X_4 - U_x)^2 + (Y_4 - U_y)^2 + (Z_4 - U_z)^2 = (r_4 - C_b)^2$$

$$\text{User's latitude} = \theta = \cos^{-1} \frac{\sqrt{U_x{}^2 + U_y{}^2}}{|U|}$$

$$\text{User's longitude} = \alpha = \tan^{-1} \frac{U_x}{U_y}$$

FIGURE 8-19 GPS satellite position calculations

Control segment. The Navstar control segment, called the *operational control system* (OCS), includes all of the fixed-location ground-based *monitor stations* located throughout the world, a *Master Control Station* (MCS), and up-link transmitters. There are passive monitor stations located in California, Hawaii, Alaska, Ascencion Island (off West Africa), Diego Garcia (Indian Ocean), Kwajalein (Pacific Ocean), among others. The monitor stations are simply GPS receivers that track the satellites as they pass overhead and accumulate ranging and *ephemeris* (orbital) data from them. This information is relayed to the Master Control Station at Falcon Air Force Base, 12 miles east of Colorado Springs, Colorado, where it is processed and determined if the actual satellite position compares to the GPS computed position. The Master Control Station is managed by the U.S. Air Force's 2nd Space Operations Squadron (2nd SOPS).

The MCS receives data from the monitor stations in real time, 24 hours a day and uses that information to determine if any satellites are experiencing clock or ephemeris

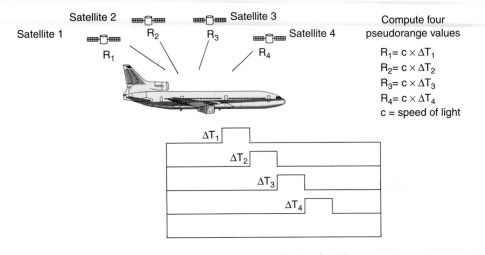

Compute four
pseudorange values

$R_1 = c \times \Delta T_1$
$R_2 = c \times \Delta T_2$
$R_3 = c \times \Delta T_3$
$R_4 = c \times \Delta T_4$
c = speed of light

Time signals transmitted by satellites

FIGURE 8-20 GPS ranging solution

changes and to detect equipment malfunctions. New navigation and ephemeris information is calculated from the monitored signals and uploaded to the satellites once or twice per day. The information calculated by the MCS, along with routine maintenance commands, are relayed to the satellites by ground-based up-link antennas. The ground antennas are located at Ascencion Island, Diego Garcia, and Kwajalein. The antenna facilities transmit to the satellites via an *S-band* radio link. In addition to its main function, the MCS maintains a 24 h computer bulletin board system with the latest system news and status.

User segment.   The GPS user segment consists of all of the GPS receivers and the user community. GPS receivers convert signals received from space vehicles into position, velocity, and time estimates. Four satellites are required to compute the four dimensions of x, y, z (position) and time. GPS receivers are used for navigation, positioning, time dissemination, mapping, guidance systems, surveying, photogrammetry, public safety, archaeology, geology, geophysics, wildlife, aviation, marine and numerous other research applications. Navigation in three dimensions, however, is the primary function of GPS.

GPS navigation receivers are made for aircraft, ships, ground vehicles, and hand-held units for individuals. GPS navigation precise positioning is possible using GPS receivers at reference locations providing corrections and relative positioning data for remote receivers. Surveying, geodetic control, and plate tectonic studies are examples. Time and frequency dissemination, based on the precise clocks on board the space vehicles and controlled by the monitor stations, is another use for GPS. Astronomical observatories, telecommunications facilities, and laboratory standards can be set to precise time signals or controlled to accurate frequencies by special purpose GPS receivers.

Differential GPS

Differential GPS makes standard GPS even more accurate. Differential GPS works by canceling out most of the natural and man-made errors that creep into normal GPS measurements. Inaccuracies in GPS signals come from a variety of sources, such as satellite clock drift, imperfect orbits, and variations in Earth's atmosphere. These imperfections are variable and difficult if not impossible to predict. Therefore, what is needed is a means to measure the actual errors as they are occurring.

TABLE 8-1   Summary of GPS Error Sources

Per Satellite Accuracy	Standard GPS	Differential GPS
Satellite clocks	1.5	0
Orbit errors	2.5	0
Ionosphere	5.0	0.4
Troposphere	0.5	0.2
Receiver noise	0.3	0.3
Multipath reception	0.6	0.6
Selective availability	30.	0
Typical Position Accuracy (meters)		
Horizontal	50	1.3
Vertical	78	2.0
3-D	93	2.8

With differential GPS, a second receiver is placed in a location whose exact position is known. It calculates its position from the satellite data and, then, compares it with its known position. The difference between the calculated and known positions is the error in the GPS signal. Differential GPS is only practical in locations where you can leave a receiver permanently, such as near an airport.

Sources of errors in GPS are satellite clocks, selective availability, ephemeris, atmospheric delays, multipath, receiver clocks, and so on. Table 8-1 summarizes GPS error sources for both standard and differential GPS.

QUESTIONS

8-1. Discuss the drawbacks of using FDM/FM modulation for satellite multiple-accessing systems.

8-2. Contrast *preassignment* and *demand assignment.*

8-3. What are the three most common multiple-accessing arrangements used with satellite systems?

8-4. Briefly describe the multiple-accessing arrangements listed in Question 8-3.

8-5. Briefly describe the operation of Comsat's SPADE system.

8-6. What is meant by *single-carrier per channel?*

8-7. What is a common-signaling channel, and how is it used?

8-8. Describe what a reference burst is for TDMA and explain the following terms: preamble, carrier recovery sequence, bit timing recovery, unique word, and correlation spike.

8-9. Describe guard time.

8-10. Briefly describe the operation of the CEPT primary multiplex frame.

8-11. What is a store-and-forward system?

8-12. What is the primary advantage of TDMA as compared to FDMA?

8-13. What is the primary advantage of FDMA as compared to TDMA?

8-14. Briefly describe the operation of a CDMA multiple-accessing system.

8-15. Describe a chip code.

8-16. Describe what is meant by an orthogonal code.

8-17. Describe cross correlation.

8-18. What are the advantages of CDMA as compared to TDMA and FDMA?

8-19. What are the disadvantages of CDMA?

8-20. What is a Gold code?

8-21. Describe frequency hopping.

8-22. What is a frequency-time matrix?

8-23. Describe digital noninterpolated interfaces.

8-24. Describe digital speech interpolated interfaces.

8-25. What is channel compression, and how is it accomplished with a DSI system?

8-26. Describe competitive clipping.

8-27. What is meant by *bit stealing?*

8-28. Describe time-assignment speech interpolation.

PROBLEMS

8-1. How many satellite transponders are required to interlink six earth stations with FDM/FM modulation?

8-2. For the SPADE system, what are the carrier frequencies for channel 7? What are the allocated passbands for channel 7? What are the actual passband frequencies (excluding guard bands) required?

8-3. If a 512-bit preamble precedes each CEPT station's transmission, what is the maximum number of earth stations that can be linked together with a single satellite transponder?

8-4. Determine an orthogonal code for the following chip code (101010). Prove that your selection will not produce any cross correlation for an in-phase comparison. Determine the cross correlation for each out-of-phase condition that is possible.

8-5. How many satellite transponders are required to interlink five earth stations with FDM/FM modulation?

8-6. For the SPADE system, what are the carrier frequencies for channel 9? What are the allocated passbands for channel 10? What are the actual passband frequencies for channel 12 (excluding the guard bands)?

8-7. If a 256-bit preamble precedes each CEPT station's transmission, what is the maximum number of earth stations that can be linked together with a single satellite transponder?

8-8. Determine an orthogonal code for the following chip code (010101). Prove that your selection will not produce any cross correlation for an in-phase comparison. Determine the cross correlation for each out-of-phase condition that is possible.

C H A P T E R   9 ⟩⟩⟩

Optical Fiber Communications

INTRODUCTION

During the past 10 years, the electronic communications industry has experienced many remarkable and dramatic changes. A phenomenal increase in voice, data, and video communications has caused a corresponding increase in the demand for more economical and larger capacity communications systems. This has caused a technical revolution in the electronic communications industry. Terrestrial microwave systems have long since reached their capacity, and satellite systems can provide, at best, only a temporary relief to the ever-increasing demand. It is obvious that economical communications systems that can handle large capacities and provide high-quality service are needed.

Communications systems that use light as the carrier of information have recently received a great deal of attention. As we shall see later in this chapter, propagating light waves through Earth's atmosphere is difficult and impractical. Consequently, systems that use glass or plastic fiber cables to "contain" a light wave and guide it from a source to a destination are presently being investigated at several prominent research and development laboratories. Communications systems that carry information through a *guided fiber cable* are called *fiber optic* systems.

The *information-carrying capacity* of a communications system is directly proportional to its bandwidth; the wider the bandwidth, the greater its information-carrying capacity. For comparison purposes, it is common to express the bandwidth of a system as a percentage of its carrier frequency. For instance, a VHF radio system operating at 100 MHz could have a bandwidth equal to 10 MHz (i.e., 10% of the carrier frequency). A microwave radio system operating at 6 GHz with a bandwidth equal to 10% of its carrier frequency would have a bandwidth equal to 600 MHz. Thus, the higher the carrier frequency, the wider the bandwidth possible and consequently, the greater the information-carrying capacity. Light frequencies used in fiber optic systems are between 10^{14} and 4×10^{14} Hz (100,000 to 400,000 GHz). Ten percent of 100,000 GHz is 10,000 GHz. To meet today's communications needs or the needs of the foreseeable future, 10,000 GHz is an excessive bandwidth. However, it does illustrate the capabilities of optical fiber systems.

HISTORY OF FIBER OPTICS

In 1880, Alexander Graham Bell experimented with an apparatus he called a *photophone*. The photophone was a device constructed from mirrors and selenium detectors that transmitted sound waves over a beam of light. The photophone was awkward, unreliable, and had no real practical application. Actually, visual light was a primary means of communicating long before electronic communications came about. Smoke signals and mirrors were used ages ago to convey short, simple messages. Bell's contraption, however, was the first attempt at using a beam of light for carrying information.

Transmission of light waves for any useful distance through Earth's atmosphere is impractical because water vapor, oxygen, and particulates in the air absorb and attenuate the signals at light frequencies. Consequently, the only practical type of optical communications system is one that uses a fiber guide. In 1930, J. L. Baird, an English scientist, and C. W. Hansell, a scientist from the United States, were granted patents for scanning and transmitting television images through uncoated fiber cables. A few years later a German scientist named H. Lamm successfully transmitted images through a single glass fiber. At that time, most people considered fiber optics more of a toy or a laboratory stunt and, consequently, it was not until the early 1950s that any substantial breakthrough was made in the field of fiber optics.

In 1951, A. C. S. van Heel of Holland and H. H. Hopkins and N. S. Kapany of England experimented with light transmission through *bundles* of fibers. Their studies led to the development of the *flexible fiberscope,* which is used extensively in the medical field. It was Kapany who coined the term "fiber optics" in 1956.

In 1958, Charles H. Townes, an American, and Arthur L. Schawlow, a Canadian, wrote a paper describing how it was possible to use stimulated emission for amplifying light waves (laser) as well as microwaves (maser). Two years later, Theodore H. Maiman, a scientist with Hughes Aircraft Company, built the first optical maser.

The *laser* (*l*ight *a*mplification by *s*timulated *e*mission of *r*adiation) was invented in 1960. The laser's relatively high output power, high frequency of operation, and capability of carrying an extremely wide bandwidth signal make it ideally suited for high-capacity communications systems. The invention of the laser greatly accelerated research efforts in fiber optic communications, although it was not until 1967 that K. C. Kao and G. A. Bockham of the Standard Telecommunications Laboratory in England proposed a new communications medium using *cladded* fiber cables.

The fiber cables available in the 1960s were extremely *lossy* (more than 1000 dB/km), which limited optical transmissions to short distances. In 1970, Kapron, Keck, and Maurer of Corning Glass Works in Corning, New York, developed an optical fiber with losses less than 2 dB/km. That was the "big" breakthrough needed to permit practical fiber optics communications systems. Since 1970, fiber optics technology has grown exponentially. Recently, Bell Laboratories successfully transmitted 1 billion bps through a fiber cable for 600 mi without a regenerator.

In the late 1970s and early 1980s, the refinement of optical cables and the development of high-quality, affordable light sources and detectors opened the door to the development of high-quality, high-capacity, and efficient fiber optics communications systems. The branch of electronics that deals with light is called *optoelectronics*.

OPTICAL FIBERS VERSUS METALLIC CABLE FACILITIES

Communications through glass or plastic fiber cables has several overwhelming advantages over communications using conventional *metallic* or *coaxial* cable facilities.

Advantages of Fiber Systems

1. Fiber systems have a greater capacity due to the inherently larger bandwidths available with optical frequencies. Metallic cables exhibit capacitance between and inductance along their conductors. These properties cause them to act as low-pass filters, which limit their transmission frequencies and bandwidths.

2. Fiber systems are immune to cross talk between cables caused by *magnetic induction*. Glass or plastic fibers are nonconductors of electricity and, therefore, do not have a magnetic field associated with them. In metallic cables, the primary cause of cross talk is magnetic induction between conductors located near each other.

3. Fiber cables are immune to *static* interference caused by lightning, electric motors, fluorescent lights, and other electrical noise sources. This immunity is also attributable to the fact that optical fibers are nonconductors of electricity. Also, fiber cables do not radiate RF energy and, therefore, cannot cause interference with other communications systems. This characteristic makes fiber systems ideally suited to military applications, where the effects of nuclear weapons (EMP—electromagnetic pulse interference) has a devastating effect on conventional communications systems.

4. Fiber cables are more resistive to environmental extremes. They operate over a larger temperature variation than their metallic counterparts, and fiber cables are affected less by corrosive liquids and gases.

5. Fiber cables are safer and easier to install and maintain. Because glass and plastic fibers are nonconductors, there are no electrical currents or voltages associated with them. Fibers can be used around volatile liquids and gases without worrying about their causing explosions or fires. Fibers are smaller and much more lightweight than their metallic counterparts. Consequently, they are easier to work with. Also, fiber cables require less storage space and are cheaper to transport.

6. Fiber cables are more secure than their copper counterparts. It is virtually impossible to tap into a fiber cable without the user knowing about it. This is another quality attractive for military applications.

7. Although it has not yet been proven, it is projected that fiber systems will last longer than metallic facilities. This assumption is based on the higher tolerances that fiber cables have to changes in the environment.

8. The long-term cost of a fiber optic system is projected to be less than that of its metallic counterpart.

Disadvantages of Fiber Systems

At the present time, there are few disadvantages of fiber systems. One significant disadvantage is the higher initial cost of installing a fiber system, although in the future it is believed that the cost of installing a fiber system will be reduced dramatically. Another disadvantage of fiber systems is the fact that they are unproven; there are no systems that have been in operation for an extended period of time. Maintenance and repair of fiber systems is also more difficult and expensive than metallic systems.

ELECTROMAGNETIC SPECTRUM

The total electromagnetic frequency spectrum is shown in Figure 9-1. It can be seen that the frequency spectrum extends from the *subsonic* frequencies (a few hertz) to *cosmic rays* (10^{22} Hz). The light frequency spectrum can be divided into three general bands:

1. *Infrared:* band of light wavelengths that are too long to be seen by the human eye

2. *Visible:* band of light wavelengths that the human eye will respond to

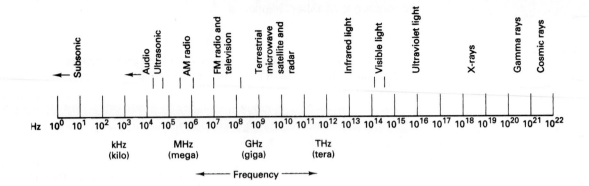

FIGURE 9-1 Electromagnetic frequency spectrum

    3. *Ultraviolet:* band of light wavelengths that are too short to be seen by the human eye

When dealing with higher-frequency electromagnetic waves, such as light, it is common to use units of *wavelength* rather than frequency. Wavelength is the length of the wave that one cycle of an electromagnetic wave occupies in space. The length of a wavelength depends on the frequency of the wave and the velocity of light. Mathematically, wavelength is

$$\lambda = \frac{c}{f} \tag{9-1}$$

where λ = wavelength (m/cycle)
         c = velocity of light (300,000,000 m/s)
         f = frequency (Hz)

With light frequencies, wavelength is often stated in *microns* (1 micron = 1 micrometer) or *nanometers* (1 nanometer = 10^{-9} meter or 0.001 micron). However, when describing the optical spectrum, the unit *angstrom* (Å) often has been used to express wavelength (1 Å = 10^{-10} meter or 0.0001 micron). Figure 9-2 shows the total electromagnetic wavelength spectrum.

OPTICAL FIBER COMMUNICATIONS SYSTEM

Figure 9-3 shows a simplified block diagram of an optical fiber communications link. The three primary building blocks of the link are the *transmitter,* the *receiver,* and the *fiber guide.* The transmitter consists of an analog or digital interface, a voltage-to-current converter, a light source, and a source-to-fiber light coupler. The fiber guide is either an ultrapure glass or plastic cable. The receiver includes a fiber-to-light detector coupling device, a photo detector, a current-to-voltage converter, an amplifier, and an analog or digital interface.

In an optical fiber transmitter, the light source can be modulated by a digital or an analog signal. For analog modulation, the input interface matches impedances and limits the input signal amplitude. For digital modulation, the original source may already be in digital form or, if in analog form, it must be converted to a digital pulse stream. For the latter case, an analog-to-digital converter must be included in the interface.

The voltage-to-current converter serves as an electrical interface between the input circuitry and the light source. The light source is either a light-emitting diode (LED) or an injection laser diode (ILD). The amount of light emitted by either an LED or an ILD is

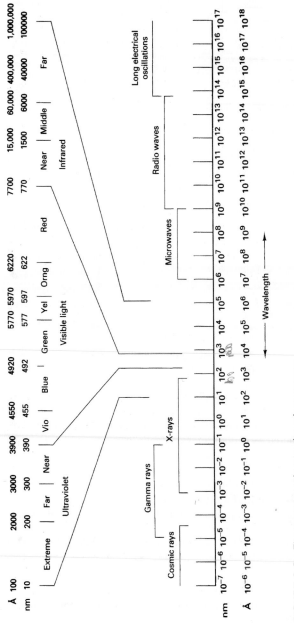

FIGURE 9-2 Electromagnetic wavelength spectrum

363

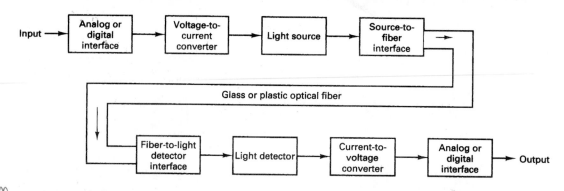

FIGURE 9-3 Fiber optic communications link

proportional to the amount of drive current. Thus, the voltage-to-current converter converts an input signal voltage to a current that is used to drive the light source.

The source-to-fiber coupler (such as a lens) is a mechanical interface. Its function is to couple the light emitted by the source into the optical fiber cable. The optical fiber consists of a glass or plastic fiber core, a cladding, and a protective jacket. The fiber-to-light detector coupling device is also a mechanical coupler. Its function is to couple as much light as possible from the fiber cable into the light detector.

The light detector is very often either a PIN (*p*-type-*i*ntrinsic-*n*-type) diode or an APD (*a*valanche *photodi*ode). Both the APD and the PIN diode convert light energy to current. Consequently, a current-to-voltage converter is required. The current-to-voltage converter transforms changes in detector current to changes in output signal voltage.

The analog or digital interface at the receiver output is also an electrical interface. If analog modulation is used, the interface matches impedances and signal levels to the output circuitry. If digital modulation is used, the interface must include a digital-to-analog converter.

Fiber Types

Essentially, there are three varieties of optical fibers available today. All three varieties are constructed of either glass, plastic, or a combination of glass and plastic. The three varieties are

1. Plastic core and cladding
2. Glass core with plastic cladding (often called PCS fiber, plastic-clad silica)
3. Glass core and glass cladding (often called SCS, silica-clad silica)

Presently, Bell Laboratories is investigating the possibility of using a fourth variety that uses a *nonsilicate* substance, *zinc chloride*. Preliminary experiments have indicated that fibers made of this substance will be as much as 1000 times as efficient as glass, their silica-based counterpart.

Plastic fibers have several advantages over glass fibers. First, plastic fibers are more flexible and, consequently, more rugged than glass. They are easy to install, can better withstand stress, are less expensive, and weigh approximately 60% less than glass. The disadvantage of plastic fibers is their high attenuation characteristic; they do not propagate light as efficiently as glass. Consequently, plastic fibers are limited to relatively short runs, such as within a single building or a building complex.

Fibers with glass cores exhibit low attenuation characteristics. However, PCS fibers are slightly better than SCS fibers. Also, PCS fibers are less affected by radiation and, therefore, are more attractive to military applications. SCS fibers have the best propagation characteristics and they are easier to terminate than PCS fibers. Unfortunately, SCS

FIGURE 9-4 Fiber optic cable configurations: (a) loose tube construction; (b) constrained fiber; (c) multiple strands; (d) telephone cable; (e) plastic-clad silica cable

↳ not used c

cables are the least rugged, and they are more susceptible to increases in attenuation when exposed to radiation.

The selection of a fiber for a given application is a function of specific system requirements. There are always trade-offs based on the economics and logistics of a particular application.

Cable Construction

There are many different cable designs available today. Figure 9-4 shows examples of several fiber optic cable configurations. Depending on the configuration, the cable may include a *core*, a *cladding*, a *protective tube*, *buffers*, *strength members*, and one or more *protective jackets*.

With the *loose* tube construction (shown in Figure 9-4a) each fiber is contained in a protective tube. Inside the protective tube, a polyurethane compound encapsules the fiber and prevents the intrusion of water.

Figure 9-4b shows the construction of a *constrained* optical fiber cable. Surrounding the fiber cable are a primary and a secondary buffer. The buffer jackets provide protection for the fiber from external mechanical influences that could cause fiber breakage or excessive optical attenuation. Kevlar is a yarn-type material that increases the tensile strength of the cable. Again, an outer protective tube is filled with polyurethane, which prevents moisture from coming into contact with the fiber core.

Figure 9-4c shows a *multiple-strand* configuration. To increase the tensile strength, a steel central member and a layer of Mylar tape wrap are included in the package. Figure 9-4d shows a *ribbon* configuration, which is frequently seen in telephone systems using fiber optics. Figure 9-4e shows both the end and side views of a plastic-clad silica cable.

The type of cable construction used depends on the performance requirements of the system and both the economic and environmental constraints.

LIGHT PROPAGATION

The Physics of Light

Although the performance of optical fibers can be analyzed completely by application of Maxwell's equations, this is necessarily complex. For most practical applications, *geometric wave tracing* may be used instead of Maxwell's equations; ray tracing will yield sufficiently accurate results.

An atom has several energy levels or states, the lowest of which is the ground state. Any energy level above the ground state is called an *excited state.* If an atom in one energy level decays to a lower energy level, the loss of energy (in electron volts) is emitted as a photon. The energy of the photon is equal to the difference between the energy of the two energy levels. The process of decay from one energy level to another energy level is called *spontaneous decay* or *spontaneous emission.*

Atoms can be irradiated by a light source whose energy is equal to the difference between the ground level and an energy level. This can cause an electron to change from one energy level to another by absorbing light energy. The process of moving from one energy level to another is called *absorption.* When making the transition from one energy level to another, the atom absorbs a packet of energy called a *photon.* This process is similar to that of emission.

The energy absorbed or emitted (photon) is equal to the difference between the two energy levels. Mathematically,

$$E_2 - E_1 = E_p \tag{9-2}$$

where E_p is the energy of the photon. Also,

$$E_p = hf \tag{9-3}$$

where h = Planck's constant = 6.625×10^{34} J-s
f = frequency of light emitted (Hz)

Photon energy may also be expressed in terms of wavelength. Substituting Equation 9-1 into Equation 9-3 yields

$$E_p = hf \tag{9-4}$$
$$= \frac{hc}{\lambda}$$

Velocity of Propagation

Electromagnetic energy, such as light, travels at approximately 300,000,000 m/s (186,000 miles per second) in free space. Also, the velocity of propagation is the same for all light frequencies in free space. However, it has been demonstrated that in materials more dense

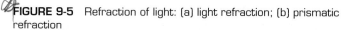

FIGURE 9-5 Refraction of light: (a) light refraction; (b) prismatic refraction

than free space, the velocity is reduced. When the velocity of an electromagnetic wave is reduced as it passes from one medium to another medium of a denser material, the light ray is *refracted* (bent) toward the normal. Also, in materials more dense than free space, all light frequencies do not propagate at the same velocity.

Refraction

Figure 9-5a shows how a light ray is refracted as it passes from a material of a given density into a less dense material. (Actually, the light ray is not bent, but rather, it changes direction at the interface.) Figure 9-5b shows how sunlight, which contains all light frequencies, is affected as it passes through a material more dense than free space. Refraction occurs at both air/glass interfaces. The violet wavelengths are refracted the most, and the red wavelengths are refracted the least. The spectral separation of white light in this manner is called *prismatic refraction.* It is this phenomenon that causes rainbows; water droplets in the atmosphere act as small prisms that split the white sunlight into the various wavelengths, creating a visible spectrum of color.

Refractive Index

The amount of bending or refraction that occurs at the interface of two materials of different densities is quite predictable and depends on the *refractive index* (also called *index of refraction*) of the two materials. The refractive index is simply the ratio of the

TABLE 9-1 Typical Indexes of Refraction

Medium	Index of Refraction*
Vacuum	1.0
Air	1.0003 ($\approx$1.0)
Water	1.33
Ethyl alcohol	1.36
Fused quartz	1.46
Glass fiber	1.5–1.9
Diamond	2.0–2.42
Silicon	3.4
Gallium-arsenide	3.6

*Index of refraction is based on a wavelength of light emitted from a sodium flame (5890 Å).

velocity of propagation of a light ray in free space to the velocity of propagation of a light ray in a given material. Mathematically, the refractive index is

$$n = \frac{c}{v}$$

where c = speed of light in free space (300,000,000 m/s)
   v = speed of light in a given material

Although the refractive index is also a function of frequency, the variation in most applications is insignificant and, therefore, omitted from this discussion. The indexes of refraction of several common materials are given in Table 9-1.

How a light ray reacts when it meets the interface of two transmissive materials that have different indexes of refraction can be explained with *Snell's law.* Snell's law simply states

$$n_1 \sin \theta_1 = n_2 \sin \theta_2 \qquad (9\text{-}5)$$

where n_1 = refractive index of material 1 (unitless)
   n_2 = refractive index of material 2 (unitless)
   θ_1 = angle of incidence (degrees)
   θ_2 = angle of refraction (degrees)

A refractive index model for Snell's law is shown in Figure 9-6. At the interface, the incident ray may be refracted toward the normal or away from it, depending on whether n_1 is less than or greater than n_2.

Figure 9-7 shows how a light ray is refracted as it travels from a more dense (higher refractive index) material into a less dense (lower refractive index) material. It can be seen that the light ray changes direction at the interface, and the angle of refraction is greater than the angle of incidence. Consequently, when a light ray enters a less dense material, the ray bends away from the normal. The normal is simply a line drawn perpendicular to the interface at the point where the incident ray strikes the interface. Similarly, when a light ray enters a more dense material, the ray bends toward the normal.

Example 9-1

In Figure 9-7, let medium 1 be glass and medium 2 be ethyl alcohol. For an angle of incidence of 30°, determine the angle of refraction.

Solution   From Table 9-1,

$$n_1 \text{ (glass)} = 1.5$$
$$n_2 \text{ (ethyl alcohol)} = 1.36$$

FIGURE 9-6   Refractive model for Snell's law

[handwritten notes to the right of Figure 9-6:] 2 units away from pt of incidence / A has traveled further than B

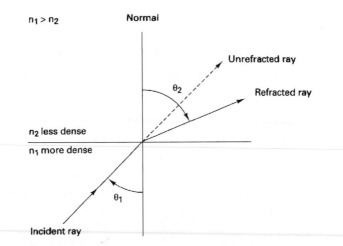

FIGURE 9-7   Light ray refracted away from the normal

Rearranging Equation 9-5 and substituting for n_1, n_2, and θ_1 gives us

$$\frac{n_1}{n_2} \sin \theta_1 = \sin \theta_2$$

$$\frac{1.5}{1.36} \sin 30 = 0.5514 = \sin \theta_2$$

$$\theta_2 = \sin^{-1} 0.5514 = 33.47°$$

The result indicates that the light ray refracted (bent) or changed direction by 3.47° at the interface. Because the light was traveling from a more dense material into a less dense material, the ray bent away from the normal.

Critical Angle

Figure 9-8 shows a condition in which an *incident ray* is at an angle such that the angle of refraction is 90° and the refracted ray is along the interface. (It is important to note that the light ray is traveling from a medium of higher refractive index to a medium with a lower refractive index.) Again, using Snell's law,

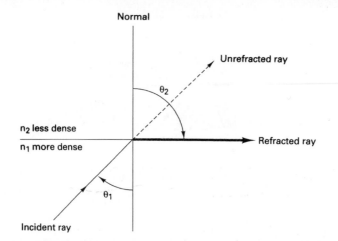

FIGURE 9-8 Critical angle refraction

$$\sin \theta_1 = \frac{n_2}{n_1} \sin \theta_2$$

With $\theta_2 = 90°$,

$$\sin \theta_1 = \frac{n_2}{n_1}(1) \qquad \text{or} \qquad \sin \theta_1 = \frac{n_2}{n_1}$$

and

$$\sin^{-1} \frac{n_2}{n_1} = \theta_1 = \theta_c \tag{9-6}$$

where θ_c is the critical angle.

The *critical angle* is defined as the minimum angle of incidence at which a light ray may strike the interface of two media and result in an angle of refraction of 90° or greater. (This definition pertains only when the light ray is traveling from a more dense medium into a less dense medium.) If the angle of refraction is 90° or greater, the light ray is not allowed to penetrate the less dense material. Consequently, total reflection takes place at the interface, and the angle of reflection is equal to the angle of incidence. Figure 9-9 shows a comparison of the angle of refraction and the angle of reflection when the angle of incidence is less than or more than the critical angle.

PROPAGATION OF LIGHT THROUGH AN OPTICAL FIBER

Light can be propagated down an optical fiber cable by either reflection or refraction. How the light is propagated depends on the *mode of propagation* and the *index profile* of the fiber.

Mode of Propagation

In fiber optics terminology, the word *mode* simply means path. If there is only one path for light to take down the cable, it is called *single mode*. If there is more than one path, it is called *multimode*. Figure 9-10 shows single and multimode propagation of light down an optical fiber.

Index Profile

The index profile of an optical fiber is a graphical representation of the value of the refractive index across the fiber. The refractive index is plotted on the horizontal axis and

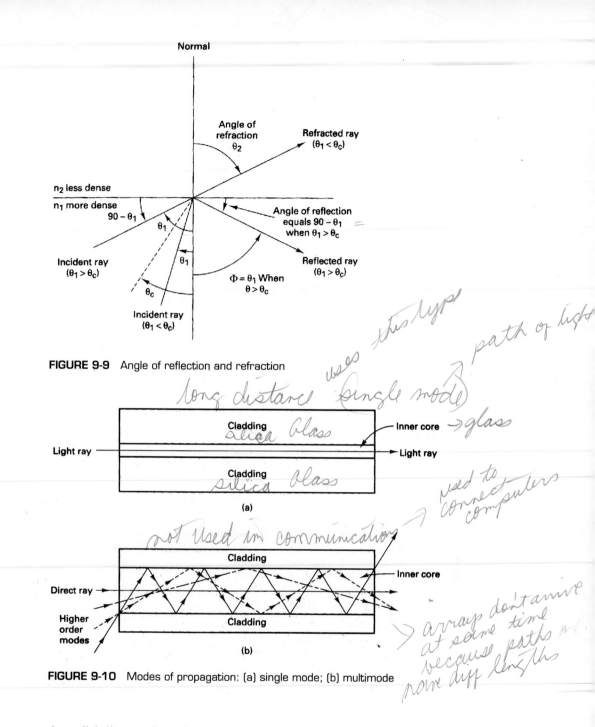

FIGURE 9-9 Angle of reflection and refraction

FIGURE 9-10 Modes of propagation: (a) single mode; (b) multimode

[handwritten annotations: uses this type — long distance (single mode) — path of light — silica glass — Inner core → glass — Cladding silica glass — not used in communication → used to connect computers — arrays don't arrive at same time because paths are diff lengths]

the radial distance from the core axis is plotted on the vertical axis. Figure 9-11 shows the core index profiles of three types of fiber cables.

There are two basic types of index profiles: step and graded. A *step-index fiber* has a central core with a uniform refractive index. The core is surrounded by an outside cladding with a uniform refractive index less than that of the central core. From Figure 9-11 it can be seen that in a step-index fiber there is an abrupt change in the refractive index at the core/cladding interface. In a *graded-index fiber* there is no cladding, and the refractive index of the core is nonuniform; it is highest at the center and decreases gradually with distance toward the outer edge.

FIGURE 9-11 Core index profiles: (a) single-mode step index; (b) multimode step index; (c) multimode graded index

OPTICAL FIBER CONFIGURATIONS

Essentially, there are three types of optical fiber configurations: single-mode step-index, multimode step-index, and multimode graded-index.

Single-Mode Step-Index Fiber

A *single-mode step-index fiber* has a central core that is sufficiently small so that there is essentially only one path that light may take as it propagates down the cable. This type of fiber is shown in Figure 9-12. In the simplest form of single-mode step-index fiber, the outside cladding is simply air (Figure 9-12a). The refractive index of the glass core (n_1) is approximately 1.5, and the refractive index of the air cladding (n_0) is 1. The large difference in the refractive indexes results in a small critical angle (approximately 42°) at the glass/air interface. Consequently, the fiber will accept light from a wide aperture. This makes it relatively easy to couple light from a source into the cable. However, this type of fiber is typically very weak and of limited practical use.

A more practical type of single-mode step-index fiber is one that has a cladding other than air (Figure 9-12b). The refractive index of the cladding (n_2) is slightly less than that of the central core (n_1) and is uniform throughout the cladding. This type of cable is physically stronger than the air-clad fiber, but the critical angle is also much higher (approximately 77°). This results in a small acceptance angle and a narrow source-to-fiber aperture, making it much more difficult to couple light into the fiber from a light source.

With both types of single-mode step-index fibers, light is propagated down the fiber through reflection. Light rays that enter the fiber propagate straight down the core or,

$$\theta_c = \sin^{-1} n_2/n_1$$
$$\theta_c = \sin^{-1} 1/1.5 = 41.8°$$
Acceptance angle = $90 - \theta_c = 48.2°$

(a)

$$\theta_c = \sin^{-1} n_2/n_1$$
$$\theta_c = \sin^{-1} 1.46/1.5 = 76.7°$$
Acceptance angle = $90 - \theta_c = 13.3°$

(b)

FIGURE 9-12 Single-mode step-index fibers: (a) air cladding; (b) glass cladding

FIGURE 9-13 Multimode step-index fiber

perhaps, are reflected once. Consequently, all light rays follow approximately the same path down the cable and take approximately the same amount of time to travel the length of the cable. This is one overwhelming advantage of single-mode step-index fibers and will be explained in more detail later in this chapter.

Multimode Step-Index Fiber

A *multimode step-index fiber* is shown in Figure 9-13. It is similar to the single-mode configuration except that the center core is much larger. This type of fiber has a large light-to-fiber aperture and, consequently, allows more light to enter the cable. The light rays that strike the core/cladding interface at an angle greater than the critical angle (ray A) are propagated down the core in a zigzag fashion, continuously reflecting off the

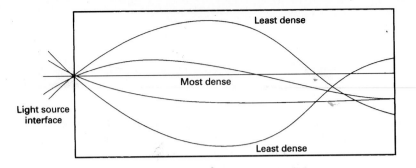

Least dense

Most dense

Light source
interface

Least dense

FIGURE 9-14 Multimode graded-index fiber

interface boundary. Light rays that strike the core/cladding interface at an angle less than the critical angle (ray B) enter the cladding and are lost. It can be seen that there are many paths that a light ray may follow as it propagates down the fiber. As a result, all light rays do not follow the same path and, consequently, do not take the same amount of time to travel the length of the fiber.

Multimode Graded-Index Fiber

A *multimode graded-index fiber* is shown in Figure 9-14. A multimode graded-index fiber is characterized by a central core that has a refractive index that is nonuniform; it is maximum at the center and decreases gradually toward the outer edge. Light is propagated down this type of fiber through refraction. As a light ray propagates diagonally across the core toward the center it is continually intersecting a less-dense-to-more-dense interface. Consequently, the light rays are constantly being refracted, which results in a continuous bending of the light rays. Light enters the fiber at many different angles. As they propagate down the fiber, the light rays that travel in the outermost area of the fiber travel a greater distance than the rays traveling near the center. Because the refractive index decreases with distance from the center and the velocity is inversely proportional to the refractive index, the light rays traveling farthest from the center propagate at a higher velocity. Consequently, they take approximately the same amount of time to travel the length of the fiber.

Comparison of the Three Types of Optical Fibers

Single-mode step-index fiber

Advantages

1. There is minimum dispersion. Because all rays propagating down the fiber take approximately the same path, they take approximately the same amount of time to travel down the cable. Consequently, a pulse of light entering the cable can be reproduced at the receiving end very accurately.

2. Because of the high accuracy in reproducing transmitted pulses at the receive end, larger bandwidths and higher information transmission rates are possible with single-mode step-index fibers than with the other types of fibers.

Disadvantages

1. Because the central core is very small, it is difficult to couple light into and out of this type of fiber. The source-to-fiber aperture is the smallest of all the fiber types.

2. Again, because of the small central core, a highly directive light source such as a laser is required to couple light into a single-mode step-index fiber.

3. Single-mode step-index fibers are expensive and difficult to manufacture.

Multimode step-index fiber

Advantages

1. Multimode step-index fibers are inexpensive and simple to manufacture.

2. It is easy to couple light into and out of multimode step-index fibers; they have a relatively large source-to-fiber aperture.

Disadvantages

1. Light rays take many different paths down the fiber, which results in large differences in their propagation times. Because of this, rays traveling down this type of fiber have a tendency to spread out. Consequently, a pulse of light propagating down a multimode step-index fiber is distorted more than with the other types of fibers.

2. The bandwidth and rate of information transfer possible with this type of cable are less than the other types.

Multimode graded-index fiber. Essentially, there are no outstanding advantages or disadvantages of this type of fiber. Multimode graded-index fibers are easier to couple light into and out of than single-mode step-index fibers but more difficult than multimode step-index fibers. Distortion due to multiple propagation paths is greater than in single-mode step-index fibers but less than in multimode step-index fibers. Graded-index fibers are easier to manufacture than single-mode step-index fibers but more difficult than multimode step-index fibers. The multimode graded-index fiber is considered an intermediate fiber compared to the other types.

ACCEPTANCE ANGLE AND ACCEPTANCE CONE

In previous discussions, the *source-to-fiber aperture* was mentioned several times, and the *critical* and *acceptance* angles at the point where a light ray strikes the core/cladding interface were explained. The following discussion deals with the light-gathering ability of the fiber, the ability to couple light from the source into the fiber cable.

Figure 9-15 shows the source end of a fiber cable. When light rays enter the fiber, they strike the air/glass interface at normal A. The refractive index of air is 1 and the refractive index of the glass core is 1.5. Consequently, the light entering at the air/glass interface propagates from a less dense medium into a more dense medium. Under these conditions and according to Snell's law, the light rays will refract toward the normal. This causes the light rays to change direction and propagate diagonally down the core at an

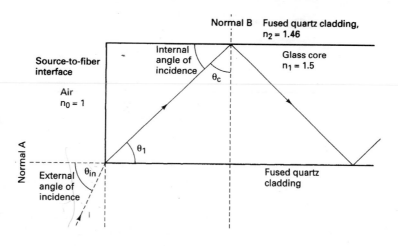

FIGURE 9-15 Ray propagation into and down an optical fiber cable

FIGURE 9-16 Geometric relationship of Equation 9-9

angle (θ_c) that is different than the external angle of incidence at the air/glass interface (θ_{in}). In order for a ray of light to propagate down the cable, it must strike the internal core/cladding interface at an angle that is greater than the critical angle (θ_c).

Applying Snell's law to the external angle of incidence yields the following expression:

$$n_0 \sin \theta_{in} = n_1 \sin \theta_1 \tag{9-7}$$

and

$$\theta_1 = 90 - \theta_c$$

Thus,

$$\sin \theta_1 = \sin (90 - \theta_c) = \cos \theta_c \tag{9-8}$$

Substituting Equation 9-8 into Equation 9-7 yields the following expression:

$$n_0 \sin \theta_{in} = n_1 \cos \theta_c$$

Rearranging and solving for $\sin \theta_{in}$ gives us

$$\sin \theta_{in} = \frac{n_1}{n_0} \cos \theta_c \tag{9-9}$$

Figure 9-16 shows the geometric relationship of Equation 9-9.

From Figure 9-16 and using the Pythagorean theorem, we obtain

$$\cos \theta_c = \frac{\sqrt{n_1^2 - n_2^2}}{n_1} \tag{9-10}$$

Substituting Equation 9-10 into Equation 9-9 yields

$$\sin \theta_{in} = \frac{n_1}{n_0} \frac{\sqrt{n_1^2 - n_2^2}}{n_1}$$

Reducing the equation gives

$$\sin \theta_{in} = \frac{\sqrt{n_1^2 - n_2^2}}{n_0} \tag{9-11}$$

and

$$\theta_{in} = \sin^{-1} \frac{\sqrt{n_1^2 - n_2^2}}{n_0} \tag{9-12}$$

Because light rays generally enter the fiber from an air medium, n_0 equal 1. This simplifies Equation 9-12 to

$$\theta_{in(max)} = \sin^{-1} \sqrt{n_1^2 - n_2^2} \tag{9-13}$$

θ_{in} is called the *acceptance angle* or *acceptance cone* half-angle. It defines the maximum angle in which external light rays may strike the air/fiber interface and still propagate

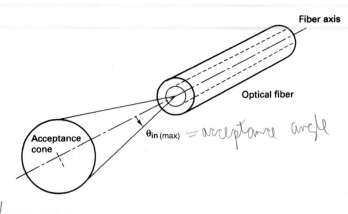

Fiber axis

Optical fiber

Acceptance cone

$\theta_{in\,(max)}$ = acceptance angle

FIGURE 9-17 Acceptance cone of a fiber cable

down the fiber with a response that is no greater than 10 dB down from the peak value. Rotating the acceptance angle around the fiber axis describes the acceptance cone of the fiber input. This is shown in Figure 9-17.

Numerical Aperture

Numerical aperture (NA) is a figure of merit that is used to describe the light-gathering or light-collecting ability of an optical fiber. The larger the magnitude of NA, the greater the amount of light accepted by the fiber from the external light source. For a step-index fiber, numerical aperture is mathematically defined as the sine of the acceptance half-angle. Thus,

$$NA = \sin \theta_{in}$$

and

$$NA = \sqrt{n_1^2 - n_2^2}$$

Also,

$$\sin^{-1} NA = \theta_{in}$$

For a graded index, NA is simply the sine of the critical angle:

$$NA = \sin \theta_c \tag{9-14}$$

Example 9-2

For this example refer to Figure 9-15. For a multimode step-index fiber with a glass core ($n_1 = 1.5$) and a fused quartz cladding ($n_2 = 1.46$), determine the critical angle (θ_c), acceptance angle (θ_{in}), and numerical aperture. The source-to-fiber medium is air.

Solution Substituting into Equation 9-6, we have

$$\theta_c = \sin^{-1} \frac{n_2}{n_1} = \sin^{-1} \frac{1.46}{1.5} = 76.7°$$

Substituting into Equation 9-13 yields

$$\theta_c = \sin^{-1} \sqrt{n_1^2 - n_2^2} = \sin^{-1} \sqrt{1.5^2 - 1.46^2} = 20.2°$$

Substituting into Equation 9-14 gives us

$$NA = \sin \theta_{in} = \sin 20.2 = 0.344$$

LOSSES IN OPTICAL FIBER CABLES

Transmission losses in optical fiber cables are one of the most important characteristics of the fiber. Losses in the fiber result in a reduction in the light power and, thus, reduce the system bandwidth, information transmission rate, efficiency, and overall system capacity. The predominant fiber losses are as follows:

1. Absorption losses
2. Material or Rayleigh scattering losses
3. Chromatic or wavelength dispersion
4. Radiation losses
5. Modal dispersion
6. Coupling losses

Absorption Losses

Absorption loss in optical fibers is analogous to power dissipation in copper cables; impurities in the fiber absorb the light and convert it to heat. The ultrapure glass used to manufacture optical fibers is approximately 99.9999% pure. Still, absorption losses between 1 dB/km and 1000 dB/km are typical. Essentially, there are three factors that contribute to the absorption losses in optical fibers: ultraviolet absorption, infrared absorption, and ion resonance absorption.

Ultraviolet absorption.   Ultraviolet absorption is caused by valence electrons in the silica material from which fibers are manufactured. Light *ionizes* the valence electrons into conduction. The ionization is equivalent to a loss in the total light field and, consequently, contributes to the transmission losses of the fiber.

Infrared absorption.   Infrared absorption is a result of *photons* of light that are absorbed by the atoms of the glass core molecules. The absorbed photons are converted to random mechanical vibrations typical of heating.

Ion resonance absorption.   Ion resonance absorption is caused by OH^- ions in the material. The source of the OH^- ions is water molecules that have been trapped in the glass during the manufacturing process. Ion absorption is also caused by iron, copper, and chromium molecules.

Figure 9-18 shows typical losses in optical fiber cables due to ultraviolet, infrared, and ion resonance absorption.

Material or Rayleigh Scattering Losses

During the manufacturing process, glass is drawn into long fibers of very small diameter. During this process, the glass is in a plastic state (not liquid and not solid). The tension applied to the glass during this process causes the cooling glass to develop submicroscopic irregularities that are permanently formed in the fiber. When light rays that are propagating down a fiber strike one of these impurities, they are *diffracted*. Diffraction causes the light to disperse or spread out in many directions. Some of the diffracted light continues down the fiber and some of it escapes through the cladding. The light rays that escape represent a loss in light power. This is called *Rayleigh scattering loss*. Figure 9-19 graphically shows the relationship between wavelength and Rayleigh scattering loss.

Chromatic or Wavelength Dispersion

As stated previously, the refractive index of a material is wavelength dependent. Light-emitting diodes (LEDs) emit light that contains a combination of wavelengths. Each wavelength within the composite light signal travels at a different velocity. Consequently, light rays that are simultaneously emitted from an LED and propagated down an optical fiber do not arrive at the far end of the fiber at the same time. This results in a distorted receive signal; the distortion is called *chromatic distortion*. Chromatic distortion can be eliminated by using a monochromatic source such as an injection laser diode (ILD).

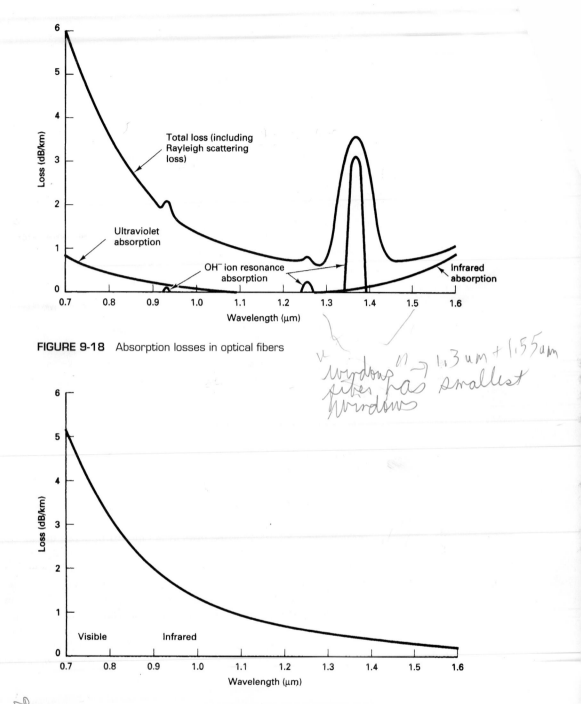

FIGURE 9-18 Absorption losses in optical fibers

(handwritten notes) "windows" → 1.3 um + 1.55 um fiber has smallest windows

FIGURE 9-19 Rayleigh scattering loss as a function of wavelength

Radiation Losses

Radiation losses are caused by small bends and kinks in the fiber. Essentially, there are two types of bends: microbends and constant-radius bends. *Microbending* occurs as a result of differences in the thermal contraction rates between the core and cladding material. A microbend represents a discontinuity in the fiber where Rayleigh scattering can occur. *Constant-radius bends* occur when fibers are bent during handling or installation.

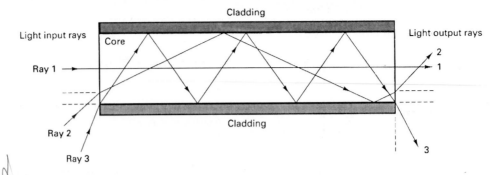

Cladding

Light input rays

Core   Light output rays

Ray 1 →   2
                                           1

Cladding

Ray 2 ↗

Ray 3   ↘ 3

FIGURE 9-20 Light propagation down a multimode step-index fiber

Light input rays	Cladding	Light output rays
Ray 1	Core	1
Ray 2		2
Ray 3		3
	Cladding	

FIGURE 9-21 Light propagation down a single-mode step-index fiber

Modal Dispersion

Modal dispersion or *pulse spreading* is caused by the difference in the propagation times of light rays that take different paths down a fiber. Obviously, modal dispersion can occur only in multimode fibers. It can be reduced considerably by using graded-index fibers and almost entirely eliminated by using single-mode step-index fibers.

Modal dispersion can cause a pulse of light energy to spread out as it propagates down a fiber. If the pulse spreading is sufficiently severe, one pulse may fall back on top of the next pulse (this is an example of intersymbol interference). In a multimode step-index fiber, a light ray that propagates straight down the axis of the fiber takes the least amount of time to travel the length of the fiber. A light ray that strikes the core/cladding interface at the critical angle will undergo the largest number of internal reflections and, consequently, take the longest time to travel the length of the fiber.

Figure 9-20 shows three rays of light propagating down a multimode step-index fiber. The lowest-order mode (ray 1) travels in a path parallel to the axis of the fiber. The middle-order mode (ray 2) bounces several times at the interface before traveling the length of the fiber. The highest-order mode (ray 3) makes many trips back and forth across the fiber as it propagates the entire length. It can be seen that ray 3 travels a considerably longer distance than ray 1 as it propagates down the fiber. Consequently, if the three rays of light were emitted into the fiber at the same time and represented a pulse of light energy, the three rays would reach the far end of the fiber at different times and result in a spreading out of the light energy in respect to time. This is called modal dispersion and results in a stretched pulse that is also reduced in amplitude at the output of the fiber. All three rays of light propagate through the same material at the same velocity, but ray 3 must travel a longer distance and, consequently, takes a longer period of time to propagate down the fiber.

Figure 9-21 shows light rays propagating down a single-mode step-index fiber. Because the radial dimension of the fiber is sufficiently small, there is only a single path for each of the rays to follow as they propagate down the length of the fiber. Consequently, each ray of light travels the same distance in a given period of time and the light rays have exactly the same time relationship at the far end of the fiber as they had when they entered the cable. The result is no *modal dispersion* or *pulse stretching*.

FIGURE 9-22 Light propagation down a multimode graded-index fiber

FIGURE 9-23 Pulse-width dispersion in an optical fiber cable

Figure 9-22 shows light propagating down a multimode graded-index fiber. Three rays are shown traveling in three different modes. Each ray travels a different path but they all take approximately the same amount of time to propagate the length of fiber. This is because the refractive index of the fiber decreases with distance from the center, and the velocity at which a ray travels is inversely proportional to the refractive index. Consequently, the farther rays 2 and 3 travel from the center of the fiber, the faster they propagate.

Figure 9-23 shows the relative time/energy relationship of a pulse of light as it propagates down a fiber cable. It can be seen that as the pulse propagates down the fiber, the light rays that make up the pulse spread out in time, which causes a corresponding reduction in the pulse amplitude and stretching of the pulse width. This is called *pulse spreading* or *pulse-width dispersion* and causes errors in digital transmission. It can also be seen that as light energy from one pulse falls back in time, it will interfere with the next pulse causing intersymbol interference.

Figure 9-24a shows a unipolar return-to-zero (UPRZ) digital transmission. With UPRZ transmission (assuming a very narrow pulse) if light energy from pulse A were to fall back (*spread*) one bit time (t_b), it would interfere with pulse B and change what was a logic 0 to a logic 1. Figure 9-24b shows a unipolar nonreturn-to-zero (UPNRZ) digital

Losses in Optical Fiber Cables

381

FIGURE 9-24 Pulse spreading of digital transmissions: (a) UPRZ; (b) UPNRZ

transmission where each pulse is equal to the bit time. With UPNRZ transmission, if energy from pulse A were to fall back one-half of a bit time, it would interfere with pulse B. Consequently, UPRZ transmissions can tolerate twice as much delay or spread as UPNRZ transmissions.

The difference between the absolute delay times of the fastest and slowest rays of light propagating down a fiber of unit length is called the *pulse-spreading constant* (Δt) and is generally expressed in nanoseconds per kilometer (ns/km). The total pulse spread (ΔT) is then equal to the pulse spreading constant (Δt) times the total fiber length (L). Mathematically, ΔT is

$$\Delta T_{(ns)} = \Delta t_{(ns/km)} \times L_{(km)} \qquad (9\text{-}15)$$

For UPRZ transmissions, the maximum data transmission rate in bits per second (bps) is expressed as

$$f_{b(bps)} = \frac{1}{\Delta t \times L} \qquad (9\text{-}16)$$

and for UPNRZ transmissions, the maximum transmission rate is

$$f_{b(bps)} = \frac{1}{2\,\Delta t \times L} \qquad (9\text{-}17)$$

Example 9-3

For an optical fiber 10 km long with a pulse-spreading constant of 5 ns/km, determine the maximum digital transmission rates for

(a) Return-to-zero.
(b) Nonreturn-to-zero transmissions.

Solution   (a) Substituting into Equation 9-16 yields

$$f_b = \frac{1}{5 \text{ ns/km} \times 10 \text{ km}} = 20 \text{ Mbps}$$

(b) Substituting into Equation 9-17 yields

$$f_b = \frac{1}{(2 \times 5 \text{ ns/km}) \times 10 \text{ km}} = 10 \text{ Mbps}$$

The results indicate that the digital transmission rate possible for this optical fiber is twice as high (20 Mbps versus 10 Mbps) for UPRZ as for UPNRZ transmission.

Coupling Losses

In fiber cables coupling losses can occur at any of the following three types of optical junctions: light source-to-fiber connections, fiber-to-fiber connections, and fiber-to-photodetector connections. Junction losses are most often caused by one of the following alignment problems: lateral misalignment, gap misalignment, angular misalignment, and imperfect surface finishes. These impairments are shown in Figure 9-25.

    Lateral misalignment.   This is shown in Figure 9-25a and is the lateral or axial displacement between two pieces of adjoining fiber cables. The amount of loss can be from a couple of tenths of a decibel to several decibels. This loss is generally negligible if the fiber axes are aligned to within 5% of the smaller fiber's diameter.

    Gap misalignment.   This is shown in Figure 9-25b and is sometimes called *end separation*. When *splices* are made in optical fibers, the fibers should actually touch. The farther apart the fibers are, the greater the loss of light. If two fibers are joined with a connector, the ends should not touch. This is because the two ends rubbing against each other in the connector could cause damage to either or both fibers.

    Angular misalignment.   This is shown in Figure 9-25c and is sometimes called *angular displacement*. If the angular displacement is less than 2°, the loss will be less than 0.5 dB.

    Imperfect surface finish.   This is shown in Figure 9-25d. The ends of the two adjoining fibers should be highly polished and fit together squarely. If the fiber ends are less than 3° off from perpendicular, the losses will be less than 0.5 dB.

LIGHT SOURCES

Essentially, there are two devices commonly used to generate light for fiber optic communications systems: light-emitting diodes (LEDs) and injection laser diodes (ILDs). Both devices have advantages and disadvantages and selection of one device over the other is determined by system economic and performance requirements.

Light-Emitting Diodes

Essentially, a *light-emitting diode* (LED) is simply a P-N junction diode. It is usually made from a semiconductor material such as aluminum-gallium-arsenide (AlGaAs) or gallium-arsenide-phosphide (GaAsP). LEDs emit light by spontaneous emission; light is emitted as a result of the recombination of electrons and holes. When forward biased, minority carriers are injected across the *p-n* junction. Once across the junction, these

FIGURE 9-25 Fiber alignment impairments: (a) lateral misalignment; (b) gap displacement; (c) angular misalignment; (d) surface finish

minority carriers recombine with majority carriers and give up energy in the form of light. This process is essentially the same as in a conventional diode except that in LEDs certain semiconductor materials and dopants are chosen such that the process is radiative; a photon is produced. A photon is a quantum of electromagnetic wave energy. Photons are particles that travel at the speed of light but at rest have no mass. In conventional semiconductor diodes (germanium and silicon, for example), the process is primarily nonradiative and no photons are generated. The energy gap of the material used to construct an LED determines whether the light emitted by it is invisible or visible and of what color.

The simplest LED structures are homojunction, epitaxially grown, or single-diffused devices and are shown in Figure 9-26. *Epitaxially grown LEDs* are generally constructed of silicon-doped gallium-arsenide (Figure 9-26a). A typical wavelength of light emitted from this construction is 940 nm, and a typical output power is approximately 3 mW at 100 mA of forward current. *Planar diffused (homojunction) LEDs* (Figure 9-26b) output approximately 500 μW at a wavelength of 900 nm. The primary disadvantage of homojunction LEDs is the nondirectionality of their light emission, which makes them a poor choice as a light source for fiber optic systems.

The *planar heterojunction LED* (Figure 9-27) is quite similar to the epitaxially grown LED except that the geometry is designed such that the forward current is

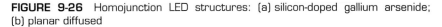

FIGURE 9-26 Homojunction LED structures: (a) silicon-doped gallium arsenide; (b) planar diffused

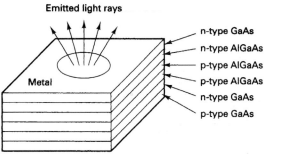

FIGURE 9-27 Planar heterojunction LED

concentrated to a very small area of the active layer. Because of this, the planar heterojunction LED has several advantages over the homojunction type. They are

1. The increase in current density generates a more brilliant light spot.
2. The smaller emitting area makes it easier to couple its emitted light into a fiber.
3. The small effective area has a smaller capacitance, which allows the planar heterojunction LED to be used at higher speeds.

Burrus etched-well surface-emitting LED. For the more practical applications, such as telecommunications, data rates in excess of 100 Mbps are required. For these applications, the etched-well LED was developed. Burrus and Dawson of Bell Laboratories developed the etched-well LED. It is a surface-emitting LED and is shown in Figure 9-28. The Burrus etched-well LED emits light in many directions. The etched well helps concentrate the emitted light to a very small area. Also, domed lenses can be placed over the emitting surface to direct the light into a smaller area. These devices are more efficient than the standard surface emitters and they allow more power to be coupled into the optical fiber, but they are also more difficult and expensive to manufacture.

Edge-emitting LED. The edge-emitting LED, which was developed by RCA, is shown in Figure 9-29. These LEDs emit a more directional light pattern than do the surface-emitting LEDs. The construction is similar to the planar and Burrus diodes except that the emitting surface is a stripe rather than a confined circular area. The light is emitted from an active stripe and forms an elliptical beam. Surface-emitting LEDs are more commonly used than edge emitters because they emit more light. However, the coupling losses with surface emitters are greater and they have narrower bandwidths.

The *radiant* light power emitted from an LED is a linear function of the forward current passing through the device (Figure 9-30). It can also be seen that the optical output power of an LED is, in part, a function of the operating temperature.

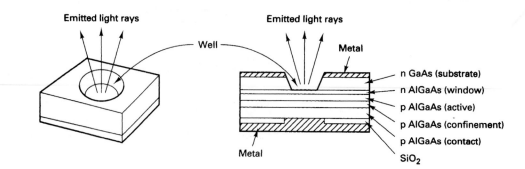

FIGURE 9-28 Burrus etched-well surface-emitting LED

FIGURE 9-29 Edge-emitting LED

FIGURE 9-30 Output power versus forward current and operating temperature for an LED

Injection Laser Diode

Lasers are constructed from many different materials, including gases, liquids, and solids, although the type of laser used most often for fiber optic communications is the semiconductor laser.

The *injection laser diode* (ILD) is similar to the LED. In fact, below a certain threshold current, an ILD acts similarly to an LED. Above the threshold current, an ILD oscillates; lasing occurs. As current passes through a forward-biased *p-n* junction diode, light is emitted by spontaneous emission at a frequency determined by the energy gap of the semiconductor material. When a particular current level is reached, the number of minority carriers and photons produced on either side of the *p-n* junction reaches a level

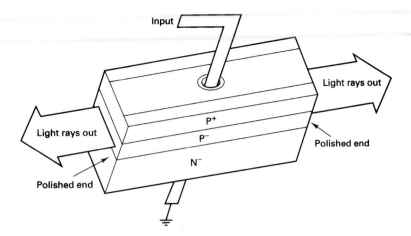

FIGURE 9-31 Injection laser diode construction

FIGURE 9-32 Output power versus forward current and temperature for an ILD

where they begin to collide with already excited minority carriers. This causes an increase in the ionization energy level and makes the carriers unstable. When this happens, a typical carrier recombines with an opposite type of carrier at an energy level that is above its normal before-collision value. In the process, two photons are created; one is stimulated by another. Essentially, a gain in the number of photons is realized. For this to happen, a large forward current that can provide many carriers (holes and electrons) is required.

The construction of an ILD is similar to that of an LED (Figure 9-31) except that the ends are highly polished. The mirror-like ends trap the photons in the active region and, as they reflect back and forth, stimulate free electrons to recombine with holes at a higher-than-normal energy level. This process is called *lasing*.

The radiant output light power of a typical ILD is shown in Figure 9-32. It can be seen that very little output power is realized until the threshold current is reached; then lasing occurs. After lasing begins, the optical output power increases dramatically, with small increases in drive current. It can also be seen that the magnitude of the optical output power of the ILD is more dependent on operating temperature than is the LED.

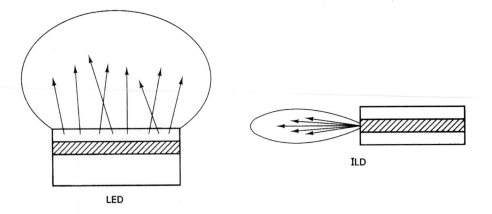

FIGURE 9-33 LED and ILD radiation patterns

Figure 9-33 shows the light radiation patterns typical of an LED and an ILD. Because light is radiated out the end of an ILD in a narrow concentrated beam, it has a more direct radiation pattern.

Advantages of ILDs

1. Because ILDs have a more direct radiation pattern, it is easier to couple their light into an optical fiber. This reduces the coupling losses and allows smaller fibers to be used.

2. The radiant output power from an ILD is greater than that for an LED. A typical output power for an ILD is 5 mW (7 dBm) and 0.5 mW (−3 dBm) for LEDs. This allows ILDs to provide a higher drive power and to be used for systems that operate over longer distances.

3. ILDs can be used at higher bit rates than can LEDs.

4. ILDs generate monochromatic light, which reduces chromatic or wavelength dispersion.

Disadvantages of ILDs

1. ILDs are typically on the order of 10 times more expensive than LEDs.

2. Because ILDs operate at higher powers, they typically have a much shorter lifetime than LEDs.

3. IDLs are more temperature dependent than LEDs.

LIGHT DETECTORS

There are two devices that are commonly used to detect light energy in fiber optic communications receivers; PIN (p-type-intrinsic-n-type) diodes and APD (avalanche photodiodes).

PIN Diodes

A *PIN diode* is a *depletion-layer photodiode* and is probably the most common device used as a light detector in fiber optic communications systems. Figure 9-34 shows the basic construction of a PIN diode. A very lightly doped (almost pure or intrinsic) layer of *n*-type semiconductor material is sandwiched between the junction of the two heavily doped *n*- and *p*-type contact areas. Light enters the device through a very small window and falls on the carrier-void intrinsic material. The intrinsic material is made thick enough so that most of the photons that enter the device are absorbed by this layer. Essentially, the PIN photodiode operates just the opposite of an LED. Most of the photons are

FIGURE 9-34   PIN photodiode construction

absorbed by electrons in the valence band of the intrinsic material. When the photons are absorbed, they add sufficient energy to generate carriers in the depletion region and allow current to flow through the device.

Photoelectric effect.   Light entering through the window of a PIN diode is absorbed by the intrinsic material and adds enough energy to cause electronics to move from the valence band into the conduction band. The increase in the number of electrons that move into the conduction band is matched by an increase in the number of holes in the valence band. To cause current to flow in a photodiode, light of sufficient energy must be absorbed to give valence electrons enough energy to jump the energy gap. The energy gap for silicon is 1.12 eV (electron volts). Mathematically, the operation is as follows.

For silicon, the energy gap (E_g) equals 1.12 eV:

$$1 \text{ eV} = 1.6 \times 10^{-19} \text{ J}$$

Thus, the energy gap for silicon is

$$E_g = (1.12 \text{ eV})\left(1.6 \times 10^{-19} \frac{\text{J}}{\text{eV}}\right) = 1.792 \times 10^{-19} \text{ J}$$

and   energy $(E) = hf$

where h = Planck's constant = 6.6256×10^{-34} J/Hz
         f = frequency (Hz)

Rearranging and solving for f yields

$$f = \frac{E}{h}$$

For a silicon photodiode,

$$f = \frac{1.792 \times 10^{-19} \text{ J}}{6.6256 \times 10^{-34} \text{ J/Hz}} = 2.705 \times 10^{14} \text{ Hz}$$

Converting to wavelength yields

$$\lambda = \frac{c}{f} = \frac{3 \times 10^8 \text{ m/s}}{2.705 \times 10^{14} \text{ Hz}} = 1109 \text{ nm/cycle}$$

Consequently, light wavelengths of 1109 nm or shorter, or light frequencies of 2.705×10^{14} Hz or higher, are required to cause enough electrons to jump the energy gap of a silicon photodiode.

Light Detectors

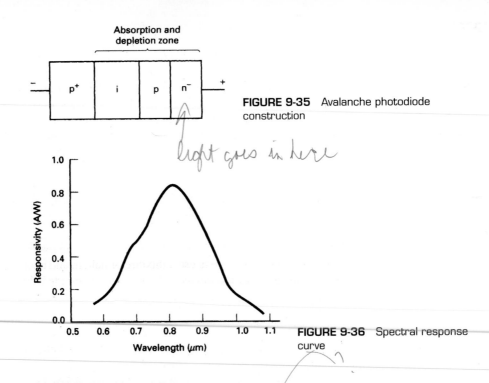

FIGURE 9-35 Avalanche photodiode construction

light goes in here

FIGURE 9-36 Spectral response curve

Avalanche Photodiodes

Figure 9-35 shows the basic construction of an *avalanche photodiode* (APD). An APD is a *pipn* structure. Light enters the diode and is absorbed by the thin, heavily doped *n*-layer. A high electric field intensity developed across the *i-p-n* junction by reverse-bias causes impact ionization to occur. During impact ionization, a carrier can gain sufficient energy to ionize other bound electrons. These ionized carriers, in turn, cause more ionizations to occur. The process continues as in an avalanche and is, effectively, equivalent to an internal gain or carrier multiplication. Consequently, APDs are more sensitive than PIN diodes and require less additional amplification. The disadvantages of APDs are relatively long transit times and additional internally generated noise due to the avalanche multiplication factor.

Characteristics of Light Detectors

The most important characteristics of light detectors are

1. *Responsivity.* Responsivity is a measure of the conversion efficiency of a photodetector. It is the ratio of the output current of a photodiode to the input optical power and has the unit of amperes/watt. Responsivity is generally given for a particular wavelength or frequency.

2. *Dark current.* Dark current is the leakage current that flows through a photodiode with no light input. Dark current is caused by thermally generated carriers in the diode.

3. *Transit time.* Transit time is the time it takes a light-induced carrier to travel across the depletion region. This parameter determines the maximum bit rate possible with a particular photodiode.

4. *Spectral response.* Spectral response is the range of wavelength values that can be used for a given photodiode. Generally, relative spectral response is graphed as a function of wavelength or frequency. Figure 9-36 is an illustrative example of a spectral response curve. It can be seen that this particular photodiode more efficiently absorbs energy in the range 800 nm to 820 nm.

Laser technology deals with the concentration of light into very small, powerful beams. The acronym was chosen when technology shifted from microwaves to light waves.

The first layer was developed by Theodore H. Maiman, a scientist who worked for Hughes Aircraft Company in California. Maiman directed a beam of light into ruby crystals with a xenon flashlamp and measured emitted radiation from the ruby. He discovered that when the emitted radiation increased beyond threshold it caused emitted radiation to become extremely intense and highly directional. Uranium lasers were developed in 1960 along with other rare-earth materials. Also in 1960, A. Javin of Bell Laboratories developed the helium laser. Semiconductor lasers (injection laser diodes) were manufactured in 1962 by General Electric, IBM, and Lincoln Laboratories.

Laser Types

Basically, there are four types of lasers: gas, liquid, solid, and semiconductor.

1. *Gas lasers.* Gas lasers use a mixture of helium and neon enclosed in a glass tube. A flow of coherent (one frequency) light waves is emitted through the output coupler when an electric current is discharged into the gas. The continuous light-wave output is monochromatic (one color).

2. *Liquid lasers.* Liquid lasers use organic dyes enclosed in a glass tube for an active medium. Dye is circulated into the tube with a pump. A powerful pulse of light excites the organic dye.

3. *Solid lasers.* Solid lasers use a solid, cylindrical crystal, such as ruby, for the active medium. Each end of the ruby is polished and parallel. The ruby is excited by a tungsten lamp tied to an alternating-current power supply. The output from the laser is a continuous wave.

4. *Semiconductor lasers.* Semiconductor lasers are made from semiconductor *p-n* junctions and are commonly called *injection laser diodes* (ILDs). The excitation mechanism is a direct-current power supply that controls the amount of current to the active medium. The output light from an ILD is easily modulated, making it very useful in many electronic communications applications.

Laser Characteristics

All types of lasers have several common characteristics: (1) they all use an active material to convert energy into laser light, (2) a pumping source to provide power or energy, (3) optics to direct the beam through the active material to be amplified, (4) optics to direct the beam into a narrow powerful cone of divergence, (5) a feedback mechanism to provide continuous operation, and (6) an output coupler to transmit power out of the laser.

The radiation of a laser is extremely intense and directional. When focused into a fine hairlike beam, it can concentrate all its power into the narrow beam. If the beam of light were allowed to diverge, it would lose most of its power.

Laser Construction

Figure 9-37 shows the construction of a basic laser. A power source is connected to a flashtube that is coiled around a glass tube that holds the active medium. One end of the glass tube is a polished mirror face for 100% internal reflection. The flashtube is energized by a trigger pulse and produces a high-level burst of light (similar to a flashbulb). The flash causes the chromium atoms within the active crystalline structure to become excited. The process of pumping raises the level of the chromium atoms from ground state to an excited energy state. The ions then decay, falling to an intermediate energy level. When the population of ions in the intermediate level is greater than the

FIGURE 9-37 Laser construction

ground state, a population inversion occurs. The population inversion causes laser action (lasing) to occur. After a period of time, the excited chromium atoms will fall to the ground energy level. At this time, photons are emitted. A photon is a packet of radiant energy. The emitted photons strike atoms and two other photons are emitted (hence, the term "stimulated emission"). The frequency of the energy determines the strength of the photons; higher frequencies cause greater strength photons.

Laser Applications

Since its inception, lasers have become commonly used devices for both commercial and industrial applications. Lasers are used in electronics communications, holography, medicine, direction finding, and manufacturing.

In electronics communications, lasers are used in audio, radio, and television transmission. Laser beams have a very narrow bandwidth and they are also highly directional. Modulated light is a necessity for optical fiber applications. In medicine, ruby lasers are used for precise applications such as eye surgery. Argon ion lasers are replacing scalpels. The military uses lasers for distance measuring and surveying. In manufacturing, the laser is used for holography to detect stains and measure irregular objects. High-power lasers are used to cut reams of cloth and drill fine holes. Because of its narrow beamwidth, laser can be used to cut fabric within the accuracy of a single thread. There is really no end in sight for the application for lasers.

QUESTIONS

9-1. Define a fiber optic system.

9-2. What is the relationship between information capacity and bandwidth?

9-3. What development in 1951 was a substantial breakthrough in the field of fiber optics? In 1960? In 1970?

9-4. Contrast the advantages and disadvantages of fiber optic cables and metallic cables.

9-5. Outline the primary building blocks of a fiber optic system.

9-6. Contrast glass and plastic fiber cables.

9-7. Briefly describe the construction of a fiber optic cable.

9-8. Define the following terms: velocity of propagation, refraction, and refractive index.

9-9. State Snell's law for refraction and outline its significance in fiber optic cables.

9-10. Define *critical angle.*

9-11. Describe what is meant by mode of operation; by index profile.

9-12. Describe a step-index fiber cable; a graded-index cable.

9-13. Contrast the advantages and disadvantages of step-index, graded-index, single-mode propagation, and multimode propagation.

9-14. Why is single-mode propagation impossible with graded-index fibers?

9-15. Describe the source-to-fiber aperture.

9-16. What are the acceptance angle and the acceptance cone for a fiber cable?

9-17. Define *numerical aperture.*

9-18. List and briefly describe the losses associated with fiber cables.

9-19. What is *pulse spreading?*

9-20. Define *pulse spreading constant.*

9-21. List and briefly describe the various coupling losses.

9-22. Briefly describe the operation of a light-emitting diode.

9-23. What are the two primary types of LEDs?

9-24. Briefly describe the operation of an injection laser diode.

9-25. What is lasing?

9-26. Contrast the advantages and disadvantages of ILDs and LEDs.

9-27. Briefly describe the function of a photodiode.

9-28. Describe the photoelectric effect.

9-29. Explain the difference between a PIN diode and an APD.

9-30. List and describe the primary characteristics of light detectors.

PROBLEMS

9-1. Determine the wavelengths in nanometers and angstroms for the following light frequencies.
(a) 3.45×10^{14} Hz
(b) 3.62×10^{14} Hz
(c) 3.21×10^{14} Hz

9-2. Determine the light frequency for the following wavelengths.
(a) 670 nm
(b) 7800 Å
(c) 710 nm

9-3. For a glass ($n_1 = 1.5$)/quartz ($n_2 = 1.38$) interface and an angle of incidence of 35°, determine the angle of refraction.

9-4. Determine the critical angle for the fiber described in Problem 9-3.

9-5. Determine the acceptance angle for the cable described in Problem 9-3.

9-6. Determine the numerical aperture for the cable described in Problem 9-3.

9-7. Determine the maximum bit rate for RZ and NRZ encoding for the following pulse-spreading constants and cable lengths.
(a) $\Delta t = 10$ ns/m, $L = 100$ m
(b) $\Delta t = 20$ ns/m, $L = 1000$ m
(c) $\Delta t = 2000$ ns/km, $L = 2$ km

9-8. Determine the lowest light frequency that can be detected by a photodiode with an energy gap = 1.2 eV.

9-9. Determine the wavelengths in nanometers and angstroms for the following light frequencies:
(a) 3.8×10^{14} Hz
(b) 3.2×10^{14} Hz
(c) 3.5×10^{14} Hz

9-10. Determine the light frequencies for the following wavelengths:
(a) 650 nm
(b) 7200 Å
(c) 690 nm

9-11. For a glass ($n = 1.5$)/quartz ($n = 1.41$) interface and an angle of incidence of 38°, determine the angle of refraction.

9-12. Determine the critical angle for the fiber described in Problem 9-11.

9-13. Determine the acceptance angle for the cable described in Problem 9-11.

9-14. Determine the numerical aperture for the cable described in Problem 9-11.

9-15. Determine the maximum bit rate for RZ and NRZ encoding for the following pulse spreading constants and cable lengths.
   (a) $\Delta t = 14$ ns/m, $L = 200$ m
   (b) $\Delta t = 10$ ns/m, $L = 50$ m
   (c) $\Delta t = 20$ ns/m, $L = 200$ m

9-16. Determine the lowest light frequency that can be detected by a photodiode with an energy gap $= 1.25$ eV.

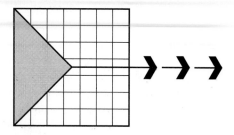

Solutions to Selected Problems

CHAPTER 1

1-1. 16 kHz = B 4000 = Baud

1-2. 3 kbps

1-6. The inputs to the I balanced modulator are sin ($\omega_c t$) and either + or −1 V. The inputs to the Q balanced modulator are −cos ($\omega_c t$) and either + or −1 V. The truth table for the I and Q channels is

Q	I	I	Q	Output Phase
0	0	$-\sin \omega_c t$	$+\cos \omega_c t$	$+135°$
0	1	$+\sin \omega_c t$	$+\cos \omega_c t$	$+45°$
1	0	$-\sin \omega_c t$	$-\cos \omega_c t$	$-135°$
1	1	$+\sin \omega_c t$	$-\cos \omega_c t$	$-45°$

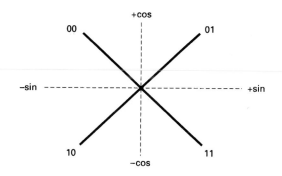

1-7. $I = [\sin(\omega_c t) - \cos(\omega_c t)][\sin(\omega_c t)]$

$I = \sin^2(\omega_c t)$

$I = \dfrac{1}{2}[1 - \cos(2\omega_c t)] = \dfrac{1}{2} = \text{logic } 1$

$$Q = [\sin(\omega_c t) - \cos(\omega_c t)][\cos(\omega_c t)]$$

$$Q = -\cos^2(\omega_c t)$$

$$Q = -\frac{1}{2}[1 - \cos(2\omega_c t)] = -\frac{1}{2} = \text{logic } 0$$

1-8. With an 8-PSK modulator, the baud is equal to one-third of the input bit rate.

$$\text{Baud} = \frac{f_b}{3} = \frac{20 \text{ Mbps}}{3} = 6.667 \text{ Megabaud}$$

With 8-PSK, the minimum bandwidth is equal to the baud, therefore, $B = 6.667$ MHz

1-9.

I	C	2-4 Level Converter	Carrier Input	Product Detector Output
0	0	-0.541	cos	-0.541 cos
0	1	-1.307	cos	-1.307 cos
1	0	+0.541	cos	+0.541 cos
1	1	+1.307	cos	+1.307 cos

Q	C	2-4 Level Converter	Carrier Input	Product Detector Output
0	0	-1.307	-sin	+1.307 sin
0	1	-0.541	-sin	+0.541 sin
1	0	+1.307	-sin	-1.307 sin
1	1	+0.541	-sin	-0.541 sin

Q	I input	C	Modulator Output Expression	Phase
0	0	0	-0.541 cos + 1.307 sin	-22.5°
0	0	1	-1.307 cos + 0.541 sin	-67.5°
0	1	0	+0.541 cos + 1.307 sin	+22.5°
0	1	1	+1.307 cos + 0.541 sin	+67.5°
1	0	0	-0.541 cos - 1.307 sin	-157.5°
1	0	1	-1.307 cos - 0.541 sin	-112.5°
1	1	0	+0.541 cos - 1.307 sin	+157.5°
1	1	1	+1.307 cos - 0.541 sin	+112.5°

1-10 With 16-QAM, the baud and minimum Nyquist frequency are both equal to $f_b/4$.

$$\text{Baud} = \frac{20 \text{ Mbps}}{4} = 5 \text{ Megabaud} \qquad f_N = \frac{20 \text{ Mbps}}{4} = 5 \text{MHz}$$

1-11.

I	I'	Output	Q	Q'	Output
0	0	−0.220	0	0	−0.220
0	1	−0.821	0	1	−0.821
1	0	+0.220	1	0	+0.220
1	1	+0.821	1	1	+0.821

Q	Q'	I	I'	16-QAM Output Expression	Phase
0	0	0	0	$+0.220 \sin - 0.220 \cos$	$-45°$
1	1	1	1	$-0.821 \sin + 0.821 \cos$	$+135°$
1	0	1	0	$-0.821 \sin + 0.220 \cos$	$+135°$
0	1	0	1	$+0.821 \sin - 0.220 \cos$	$-45°$

1-12. **a.** QPSK = 2 bps/Hz   **b.** 8-PSK = 3 bps/Hz   **c.** 16-QAM = 4 bps/Hz

1-13. Input data   0 0 1 1 0 0 1 1 0 1 0 1 0 1
XNOR out   1 0 1 1 1 0 1 1 1 0 0 1 1 0 0

1-14. **a.** The carrier power is

$$C_{(dBm)} = 10 \log \frac{(10^{-13})}{0.001} = -100 \text{ dBm} \quad N_{(dBm)} = 10 \log \frac{(0.06 \times 10^{-15})}{0.001} = -132.2 \text{ dBm}$$

c. The noise power density is

$$N_0 = N_{(dBm)} - B_{(dB)} = -132.2 \text{ dBm} - 10 \log(60000) = -180 \text{ dBm}$$

d. The energy-per-bit is

$$E_{b(dBJ)} = 10 \log \frac{(10^{-13})}{30000} = -174.77 \text{ dBJ}$$

e. The carrier-to-noise ratio is

$$\frac{C}{N} (dB) = 10 \log \frac{(10^{-13})}{(0.06 \times 10^{-15})} = 32.23 \text{ dB}$$

f. The energy-per-bit-to-noise density ratio is

$$\frac{E_b}{N_0}(dB) = \frac{C}{N} + 10 \log \frac{B}{f_b} = 32.23 \text{ dB} + 10 \log \frac{60000}{30000} = 35.23 \text{ dB}$$

1-15. The minimum E_b/N_0 for a $P(e)$ of 10^{-6} is 14 dB. Therefore,

$$14 \text{ dB} = 11 \text{ dB} + 10 \log \frac{B}{20 \text{ Mbps}} \qquad 3 \text{ dB} = 10 \log \frac{B}{20 \text{ Mbps}}$$

$$B = 10^{-0.3}(20000000) = 40 \text{ MHz}$$

CHAPTER 2

2-1.

	D	A	T	A	Sp	C	O	M	M	U	N	I	C	A	T	I	O	N	S	ETX	BSC
b_0	0	1	0	1	0	1	1	1	1	1	0	1	1	1	0	1	1	0	1	1	0
b_1	0	0	0	0	0	1	1	0	0	0	1	0	1	0	0	0	1	1	1	1	0
b_2	1	0	1	0	0	0	1	1	1	1	1	0	0	0	1	0	1	1	0	0	0
b_3	0	0	0	0	0	0	1	1	1	0	1	1	0	0	0	1	1	1	0	0	0
b_4	0	0	1	0	0	0	0	0	0	1	0	0	0	0	1	0	0	0	1	0	0
b_5	0	0	0	0	1	0	0	0	0	0	0	0	0	0	0	0	0	0	0	0	1
b_6	1	1	1	1	0	1	1	1	1	1	1	1	1	1	1	1	1	1	1	0	0
VRC	1	1	0	1	0	0	0	1	1	1	1	0	0	1	0	0	0	1	1	1	1

2-2. $G(X) = X^7 + X^4 + X^2 + X^0 = 10010101$

$P(X) = X^5 + X^4 + X^1 + X^0 = 110011$

$G(X) \times P(X) = X^{12} + X^9 + X^7 + X^5$

$G(X) \times P(X) = 1001010100000$

2-3. A single ASCII character has seven bits. The minimum number of Hamming bits required for a particular code is determined from the following formula:

$2^N \geq M + N + 1$ where M = number of data bits per word

N = number of Hamming bits per word

Substituting into the above equation will yield the minimum number of Hamming bits.

First try 3 Hamming bits: $2^3 \geq 7 + 3 + 1$ $8 \geq 11$ (No)

Next try 4 Hamming bits: $2^4 \geq 7 + 4 + 1$ $16 \geq 12$ (Yes)

2-4. ASCII character B = 42H = 1000010 binary and from $2^N \geq M + N + 1$, four Hamming bits are required for each character. Therefore, the encoded character will have the following format:

bit position	11	10	9	8	7	6	5	4	3	2	1
	H	1	H	0	H	0	H	0	0	1	0

To determine the logic conditions of the Hamming bits, XOR all bit positions that contain a logic 1.

bit 2	0010
bit 10	1010
XOR	1000 = Hamming code

The encoded ASCII character B will have the following bit sequence:

bit position	11	10	9	8	7	6	5	4	3	2	1
code	1	1	0	0	0	0	0	0	0	1	0

CHAPTER 3

3-1.

	b_0	b_1	b_2	b_3	b_4	b_5	b_6	b_7
B8H	1	0	1	1	1	0	0	0

nr = 5 poll ns = 4 I-frame

confirms reception of frames through 4

the number of the frame currently being transmitted

3-2.

	b_0	b_1	b_2	b_3	b_4	b_5	b_6	b_7
31H	0	0	1	1	0	0	0	1

nr = 1 final ready to supervisory

confirms reception of frames through 0

receive frame

3-3. 1110001000011111 11110011111 0100111101011111 11111 1001011

         0   0   0   0
         └───────────────┴───── inserted zeros ─────┴──────┘

3-4. 0101111101000110111110111011101011111010101110001111100

          *   *   *   *
          └──────────────┴── deleted zeros ─┴──────────────┘

3-5.

Input

Output

CHAPTER 4

4-1. $f_s \geq 2f_a$ where f_s = Nyquist sample rate, f_a = sampled signal

a. $f_s \geq 2(4 \text{ kHz}) \geq 8 \text{ kHz}$ **b.** $f_s \geq 2(10 \text{ kHz}) \geq 20 \text{ kHz}$

4-2. $C_{max} = \dfrac{i\,dt}{dv}$ or $C_{max} = \dfrac{\tau}{R}$

$$C_{max} = \frac{(20\text{ mA})(10\ \mu s)}{10\text{ V}} = 0.02\ \mu F = \frac{10\ \mu s}{4(40)} = 0.62\ \mu F$$

The smaller value of C_{max} must be used to satisfy both conditions.

4-3. $f_s \geq 2f_a$ where f_s = Nyquist sample rate, f_a = sampled signal
20 kHz $\geq 2f_a$; therefore, f_a must be 10 kHz or less.

4-4. The alias frequency equals the second harmonic of the sample frequency minus the modulating signal frequency. For this problem, the second harmonic frequency is 8 kHz and the modulating signal frequency is 1.5 kHz. Therefore, there is no alias frequency because 8 kHz − 1.5 kHz = 6.5 kHz, which does not fall within the modulating signal frequency range of 0 kHz to 4 kHz.

4-5. DR = $2^n - 1$ where n is the number of magnitude bits
DR = $2^9 - 1 = 511$ 20 log 511 = 54 dB

4-6. 80 dB is an absolute factor of 10,000 for DR. n is determined from the following formula:

$$n = \frac{\log(DR - 1)}{\log 2} = \frac{\log 9{,}999}{\log 2} = 13.21$$

Therefore, 13.21 is rounded up to 14 magnitude bits. However, the sign bit is used for calculating the coding efficiency. Coding efficiency is determined from the following formula:

$$\text{coding efficiency} = \frac{\text{minimum number of bits}}{\text{actual number of bits}} \times 100 = \frac{14.21}{15} \times 100 = 94.73\%$$

4-7. **a.** −2.12 V   **b.** −0.12 V   **c.** +0.04 V   **d.** −2.52 V   **e.** +0 V

4-8. Signal-to-quantization noise ratio is determined from the following formula:

$$SQR = \frac{v^2}{q^2/12} = \frac{v^2}{(0.2)^2/12} = 1200$$

$$SQR_{(dB)} = 10\log 1200 = 30.8\text{ dB} \quad \text{or} \quad SQR_{(dB)} = 10.8\text{ dB} + 20\log\frac{2}{0.2} = 30.8\text{ dB}$$

4-9. Resolution $= \dfrac{V_{max}}{2^n - 1} = \dfrac{1.27}{2^7 - 1} = 0.01$ V

Quantization error $= \dfrac{\text{resolution}}{2} = \dfrac{0.01}{2} = 0.005$ V

4-10. **a.** The 12-bit liner code is determined as follows:

$$12\text{-bit linear code} = \frac{V_{in}}{\text{resolution}} = \frac{1.465}{0.03} = +48.833$$

rounded up to 49 = 1 0 0 0 0 0 1 1 0 0 0 1

b. The 8-bit compressed code is determined as follows:
12-bit linear code = 1 0 0 0 0 0 1 1 0 0 0 1
(7 − 5 = 2) A B C D X
8-bit code = 1 0 1 0 1 0 0 0

c. The decoded 12-bit code is determined as follows:
8-bit code = 1 0 1 0 1 0 0 0
(7 − 2 = 5)
1 0 0 0 0 0 1 1 0 0 0 X
|
12-bit code = 1 0 0 0 0 0 1 1 0 0 0 1

d. 100000110001 = 49   and   49(0.03) = 1.47 V

e. For an input voltage of + 1.465 V, there is no compression error. The only error is the quantization error $Q_e = 0.005$ V.

4-11. **a.** 1 0 0 0 0 0 0 0 0 0 0 1 = +0.01 V to +0.03 V
b. 0 0 0 0 0 0 0 0 0 0 0 0 = −0.01 V to 0 V
c. 1 1 0 0 0 0 0 0 0 0 0 0 = +10.23 V to +10.25 V
d. 0 1 0 0 0 0 0 0 0 0 0 0 = −10.23 V to −10.25 V
e. 1 0 0 1 0 0 0 0 0 0 0 1 = +5.13 V to +5.15 V
f. 1 0 1 0 1 0 1 0 1 0 1 0 = +13.63 V to +13.65 V

4-12. **a.** 1 0 0 0 1 0 0 0   **b.** 1 0 0 0 1 0 0 1   **c.** 1 0 0 1 0 0 0 0
      d. 0 0 1 0 0 0 0 0   **e.** 0 1 1 1 0 0 0 0   **f.** 0 1 1 1 0 0 0 0

CHAPTER 5

5-1. **a.** The number of bits-per-frame is $[(24 \times 7) + 1] = 169$

$$\text{bps} = \frac{9000 \text{ frames}}{\text{second}} \times \frac{169 \text{ bits}}{\text{frame}} = 1.521 \text{ Mbps}$$

b. The minimum Nyquist frequency using BPRZ-AMI encoding is equal to one-half the line speed. Therefore,

$$f_N = \frac{1.521 \text{ Mbps}}{2} = 760.5 \text{ kHz}$$

5-2. **a.** The minimum sample rate is equal to twice the highest input frequency.
$$f_s = 2(4 \text{ kHz}) = 8 \text{ kHz}$$

b. The number of bits per frame is $3^2 \times 8 = 256$; therefore, the line speed is
$$\text{line speed} = \frac{8000 \text{ frames}}{\text{second}} \times \frac{256 \text{ bits}}{\text{frame}} = 2.048 \text{ Mbps}$$

c. With UPNRZ encoding, the minimum Nyquist frequency is equal to one-half the line speed. Therefore,
$$f_N = \frac{2.048 \text{ Mbps}}{2} = 1.024 \text{ MHz}$$

5-3.

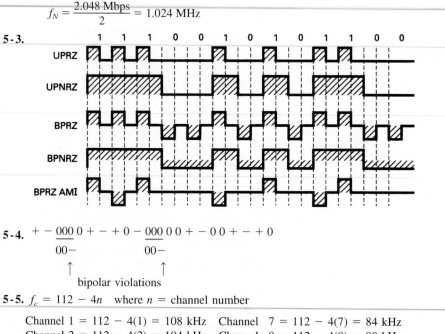

5-4. $+ - \underline{000}\ 0 + - + 0 - \underline{000}\ 0\ 0 + - 0\ 0 + - + 0$
         $\underline{00-}$ $\underline{00-}$
        ↑   ↑
       bipolar violations

5-5. $f_c = 112 - 4n$ where n = channel number

Channel 1 = 112 − 4(1) = 108 kHz   Channel 7 = 112 − 4(7) = 84 kHz
Channel 2 = 112 − 4(2) = 104 kHz   Channel 8 = 112 − 4(8) = 80 kHz
Channel 3 = 112 − 4(3) = 100 kHz   Channel 9 = 112 − 4(9) = 76 kHz
Channel 4 = 112 − 4(4) = 96 kHz   Channel 10 = 112 − 4(10) = 72 kHz
Channel 5 = 112 − 4(5) = 92 kHz   Channel 11 = 112 − 4(11) = 68 kHz
Channel 6 = 112 − 4(6) = 88 kHz   Channel 12 = 112 − 4(12) = 64 kHz

CHAPTER 6

6-1. $N = KTB$ $N_{\text{(dBm)}} = 10 \log \dfrac{KTB}{0.001}$

$T = 273 + 27 = 300°$

$N = (1.38 \times 10^{23})(300)(30,000,000) = 1.242 \times 10^{-13} \text{ W}$

$N = 10 \log \dfrac{1.242 \times 10^{-13}}{0.001} = -99.23 \text{ dBm}$

6-2. $L_p = 20 \log [4 \pi (3.4 \text{ GHz})(20 \text{ km})]^2 = 129 \text{ dB}$ or $L_p = 92.4 \text{ dB} + 10 \log 3.4 + 20 \log$
      $20 = 129 \text{ dB}$

6-3. $F_m = 30 \log[D_{(\text{km})}] + 10 \log[6ABf_{(\text{GHz})}] - 10 \log(1 - R) - 70$

$= 30 \log(60) + 10 \log[(6)(4)(0.125)(6)] - 10 \log(1 - 0.9995) - 70$

$= 53.34 + 12.55 + 33.01 - 70 = 28.9 \text{ dB}$

6-4. $T = 273 + 290 = 563°$

$N = 10 \log \dfrac{[(1.38 \times 10^{-23})(563)(20 \times 10^6)]}{0.001} = -98.09 \text{ dBm}$

6-5. $\dfrac{C}{N} + N = C_{\min} = 30 \text{ dB} + (-115 \text{ dBm}) = -85 \text{ dBm}$

$P_t = C_{\min} + G_S = -85 \text{ dbm} + 120 \text{ dB} = 35 \text{ dBm}$

6-6. $\text{Loss} = 10 \log(1 - R) = 10 \log(1 - 0.9998) = 37 \text{ dB}$

6-7. $\text{Loss} = 10 \log(6ABf) = 10 \log[(6)(0.25)(0.125)(4)] = -1.25 \text{ dB}$

6-8. $F_m = 30 \log D_{(\text{km})} + 10 \log[6ABf_{(\text{GHz})}] - 10 \log(1 - R) - 70$

$= 30 \log 50 + 10 \log[(6)(1)(0.125)(7.4)] - 10 \log(1 - 0.99998) - 70$

$= 50.97 + 7.44 + 50 - 70 = 38.41 \text{ dB}$

Antenna gain is determined from the chart as
$A_t = A_r = 43.1 \text{ dB} + 6 \text{ dB} = 49.1 \text{ dB}$

$L_p = 92.4 + 20 \log 7.4 + 20 \log 50 = 92.4 + 17.38 + 33.9 = 143.76 \text{ dB}$

$L_b = 3 \text{ dB}$ for a frequency diversity system

$L_f = \dfrac{4.7 \text{ dB}}{100 \text{ m}} \times 200 \text{ m} = 9.4 \text{ dB}$

$B = 2 \times 8294 \text{ MHz}$

$N = 10 \log \dfrac{[(k)(290)(16.568 \text{ MHz})]}{0.001} = -101.78 \text{ dBm}$

$C_{\min} = \dfrac{C}{N} + N = 30 + (-101.78 \text{ dB}) = -71.78 \text{ dBm}$

$G_S = F_m + L_p + L_f + L_b - A_t - A_r = 38.41 + 143.76 + 9.4 + 3 - 2(49.1)$

$= 96.37 \text{ dB}$

$Pt = C_{\min} + G_S = -71.78 \text{ dBm} + 96.37 \text{ dB} = 24.59 \text{ dBm}$

6-9. $F_T = 4 + 4 - 110 + 10 - 1100 + 4 - 125 = 4.51 \qquad NF_{(\text{dB})} = 10 \log 4.51 = 6.54 \text{ dB}$

6-10. C/N at receiver input $= C/N_{\text{detector}} + $ noise figure

$C/N = 20 \text{ dB} + 4 \text{ dB} = 24 \text{ dB}$

$C_{\min} = 24 \text{ dB} + (-102 \text{ dBm}) = -78 \text{ dBm}$

CHAPTER 7

7-1. Elevation angle $= 51°$, azimuth $= 33°$ west of south

7-2. For 8-PSK the minimum bandwidth $f_N = f_b/3 = 40 \text{ MHz}$.

$\dfrac{E_b}{N_0} = \dfrac{C}{N} + 10 \log \dfrac{B}{f_b} = 20 \text{ dB} + 10 \log \dfrac{40 \text{ MHz}}{120 \text{ Mbps}} = 20 \text{ dB} + (-4.77 \text{ dB}) = 15.23 \text{ dB}$

$N_0 = 10 \log \dfrac{KT_e}{0.001} = 10 \log \dfrac{(k)(400)}{0.001} = -172.6 \text{ dBm}$

$N = 10 \log \dfrac{[KT_e B]}{0.001} = 10 \log \dfrac{(k)(400)(40 \text{ MHz})}{0.001} = -96.56 \text{ dBm}$

$C_{\min} = 20 \text{ dB} + (-96.56 \text{ dBm}) = -76.56 \text{ dBm}$

$E_b = \dfrac{C_{\min}}{f_b} = -76.56 \text{ dB} - 10 \log 120 \text{ Mbps} = -76.56 + (-80.79) = -157.29 \text{ dBm}$

7-3. **a.** 11.74 dB **b.** 8.75 dB

7-4. **a.** $f_N = f_b/3 = 60 \text{ Mbps}/3 = 20 \text{ MHz}$

$\dfrac{E_b}{N_0} = \dfrac{C}{N} + 10 \log \dfrac{B}{f_b} = 15 \text{ dB} + 10 \log \dfrac{(2)(20 \text{ MHz})}{60 \text{ Mbps}} = 19.24 \text{ dB}$

b. $f_N = f_b/2 = 40$ Mbps$/2 = 20$ MHz

$$\frac{E_b}{N_0} = \frac{C}{N} + 10 \log \frac{B}{f_b} = 16 \text{ dB} + 10 \log \frac{(2)(20 \text{ MHz})}{40 \text{ Mbps}} = 13 \text{ dB}$$

The 8-QAM system would have a $P(e)$ between 10^{-4} and 10^{-5}. The QPSK system would have a $P(e)$ better than 10^{-5}.

7-5. Radiated power = 28 dBW, EIRP = 68 dBW

7-6. $N_{(\text{dBW})} = 10 \log KTB = 10 \log [(K)(600)(20 \text{ MHz})] = -127.8$ dBw

7-7. -200.8 dBW

7-8. From the table, C/N = 18.5 dB

7-9. 26.18 dB

7-10. $N_{0(\text{dBW})} = 10 \log[(K)(T)] = 10 \log[(K)(180)] = -206$ dBW

$$\frac{C}{N_0} = -70 \text{ dBW} - (-206 \text{ dB}) = 136 \text{ dB}$$

7-11. 19.77 dB

7-12. $\dfrac{G}{T_e} = 10 \log A_r - 10 \log T_e$

$$\frac{G}{T_e} = 50 \text{ dB} - 10 \log 200 = 27 \text{ dB}$$

$$N_0 = 10 \log KT_e = 10 \log[(K)(200)] = -205.6 \text{ dBW}$$

$$N = 10 \log KT_eB = 10 \log[(K)(200)(20 \text{ MHz})] = -132.6 \text{ dBW}$$

7-13. 12.5 dB overall

7-14. Up-link budget:

$$\text{EIRP} = P_t + A_t - L_{\text{bo}} - L_{bt} = 10 \log 1000 + 60 \text{ dB} - 3 \text{ dB} - 3 \text{ dB} = 84 \text{ dBW}$$

$$C' = \text{EIRP} - L_p - L_u = 84 \text{ dBW} - 203.5 \text{ dB} - 0.8 \text{ dB} = -120.3 \text{ dBW}$$

$$\frac{C}{N_0} = C' + \frac{G}{T_e} + 228.6 = -120 - 4.6 + 228.6 = 103.7 \text{dB}$$

$$\frac{E_b}{N_0} = \frac{C}{N_0} - 10 \log 90 \text{ Mbps} = 24.2 \text{ dB}$$

For a minimum bandwidth system,

$$\frac{C}{N} = \frac{E_b}{N_0} - 10 \log \frac{B}{T_e} = 24.2 \text{ dB} - 10 \log \frac{30 \text{ MHz}}{90 \text{ Mbps}} = 29 \text{ dB}$$

Down-link budget:

$$\text{EIRP} = 10 \log 10 + 33.4 - 0.8 - 0 = 44 \text{ dBW}$$

$$C' = 44 - 205 - 0.6 = -161 \text{ dBW}$$

$$\frac{C}{N_0} = C' + A_r - T_e + 228.6 = -161 \text{ dBW} + 59 - 23 + 228.6 = 103.6 \text{ dB}$$

$$\frac{E_b}{N_0} = 103.6 - 10 \log 90 \text{ Mbps} = 24.06 \text{ dB}$$

$$\frac{C}{N} = 24.06 - 10 \log \frac{30 \text{ MHz}}{90 \text{ Mbps}} = 28.83 \text{ dB}$$

CHAPTER 8

8-1. 15 transponders

8-2. Channel 1 carrier frequency = 52.0225 MHz. Each successive channel is separated from the previous channel by 45 kHz. Therefore, channel 7 is 6 × 45 kHz above channel 1: 52.0225 MHz + 6(45 kHz) = 52.2925 MHz. With QPSK, $B = f_b/2 = 64$ kbps$/2 = 32$ kHz. However, each channel is allocated 45 kHz, ± 22.5 kHz. Therefore, the frequency limits for channel 7 are upper limit = 53.315 MHz and lower limit = 52.27 MHz.

8-3. 44 stations

8-4. Chip code = 1 0 1 0 1 0   Orthogonal code = 1 0 1 1 0 1

$$
\begin{array}{l}
1\ 0\ 1\ 0\ 1\ 0 \\
\underline{1\ 0\ 1\ 1\ 0\ 1} \\
+\,+\,+\,-\,-\,- \quad = 0\ \text{V}
\end{array}
\qquad
\begin{array}{l}
1\ 0\ 1\ 0\ 1\ 0 \\
\underline{1\ 0\ 1\ 1\ 0\ 1\ 1\ 0\ 1\ 1} \\
-\,-\,+\,+\,+\,- \quad = 0\ \text{V}
\end{array}
\qquad
\begin{array}{l}
1\ 0\ 1\ 0\ 1\ 0 \\
\underline{1\ 0\ 1\ 1\ 0\ 1\ 1\ 0\ 1} \\
+\,+\,+\,-\,-\,- \quad = 0\ \text{V}
\end{array}
$$

$$
\begin{array}{l}
1\ 0\ 1\ 0\ 1\ 0 \\
\underline{1\ 0\ 1\ 1\ 0\ 1\ 1} \\
-\,-\,+\,+\,+\,- \quad = 0\ \text{V}
\end{array}
\qquad
\begin{array}{l}
1\ 0\ 1\ 0\ 1\ 0 \\
\underline{1\ 0\ 1\ 1\ 0\ 1\ 1\ 0\ 1\ 1\ 0} \\
+\,-\,-\,-\,+\,+ \quad = 0\ \text{V}
\end{array}
$$

$$
\begin{array}{l}
1\ 0\ 1\ 0\ 1\ 0 \\
\underline{1\ 0\ 1\ 1\ 0\ 1\ 1\ 0} \\
+\,-\,-\,-\,+\,+ \quad = 0\ \text{V}
\end{array}
\qquad
\begin{array}{l}
1\ 0\ 1\ 0\ 1\ 0 \\
\underline{1\ 0\ 1\ 1\ 0\ 1\ 1\ 0\ 1\ 1\ 0\ 1} \\
+\,+\,+\,-\,-\,- \quad = 0\ \text{V}
\end{array}
$$

CHAPTER 9

9-1. **a.** 869 nm, 8690 A   **b.** 828 nm, 8280 A   **c.** 935 nm, 9350 A

9-2. $f = c/\lambda$

a. 4.4776119×10^{14} Hz   **b.** 3.8461538×10^{14} Hz   **c.** 4.2253521×10^{14} Hz

9-3. 38.57°

9-4. $\theta_c = \sin^{-1} \dfrac{n_2}{n_1} = \sin^{-1} \dfrac{1.38}{1.5} = 66.92$

9-5. 36°

9-6. $\text{NA} = \sqrt{n_2^2 - n_1^2} = \sqrt{1.5^2 - 1.38^2} = 0.588$

9-7. **a.** RZ = 1 Mbps, NRZ = 500 kbps   **b.** RZ = 50 kbps, NRZ = 25 kbps

c. RZ = 250 kbps, NRZ = 125 kbps

9-8. $f = E/h$ $E_g = 1.2$ eV$(1.6 \times 10^{-19}$ j/eV$) = 1.92 \times 10^{-19}$ J

$$f = \frac{1.92 \times 10^{-19}}{6.6256 \times 10^{-34}} = 2.8978597 \text{ Hz}$$

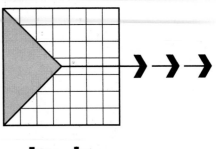

Index